THERAPIST'S GUIDE TO EVIDENCE-BASED RELAPSE PREVENTION

THERAPIST'S GUIDE TO EVIDENCE-BASED RELAPSE PREVENTION

EDITED BY

KATIE A. WITKIEWITZ
University of Illinois at Chicago
Chicago, Illinois

G. ALAN MARLATT
University of Washington
Seattle, Washington

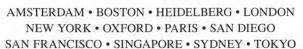

AMSTERDAM • BOSTON • HEIDELBERG • LONDON
NEW YORK • OXFORD • PARIS • SAN DIEGO
SAN FRANCISCO • SINGAPORE • SYDNEY • TOKYO

ELSEVIER   Academic Press is an imprint of Elsevier

Academic Press is an imprint of Elsevier
30 Corporate Drive, Suite 400, Burlington, MA 01803, USA
525 B Street, Suite 1900, San Diego, California 92101-4495, USA
84 Theobald's Road, London WC1X 8RR, UK

This book is printed on acid-free paper. ∞

Library of Congress Cataloging-in-Publication Data
APPLICATION SUBMITTED

British Library Cataloguing-in-Publication Data
A catalogue record for this book is available from the British Library.

ISBN 13: 978-0-12-369429-4
ISBN 10: 0-12-369429-9

For information on all Academic Press publications
visit our Web site at www.books.elsevier.com

Printed in the United States of America
07 08 09 10 9 8 7 6 5 4 3 2 1

**Working together to grow
libraries in developing countries**

www.elsevier.com | www.bookaid.org | www.sabre.org

ELSEVIER   BOOK AID International   Sabre Foundation

CONTENTS

SECTION I

INTRODUCTION AND OVERVIEW

1

OVERVIEW OF RELAPSE PREVENTION 3
KATIE WITKIEWITZ AND G. ALAN MARLATT

2

HIGH-RISK SITUATIONS: RELAPSE AS A DYNAMIC PROCESS 19
KATIE WITKIEWITZ AND G. ALAN MARLATT

SECTION II

APPLICATION OF RELAPSE PREVENTION TO
SPECIFIC PROBLEM AREAS

12

RELAPSE PREVENTION WITH HISPANIC AND OTHER RACIAL/ETHNIC POPULATIONS: CAN CULTURAL RESILIENCE PROMOTE RELAPSE PREVENTION? 259

FELIPE GONZÁLEZ CASTRO, ERICA NICHOLS, AND KARISSA KATER

13

RELAPSE PREVENTION FOR ADOLESCENT SUBSTANCE ABUSE: OVERVIEW AND CASE EXAMPLES 293

DANIELLE E. RAMO, MARK G. MYERS, AND SANDRA A. BROWN

14

RELAPSE PREVENTION WITH OLDER ADULTS 313

FREDERIC C. BLOW, LAURIE M. BROCKMANN, AND KRISTEN L. BARRY

15

UTILIZING RELAPSE PREVENTION WITH OFFENDER POPULATIONS: WHAT WORKS 339

CRAIG DOWDEN AND DON A. ANDREWS

16

DRINKING AS AN EPIDEMIC—A SIMPLE MATHEMATICAL MODEL WITH RECOVERY AND RELAPSE 353

FABIO SÁNCHEZ, XIAOHONG WANG, CARLOS CASTILLO-CHÁVEZ, DENNIS M. GORMAN, AND PAUL J. GRUENEWALD

CONTRIBUTORS

Numbers in parentheses indicate the pages on which the authors' contributions begin.

Don A. Andrews (339), Carleton University, Ottawa, Ontario, Canada K1S5B6

Kristen L. Barry (313), Department of Psychiatry, University of Michigan, Ann Arbor, Michigan 48109; and VA National Serious Mental Illness Treatment Research and Evaluation Center, Ann Arbor, Michigan 48109

Frederic C. Blow (313), Department of Psychiatry, University of Michigan, Ann Arbor, Michigan 48109; and VA National Serious Mental Illness Treatment Research and Evaluation Center, Ann Arbor, Michigan 48109

Laurie M. Brockmann (313), VA National Serious Mental Illness Treatment Research and Evaluation Center, Ann Arbor, Michigan 48109

Milton Z. Brown (191), Alliant International University, San Diego, California 92131-1799

Sandra A. Brown (293), Veteran Affairs Medical Center, San Diego, University of San Diego, San Diego, California 92093

Carlos Castillo-Chávez (353), Department of Mathematics, Arizona State University, Tempe, Arizona 85287-1804

Felipe González Castro (259), Department of Psychology, Arizona State University, Tempe, Arizona 85287-1104

Richard F. Catalano (237), School of Social Work, University of Washington, Seattle, Washington 98115

Alex Chapman (191), Department of Psychology, Simon Fraser University, Burnaby, British Columbia, Canada V5A1S6

Dennis C. Daley (37), University of Pittsburgh Medical Center, Pittsburgh, Pennsylvania 15213

Antoine Douaihy (37), Western Psychiatric Institute and Clinic, Pittsburgh, Pennsylvania 15213

Craig Dowden (339), Carleton University, Ottawa, Ontario, Canada K1K2B8

Corey Fagan (91), Department of Psychology, University of Washington, Seattle, Washington 98195-1525

Charles B. Fleming (237), School of Social Work, University of Washington, Seattle, Washington 98115

Dennis M. Gorman (353), School of Rural Public Health, Texas A&M Health Science Center, Bryan, Texas 77802

Paul J. Gruenewald (353), Prevention Research Center, Berkeley, California 94704

Kevin P. Haggerty (237), School of Social Work, University of Washington, Seattle, Washington 98115

Karissa Kater (259), Department of Psychology, Arizona State University, Tempe, Arizona 85287-1104

Mark A. Lau (73), Centre for Addiction and Mental Health, University of Toronto, Toronto, Ontario, Canada M5T 1R8

Diane E. Logan (91), Department of Psychology, University of Washington, Seattle, Washington 98195-1525

G. Alan Marlatt (3, 19, 91), Department of Psychology, University of Washington, Seattle, Washington 98195-1525

Mark G. Myers (293), Veteran Affairs Medical Center, San Diego, University of San Diego, San Diego, California 92161

Lisa M. Najavits (141), Harvard Medical School, Boston, Massachusetts 02115

Thach (Franchesca) Nguyen (91), Department of Psychology, University of Washington, Seattle, Washington 98195-1525

Erica Nichols (259), Department of Psychology, Arizona State University, Tempe, Arizona 85287-1104

Tae Woo Park (37), Western Psychiatric Institute and Clinic, Pittsburgh, Pennsylvania 15213

Danielle E. Ramo (293), University of California, San Diego, San Diego State University, La Jolla, California 92093

Fabio Sánchez (353), Biological Statistics and Computational Biology, Cornell University, Ithaca, New York 14853

Tanya R. Schlam (169), Department of Psychology, Rutgers University, Piscataway, New Jersey 08854

Zindel V. Segal (73), Centre for Addiction and Mental Health, University of Toronto, Toronto, Ontario, Canada M5T 1R8

Steven M. Silverstein (117), Department of Psychiatry, Robert Wood Johnson Medical School, Piscataway, New Jersey 08854; University Behavioral Health Care (UMDNJ)

Martie L. Skinner (237), School of Social Work, University of Washington, Seattle, Washington 98115

Keith R. Stowell (37), Western Psychiatric Institute and Clinic, Pittsburgh, Pennsylvania 15213

Xiaohong Wang (353), Department of Mathematics, Arizona State University, Tempe, Arizona 85287-1804

Tony Ward (215), School of Psychology, University of Wellington, Wellington, New Zealand

Ursula Whiteside (91), Department of Psychology, University of Washington, Seattle, Washington 98195-1525V

G. Terence Wilson (169), Department of Psychology, Rutgers University, Piscataway, New Jersey 08854

Katie Witkiewitz (3, 19, 91), Department of Psychology, University of Illinois at Chicago, Chicago, Illinois 60607

Philip T. Yanos (117), Department of Psychology, John Jay College of Criminal Justice, City University of New York, New York, New York 10019

Pamela M. Yates (215), Cabot Consulting and Research Services, Ottawa, Ontario, Canada K2C1N0

Douglas Ziedonis (117), Department of Psychiatry, University of Massachusetts Medical School, Worcester, Massachusetts 01655

PREFACE

Relapse, the process of returning to symptomatic behavior after a period of symptom remission, is the most widely noted outcome following treatment for psychological and substance abuse disorders. It has been demonstrated that at least a minor transgression, and at worst a complete reversal of behavioral gains, is the most common outcome following attempts at behavior change. Given this common outcome it is critical that effective treatments incorporate strategies for preventing lapses following symptom remission. One of the major goals of relapse prevention therapy is to help clients identify their personal high-risk situations and provide coping skills training to increase the use of effective coping strategies in those situations. The widespread application of relapse prevention techniques to several different behavioral targets (e.g., dieting, smoking, sex offending, psychotic symptoms, worrying, depression) demonstrates the importance of a comprehensive book for clinicians who work with a broad range of client populations.

It has been over 20 years since the publication of the original text on relapse prevention (RP): *Relapse Prevention: Maintenance Strategies in the Treatment of Addictive Behaviors* (Marlatt & Gordon, 1985). As can be seen in the title of the book, "relapse prevention" was initially designed as an adjunct treatment to help prevent addictive behavior relapse. RP was based on the cognitive-behavioral model of alcohol relapse and can be characterized as a tertiary prevention and intervention strategy designed specifically to prevent initial lapses and provide lapse management skills to enact if a lapse occurs. As described in great detail in Chapters 1 and 2, relapse prevention and the cognitive-behavioral model of relapse centers on high-risk situations and an individual's response in those situations. Chapter 2 also presents the revised cognitive behavioral model of relapse that we initially proposed in 2004 (Witkiewitz & Marlatt, 2004). The dynamic model of relapse is based on the underlying processes of the cognitive-behavioral model of relapse and adds to the model an emphasis on the timing and interrelatedness of events. In this chapter we provide a basic overview of the new model as well as a discussion of the aspects of the model that are directly relevant to clinical practice. Chapter 2 concludes with a case illustration of how the dynamic model of relapse may be incorporated into case conceptualization and treatment.

Since the original publication of *Relapse Prevention*, reviews have questioned whether the original RP techniques are effective for other addictive disorders (Carroll, 1996; Irvin, Bowers, Dunn & Wang, 1999). As described in the empirical review of the literature presented throughout this book, it is clear that RP techniques are highly effective for addictive and many nonaddictive disorders. Reading through the initial drafts of the chapters presented in this book we observed the discrepancy between the previous reviews and the current literature may be partially due to an inconsistency in terminology across the diverse areas that employ RP techniques. Thus, we hope this text will clarify definitions of RP techniques and bring together practitioners who are working in these diverse areas.

This text introduces many new techniques and ideas for the prevention of relapse. One of the overarching themes throughout many chapters of the book is the highrates of co-morbidity and the need to incorporate techniques that are applicable to symptoms of more than one disorder. A main emphasis of many chapters (see Daley et al., Brown & Chapman; Lau & Segal; Schlam & Wilson; and Whiteside et al.) is the application of mindfulness training as a key component for relapse prevention. Throughout these chapters we are introduced to mindfulness as an intervention and way of being that may prevent lapses or minimize the severity of a lapse.

The first section of the book, Chapters 1 and 2, include a description of the cognitive-behavioral model of relapse, a general introduction to relapse prevention techniques, and an overview of the empirical support for relapse prevention interventions. Chapter 2 also provides a detailed description of the dynamic model of relapse and clinical application of the revised model.

Section II focuses on specific problem areas and specific applications of relapse prevention techniques within other cognitive-behavioral interventions. In Chapter 3 Douaihy, Daley, Stowell, and Park provide a general overview of RP strategies for substance use disorders, encapsulating a description of the recent empirical evidence supporting RP for alcohol, nicotine, cocaine, and heroin/opioids. One of the many goals of this book was to introduce RP applied to nonaddictive disorders, a topic that has received scant coverage across disciplines. If you are interested in a more thorough discussion of RP for specific substance use disorders we highly recommend the 2nd edition of the *Relapse Prevention* text edited by G. Alan Marlatt and Dennis Donovan and published by Guilford Press.

Chapters 4 and 5 could be characterized as a subsection on mindfulness based approaches to psychological disorders. In Chapter 4, Lau and Segal describe their mindfulness-based cognitive therapy (MBCT) program. MBCT has proven to be very useful and effective as a relapse prevention approach for depression. In Chapter 5, Whiteside and colleagues provide an overview of the research and treatment of generalized anxiety disorder, with a particular emphasis on chronic, pathological worry. Both chapters argue that mindfulness strategies are key components in the identification of high-risk situations and managing negative affective states.

In Chapter 6, Ziedonis, Yanos, and Silverstein provide a thorough description of relapse prevention and other cognitive-behavioral treatments (e.g., dual recovery therapy and social skills training) for schizophrenia. They point out that adopting a RP model is especially useful considering the high co-morbidity of substance use with schizophrenia. Likewise, in Chapter 7, Najavits highlights the often high co-morbidity between substance use and PTSD. Najavits provides a thorough description of her highly effective Seeking Safety program, which was designed to continually attend to both PTSD and substance use disorders. She also provides a description of the similarities and differences between Seeking Safety and RP.

Chapters 8 and 9 provide descriptions of RP for two disorders that are less commonly described within a RP framework. In Chapter 8, Schlam and Wilson describe RP as an essential element of CBT for eating disorders, including descriptions of RP techniques for anorexia nervosa, bulimia nervosa, and eating disorders not otherwise specified. In Chapter 9, M. Brown and Chapman introduce the RP model as part of a Dialectical Behavior Therapy (DBT) intervention for self-harm behavior. Both Chapters 8 and 9 describe the importance of mindfulness strategies in the management of eating disorder and self-harm behaviors.

The application of RP to the treatment of sexual offending has received a great deal of attention and resistance throughout the years. In Chapter 10, Yates and Ward describe the extant literature on RP for sexual offending, as well as the controversies associated with the application of RP for a diverse group of sex offenders. Yates and Ward then focus the chapter on their self-regulation model of offense and the relapse process. The parallels between the descriptions of the self-regulation model in Chapter 10 and the dynamic model of relapse in Chapter 2 highlights the tendency for the field to be moving in the direction of recognizing individual heterogeneity in the relapse process.

Section III focuses on specific populations and the adaptation of RP techniques for diverse populations with substance use disorders. Chapter 11, by Catalano, Haggerty, Fleming, and Skinner, describes the Focus on Families intervention, which integrates RP training with the prevention of child and drug abuse within a group of parents in methadone treatment. The primary goal of Focus on Families is to reduce parents' illicit drug use by teaching them relapse prevention and coping skills, while also teaching parents how to manage their families better, with the goal of preventing drug abuse among their children.

In Chapter 12, Castro, Nichols, and Kater review the sociocultural and political reasons for studying health-related disparities and describe the fundamental approaches for designing and conducting culturally relevant relapse prevention interventions with Hispanic and other racial/ethnic clients in treatment for the abuse of illegal drugs. Likewise, in Chapter 13, Ramo, Myers, and S. Brown describe RP for adolescents with substance use disorders. On the other end of the life span, in Chapter 14, Blow, Brockmann, and Barry describe RP for older adults.

The book concludes with two chapters that introduce methodologies for establishing the effectiveness of RP interventions. In Chapter 15, Dowden and Andrews provide a meta-analysis of relapse prevention with offender populations, concluding that RP effectively prevents offender recidivism under specific conditions. In Chapter 16, Sánchez, Wang, Castillo-Chávez, Gorman, and Gruenewald, present a mathematical model of alcohol relapse, which draws a parallel between drinking relapse and "outbreaks" of an epidemic, drawing a distinction between people who are recovered from alcohol dependence, currently drinking and susceptible to relapse.

We are very excited about this collection of chapters and we are especially thrilled to see the wide range of RP applications and unique RP strategies for specific disorders and populations. The idea behind this book was sparked by Mara Conner at Elsevier, for whom we are eternally grateful. We also thank our publisher Nikki Levy, our developmental editor Barbara Makinster, and our project manager Christie Jozwiak at Elsevier, who were incredibly patient throughout the process of pulling together the chapters and making final edits on the book.

SECTION I

INTRODUCTION AND OVERVIEW

Relapse, the process of returning to symptomatic behavior after a period of symptom remission, is the most widely noted outcome following treatment for psychological and substance abuse disorders. It has been demonstrated that at least a minor transgression, and at worst a complete reversal of behavioral gains, is the most common outcome following attempts at behavior change. Relapse prevention (RP), which is based on the cognitive-behavioral model of relapse, is a tertiary prevention and intervention strategy designed to prevent initial lapses and provide lapse management skills to enact if a lapse occurs. One of the major goals of relapse prevention therapy is to help clients identify their personal high-risk situations and provide coping skills training to increase the use of effective coping strategies in those situations.

In this text, you will learn about the widespread application of relapse prevention techniques to several different behavioral targets (including substance abuse, self-harm, eating disorders, sexual and criminal offending, substance use, psychotic symptoms, post-traumatic stress disorder, anxiety, and depression), and a broad range of client populations (including adolescents, medical populations, minority groups, and older adults). Section I includes a description of the cognitive–behavioral model of relapse, a general introduction to relapse prevention techniques, and an overview of the empirical support for relapse prevention interventions. We will also introduce a revised version of the relapse prevention model that was put forth initially by Marlatt and Gordon (1985). Section II includes chapters by experts in the field who have provided detailed illustrations of relapse prevention and cognitive behavioral techniques for a wide variety of problem behaviors. Drawing from the empirical literature and clinical experiences, Section II provides a balanced, comprehensive, and practical guide to incorporating relapse prevention techniques into a clinical practice. Section III provides an overview of relapse prevention techniques for specific client populations, with a focus on client characteristics, treatment settings, and provider populations. The focus of each chapter transcends behavioral problem areas; the chapters focus on the idiosyncrasies of unique client populations. Finally, Section IV concludes with an empirically derived model of relapse to alcohol use disorders and an epilogue highlighting directions for future research.

In each chapter, the authors present theoretical and empirical support for the implementation of relapse prevention techniques for the particular problem area or special population. Each chapter also includes specific strategies, a step-by-step overview of "how to" incorporate relapse prevention skills into a clinical practice and specific tactics, metaphors, and/or analogies that can be incorporated into the treatment. For the chapters in Section II the authors have included at least two case examples, including the overall treatment rational, specific issues and problems that arose during treatment, the outcomes of the intervention, and the ways in which the case examples may be more or less similar to typical presentations of the problem behavior.

1

OVERVIEW OF RELAPSE PREVENTION

KATIE WITKIEWITZ

Department of Psychology
University of Illinois at Chicago
Chicago, Illinois

G. ALAN MARLATT

Department of Psychology
University of Washington
Seattle, Washington

"Relapse prevention" was a phrase coined in the late 1970s to describe a theoretical model and to provide an umbrella term for a set of cognitive-behavioral intervention strategies that were designed to prevent the progression from lapse to relapse in individuals with alcohol dependence (Marlatt & George, 1984; Marlatt & Gordon, 1985). Marlatt and colleagues developed the overall model based on a series of studies in which they identified triggers for alcohol lapses following behavioral intervention (Chaney, O'Leary & Marlatt, 1978; Fromme, Kivlahan & Marlatt, 1986; Marlatt, 1987; Rohsenow & Marlatt, 1981). In this chapter we provide a concise overview of the original model and specific relapse prevention intervention strategies.

COGNITIVE-BEHAVIORAL MODEL OF RELAPSE

Relapse has been defined as both an event, "any drinking" (Sutton, 1979), and a process (Miller, Walters & Bennett, 2001; Stout, 2000; Witkiewitz & Marlatt, 2004). Within the relapse process two possible outcomes have been described: lapse and prolapse. A lapse is the initial set-back or the first instance of a previously changed behavior, whereas a prolapse is the process of "getting back on track" in the direction of positive behavior change.

Research on determinants of relapse began in the late 1970s, during a follow-up of a group of male alcoholic patients who were treated with aversion therapy while participating in a residential treatment program (Marlatt, 1978). To increase the generalization of the aversion effects, treatment sessions were conducted in a simulated bar. In the follow-up assessment interviews, we gathered as much information as possible about the details of the initial lapse for those patients who took at least one drink following the completion of treatment. During the first 90 days post-treatment, 48 patients out of the sample of 65 consumed alcohol. Patients were asked a variety of questions about the events leading to the initial lapse, including information about the physical location, time of day, presence of others, external or environmental factors that may have played a role, and the patient's emotional feelings on the day of the first drink. We attempted to categorize the list of relapse precipitants into independent, operationally defined categories. In our first analysis, the first two categories, accounting for over half the cases, involved an interpersonal encounter. In the first category (29% of the initial lapse episodes), the patient reported feeling frustrated in some goal-directed activity (usually precipitated by another individual who negatively evaluated the patient), and reported feelings of anger. Rather than expressing the anger openly, the patients ended up drinking alcohol instead. As for the second category (23%), patients reported being unable to resist social pressure from others to return to drinking. Temptation situations were also quite common (21%), such as passing by a favorite bar, although it is possible that the sudden temptation and resulting urge to drink was determined by other environmental or emotional factors that were not identified in the interview. These results were consistent with earlier research we conducted on determinants of drinking among social drinkers. These studies showed feelings of anger (Marlatt, Kosturn & Lang, 1975), anticipation of negative interpersonal evaluation (Higgins & Marlatt, 1975), and social modeling as a form of social pressure to drink (Caudill & Marlatt, 1975) all served as strong determinants of increased drinking in nonalcoholic subjects. These findings served as the impetus for the development of a cognitive-behavioral model of the relapse process over the next few years (Marlatt, 1979; Marlatt & Gordon, 1980).

The first treatment outcome study to evaluate the efficacy of relapse prevention in the treatment of alcohol dependence was published in 1978 (Chaney, O'Leary & Marlatt, 1978). The study was conducted in an inpatient treatment center for male alcoholics as an "add-on" intervention. The RP training consisted of eight semi-weekly sessions, each 90 minutes long. Patients met in groups of three to five, and were instructed by two therapists (male and female team). The goal of the RP program was to teach patients effective coping skills to deal with high-risk trigger situations that might precipitate relapse. The groups incorporated direct instructions, modeling, behavioral rehearsal and coaching, both for the actual behavioral response (e.g., anger management) and the cognitive processes involved in selecting an effective coping response. Patients were instructed how to define the problematic high-risk situation and how to generate alternatives, and to think about the consequences (both short-term and long-term) of their actions.

Finally, the behavioral rehearsal phase provided practice in carrying out adaptive responses and served as a role-play to assess the adequacy of the problem-solving process.

In the study design, patients were randomly assigned to either the RP condition or to one of two control groups: a discussion-only group or a treatment-as-usual condition (receiving only the regular 28-day inpatient treatment). The purpose of the discussion-only condition (similar in format to psychodynamic "insight therapy" in which patients were asked to describe their feelings that were elicited by various high-risk situations, but without any attempt to teach coping skills) was to control for the additional time and attention patients received in the RP groups. All patients were followed up on a continuous basis for one year post-treatment. Results showed that the RP group proved to be significantly more effective than either control group, demonstrating enhanced improvement on such outcome measures as number of drinks consumed during the follow-up period, days of continuous drinking before regaining abstinence, and number of days of intoxication. Results showed continued improvement over the one-year post-treatment assessment period, and resembled a typical learning curve pattern in that more lapses occurred in the early stages of acquiring new coping skills, followed by a stabilization period as the new learning consolidates over time. This pattern of results was reported in other similar studies of the effects of RP that were summarized in later publications (Marlatt & George, 1984; Marlatt & Gordon, 1985).

HIGH-RISK SITUATIONS

As described earlier, the primary basis of the cognitive-behavioral model of relapse is the identification of a high-risk situation. A high-risk situation is defined as any experience, emotion, setting, thought, or context that presents an increased risk for a person to engage in some transgressive behavior. Marlatt and colleagues (Marlatt, 1996; Marlatt & Nathan, 1978) developed a taxonomy of high-risk situations that included three hierarchically arranged levels of categories used in the classification of relapse episodes. The *first level* of the hierarchy distinguishes between the intrapersonal and interpersonal precipitants for relapse. The *second level* consists of eight subdivisions, including five within the intrapersonal category: coping with negative emotional states, coping with negative physical-psychological states, enhancement of positive-emotional states, testing personal control, and giving in to temptations and urges; and three within the interpersonal category: coping with interpersonal conflict, social pressure, and enhancement of positive emotional states. The *third level* of the taxonomy provides a more detailed inspection of five of the eight Level 2 subdivisions (e.g., coping with negative emotional states is segregated into coping with frustration and/or anger and coping with other negative emotional states).

Since the original publication of the relapse taxonomy there have been several critiques (Donovan, 1996; Edwards, 1987; Kadden, 1996; Maisto, Connors &

Zywiak, 1996) of the classification system and few clinicians have used the taxonomy as it was originally intended. However, the inter- and intrapersonal determinants of relapse set forth by the relapse taxonomy have been shown to be reliable and valid, with high clinical utility (Larimer, Palmer & Marlatt, 1999; Stout, Longabaugh & Rubin, 1996; Zywiak, Connors, Maisto & Westerberg, 1996). In the next section we provide a brief review of relapse precipitants and the empirical basis for their inclusion in the cognitive-behavioral model, and in the following section we describe specific RP intervention strategies related to each of the relapse precipitants.

Negative Emotional States

In the original relapse taxonomy (Marlatt & Gordon, 1985) and in the replication of the taxonomy (Lowman, Allen & Stout, 1996), negative affect was the best predictor of outcomes. Negative emotions may manifest differently for different individuals, thus it is hard to pinpoint one emotional state (e.g., anxiety, depression, anger) that is most predictive of relapse. Furthermore, it may not be absolute level of emotion that predicts lapses, but rather one's situational ability to regulate that emotion (Baker, Piper, McCarthy, Majeskie & Fiore, 2003; Burish, Maisto & Shirley, 1982; Marlatt, Kosturn & Lang, 1975). One study demonstrated that high emotional arousal during an alcohol intervention can have iatrogenic effects (Moos & Moos, 2005), presumably the heightened emotional responding combined with a lack of skills for regulating the emotion will set a client up for failure. Thus, clinicians should be prepared to provide interventions that decrease negative emotional states as well as teach skills for regulating one's emotions (see Brown & Chapman, this volume).

Positive Emotional States

When the original relapse taxonomy was proposed there was much less research on the role of positive emotions in the relapse process. In the replication of the taxonomy the researchers found positive emotions, particularly in social contexts, to be positively related to relapse (Lowman, Allen & Stout, 1996). Other studies have concluded that positive affect is related to less severe lapses (Currie, Hodgins, el-Guebaly & Campbell, 2001) and lower relapse rates (Alterman, O'Brien, McLellan & McKay, 2001). For individuals within nonsubstance-related problems positive emotions are predictive of better health outcomes (Richman et al., 2005; Zautra, Johnson & Davis, 2005).

Coping

Within a few seconds of entering a high-risk situation or in the anticipation of a future high-risk situation the key relapse prevention strategy is the implementation of an effective coping skill. Coping, in general, has been shown to be a critical predictor of substance use treatment outcomes and is often the strongest predictor of behavioral lapses in the moment (Carels, Douglass, Cacciapaglia &

O'Brien, 2004; Maisto, Zywiak & Connors, 2006; Monti, Rohsenow, Michalec, Martin & Abrams, 1997; Moser & Annis, 1996). Importantly, studies have identified types of coping that may be more effective than others. For example, active cognitive and behavioral approach coping strategies have been shown to be significantly related to abstinence outcomes, whereas the exclusive use of avoidant coping strategies tends to be related to more negative outcomes (Maisto, Zywiak & Connors, 2006; Moser & Annis, 1996).

Outcome Expectancies

Anticipation of the effects of a substance has been described as one of the primary cognitions related to substance use and relapse, regardless of whether the expectancies are explicit (Jones & McMahon, 1994; Wiers et al., 2002) or implicit (Palfai, Monti, Colby & Rohsenow, 1997). Outcome expectancies may be influencing substance use behavior via the relationship between negative emotional states and beliefs about substances relieving negative affect, particularly among treatment-seeking individuals (Abrams & Kushner, 2004; Demmel, Nicolai & Gregorzik, 2006; Leigh & Stacy, 1994). Interestingly both negative and positive outcome expectancies are related to relapse, with negative expectancies being protective against relapse (Jones & McMahon, 1994) and positive expectancies being a risk factor for relapse (Gwaltney, Shiffman, Balabanis & Paty, 2005). When individuals endorse positive outcome expectancies at the beginning of treatment, some evidence supports the use of an intervention to challenge expectancies (Corbin, McNair & Carter, 2001), which can be accomplished by linking outcome expectancies to other cognitive and behavioral indices (e.g., tension reduction expectancies related to coping with stress).

Self-Efficacy

The client's personal belief in their ability to control their substance use (abstaining or moderate use) is a reliable predictor of lapses immediately following treatment (Demmel & Rist, 2005; Gwaltney, Shiffman, Balabanis & Paty, 2005) and over long-term outcomes (Maisto, Clifford, Longabaugh & Beattie, 2002; Moos & Moos, 2006). Brown and colleagues (Brown, Seraganian, Tremblay & Annis, 2002) studied changes in self-efficacy during an RP intervention and demonstrated that increased self-efficacy following RP was related to improved outcomes. There is most likely a bidirectional relationship between self-efficacy and outcomes, whereby individuals who are more successful report greater self-efficacy and individuals who have lapsed report lower self-efficacy. Evidence from a daily monitoring study showed decreases in self-efficacy preceded a first lapse on the following day and daily variation in self-efficacy predicted transitions from lapse to heavier use (Gwaltney, Shiffman, Balabanis & Paty, 2005). A similar study showed baseline self-efficacy was as predictive of first lapse as daily measures of self-efficacy (Shiffman et al., 2000). Thus, assessment of self-efficacy during treatment and interventions designed to enhance self-efficacy are critical components of any RP intervention.

Abstinence-Violation Effect

The abstinence violation effect (AVE), which is defined as attributions of failure and feelings of guilt or shame following the breach of self-imposed rules, was a component of the original cognitive behavioral model. There is scant research supporting the AVE in the prediction of alcohol relapse (Larimer, Palmer & Marlatt, 1999), and mixed findings in the prediction of smoking relapse (Curry, Marlatt & Gordon, 1987; Shiffman et al., 1996). The AVE is widely acknowledged as a predictor of recidivism in the areas of domestic violence (King & Polaschek, 2003) and sexual offending (see Wheeler, George & Marlatt, in press; Yates & Ward, this volume), and a predictor of eating-related disorders (Carels, Douglass, Cacciapaglia & O'Brien, 2004; Grilo & Shiffman, 1994). The core belief of the AVE, whether a person attributes any transgression of behavior as a complete failure, should always be assessed and challenged as part of treatment.

Craving

The role of craving in substance use and nonsubstance (e.g., gambling) relapse has been widely studied. Yet the construct of craving is poorly understood and recent addiction research has failed to find a significant association between subjective craving and objective measures of relapse (Drummond, Litten, Lowman & Hunt, 2000). As mentioned earlier in the section on outcome expectancies, craving has been described as a cognitive experience focused on the desire to use a substance and is often highly related to expectancies for the desired effect of the substance, whereas urge has been defined as the behavioral intention or impulse to use a substance. One RP strategy that has recently received attention (which is described later) is the application of mindfulness and acceptance techniques for managing craving and urges (Marlatt & Ostafin, 2006; Witkiewitz, Marlatt & Walker, 2005). From this perspective, craving is seen as attachment to a desired experience that has previously been achieved via the transgressive behavior (e.g., winning at blackjack, numbing associated with alcohol use, and perceived stress reduction associated with smoking). If a person is attached to an experience and the expectation is that they can have that experience only by lapsing, then of course the individual will encounter craving and urges to engage in that behavior. At least three ways are available to prevent a lapse in this situation: letting go of attachment to the experience, reducing positive outcome expectation for the lapse leading to the desired experience, or pharmacologically reducing the experience of craving with an "anti-craving" medication (O'Brien, 2005).

Interpersonal Precipitants

As described by Stanton (2005), the role of interpersonal processes and social support is a critical component of RP that was largely missing from our revised RP model described in 2004 (Stanton, 2005; Witkiewitz & Marlatt, 2004;

Witkiewitz & Marlatt, 2005). Stanton (2005) reviewed empirical research on the role of social support in lapse events and provided an overview of interpersonal dynamics as a high-risk situation for relapse. In our reply, we noted that the relationship between interpersonal factors and relapse is not entirely clear given disparate findings in the field (Armeli, Todd & Mohr, 2005; Hardoon, Gupta & Derevensky, 2004; McCrady, Epstein & Kahler, 2004; Quigley & Marlatt, 1999; Room, Matzger & Weisner, 2004). Positive social support, in the form of support for abstinence or reduced use, is likely to be related to improved outcomes, but support for drinking and more general forms of support can be related to increased rates of relapse. An extension of RP that incorporates spouses or significant others into a conjoint treatment has been developed and has strong empirical support (McCrady, Epstein & Hirsch, 1999).

RELAPSE PREVENTION INTERVENTIONS

REVIEWS OF RELAPSE PREVENTION

The RP approach has provided an important heuristic and treatment framework for clinicians working with several types of addictive behavior. Incorporating studies of RP for smoking, alcohol, marijuana, and cocaine addiction, Carroll (1996) concluded that RP was more effective than no-treatment control groups and equally effective as other active treatments (e.g., supportive therapy, social support group, interpersonal psychotherapy) in improving substance use outcomes. Irvin and colleagues (1999) conducted a meta-analysis on the efficacy of RP techniques in the improvement of substance abuse and psychosocial outcomes (Irvin, Bowers, Dunn & Wang, 1999). Twenty-six studies representing a sample of 9,504 participants were included in the review, which focused on alcohol use, smoking, polysubstance use, and cocaine use. The overall treatment effects demonstrated that RP was a successful intervention for reducing substance use and improving psychosocial adjustment. In particular, RP was more effective in treating alcohol and polysubstance use than it was in the treatment of cocaine use and smoking, although these findings need to be interpreted with caution due to the small number of studies evaluating cocaine use. RP was equally effective across different treatment modalities, including individual, group, and marital treatment delivery, although all these methods were most effective in treating alcohol use.

The Relapse Replication and Extension Project (RREP), initiated by the Treatment Research Branch of the United States National Institute of Alcohol Abuse and Alcoholism (NIAAA), was specifically designed to investigate the cognitive-behavioral model of relapse developed by Marlatt and colleagues (Marlatt & Gordon, 1985). The RREP focused on the replication and extension of the high-risk situation in relation to relapse, and the reliability and validity of the taxonomic system for classifying relapse episodes. As in the original studies of relapse episodes, the RREP found that negative emotional states and exposure to social pressure to drink were most commonly identified as high-risk situations for relapse (Lowman et al., 1996). However, in many ways the RREP failed to replicate the original relapse taxonomy and the RREP investigators recommended several important changes to the taxonomy (Connors, Maisto & Zywiak, 1996; Donovan, 1996; Maisto, Connors & Zywiak, 1996), many of which have been incorporated in our revised model of relapse (Witkiewitz & Marlatt, 2004) as described in the next chapter of this volume.

IS IT RP?

Substance Abuse Treatment

In 1998 the National Institute of Drug Abuse (NIDA) held the National Conference on Drug Addiction Treatment: From Research to Practice and prepared a guide that is freely downloadable from http://www.nida.nih.gov/PDF/PODAT/PODAT.pdf. We recommend visiting the web site and taking advantage of a number of useful clinical resources, including treatment and assessment protocols. The recommended treatments in the guide included relapse prevention, supportive-expressive psychotherapy, individualized drug counseling, motivational enhancement therapy, behavioral therapy for adolescents, multidimensional family therapy for adolescence, multisystemic therapy, combined behavioral and nicotine replacement therapy, community reinforcement approach plus vouchers, voucher-based reinforcement therapy, day treatment with abstinence contingencies and vouchers, and the Matrix model. Other treatments that were not specifically named in this review, but have been shown to be highly effective in the treatment of alcohol and drug use (Miller & Wilbourne, 2002) include behavioral couples therapy, behavioral self-control training, coping skills training, social skills training, and twelve-step approaches.

The majority of the treatments described by NIDA (1998) and Miller and Wilbourne (2002) incorporate at least some aspects of the cognitive-behavioral model of relapse and the RP strategies described by Marlatt and Gordon (1985). For example, the Matrix model (Rawson et al., 1989) draws heavily on the original cognitive-behavioral model, but is delivered as a 16-week manualized intensive outpatient treatment for stimulant users. The treatment is designed to teach immediate skills needed to stop substance use, provide an understanding of factors critical to preventing relapse, educate family members, reinforce and encourage positive changes, introduce patients to self-help programs, and monitor substance use via biochemical testing. There have been numerous studies over the past 15 years providing strong empirical support for the Matrix approach (see Carroll & Rawson, 2005 for a review).

Coping skills training is a major component of most RP interventions and has also been used as a stand-alone treatment (Kadden & Cooney, 2005). Coping skills training often incorporates an emphasis on avoiding high-risk situations altogether, avoiding decisions that could result in a person being in a high-risk situation (referred to as "apparently irrelevant decisions"), and training in coping strategies to provide a means for preventing lapses when a person is in a high-risk situation. Kadden (2005) has published a protocol on coping skills training, which can be downloaded from http://www.bhrm.org/guidelines/CBT-Kadden.pdf.

ESSENTIAL ELEMENTS OF RP

In general, how a therapist conducts an RP intervention will be influenced by a number of factors specific to each individual client and client problem. As shown throughout this book there are many techniques that are uniquely suited for certain problem areas and there are a few core elements of RP that are common across many areas. First, RP is grounded by a biopsychosocial model (Donovan, 1996), in which there are multiple factors influencing behavior: biological factors (including genetic, cellular, neuronal, and physiological influences), psychological factors (including cognitions and learning history), and social factors (including interpersonal relationships and social support systems).

The initial goal of any RP intervention is to identify and discuss high risk situations for lapse and relapse. Often this will necessitate some psychoeducation regarding the lapse process and assessment of prior lapse/relapse episodes. Working in collaboration the therapist and client should identify potential triggers and attempt to make connections between the triggers (e.g., is the client primarily triggered by affective, social, or physical stimuli). Some clients will have insight into their triggers and be able to easily identify high-risk situations. Other clients may have little to no insight into their lapse triggers and will require a more detailed interview to generate potential high-risk situations. For clients who struggle to identify triggers it may be helpful to describe the theory of apparently irrelevant decisions (Jenkins-Hall & Marlatt, 1989), which is based on the notion that individuals make decisions that initiate the lapse process well before they realize the process was triggered.

After high-risk situations are identified it is critical to examine each situation paying special attention to related triggers and potential strategies for coping with the situation. Craving is defined for clients as a longing or desire to use a substance and urges are defined as the intention to use substances. Clients often find they have a strong craving with no intention to use or may also experience strong craving and a strong intention to use. Experiencing both craving and an urge to use makes the client vulnerable to relapse unless the client uses a coping strategy to reduce or eliminate the urge. Many people find that being aware of situations that tend to elicit cravings and developing ways of coping with cravings in those situations can greatly reduce the risk of relapse. It is also important to validate the client's experience and recognize that using substances can be a means of coping with difficult times and emotions, but oftentimes substance use is a temporary solution that may cause more problems. One of the main goals of RP is to develop *effective* means for coping with risky situations, craving, and diffi-cult emotions.

Coping with Lapses

The occurrence of a lapse cannot be viewed as a totally benign event and the most dangerous period is the time immediately following the initial lapse. In the following section we provide a few recommended strategies/emergency proce-dures to be used in case a lapse occurs. The strategies are listed in order of tem-poral priority, with the most important immediate steps listed first.

(1) *Stop, look, and listen.* The first thing to do when a lapse occurs is to *stop* the ongoing flow of events and to *look* and *listen* to what is happening. The lapse is a warning signal indicating that the client is in danger.

(2) *Keep calm.* Just because the client slipped does not indicate failure. Look upon the slip as a single event, something that can be avoided in the future. A slip is a mistake, an opportunity for learning, not a sign of total failure.

(3) *Renew commitment.* After a lapse, the most difficult problem to deal with is motivation. The client may feel like giving up and may need a reminder of the long-range benefits to be gained from this change. Clients should be encouraged to reflect optimistically on their past successes in being able to quit the old habit, instead of focusing on current setbacks.

(4) *Review the situation leading up to the lapse.* Look at the slip as a specific unique event. The following questions may help clarify the lapse episode: What events led up to the slip? Were there any early warning signals that preceded the lapse? What was the nature of the high-risk situation that trig-gered the slip? Each of these questions may yield valuable information con-cerning sources of stress and high-risk situations for the client. The fact that a slip occurred often is an event that tells you that something is going on that needs attending to.

(5) *Make an immediate plan for recovery.* After a slip, renewed commitments should be turned into a plan of action to be carried out immediately. Thera-pists can help clients identify Emergency Action Plans, which may include a crisis hotline telephone number, an alternative activity, or a trustworthy friend.

(6) *Dealing with the Abstinence Violation Effect.* The cognitive restructuring process designed to assist clients to cope with a lapse after a period of absti-nence or controlled use includes the following points:

a. Teach clients not to view the cause of the lapse as a personal failure or as a lack of willpower, but instead ask them to pay attention to the environ-mental and psychological factors in the high-risk situation, to review what coping skills they had available but didn't implement, and to notice how they felt decreased self-efficacy when they couldn't deal with the situation adequately.

b. Clients may need help to deal with the inevitable feelings of guilt and shame and the cognitive dissonance that usually accompany a lapse. Guilt and shame reactions are particularly dangerous because they are likely to motivate further substance use or other addictive behaviors as a means of coping with these unpleasant reactions to the slip.

c. After the lapse has occurred, the RP approach is to react to the client with compassion and understanding, but with the encouragement to learn everything possible about how to cope with similar situations in the future by a thorough debriefing of the lapse and its consequences.

d. Help clients identify any of the cognitive distortions they may succumb to in exposing themselves to the high-risk situation, limiting their ability to engage in an effective coping response, and finally, making the decision to choose to take that first drink, dose of drugs, or to engage in criminal activity.

RP FOR CO-OCCURRING DISORDERS

As described in detail in the next chapter, relapse is a complex process and the prevention of relapse requires individualized attention to the entire process. This is especially true for individuals with co-occurring disorders, who may be remitted from one or both disorders, and who may experience unique challenges on the path to recovery (Drake, Wallach & McGovern, 2005). For example, individuals with severe mental illness and substance use disorders have increased vulnerability for relapse because of cognitive and/or social skills deficits; dependence on others for care, housing, and/or employment; and numerous other contextual factors. A recent review by Bradizza and colleagues (Bradizza, Stasiewicz & Paas, 2006) reported rates of mood and comorbid substance use disorders range from 16% (comorbid depression and alcohol use disorder) to 56% (bipolar and alcohol or drug use disorder), odds of those diagnosed with any anxiety disorder being diagnosed with an alcohol use disorder was 50%, and 20 to 65% of individuals with severe mental illness were also diagnosed with an alcohol or drug use disorder.

The interested reader is referred to a recent special issue of the journal *Psychiatric Services*, which provides an excellent overview on the research and treatment of individuals with co-occurring substance abuse and severe mental illness (Drake, Wallach & McGovern, 2005; McGovern, Wrisley & Drake, 2005; Xie, McHugo, Fox & Drake, 2005). As described by many of the authors in the series it is often necessary to adapt the skills training modules of RP to accommodate the pervasive cognitive and social deficits because "individual relapse prevention skills by themselves seem insufficient to sustain abstinence" (Harris, Fallot & Berley, 2005, p. 1292). Oftentimes the housing and support needs for individuals with co-occurring disorders need to be a primary component of treatment. Unemployment and poor cognitive abilities may also be an indicator of major neuropsychological deficits, which may cause heightened sensitivity to substance cues and/or the biological effects of a substance (Drake, Wallach & McGovern, 2005).

SUMMARY AND CONCLUSIONS

As described in the following chapters of this book, relapse prevention (RP) has been an adjunct to the treatment of several behavior disorders and a useful tool for navigating the rough waters of maintaining behavior change. In the process of editing this book we have been amazed by the robustness of the research in this area and excited by the promising new findings presented throughout the remaining chapters. In the next chapter we provide an overview of the dynamic reconceptualization of the original relapse model proposed by Marlatt and colleagues. We view the new model as an "addition" to the existing model and it is not meant to replace the original model, which has been widely supported and implemented over the past 20 years.

REFERENCES

Abrams, K., Kushner, M.G. (2004). The moderating effects of tension-reduction alcohol outcome expectancies on placebo responding in individuals with social phobia. *Addictive Behaviors* **29**(6):1221–1224.

Alterman, A.I., O'Brien, C.P., McLellan, A., McKay, J.R. (2001). Cocaine and opioid abuse/dependence disorders. In Sutker, P.B., Adams, H.E., eds., *Comprehensive handbook of psychopathology, 3e*, 623–640. NY, US: Kluwer Academic/Plenum Publishers.

Armeli, S., Todd, M., Mohr, C. (2005). A daily process approach to individual differences in stress-related alcohol use. *Journal of Personality* **73**(6):1–30.

Baker, T.B., Piper, M.E., McCarthy, D.E., Majeskie, M.R., Fiore, M.C. (2003). Addiction motivation reformulated: An affective processing model of negative reinforcement. *Psychological Review* **111**:33–51.

Bradizza, C.M., Stasiewicz, P.R., Paas, N.D. (2006). Relapse to alcohol and drug use among individuals diagnosed with co-occurring mental health and substance use disorders: A review. *Clinical Psychology Review* **26**(2):162–178.

Brown, T.G., Seraganian, P., Tremblay, J., Annis, H. (2002). Process and outcome changes with relapse prevention versus 12-step aftercare programs for substance abusers. *Addiction* **97**(6): 677–689.

Burish, T.G., Maisto, S.A., Shirley, M.C. (1982). Effect of alcohol and stress on emotion and physiological arousal. *Motivation and Emotion* **6**(2):149–159.

Carels, R.A., Douglass, O.M., Cacciapaglia, H.M., O'Brien, W.H. (2004). An ecological momentary assessment of relapse crises in dieting. *Journal of Consulting and Clinical Psychology* **72**(2):341–348.

Chaney, E.F., O'Leary, M.R., Marlatt, G. (1978). Skill training with alcoholics. *Journal of Consulting and Clinical Psychology* **46**(5):1092–1104.

Connors, G.J., Maisto, S.A., Zywiak, W.H. (1996). Section IIB. Extensions of relapse predictors beyond high-risk situations: Understanding relapse in the broader context of post-treatment functioning. *Addiction* **91**(Suppl):S173–S189.

Corbin, W.R., McNair, L.D., Carter, J.A. (2001). Evaluation of a treatment-appropriate cognitive intervention for challenging alcohol outcome expectancies. *Addictive Behaviors* **26**(4): 475–488.

Currie, S.R., Hodgins, D.C., el-Guebaly, N., Campbell, W. (2001). Influence of depression and gender on smoking expectancies and temptations in alcoholics in early recovery. *Journal of Substance Abuse* **13**(4):443–458.

Curry, S., Marlatt, G., Gordon, J.R. (1987). Abstinence violation effect: Validation of an attributional construct with smoking cessation. *Journal of Consulting and Clinical Psychology* **55**(2): 145–149.

Demmel, R., Nicolai, J., Gregorzik, S. (2006). Alcohol expectancies and current mood state in social drinkers. *Addictive Behaviors* **31**(5):859–867.

Demmel, R., Rist, F. (2005). Prediction of treatment outcome in a clinical sample of problem drinkers: Self-efficacy and coping style. *Addictive Disorders & Their Treatment* **4**(1):5–10.

Donovan, D.M. (1996). Commentary on replications of Marlatt's taxonomy: Marlatt's classification of relapse precipitants: Is the emperor still wearing clothes? *Addiction* **91**(Suppl):S131–S137.

Drake, R.E., Wallach, M.A., McGovern, M.P. (2005). Special section on relapse prevention: Future directions in preventing relapse to substance abuse among clients with severe mental illnesses. *Psychiatric Services* **56**(10):1297–1302.

Drummond, D., Litten, R.Z., Lowman, C., Hunt, W.A. (2000). Craving research: Future directions. *Addiction* **95**(Suppl 2):S247–S255.

Edwards, G. (1987). Book Review of *Relapse Prevention*, edited by G. Alan Marlatt and J.R. Gordon. *British Journal of Addiction* **82**:319–323.

Fromme, K., Kivlahan, D.R., Marlatt, G. (1986). Alcohol expectancies, risk identification, and secondary prevention with problem drinkers. *Advances in Behaviour Research & Therapy* **8**(4): 237–251.

Grilo, C.M., Shiffman, S. (1994). Longitudinal investigation of the abstinence violation effect in binge eaters. *Journal of Consulting & Clinical Psychology* **62**(3):611–619.

Gwaltney, C.J., Shiffman, S., Balabanis, M.H., Paty, J.A. (2005). Dynamic self-efficacy and outcome expectancies: Prediction of smoking lapse and relapse. *Journal of Abnormal Psychology* **114**(4):661–675.

Hardoon, K.K., Gupta, R., Derevensky, J.L. (2004). Psychosocial variables associated with adolescent gambling. *Psychology of Addictive Behaviors* **18**(2):170–179.

Harris, M., Fallot, R.D., Berley, R.W. (2005). Special section on relapse prevention: Qualitative interviews on substance abuse relapse and prevention among female trauma survivors. *Psychiatric Services* **56**(10):1292–1296.

Jenkins-Hall, K.D., Marlatt, G. (1989). Apparently irrelevant decisions in the relapse process. In Laws, D.R., ed., *Relapse prevention with sex offenders*, 47–55. NY, US: Guilford Press.

Jones, B.T., McMahon, J. (1994). Negative alcohol expectancy predicts post-treatment abstinence survivorship: The whether, when and why of relapse to a first drink. *Addiction* **89**(12): 1653–1665.

Kadden, R.M. (1996). Commentary on replications of Marlatt's taxonomy: Is Marlatt's relapse taxonomy reliable or valid? *Addiction* **91**(Suppl):S139–S145.

King, L.L., Polaschek, D.L. (2003). The abstinence violation effect: Investigating lapse and relapse phenomena using the relapse prevention model with domestically violent men. *New Zealand Journal of Psychology* **32**(2):67–75.

Larimer, M.E., Palmer, R.S., Marlatt, G. (1999). Relapse prevention: An overview of Marlatt's cognitive-behavioral model. *Alcohol Research & Health* **23**(2):151–160.

Leigh, B.C., Stacy, A.W. (1994). Self-generated alcohol outcome expectancies in four samples of drinkers. *Addiction Research* **1**(4):335–348.

Lowman, C., Allen, J., Stout, R.L. (1996). Section II. Marlatt's taxonomy of high-risk situations for relapse: Replication and extension. *Addiction* **91**(Suppl):S51–S71.

Maisto, S.A., Clifford, P.R., Longabaugh, R., Beattie, M. (2002). The relationship between abstinence for one year following pretreatment assessment and alcohol use and other functioning at two years in individuals presenting for alcohol treatment. *Journal of Studies on Alcohol* **63**(4):397–403.

Maisto, S.A., Connors, G.J., Zywiak, W.H. (1996). Section IIA. Replication and extension of Marlatt's taxonomy: Construct validation analyses on the Marlatt typology of relapse precipitants. *Addiction* **91**(Suppl):S89–S97.

Maisto, S.A., Zywiak, W.H., Connors, G.J. (2006). Course of functioning 1 year following admission for treatment of alcohol use disorders. *Addictive Behaviors* **31**(1):69–79.

Marlatt, G.A. (1987). Alcohol, the magic elixir: Stress, expectancy, and the transformation of emotional states. In Gottheil, E., Druley, K., Pashko, S., Weinstein, S.P., eds., *Stress and addiction*, 302–322. PA, US: Brunner/Mazel, Inc.

Marlatt, G.A. (1996). Section I. Theoretical perspectives on relapse: Taxonomy of high-risk situations for alcohol relapse: Evolution and development of a cognitive-behavioral model. *Addiction* **91**(Suppl):S37–S49.

Marlatt, G.A., George, W.H. (1984). Relapse prevention: Introduction and overview of the model. *British Journal of Addiction* **79**:261–273.

Marlatt, G.A., Gordon, J. (1985). *Relapse Prevention*. New York: Guilford.

Marlatt, G.A., Kosturn, C.F., Lang, A.R. (1975). Provocation to anger and opportunity for retaliation as determinants of alcohol consumption in social drinkers. *Journal of Abnormal Psychology* **84**(6):652–659.

Marlatt, G.A., Nathan, P.E. (1978). *Behavioral approaches to alcoholism*. New Brunswick, NJ: Rutgers Center of Alcohol Studies.

Marlatt, G.A., Ostafin, B.D. (2006). Being Mindful of Automaticity in Addiction: A Clinical Perspective. In Wiers, R.W., Stacy, A.W., eds., *Handbook of implicit cognition and addiction*, 489–495. Thousand Oaks, US: Sage Publications, Inc.

McCrady, B.S., Epstein, E.E., Hirsch, L.S. (1999). Maintaining change after conjoint behavioral alcohol treatment for men: Outcomes at 6 months. *Addiction* **94**(9):1381–1396.

McCrady, B.S., Epstein, E.E., Kahler, C.W. (2004). Alcoholics Anonymous and relapse prevention as maintenance strategies after conjoint behavioral alcohol treatment for men: 18-month outcomes. *Journal of Consulting and Clinical Psychology* **72**(5):870–878.

McGovern, M.P., Wrisley, B.R., Drake, R.E. (2005). Special section on relapse prevention: Relapse of substance use disorder and its prevention among persons with co-occurring disorders. *Psychiatric Services* **56**(10):1270–1273.

Miller, W.R., Walters, S.T., Bennett, M.E. (2001). How effective is alcoholism treatment in the United States? *Journal of Studies on Alcohol* **62**, 211–220.

Miller, W.R., Wilbourne, P.L. (2002). Mesa Grande: A methodological analysis of clinical trials of treatment for alcohol use disorders. *Addiction* **97**(3):265–277.

Monti, P.M., Rohsenow, D.J., Michalec, E., Martin, R.A., Abrams, D.B. (1997). Brief coping skills treatment for cocaine abuse: Substance use outcomes at three months. *Addiction* **92**(12): 1717–1728.

Moos, R.H., Moos, B.S. (2005). Paths of entry into Alcoholics Anonymous: Consequences for participation and remission. *Alcoholism: Clinical and Experimental Research* **29**(10):1858–1868.

Moos, R.H., Moos, B.S. (2006). Rates and predictors of relapse after natural and treated remission from alcohol use disorders. *Addiction* **101**(2):212–222.

Moser, A.E., Annis, H.M. (1996). The role of coping in relapse crisis outcome: A prospective study of treated alcoholics. *Addiction* **91**(8):1101–1114.

O'Brien, C.P. (2005). Anticraving medications for relapse prevention: A possible new class of psychoactive medications. *American Journal of Psychiatry* **162**(8):1423–1430.

Palfai, T.P., Monti, P.M., Colby, S.M., Rohsenow, D.J. (1997). Effects of suppressing the urge to drink on the accessibility of alcohol outcome expectancies. *Behaviour Research and Therapy* **35**(1):59–65.

Quigley, L.A., Marlatt, G. (1999). Relapse prevention: Maintenance of change after initial treatment. In McCrady, B.S., Epstein, E.E., eds., *Addictions: A comprehensive guidebook*, 370–384. NY, US: Oxford University Press.

Richman, L.S., Kubzansky, L., Maselko, J., Kawachi, I., Choo, P., Bauer, M. (2005). Positive emotion and health: Going beyond the negative. *Health Psychology* **24**(4):422–429.

Rohsenow, D.J., Marlatt, G. (1981). The balanced placebo design: Methodological considerations. *Addictive Behaviors* **6**(2):107–122.

Room, R., Matzger, H., Weisner, C. (2004). Sources of informal pressure on problematic drinkers to cut down or seek treatment. *Journal of Substance Use* **9**(6):280–295.

Shiffman, S., Balabanis, M.H., Paty, J.A., Engberg, J., Gwaltney, C.J., Liu, K.S. et al. (2000). Dynamic effects of self-efficacy on smoking lapse and relapse. *Health Psychology* **19**(4): 315–323.

Shiffman, S., Hickcox, M., Paty, J.A., Gnys, M., Kassel, J.D., Richards, T.J. (1996). Progression from a smoking lapse to relapse: Prediction from abstinence violation effects, nicotine dependence, and lapse characteristics. *Journal of Consulting & Clinical Psychology* **64**(5):993–1002.

Stanton, M. (2005). Relapse prevention needs more emphasis on interpersonal factors. *American Psychologist* **60**(4):340–341.

Stout, R.L. (2000). What is a drinking episode? *Journal of Studies on Alcohol* **61**:455–461.

Stout, R.L., Longabaugh, R., Rubin, A. (1996). Section IIA. Replication and extension of Marlatt's taxonomy: Predictive validity of Marlatt's relapse taxonomy versus a more general relapse code. *Addiction* **91**(Suppl):S99–S110.

Sutton, S.R. (1979). Interpreting relapse curves. *Journal of Consulting and Clinical Psychology* **47**:96–98.

Wheeler, J.G., George, W.H., Marlatt, G.A. (In press). Relapse prevention for sexual offenders: Considerations for the "Abstinence Violation Effect." *Sexual Abuse: Journal of Research and Treatment*.

Wiers, R.W., Stacy, A.W., Ames, S.L., Noll, J.A., Sayette, M.A., Zack, M. et al. (2002). Implicit and explicit alcohol-related cognitions. *Alcoholism: Clinical and Experimental Research* **26**(1): 129–137.

Witkiewitz, K., Marlatt, G. (2004). Relapse prevention for alcohol and drug problems: That was Zen, this is Tao. *American Psychologist* **59**(4):224–235.

Witkiewitz, K., Marlatt, G. (2005). Emphasis on interpersonal factors in a dynamic model of relapse. *American Psychologist* **60**(4).341–342.

Witkiewitz, K., Marlatt, G., Walker, D. (2005). Mindfulness-based relapse prevention for alcohol and substance use disorders. *Journal of Cognitive Psychotherapy* **19**(3):211–228.

Xie, H., McHugo, G.J., Fox, M.B., Drake, R.E. (2005). Special section on relapse prevention: Substance abuse relapse in a ten-year prospective follow-up of clients with mental and substance use disorders. *Psychiatric Services* **56**(10):1282–1287.

Zautra, A.J., Johnson, L.M., Davis, M.C. (2005). Positive affect as a source of resilience for women in chronic pain. *Journal of Consulting & Clinical Psychology* **73**:212–220.

Zywiak, W.H., Connors, G.J., Maisto, S.A., Westerberg, V.S. (1996). Section IIA. Replication and extension of Marlatt's taxonomy: Relapse research and the reasons for drinking questionnaire: A factor analysis of Marlatt's relapse taxonomy. *Addiction* **91**(Suppl):S121–S130.

2

HIGH-RISK SITUATIONS: RELAPSE AS A DYNAMIC PROCESS

KATIE WITKIEWITZ

Department of Psychology
University of Illinois
Chicago, Illinois

G. ALAN MARLATT

Department of Psychology
University of Washington
Seattle, Washington

Relapse has been described as complex (Donovan, 1996; Shiffman, 1989), and this statement has been supported by numerous empirical investigations (Gwaltney, Shiffman, Balabanis & Paty, 2005; Hufford, Witkiewitz, Shields, Kodya & Caruso, 2003; Piasecki, Fiore, McCarthy & Baker, 2002; Warren, Hawkins & Sprott, 2003). The reconceptualization of the cognitive behavioral model of relapse, as described previously (Witkiewitz & Marlatt, 2004) and in this chapter, tries to accommodate this complexity by characterizing relapse as a fluid process of behavior change. The dynamic model of relapse is based on the underlying processes of the cognitive-behavioral model of relapse originally proposed by Marlatt (Marlatt, 1982; Marlatt & Gordon, 1985) and adds to the model an emphasis on the timing and interrelatedness of events. In this chapter we provide a basic overview of the new model as well as a discussion of the aspects of the model that are directly relevant to clinical practice.

Therapist's Guide to Evidence-Based
Relapse Prevention

19

COGNITIVE BEHAVIORAL MODEL OF
RELAPSE, REVISED

As described in the previous chapter and Marlatt's original writings on relapse (George & Marlatt, 1983; Marlatt & Gordon, 1985; Marlatt & Nathan, 1978) the main goal of a relapse prevention intervention and the central component of the cognitive-behavioral model of relapse is the identification of an individual's high-risk situations. High-risk situations are events, places, persons, emotions, behaviors, or cognitions that place an individual at increased risk for lapse or relapse. Importantly, across many of the problem behaviors described in this book the range of intensity and severity of high-risk situations can be highly variable and result in markedly different consequences. For example consider the problem of situational cues for individuals with eating disorders compared to individuals with an illicit drug use disorder. It is necessary for survival that people consume food and individuals are likely to habituate to most food cues, although some physical food cues (especially "forbidden" foods) will likely result in increased risk. For illicit drug use it is not necessary to be in contact with drugs, and individuals may be able to avoid physical drug cues, thus being in contact with any drug cue will be more likely to increase risk for a lapse. For both groups of individuals the emotional and physical cues can be severe and may be particularly strong when an individual is experiencing withdrawal (e.g., hunger or physical withdrawal from a drug). Given the large range of high-risk situations for each individual a large component of any treatment should incorporate a thorough functional assessment of high-risk situations at the individual level.

As shown in Figure 2.1, the dynamic model of relapse is almost wholly encompassed by a circle labeled "high-risk situations". The two other circles, tonic and phasic processes, are important for the timing of a lapse-relapse sequence and will be described in detail later. The model itself incorporates several interacting relapse risk factors, which are each predictive of the transgressive behavior (e.g., "substance use behavior") as well as each other. Reading the model from left to right, it starts with distal risks, which incorporate factors that predispose an individual to lapse and may be considered the background factors people bring with them to treatment. Distal risks are directly predictive of cognitive processes, physical withdrawal, coping, and lapses. Affective states are not directly predicted from distal risks, but are related indirectly through their relationship with cognitions, coping, and physical withdrawal. Cognitions and coping behaviors are also interrelated.

Feedback loops (indicated by double-headed arrows) are used to characterize the bidirectional relationship between cognitions and lapse, as well as affective state and lapse. Coping is shown as directly interrelated with lapse. The difference between a feedback loop and interrelatedness in the model is primarily a consideration of the distinction between the two processes. For example, a feedback look is used to describe the relationship between affective state and lapse

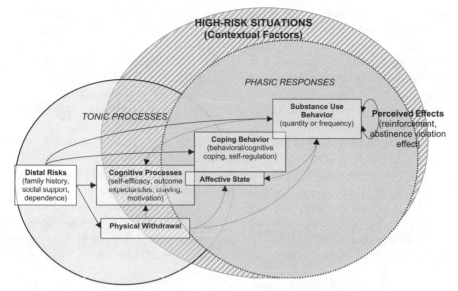

FIGURE 2.1: Dynamic Model of Relapse

because it is hypothesized that although the two are very highly related in either direction, there is a great deal of separation between the two with regard to operational definitions (e.g., anxiety is not a necessary condition for lapse and varying levels of anxiety at different times may or may not be related to lapse). An individual may be experiencing a great deal of negative affect, but not lapse. On the other hand, coping and lapse are shown as interrelated because "effective" coping often is defined primarily by whether the person lapses or not in a given high-risk situation. Thus, interrelatedness is indicated by the reliance of lapse outcome on evaluation of coping skills: an individual who lapses did not cope effectively in that particular high-risk situation and not lapsing in a particular high-risk situation is indicative of effective coping of some form.

HIGH-RISK SITUATIONS

High-risk situations, which are the contextual core of the model, can be either static or dynamic. Static situations are always risky (or not risky) for an individual and regardless of other factors the person will always be influenced by the situation in the same way. For example, the second author (GAM) had a client who lapsed following a visit to the street corner where the client previously had procured cocaine. The client reported that he would always lapse when he visited that particular environment. More often high-risk situations are dynamically influenced by a number of factors and are dependent upon initial conditions to be optimally risky. For example, hassles can be a high-risk situation for depressive relapse (Segal, Pearson & Thase, 2003), but daily hassles *may not be risky* for all individuals, particularly among those with higher self-esteem (Abela, Webb, Wagner, Moon-Ho & Adams, 2006). On the other hand, physical smoking cues are often risky for smokers who are trying to quit and are *especially risky* if the individual is also experiencing negative affect (Shiffman, Paty, Gnys, Kassel & Hickcox, 1996).

Static high-risk situations are often easier targets for intervention in that individually tailored lapse management plans can be developed and practiced with little ongoing modification. Dynamic high-risk situations are more likely to catch an individual off-guard and can seemingly appear out of nowhere. Responding to these situations and planning for these situations can be much more difficult. The remainder of this chapter focuses on dynamic high-risk situations and how therapists may use empirically derived theories of behavior and a complex conceptualization of relapse to better prepare clients for relapse risk.

TONIC PROCESSES

Reading Figure 2.1 from left to right, the first circle is designated *tonic processes*, a term borrowed from medicine, neuroscience, and other fields. Tonic activity is defined as continuous or sustained activity (Grace, 2000) and in the dynamic model of relapse a tonic process is defined as chronic vulnerability (Witkiewitz & Marlatt, 2004). Within the dynamic model tonic processes include distal risks, cognitions, physical withdrawal, and affect. As described earlier, distal risks are predisposing factors for lapse. Some examples of distal risk include genetic factors and the severity and duration of the problem behavior. Cognitions that can be described as tonic processes include cognitive attributions (including one's beliefs about abstinence), outcome expectancies, and baseline self-efficacy.

Physical withdrawal, self-efficacy, and negative affect, although often regarded as state variables, are considered partially tonic because there are set-points or baseline levels of physical withdrawal, self-efficacy, and affectivity for each individual. Increases (or spikes) in withdrawal and negative affect are considered as phasic processes, to be described next. For example, Gwaltney and colleagues (Gwaltney, Shiffman, Balabanis & Paty, 2005) found baseline self-efficacy to be uniquely predictive of smoking lapses in addition to the lapses predicted from daily variations in self-efficacy. Withdrawal dynamics have been described by Baker and his colleagues (Piasecki, Fiore, McCarthy & Baker, 2002) and are reviewed in detail later. These authors have data to support a model of withdrawal symptoms that takes into account both phasic withdrawal and underlying vulnerability for lapse given history of physical withdrawal experiences. With regard to affectivity it has long been known that individuals with affective disorders (e.g., anxiety or depression) are at increased risk for lapses, including alcohol lapses (Cornelius et al., 2004), smoking lapse (Kahler et al., 2002), and many types of illicit drug lapses (McLellan & Druley, 1977).

PHASIC PROCESSES

The second circle in Figure 2.1 is labeled phasic responses, which is defined as risk factors that are encountered as transient states or activating factors that precede a lapse (Witkiewitz & Marlatt, 2004). With regard to dopamine system activation and drug craving, Grace (2000) refers to a phasic release as a spike of dopamine into the synapse that causes "behaviorally relevant actions of dopamine system activation, such as those related to reward mechanisms" (p. 121). We postulate that this system and the cognitive-behavioral mechanisms described in the dynamic model of relapse are two sides of the same coin. For example, with respect to alcohol, situational cues may activate the dopamine system and make it more difficult for an individual to resist drinking. In support of this example it has been shown that combined therapy, which targets both neurobiology and cognitive-behavioral mechanisms, is the most effective treatment for individuals with alcohol dependence (Anton et al., 2006). The following section describes each of these mechanisms in detail.

As shown in the figure, physical withdrawal is included as a tonic and phasic process. In line with Baker and colleagues (2003) we define phasic withdrawal as physical and/or behavioral deprivation of a drug that lends itself to intense craving or urges to engage in the transgressive behavior. Piasecki and colleagues (Piasecki, Fiore, McCarthy & Baker, 2002) have done several investigations of the withdrawal process in smoking lapses and have demonstrated that self-reported withdrawal symptoms are highly variable within individuals, and the course of physical withdrawal after a quit attempt is highly variable between individuals. Thus most individuals experience volatility in withdrawal symptoms and few individuals report the same course of withdrawal symptoms over time. Interestingly in early clinical studies withdrawal was not shown to be a strong predictor of relapse (Patten & Martin, 1996), but withdrawal symptoms are a reliable predictor of smoking lapses when analyses take into account individual differences in withdrawal symptom profiles (Piasecki, 2006). Furthermore, relapse can be predicted by multiple measures of withdrawal, including phasic elevation and volatility in symptoms from day-to-day, as well as absolute magnitude of symptoms.

Negative affective states are consistently cited as primary predictors of lapse (Donovan, 1996; Drapkin, Wing & Shiffman, 1995; Marlatt & Gordon, 1985; O'Connell et al., 1998). As described earlier, continuous levels of higher negative affect are related to increased risk for relapse and momentary spikes in negative affect are especially related to lapse (Shiffman & Waters, 2004). Interestingly, when smokers are asked retrospectively about the cause of their lapse, the majority will cite the relief of negative affect and stress as the primary motive, but momentary prospective data does not consistently support this attribution (Shiffman et al., 2002). One hypothesis is that negative affect is so highly correlated with withdrawal symptoms that individuals are more likely to cite negative affect as the cause of relapse when assessed retrospectively, but prospectively describe acute withdrawal immediately preceding a lapse (Baker et al., 2004; Piasecki, 2006). Clinically relapse prevention interventions typically are designed to help clients identify negative affective states to prevent lapses, but the research data suggest a different emphasis may be necessary. Rather than just identifying negative affect state clients should also learn to identify the likely precursors to spikes in negative affect (e.g., arguments with a spouse or being stuck in traffic), vulnerability based on trait affectivity, as well as daily variation and increases in physical withdrawal.

Cognitive processes can be indirectly or directly related to lapse via a phasic response. Emerging research on implicit cognitions is particularly relevant when describing transient cognitive states (Palfai & Ostafin, 2003; Wiers, 2002; Wiers et al., 2002). For example, Gemar and colleagues (2001) used the implicit attitudes test to study negative mood and negative cognitive distortions in a group of formerly depressed individuals compared to a nondepressed and currently depressed group. The results suggest that even a minor negative mood induction predicted increased negative automatic processing for the formerly and currently depressed, but not for the never depressed controls. These studies point to a phasic model of cognitions in which thoughts related to the transgressive behavior can be so insidious as to go undetected by the client and certainly untapped by the clinician.

Coping in the moment of a high-risk situation has been shown to be a primary defense against relapse across many behavioral disorders (Carels, Douglass, Cacciapaglia & O'Brien, 2004; Lam, Hayward, Watkins, Wright & Sham, 2005; Lamberti, 2001; Moos & Moos, 2006; Smyth & Wiechelt, 2005; Stetson et al., 2005). Interestingly, changes in coping as part of a cognitive-behavioral intervention does not necessarily mediate outcomes, thus the mechanism of phasic coping remains unclear (Morgenstern & Longabaugh, 2000). One hypothesis is that coping and other cognitive and behavioral relapse precipitants (e.g., self-efficacy) are often highly intertwined and it is nearly impossible to determine which changes first in the prevention of lapse. Does active coping increase an individual's self-efficacy for lapse prevention? On the contrary, do decreases in self-efficacy immediately preceding a lapse result in less utilization of coping strategies? Further research using momentary assessment may help untangle these overlapping relationships and guide clinical practice (Gwaltney, Shiffman, Balabanis & Paty, 2005). Until more is learned about the details of the process it is safe to conclude that learning effective coping strategies is a critical component of any relapse prevention intervention and having greater coping resources cannot be harmful.

DYNAMICAL SYSTEMS PROCESSES

For almost 30 years addictive behaviors researchers have been referring to relapse as complex and some theoretical writings have mused about addiction and relapse as chaotic processes (Ehlers, 1992; Skinner, 1989; Zeeman, 1977). Chaos theory has become a popular phrase that is used often to describe phenomenon that are derived from the more general nonlinear dynamical systems theory. In the following section we highlight a few general processes in light of the recent empirical work that has provided support for a nonlinear dynamical conceptualization of relapse.

Sensitivity to initial conditions is one of the hallmark characteristics of chaos theory. Although many early mathematicians had been working on problems related to sensitive dependence on initial conditions, it was not until after a paper published in 1963 by Edward Lorenz that the phenomenon became more popular in math and science circles (Lorenz, 1963). Lorenz, who often is cited as the scientist that discovered the butterfly effect, was studying computer algorithms of weather patterns. As the story goes, Lorenz was simulating weather patterns using the same starting values and would arrive at the same weather patterns; however when he mistakenly altered a starting value by a small increment he simulated major changes in the predicted weather pattern. Thus, a small change in the initial conditions of the system produced major changes in the overall behavior of the system (Lorenz, 1993). The phrase "a butterfly flaps its wings in Tokyo and there is a tornado in Texas" is the classic example of Lorenz's finding.

Applied to the relapse process one must first consider: what is the initial condition? Skinner (1989) hypothesized genetic heritability as the initial condition, whereas Hufford and colleagues (Hufford, Witkiewitz, Shields, Kodya & Caruso, 2003) focused more generally on distal risks as the initial condition. Hufford et al. (2003) found minor changes in distal risks were related to large, divergent changes in outcome. It is likely that the initial conditions are actually multi-dimensional over the duration of a behavioral problem and throughout the relapse process. In a recent study by Witkiewitz and colleagues (2006), we found sensitivity to baseline levels of self-efficacy in the prediction of drinking behavior at six and 12 months following treatment as the initial condition. In this study, small changes in baseline self-efficacy were related to major changes in percent of days abstinent following treatment, with the direction of that change determined by post-treatment self-efficacy. As demonstrated in numerous other studies lower self-efficacy was associated with fewer abstinent days.

Bifurcation and divergence are two properties of nonlinear dynamical systems that follow from initial conditions. Essentially the sensitivity in initial conditions manifests in bifurcations and subsequent divergence. Bifurcations can be defined as sudden changes that result in qualitatively different behaviors, and divergence can be defined as the path of behavior following the bifurcation. A simple metaphor is to consider the bifurcation as the fork in the road that provides two optional paths and divergence as the exponentially increasing distance between the two options after the fork. For example, individuals who are not in a lapse state (either abstaining or free from symptoms in the case of depression or psychosis) may experience some shock to the system (e.g., a negative event) and then either respond by maintaining the nonlapsed state or lapsing. If the individual lapsed, which is a qualitative change in the behavior, then a bifurcation occurred and the path of behavior after that lapse would be of primary interest. Based on clinical experience we tend to see one of two divergent pathways, either the person gets back on track after the lapse (i.e., prolapse) or they continue toward relapse. We hypothesize that this bifurcation point is a critical period for intervention, where the implementation of an effective coping strategy after the initial lapse can divert a major relapse. It is not always the case that a bifurcation point will occur during the course of treatment, but educating clients about these processes may better prepare them for dealing with lapse crises as they occur.

EMPIRICAL BASIS FOR DYNAMIC MODEL

CATASTROPHE MODELS

The Hufford et al. (2003) and Witkiewitz et al. (2006) studies used catastrophe theory, which is a type of nonlinear dynamical system (could be described as a cousin of chaos theory), to study drinking behavior following treatment for an alcohol use disorder. Catastrophe theory may be particularly useful for characterizing the nonnormality and discontinuity often observed in treatment outcome data (Hufford et al., 2003; Witkiewitz & Marlatt, 2004). Catastrophe theory is based on the topology of discontinuous change (Thom, 1975) and it is used to study behavior of a system that is driven toward equilibrium states. The cusp catastrophe model (the simplest form of the seven catastrophe types described by Thom, 1975) is characterized by three states: two stable states and one unstable state. The movement between these states depends on specific critical points as well as two variables controlling those critical points. The area between the two critical points is defined as the region of indeterminacy, because the state of the behavior cannot be known unless prior status is also known. Transitioning between the two stable states of behavior is called a phase transition.

Applying these concepts to relapse, it is hypothesized that at critical points of risk factors there are sudden changes in behavior. Thus, individuals with the same level of absolute risk may display qualitatively distinct behavior, depending on the direction of change and prior status. Current research on catastrophe models of relapse is limited by available methods for analyzing relapse dynamics as well as the lack of empirical data to provide a rigorous test of the model (McKay, Franklin, Patapis & Lynch, 2006). Potentially these methods could guide treatment by establishing cusp points or moments of instability during the relapse process given a set of observed risk factors.

WITHDRAWAL DYNAMICS

Baker, Piasecki, and colleagues (Baker, Piper, McCarthy, Majeskie & Fiore, 2004; Piasecki, Fiore, McCarthy & Baker, 2002) have done numerous investigations of the smoking relapse process in an effort to gain a better understanding of withdrawal symptoms, severity, and correlates with other predictors of smoking lapses (primarily negative affect). Their empirical work suggests withdrawal symptoms are highly variable across individuals and within individuals across time. Therefore clinicians may not be capable of preparing clients for volatile and overwhelming withdrawal symptoms following a quit attempt. Furthermore, for smoking lapses few precessation variables were predictive of postcessation withdrawal symptom dynamics, suggesting great susceptibility to events and situations during the recovery process.

Notably, "if one were to postulate a universal element of withdrawal that constitutes the aversive setting event for further drug self-administration or relapse [across all addictive drugs], it would be negative affect" (p. 36; Baker et al., 2004). This statement may be especially true for highly addictive drugs that do not produce intense physical withdrawal symptoms (e.g., cocaine and buprenorphine; Baker et al., 2004). The motivational model of Baker and colleagues (2004) thus emphasizes affective processing as the main driving force for drug use motivation. Recent data suggests withdrawal-related negative affect as a robust precipitant of lapses may be counteracted by prompting emotion regulation strategies (Piper & Curtin, 2006). Thus, behavioral treatments designed to improve negative affect regulation in high-risk situations could help prevent lapses in those situations. Interestingly, pharmacological agents designed to reduce withdrawal (such as the nicotine patch) may only ameliorate physical sensations of withdrawal and offer very little in the way of treating the affective-withdrawal symptom patterns (Piasecki, 2006). Given these findings it is not surprising that combined interventions, which include pharmacological and behavioral components, are the most effective at preventing smoking lapses following a quit attempt (Fiore et al., 2000).

DYNAMIC SELF-EFFICACY

Social learning theory was the primary basis for the original cognitive-behavioral model of relapse (Marlatt, Baer & Quigley, 1995), yet until recently few studies had investigated the role of individual variation in self-efficacy immediately preceding a lapse. Advancements in assessment technology and data analytic techniques has allowed researchers to quantify self-efficacy in the moments immediately preceding and following a lapse (Gwaltney, Shiffman, Balabanis & Paty, 2005; Shiffman et al., 2000). Using ecological momentary assessment these researchers have been able to demonstrate dynamic changes in abstinence self-efficacy across situations (Gwaltney, Shiffman, Balabanis & Paty, 2005) and over time (Gwaltney, Shiffman, Balabanis & Paty, 2005). Thus, reductions in self-efficacy in the days and moments preceding a smoking lapse may serve as warning signs for increased lapse likelihood in the context of a high-risk situation.

Focusing on situation-specific self-efficacy, Gwaltney et al. (2002) found that individuals make situation-specific ratings of their abstinence self-efficacy and the situations that elicit the lowest momentary self-efficacy ratings are the highest risk situations for a lapse, regardless of overall self-efficacy (Gwaltney et al., 2002). Based on these results, interventions that are designed to increase self-efficacy may be successful only when delivered at times the individual is in a situation that elicits low self-efficacy ratings. As part of a relapse prevention, intervention clients could be trained to monitor self-efficacy judgments on a daily basis and clinicians could help clients generate coping plans for low self-efficacy situations.

The results from Shiffman, Gwaltney, and colleagues are based on correlational research questions and the observed behavior of individuals who recently quit or were planning to quit smoking, thus one may ask whether their findings would be supported if self-efficacy was experimentally manipulated. To address this question Shadel and Cervone (2006) conducted an experimental test of self-efficacy appraisals in an experimental context. Specifically, the researchers assessed whether cognitively primed schemas of "abstainer selves" versus a smoking self-schema would be related to self-efficacy and craving in smokers exposed to smoking cues (an analog for a high-risk situation). The results strongly supported the previous findings: higher levels of self-efficacy were consistently related to decreases in self-reported craving. Furthermore the researchers demonstrated an effect of the priming conditioning, with evidence that self-efficacy to resist smoking in high-craving situations was partially mediated by self-schema. Individuals who were primed with an abstainer self-schema experienced less craving and reported higher self-efficacy as compared to those primed with a smoker self-schema under the same cue conditions. These findings have potential implications for relapse prevention in that it may be possible to change self-schemas toward the "abstainer self" as part of a schema-based intervention (Shadel & Cervone, 2006).

SUDDEN GAINS AND QUANTUM CHANGES

Tang, DeRubeis, and others (Gaynor, Weersing, Kolko, Birmaher, Heo & Brent, 2003; Stiles et al., 2003; Tang & DeRubeis, 1999; Tang, DeRubeis, Beberman & Pham, 2005) have identified some individuals who undergo sudden improvements in depression severity in between treatment sessions and demonstrated that those who make large gains are significantly less depressed at the end of treatment and over a year following treatment. In the original Tang and DeRubeis (1999) study sudden gains was defined as a change in Beck Depression Inventory scores of 11 points or more from one session of cognitive-behavior therapy to the next. This finding was replicated using alternative definitions of "sudden gains" (Tang et al., 2005) and other treatment methods (Gaynor et al., 2003). These findings are relevant because they demonstrate the same effect of "falling off the wagon" that is often attributed to relapse, but in the opposite direction.

Likewise, Miller and C'De Baca (2002) have described "quantum changes" in the area of substance abuse. Miller (2004) defines quantum change as the "sudden, dramatic, and enduring transformations that affect a broad range of personal emotion, cognition, and behavior" (p. 453). The research on sudden gains and quantum changes are each describing a nonlinear, discontinuous change in behavior during the course of psychotherapy. People do not change in predictable, continuous ways. They take a few steps forward and a few more steps back and then a few more steps forward, yet oftentimes clients expect changes to be instantaneous and constant. Drawing from the current research on relapse dynamics and sudden gains it makes good clinical sense to educate clients about the discontinuity in the change process.

CLINICAL CASE ILLUSTRATION

We conclude with a case summary that provides an example of how the dynamic model of relapse may be used in clinical practice.

CASE SUMMARY

Jill B. was a 49-year-old unemployed, divorced, Caucasian female who initially presented at a low-fee voluntary outpatient general psychotherapy clinic needing help in reducing her drinking. Jill had a long history of polysubstance abuse but she had not used illicit drugs for over 15 years and she had successfully moderated her drinking for almost 13 years. It was only in the past two years, following her second divorce, that she started drinking heavily again. Up until six months prior to her presentation at the clinic she was successfully employed as a business executive earning a substantial income. She attributes the loss of her job to fatigue and irritability. After losing her job, Jill's daily ritual was to wake up in the morning feeling determined to not drink that day. She would then exercise, write in her journal and work on job-hunting in the afternoon. By late-afternoon she would start thinking about how much she "deserved a drink," and this entitlement was based on either celebration (e.g., landing an interview) or devastation (e.g., being turned down for another job). She would proceed to walk to a local market, purchase an expensive bottle of wine and then drink the bottle throughout the afternoon and evening.

After several weeks of functional analysis we conceptualized her pattern as including abrupt changes in affect (either positive or negative) and activation of an alcoholic "deserving a drink" self-schema. It became clear that the abrupt changes in effect often occurred in the early evening and were possibly triggered by her thinking about going to happy hour after work. The sheer awareness of this pattern helped Jill moderate her drinking substantially. We then worked on affect regulation strategies and building the self-schema of being a successful professional who was currently unemployed. By the end of treatment she was able to restrict her drinking to one to two glasses of wine on weekend evenings in the presence of friends.

This case highlights several aspects of the dynamic model. The phasic interrelation between affect and cognition (outcome expectancies) was notable and largely activated by a tonic self-schema. The process unfolded during the high-risk situation of the time being 5 P.M. and Jill's thoughts about happy hour. Given this outline of processes an intervention was developed that introduced a new self-schema (removing the tonic influence) and provided training in affective regulation (reducing the phasic influence of abrupt changes in affect). Considering Jill encountered her high risk situation daily (every time she noticed the time was after 5 P.M.), it was particularly helpful to focus on the total process rather than solely targeting avoidance of, or coping with, the high-risk situation.

SUMMARY OF CLINICAL IMPLICATIONS

Research on the dynamic model of relapse is truly in its infancy and considerably more empirical tests need to be conducted on the hypothesized mechanisms and components of the model. We have presented a theoretical organization of relapse risk factors and how these variables may influence a complex relapse process, but we recognize that much more basic and clinical research needs to be conducted. It is our hope that practitioners will take the empirical data on basic mechanisms of relapse processes and convert that knowledge into empirically based RP techniques. Undoubtedly the processes described in this chapter are not likely to be the same for all individuals entering treatment and an idiographic assessment is a critical component of any RP intervention.

DYNAMIC RELAPSE MODEL AND NONSUBSTANCE USE BEHAVIOR

As alluded to throughout this chapter and seen throughout this book, the dynamic model of relapse has direct application to other types of lapsing behaviors. The important consideration for researchers or clinicians who are interested in applying aspects of the dynamic model to nonsubstance use behavior is to review the relevant literature specific to that lapsing behavior and make testable hypotheses regarding the factors that may be dynamically influencing the relapse process. For depression and anxiety relapse it is likely that negative affect and lapse is interrelated (not just a feedback loop as described earlier) in the same way that coping and lapse were interrelated in the substance use model. For schizophrenia the influence of social factors (including social support and social skills) and/or biological factors (e.g., medication issues) are likely to be primary antecedents to lapse episodes. Researchers and clinicians are encouraged to take the dynamic model we described in the current chapter as one means for characterizing the relapse process, but certainly the distal and proximal risk factors, and tonic and phasic processes are likely to be highly unique to each type of lapsing behavior.

REFERENCES

Abela, J.R.Z., Webb, C.A., Wagner, C., Moon-Ho, R.H., Adams, P. (2006). The role of self-criticism, dependency, and hassles in the course of depressive illness: A multiwave longitudinal study. *Personality and Social Psychology Bulletin* **32**(3):328–338.

Anton, R.F., O'Malley, S.S., Ciraulo, D.A., Cisler, R.A., Couper, D., Donovan, D.M. et al. (2006). Combined pharmacotherapies and behavioral interventions for alcohol dependence. *JAMA* **295**:2003–2017.

Baker, T.B., Piper, M.E., McCarthy, D.E., Majeskie, M.R., Fiore, M.C. (2004). Addiction motivation reformulated: An affective processing model of negative reinforcement. *Psychological Review* **111**:33–51.

Carels, R.A., Douglass, O.M., Cacciapaglia, H.M., O'Brien, W.H. (2004). An ecological momentary assessment of relapse crises in dieting. *Journal of Consulting and Clinical Psychology* **72**(2):341–348.

Cornelius, J.R., Maisto, S.A., Martin, C.S., Bukstein, O.G., Salloum, I.M., Daley, D.C. et al. (2004). Major depression associated with earlier alcohol relapse in treated teens with AUD. *Addictive Behaviors* **29**(5):1035–1038.

Donovan, D.M. (1996). Section I. Theoretical perspectives on relapse: Assessment issues and domains in the prediction of relapse. *Addiction* **91**(Suppl):S29–S36.

Drapkin, R.G., Wing, R.R., Shiffman, S. (1995). Responses to hypothetical high risk situations: Do they predict weight loss in a behavioral treatment program or the context of dietary lapses? *Health Psychology* **14**(5):427–434.

Ehlers, C.L. (1992). The new physics of chaos: Can it help us understand the effects of alcohol? *Alcohol Health & Research World* **16**:169–176.

George, W.H., Marlatt, G. (1983). Alcoholism: The evolution of a behavioral perspective. *Recent Developments in Alcoholism* **1**:105–138.

Grace, A.A. (2000). The tonic/phasic model of dopamine system regulation and its implications for understanding alcohol and psychostimulant craving. *Addiction* **95**(Suppl. 2):S119–S128.

Gwaltney, C.J., Shiffman, S., Balabanis, M.H., Paty, J.A. (2005). Dynamic self-efficacy and outcome expectancies: Prediction of smoking lapse and relapse. *Journal of Abnormal Psychology* **114**(4):661–675.

Hufford, M.R., Witkiewitz, K., Shields, A.L., Kodya, S., Caruso, J.C. (2003). Relapse as a nonlinear dynamic system: Application to patients with alcohol use disorders. *Journal of Abnormal Psychology* **112**(2):219–227.

Kahler, C.W., Brown, R.A., Ramsey, S.E., Niaura, R., Abrams, D.B., Goldstein, M.G. et al. (2002). Negative mood, depressive symptoms, and major depression after smoking cessation treatment in smokers with a history of major depressive disorder. *Journal of Abnormal Psychology* **111**(4):670–675.

Lam, D.H., Hayward, P., Watkins, E.R., Wright, K., Sham, P. (2005). Relapse prevention in patients with bipolar disorder: Cognitive therapy outcome after 2 years. *American Journal of Psychiatry* **162**(2):324–329.

Lamberti, J. (2001). Seven keys to relapse prevention in schizophrenia. *Journal of Psychiatric Practice Vol* 7(4):253–259.

Lorenz, E.N. (1963). Deterministic nonperiodic flow. *Journal of Atmospheric Sciences* **20**: 130–141.

Lorenz, E.N. (1993). *The essence of chaos.* Seattle, WA: University of Washington Press.

Marlatt, G.A. (1982). Research and treatment with alcohol problems: Frontiers for the eighties. *Bulletin of the Society of Psychologists in Substance Abuse* 1(4):145–150.

Marlatt, G.A., Baer, J.S., Quigley, L.A. (1995). Self-efficacy and addictive behavior. In Bandura, A., ed., *Self-efficacy in changing societies*, 289–315. New York: Cambridge University Press.

Marlatt, G.A., Gordon, J. (1985). *Relapse Prevention.* New York: Guilford.

Marlatt, G.A., Nathan, P.E. (1978). *Behavioral approaches to alcoholism.* New Brunswick, NJ: Rutgers Center of Alcohol Studies.

McKay, J.R., Franklin, T.R., Patapis, N., Lynch, K.G. (2006). Conceptual, methodological, and analytical issues in the study of relapse. *Clinical Psychology Review* 26(2):109–127.

McLellan, A., Druley, K.A. (1977). Non-random relation between drugs of abuse and psychiatric diagnosis. *Journal of Psychiatric Research* 13(3):179–184.

Miller, W.R. (2004). The phenomenon of quantum change. *Journal of Clinical Psychology* 60(5):453–460.

Miller, W.R., C'De Baca, J. (2002). Quantum change: When epiphanies and sudden insights transform ordinary lives. *Journal of Psychiatry & Law* 30(3) *Fall*:395–399.

Moos, R.H., Moos, B.S. (2006). Rates and predictors of relapse after natural and treated remission from alcohol use disorders. *Addiction* 101(2):212–222.

Morgenstern, J., Longabaugh, R.L. (2000). Cognitive–behavioral treatment for alcohol dependence: A review of evidence for its hypothesized mechanisms of action. *Addiction* 95:1475–1490.

O'Connell, K.A., Gerkovich, M.M., Cook, M.R., Shiffman, S., Hickcox, M., Kakolewski, K.E. (1998). Coping in real time: Using Ecological Momentary Assessment techniques to assess coping with the urge to smoke. *Research in Nursing & Health* 21(6):487–497.

Palfai, T.P., Ostafin, B.D. (2003). The influence of alcohol on the activation of outcome expectancies: The role of evaluative expectancy activation in drinking behavior. *Journal of Studies on Alcohol* 64(1):111–119.

Patten, C.A., Martin, J.E. (1996). Does nicotine withdrawal affect smoking cessation? Clinical and theoretical issues. *Annals of Behavioral Medicine* 18:190–200.

Piasecki, T.M., Fiore, M.C., McCarthy, D.E., Baker, T.B. (2002). Have we lost our way? The need for dynamic formulations of smoking relapse proneness. *Addiction* 97(9):1093–1108.

Segal, Z.V., Pearson, J.L., Thase, M.E. (2003). Challenges in preventing relapse in major depression report of a National Institute of Mental Health Workshop on state of the science of relapse prevention in major depression. *Journal of Affective Disorders* 77(2):97–108.

Shiffman, S. (1989). Conceptual issues in the study of relapse. In Gossop, M., ed., *Relapse and addictive behaviour*, 149–179. New York: Tavistock/Routledge.

Shiffman, S., Balabanis, M.H., Paty, J.A., Engberg, J., Gwaltney, C.J., Liu, K.S. et al. (2000). Dynamic effects of self-efficacy on smoking lapse and relapse. *Health Psychology* 19(4):315–323.

Shiffman, S., Gwaltney, C.J., Balabanis, M.H., Liu, K.S., Paty, J.A., Kassel, J.D. et al. (2002). Immediate antecedents of cigarette smoking: An analysis from ecological momentary assessment. *Journal of Abnormal Psychology* 111(4):531–545.

Shiffman, S., Paty, J.A., Gnys, M., Kassel, J.A., Hickcox, M. (1996). First lapses to smoking: Within-subjects analysis of real-time reports. *Journal of Consulting & Clinical Psychology* 64(2): 366–379.

Shiffman, S., Waters, A.J. (2004). Negative affect and smoking lapses: A prospective analysis. *Journal of Consulting & Clinical Psychology* 72(2):192–201.

Skinner, H.A. (1989). Butterfly wings flapping: Do we need more "chaos" in understanding addictions. *British Journal of Addiction* 84:353–356.

Smyth, N.J., Wiechelt, S.A. (2005). Drug use, self-efficacy, and coping skills among people with concurrent substance abuse and personality disorders: Implications for relapse prevention. *Journal of Social Work Practice in the Addictions* **5**(4):63–79.

Stetson, B.A., Beacham, A.O., Frommelt, S.J., Boutelle, K.N., Cole, J.D., Ziegler, C.H. et al. (2005). Exercise slips in high-risk situations and activity patterns in long-term exercisers: An application of the relapse prevention model. *Annals of Behavioral Medicine* **30**(1):25–35.

Thom, R. (1975). *Stabilité structurelle et morphogenèse* (Structural stability and morphogenesis). Reading: Benjamin.

Warren, K., Hawkins, R.C., Sprott, J.C. (2003). Substance abuse as a dynamical disease: Evidence and clinical implications of nonlinearity in a time series of daily alcohol consumption. *Addictive Behaviors* **28**(2):369–374.

Wiers, R.W. (2002). Half full or half empty, what are we drinking? Some comments on the discussion of the causal role of alcohol expectancies as a mechanism of change. *Addiction* **97**(5): 599–600.

Wiers, R.W., Stacy, A.W., Ames, S.L., Noll, J.A., Sayette, M.A., Zack, M. et al. (2002). Implicit and explicit alcohol-related cognitions. *Alcoholism: Clinical and Experimental Research* **26**(1): 129–137.

Witkiewitz, K., Marlatt, G. (2004). Relapse prevention for alcohol and drug problems: That was Zen, this is Tao. *American Psychologist* **59**(4):224–235.

Zeeman, E.C. (1977). Catastrophe theory. *Scientific American* **234**:65 83.

SECTION II

APPLICATION OF RELAPSE PREVENTION TO SPECIFIC PROBLEM AREAS

3

RELAPSE PREVENTION: CLINICAL STRATEGIES FOR SUBSTANCE USE DISORDERS

ANTOINE DOUAIHY,
KEITH R. STOWELL, AND
TAE WOO PARK

Western Psychiatric Institute and Clinic
Pittsburgh, Pennsylvania

DENNIS C. DALEY

University of Pittsburgh Medical Center
Pittsburgh, Pennsylvania

INTRODUCTION

Overall, an estimated 22.5 million Americans aged 12 and older in 2004 were classified with substance dependence or abuse (9.4% of the population) according to the 2003 data from the National Survey on Drug Use and Health (SAMSHA, 2004). Including the cost of healthcare, productivity loss, and crime, the yearly costs associated with illicit drug use and alcohol use disorders was estimated at $180 billion and $185 billion, respectively (Harwood, 2004). Of course, the economic costs cannot completely capture the heavy emotional and psychological burden that substance use disorders (SUDs) can have on individuals, their families, and significant others.

Existing data indicate that individuals with SUDs face the possibility of relapse once they stop using alcohol or other drugs even if they have a successful treatment episode (NIAAA, 2000). For many individuals with SUDs, substance use leads to a chronic cycle of relapse, treatment reentry, and recovery, often lasting for decades. Therefore, greater emphasis has been placed on identifying clinical strategies to reduce the likelihood of a relapse and to manage actual relapse in order to minimize adverse effects in cases in which an individual returns to substance use following a period of recovery.

Relapse prevention (RP) is a cognitive-behavioral approach that combines behavioral skills training procedures with cognitive intervention techniques to assist persons in maintaining desired behavioral changes. Based in part upon the principles of health psychology and social-cognitive theory, the typical treatment goal of RP in SUDs is either to refrain totally from using substances or to reduce the harm of or risk of ongoing lapse, therefore preventing further relapse. RP strategies often are incorporated into individual and group treatment approaches (see NIAAA and NIDA treatment manuals on psychosocial treatments). In addition, RP programs are sometimes offered as part of a rehabilitation, partial hospital, intensive outpatient, or outpatient program. For example, the MATRIX model of treatment provides numerous RP groups in addition to individual sessions, early recovery skills groups, family education, and a social support group (Rawson, Obert, McCann & Ling, 2005). Both the Individual Drug Counseling (NIDA, 1999) and Group Drug Counseling (NIDA, 2002) models of treatment focus considerable attention on RP issues in the context of individual and group treatment sessions. Many structured residential and ambulatory programs incorporate a RP track into their group program to educate clients and help them learn coping skills to reduce relapse risk as well as to intervene early in a lapse or relapse.

This chapter summarizes the major tenets of RP including the concepts of lapse, relapse, and recovery, and the hypothesized common relapse precipitants and determinants. We also provide a discussion on treatment outcome literature and empirical data incorporating RP techniques. Models of RP are reviewed. We also present highlights of RP assessment and intervention strategies representing the most common principles espoused in the RP models. Finally, we propose future research initiatives and their relevance to clinical settings.

OVERVIEW OF LAPSE, RELAPSE, AND RECOVERY

One of the most difficult issues that continues to create an ongoing debate is the way *relapse* is defined. So what really constitutes relapse? As Einstein (1994) stated: "At what point is a return to a defined pattern of single/multiple substance use relapse as well as what are the coping/adaptational and treatment implications of the definition(s)?" The complexity of this issue has evolved throughout the years and multiple definitions and meanings of the term relapse were suggested (Litman et al., 1983; Miller, 1996; Saunders et al., 1989; Wilson, 1992). Marlatt has identified a conceptual distinction between *lapse*, which he described as the initial episode of alcohol or other drug use after a period of abstinence (Marlatt & Gordon, 1985), and a *relapse*, as continued use after the initial lapse, "a break-down or setback in the person's attempt to change or modify any target behavior" (Marlatt, 1985a, p. 3). Other definitions have included: (1) a process that slowly and gradually leads to the initiation of substance use or engagement in the behavior after a period of abstinence; (2) descriptive presence or absence of the behavior, the behavior exceeding a certain threshold, and a judgment about the behavior in the context of individual and societal standards (Miller, 1996); (3) a consequence of substance use resulting in the need for subsequent treatment (e.g., recidivism) (Donovan, 1996); (4) an "unfolding process in which the resumption of substance use is the last event in a long series of maladaptive responses to internal or external stressors or stimuli" (NIDA's Cue Extinction (CE) model; NIDA, 1993, p. 39); (5) a complex multidimensional composite indices of outcome/relapse, taking into account the different aspects of return to problematic behavior and the presence or absence of related consequences that go beyond the simple concept of abstinence-lapse-relapse and fit more into the concept of a harm reduction approach (Marlatt & Witkiewitz, 2002; Zweben & Cisler, 2003).

It has been shown that a lapse does not necessarily herald a full-blown relapse in users of opiates (Gossop et al., 1989) and tobacco (Gwantley et al., 2005). Milby et al. (2004) compared behavioral day treatment (DT) with the same day treatment plus abstinent contingent housing and work (DT+) in cocaine users and found that the DT+ subjects who lapsed were actually less likely to relapse. This indicates that the lapse event could be perceived as a crossroads. Based on different rates of relapse using different definitions and diverse conceptual and methodological approaches involved in understanding the process of relapse, it is clear that relapse is better understood as both a dichotomous outcome and a process involving a series of prior related events and the predictors of these events interfering with behavior change (Daley & Marlatt, 2005, 2006a; Wang et al., 2002). Therefore a dynamic, not static, conceptual and clinical assessment model would potentially capture all the elements of relapse as it unfolds across time (Donovan, 1996a; Hufford, Witkiewitz et al., 2003; Shiffman et al., 2000; Witkiewitz & Marlatt, 2004). Determining and addressing both the immediate variables and the distal variables remain essential to the process of preventing a lapse episode from evolving into a full-blown relapse (Miller et al., 1996; Moser & Annis et al., 1996; Vielva & Iraurgi et al., 2001). In addition, a recent review exploring gender differences in alcohol and substance use relapse showed that for women, marriage and marital stress were risk factors for alcohol relapse and among men, marriage lowered relapse risk (Walitzer & Dearing, 2006). In contrast to the lack of gender differences in alcohol relapse rates, this review also showed that women appear to be less likely to experience relapse to substance use, relative to men.

Multiple epidemiological studies of people with lifetime substance dependence suggest that 58 percent eventually enter sustained recovery (i.e., no symptoms for the past year), a rate that is considerably better than the 39 percent average rate of recovery across psychiatric disorders (Kessler, 1994; McLellan, Lewis & O'Brien, 2000; Robins & Rigier, 1991). Of the people who eventually achieved a state of sustained recovery, the majority did so after participating in treatment (Cunningham, Lin, Ross & Walsh, 2000).

Recovery is defined as a long-term and ongoing process rather than an endpoint (Dimeff & Marlatt, 1995; NIDA, 1999). Specific areas of change during the process of recovery include physical, psychological, behavioral, interpersonal, spiritual, socio-cultural, familial, and financial (Daley & Marlatt, 2006a, 2006b). Recovery tasks depend on the stage and recovery the individual is in (Washton, 2001, 2002). Recovering from SUD involves psychoeducation, focusing on involvement in a program of change including learning coping skills, and staying engaged in treatment for long enough to benefit from it. The program of change may also incorporate psychotherapy, pharmacotherapy, case management, participation in self-help groups, and self-management goals. As recovery progresses, clients rely more on themselves after initially utilizing support from family, significant others, and health care professionals, with the goal of improving their overall quality of life. In fact, Flynn et al. (2003) studied a group of opiate users five years after treatment and compared those who were in recovery and those who were not. The subjects in recovery were more likely to benefit from family and friends as a support group and were more likely to agree that their social network did not include people with SUDs. The subjects in recovery were nearly four times more likely to perceive themselves as improving their overall personal growth and ability to lead a constructive and fulfilling lifestyle.

TREATMENT OUTCOMES AND RELAPSE RATES

Despite the fact that longitudinal studies have repeatedly demonstrated that substance abuse treatment is associated with major reductions in substance abuse, other studies demonstrated that after discharge from treatment, relapse and eventual readmission are also common, particularly when addiction is coexisting with psychiatric disorders (Godley, Godley et al., 2002; Lash, Petersen et al., 2001). In addition, co-occurring psychiatric disorders are associated with higher substance use severity, more intensive level of care placements, lower treatment participation, and worse outcomes (American Society of Addiction Medicine, 2003; Angst, Sellaro et al., 2002; Daley & Moss, 2002; Grella, 2003; Mueser et al., 2003).

Miller and Hester (1980) reviewed more than 500 alcoholism outcome studies and reported that three-quarters of subjects relapse within one year. More recently, McLellan and colleagues (2000) reviewed more than 100 clinical trials of drug addiction treatments and noted that in one-year post-discharge follow-up studies, 40 to 60 percent of individuals discharged from treatment were continuously abstinent and 15 to 30 percent had not used substances addictively. Several publications by the Center for Substance Abuse Treatment (CSAT, 1999, 2000a, 2000b) describe positive outcomes for substance abusers who have received professional treatment including reduced rates of substance use, reduced rates of criminal behaviors, improved psychological functioning, and family productivity. Most relapses occur within the first year of treatment, with two-thirds occurring within the first 90 days (Daley, 2003). Though this may be the case, the risk of relapse may be present even after a long period of abstinence.

The cycle of relapse, treatment reentry, and recovery has been evident in statistics for people admitted to the U.S. public treatment system in 1999, in which 60 percent were reentering treatment, including 23 percent for the second time, 13 percent for third time, 7 percent for the fourth time, 4 percent for the fifth time, and 13 percent for six or more times (Office of Applied Studies, 2000). Even though retention and treatment dosage may predict better outcomes for a given episode of care (Simpson et al., 2002), multiple episodes of care can also be a marker for people who have not been responsive to prior treatment and hence have a worse prognosis (Hser, Joshi, Anglin et al., 1999). More studies have indicated that individuals move along various pathways in the addiction-recovery cycle, e.g., using in the community, treatment, abstinence, incarceration, abstinence in the community, and death (Hser et al., 1997; Hser, Hoffman et al., 2001). Multiple episodes of care over several years seem to be the norm (Dennis et al., 2005). It has been suggested that treatment episodes may have a cumulative effect on the recovery process (Hser, 1997). Scott, Foss et al. (2005) recently clearly demonstrated the importance of better understanding of the factors influencing transitions in the recovery cycle, shifting the focus to better identify the chronic and cyclical nature of addiction, evaluate long-term recovery management models to shorten the cycle through correcting the mislabel of relapse as failure and identifying it as a part of the process of treatment. Patients who remain in treatment the longest generally have the best outcomes (NIDA, 1997a, 1997b).

EFFECTIVENESS AND EFFICACY OF RP

Several studies and reviews have shown that RP does help improve recovery and reduce relapse rates. Carroll (1996) reviewed randomized controlled trials on the effectiveness of RP among smokers (12 studies), alcohol abusers (6 studies), cocaine abusers (3 studies), opiate addicts (1 study), and other drug abusers (2 studies), using the RP strategies recommended by Marlatt and Gordon (1985). Carroll concluded that there is strong evidence that RP was more effective than no-treatment control groups and equally effective as other active treatment such as supportive therapy and interpersonal psychotherapy in improving substance use outcomes, including reduction in severity of relapses when they occur and durability of effects. Individuals with higher levels of impairment along dimensions such as psychiatric severity appear to benefit most from RP compared with those with less severe levels of impairment. Moreover, Goldstein and colleagues (1989) had found a significant delayed effect for an RP condition as compared to an educational support control condition at six months for smokers treated in a 10-week group program (Goldstein, Niaura et al., 1989). Later, Carroll and colleagues (1994) also found, while comparing RP with an operationalized clinical management condition and pharmacotherapy using desipramine hydrochloride or placebo, a significant psychotherapy-by-time effect at one-year follow-up, indicating a delayed response to treatment among patients who received RP. Then, Rawson and colleagues also identified a "sleeper effect" for RP in patients with cocaine dependence (Rawson et al., 2002). These findings of delayed effects of RP are consistent with the notion that learning new coping skills to deal with high-risk situations takes time and leads to a decreased probability of relapse over time. Polivy and Herman (2002) have demonstrated that 90 percent of individuals who attempt to change their behavior struggle with lapses and do not achieve change on their first attempt.

Irvin and colleagues (1999) conducted a meta-analysis of 26 published and unpublished clinical trials on RP techniques between 1978 and 1995, involving a total sample of 9,504 participants. These studies have assessed the efficacy of RP and were also consistent with Marlatt and Gordon's approach to RP. The strongest treatment effects were for alcohol and polysubstance use outcomes, reducing substance use and improving psychosocial adjustment. The effects were weaker for smoking and cocaine. Some studies' empirical limitations could be responsible for the inconsistent support for the effects of RP on smoking cessation. Other randomized trials of RP for smoking showed that additional supportive elements such as stress management, emotion regulation techniques, and abstinence "resource renewal" may be needed in addition to RP in a smoking intervention (Hajek, Stead et al., 2005; Piasecki et al., 2002). The results of these studies indicate that more research should focus on modifying and improving RP techniques in the context of other substance use such as cocaine, nicotine, and opioids. The analysis also showed that individual, group, and marital modalities were equally effective. Another finding was that medication seems to be very helpful in reducing relapse rates in the context of alcohol problems.

Recent randomized controlled trials support the reported efficacy of combined CBT-like therapies and naltrexone for alcohol-dependent individuals (Anton et al., 2005). The COMBINE (Effect of Combined Pharmacotherapies and Behavioral Interventions) study suggested that medical management of an alcohol-dependent patient with a physician providing treatment with naltrexone and basic advice and information is as effective as cognitive-behavioral therapy (CBT). That trial enrolled 1,383 alcohol-dependent subjects and randomly assigned them to one of eight groups that could include naltrexone, acamprosate, or both of the drugs, with or without what was identified as a cognitive-behavioral intervention (CBI). One group received the CBI alone, without placebo. The patients who received a medication received medical management that was fairly rigorous (9 appointments over 16 weeks), during which the physician or a nurse discussed the patient's diagnosis and progress and suggested attendance to AA. Those who got the CBI received up to 20 sessions, which was comparable with a streamlined version of outpatient alcoholism treatment. Subjects receiving medical management with naltrexone, CBI, or both fared better on drinking outcomes, whereas acamprosate showed no evidence of efficacy, with or without CBI. Putting it more into clinical significance, the percentages of subjects with a good clinical outcome were 58 percent for those who received only medical management and placebo, 74 percent for those who received medical management with naltrexone only, 74 percent for those who received medical management with naltrexone and cognitive-behavioral treatment, and 71 percent for those who received medical management with placebo and cognitive behavioral treatment. The subjects were also followed for a year after the 16-week treatment, and although the patterns of efficacy remained much the same, there was appreciable fall-off for all groups. (Anton et al., 2006; The Combine Study, 2003). In a recently completed trial, 121 cocaine-dependent individuals were randomized to one of four conditions in a 2 × 2 factorial design: disulfiram plus CBT, disulfiram plus Interpersonal Therapy (IPT) that did not include RP companants, placebo plus CBT, and placebo plus IPT. This study showed a significant main effect for CBT over IPT. The patients assigned to CBT reduced their cocaine use more significantly than those assigned to IPT, and patients assigned to disulfiram reduced their cocaine significantly more than those assigned to placebo. In addition, the CBT × time effect remained statistically significant after controlling for retention, which was a significant predictor of better drug use outcomes (Carroll, Fenton et al., 2004).

Furthermore, the results of a study randomizing 128 cocaine users to either CBT or 12-step facilitation (TSF) suggested that CBT was more effective than TSF overall. Several matching hypotheses were supported. CBT was differentially effective for individuals with a history of depression, whereas TSF was more effective for participants with low levels of abstract reasoning skills (Maude-Griffin et al., 1998).

The literature evaluating the efficacy and effectiveness of RP with stimulant users has been nearly all conducted with cocaine users as the study participants. Some data support the view that the response to RP treatment is quite comparable between cocaine-dependent individuals and those dependent on methamphetamines (Rawson et al., 2000). Rawson and colleagues (2004) conducted a study with methamphetamine-dependent individuals assessing the effectiveness of the Matrix treatment protocol (based on cognitive behavioral principles described in Marlatt and Gordon, 1985, used as an outpatient intensive approach for the treatment of stimulant users: Rawson et al., 1989, 1995, 2002; Shoptaw et al., 2004) versus "treatment as usual" in eight community treatment organizations. The in-treatment gains made by participants with the Matrix approach suggest that the treatment approach has positive empirical evidence for treating methamphetamine-dependent individuals when compared to a group of community treatment programs. Rawson et al. (2002) recently compared group CBT, voucher contingency management (CM), and a CBT/CM in combination with standard methadone maintenance treatment for cocaine-using methadone maintenance patients. During the acute phase of treatment, the CM group had significantly better cocaine use outcomes. However, during the follow-up period, a CBT sleeper effect emerged again, where the CBT group had better outcomes at the 26-week and 52-week follow-up than the CM group. Another similar study in the context of intensive methadone maintenance showed similar results with best one-year outcomes for the CM + CBT combination (Epstein, Hawkins et al., 2003). Two trials have compared the delivery of RP in individual versus group format. Schmitz et al. (1997) and Marques & Formigoni (2001) found no differences in-group versus individually delivered CBT. These results suggest that CBT/RP can be effectively implemented in either format. Furthermore, a recent study has demonstrated that stress-induced cocaine craving is predictive of cocaine relapse outcomes. Therefore treatments addressing stress-induced cocaine craving could be of benefit in improving relapse outcomes in cocaine dependence (Sinha, Garcia, Paliwal et al., 2006).

The empirical literature on testing RP strategies (12 trials) for cannabis abuse has also incorporated treatment components focusing on aversion training, motivational enhancement, contingency reinforcement, and case management. A multisite study involving 450 marijuana-dependent individuals demonstrated that a nine-session individual approach that integrated cognitive behavior therapy and motivational interviewing was more effective than a two-session motivational interviewing approach, which in turn was more effective than a delayed-treatment control condition (MTP Research Group, 2004). The relatively modest long-term outcomes reported in the trials conducted thus far suggest that intervention protocols need to be developed to effectively meet the needs of this population.

Several studies included spouses in the RP intervention (Maisto et al., 1995; O'Farrell et al., 1993). A recent study evaluated conjoint treatments in 90 men with alcohol problems and their female partners. The subjects were randomly assigned to one of three outpatient conjoint treatments: alcohol behavioral couples therapy (ABCT), ABCT with relapse prevention techniques (RP/ABCT) (as per Marlatt and Gordon, 1985), or ABCT with interventions encouraging Alcoholics Anonymous (AA) involvement (AA/ABCT). Couples were followed for 18 months after treatment. Across the three treatments, drinkers who provided follow-up data maintained abstinence on almost 80 percent of days during follow-up, with no differences in drinking or marital happiness outcomes between groups. In the RP/ABCT treatment, attendance at post-treatment booster sessions was related to post-treatment abstinence. AA attendance was positively related to abstinence during follow-up treatment in both concurrent and time-lagged analyses (McCrady, Epstein et al., 2004). Despite strong evidence for efficacy of psychosocial treatments of alcohol use disorders, aggregate rates of continuous abstinence after treatment are well below 50 percent and relapses are more common than abstinence, indicating the need for continued efforts to develop more efficacious treatments (McCrady & Nathan et al., in press).

There are no efficacy studies evaluating RP strategies specifically for abuse of club drugs, hallucinogens, inhalants, and steroids (Kilmer et al., 2005). Despite several limitations to studies on RP, such as the use of RP as a component of multimodal treatment packages, poor emphasis on the level of readiness to change and motivation level, and small sample sizes, the literature generally favors the efficacy and effectiveness of RP and shows that RP strategies enhance the recovery of individuals with SUDs.

RELAPSE REPLICATION AND EXTENSION PROJECT

In a series of studies sponsored by the NIAAA called the Relapse Replication Extension Project (RREP), aspects of RP including Marlatt's taxonomy for relapse determinants were explored. Using this taxonomy, Longabaugh et al. (1996) compared the reliability of independent classifications of 149 relapse episodes by trained raters at three research laboratories. They concluded that the inter-rater reliability of Marlatt's coding system was not adequately demonstrated. The best across-site agreement was 81 percent for the negative emotional state category. In contrast, overall inter-rater reliabilities were found to be 88 percent (Marlatt, 1978) and 91.7 percent (Hodgkins et al., 1995) in two other studies examining Marlatt's taxonomy. Several studies in the RREP showed that the taxonomy had minimal ability to predict drinking outcomes (Maisto, 1996; Stout, 1996). The studies examined whether the determinant for a baseline relapse episode could predict the nature of future relapse episodes and overall drinking outcomes. Marlatt (1996) delineated several flaws in these studies, pointing out problems with the criteria for a baseline relapse (a relapse defined as drinking that followed only 4 days of abstinence) and the studies' failure to capture the "dynamic interplay of cognitive and behavioral factors in the ongoing process of relapse and recovery." On the basis of the findings, a major reconceptualization of the relapse taxonomy was recommended (Donovan, 1996; Kadden, 1996). Longabaugh et al. (1996) suggested a revision of the taxonomy categories to include greater distinction between inter- and intrapersonal determinants and more emphasis on cravings.

An expanded model of Marlatt's relapse precipitant taxonomy has been recommended (Donovan, 1996b; Stout, Longabaugh et al., 1996). It would allow the inclusion of multiple variables exerting differential levels of influence across time in the relapse process. A new reconceptualization of cognitive behavioral model of relapse that focuses on the dynamic interactions between multiple risk factors and situational determinants will be discussed later (Witkiewitz & Marlatt, 2004). In this model, multiple reasons, in combination and interaction, are identified by subjects as being important in the relapse process (Miller et al., 1996; Zywiak, Connors et al., 1996).

MODELS OF RELAPSE PREVENTION

As discussed earlier, most of the RP interventions have a multicomponent character. That is, many of these clinical trials have embedded RP strategies in more broadly encompassing cognitive behavioral skills training including relaxation training, increasing pleasant activities, self talk, and problem-solving skills. Other treatment studies such as motivational enhancement therapy, contingency management, individual and group drug counseling approaches, and case management typically have included RP modules (NIDA, 2000; NIDA, 2001). Specific RP models that focus primarily on cognitive-behavioral skills to cope with high-risk situations, craving management, cognitive restructuring, and lifestyle interventions are seen as most relevant to enhance the client's ability to maintain abstinence (Dimeff & Marlatt, 1995; Washton, 2001, 2002). Furthermore, psychopharmacological interventions including anticraving medications combined with RP are evaluated as a part of an overall treatment strategy to reduce relapse risk and improve abstinence rates (Anton, Moak et al., 2005; Lewis et al., 2000; NIAAA, 2000).

Various models of RP are described in the literature and many of these have been adapted for use in clinical trials. They include the following:

- Marlatt and Gordon's cognitive-behavioral approach (1985; Marlatt, Barrett et al., 1999; Marlatt & Donovan, 2005).
- Annis's cognitive behavioral approach (1991), which incorporates concepts of Marlatt's model with Bandura's self-efficacy concept.
- Daley's psychoeducational approach (Daley, 2004; Daley & Marlatt, 2005), which adapted Marlatt's classification of relapse determinants to a treatment protocol that can be used in individual and group settings.
- Gorski's neurologic impairment model, which incorporates elements from the disease model of addiction and relapse, as well as Marlatt's model (2000).
- Zackon, McAuliffe, and Chien's recovery training and self-help model (NIDA, 1994).
- The MATRIX model of treatment, which includes RP as a central component of treatment (Matrix Center, 1989; Rawson, Obert et al., 1993a; Obert, McCann et al., 2000; Rawson et al., 2005; Shoptaw, Reback et al., 1998).
- Washton's intensive outpatient model (2001, 2002), which includes significant attention to RP during the third phase of treatment.
- The coping/social skills training (CSST) model of Monti and colleagues (1993, 2002).
- The cue exposure model developed by Childress and colleagues (NIDA, 1993).

No single model of RP could ever encompass all individuals at different levels of behavior change. Therefore a comprehensive evaluation of the determinants of relapse and underlying processes may be more helpful to identify RP strategies.

THE COGNITIVE-BEHAVIORAL MODEL OF RELAPSE
(MARLATT & GORDON, 1985)

A schematic representation of this model is presented in Figure 3.1. The model assumes that the person experiences a sense of perceived control while maintaining abstinence (or complying with other rules governing the target behavior). The target behavior is "under control" so long as it does not occur. This perceived control would continue until the person encounters a high-risk situation, a situation that poses a threat to the person's sense of control and increases the risk of potential relapse. The high-risk situations associated with the highest relapse rates include negative emotional states, interpersonal conflict, and social pressure. This model centers on the individual's response to the high-risk situation. If the individual is able to execute an effective coping response and has high self-efficacy in a high-risk situation (e.g., assertive in counteracting social pressures), the probability of relapse decreases. The combination of being unable to cope effectively in a high-risk situation and positive outcome expectancies for the effects of the habitual coping behavior (substance use) greatly increase the probability that an initial lapse will occur. Whether the first lapse is followed by a full-blown relapse depends in part on the person's attributions as to the cause of the lapse and the reactions associated with its occurrence.

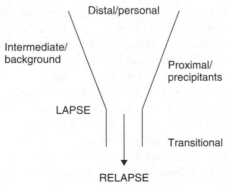

FIGURE 3.1: A heuristic framework for conceptualizing the levels of assessment involved in Shiffman's model of relapse predictors. Addiction (1996) 91 (Supplement), S29-S36 Reprinted with Permission

Individuals who choose to indulge may be vulnerable to the abstinence violation rule or AVE. The AVE is characterized by two key cognitive-affective elements: cognitive dissonance (i.e., conflict and guilt) and a personal attribution effect (i.e., blaming the self as a cause of the relapse). Persons who experience an intense AVE following a lapse often experience a motivation crisis (demoralization reaction) that undermines their commitment to abstinence goals. If the individual views the lapse as external, unstable, and controllable, then the likelihood of a relapse is decreased. The lapse is more likely to progress to a relapse if the person views it as an irreparable failure. However, the results of studies investigating AVE have been mixed (Brike et al., 1990; Grilo & Shiffman, 1994; Mooney et al., 1992; Shiffman, Hickcox et al., 1996). Other factors such as the individual's restorative coping abilities, the reaction of family and friends, and the individual's commitment to return to abstinence must be considered.

RECONCEPTUALIZED MODEL OF RELAPSE
(WITKIEWITIZ & MARLATT, 2004)

The current reconceptualization of relapse has incorporated and expanded on the dynamic interplay of multiple factors from the biopsychosocial model, from distal to proximal. This model proposes a dynamic interaction between several factors leading up to, and during, a high-risk situation. This model is explained in detail in Chapter 2.

RELAPSE-RELATED DOMAINS
OF ASSESSMENT

Shiffman's (1989) model of assessment of relapse predictors involves three levels of assessment to be considered to understand and predict the likelihood of relapse. The first level included distal personal characteristics that are longstanding, enduring, and unchanging. The second level involves intermediate or background variables that fluctuate over time, but do so gradually and may potentially contribute to an increased risk of relapse. The third level involves very proximal precipitants that occur at or immediately prior to the lapse; these factors are transient and occur within the context of a high-risk situation. Other factors not incorporated in Shiffman's model but essential to understanding the probability of movement from lapse to relapse are the transitional variables. They usually occur after an initial use of substance or recurrence of an addictive behavior and either promote continued engagement in the behavior or lead to postlapse cessation, thus mediating the transition from lapse to relapse. These levels and the dynamic interplay among variables from these levels are comparable to those incorporated into the reconceptualized model of the relapse process described earlier (Witkiewitz & Marlatt, 2004). This heuristic assessment model is presented in Figure 3.2

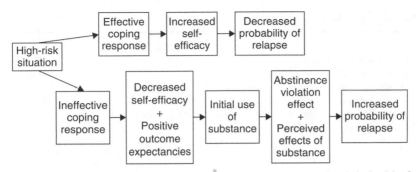

FIGURE 3.2: Cognitive Behavioral Model of Relapse. American Psychologist May-June 2004 Reprinted with permission

(Donovan, 1996a), and Table 3.1 (Donovan, 1996a) presents variables within each of the assessment domains of this model. The consideration of how these variables may interact within a high-risk situation and how changes in proximal risks can alter behaviors leading up to high-risk situations will enable patients and their clinicians to assess their own (client's) relapse vulnerability.

RP INTERVENTIONS TO MINIMIZE LAPSE AND RELAPSE RISK

Each lapse or relapse gives the client an opportunity to explore and understand what precipitated it, and where the focus on potential risk factors should be (e.g., particular high-risk situations, lack of appropriate coping skills, low self-efficacy) to avoid an abstinence violation effect. Viewing lapse as a "teachable moment," a part of a learning process may thus reduce the experience of a full-blown relapse (Marlatt & Gordon, 1985). This section discusses practical relapse prevention techniques and strategies that can be utilized in many treatment settings. These interventions reflect the experiences of clinicians, researchers, and other health care providers, who have generated the specific models of RP and the client-oriented RP recovery materials and workbooks. RP interventions are characterized by an emphasis on understanding substance use within the context of its antecedents and consequences, on the development of skills that can be used in high-risk situations to foster abstinence, and on lifestyle interventions. These interventions can be a part of a self-management recovery program and a joint recovery program involving support of family and significant others. The literature has emphasized the importance of individualizing RP interventions, taking into account the client's stage of change, level of motivation, severity of substance use and coexisting problems, gender, ego functioning, and socio-cultural environment.

TABLE 3.1:   Assessment Domains Related to Relapse

Distal personal factors
  Family history of alcoholism
  "Type" of alcoholism
  Nature/severity of concurrent psychiatric disorders
  Nature/severity of concurrent substance use disorders
  Presence of cognitive impairment or reduced problem solving abilities
  Severity of alcohol dependence
  Conditioned reactivity to alcohol-related cues
Intermediate background factors
  Major life events
  Enduring life strain
  Everyday life problems
  Social and environmental supports
  Stress-coping skills/anticipatory coping skills
  General sense of personal efficacy
  General expectancies concerning the effects of substance
  Motivation for self-improvement
Proximal precipitating factors
  High-risk situations
  Cognitive vigilance and internal dialogue
  Emotional states
  Temptation-coping skills
  Situational response efficacy
  Conditioned cue reactivity
  Salience of expected/desired substance effects
  "Craving"
  Commitment to abstinence
Transitional factors
  Abstinence violation effect
  • Emotional states
  • Attributional tendencies
  Restorative coping skills
  Reaction of support system
  Commitment to return to abstinent state

Addiction (1996) 91 (Supplement), S29–S36. Reprinted with permission.

CLINICAL STRATEGIES TO REDUCE RELAPSE RISK

STRATEGY 1: HELP CLIENTS UNDERSTAND RELAPSE AS A PROCESS AND EVENT, AND LEARN TO IDENTIFY EARLY WARNING SIGNS

The understanding of addiction as a chronic cyclical condition often involving several transitions between relapse and recovery helps the client look at relapse as a process occurring in a certain context and see that early warning signs often precede an actual lapse or relapse. Attitudinal, emotional, cognitive, and/or behavioral changes seem to occur days, weeks and even longer before resuming the use of substances (Daley, 2004). These changes develop progressively. Warning signs can be conceptualized as links in a relapse chain (Brownell & Rodin, 1990; Daley & Marlatt, 1997b, 2006a, 2006b). Warning signs may be subtle and idiosyncratic such as an increase in dishonesty, poor involvement in church community, an increased period of irritability and short fuse and involvement in interpersonal conflicts, and a tendency to undermine the recovery program. Other warning signs that could be overt include stopping or reducing involvement in treatment and self-help groups and worsening of cravings.

Reviewing with the client the relapse history, relapse calendar (use of daily inventory that helps identify relapse risk factors, relapse warning signs, or significant life events that could lead to relapse) is essential (Gorski & Miller, 1988, Project Match). Gorski (1995) has also suggested reviewing the three most recent attempts at recovery followed by the standard warning sign list, the most outstanding personal warning signs, and then sentence completion tasks to examine threats to recovery; developing a final warning sign list using cognitive, behavioral, and emotional strategies targeting these warnings; and finally formulating a recovery plan to complete the intervention. "Understanding the Relapse Process" was identified as the most useful topic as a part of evaluating Daley's Psychoeducational Model of RP (1989) and a workbook used in conjunction with the program.

STRATEGY 2: HELP CLIENTS IDENTIFY THEIR HIGH-RISK SITUATIONS AND DEVELOP COGNITIVE AND BEHAVIORAL COPING RESPONSES

Recognizing and coping with high-risk situations prevent a single lapse from developing into a full-blown relapse. High-risk situations include interpersonal and intrapersonal factors. Coping skills, rather than the high-risk situation, predict relapse. As discussed earlier, assessing the client's coping strategies is crucial to RP. Individuals who successfully avoided relapse initially have relied on behavioral avoidance of potential high-risk situations, and if they are challenged, they elicit social support to foster continued abstinence. Greater reliance on cognitive coping happens after longer periods of abstinence, which include thinking more about the negative consequences of drinking in the past, and consequently thinking about the positive impact of maintaining abstinence (Litman, Stapleton, Oppenheim et al., 1984). Developing a greater diversity and range of available coping abilities and learning to be more flexible about shifting adaptively among them when necessary could help maintain sobriety (Litman, 1986). In addition to teaching specific RP skills to deal with high-risk situations, the clinician should also incorporate global RP self-control strategies that go beyond the analysis of the initial lapse and include skills-training strategies (e.g., behavioral rehearsal, covert modeling, assertiveness training), coping cognitive reframing (e.g., coping imagery to deal with early warning signs, restructuring of the AVE), and lifestyle balancing strategies (e.g., meditation, mindfulness, and exercise) (Marlatt, 1985). Preparing clients to interrupt lapses and relapses as early as possible in the process to minimize damage caused by setbacks can be done using an emergency plan to follow if they lapse or relapse. A person heading for a relapse usually makes a number of mini decisions over time, each of which brings the person closer to creating a high-risk situation or giving in. These choices are called "apparently irrelevant decisions" and they need to be identified and addressed with clients in recovery.

STRATEGY 3: HELP CLIENTS ENHANCE COMMUNICATION SKILLS, INTERPERSONAL RELATIONSHIPS, AND SOCIAL NETWORKS

If we only focus on reducing or totally eliminating substance clients' substance abuse without helping them with their relationships, we may be "hanging them out to dry" (McCollum, 2004). Families are more likely to support the client's efforts in change/recovery if they are involved in the treatment process. Practicing communication skills such as paraphrasing, empathizing, and validating can help the substance abusing client and his or her partner better address conflicts and stressors in their relationship and their lives. These skills are believed to reduce the risk of relapse. Enhancing problem-solving skills and caring behaviors seem to have a positive effect on relationships therefore fostering substance use recovery. Clients are encouraged to get involved in self-help support groups. Clients need to identify whom to include or exclude from their recovery network. Behavioral rehearsal can help the client practice ways to make special requests for support. Rehearsal can also help clients deal with their ambivalence about asking for help or support from others. This process helps the client become better prepared to deal with negative responses from others. Formulating an action plan is necessary, and it should incorporate how to identify and manage early warning signs, cues, and high-risk situations; how to interrupt a lapse and how to intervene if a relapse occurs; how to analyze the drug use and its context and approach the process as a learning opportunity. Working with clients on identifying and preparing to handle direct and indirect social/peer pressures to engage in substance use is a part of the recovery action plan.

STRATEGY 4: HELP CLIENTS MANAGE NEGATIVE EMOTIONAL STATES

The relapse determinant most frequently endorsed by clients with alcohol addiction was depressed mood (Strowig, 2000). Negative emotional states including anxious mood, tense situations, and depressed mood are factors in a substantial number of relapses (Hodgins et al., 1995). Other negative affective states associated with relapse include anger and boredom (Daley, 2004). The acronym

HALT, frequently cited by members of AA and NA, speaks to the importance of identifying negative emotions and preventing them ("don't get too Hungry, Angry, Lonely, or Tired"). Clinicians should help clients learn stress management techniques to cope with stress in recovery and work toward a more balanced lifestyle. Educating the clients on the role of negative emotional states in recovery as well as identifying situations and self-statements with the potential to trigger negative emotions prepares the client to adapt his or her cognitive-behavioral coping skills. Clients with significant mood or anxiety symptoms may need to be evaluated for a mood or an anxiety disorder (Daley & Moss, 2002; Westermyer, Weiss, & Zeidonis, 2003).

STRATEGY 5: HELP CLIENTS IDENTIFY AND MANAGE CRAVINGS AND "CUES" THAT PRECEDE CRAVINGS

Different aspects of cravings have been postulated (Anton et al., 1995; Verheul et al., 1999). Widely accepted are the notions of reward or positive craving that arise as a conditioned cue to drink in order to experience the hedonic effects of alcohol, and relief or negative cravings, a conditioned cue to avoid the unpleasant effects associated with the absence of alcohol (Verheul et al., 1999). Environmental cues may trigger cravings that become evident in cognitive (e.g., increased thoughts of using) and physiologic (e.g., anxiety) changes. The advice given in AA, NA, and CA for alcoholics and addicts to "avoid places, people, and things" associated with their substance use was identified as a way to minimize exposure to cues that trigger cravings that could be difficult to resist, leading to a relapse. Cue exposure (CE) treatment reduces the intensity in the client's reactions to the cues (NIDA, 1993). CE aims to enhance behavioral and cognitive coping skills as well as the patient's confidence in his or her ability to resist the desire to use. Systematic relaxation, visual imagery, behavioral alternatives, and cognitive strategies are used in CE. Monitoring and recording cues and how they trigger cravings can help clients become more vigilant and prepare them to deal with them.

STRATEGY 6: HELP CLIENTS IDENTIFY AND CHALLENGE COGNITIVE DISTORTIONS

Teaching clients to identify their negative thinking patterns or cognitive errors such as catastrophizing, jumping to conclusions, and overgeneralizing, and to evaluate how these affect recovery and relapse is beneficial. Clients then can be taught to use counter-thoughts to challenge their thinking errors or specific negative thoughts. Many of the AA and NA slogans were identified to help alcoholics and drug addicts alter their thinking and overcome desires to use. Slogans such as "this too will pass," "let go and let God," and "one day at a time" are often helpful for clients to work through thoughts of using.

TABLE 3.2:   Medications to Assist Recovery and Reduce Relapse Risk

Substance	Medication
Alcohol	Disulfiram (Antabuse),[1] Naltrexone oral (ReVia)[1] and Injectable form (Vivitrol),[1] Topiramate (Topamax),[2] Ondansetron (Zofran)[2], Quetiapine,[2] (Seroquel) Acamprosate (Campral),[1] Aripiprazole (Abilify),[2] Memantine[2] (Namenda)
Heroin/ Opioids	Methadone,[1] Burprenorphine[1] (Subutex, Suboxone), Naltrexone,[1] LAAM[1]
Nicotine	Bupropion SR (Zyban),[1] Nicotine Replacement therapy,[1] Clonidine (Catapres),[2] Nortriptyline (Pamelor),[2] Rimonabant, Varenicline[1] (Chantese)
Cocaine[3]	Disulfiram, Topiramate, Modafinil (Provigil),[2] Propranolol (Inderal),[2] Naltrexone, Baclofen (Lioresal),[2] Tiagabine (Gabitul), TA-CD (Cocaine Vaccine)

[1]FDA approved for this indication.
[2]FDA approved for another indication.
[3]No FDA indication.

STRATEGY 7: CONSIDER THE USE OF MEDICATIONS

In the treatment of addictions, there are two goals for the use of medications: to help clients attain an initial period of abstinence after treating withdrawal syndromes and to assist clients with relapse prevention. There is now a range of medications available for each of the major classes of addictive drugs: alcohol, opioids, and nicotine (see Table 3.2). Some clinicians believe that medications might diminish the client's motivation to help himself or herself or to participate in self-help groups. Perhaps more importantly, the best use of medications may be in combination with one another and with psychosocial interventions. Treatment with both acamprosate and naltrexone has been shown to be efficacious in reducing relapse risk (Mann et al., 2004; Steeton & Wheelan, 2001). Furthermore, studies show that individuals who relapse and fail to be totally abstinent while on these drugs still drink a lot less, which presumably means fewer negative consequences. Naltrexone may be the drug that should be used for a harm reduction approach. Even the combination of acamprosate and naltrexone seems to be efficacious and safe (Kiefer & Wiedemann, 2004). It was hypothesized that naltrexone would specifically attenuate reward craving, whereas acamprosate would diminish relief craving. The combination may act simultaneously on two different aspects of craving and have a more incisive effect on the risk of relapse than either treatment alone. The old concept of total abstinence as the only goal for treatment of alcohol abuse stemmed from two sources: (1) AA and (2) the use of the medication disulfiram (Antabuse), which makes a person feel very sick when he or she drinks (aversive response to drinking alcohol). All the medications approved in the United States to treat alcohol dependence reduce drinking even among non-abstinent individuals. A recent study investigating the supervised, long-term administration of alcohol deterrents—specifically disulfiram and calcium carbiamide—with a focus on the psychological rather the pharmacological action of alcohol deterrents found a psychological role that alcohol deterrents may play in relapse prevention. The results support the theory that prolonged abstinence achieved with disulfiram automatically leads to the con-solidation of the habit of abstinence: "the longer people abstain, the longer they will abstain" (Krampe et al., 2006). Promising agents for the treatment of alcohol dependence include topiramate and aripiprazole.

At present, no medication is FDA approved for the indication of cocaine dependence. Potential relapse-prevention medications include GABAergic medi-cations, such as baclofen, tiagabine, topiramate, and the glutamatergic medica-tion, modafinil. Surprisingly disulfiram may also have efficacy for cocaine relapse prevention. A vaccine capable of stimulating the production of cocaine-specific antibodies has shown promise in some preliminary studies for the prevention of relapse to cocaine use.

Three types of medications are available to treat nicotine dependence. Sustained-release bupropion (Zyban) and nicotine replacement therapies (NRT) can be given in a coordinated fashion to provide good outcomes. The newly approved drug varenicline (Chantix) may help a significantly higher percentage of patients to quit smoking than bupropion. The drug is not approved for adoles-cents. It is a novel selective nicotinic receptor partial agonist that helps ease withdrawal craving and partly blocks the nicotine effect of smoking. The label will recommend not combining the drug with bupropion or the nicotine patch. Second-line pharmacotherapies (e.g., clonidine, nortriptyline) that have empirical support as cessation aids (Hall et al., 2002), but which do not have an FDA indication for treatment of tobacco dependence, may have more aversive side effects compared to first-line therapies. Research shows that the combined effects of the pharmacological and behavioral treatments are additive (Hughes et al., 1995). Five NRTs are proven effective (Fiore et al., 2000).

Medications can be useful in preventing relapse to opioid dependence. Medi-cations can provide antagonism to the reinforcing effects of opioid drugs and can provide stable replacement for illegal drugs (Hart, McCance-Katz et al., 2001). They include opioid agonists such as methadone and LAAM, opioid antagonist such as naltrexone, and a mixed agonist/antagonist medication called buprenor-phine. Buprenorphine's partial mu opioid agonist properties provide a wide safety margin, with relatively slim chances for severe overdose effects. Second, its long duration of action allows for flexible, client-tailored dose administration multiple times daily, once daily, or at longer intervals. Another advantage is the less likeli-hood of diversion with the combination formulation of buprenorphine and nal-oxone (Suboxone). Despite some clinical trials with good outcomes, this class of medications is still underused by physicians. Medications are most useful in conjunction with psychosocial and behavioral treatments.

RP IN THE CONTEXT OF SUDs WITH COMORBID PSYCHIATRIC DISORDERS

Substance-abusing adults with comorbid mental health disorders place greater demands on treatment providers, with more admissions for mental health and substance abuse treatment, which underscores the importance of understanding the complexity of the underlying relapse mechanism for these patients and the impact on the dual recovery process (Brown et al., 1995; Daley & Moss, 2002; Wu, Kouzis, & Leaf, 1999). The increased likelihood, intensity, duration, and chronicity of aversive emotional states inherent to psychiatric disorders may increase the risk and influence motivation for a return to substance use (Abrantes, Brown et al., 2003). In addition, negative emotional states may also be related to the increase in severity of substance consumption following post-treatment relapse. Social isolation seen in depression and PTSD has also been associated with increased frequency and intensity of substance use.

A recent study exploring the context of relapse for substance-dependent adults with and without comorbid psychiatric disorders found that negative affective states preceded post-treatment use episodes more frequently in adults with dual disorders. The majority of adults with dual diagnosis reported intrapersonal determinants, whereas the majority of adults with SUD reported interpersonal determinants. The majority of adults with dual disorders typically first resume substance use when they are alone and most often in intrapersonal/environmental contexts. More passive distressing affective states such as sadness, remorse, and insecurity are as important to address since they can be associated with resuming substance use (Tate et al., 2004). The results underscore the importance of interventions targeting psychiatric symptom management, early identification of psychiatric relapse signs, and medication use to reduce the frequency of these contexts for substance-dependent individuals with mood disorders or PTSD to minimize the risk of relapse.

Furthermore, a recent study showed that depressive symptoms are an important factor affecting successful substance abuse treatment outcomes (Dodge, 2005). In standard drug treatment centers, there is a tendency to pay less attention to the management of depressive symptoms and regulation of emotional distress (Carroll, 1998). The recent data indicated the need for interventions designed to target the negative sequelae of depressive symptoms and subjective distress (drug cue-induced craving) to optimize treatment outcomes. In addition, pharmacological interventions have been demonstrated to improve outcomes for patients with comorbid depression and SUDs (Bradizza et al., 2006; Cornelius et al., 1997; Mueller et al., 1997; Nunes at Levin, 2004). Valproate, a mood stabilizer, has been shown to significantly decrease heavy drinking in patients with comorbid bipolar disorder and alcohol dependence (Salloum et al., 2005). A recent pilot study using divalproex in individuals with bipolar disorder with co-occurring cocaine dependence appears to reduce self-reported cocaine and other substances of abuse (Salloum et al., in press). Behavioral interventions focused on depression also have been shown to increase drug abstinence in depressed alcoholics and among cocaine-abusing opiate dependent individuals with depression (Brown, Evans et al., 1997; Gonzalez, Feingold et al., 2003).

Thus pharmacological and psychosocial treatments that focus on regulation of affective symptoms need to be integrated in treatment of SUDs. Incorporating strategies to enhance treatment entry and improve adherence to treatment in this population should be an integral part of treatment (Daley & Zuckoff, 1999; Higgins & Silverman, 1999).

FUTURE RESEARCH DIRECTIONS

The new theoretical conceptualization of RP provides a careful consideration of why the interaction between interpersonal and intrapersonal factors is complex and dynamic. Withdrawal syndromes also contribute to the relapse vulnerability. Since this relationship is poorly understood, it is an important area of future research. Furthermore, incorporating more dynamic data collection such as Ecological Momentary Assessment (EMA) and analyses (Hufford, Witkiewitz et al., 2003) in understanding the relationship between risk factors and relapse is very much needed. This new model needs to be empirically tested in special populations such as individuals with co-occurring disorders and ethnic minority groups. Learning more about identifying different types of stress that predict reduced relapse risk and incorporating social support, family-based, and coping interventions may improve outcomes. Clinical researchers should focus more on redoubling their efforts to better disseminate RP techniques to community-based providers of substance abuse services. Witkiewitz and Marlatt raised the importance of better understanding the basic processes underlying the measured outcomes instead of focusing solely on testing the efficacy of an intervention, which remains essential. The integration of RP techniques with Motivational Interviewing (MI)/adaptations of MI and pharmacotherapy or spirituality/mindfulness meditation (Leigh & Marlatt, 2005; Marlatt, 2002) warrants further investigation. Neuroimaging and behavioral studies are needed to better elucidate the underlying neuronal substrates of cue reactivity, craving, and decision-making, and the implications for relapse prevention.

CLINICAL CASE ILLUSTRATIONS

SUCCESSFUL CASE EXAMPLE

Nancy is a 37-year-old married mother of two with a five-year history of cocaine dependence. The next to last of three children in a middle class family, she described her mother as alcoholic, depressed, and emotionally unavailable. Her father divorced her mother when Nancy was 10 years old and her relationship with him grew more distant. Nancy reported that she felt neglected by her family and had difficulty making and maintaining friendships and struggled throughout college, never completed it, and ended up with many odd jobs that were unfulfilling.

Nancy started using cocaine in an attempt to deal with depression, anger, and feeling "unworthy" of her family. Her relationship with her husband became more problematic since she started being dishonest about her drug use and taking money from the family's savings to buy cocaine. As things got worse, she was more unavailable at home and her children felt neglected and extremely angry with her. When her husband confronted Nancy about her behaviors and drug use and asked her to seek help, she decided to move out, which led to the break up of the family and eventually to divorce. Nancy's social contacts were mainly with other drug users who took advantage of her. She distanced herself from her siblings who have attempted to reach out to her to no avail.

Nancy felt so demoralized, humiliated, and hurt about losing her family, she finally decided to seek treatment. Initially she tried only halfheartedly and dropped out many times prematurely, believing "she cannot stay clean." When she started feeling significant shame and guilt over the impact of her addiction on her family, especially her children whom she stopped seeing regularly, Nancy was willing to make a change even though she realized how challenging recovery would be.

Treatment focused initially on engagement, enhancing motivation and commitment to change, and adhering to treatment. Nancy initially agreed to get involved in a residential addiction rehabilitation program since she was unable to stay drug-free even though she was adherent to outpatient therapy sessions. Nancy resumed outpatient individual and group therapy after she finished rehabilitation and got involved in NA. She realized that sometimes she criticized people at NA and created reasons to avoid going to meetings regularly.

As treatment and involvement in NA continued, Nancy started understanding the relapse process and the importance of a recovery plan. In therapy, she started to identify her core beliefs (I am a failure, I am a bad person, I am vulnerable, and I don't deserve love) and ensuing conditional assumptions (if I try to stop using, I will fail; if I numb my feelings, I will be ok) and became more aware that certain situations led to her automatic thoughts, emotions, and resulting behaviors (avoiding negative emotions; avoiding assertion; using drugs; feeling hopeless, lonely, anxious, angry) that she coped with by using drugs, leading to a vicious cycle. She also realized that she had poor coping abilities (not capable of tolerating changes in moods and feelings: increased moodiness, strong feelings of anger, increased feelings of boredom, sudden feelings of euphoria; unable to solve problems; unable to assert herself; and being unrealistic about some situations).

The therapeutic approach with Nancy included identifying her thinking and the sequence of events leading to an episode of substance use, and targeting points of intervention. Relapse cues preceding relapse included behavior changes such as stopping at a bar to socialize and drink soda, displaying increased stress symptoms such as smoking more cigarettes; attitude changes such as not caring about sobriety, not caring about what happens, becoming too negative about life and making changes; thought changes such as "since my life is crappy, I deserve to use to feel better"; thinking about using as a reward for being clean for six months; thinking my drug problem is "cured"; and changes in feelings. Nancy was able to spot some of her relapse warning signs such as skipping NA meetings, being angry about not seeing her children very often and wanting to use to feel better, arguing with her ex-husband, and so on, and addressed these by bringing them out in the open to discuss them with an NA sponsor that she felt comfortable sharing with, asking her sisters for support and help, remembering what she put her family through, and remembering that staying sober improved her relationships with her children and made her feel like a better mother.

Nancy has also started identifying her high-risk situations and how to cope with them, such as negative emotions (anger, boredom, guilt, shame), interpersonal problems such as conflicts with her ex-husband, inability to solve problems or manage stress, strong cravings for drugs, and doubts about following a recovery program and staying in treatment and dealing with past issues related to her relationships with her parents and emotional neglect. Nancy has maintained sobriety through continuing to work a recovery program that also incorporated reconnecting with her children and her family and staying involved in NA and therapy.

UNSUCCESSFUL CASE EXAMPLE

Kevin is a 50-year-old divorced employed father of three daughters. He sought treatment for depression, chronic anxiety, family problems, and alcohol dependence. During the first six months of treatment, he canceled most of his outpatient sessions and continued to drink alcohol on a daily basis despite worsening of his depressive and anxiety symptoms. When he finally realized the impact of his alcohol use on his depression and anxiety and his family problems, he decided to enter the hospital for detoxification and psychiatric treatment. His motivation for change was still low.

Once Kevin was stabilized psychiatrically and detoxified, he was referred to outpatient treatment. After being sober for three weeks, he started drinking again and got a DUI that made him concerned about the possibility of losing his job. He attempted to minimize the extent of his use of alcohol to his therapist. He also became less consistent with his therapy sessions and started having conflicts with his daughters, who confronted him about his drinking and threatened to stop seeing him if he continued to drink. Kevin made the decision to stop drinking on his own without considering a rehabilitative program that was suggested by his therapist. He insisted on feeling that he "can do it" on his own, and was reluctant to consider attending AA meetings. He was able to stay sober for almost a month but told his therapist, "I don't need therapy for my alcohol problem, I should be strong enough to do it myself, I am too busy to go to therapy and AA, and anyway, talking about alcohol makes me crave a drink."

Kevin's therapist tried to help him challenge his beliefs and automatic thoughts that resulted from these beliefs such as "Why bother, I can handle it if I drink, I won't have more than three drinks, and anyway my kids don't care about me." However, Kevin was resistant to the therapist's interventions and also made statements about "not liking you" (the therapist). When the therapist attempted to inquire about times the patient felt cravings for alcohol, Kevin became defensive saying that he could handle them without using any particular coping strategy. Kevin also talked about feeling angry and frustrated with his family and anxious about losing his job, and canceled numerous appointments with his therapist. During the sessions he attended, Kevin was not willing to explore his poor adherence to treatment and relapse warning signs or high-risk situations, and whether these indicated that he was headed for a relapse. The therapist tried to focus the sessions more on addressing Kevin's ambivalence about wanting to make a change and enhancing his motivation for change. The therapist was very concerned that Kevin was at high risk for a relapse since he did not follow any recovery plan and was not even willing to continue taking his antidepressant medication "because I feel groggy and I don't need them." The therapist felt unable to form a strong alliance with Kevin and was concerned that he would drop out of treatment. One strategy that the therapist used was the advantage-disadvantage analysis, exploring with Kevin the benefits of achieving a goal, while also reframing disadvantages (decisional balance). Asking Kevin about involving his daughters in his treatment was rejected. Kevin eventually relapsed after being sober for six weeks and decided to quit therapy despite many attempts by the therapist to reach out to him to reengage in treatment.

CONCLUSIONS

Relapse is a major clinical challenge in the treatment of addictive disorders. Several sources have recently described relapse as complex, dynamic, and multidimensional (Buhringer, 2000; Donovan, 1996; Marlatt, 1996b). RP interventions aim to help clients maintain change over time and address the most common relapse risk factors and other issues raising vulnerability to relapse. RP also aims to increase the likelihood of initiating effective coping efforts in response to stressors and negative emotional states that are common precursors of substance relapse. Clinical RP strategies can be used throughout the continuum of care and can be supplemented by other treatment, for addictive disorders, such as pharmacotherapy, motivational interventions, contingency management, family-based interventions, self-help groups, and spirituality. User-friendly, interactive recovery materials, such as books, workbooks, videos, and audiotapes, support most clinical models of RP. Future research focusing on better assessment of the dynamic interplay of relapse factors will add to the understanding of the process of relapse and its prevention.

ACKNOWLEDGEMENTS

The preparation of this chapter was supported in part by a grant from the National Institute on Drug Abuse (U10 DA020036)

REFERENCES

Abrantes, A.M., Brown, S.A., Tomlinson, K.L. (2003). Psychiatric comorbidity among inpatient substance abusing adolescents. *Journal of Child & Adolescent Substance Abuse* **13**:83–101.

American Society of Addiction Medicine. (2001). *Patient placement criteria for the treatment of substance-related disorders, 2e.* Chevy Chase: American Society of Addiction Medicine.

Angst, J., Sellaro, R., Ries, M.K. (2002). Multimorbidity of psychiatric disorders as an indicator of clinical severity. *European Archives of Psychiatry and Clinical Neuroscience* **252**:147–154.

Annis, H. (1986). A relapse prevention model for treatment of alcoholics. In Miller, W., Heather, N., eds., *Treating addictive behaviors: Processes of change.* New York: Plenum Books.

Annis, H. (1991). A cognitive-social learning approach to relapse: Pharmacotherapy and relapse prevention counseling. *Alcohol and Alcoholism* **1**(Suppl):527–530.

Annis, H., Davis, C.S. (1988). Self-efficacy and the prevention of alcoholic relapse: Initial findings from a treatment trial. In Baker, T.B., Cannon, D.S., eds., *Assessment and treatment of addictive disorders*, 88–112. New York: Praeger.

Annis, H.M. (1982). *Inventory of drinking situations.* Toronto: Addiction Research Foundation.

Annis, H.M., Graham, J.M. (1988). *Situation confidence questionnaire user's guide.* Toronto: Addiction Research Foundation of Ontario.

Anton, R.F., Moak, D.H., Latham, P., Waid, L.R., Myrick, H., Voronin, K. et al. (2005). Naltrexone combined with either cognitive behavioral or motivational enhancement therapy for alcohol dependence. *Journal of Clinical Psychopharmacology* **25**:349–357.

Anton, R.F., O'Malley, S.S., Ciraulo, D.A., Cisler, R.A., Couper, D., Donovan, D.M. et al. (2006). Combined pharmacotherapies and behavioral interventions for alcohol dependence. *JAMA* **295**:2003–2017.

Aspen, R.F., Kranzler, H.R., Meyer, R.E. (1995). Neurobehavioral aspects of the pharmacotherapy of alcohol dependence. *Clinical Neuroscience* **3**:145–154.

Baker, T.B., Curtin, J.J. (2002). How will we know a lapse when we see one? Comment on Leri and Stewart experimental and clinical. *Psychopharmacology* **10**:350–352.

Baker, T.B., Piper, M.E., McCarthy, D.E., Majeskie, M.R., Fiore, M.C. (2004). Addiction motivation reformulated: An affective processing model of negative reinforcement. *Psychological Bulletin* **111**:33–51.

Bandura, A. (1977). Self-efficicay: Toward a unifying theory of behavioral change. *Psychological Review* **84**:191–215.

Beattie, M.C., Longabaugh, R. (1999). General and alcohol-specific social support following treatment. *Addictive Behaviors* **24**:593–606.

Birke, S.A., Edemann, R.J., Davis, P.E. (1990). An analysis of the abstinence violation effect in a sample of illicit drug users. *British Journal on Addictions* **85**:1299–1397.

Bradizza, C.M., Stasiewicz, P.R., Paas, N.D. (2006). Relapse to alcohol and drug use among individuals diagnosed with co-occurring mental health and substance use disorders: A review. *Clinical Psychology Review* **26**:162–178.

Breslin, B., Sobell, L.C., Sobell, M.B., Buchan, G., Kwan, E. (1996). Aftercare telephone contacts with problem drinkers can serve a clinical and research function. *Addiction* **91**:1359–1364.

Breslin, C., Sobell, M.B., Sobell, L.C., Sdao-Jarvia, K., Sagorsky, L. (1996). Relationship between posttreatment drinking and alternative responses to high-risk situations proposed during treatment by problem drinkers. *Journal of Substance Abuse* **8**:479–486.

Brown, P.J., Recupero, P.R., Stout, R. (1995). PTSD substance abuse comorbidity and treatment utilization. *Addictive Behaviors* **20**:251–254.

Brown, R., Evans, D., Miller, I. (1997). Cognitive-behavioral treatment for depression in alcoholism. *Journal of Consulting and Clinical Psychology* **65**:715–726.

Brown, S.A., Goldman, M.S., Christiansen, B.A. (1985). Do alcohol expectancies mediate drinking patterns of adults? *Journal of Consulting and Clinical Psychology* **53**:512–519.

Brown, S.A., Vik, P.W., Craemer, V.A. (1989). Characteristics of relapse following adolescent substance abuse treatment. *Addictive Behaviors* **14**:291–300.

Brownell, K., Rodin, J. (1990). *The weight maintenance survival guide*. Dallas: The LEARN Education Center.

Buhringer, G. (2000). Testing CBT mechanisms of action: Humans behave in a more complex way than our treatment studies would predict. *Addiction* **95**:1715–1716.

Burgess, E.S., Brown, R.A., Kahler, C.W., Niaura, R., Abrams, D.P., Goldstein, M.G., Miller, I.W. (2002). Patters of change in depressive symptoms during smoking cessation: Who's at risk for relapse? *Journal of Consulting and Clinical Psychology* **70**:356–361.

Burke, B.L., Arkowtiz, H., Menchola, M. (2003). The efficacy of motivational interviewing: A meta-analysis of controlled clinical trials. *Journal of Consulting and Clinical Psychology* **71**:843–861.

Carrol, K. (1998). *A cognitive-behavioral approach: Treating cocaine addiction* (NIH Publication No 98-4308). Rockville: National Institute on Drug Abuse.

Carrol, K.M., Rounsaville, B.J., Gawin, F.H. (1991). A comparative trial of psychotherapies for ambulatory cocaine abusers: Relapse prevention and interpersonal psychotherapy. *American Journal of Drug and Alcohol Abuse* **17**:229–249.

Carroll, K.M. (1996). Relapse prevention as a psychosocial treatment: A review of controlled clinical trials. *Experimental and Clinical Psychopharmacology* **4**:46–54.

Carroll, K.M., Fenton, L.R., Ball, S.A., Nich, C., Frankforter, T.L., Shi, J. et al. (2004). Efficacy of disulfiram and cognitive-behavioral therapy for cocaine-dependent outpatients. *Archives of General Psychiatry* **64**:264–272.

Carroll, K.M., Rounsaville, B.J., Nich, C. et al. (1994). One-year follow-up of psychotherapy and pharmacotherapy for cocaine dependence. Delayed emergence of psychotherapy effects. *Archives of General Psychiatry* **51**:989–997.

Center for Substance Abuse Treatment (CSAT). (1999). Treatment succeeds in fighting crime. In *Substance Abuse Brief.* Rockville: CSAT, SAMHSA.

Center for Substance Abuse Treatment (CSAT). (2000a). Substance abuse treatment reduces family dysfunction, improves productivity. In *Substance Abuse Brief.* Rockville: CSAT, SAMHSA.

Center for Substance Abuse Treatment (CSAT). (2000b). Treatment cuts medical costs. In *Substance Abuse Brief.* Rockville: CSAT, SAMHSA.

Chung, T., Langenbucher, J., Labouvie, E., Pandina, R.J., Moos, R.H. (2001). Changes in alcoholic patients' coping responses predict 12-month treatment outcomes. *Journal of Consulting and Clinical Psychology* **69**:92–100.

Connors, G.J., Tarbox, A.R., Faillace, L.A. (1993). Changes in alcohol expectancies and drinking behavior among treated problem drinkers. *Journal of Studies on Alcohol* **54**: 676–683.

Cornelius, J.R., Salloum, I.M., Ehler, J.G., Jarrett, P.J., Cornelius, M.D., Perel, J.M., Thase, M.E., Black, A. (1997). Fluoxetine in depressed alcoholics: A double-blind, placebo-controlled trial. *Archives of General Psychiatry* **54**:700–705.

Cunningham, J.A., Lin, E., Ross, H.E., Walsh, G.W. (2000). Factors associated with untreated remissions from alcohol abuse or dependence. *Addictive Behaviors* **25**:317–321.

Daley, D.C. (1988). *Relapse prevention: Treatment alternatives and counseling aids*. Bradenton, FL: Human Services Institute.

Daley, D.C. (1989a). Five perspectives on relapse in chemical dependency. *Journal of Chemical Dependency Treatment* **2**:3–26.

Daley, D.C., ed. (1989b). *Relapses: Conceptual, research and clinical perspectives*. New York: Haworth Medical Publishing.

Daley, D.C., Marlatt, G.A. (1997a). *Therapists guide for managing your alcohol or drug problem*. San Antonio: Psychological Corporation.

Daley, D.C., Marlatt, G.A. (1997b). *Managing your alcohol or drug problem*. San Antonio: Psychological Corporation.

Daley, D.C., Marlatt, G.A. (2005). Relapse prevention: Cognitive and behavioral interventions. In Lowinson, J., Ruiz, P., Millman, R.B. et al., eds., *Substance abuse: A comprehensive textbook, 4e*, 772–785. Baltimore: Williams & Wilkins.

Daley, D.C., Marlatt, G.A. (2006a). *Overcoming your alcohol and drug problem: Effective recovery strategies. Client Workbook, 2e.* NY: Oxford University Press.

Daley, D.C., Marlatt, G.A., Spotts, C.E. (2003). Relapse prevention: Clinical models and intervention strategies. In Graham, A.W. et al., eds., *Principles of addiction medicine, 3e*, 467–485. Chevy Chase: American Society of Addiction Medicine.

Daley, D.C., Zuckoff, A. (1999). *Improving treatment compliance: Counseling and system strategies for substance use and dual disorders.* Center City: Hazelden.

Dawson, D.M. (1996). Marlatt's classification of relapse precipitants: Is the emperor still wearing clothes? *Addiction* **91**:131–137.

Dennis, M.L., Scott, C.K., Funk, R., Foss, M.A. (2005). The duration and correlates of addiction treatment careers. *Journal of Substance Abuse Treatment* **28**:S51–S62.

DiClemente, C.C., Carbonari, J.P., Montgomery, R.P., Hughes, S.O. (1994). The Alcohol Abstinence Self-Efficacy scale. *Journal of Studies on Alcohol* **55**:141–148.

Dimeff, L.A., Marlatt, G.A. (1995). Relapse prevention. In Hester, R., Miller, W., eds., *Handbook of alcoholism treatment approaches, 2e*, 176–194. Boston: Allyn & Bacon.

Dobkin, P.L., Civita, M., Paraherakis, A., Gill, K. (2002). The role of functional social support in treatment retention and outcomes among outpatient adult substance abusers. *Addiction* **97**:347–356.

Dodge, R., Sindelar, J., Sinha, R. (2005). The role of depression symptoms in predicting drug abstinence outpatient substance abuse treatment. *Journal of Substance Abuse Treatment* **28**:189–196

Donovan, D.M. (1996a). Assessment issues and domains in the prediction of relapse. *Addiction* **91**: S29–S36.

Donovan, D.M., Marlatt, G.A., eds. (2005). *Assessment of addictive behavior, 2e.* New York: Guilford Press.

Drobes, D.J., Meier, E.A., Tiffany, S.T. (1994). Assessment of the effects of urges and negative affect on smokers' coping skills. *Behaviour Research and Therapy* **32**:165–174.

Einstein, S. (1994). Relapse revisited: Failure by whom and what? *International Journal of Addictions* **29**:409–413.

Epstein, D.F., Hawkins, W.F., Covi, L., Umbricht, A., Preston, K.L. (2003). Cognitive behavioral therapy plus contingency management for cocaine use: Findings during treatment and across 12-month follow-up. *Psychology of Addictive Behaviors* **17**:73–82.

Etter, J.F., Bergman, M.M., Humair, J.P., Perneger, T.V. (2000). Development and validation of a scale measuring self-efficacy of current and former smokers. *Addiction* **95**:613–625.

Fals-Stewart, W., O'Farrell, T.J., Birchler, G.R. (2004). Behavioral couples therapy for substance abuse: Rationale, methods, and findings. In *National Institute on Drug Abuse. Science Practice & Perspectives, Volume 2.* Rockville: NIDA, National Institutes of Health.

Finney, J.W., Monahan, S.C. (1996). The cost-effectiveness of treatment for alcoholism: A second approximation. *Journal of Studies on Alcohol* **52**:517–540.

Fiore, M.C., Bailey, W.C., Cohen, S.J., Dorfman, S.F., Gritz, E.R., Heyman, R.B. et al. (2000). Treating tobacco use and dependence: Clinical practice guideline. Rockville: US Department of Health and Human Services, Public Health Service.

Flynn, P.M., Joe, G.W., Broome, K.M., Simpson, D.D., Brown, B.S. (2003). Recovery from opioid addiction in DATOS. *Journal of Substance Abuse Treatment* **25**:177–186.

Godley, M.D., Godley, S.H., Dennis, M.L., Funk, R., Passetti, L. (2002). Preliminary outcomes from the assertive continuing care experiment for adolescents discharged from residential treatment. *Journal of Substance Abuse Treatment* **23**:21–32.

Goldstein, M.G., Niaura, R., Follick, M.J. et al. (1989). Effects of behavioral skills training and schedule of nicotine gum administration on smoking cessation. *American Journal of Psychiatry* **146**:56–60.

Gonzalez, G., Feingold, A., Oliveto, A., Gonasi, K., Osten, T. (2003). Comorbid major depressive disorder as a prognostic factor in cocaine-abusing buprenorphine-maintained patients treated with desipramine and contingency management. *American Journal of Drug and Alcohol Abuse* **29**:497–514.

Gorski, T. (1995). *Relapse prevention therapy workbook: Managing core personality and lifestyle issues*. Independence: Herald House.

Gorski, T. (2000). *The CENAPS model of relapse prevention therapy (CMRPT). Approaches to drug abuse counseling*. Rockville: National Institute on Drug Abuse.

Gossop, M., Green, L., Phillips, G., Bradley, B.P. (1989). Lapse, relapse and survival among opiate addicts after treatment: A prospective follow-up study. *British Journal of Psychiatry* **154**: 348–353.

Gossop, M., Stewart, D., Browne, N., Marsden, J. (2002). Factors associate with abstinence, lapse or relapse to heroin use after residential treatment: Protective effect of coping responses. *Addiction* **97**:1259–1267.

Grace, A.A. (1995). The tonic/phasic model of dopamine system regulation: Its relevance for understanding how stimulant abuse can alter basal ganglia function. *Drug and Alcohol Dependence* **37**:111–129.

Greenfield, S., Hufford, M., Vagge, L., Muenz, L., Costello, M., Weiss, R. (2000). The relationship of self-effficacy expectancies to relapse among alcohol dependence men and women: A prospective study. *Journal of Studies on Alcohol* **61**:345–351.

Grella, C.E. (2003). Effects of gender and diagnosis on addiction history, treatment utilization, and psychosocial functioning among a dually diagnosed sample in drug treatment. *Journal of Psychoactive Drugs* **35**:169–179.

Grella, C.E., Hser, Y., Hseih, S. (2003). Predictors of drug treatment re-entry following relapse to cocaine use in DATOS. *Journal of Substance Abuse Treatment* **25**:145–154.

Grilo, G.M., Shiffman, S. (1994). Longitudinal investigation of the abstinence violation effect in binge eaters. *Journal of Consulting and Clinical Psychology* **62**:611–619.

Gwaltney, C.J., Shiffman, S., Paty, J.A., Liu, K.S., Kassel, J.D., Gnys, M., Hickcox, M. (2002). Using self-efficacy judgments to predict characteristics of lapses to smoking. *Journal of Consulting and Clinical Psychology* **70**:1140–1149.

Hajek, P., Stead, L.F., West, R., Jarvis, M., Lancaster, T. (2005). Relapse prevention interventions for smoking cessation. *The Cochrane Database of Systematic Reviews*.

Hall, S.M., Humfleet, G.L., Reus, V.I., Munoz, R.F., Hartz, D.T., Maude-Griffin, R. (2002). Psychological intervention and antidepressant treatment in smoking cessation. *Archives of General Psychiatry* **59**:930–936.

Hart, C., McCance-Katz, E.F., Kosten, T.R. (2001). Pharmacotherapies used in common substance use disorders. In Tims, F.M., Leukefeld, C.G. et al., eds., *Relapse and recovery in addictions*, 303–333. New Haven: Yale University Press.

Harwood, H. (2004). The economic costs of drug abuse in the United Status: 1992–2002. Report prepared by The Lewin Group for the Office of National Drug Control Policy.

Hawkins, R.C., Hawkins, C.A. (1998). Dynamics of substance abuse: Implications of chaos theory for clinical research. In Chamberlain, L., Butz, M.R., eds., *Clinical chaos: A therapist's guide to non-linear dynamics and therapeutic change*, 89–101. Philadelphia: Brunner/ Mazel.

Heather, N., Stallard, A. (1989). Does the Marlatt model underestimate the importance of conditioned craving in the relapse process? In Gossop, M., ed., *Relapse and addictive behavior*, 180–208. London: Routledge.

Higgins, S.T., Silverman, K., eds. (1999). *Motivating behavior change among illicit drug abusers: Research on contingency management*. Washington: American Psychological Association.

Hodgins, D.C., Guebaly, N., Armstrong, S. (1995). Prospective and retrospective reports of mood states before relapse to substance use. *Journal of Consulting and Clinical Psychology* **63**: 400–407.

Hser, Y., Hoffman, V., Grella, C.E., Anglin, M.D. (2001). A 33-year follow-up of narcotics addicts. *Archives of General Psychiatry* **58**:503–508.

Hser, Y.I., Anglin, M.D., Grella, C., Longshore, D., Prendergast, M.L. (1997). Drug treatment careers: A conceptual framework and existing research findings. *Journal of Substance Abuse Treatment* **14**:543–558.

Hser, Y.I., Joshi, V., Anglin, M.D., Fletcher, B. (1999). Predictive post-treatment cocaine abstinence: What works for first-time admissions and treatment repeaters. *American Journal of Public Health* **89**:666–671.

Hufford, M.H., Witkiewitz, K., Shields, A.L., Kodya, S., Caruso, J.C. (2003). Applying nonlinear dynamics to the prediction of alcohol use disorder treatment outcomes. *Journal of Abnormal Psychology* **112**:219–227.

Hughes, J.R. (1995). Combining behavioral therapy and pharmacotherapy for smoking cessation: An update. *NIDA Research Monograph* **150**:92–109.

Irvin, J.E., Bowers, C.A., Dunn, M.E., Wang, M.C. (1999). Efficacy of relapse prevention: A meta-analytic review. *Journal of Consulting and Clinical Psychology* **67**:563–570.

Jones, B.T., Corbin, W., Fromme, K. (2001). A review of expectancy theory and alcohol consumption. *Addiction* **96**:57–72.

Jones, B.T., McMahon, J. (1996). A comparison of positive and negative alcohol expectancy value and their multiplicative composite as predictors of post-treatment abstinence survivorship. *Addiction* **91**:89–99.

Kadden, R. (1996). Is Marlatt's taxonomy reliable or valid? *Addiction* **91**:139–146.

Kassel, J.D., Shiffman, S. (1992). What can hunger tell us about drug craving? A comparative analysis of two constructs. *Advances in Behaviour Therapy and Research* **14**:141–167.

Kassel, J.D., Stroud, L.R., Paronis, C.A. (2003). Smoking, stress, and negative affect: Correlation, causation, and context across stages of smoking. *Psychological Bulletin* **129**:270–304.

Kenford, S.L., Smith, S.S., Wetter, D.W., Jorenby, D.E., Fiore, M.C., Baker, T.B. (2002). Predictive relapse back to smoking: Contrasting affective and physical models of dependence. *Journal of Consulting and Clinical Psychology* **70**:216–227.

Kessler, R.C., McGonagle, K.A., Shanyang, Z., Nelson, C.B., Hughes, M., Eshleman, S. et al. (1994). Lifetime and 12-month prevalence of DSM-III-R psychiatric disorders in the United States. *Archives of General Psychiatry* **51**:8–19.

Khantzian, E.F. (1974). Opiate addiction: A critique of theory and some implications for treatment. *American Journal of Psychotherapy* **28**:59–70.

Kiefer, F., Wiedemann, K. (2004). Combined therapy: What does acamprosate and naltrexone combination tell us? *Alcohol & Alcoholism* **39**:542–547.

Kilmer, J.R., Cronce, J.M., Palmer, R.S. (2005). Relapse prevention for abuse of club drugs, hallucinogens, inhalants, and steroids. In Marlatt, G.A., Donovan, D.M., Relapse Prevention (2nd edition). NY: Guilford Press, 208–247.

Krampe, H., Stawicki, S., Wagner, T. et al. (2006). Follow-up of 180 alcoholic patients for up to 7 years after outpatient treatment: Impact of alcohol deterrents on outcome. *Alcoholism: Clinical and Experimental Research* **30**:86–95.

Lash, S.J., Petersen, G.E., O'Connor Jr, E.A., Lehmann, L.P. (2001). Social reinforcement of substance abuse aftercare group therapy attendance. *Journal of Substance Abuse Treatment* **20**:3–8.

Leigh, J., Bowen, S., Marlatt, G.A. (2005). Spirituality, mindfulness and substance abuse. *Addictive Behaviors* **30**:1335–1341.

Li, T.K. (2000). Clinical perspectives for the study of craving and relapse in animal models. *Addiction* **95**:55–60.

Litman, G.K., Stapleton, J., Oppenheim, A.N., Peleg, M., Jackson, P. (1983). Situations related to alcoholism relapse. *British Journal of Addiction* **78**:381–389.

Litman, G.K., Stapleton, J., Oppenheim, A.N., Peleg, M., Jackson, P. (1984). Relationship between coping behaviours, their effectiveness and alcoholism relapse and survival. *British Journal of Addiction* **79**:283–291.

Litman, G.K. (1986). Alcohol survival: The prevention of relapse. In Miller, W.R., Heather, N., eds., *Treating addiction disorders: Processes of change*, 391–405. New York: Plenum Press.

Litt, M.D., Cooney, N.L., Morse, P. (2000). Reactivity to alcohol-related stimuli in the laboratory and in the field: predictors of craving in treated alcoholics. *Addiction* **95**:889–900.

Litt, M.D., Kadden, R.M., Cooney, N.L., Kabela, E. (2003). Coping skills and treatment outcomes in cognitive-behavioral and interactional group therapy for alcoholism. *Journal of Consulting and Clinical Psychology* **71**:118–128.

Longabaugh, R., Morgenstern, J. (1999). Cognitive behavioral coping skills therapy for alcohol dependence: Current status and future directions. *Alcohol Research and Health: The Journal of the NIAAA* **23**(2):78–85.

Longabaugh, R., Rubin, A., Stout, R.L., Zwyiak, W.H., Lowman, C. (1996). The reliability of Marlatt's taxonomy for classifying relapses. *Addiction* **91**:73–88.

Lowman, C., Hunt, W.A., Litten, R.Z., Drummond, D.C. (2000). Research perspectives on alcohol craving: An overview. *Addiction* 45–54.

Maisto, S.A., Connors, G.J., Zwyiak, W.H. (1996). Construct validation analyses on the Marlatt typology of relapse precipitants. *Addiction* **91**:89–98.

Maisto, S.A., McKay, J.R., O'Farrell, T.J. (1995). Relapse precipitants and behavioral marital therapy. *Addictive Behaviors* **20**(3):383–393.

Mann, K., Lehert, P., Morgan, M.Y. (2004). The efficacy of acamprosate in the maintenance in alcohol-dependent individuals: Results of a meta-analysis. *Alcoholism: Clinical and Experimental Research* **28**:51–63.

Marlatt, G.A. (1978). Craving for alcohol, loss of control, and relapse: A cognitive-behavioral analysis. In Nathan, P.E., Marlatt, G.A., Loberg, T., eds., *New directions in behavioral research and treatment*, 271–314. New Brunswick: Rutgers Center of Alcohol Studies.

Marlatt, G.A. (1985a). Relapse prevention: Theoretical rationale and overview model. In Marlatt, G.A., Gordon, G., eds. *Relapse prevention: A self-control strategy for the maintenance of behavioral change*, 3–70. New York: Guildford.

Marlatt, G.A. (1985b). Relapse prevention: Theoretical rationale and overview of the model. In Marlatt, G.A., Gordon, J.R., eds. *Relapse Prevention,* 208–250. New York: Guilford Press.

Marlatt, G.A. (1996). Taxonomy of high-risk situations for alcohol relapse: Evolution and development of a cognitive-behavioral model. *Addiction* **91**:S37–S49.

Marlatt, G.A. (2002). Buddhist philosophy and the treatment of addictive behaviors. *Cognitive and Behavioral Practice* **9**:44–49.

Marlatt, G.A., Barrett, K., Daley, D.C. (1999). Relapse prevention. In Galanter, M., Kleber, H.D., eds., *Textbook of Substance Abuse, 2e*. Washington: American Psychiatric Press.

Marlatt, G.A., Demming, B., Reid, J.B. (1973). Loss of control drinking in alcoholics: An experimental analogue. *Journal of Abnormal Psychology* **81**(3):233–241.

Marlatt, G.A., Gordon, J.R., eds. (1985). Relapse prevention: Maintenance strategies in the treatment of addiction behaviors. New York: Guilford Press.

Marlatt, G.A., Kristellar, J. (1999). Mindfulness and meditation. In Miller, W.R., ed., *Integrating spirituality in treatment: Resources for practitioners*, 67–84. Washington: American Psychological Association Books.

Marlatt, G.A., Witkiewitz, K. (2002). Harm reduction approaches to alcohol use: Health promotion, prevention, treatment. *Addictive Behaviors* **27**:867–886.

Marlatt, G.A., Witkiewitz, K., Dillworth, T., Bowen, S.W., Parks, G., Macpherson, L.M. (2004). Vipassana meditation as a treatment for alcohol and drug use disorders. In Hayes, S.C., Follette, V.M., Linehan, M.M., eds., *Mindfulness and acceptance: Expanding the cognitive-behavioral tradition*, 261–287. New York: Guilford Press.

Marques, A.C., Formignoi, M.L. (2001). Comparison of individual and group cognitive behavioral therapy for alcohol and/or drug dependent patients. *Addiction* **96**:832–837.

Martin, G.M., Pollock, N.K., Cornelius, J.R., Lynch, K.G., Martin, C.S. (1995). The Drug Avoidance Self-Efficacy Scale. *Journal of Substance Abuse* **7**:151–163.

Maude-Griffin, P.M., Hohenstein, J.M., Humfleet, G.L., Reilly, P.M., Tusel, D.J., Hall, S.M. (1998). Superior efficacy of cognitive-behavioral therapy for crack cocaine abusers: Main and matching effects. *Journal of Consulting and Clinical Psychology* **66**:832–837.

McClellan, A.T., Lewis, D.C., O'Brien, C.P. et al. (2000). Drug dependence, a chronic medical illness: Implications for treatment, insurance, and outcomes evaluation. *Journal of the American Medical Association* **284**:1689–1695.

McCollum, E., McMahon, M., Watson, M.F. (2004). Response: Families, models, relationships. In National Institute on Drug Abuse. *Science Practice & Perspectives, Volume 2*. Rockville: NIDA, National Institutes of Health.

McCrady, B.S., Epstein, E.E., Kahler, C.W. (2004). Alcoholics Anonymous and relapse prevention as maintenance strategies after conjoint behavioral alcohol treatment for men: 18-month outcomes. *Journal of Consulting and Clinical Psychology* **72**:870–878.

McCrady, B.S., Nathan, P.E. (In press). Impact of treatment factors on outcomes of treatment for substance use disorders. In Beutler, L., Castonguay, L., eds., *Empirically supported principles of therapeutic change: Integrating common and specific therapeutic factors across major psychological disorders*. New York: Oxford University Press.

McKay, J.R., Merikle, E., Mulvaney, F.D., Weiss, R.V., Koppenhaver, J.M. (2001). Factors accounting for cocaine use two years following initiation of continuing care. *Addiction* **96**:213–225.

McLellan, A.T., Lewis, D.C., O'Brien, C.P., Kleber, H.D. (2000). Drug dependence, a chronic medical illness: implications for treatment, insurance, and outcomes evaluation. *Journal of the American Medical Association* **284**.1689 1695.

McMahon, R.C. (2001). Personality, stress, and social support in cocaine relapse prediction. *Journal of Substance Abuse Treatment* **21**:77–87.

Milby, J.B., Schumacher, J.E., Vuchinich, R.E., Wallace, D., Plant, M.A., Freedman, M.J. et al. (2004). Transitions during effective treatment for cocaine-abusing homeless persons: Establishing abstinence, lapse, and relapse, and reestablishing abstinence. *Psychology of Addictive Behaviors* **18**:250–256.

Miller, W., Hester, R. (1980). Treating the problem drinker: Modern approaches. *The addictive behaviors treatment of alcoholism, drug abuse, smoking and obesity*. New York: Pergamon Press.

Miller, W.R. (1996). What is a relapse? Fifty ways to leave the wagon. *Addiction* **91**:S15–S27.

Miller, W.R., Rollnick, S. (2002). *Motivational interviewing: Preparing people for change, 2e*. New York: Guilford Press.

Miller, W.R., Westerberg, V.S., Harris, R.J. et al. (1996). What predicts relapse? Prospective testing of antecedent models. *Addiction* **91**:S155–S171.

Monti, P., Adams, D., Kadden, R. et al. (1996). *Treatment alcohol dependence*. New York: Guilford Press.

Monti, P.M., Kadden, R.M., Rohsenow, D.J., Cooney, N.L., Abrams, D.B. (2002). *Treating alcohol dependence: A coping skills training guide, 2e*. NY: Guilford Press.

Monti, P.M., Rohsenow, D.J., Rubonis, A.V. et al. (1993). Cue exposure with coping skills treatment for male alcoholics: A preliminary investigation. *Journal of Clinical and Consulting Psychology* **61**:1011–1019.

Monti, P.M., Rohsenow, D.J., Swift, R.M., Gulliver, S.B., Colby, S.M., Mueller, T.I. et al. (2001). Naltrexone and cue exposure with coping and communication skills training for alcoholics: Treatment process and 1-year outcomes. *Alcoholism: Clinical and Experimental Research* **25**:1634–1647.

Mooney, J.P., Burling, T.A., Hartman, W.M., Brenner-Liss, D. (1992). The abstinence violation effect and very low calorie diet success. *Addictive Behaviors* **17**:319–324.

Moos, R.H., Holahan, C.J. (2003). Dispositional and contextual perspectives on coping: Toward an integrative framework. *Journal of Clinical Psychology* **59**:1387–1403.

Moser, A.E., Annis, H.M. (1996). The role of coping in relapse crisis outcome: A prospective study of treated alcoholics. *Addiction* **91**:1101–1114.

MTP Research Group (2004). Brief treatments for cannabis dependence: Findings from a randomized multi-site trial. *Journal of Consulting and Clinical Psychology* **72**:455–466.

Mueller, T.I., Stout, R.L., Rudden, S., Brown, R.A., Gordon, A., Solomon, D.A. (1997). A double-blind placebo-controlled pilot study of carbamazepine for the treatment of alcohol dependence. *Alcoholism: Clinical and Experimental Research* **21**:86–92.

Mueser, K.T., Noordsy, D.L., Drake, R.E., Fox, L. (2003). *Integrated treatment for dual disorders: A guide to effective practice.* NY: Guilford Press.

National Institute on Alcohol Abuse and Alcoholism (NIAAA). (2000). Highlights from the 10th special report to Congress. *Alcohol Research & Health* **24**.

National Insitute on Drug Abuse (NIDA). (1993). *Cue extinction techniques: NIDA technology transfer package.* Rockville: NIDA, National Institutes of Health.

National Institute on Drug Abuse (NIDA). (1994). *Recovery training and self-help, 2e.* Rockville: NIDA, National Institutes of Health.

National Institute on Drug Abuse (NIDA). (1999). *Principles of drug addiction: A research-based guide.* Rockville: NIDA, National Institutes of Health.

National Institute on Drug Abuse (NIDA). (2000). *Individual drug counseling for cocaine addiction: The cocaine collaborative model.* Rockville: NIDA, National Institutes of Health.

National Institute on Drug Abuse (NIDA). (2001). *Group drug counseling for cocaine dependence: The cocaine collaborative model.* Rockville: NIDA, National Institutes of Health.

Niaura, R. (2000). Cognitive social learning and related perspectives on drug craving. *Addiction* **95**:155–163.

Nunes, E., Levin, F. (2004). Treatment of depression in patients with alcohol or other drug dependence. *Journal of the American Medical Association* **291**:1887–1896.

O'Farrell, T.J., Choquette, K.A., Cutter, H.S.G., Brown, E.D., McCourt, W.F. (1993). Behavioral marital therapy with and without additional couples relapse prevention sessions for alcoholics and their wives. *Journal of Studies on Alcohol* **54**:652–666.

Obert, J.L., McCann, M.J., Marinelli-Casey, P. et al. (2000). The matrix model of outpatient stimulant abuse treatment: History and description. *Journal of Psychoactive Drugs* **32**:157–164.

Office of Applied Studies (2000). *National household survey on drug abuse: Main findings 1998.* Rockville: Substance Abuse and Mental Health Services Administration.

Palfai, T.P., Ostafin, B.D. (2003). Alcohol-related motivational tendencies in hazardous drinkers: Assessing implicit response tendencies using the modified-IAT. *Behaviour Research and Therapy* **41**:1148–1162.

Piasecki, T.M., Fiore, M.C., McCarthy, D.E., Baker, T.B. (2002). Have we lost our way? The need for dynamic formulations of smoking relapse proneness. *Addiction* **97**(9):1098–1108.

Polivy, J., Herman, C.P. (2002). If at first you don't succeed: False hopes of self-change. *American Psychologist* **109**:74–86.

Prochaski, J.O., DiClementa, C.C. (1984). *The transtheoretical approach: Crossing the traditional boundaries of therapy.* Malabar: Krieger.

Rawson, R., McCann, M., Flammino, F., Shoptaw, S., Miotto, K., Reiber, C. et al. (2002). A comparison of contingency management and cognitive-behavioral approaches for cocaine- and methamphetamine-dependent individuals. *Archives in General Psychiatry* **59**:817–824.

Rawson, R.A. and the Methamphetamine Treatment Project Corporate Authors. (2004). A multi-site comparison of psychosocial approaches for the treatment of methamphetamine dependence. *Addiction* **99**:708–717.

Rawson, R.A., Huber, A., Brethen, P.B., Obert, J.L., Bulati, V., Shoptaw, S., Ling, W. (2000). Methamphetamine and cocaine users: Differences in characteristics and treatment retention. *Journal of Psychoactive Drugs* **32**:233–238.

Rawson, R.A., Huber, A., McCann, M.J., Shoptaw, S., Farabee, D., Reiber, C. et al. (2002). A comparison of contingency management and cognitive-behavioral approaches during methadone maintenance for cocaine dependence. *Archives of General Psychiatry* **59**:817–824.

Rawson, R.A., Obert, J.L., McCann, M.J. et al. (1993). Relapse prevention models for substance abuse treatment. *Psychotherapy* **30**:284–298.

Rawson, R.A., Obert, J.L., McCann, M.J., Ling, W. (2005). The matrix model of intensive outpatient alcohol and drug treatment: A 16-week individualized program. Center City, MN: Hazelden.

Rawson, R.A., Obert, J.L., McCann, M.J., Smith, D.P., Scheffey, E.H. (1989). *The neurobehavioral treatment manual*. Beverly Hills: Matrix.

Rawson, R.A., Shoptaw, S.J., Obert, J.L., McCann, M.J., Hasson, A.L., Marinelli Casey, P.M. et al. (1995). An intensive outpatient approach for cocaine abuse treatment: The Matrix Model. *Journal of Substance Abuse Treatment* **12**:117–127.

Robins, L.N., Regier, D.A. (1991). *Psychiatric disorders in America*. New York: MacMillan.

Robinson, T.E., Berridge, K.C. (2000). The psychology and neurobiology of addiction: An incentive-sensitization. *Addiction* **95**:91–118.

Salloum, I.M., Cornelius, J.R., Daley, D.C., Kirsici, L., Himmelhoch, J.M., Thase, M.E. (2005). Efficacy of valproate maintenance in patients with bipolar disorder and alcoholism. *Archives of General Psychiatry* **62**:37–45.

Salloum, I.M., Douaihy, A., Cornelius, J.R., Kirisci, L., Kelly, T.M., Hayes, J. (In press). Divalproex utility in bipolar disorder with co-occurring cocaine dependence: A pilot study. *Addictive Behaviors*.

SAMHSA (2004). Results from the 2003 National Survey on Drug Use and Health (NSDUH Series H-25), Office of Applied Studies, Substance Abuse and Mental Health Service Administration, Rockville, MD.

Sandahl, C. (1984). Determinants of relapse among alcoholics: A cross-cultural replication study. *International Journal of the Addictions* **19**:833–848.

Sayette, M.A., Shiffman, S., Riffany, S.T., Niaura, R.S., Martin, C.S., Shadel, W.G. (2000). The measurement of drug craving. *Addiction* **95**:189–210.

Schmitz, J.M., Oswald, L.M., Jacks, S., Rustin, T., Rhoades, H.M., Grabowsky, J. (1997). Relapse prevention treatment for cocaine dependence: Group versus individual format. *Addictive Behaviors* **22**:405–418.

Schroter, M., Collins, S.E., Frittrang, T., Buchkremer, G., Batra, A. (2005). Randomized controlled trial of relapse prevention and a standard behavioral intervention with adult smokers. *Addictive Behaviors*. Available online 1 September 2005.

Scott, C.K., Foss, M.A., Dennis, M.L. (2005). Pathways in the relapse–treatment–recovery cycle over 3 years. *Journal of Substance Abuse Treatment* **28**:S63–S72.

Shiffman, S. (1987). Maintenance and relapse: Coping with temptation. In Nirenberg, T.D., Maisto, S.A., eds., *Developments in the assessment and treatment of addictive behaviors*, 353–385. Norwood: Ablex.

Shiffman, S. (1989). Conceptual issues in the study of relapse. In Gossop, M., ed., *Relapse and addictive behaviour*, 148–179. London: Tavistock/Routledge.

Shiffman, S., Balabanis, M.H., Paty, J.A., Engberg, J., Gwaltney, C.J., Liu, K.S. et al. (2000). Dynamic effects of self-efficacy on smoking lapse and relapse. *Health Psychology* **19**:315–323.

Shiffman, S., Hickcox, M., Paty, J.A., Gnys, M., Kassel, J.D., Richards, T.J. (1996). Progression from a smoking lapse to relapse: Prediction from abstinence violation effects, nicotine dependence, and lapse characteristics. *Journal of Consulting and Clinical Psychology* **64**:993–1002.

Shiffman, S., Paty, J.A., Gnys, M., Kassel, J.D., Hickcox, M. (1996). First lapses to smoking: Within subject analysis of real time reports. *Journal of Consulting and Clinical Psychology* **2**:366–379.

Shiffman, S., Waters, A.J. (2004). Negative affect and smoking lapses: A prospective analysis. *Journal of Consulting and Clinical Psychology* **72**:191–201.

Shoptaw, S., Reback, C.J., Frosch, D.L. et al. (1998). Stimulant abuse treatment as HIV prevention. *Journal of Addictive Diseases* **17**:19–32.

Simpson, D.D., Joe, G.W., Broome, K.M. (2002). A national 5-year follow-up of treatment outcomes for cocaine dependence. *Archives of General Psychiatry* **59**:538–544.

Sinha, R., Garcia, M., Paliwal, P., Kreek, M.J., Rounsaville, B. (2006). Stress-induced cocaine craving and hypothalamic-pituitary-adrenal responses are predictive of cocaine relapse outcomes. *Archives of General Psychiatry* **63**:324–331.

Sklar, S.M., Annis, H.M., Turner, N.E. (1997). Development and validation of the Drug-Taking Confidence Questionnaire: A measure of coping self-efficacy. *Addictive Behaviors* **22**:655–670.

Stacy, A.W., Ames, S.L., Leigh, B.C. (2004). An implicit cognition assessment approach to relapse, secondary prevention, and media effects. *Cognitive and Behavioral Practice* **11**:139–148.

Stout, R.L., Longabaugh, R., Rubin, R. (1996). Predictive validity of Marlatt's taxonomy versus a more general relapse code. *Addiction* **91**:99–110.

Streeton, C., Whelan, G. (2001). Naltrexone, a relapse prevention maintenance treatment of alcohol dependence: A meta-analysis of randomized controlled trials. *Alcohol and Alcoholism* **36**:544–552.

Strowig, A.B. (2000). Relapse determinants reports by men treated for alcohol dependence. *Journal of Substance Abuse Treatment* **19**:469–474.

Saunders, B., Allsop, S. (1989). Relapse: A critique. In Gossop, M., ed., *Relapse and addictive behaviour*, 249–277. London: Routledge.

Swendsen, J., Tennen, H., Carney, M.A., Affleck, G., Willard, A., Hromi, A. (2000). Mood and alcohol consumption: An experience sampling test of self-medication hypothesis. *Journal of Abnormal Psychology* **109**:198–204.

Tate, S.R., Brown, S.A., Unrod, M., Ramo, D.E. (2004). Context of relapse for substance-dependent adults with and without comorbid psychiatric disorders. *Addictive Behaviors* **29**:1707–1724.

The COMBINE Study Group. (2003a). Testing combined pharmacotherapies and behavioral interventions for alcohol dependence (the COMBINE study): Rationale and methods. *Alcoholism, Clinical and Experimental Research* **27**:1107–1122.

The COMBINE Study Group. (2003b). Testing combined pharmacotherapies and behavioral interventions for alcohol dependence (the COMBINE study): A pilot feasibility study. *Alcoholism, Clinical and Experimental Research* **27**:1123–1131.

The Matrix Center. (1989). *The neurobehavioral treatment model volume II: Group sessions.* Beverly Hills: Matrix Center.

Tiffany, S.T. (1990). A cognitive model of drug urges and drug use behavior: Role of automatic and non-automatic processes. *Psychological Review* **97**:147–168.

Tiffany, S.T., Carter, B.L., Singleton, E.G. (2000). Challenges in the manipulation, assessment and interpretation of craving relevant variables. *Addiction* **95**:177–187.

Verheul, R., van den Brink, W., Geerlings, P. (1999). A three-pathways psychobiological model of craving for alcohol. *Alcohol and Alcoholism* **34**:197–222.

Vivelva, I., Iraurgi, I. (2001). Cognitive and behavioural factors as predictors of abstinence following treatment for alcohol dependence. *Addiction* **96**:297–303.

Walitzer, K.S., Dearing, R. (2006). Gender differences in alcohol and substance use relapse. *Clinical Psychology Review* **26**:128–148.

Wang, S.J., Winchell, C.J., McCormick, C.G., Nevius, S.E., O'Neill, R.T. (2002). Short of complete abstinence: An analysis exploration of multiple drinking episodes in alcoholism treatment trials. *Alcohol: Clinical and Experimental Research* **26**:1803–1809.

Washton, A.M. (2001). Group therapy: A clinician's guide to doing what works. In Coombs, R., ed., *Addiction recovery tools: A practical handbook.* Newbury Park: Sage Publications.

Washton, A.M. (2002). Outpatient groups at different stages of substance abuse treatment: Preparation, initial abstinence, and relapse prevention. In Brook, D.W., Spitz, H.I., eds., *The group therapy of substance abuse.* New York: Haworth Medical Publishing.

Westermyer, J.J., Weiss, R.D., Zeidonis, D.M., eds. (2003). *Integrated treatment for mood and substance use disorders.* Baltimore, MD: The Johns Hopkins University Press.

Wilson, P.H. (1992). Relapse prevention: Conceptual and methodological issues. In Wilson, P.H., ed., *Principles and practice of relapse prevention*, 1–22. New York: Guilford Press.

Winters, J., Fals-Stewart, W., O'Farrell, T.J., Birchler, G.R., Kelley, M.L. (2002). Behavioral couples therapy for female substance-abusing patients: Effects on substance use and relationship adjustment. *Journal of Consulting and Clinical Psychology* **70**:344–355.

Witkiewitz, K., Marlatt, G.A. (2004). Relapse prevention for alcohol and drug problems: That was Zen, this is Tao. *American Psychologist* **59**:224–235.

Wu, L.T., Kouzis, A.C., Leaf, P.J. (1999). Influence of comorbid alcohol and psychiatric disorders on utilization of mental health services in the national comorbidity survey. *American Journal of Psychiatry* **16**:1230–1236.

Zweben, A., Cisler, R.A. (2003). Clinical and methodological utility of a composite outcome measure for alcohol treatment research. *Alcohol: Clinical and Experimental Research* **27**:1680–1685.

Zywiak, W.H., Connors, G.J., Maisto, S.A., Westerberg, V.S. (1996). Relapse research and the Reasons for Drinking Questionnaire: A factor analysis of Marlatt's relapse taxonomy. *Addiction* **91**:S121–S130.

INTERNET RESOURCES

- http://adai.washington.edu/ebp
- www.drugabuse.gov/ADAC/ADAC1.html
- www.csat.samsha.gov/publications.html
- www.harmreduction.org
- www.drugabuse.gov/TB/Clinical/ClinicalToolbox.html
- www.drdennisdaley.com

4

MINDFULNESS-BASED COGNITIVE THERAPY AS A RELAPSE PREVENTION APPROACH TO DEPRESSION

MARK A. LAU AND ZINDEL V. SEGAL

Centre for Addiction and Mental Health
University of Toronto
Toronto, Ontario

INTRODUCTION TO MINDFULNESS-BASED COGNITIVE THERAPY (MBCT)

And the faculty of voluntarily bringing back a wandering attention, over and over again, is the very root of judgment, character, and will. No one is *compos sui* if he have it not. An education which should improve this faculty would be *the* education *par excellence*. But it is easier to define this ideal than to give practical instructions for bringing it about. (James, 1890, p. 401)

Approximately 100 years after William James wrote this passage, Zindel Segal, John Teasdale, and Mark Williams were faced with addressing a similar issue in designing a new psychosocial intervention, mindfulness-based cognitive therapy (MBCT), to reduce depressive relapse or recurrence. After a careful theoretical analysis (Teasdale, Segal & Williams, 1995), they found themselves looking, in part, for ways to educate at-risk individuals to voluntarily bring back a "wandering attention" captured by ruminative thought patterns implicated in depressive relapse. The solution lay, in large part, in mindfulness training as developed by Jon Kabat-Zinn and his colleagues at the University of Massachusetts Medical Center (Kabat-Zinn, 1990). Integrating mindfulness training with traditional cognitive therapy (CT) techniques (Beck, Rush, Shaw & Emory, 1979) resulted in the creation of MBCT as described in the treatment manual, *Mindfulness-Based Cognitive Therapy for Depression: A New Approach to Preventing Relapse*

(Segal et al., 2002). Thus, in this chapter, we present MBCT, a novel, theory-driven, psychological intervention designed to reduce relapse in recurrent major depression.

DEFINITION OF MINDFULNESS

Broadly conceptualized, mindfulness has been described as a nonelaborative, nonjudgmental, present-centered awareness in which each thought, feeling, or sensation that arises in the attentional field is acknowledged and accepted as it is (Kabat-Zinn, 1990; Segal, Williams & Teasdale, 2002; Shapiro & Schwartz, 1999). In mindfulness, thoughts and feelings are observed as events in the mind, without over-identifying with them, and without reacting to them in an automatic, habitual pattern of reactivity. This is thought to introduce a space between one's perception and response, enabling one to respond to situations reflectively versus reflexively.

More recently, Bishop et al. (2004) have operationally defined a two-component model of mindfulness: (1) the self-regulation of attention of immediate experience, thereby allowing for increased recognition of mental events in the present moment; and (2) adopting an orientation of curiosity, openness, and acceptance toward one's experiences in each moment. These two elements are represented in many discussions of mindfulness and psychotherapy (e.g., Brown & Ryan, 2004; Germer, 2005a; Hayes & Feldman, 2004), and there is empirical support for these two components based on behavioral (Anderson, Lau, Segal & Bishop, 2006) and self-report (Lau et al., 2006) data.

The term mindfulness also commonly refers to the practice of cultivating mindfulness (Germer, 2005a), which typically is developed through various meditation techniques that originate from Buddhist spiritual practices (Hanh, 1976). Interestingly, the past 20 years has witnessed a surge in the clinical use of mindfulness including, in particular, the integration of mindfulness with cognitive-behavioral psychotherapies. This has resulted in mindfulness being cultivated in psychotherapy in two ways that are different but not mutually exclusive. First, mindfulness-informed psychotherapy uses a theoretical framework informed by insights derived from both Buddhist and Western psychology, as well as the personal experience of therapists. Mindfulness-informed treatments include: behavioral activation for depression (Martell et al., 2001) and Acceptance and Commitment Therapy (ACT) (Hayes, Strosahl & Wilson, 1999). Second, mindfulness-based psychotherapy explicitly educates patients in the practice of mindfulness. These treatments can vary in the degree to which they are based on mindfulness training. On the one hand, Dialectical Behavior Therapy (DBT) (Linehan, 1993), a treatment for borderline personality disorder (BPD), incorporates some formal meditation practice, the degree of which is limited, in part, by the perceived capacity or willingness of this patient group to be aware of and attend to present experience. On the other hand, mindfulness-based stress reduction (MBSR) (Kabat-Zinn, 1990) is an intensive eight- to ten-week mindfulness training course that is based almost entirely on formal and informal mind-fulness practices. MBCT (Segal et al., 2002) places close to MBSR on this continuum as it draws heavily on the MBSR program in combination with CT techniques.

EMPIRICAL SUPPORT FOR MBCT IN PREVENTING DEPRESSIVE RELAPSE

Two randomized controlled clinical trials (Ma & Teasdale, 2004; Teasdale, Segal, Williams, Ridgeway, Soulsby & Lau, 2000) support the efficacy of MBCT in preventing depressive relapse. The first multicenter trial (n = 145) was con-ducted at three sites (Toronto, Canada; Cambridge, England; Bangor, Wales) and the second trial (n = 75) was a single site replication (Cambridge, England). In both trials, individuals who had recovered from at least two episodes of depres-sion and were symptom-free and off medication for at least three months before the study were randomized to receive either MBCT or to continue with treatment as usual (TAU). In the MBCT group, individuals participated in eight weekly group sessions plus four follow-up sessions scheduled at one-, two-, three-, and four-month intervals. Individuals in both groups were followed for a total of 60 weeks from the time of enrollment.

The primary outcome measure was whether and when patients experienced relapse or recurrence defined as meeting DSM-IIIR criteria for a major depressive episode (American Psychiatric Association, 1987), as assessed by the Structured Clinical Interview for Diagnosis (SCID) (Spitzer, Williams, Gibbon & First, 1992) administered at bimonthly assessments throughout the trial. In both trials, the samples were stratified according to the number of previous episodes (two vs. three or more). The results from the first study revealed a significantly dif-ferent pattern of results for individuals with two versus three or more episodes. For those individuals with only two previous episodes (23% of the sample), the relapse rates between the MBCT and TAU groups were not statistically different. On the other hand, for the group with three or more episodes (77% of the sample), there was a statistically significant difference in relapse rates between those who received a "minimum effective dose" (at least four of the eight weekly MBCT sessions) of MBCT (37%) and TAU (66%) groups over the 60-week study period. The difference in relapse rates between TAU and MBCT remained statistically significant when all those allocated to the MBCT condition were considered (irrespective of whether or not they received a "minimally adequate dose" of MBCT—this is called the Intention to Treat sample, or ITT). For this sample, the relapse rate was 40 percent.

The benefits of MBCT could not be accounted for by a greater use of anti-depressant medication as those in the MBCT group actually used less medication than those in the TAU group. Similarly, Ma and Teasdale (2004) reported relapse rates, based on ITT analyses, for individuals with three or more depressive epi-sodes (73% of the sample) of 36 percent for MBCT versus 78 percent for TAU, whereas there was no prophylactic advantage of MBCT for individuals with a history of only two depressive episodes.

Although these results support MBCT's efficacy in reducing depressive relapse, the study design did not permit ruling out confounding explanations for the treatment benefits of nonspecific factors such as group participation and/or therapeutic attention. There is indirect support, however, that the effects of MBCT are consistent with the underlying theoretical rationale of MBCT, which derives in large part from answering the two fundamental questions described later in this chapter. First, the demonstration that MBCT was more effective than TAU for individuals with a history of three or more episodes is consistent with the view that MBCT helps individuals disrupt autonomous relapse processes that involve the automatic reactivation of depressogenic thinking patterns by dysphoria at times of potential relapse (see pp. 75–76; Segal et al., 2002). Convergent with this finding is that MBCT was more effective than TAU for depression onsets where no antecedent major life stressors were reported, but that there was no difference between MBCT and TAU for depressive episodes that were preceded by a major life stressor (Ma & Teasdale, 2004). Thus, MBCT appears to be more effective in reducing relapse rates in those individuals whose depressive relapse is more likely to be due to autonomous processes rather than a major life stressor.

Second, MBCT was designed to prevent depressive relapse by increasing the ability to decenter from negative thinking patterns. Direct support for this comes from Teasdale, Moore, Hayhurst, Pope, Williams, and Segal (2002), who investigated the ability to decenter in a subset of participants from the original multicenter trial (Teasdale et al., 2000). Decentering was operationalized using the Measure of Awareness and Coping in Autobiographical Memory (MACAM) (Moore, Hayhurst & Teasdale, 1996), which involves analyzing the autobiographical memories stimulated by depression-related cues and measures the ability to see negative thoughts and feelings as passing mental events rather than as an aspect of self. MBCT was associated with increased metacognitive awareness in relation to negative thoughts and feelings. Furthermore, encouraging preliminary support specifically for the importance of the mindfulness component of MBCT comes from a qualitative study of seven participants from the first multicenter trial who identified the development of mindfulness skills as one of MBCT's key elements that contributed to reduced relapse risk (Mason & Hargreaves, 2001).

OVERVIEW OF MBCT

HISTORICAL BACKGROUND

The impetus for developing MBCT came from the growing literature that depression is best viewed as a chronic, lifelong, recurrent disorder. Major depressive disorder (MDD) remains a daunting mental health challenge, with lifetime prevalence rates estimated between 2.9 and 12.6 per 100 and lifetime risk estimated at 17 to 19 percent (Kessler et al., 1994). According to the World Health Organization (WHO), when the burden of ill health imposed by all diseases worldwide was considered, unipolar major depression imposed the fourth greatest burden (Murray & Lopez, 1998). Alarmingly, this burden is projected to increase both absolutely and relatively such that by the year 2020 depression will impose the second greatest burden of ill health, very close behind the top cause, ischemic heart disease.

A major reason for the scale of the burden caused by MDD is that, as well as being a condition with a high rate of incidence, MDD is now viewed as a chronic, lifelong illness with a high risk for relapse and/or recurrence (Berti Ceroni, Neri & Pezzoli, 1984; Keller, Lavori, Lewis & Klerman, 1983; for review see Judd, 1997). For example, those who recover from an initial episode of depression have a 50 percent chance of a second episode, and for those with a history of two or more episodes, then the relapse/recurrence risk increases to 70 to 80 percent. Those who suffer from one depressive episode will "experience an average of 4 lifetime major depressive episodes of 20 weeks duration each" (Judd, 1997, p. 990).

Such data point to effective prevention of relapse and recurrence as a central challenge in the overall management of major depressive disorder. Currently, maintenance pharmacotherapy is the best validated and most widely used approach to prophylaxis in depression (e.g., Kupfer et al., 1992). In this approach, patients who have recovered following treatment of the acute episode by antidepressant medication continue to take their medication as a way to reduce risk of further episodes. However, the protection from maintenance pharmacotherapy lasts only as long as patients continue to take their antidepressant medication. By contrast, it appears that CT as an acute treatment for depression also has long-term effects in preventing future relapse (Blackburn, Eunson & Bishop, 1986; Evans et al., 1992; Hollon et al., 2005; Shea et al., 1992; Simons, Murphy, Levine & Wetzel, 1986). These data were consistent with the possibility that a maintenance version of CT could be developed that might offer a psychosocial alternative to pharmacotherapy in preventing depressive relapse. Yet, instead of making modifications to CT, Segal et al. (2002) developed MBCT based on the answers to two central questions: (1) What are the psychological mechanisms underlying cognitive vulnerability to depressive relapse, and (2) how might CT reduce depressive relapse?

A COGNITIVE VULNERABILITY MODEL
OF DEPRESSIVE RELAPSE

This model attempts to explain the increased risk of relapse/recurrence with increased number of previous depressive episodes. There is evidence that distinct processes are involved in the onset of first versus recurrent depressive episodes

Sayle
+
Recurry
episodes

(Lewinsohn, Allen, Seeley & Gotlib, 1999). Whereas major life stressors are a stronger predictor of first depression onsets versus recurrent episodes, dysphoric mood and dysfunctional thinking styles are more highly correlated with a history of previous depressive episodes, and this correlation is a stronger predictor of recurrent episodes than first onset episodes. These results are part of a larger body of support for John Teasdale's (1988) differential activation hypothesis (DAH) as a variable risk factor for depressive relapse (Lau, Segal & Williams, 2004). The DAH maintains that repeated associations between depressed mood and patterns of negative thinking during episodes of depression lead to a higher likelihood of reactivation of dysfunctional thinking in dysphoric mood states. In other words, less environmental stress is required to provoke relapse. Rather, the processes mediating relapse may become more autonomous with increasing experience of depression (Teasdale et al., 1995). Specifically, it is the reinstatement of negative thinking patterns activated in dysphoric mood that can serve to maintain depression. Data consistent with this view derive from the demonstration that a ruminative response style to depression can perpetuate depression (Nolen-Hoeksema, 1991).

This model suggests that relapse risk might be reduced first by increasing one's awareness of negative thinking at times of potential relapse and, second, by responding in ways that allow one to uncouple from the reactivated negative thought streams. Moreover, any intervention designed to reduce relapse risk should lead to a change in the patterns of cognitive processing that become activated in dysphoric states. It is not essential, or even desirable, that the treatment should aim to eliminate the experience of sadness. Rather, the aim should be to normalize the pattern of thinking in states of mild sadness so that these moods remain mild and do not escalate to more severe affective states.

HOW COGNITIVE THERAPY REDUCES DEPRESSIVE RELAPSE/RECURRENCE

A growing body of literature demonstrates that treating acute depression with CT significantly reduces subsequent relapse risk as compared to discontinuation pharmacotherapy (Blackburn et al., 1986; Evans et al., 1992; Hollon et al., 2005; Shea et al., 1992; Simons et al., 1986). With respect to designing a novel prophylactic intervention for depression, it was important to understand how CT might achieve these effects. Beck et al.'s (1979) cognitive model proposed that depression vulnerability was related to underlying dysfunctional attitudes. Thus, it would follow that CT reduces depressive relapse risk by modifying those dysfunctional attitudes. However, Barber & DeRubeis (1989) argued that this view was not broadly supported. For example, in the previously mentioned studies, CT and pharmacotherapy typically did not differ on post-treatment measures of dysfunctional attitudes.

Alternatively, Ingram & Hollon (1986) proposed that CT has its prophylactic effects by facilitating the individual's ability to decenter or distance from his or her depressive thoughts such that they are no longer seen as absolutely true. Although the concept of decentering had been recognized in previous discussions of CT (e.g., Beck et al., 1979), it typically had been viewed as simply a means to the end of thought content change. Conversely, a shift in one's cognitive perspective known as decentering or disidentification might lead to a change in one's relationship to negative thoughts and feelings such that one can see negative thoughts and feelings simply as passing events in the mind rather than reflections of reality. At the time MBCT was being developed by Segal and colleagues, this view of how CT prevented depressive relapse was more consistent both with their clinical experience and their theoretical analysis.

Thus, this cognitive vulnerability model of depressive relapse suggested developing a treatment that would first develop skills in becoming aware of negative thoughts and feelings that are reactivated by dysphoric mood, and second, to develop a different relationship to those thoughts and feelings in order to interrupt negative thought patterns. Moreover, the emphasis on developing a different relationship to one's thoughts and feelings versus specifically changing thought content opened up the possibility to consider additional treatment approaches to CT. One such approach was the MBSR program (Kabat-Zinn, 1990), which facilitated awareness of moment-by-moment experience and fostered a decentered relationship to one's thoughts and feelings in the service of helping individuals who suffered from intractable chronic pain. Thus, Teasdale et al. (1995) proposed an integrated treatment that combined mindfulness meditation training with elements of CT in order to prevent the consolidation of negative thinking patterns that contribute to depressive relapse.

KEY PRINCIPLES

MBCT consists primarily of an integration of traditional MBSR exercises with standard CT techniques. MBSR exercises included in MBCT are formal mindfulness meditation practices such as the body scan, mindful stretching, mindfulness of breath/body/sounds/thoughts, as well as informal practices that encourage the application of mindfulness skills in everyday life (e.g., eating a meal mindfully, monitoring physical sensations, thoughts and feelings during pleasant and unpleasant experiences). The CT techniques include psychoeducation about depression symptoms and automatic thoughts, exercises designed to demonstrate the cognitive model and how the nature of one's thoughts can change depending on the situation, questioning of automatic thoughts, identifying activities that provide feelings of mastery and/or pleasure as well as creating a specific relapse prevention plan. In addition, MBCT includes the introduction of the three-minute breathing space to facilitate present moment awareness in everyday upsetting situations (Segal et al., 2002).

MBCT also includes a modified version of the inquiry process used in MBSR as a way of responding to participants' comments on their meditation experiences. This inquiry process is somewhat similar to Socratic questioning as defined by Padesky (1993), which serves to help individuals generate their own solutions to life's problems. In MBCT, inquiry facilitates awareness of automatic reactions in order to help people to discover aspects of themselves in the service of helping them understand how meditation might help them prevent depressive relapse. Finally, participants in the MBCT program are asked to engage in a daily meditation practice and homework exercises directed at integrating the application of awareness skills into daily life.

Together the skills taught in MBCT can facilitate awareness of negative thinking patterns with an accepting attitude in order to help the individual respond in a flexible and deliberate way to these thinking patterns at times of potential relapse. What follows is a brief description of how these goals are accomplished over the course of the eight-week treatment.

AWARENESS OF PRESENT EXPERIENCE
WITH ACCEPTANCE

The first four MBCT sessions are devoted, in large part, to facilitating non-judgment awareness of present experience. This is accomplished, in large part, via the formal meditation practices, which help participants to learn a number of important skills including concentration, awareness of thoughts, feelings, and bodily sensations as well as being in the present moment. Together, these skills facilitate the participants' ability to deconstruct their experience into the component elements of physical sensations and the accompanying thoughts and emotions. This awareness is enhanced and made more specific to depression using a CT exercise, which teaches that one's reactions to situations are influenced by one's thoughts or interpretations of events. Furthermore, the implicit message of this exercise is that thoughts are not facts, which is made more explicit later in session six.

AWARENESS OF DEPRESSION-RELATED EXPERIENCE

Specific awareness of depression-related experience is facilitated through psychoeducation regarding the nature of depressive symptoms as well as the types of negative thinking that can occur in depression in order to facilitate one's ability to detect experiences that might indicate potential relapse.

DEVELOP MORE FLEXIBLE, DELIBERATE RESPONSES
AT TIMES OF POTENTIAL RELAPSE

The second half of the program is directed toward developing more flexible, deliberate responses at times of potential relapse. In session five, acceptance as a skillful first step in dealing with one's experience is made explicit. Up until

this time, participants have been implicitly practicing acceptance in their meditations by being encouraged to bring awareness to their experience with an attitude
of nonjudgment. Acceptance is made explicit as a first step in dealing with difficulties, for example, by introducing specific instructions that encourage acceptance near the end of the three-minute breathing space. In session six, the theme
is "thoughts are not facts." This theme is made explicit, in part, via a CT exercise
that involves describing one's thoughts after a coworker rushes off without stopping to talk, depending on whether one was in a good mood or already upset
when this happened. This exercise is designed to illustrate that one's interpretations can depend on one's mood and may not necessarily represent reality. Thus,
the suggestion is to take a step back and question the veracity of one's thoughts.
In session seven, participants engage in specific CT relapse prevention strategies
geared toward creating a deliberate action plan that can be utilized at the time
of potential relapse (such as involving family members in an "early warning"
system, keeping written suggestions to engage in activities that are helpful in
interrupting relapse-engendering processes, or to look out for habitual negative
thoughts).

HOW MBCT IS SIMILAR AND DIFFERENT WITH CT AND MBSR

As the name suggests, Mindfulness-Based Cognitive Therapy shares similarities with more traditional CT. The most important of these is the focus on relapse
prevention, which depends on identifying triggers and potential warning signs of
an incipient relapse as well as developing an action plan of how the patient can
best take care of themselves in this event. Other similarities include a focus on
educating patients about the symptoms of depression including the experience of
automatic thoughts, monitoring thoughts and feelings in unpleasant situations,
and rating activities for the degree of pleasure and mastery they evoke.

However, MBCT significantly differs from CT in a number of important ways.
The most important difference is MBCT's emphasis of an acceptance-based
approach versus CT's change-based orientation. To illustrate the difference
between acceptance-based and a change-based approach, consider the negative
thought "I am unlovable." Mindfulness practice invites the meditator to notice
and accept this thought as an event occurring in the mind rather than as a truth
that defines the self. Thus mindfulness offers the potential of relating differently
to pain and distress; specifically, it can alter one's attitude or relation to thoughts,
such that they are less likely to influence subsequent feelings and behaviors. In
contrast, CT involves the evaluation and the possibility of restructuring cognitions and beliefs in the service of acquiring more functional ways of viewing the
world. Further differences between MBCT and CT are that there is no attempt
in MBCT to induce or expose the individual to problematic situations. Rather,

patients are encouraged to bring awareness and openness to their experience as it unfolds moment by moment. Finally, MBCT includes minimum guidelines about the current meditation practice of the therapist, which are discussed in more detail later.

In terms of how MBCT compares with MBSR, MBCT is a hybrid of the original MBSR course in that it draws heavily from the core mindfulness meditation practices of MBSR. However, while MBSR is provided to groups, heterogeneous with respect to medical condition, with the purpose of providing skills to better deal with stress, MBCT was developed specifically to reduce relapse risk for remitted depressed individuals. Thus, MBSR and MBCT diverge most importantly with respect to the various techniques (e.g., psychoeducation) geared to helping the patient better deal with stress versus depression.

ASSESSMENT

MBCT was specifically designed and evaluated for remitted depressed patients. Eligibility for participation in an MBCT group is determined during an initial assessment interview. First, depression status is assessed using a diagnostic interview (e.g., Structured Clinical Interview for Diagnosis for DSM-IV (SCID-IV); First, Spitzer, Gibbon & Williams, 1996) and symptom severity measures (e.g., Hamilton Rating Scale for Depression, HRSD; Hamilton, 1960). Second, willingness to be patient and persist with the demands of the program is determined. Third, persons are not accepted into the program if they are actively suicidal *and* have no other form of counseling support, or they are currently abusing drugs or alcohol. The purpose of MBCT is to help remitted depressed patients stay well, yet this is a population with a high risk of relapse. Thus, assessment at the end of the program (e.g., SCID-IV, HRSD) is directed toward ensuring that participants are not experiencing a return of depressive symptoms.

IMPLEMENTATION

The MBCT program as originally developed (Segal et al., 2002) and subsequently evaluated in two clinical trials as described earlier included an initial individual interview, eight weekly two-hour group sessions, typically led by one instructor, with up to 12 recovered depressed patients, and four follow-up group sessions over the next year. However, MBCT as currently delivered in our center has undergone two minor modifications. First, session length now ranges from 2 to 2.5 hours to allow sufficient time to cover all the session material. Second, instead of four follow-up sessions, a full weekend day of meditation is offered, typically between the sixth and seventh session of the program. Graduates of previous MBCT programs are also invited to attend the day of meditation practice.

WHO IS QUALIFIED TO PROVIDE MBCT?

The integration of mindfulness meditation with CT in MBCT and providing the treatment in a group format has important training implications for potential MBCT instructors. Segal and colleagues (2002) recommend that potential MBCT instructors have (1) recognized training in counseling or psychotherapy, or as a mental health professional; (2) training in cognitive therapy and running groups; (3) participation in a week-long teacher development intensive workshop on MBCT; and (4) very importantly, an ongoing meditation practice. Jon Kabat-Zinn and his colleagues have always maintained the importance of having an ongoing daily meditation practice as well as having attended meditation retreats of at least a week to 10 days before using mindfulness training with others. This recommendation derives from the view that instructors teach from their own experience and should embody the attitudes that they invite participants to practice. Most importantly, personal experience with meditation is necessary in order to best respond to difficulties brought up by the participants, rather than trying to answer with intellectual knowledge alone. Furthermore, instructors model "being present" during the classes, for example, by paying attention to what is experienced in the group moment-by-moment rather than giving instructions for exercises that will happen later in the session.

SESSION STRUCTURE

The first MBCT group session includes introductions, a review of rules (e.g., confidentiality), an introduction to meditation via eating a raisin mindfully, the body scan, a short breathing meditation, and the opportunity to discuss one's experience of these meditations. The subsequent seven sessions follow a consistent format. Each session begins with a meditation (e.g., body scan or sitting with breath, body, sounds, thoughts) to facilitate the transition from "doing" mode to a mode of "non-doing," or being present in the moment. The group members then have the opportunity to discuss, and ask questions about, their experiences with the meditation they just practiced as well as with the homework from the previous week. New material is then introduced through experiential exercises and discussed.

TYPICAL DIFFICULTIES AND ROADBLOCKS

The implementation of MBCT presents challenges to both the participant and the instructor stemming, in large part, from combining acceptance and change-based strategies in the same treatment. For the participant, there is the paradox of learning to develop a mode of nonstriving, nonjudgment and acceptance of one's experience in the service of the goal of reducing depressive relapse risk. For example, the participant is asked before the group begins not to judge their progress until the end of the eight-week program. Nevertheless, it is common for participants to bring a goal orientation to their meditation, which is reflected in such judgments as "Am I doing it right?, My mind wouldn't stay still, and I just got too upset." In fact, these are examples of characteristic responses to practicing meditation (e.g., attachment, aversion, boredom) that can ultimately interfere with one's motivation to practice. Thus, it is the instructor's role to facilitate awareness of these automatic responses and to teach the individual skillful means to deal with these barriers to practice.

The challenges faced by the instructor can vary depending on the instructor's familiarity with mindfulness meditation versus CT. Those with more experience in teaching meditation and little exposure to CT may be challenged by the directed nature of CT interventions or may need additional training in these interventions. On the other hand, the introduction of mindfulness-based treatments can present a challenge to change-oriented cognitive and behavioral therapists, largely because of the acceptance-based nature of mindfulness (Lau & McMain, 2005). One area where this difficulty presents most commonly is in conducting the inquiry into the participants' experiences of their meditation practice. It is very easy for a therapist with a change-based orientation to use the discussion as a springboard for teaching the patient another way to fix things. Yet, this is very different from the purpose of meditation. Rather, the goal of the instructor is to model the skills that are being taught in the group, namely, acceptance of experience as it unfolds, by bringing an open, curious, and gentle awareness to the person's experience in the service of helping them to clarify their experience. For example, disclosure of a judgment of one's meditation experience may serve as a marker for the instructor to further explore the person's reaction by investigating where it is experienced in the body and what happens to thoughts and feelings in relation to their physical experience. The ability to do this very often depends on the depth of the instructor's own meditation experience.

CLINICAL CASE ILLUSTRATION

In MBCT, the opportunities to track an individual's progress with the treatment are limited. There is an opportunity to establish the participant's pregroup functioning level in the precourse interview and to discuss progress in the postcourse interview. However, during the group, information on a participant's progress varies widely according to the individuals' level of disclosure in the group. In spite of this caveat, we will briefly present two case examples to illustrate what a successful and unsuccessful response might look like.

SUCCESSFUL RESPONSE TO MBCT

John was a 25-year-old single man who lived with his aunt and worked part time at a grocery store. He had experienced four previous depressive episodes and met criteria for Social Phobia, Generalized at the time of the initial interview. When depressed he described periods when his mood would spiral down, leading to suicidal ideation, which led to nonlethal attempts. One of the few times that John spoke up was in session 3 to say that he was experiencing anxiety during the meditation that had just been completed and as he was speaking. The instructor inquired as to what physical sensations Peter was aware of and where in his body he experienced them. The instructor then invited him to bring a gentle awareness to his experience of these sensations. In this case, when he did this, the sensations and the feeling of anxiety dissipated. At the post-MBCT interview, John reported that he found the program very important to him, giving it a rating of 10/10 in that it gave him tools to help him better manage his depressed and anxious feelings. He noted that he no longer was experiencing suicidal ideation, nor having problems with anxiety and depression. He was maintaining a meditation practice of 40 minutes/day, usually in the mornings, and meditated at a Buddhist temple once a week. He found that if he did not meditate on a given day he noticed the difference. Finally, he claimed that the program had "changed his life."

UNSUCCESSFUL RESPONSE TO MBCT

Mary, in her early fifties, was a single woman living alone in Toronto. She had experienced two previous depressive episodes, the first in her late teens and the second in her mid-forties. She also reported experiencing a low level of depression throughout her life when not in episode. At the time of initial assessment she did not meet criteria for Major Depressive Disorder nor dysthymia but, nevertheless, was experiencing residual depressive symptoms. Over the course of the group she was an active participant in the group discussions, often describing her meditation experience as "unremarkable." However, at the end of session 5 she appeared to be upset. The instructor phoned all group members after this session to deal with some practical matters regarding the session handouts. He inquired how Mary was finding the group. She reported that she was frustrated with the program as she expected more significant experiences as part of her meditation practice. Given that this was not happening, her motivation to practice was decreasing. At the post-MBCT interview, Mary reported that she continued to hope that the program might give her something to work with in order to better manage her ongoing depressive symptoms, which were unchanged from the start of the group. She was able to practice on some weeks, but was not as consistent as she would like to be. One possible explanation for this participant's lack of success with MBCT was her high expectations regarding the potential impact of meditation. Although a personality assessment was not done, from Mary's behavior and comments throughout the group, she likely held high expectations or standards throughout the rest of her life as well.

SPECIAL TOPICS

MBCT FOR PEOPLE WITH CO-OCCURRING DISORDERS

The efficacy of MBCT for individuals for co-occurring disorders comes from the two outcome trials described earlier, and from our own clinical experience. In the original studies, individuals with a history of schizophreniphorm disorders, current substance abuse, eating disorder, obsessive-compulsive disorder (OCD), organic mental disorder, pervasive developmental delay, or BPD were excluded for various reasons. Patients with eating disorders frequently experience secondary depression, however, MBCT was not designed to deal with the primary eating disorder. Those with OCD, BPD, and current substance abuse were excluded due to anticipated difficulties in engaging with the mindfulness strategies. For example, Linehan (1993) holds the opinion that patients with BPD are less able to productively engage in lengthy sitting practice.

Of course, individuals with a history of depression often experience a range of comorbid disorders such as anxiety or bipolar disorder. Our clinical experience suggests that individuals with most of these co-occurring disorders can benefit from MBCT, including, for example, John as described earlier. One possible exception, however, are individuals who have a history of trauma. Prescribing mindfulness practices in this instance should be guided by clinical judgment (Germer, 2005b). The ability for one to stabilize their attention in the face of traumatic memories is a necessary prerequisite for a mindfulness approach since being overwhelmed or destabilized by these memories can significantly detract from the usefulness of mindful exposure to the trauma.

SPECIAL POPULATIONS

One of the most frequently asked questions about MBCT is how effective it might be for the treatment of acute depression. It is important to emphasize that MBCT was specifically designed for treating remitted patients. How concentration difficulties, intensity of rumination, and decreased motivation associated with acute depression may interfere with the ability to benefit from the meditative practices remains to be evaluated in clinical trials.

However, MBCT is currently being evaluated in the treatment of recurrent suicidal ideation. The differential activation hypothosis (DAH), proposed as one account of the cognitive vulnerability model of depressive relapse underlying the development of MBCT, has been extended to the problem of suicidal relapse/recurrence (Lau et al., 2004). Furthermore, pilot work supports MBCT's usefulness for the prevention of recurrent suicidal behavior and an ongoing controlled clinical trial may provide further support (Williams, Duggan, Crane & Fennell, 2006).

CONCLUSIONS AND FUTURE DIRECTIONS

In sum, MBCT reduced relapse/recurrence rates by about 50 percent for individuals with a history of three or more depressive episodes over a one year follow-up as compared to TAU. These benefits were obtained with an average investment of less than five hours of instructor time per patient making this group skills-based program a cost-efficient approach for preventing depressive relapse. Moreover, the demonstration of MBCT's benefits in two randomized-controlled trials conducted by the treatment developers establishes MBCT as a *probably efficacious* treatment for the prevention of depressive relapse (Chambless & Hollon, 1998).

Future trials by an independent research team are required to establish MBCT as an *efficacious* treatment. Furthermore, MBCT's efficacy is currently being compared with continuation pharmacotherapy. Comparing MBCT with other treatments that control for nonspecific factors such as group participation, expectation of change, or therapeutic attention will help to determine whether MBCT's benefits can be attributed to the specific meditation/CT skills taught in this program. Recent efforts to operationally define mindfulness (e.g., Bishop et al., 2004) and the development of mindfulness self-report measures (e.g., Brown & Ryan, 2003; Lau et al., 2006) will permit the evaluation of the unique contribution of mindfulness meditation to enhancing mindfulness and reducing relapse risk. A related issue is determining the relationship of the treatment provider's meditation practice to outcome as many clinicians do not currently have a meditation practice. Finally, who benefits from MBCT needs to be clarified given the lack of demonstrated efficacy for individuals with just two previous depressive episodes.

REFERENCES

Anderson, N.D., Lau, M.A., Segal, Z.V., Bishop, S.R. (2006). Mindfulness-based stress reduction and attentional control. Manuscript under review.

American Psychiatric Association. (1987). *Diagnostic and statistical manual of mental disorders, 3e*. Washington, DC.

Barber, J.P., DeRubeis, R.J. (1989). On second thought: Where the action is in cognitive therapy for depression. *Cognitive Therapy and Research* **13**:441–457.

Beck, A.T., Rush, A.J., Shaw, B.F., Emery, G. (1979). *Cognitive therapy of depression*. New York: Guilford Press.

Berti Ceroni, G., Neri, C., Pezzoli, A. (1984). Chronicity in major depression. A naturalistic prospective study. *Journal of Affective Disorders* **7**:123–132.

Bishop, S.R., Lau, M.A., Shapiro, S., Carlson, L., Anderson, N.D., Carmody, J. et al. (2004). Mindfulness: A proposed operational definition. *Clinical Psychology: Science and Practice* **11**:230–241.

Blackburn, I.M., Eunson, K.M., Bishop, S. (1986). A two-year naturalistic follow-up of depressed patients treated with cognitive therapy, pharmacotherapy, and a combination of both. *Journal of Affective Disorders* **10**:67–75.

Brown, K.W., Ryan, R.M. (2003). The benefits of beings present: Mindfulness and its role in psychological well-being. *Journal of Personality and Social Psychology* **84**:822–848.

Brown, K., Ryan, R.M. (2004). Perils and promise in defining and measuring mindfulness: Observations from experience. *Clinical Psychology: Science and Practice* **11**:242–248.

Chambless, D.L., Hollon, S.D. (1998). Defining empirically supported therapies. *Journal of Consulting and Clinical Psychology* **66**:7–18.

Evans, J.D., Hollon, S.D., DeRubeis, R.J., Piasecki, J.M., Grove, W.M., Garvey, M.J. et al. (1992). Differential relapse following cognitive therapy and pharmacotherapy for depression. *Archives of General Psychiatry* **49**:802–808.

First, M.B., Spitzer, R.L., Gibbon, M., Williams, J.B.W. (1996). Structured Clinical Interview for DSM-IV Axis I Disorders—Patient Edition (SCID-I/P, Version 2.0).

Germer, C.K. (2005a). Mindfulness: What is it: What does it matter? In Germer, C.K., Siegel, R.D., Fulton, P.R., eds., *Mindfulness and Psychotherapy*. New York: Guilford Press.

Germer, C.K. (2005b). Teaching mindfulness in therapy. In Germer, C.K., Siegel, R.D., Fulton, P.R., eds., *Mindfulness and Psychotherapy*. New York: Guilford Press.

Hamilton, M. (1960). A rating scale for depression. *Journal of Neurology, Neurosurgery and Psychiatry* **23**:56–62.

Hanh, T.N. (1976). *The miracle of mindfulness: A manual for meditation*. Boston: Beacon Press.

Hayes, S.C., Feldman, G. (2004). Clarifying the construct of mindfulness in the context of emotion regulation and the process of change in therapy. *Clinical Psychology: Science and Practice* **11**:255–262.

Hayes, S.C., Strosahl, K., Wilson, K.G. (1999). *Acceptance and commitment therapy: An experiential approach to behavior change*. New York: Guilford Press.

Hollon, S., DeRubeis, R.J., Shelton, R.C., Amsterdam, J.D., Salomon, R.M., O'Reardon, J.P. et al. (2005). Prevention of relapse following cognitive therapy vs medications in moderate to severe depression. *Archives of General Psychiatry* **62**:417–422.

Ingram, R.E., Hollon, S.D. (1986). Cognitive therapy of depression from an information processing perspective. In Ingram, R.E., ed., *Information processing approaches to clinical psychology*, 259–281. San Diego: Academic Press, Inc.

Judd, L.J. (1997). The clinical course of unipolar major depressive disorders. *Archives of General Psychiatry* **54**:989–991.

James, W. (1890). *Principles of Psychology*. New York: Holt.

Kabat-Zinn, J. (1990). *Full Catastrophe Living: Using the Wisdom of Your Mind to Face Stress, Pain and Illness*. New York: Dell Publishing.

Keller, M.B., Lavori, P.W., Lewis, C.E., Klerman, G.L. (1983). Predictors of relapse in major depressive disorder. *Journal of the American Medical Association* **250**:3299–3304.

Kessler, R.C., McGonagle, K.A., Zhao, S., Nelson, C.B., Hughes, M., Eshlerman, S. et al. (1994). Lifetime and twelve-month prevalence of DSM-III-R psychiatric disorders in the United States: Results from the National Comorbidity Study. *Archives of General Psychiatry* **51**:8–19.

Kupfer, D.J., Frank, E., Perel, J.M., Cornes, C., Mallinger, A.G., Thase, M.E. et al. (1992). Five-year outcomes for maintenance therapies in recurrent depression. *Archives of General Psychiatry* **49**:769–773.

Lau, M.A., McMain, S. (2005). Integrating mindfulness meditation with cognitive behavior therapies: The challenge of combining acceptance and change based strategies. *Canadian Journal of Psychiatry* **50**:863–869.

Lau, M.A., Segal, Z.V., Williams, J.M.G. (2004). Teasdale's differential activation hypothesis: Implications for mechanisms of depressive relapse and suicidal behaviour. *Behaviour Research and Therapy* **42**:1001–1017.

Lau, M.A., Bishop, S.R., Segal, Z.V., Buis, T., Anderson, N.D., Carlson, L. et al. (2006). The Toronto Mindfulness Scale: Development and Validation. *Journal of Clinical Psychology*, **62**:1445–1467.

Lewinsohn, P.M., Allen, N.B., Seeley, J.R., Gotlib, I.H. (1999). First onset versus recurrence of depression: Differential processes of psychosocial risk. *Journal of Abnormal Psychology* **108**:483–489.

Linehan, M.M. (1993). *Cognitive-behavioral treatment of borderline personality disorder.* New York: Guilford Press.

Ma, S.H., Teasdale, J.D. (2004). Mindfulness-based cognitive therapy for depression: Replication and exploration of differential relapse prevention effects. *Journal of Consulting and Clinical Psychology* **72**:31–40.

Mason, O., Hargreaves, I. (2001). A qualitative study of mindfulness-based cognitive therapy for depression. *British Journal of Medical Psychology* **74**:197–212.

Martell, C.R., Addis, M.E., Jacobson, N.S. (2001). *Depression in Context: Strategies for Guided Action.* New York: W.W. Norton & Company, Inc.

Moore, R.G., Hayhurst, H., Teasdale, J.D. (1996). *Measure of awareness and coping in autobiographical memory: Instructions for administering and coding.* Unpublished manuscript, Department of Psychiatry, University of Cambridge.

Murray, C.L., Lopez, A.D. (1998). *The global burden of disease: A comprehensive assessment of mortality and disability from disease, injuries and risk factors in 1990 and projected to 2020.* Boston: Harvard University Press.

Nolen-Hoeksema, S. (1991). Responses to depression and their effects on the duration of depressive episodes. *Journal of Abnormal Psychology* **100**:569–582.

Padesky, C.A. (1993, September 24). Socratic questioning: Changing minds or guiding discovery? Keynote address to European Congress of Behavioural and Cognitive Therapies, London.

Segal, Z.V., Williams, J.M.G., Teasdale, J.D. (2002). *Mindfulness-based cognitive therapy for depression: A new approach for preventing relapse.* New York: Guilford Press.

Shapiro, S.L., Schwartz, G.E. (1999). Intentional systemic mindfulness: An integrative model for self-regulation and health. *Advances in Mind-Body Medicine* **15**:128–134.

Shea, M.T., Elkin, I., Imber, S.D., Sotsky, F.M., Watkins, J.T., Collins, J.F. et al. (1992). Course of depressive symptoms over follow-up: Findings from the NIMH Treatment of Depression Collaborative Research Program. *Archives of General Psychiatry* **49**:782–787.

Simons, A.D., Murphy, G.E., Levine, J.L., Wetzel, R.D. (1986). Cognitive therapy and pharmacotherapy for depression: Sustained improvement over one year. *Archives of General Psychiatry* **43**:43–50.

Spitzer, R.L., Williams, J.B.W., Gibbon, M., First, M.B. (1992). The Structured Clinical Interview for DSM-III-R (SCID). I: History, rationale, and description. *Archives of General Psychiatry* **49**:624–629.

Teasdale, J.D. (1988). Cognitive vulnerability to persistent depression. *Cognition and Emotion* **2**:247–274.

Teasdale, J.D., Segal, Z.V., Williams, J.M.G. (1995). How does cognitive therapy prevent relapse and why should attentional control (mindfulness) training help? *Behaviour Research and Therapy* **33**:25–39.

Teasdale, J.D., Moore, R.G., Hayhurst, H., Pope, M., Williams, S., Segal, Z.V. (2002). Metacognitive awareness and prevention of relapse in depression: Empirical evidence. *Journal of Consulting and Clinical Psychology* **70**:275–287.

Teasdale, J.D., Segal, Z.V., Williams, J.M.G., Ridgeway, V.A., Soulsby, J.M., Lau, M.A. (2000). Prevention of relapse/recurrence in major depression by mindfulness-based cognitive therapy. *Journal of Consulting and Clinical Psychology* **68**:615–623.

Williams, J.M.G., Duggan, D.S., Crane, C., Fennell, M.J.V. (2006). Mindfulness-based cognitive therapy for prevention of recurrence of suicidal behaviour. *Journal of Clinical Psychology* **62**:201–210.

INTERNET RESOURCES

- Mindfulness-based cognitive therapy:
www.mbct.com; www.mbct.co.uk; www.bangor.ac.uk/mindfulness; www.beyondblue.org.au

- Mindfulness-based stress reduction:
  www.umassmed.edu/cfm
- MBSR meditation tapes by Jon Kabat-Zinn:
  www.stressreductiontapes.com
- Insight Meditation:
  www.dharma.org
- Mindfulness and Acceptance Special Interest Group of the Association for Behavioral and Cognitive Therapies:
  listserv.kent.edu/archives/mindfulness/html

5

RELAPSE PREVENTION FOR RETURN OF PATHOLOGICAL WORRY IN CBT-TREATED GAD

URSULA WHITESIDE,
THACH (FRANCHESCA) NGUYEN,
DIANE E. LOGAN,
COREY FAGAN, AND G. ALAN MARLATT

Department of Psychology
University of Washington
Seattle, Washington

KATIE WITKIEWITZ

Department of Psychology
University of Illinois at Chicago
Chicago, Illinois

INTRODUCTION TO GAD AND CLIENT POPULATION

Generalized anxiety disorder (GAD) is a perplexing disorder that is difficult to conceptualize and define, as evidenced by the changing diagnostic criteria across the most recent iterations of the *Diagnostic and Statistical Manual of Mental Disorders* (DSM; American Psychiatric Association, 1980, 1987, 1994), in addition to current discussions about further criteria modification and reclassification of GAD from an anxiety disorder to a mood disorder. The two most common diagnostic classification systems for mental health, the *International Classification of Diseases and Related Health Problems-10* (ICD-10; World Health Organization, 1992) and the text-revision of the fifth DSM (DSM-IV-TR;

APA, 2000), include nonidentical GAD criteria and are found to have less than ideal diagnostic agreement (e.g., only 50% diagnosis agreement between the two interviews; Slade & Andrews, 2001). Utilizing just one diagnostic system, the DSM-IV (APA, 1994), diagnostic reliability for GAD has been shown to be fair (e.g., .44 agreement on 7 to 10 day test/retest; Zanarini et al., 2000).

GAD is also considered by some to be the most challenging anxiety disorder to treat (Brown, Barlow & Liebowitz, 1994). Indeed, our best treatments result in significant improvement for only half of clients (i.e., approximately 50% have post-treatment anxiety levels in the "normal" range; Borkovec, 2002). GAD individuals have also been reported to be among the most treatment resistant (Antony, 2002) and to have considerably higher lapse and relapse rates than individuals with other anxiety disorders (e.g., Rodriguez et al., 2006). Part of the difficulty in treating GAD can be attributed to its high comorbidity rates. GAD most frequently co-occurs with depression (major depression and dysthymia), other anxiety disorders (particularly social anxiety disorder and panic disorder; Noyes et al., 1992; Reich, Noyes & Yates, 1988; Wittchen et al., 1994) and other alcohol and substance use disorders (Regier et al., 1998).

GAD is distinguished by the presence of uncontrollable worry (see "What is Pathological Worry?"). For a diagnosis of GAD, one must experience excessive anxiety and difficult-to-control worry regarding a number of events or activities. Further, this worry must be accompanied by three or more physical symptoms: restlessness or feeling keyed up or on edge, fatigue, difficulty concentrating, irritability, muscle tension, and sleep disturbance (APA, 2000). If these symptoms are present and have persisted for more days than not over the past six months and cannot be better explained by another disorder (see "Assessment of GAD"), a GAD diagnosis is warranted.

Nearly 7 million Americans meet GAD criteria, two-thirds of whom are women (Kessler, Chui, Demler & Walters, 2005; Robins & Regier, 1991). In the general community, 2 percent of Americans have GAD (or have had in the past 12 months) and 4 percent have had GAD at some point in their lifetimes (Grant et al., 2005; Kessler et al., 2005). It appears that GAD exists in similar rates across the world (e.g., Alonso et al., 2004; Andrade, Walters, Gentil & Laurenti, 2002). Comorbidity rates of GAD with other psychological disorders range from 47 percent up to 90 percent (Borkovec & Roemer, 1996; Brown, Barlow & Liebowitz, 1994; Costello, Egger & Angold, 2004; Dadds et al., 1997; Gould & Otto, 1996; Kendall et al., 2004; Mendlowicz & Stein, 2000; Story, Zucker & Craske, 2004).

ASSESSMENT OF GAD

WHAT OTHER DISORDERS OR PROBLEMS CAN BE CONFUSED WITH GAD?

What differentiates GAD from other anxiety-related disorders such as obsessive-compulsive or post-traumatic stress disorders is the pervasive nature of GAD worry. GAD individuals worry about topics across a number of contexts such as work, interpersonal, school, and ordinary daily tasks and routines. Therefore GAD worry does not include worry restricted to the area of another psychological disorder (e.g., excessive worry about having a panic attack in panic disorder or of gaining weight in anorexia). In contrast to GAD, the obsessive worry found in Obsessive Compulsive Disorder (OCD) is likely to be accompanied by urges and impulses, which when acted upon reduce anxiety (APA, 2000).

What also distinguishes GAD from other anxiety disorders is the somatic symptom presentation. Unlike other anxiety disorders (e.g., panic disorder and social phobia), GAD individuals experience more central nervous system arousal (e.g., high levels of muscle tension, irritability, fatigue) and fewer symptoms of autonomic arousal, characteristic of other anxiety disorders (e.g., sweating, accelerated heart rate; Brown, Antony & Barlow, 1995; Joormann & Stover, 1999; Noyes et al., 1992; Reich, Noyes & Yates, 1988). Although the somatic symptoms of GAD overlap with those of mood disorders such as major depression and dysthymia, other mood disorder symptoms are not present (e.g., hopelessness, suicide ideation; Brown, Barlow & Liebowitz, 1994). Physiological symptoms common to GAD can also be caused by an existing medical condition (e.g., hyperthyroidism; pheochromocytoma, i.e., tumor(s) of the adrenal gland leading to overproduction of adrenaline; APA, 2000). Clients are recommended to have a check-up with their primary care physician to rule out this possibility. Clinicians should also assess for the use of drug substances, which can also cause anxious states (e.g., over-caffeination, drug withdrawal, or chronic substance abuse; APA, 2000).

DIAGNOSTIC AND TREATMENT PROGRESS AND OUTCOME ASSESSMENTS

Included is a list of assessment measures used for diagnostic assessment, intake evaluation, and ongoing and outcome assessment (see Table 5.1). The list of self-report assessment measures is compiled from those recommended for GAD in *Practitioner's Guide to Empirically Based Measures of Anxiety* (Roemer, 2001). This useful, inexpensive, and widely utilized resource includes the actual measures in the appendices of the book.

GAD TREATMENT AND THE INCORPORATION OF RELAPSE PREVENTION

The remainder of this chapter is a synopsis of the concerns and strategies associated with treating and preventing relapse of pathological worry, the distinguishing characteristic of GAD. We focus on treatment of GAD with cognitive behavioral treatments (CBT), currently the most empirically supported GAD treatment. Models of CBT for GAD often include pieces of the original relapse

TABLE 5.1:   Diagnostic and Treatment Progress and Outcome Assessments

The following is a list of two semistructured diagnostic interviews and seven paper and pencil assessment measures. The paper and pencil measures were collected from Roemer's (2001) chapter on GAD assessments in *Practitioner's Guide to Empirically Based Measures of Anxiety*. This useful resource includes the actual measures in the appendices of the book.

Assessment	Description	Citation
Structured Clinical Interview for DSM-IV-TR (SCID-I)	This SCID is based on DSM-IV and is one of the most common semistructured diagnostic interviews used for research. Clinician-friendly versions can be ordered. Information regarding the SCID-I can be found at http://www.scid4.org/ and tapes can be ordered through the American Psychiatric Press, Inc., by calling 1-800-368-5777 or visiting http://www.appi.org.	First, Spitzer, Gibbons & Williams, 2002
Anxiety Disorder Interview Schedule for DSM-IV (ADIS-IV)	This structured, interviewer-administered assessment is designed to assess for anxiety, mood, somatoform, substance use disorders, in addition to psychotic disorders and medical problems. Clinician manual and interview set available from online booksellers (Brown, DiNardo & Barlow, 1993).	Brown, Dinardo & Barlow, 1993, 1994
Consequences of Worrying Scale (COWS)	This 29-item questionnaire assesses which consequences an individual expects when they worry. It includes both positive and negative consequences measured by a five-point Likert-scale.	Davey, Tallis & Capuzzo, 1996
GAD Questionnaire-IV (GADQ-IV)	This measure screens for GAD based on DSM-IV criteria on a nine-point Likert scale, and includes room for individuals to list the primary topics of their worry.	Newman, Zuellig, Kachin & Constantino, 2002
Intolerance of Uncertainty Scale (IUS)	Intolerance of uncertainty is measured through 27 items addressing individual responses to uncertainty, including attempts to control the future, frustration at unpredictability, and impacts on character.	Freeston, Rheaume, Letarte, Dugas & Ladouceur, 1994
Penn State Worry Questionnaire (PSWQ)	This 16-item measure assesses the amount of trait worry as measured by identification with statements on a five-point Likert scale.	Meyer, Miller, Metzger & Borkovec, 1990
Why Worry Scale (WW-II)	This revised scale updated the original Why Worry Scale and consists of 25 items in five subsections to measure the negative and positive expectations of worrying.	Freeston, Rheaume, Letarte, Dugas & Ladouceur, 1994
Worry Domains Questionnaire (WDQ)	The WDQ measures how much individuals worry about five particular life domains, including finances, work, the future, relationships, and confidence. The 25 items are measured on five-point Likert scales.	Tallis, Eysenck & Matthews, 1992
Worry Scale for Older Adults (WS)	The WS was designed specifically for use with older adult populations, measuring the amount they worry about three domains: health, social, and financial. The 35 items are measured on five-point Likert scales.	Wisocki, 1998

prevention model that have been modified for GAD. We will review these current CBT relapse prevention approaches, as well as new CBT approaches incorporating mindfulness models that may also prevent relapse. Broadly, and as a combined group, the different versions of CBT for GAD consist of multiple overlapping strategies and interventions found to reduce pathological worry and prevent reoccurrence or relapse. Research supporting these treatments will also be reviewed.

EMPIRICAL SUPPORT OF CBT FOR GAD

Borkovec and Ruscio (2001) reviewed 13 highly controlled treatment trials of GAD, finding CBT to be associated with significant reductions in GAD symptoms, which are maintained or continue to decline after treatment termination. CBT has been shown to be more effective for symptom reduction maintenance than applied relaxation, nondirective therapy, and behavioral therapy (Borkovec & Roemer, 1996; Dugas, Rodomsky & Brillon, 2004; Gould & Otto, 1996). Moreover, CBT is considered as effective as pharmacological treatment in reducing symptoms of anxiety and is associated with greater maintenance of treatment gains and greater reductions in comorbid depression (Chambless & Gillis, 1993; Gould, Otto, Pollack & Yap, 1997). Further, support of CBT for GAD is provided by the longest psychotherapy outcome trial of GAD: Durham and colleagues (2003) followed a group of individuals treated for GAD for up to 14 years. CDT, in comparison to analytical psychotherapy, medication, and placebo, faired better in terms of overall reductions in symptom severity.

RELAPSE PREVENTION AND CBT TREATMENTS
FOR GAD

What follows is a broad overview of the efforts made to incorporate relapse prevention models and strategies into CBT for GAD. For a more exhaustive list, see Figure 5.1. The goal of relapse prevention strategies is to teach the client to view any type of lapse or relapse as an opportunity for new learning that will prepare the client for future lapses and relapses. Instructions for relapse prevention for GAD can be laid out in three broad steps (Rygh & Sanderson, 2004). While still in treatment, clients must identify situations in which they will be at high risk for a return of dysfunctional worry (e.g., start of son's football season, not completing a work project on time, or other times in the recent or distant past where worry has surged). In the second step, clients outline personal warning signs or "automatic" responses to these high-risk situations (e.g., muscle-tension, increase in time spent worrying, headaches, insomnia). Essentially, steps one and two involve helping clients to develop a list of personal warning signs (Gorski & Miller, 1982) that indicate a potential resurgence of GAD-type reactions, such as specific cognitive and somatic states, and their correlates (e.g., external situations). In the third step, plans for implementation of relapse prevention are outlined. Here, the client and therapist tailor personalized and situation-specific strategies for potential high-risk situations and automatic responses. These tailored strategies are based on skills learned during treatment and include back-up plans for what to do if the first strategy fails.

Overholser and Nasser (2000) emphasize that the earlier in treatment relapse prevention is addressed, the better. This is consistent with research suggesting that over-learning of new behaviors is one of the best ways to prevent the reemergence of unwanted behaviors. Of note, during a lapse or relapse (see Chapter 1 for discussion of difference between lapse and relapse) underestimations of ability to cope or apply what was learned during treatment may appear (e.g., "I'm too stressed right now to work on my worry, I can't handle this"). The likelihood of this situation is discussed and plans to combat these thoughts with cognitive restructuring should be prepared ("I've done hard things before—I can do this, This is actually the perfect opportunity to test what I learned in treatment"; Rygh & Sanderson, 2004). It is also recommended that therapists make booster sessions available to clients during times of lapse or relapse (Rygh & Sanderson, 2004). CBT relapse prevention strategies for GAD largely focus on preparing clients for lapses and relapses to chronic worry and teaching them to use these setbacks to their advantage—as an opportunity to practice skills and identify weaknesses, as well as to increase self-control and reliance.

RECOVERY AND RELAPSE FOLLOWING CBT

Individuals who meet criteria for GAD are likely to experience either partial or full recovery over time whether or not treatment is involved (Fifer et al., 1994; Maier et al., 2000; Yonkers et al., 1996). However, relapse following full recovery is also highly probable. For example, across a naturalistic study of GAD individuals identified in a primary care setting, recovery and partial recovery rates appeared somewhat positive—with about 40 and 55 percent, respectively (Rodriguez et al., 2006)—and yet, 50 percent of those reaching full recovery would go on to experience a lapse or relapse of GAD symptoms within two years (Rodriguez et al., 2006). Further, recovery rates such as these (among primary care patients) are significantly better than for those identified through secondary settings (such as psychiatric patients; Rodriguez et al., 2006; Yonkers et al., 1996; Yonkers et al., 2000;).

It has been found that poorer outcome predictors of CBT tend to be related to the presence of another axis I disorder (e.g., major depressive disorder, or another anxiety disorder), social isolation and marital tension (Durham, Allan & Hackett 1997; Rodriguez et al., 2006). In addition to severity of disorder (e.g., primary versus secondary care patients), greater interpersonal difficulties and poorer life satisfaction, and being female are all related to poorer treatment outcomes (Rodriguez et al., 2006; Yonkers et al., 2000, 2003). Across research on GAD treatment, and even in our most tightly controlled clinical trials (including CBT, pharmacotherapy, psychosocial, and psychoanalytic treatments), GAD individuals rarely achieve full and/or unremitting recovery (e.g., Durham et al., 1997; Rodriguez et al., 2006; Yonkers et al., 2003). What follows is a GAD case example of CBT treatment and the common struggles with lapse and relapse that might occur.

CASE EXAMPLE

The following case example demonstrates the application of standard CBT for GAD and illustrates how relapse could occur following successful CBT treatment. This client is not one specific client, but instead a mixture of the authors' experiences told from the first person. This case is typical of those we might see in our offices.

JENNIFER

Jennifer, a 29-year-old female of mixed racial background (Chinese-American and Caucasian-American), contacted me after being referred by an academic advisor in the psychology department. At her intake session, Jennifer described being incredibly concerned about her classes. As an older, returning student in the process of applying for graduate school, she felt that she needed to ace all of her classes—in fact, she was doing so. Sitting across from her in the room I noted how Jennifer held her body: her shoulders were high and her arms were crossed tightly across her chest, she constantly toe-tapped and a small, tight smile was pasted across her face. Jennifer also reported a great deal of distress and concern across a number of areas: her relationship with her girlfriend of several years, the school loans that she was accruing, being overweight and not having time to exercise, transportation issues, her parents getting older, her younger brother who was just starting college. These are common concerns, but her worries appeared to be consuming her. Jennifer worried about the relatively broad, "I worry I don't have what it takes to make it in graduate school," to the fairly narrow and specific, "I have three colors I use for highlighting my books—I'm always worrying that I'll lose one of them and my study session will be wasted before I can get a new one. I can't waste any time right now or I'll blow my shot (at grad school)." Jennifer was spending a great deal of her time worrying about these and other issues, and she found it hard to concentrate because she would repeatedly be distracted by worries. Jennifer said, "I don't like the anxiety, but I will mess everything up for my future if I am not always on top of things."

At the onset of our CBT treatment, we started self-monitoring—Jennifer began listing and categorizing the things that she worried about throughout the week and estimating the percentage of a given day that she had spent worrying. In the following weeks, cognitive restructuring and progressive muscle relaxation (PMR) were introduced. Jennifer liked the PMR and began to practice it every night before she went to sleep. After an initial struggle with cognitive restructuring, she was examining her thoughts for inaccuracies ("Well, I guess my life is *not* actually over if I don't get into graduate school") and miscalculations ("When I think about it, it is quite unlikely that my official transcripts will be lost in the mail"). After 10 weeks of treatment Jennifer was markedly improved—not only by her self-report, but it was also apparent in the way she held her body. She was relaxed and cracked jokes. Jennifer no longer looked like she was ready to bolt out of the room at a moment's notice. We were well into the winter break by then when Jennifer decided to end treatment because she felt "cured." In her last session, we discussed ways to prevent her worry from returning to its original strength (see Figure 5.1). I oriented her to the function of booster sessions (i.e.,

---

Overlapping Relapse Prevention Approaches in Treatment for GAD

- Provide Psychoeducation about Relapse Prevention and Common Cognitive Errors Following Treatment

  o Teach the difference between a lapse (temporary setback) and a relapse (return to pathological worry for six months or more)

  o Address the Abstinence Violation Effect (AVE) for GAD—"If you experience a lapse/relapse, all is not lost!"

  o Use lapses and relapses in pathological worry as an opportunity, rather than a failure, for practicing coping skills, building mastery, and preventing future setbacks on the way to building a better life

  o Provide theoretical rational for function of worry—that worry may be an attempt to avoid one's own distress.

  o Emphasize the fact that anxiety and nonpathological worry are part of the human experience and increases are to be expected at times

- Make Plans for After Treatment

  o Prepare for lapses or temporary setbacks

  o Develop a plan for recovering from a lapse

  o Identify potential warning signs or cues for worry

  o Continue self-monitoring of worry

  o Focus on prevention of relapse by discussing how to prevent old "coping mechanisms" such as worry and avoidance

---

FIGURE 5.1:   Overlapping Relapse Prevention Approaches in Treatment for GAD

- Practice During and After Treatment

  o Consolidate and review skills learned during therapy

  o Practice exposure to emotions by imagining situations that may trigger a lapse in the future

  o Imagine, discuss, and plan for desired life after therapy

  o Focus on integration of awareness of emotions and reactions to emotions and rationalization in decision making—a style likely to prevent relapse

  o Somatic awareness exercises

Adapted from Dugas (unpublished manual); Ladouceur, 2004; Ladouceur et al., 2000; Mennin, 2004; Overholser & Nasser, 2000; Roemer & Orsillo, 2005.

FIGURE 5.1: *Continued*

to help maintain change or get back on course) and I invited her to utilize this option.

Six weeks later Jennifer called to make an appointment. Graduate school interviews, a high-risk situation we had planned for, were upon her. During the previous weekend, she had attended her first interview. During her trip, she began worrying constantly, often jumping from topic to topic. She worried during the cross-country plane ride ("I'm sure I forgot something important"), in the taxi from the airport ("I just know I'm going to get lost and show up late"), and on the couch where she slept at a graduate student's apartment ("I have to remember to write and thank her for letting me stay here tonight. I can't forget"). Her overwhelming worry had returned, and at levels she experienced as higher than they had been at the onset of her treatment with me. She had returned to see me, it turned out, because she was distressed about her level of distress and the impact it had and might have on her interviews. Jennifer remembered all the strategies we had practiced in treatment (PMR, cognitive restructuring, self-monitoring), but currently found her anxiety so high that she could not implement these strategies for longer than a half-minute.

We turn now to discuss the distinguishing factor of GAD—pathological worry—providing insights into why this type of worry, the type Jennifer had lapsed to, may be so difficult to change.

WHAT IS PATHOLOGICAL WORRY?

Worry is defined as "a troubled state of mind arising from the frets and cares of life; harassing anxiety or solicitude" (Oxford English Dictionary, 2006). Roemer, Orsillo & Barlow (2002) describe worry generally as the first stage of problem-solving. This stage—often considered a form of problem identification or generation—includes the recognition of a potential problem followed by the cognitive formulation of multiple possible negative outcomes or disasters (and in the absence of active attempts to solve or cope with the problem; Barlow, 2002; Roemer, Orsillo & Barlow, 2002). The pathological worry found in GAD can be distinguished from nonpathological worry: individuals experiencing "normal" worry are able set worries aside. Physical symptoms of pathological worry, such as muscle tension, irritability, and disturbed sleep, are also less likely to coincide with normal worry. In contrast to normal worry, pathological worry is more marked, all-encompassing, upsetting, and it occurs more frequently and for longer periods of time (APA, 2000).

In the general population, individuals worry most about interpersonal and family issues (Roemer, Molina & Borkovec, 1997). In comparison, GAD persons, such as our case example Jennifer, tend to spend significantly more time worrying and worry proportionately more about a larger range of topics and relatively unimportant events (e.g., being late for appointments, car repairs, and potential health problems of family members; Roemer et al., 1997; Sanderson & Barlow, 1990). Ninety-one percent of GAD individuals recognize that they over-worry, reporting that they worry excessively about minor events (Sanderson & Barlow, 1990). Although 10 percent of the general population experience worry that is excessive or chronic in nature, they do not meet full GAD diagnostic criteria (Gould & Otto, 1996). What separates these 10 percent and the rest of the non-GAD population from GAD individuals (who are by definition chronic worriers) is, again, the uncontrollable nature of the worry in GAD individuals—the sense that one could not stop worrying even when they tried to, that one's worry is out of control.

CAN WORRYING BE HELPFUL?

GAD sufferers often believe worry is necessary and effective problem solving. In reality, problem solving and effective coping are distinct constructs from worry (Roemer et al., 2002). As discussed, worry (ideally) functions to prepare the individual for attempts to cope or problem-solve. However, worry does not guarantee that attempts to problem-solve will occur or be successful (Roemer et al., 2002).

Pathological worriers are known to engage in ongoing scanning for, and pay sharp attention to, potential threats (Mathews, 1990). That is, GAD individuals are particularly skilled at identifying problems that might arise and ways in which situations could go wrong (Roemer et al., 2002). Yet, they often lack confidence in their ability to cope effectively with these uncertain situations and in their capability to influence situations so that they might result in a positive outcome (Ladouceur, Blais, Freeston & Dugas, 1998). GAD individuals have been identified as having particular difficulty dealing with uncertainty: this behavior has been branded *intolerance of uncertainty* (Ladouceur, Talbot & Dugas, 1997). Ironically, the occurrence of these uncertain or potential threats that GAD individuals worry about are usually very unlikely (e.g., his or her child being kidnapped).

WHY IS PATHOLOGICAL WORRY SO DIFFICULT TO STOP?

WORRY IS MAINTAINED THROUGH NEGATIVE REINFORCEMENT

Worry is thought to be maintained through several negative reinforcement mechanisms. Negative reinforcement occurs when removing something increases the likelihood of a behavior. As discussed, chronic worriers are likely to worry about a number of possibly, but unlikely, negative outcomes. Of course, these negative outcomes rarely occur. The worrier may think "It worked!" or "Worry ing helps." A superstitious effect is created through the negative reinforcement of worry (Borkovec & Roemer, 1996). Because the feared event often does not occur, this state of chronic worry may be maintained (Mathews, 1990). This mechanism was at work with the case example of Jennifer, who felt she had to worry to stay on top of things. However, though initially recovered after addressing this issue, Jennifer's worry returned and appeared to be maintained by another mechanism.

Negative reinforcement is thought to work in a second way—one that is likely more difficult to change. Worry and GAD are associated with decreased autonomic flexibility, characterized largely by low heart rate variability and decreased cardiac vagal tone (Hoehn-Saric & McLeod, 2000; Hofmann et al., 2005; Lyonfields, Borkovec & Thayer, 1995; Thayer, Friedman & Borkovec, 1996). This pattern of reactivity is hypothesized to be reinforcing to the individual experiencing it (i.e., if the alternative is high anxious arousal) and thus increases the likelihood of continued worry. Individuals who worry excessively are hypothesized to do so because worry prevents dramatic upward swings in anxiety (as evidenced by self-report and physiological indicators). It seems that while worry will not induce a relaxed state, it can permit for a more even state (Borkovec & Hu, 1990; Wells & Papageorgiou, 1995).

These types of findings led Borkovec to theorize that GAD worry functions as a type of avoidance (i.e., avoidance of emotionally dysregulated states; Borkovec & Hu, 1990; Borkovec, Alaine & Behar, 2004). Roemer and Orsillo high-light that this conceptualization of GAD worry overlaps with the construct of *experiential avoidance*, which is considered by many to be the root of psychological problems (Orsillo, Roemer, Lerner & Tull, 2004). Experiential avoidance is highly correlated with GAD and occurs when one is unwilling or currently lacks skills to pay attention to private experiences such as emotions, bodily sensations, and thoughts (Hayes, Strosahl & Wilson, 1999; Roemer, Salters, Raffa & Orsillo, 2005).

WORRY OBSTRUCTS PRESENT MOMENT FOCUS

To review, CBT for GAD has been successful for many, yet has left others not fully recovered or prone to relapse. Given, among this second group, the poor response and high relapse rates following our most effective treatment, a major lifestyle change may be necessary to step out of the negatively reinforcing cycle of GAD. That is, due to the chronic and future-focused nature of pathological worry, a dramatic change in the way one responds to his or her body, environment, and cognitions may be required.

Uncontrollable worry, as present in GAD, obstructs one's attention to current tasks (APA, 2000). It is estimated that the average GAD sufferer spends more than 50 percent of his or her waking time in a worried state (Gould & Otto, 1996; Sanderson & Barlow, 1990). While in a worried state, attention is directed toward perceived threats (e.g., "Will I be late?, What if I run out of gas?, What if I suffocate myself in my sleep?"; Barlow, 2002). Across time, this type of inattention (i.e., worry that keeps one from being engaged in the current moment) can lead to problems in daily functioning, contribute to financial difficulties, and disrupt family routine, leisure activities, interpersonal relationships (Borkovec, Shadick & Hopkins, 1991; Dozois & Westra, 2004).

This was true for Jennifer (the preceding case study), who was so distracted by anxiety and worry during her first graduate school interview that she essentially "blanked out" several times and was unable to complete her sentence when having a conversation with a potential advisor.

MINDFULNESS AND CBT FOR WORRY: HOPE FOR IMPROVED RESPONSE AND REDUCED RELAPSE

THE GOAL OF MINDFULNESS IS PRESENT MOMENT FOCUS

Essentially, worry can be conceptualized as a failure to focus on the present moment—that is, a failure of mindfulness. Mindfulness is described as the act of "paying attention in a particular way: on purpose, in the present moment and non-judgmentally" (Kabat-Zinn, 1994, p. 4). The current conceptualization of pathological worry, as a negatively reinforced behavior, which by nature is non-mindful and prevents full engagement in life, has informed recent GAD treatment development. These treatment researchers posit that a mindful lifestyle is necessary for recovery and maintained recovery from GAD. Before turning to these recent developments in treatment for GAD, a brief synopsis of the history of mindfulness in CBT treatments and in relapse prevention will be provided.

The original addiction-based model of relapse prevention included recommendations for the incorporation of Eastern techniques and mindfulness-based practices such as meditation (Marlatt & Gordon, 1985). It would be difficult *not* to notice that over the past several decades the field of clinical psychology has experienced a widespread influx of mindfulness-based additions to existing cognitive behavioral therapies. Mindfulness-based treatments are considered the "new" wave of treatments—treatments spanning a number of varied problem behaviors (e.g., borderline personality disorder, anxiety, depression; Hayes, Strosahl & Wilson, 1999; Linehan, 1993a, 1993b; Segal, Williams & Teasdale, 2002). These approaches each describe mindfulness as a fundamental change in the way one views and reacts to his or her problem behavior and other life circumstances.

WITH PRACTICE, MINDFULNESS IMPROVES OVER TIME

In essence, the adaptation of mindfulness to one's life is a way of retraining the brain. Research suggests that worry and mindfulness activate different parts of the left frontal lobe of the brain (e.g., see Davidson et al., 2003; Hofmann et al., 2005). These different activation areas are associated with different correlates such as moods and behaviors. It can be hypothesized then that changing the way one responds behaviorally to situations will result in changes in activation areas of one's brain. An example of a change in behavior would be responding to increased work stress with mindfulness of the present moment rather than with worry. Given that GAD individuals often have carried a worried and avoidant mind-set for many years, it is reasonable to expect that this pattern will likely not disappear completely over the course of a five- to 12-session CBT treatment.

When Jennifer (see preceding case study) returned to treatment, a mindfulness approach was adopted to help her stay focused in the present rather than on her worry. At the beginning of mindfulness training, a chronic worrier may have to redirect his or her attention away from worry and back to the present moment 20 times in one minute. Indeed Jennifer initially found mindfulness practice incredibly frustrating, judging herself as not competent to learn the practice. In these times, it is important to reassure clients that what they are experiencing is normal and that it should be talked over in the therapy. Over time and with practice, the number of times clients have to, in essence, "bring themselves back" to the present moment decreases. It would make sense then, that adapting a mindful lifestyle for GAD individuals would result in continued improvement over time (as the brain became retrained). Relapse presumably would be less likely when one has trained him- or herself to be continuously aware of thoughts, emotions, behaviors, environment, and physiological sensations.

However, adjusting to a mindful lifestyle takes time. In clinical experience, the implementation of mindfulness is a dispersion process; when a drop of blue ink falls into a glass of water, the water is not instantly and uniformly blue. But over time, as one spends more and more time practicing mindfulness, it spreads throughout one's life such that larger percentages of time are spent in a mindful state. Mindfulness treatment strategies can be hypothesized to improve GAD treatment outcomes in multiple ways (see "Potential Ways Mindfulness Works in GAD Treatment"), but first a description of these strategies is provided. We turn now to the implementation of mindfulness-based strategies for further relapse prevention of Jennifer's worry.

STRATEGIES FOR IMPLEMENTING MINDFULNESS INTO GAD CBT TREATMENT

What follows are four treatment strategies common to CBT. Into each strategy a common foundation of mindfulness. These CBT strategies have been enhanced, based on recent literature and clinical experience, to represent current directions in treatment development and relapse prevention for GAD. Experiences from the case study of Jennifer, once she returned to treatment, are woven into the strategies.

PSYCHOEDUCATION

Psychoeducation, in essence, is client orientation—or, explaining what to expect or do and why it is important. Psychoeducation for mindfulness-based CBT includes explanations for worry, its maintenance and consequences, how emotion awareness is relevant and important, and the rationale for the implementation of mindfulness into treatment. Upon returning to treatment, Jennifer found the second explanation for worry (that it functions to avoid emotions) more helpful than the original conceptualization (that worry maintains because she felt it was necessary to worry). Roemer and Orsillo (2005) suggest several steps for educating the client on how worry functions for them and how it does not. This includes identification of the short-term benefits (e.g., as sense of control, reduced anxiety) and long-term consequences of excessive worry (i.e., a life not lived fully). Using examples from the client's life, the therapist and client can identify ways in which the client is directing his or her attention toward potential threats (e.g., worries about the possibility of their child getting hurt while playing soccer rather than being engaged in the child's game). These examples can be used to explain the function of worry—a way of being nonmindful or avoiding uncomfortable emotional states, a way of trying to control a situation or emotion(s). The definition of mindfulness and the rationale for the use of mindfulness can then be introduced (see "Potential Ways Mindfulness Works in GAD Treatment").

GAD individuals may also benefit from learning about other pathological worriers. That is, GAD sufferers are more likely to experience greater intensity and less understanding of emotions, are more prone to feel negatively about their emotions, and tend to have more difficulty managing their emotional reactions or calming themselves after experiencing strong negative emotions (Mennin, Heimberg, Turk & Fresco, 2005). Therefore, education and training around emotions and the importance of emotion awareness is implemented (and can be tracked on the diary card; see Figure 5.2). Clients can be taught that emotions function to communicate to the self or others, prepare us to react to a situation, and provide a richer life experience (see Linehan, 1993b).

SELF-MONITORING

CBT treatments for GAD have long included self-monitoring, such as tracking the percentage of the day one spends worrying. Mindfulness-related self-monitoring can be built into existing monitoring forms (see Figure 5.2, based on Linehan, 1993a). Clients can also begin monitoring emotions, responses to emotions, and how difficult or easy it is to identify what emotion they are having (Roemer & Orsillo, 2005). Over time, this type of self-monitoring leads to increased awareness of one's internal experience, which may not have received much attention in the past. Vulnerability factors, such as amount of sleep and alcohol consumption, can be tracked in order to see how they relate to overall levels of worry, stress, and mindfulness. During treatment, the self-monitoring tracking can serve dual purposes, first increasing the client's awareness of his or her daily behaviors and second, providing the client and therapist with information about how much progress is being made and what factors are contributing to progress.

For relapse prevention following treatment, clients can continue to self-monitor. This may help clients maintain mindful self-awareness and increased understanding of their patterns of behavior. Self-monitoring is a useful way to keep on the lookout for high-risk situations, particularly through monitoring vulnerability factors (see Figure 5.2, diary card) such as sleep and stress levels. Continued behavioral monitoring allows the client to see how emotions and behaviors are related (e.g., increase in stress is related to increase in worrying). Diary cards can be continuously tailored to relevant client behaviors and new goals. Indeed, our client Jennifer found this diary card quite helpful in that she felt more like a scientific observer of her thoughts and feelings. She began to see relationships between emotions and vulnerability factors and stress show up on her diary card, thus allowing her to be on guard for a resurgence of problematic worry.

| Weekly Diary Card | Initials | | | | | Filled out in Session? Y   N (Circle)DC40 | | How often did you fill out this out?DC41 _1__ Daily 3____ 2-3x _2__ 4-6x 4____Once | | Started: DATE Date____/____/____ | | |
| ID # | | | | | |

Circle Start Day	Highest Level			Average Level			Vulnerability Factors					Emotions: Experienced (E) or Avoided (A)℞ DC28DC27				
Day Of Week DC01	WorryD C02	Bodily Anx*Har mDC03	Mindful ActionD C04	WorryDC 02	Bodily Anx*Ha rmDCO3	Mindful ActionD C04	Sleep		Alcohol	Daily Stress	Pleasant Activities	Presc. Meds	Fear	Sad	Joy	Shame or Guilt	Anger
	0-5	0-5	0-5	0-5	0-5	0-5	# hrs DC11	Qual℃ DC11a	Y or N	DC13 0-5	Y or NDC14	Y or N	0-5DC19	0-5	0-5	0-5	0-5
(1) MON																	
(2) TUE																	
(3) WED																	
(4) THUR																	
(5) FRI																	
(6) SAT																	
(7) SUN																	

LEGEND:

(0 – 5) means select a number between 0 and 5:
0 = Least possible or None
5 = Most possible

* Bodily Anxiety: This includes bodily sensations of anxiety, (e.g., physiological sensations, muscle tension, rapid breathing, heart pounding, dry mouth, nausea, dizziness

℃ Quality of Sleep: Indicate Good (G), Fair (F), or Poor (P)

℞ Level of Contact with Emotions: Indicate Experienced (E) and rate (0-5) or indicate Avoided (A) DC28DC27

NOTES:

Adapted from Linehan, 1993a

FIGURE 5.2:   Sample Diary Card

MINDFULNESS TRAINING AND
RELAXATION TRAINING

Relaxation training, such as diaphragmatic breathing and progressive muscle relaxation are taught as ways to practice being more aware of the body and self, as well as to practice engagement in the present moment. Of course, these strategies have long been a part of CBT treatment for anxiety disorders. Therapists can emphasize that these exercises are to be conducted in a mindful manner—that is, without judgment of self or exercise, with compassion for self, and in order to gain distance from one's thoughts and feelings (Roemer & Orsillo, 2005). Other mindfulness breathing exercises can be taught, such as noticing one's breath as it enters and leaves the nostrils or lungs, noticing any thoughts that arise, and directing one's attention back to the sensations of the breath. The type of mindfulness exercise is not dictated, but some type of regular practice (at least 15 minutes a day) is suggested.

Jennifer found a body scanning exercise to be most helpful. She practiced this the nights before her interviews and right before the interviews. First, she would scan her body to examine where she felt the anxiety the strongest. Jennifer felt it most prominently in her stomach. She then directed her attention to this area and to the sensations she experienced there. When worry crept into her mind, she would simply notice it and direct her attention back to those sensations. She found that after she did this for five to 10 minutes, that the sensations in her stomach had reduced and, as a result of this, she felt less anxious (see "Mindfulness, Experiential Avoidance, and Exposure", p. 106). Mindfulness exercises can and should eventually take on a more natural integration into one's life. For example, one may be more mindful while driving or riding the bus to work, or prepping for an important conversation with a partner by planning to pay careful attention to the spouse's facial expressions and body posture as well as to one's internal reactions and emotions before acting on them.

MINDFUL ACTION

Mindful action is a term coined to describe moving in the direction of one's overarching goals while being conscious and participatory in one's current life (Roemer & Orsillo, 2002). Further, mindful action means that that no matter the current emotional, cognitive, or bodily state, behavior should focus on one's values and goals rather than trying to escape that state. Jennifer wanted to cancel her graduate school interviews because she felt she could not tolerate the anxiety she had experienced at her first interview. However, Jennifer's current life goal was to get into graduate school, she chose to act mindful and go despite her overwhelming worry. Essentially, rather than working diligently to reduce ones' anxiety, the focus of mindful action is to act in a valued way regardless of one's internal experience. This is similar to Linehan's opposite action, where if acting on an emotion will not be effective, the individual is encouraged to "act opposite" (Linehan, 1993b). To do this, a focus on the present moment is necessary. Essentially, individuals must throw themselves into a chosen activity. Mindfulness is required for this skill to work properly and it is important for mindful action to be tracked on the diary card.

POTENTIAL WAYS MINDFULNESS WORKS IN GAD TREATMENT

MINDFULNESS, EXPERIENTIAL AVOIDANCE, AND EXPOSURE

Worry in GAD is considered a type of experiential avoidance that functions short term to reduce anxiety (Mennin, Heimberg, Turk & Fresco, 2002; Roemer & Orsillo, 2002). The current understanding of worry (as an avoidance of emotional states, particularly internal sensations associated with those emotions) lends itself to an exposure therapy approach. Exposure treatments are understood to work such that by presenting the client with avoided situations, new corrective learning can occur (e.g., "Worrying does not prevent bad things from happening," "My emotions are tolerable"). Repeatedly returning to the emotion underlying current worries can be a way of problem solving, particularly when worries are about low-likelihood events or uncontrollable circumstances. That is, if one experiences the emotion or bodily sensations underlying that worry, it is possible that that emotion or anxiety will diminish and worry will no longer serve the function of negative reinforcement. With practice, this can become an almost automatic response to bodily sensations and emotions and help prevent relapse to pathological worry. One might learn (either consciously or unconsciously) that being present and experiencing an emotion about something can resolve the situation faster and more effectively than worrying can. Further, continued exposure to the present moment and current emotions reduces the opportunity for further negative reinforcement of worry through lowered physiological arousal.

MINDFULNESS PROVIDES A FOUNDATION FOR SKILL ACQUISITION AND IMPLEMENTATION

Mindfulness has been considered the foundation upon which to build new skills for managing anxiety and other emotions (e.g., Hayes, Strosahl, & Wilson, 1999; Linehan, 1993a, 1993b). For example, mindfulness is the first skill taught in DBT therapy. It is thought that the practice of mindfulness allows one to most effectively learn and implement the other sets of skills that will be learned (i.e., interpersonal effectiveness, emotion regulation, and distress tolerance). Learning how to be more interpersonally effective is an important skill, but it works much better if the person practices it with awareness of what is going on with the other person and with him or herself (e.g., awareness of eye contact, facial expressions, and voice tone of themselves and of the people with whom they are communicating).

MINDFULNESS FOR APPROACHING THOUGHTS AND REDUCING THOUGHT/ACTION FUSION

GAD individuals are prisoners to their own thoughts—primarily their worries. They often experience something termed "thought/action fusion." That is, there is no distance between the individual and his or her thoughts. Thoughts are believed wholeheartedly and are not appraised. Both mindfulness and cognitive modification interrupt this fusion. The cognitive modification component of CBT teaches one to evaluate the accuracy of beliefs and worries. Another type of ammunition for approaching worry is changing one's relationship to thoughts. Mindfulness strategies approach worry thoughts from another stance—instead of trying to change, suppress, or otherwise modify thoughts, one becomes an observer of one's thoughts, nonjudgmentally watching them or categorizing them (e.g., "Not a thought effective to my long term goals," or "There went a whole train of worry thoughts—what triggered that?").

MINDFULNESS INCREASES AWARENESS OF IMMINENT LAPSE AND PREVENTS RELAPSE

Relapse, whether it is to worry, alcohol, or other problem behaviors, often coincides with major life stressors. Though this might have been discussed during the relapse prevention portion of treatment, when significant stress pops up in real life it is sometimes difficult to recognize that this is a high-risk situation for relapse. Practicing mindful awareness, one might notice "Ah, this is the type of situation where I'm likely to start worrying again." If this occurs before the onset of major worry (before a lapse occurs), it could prevent a lapse. Mindful behavior (or Mindful Action) during a lapse may help one react in a deliberate fashion, preventing a full relapse. In general, mindfulness can help avoid or solve problem situations that might lead to a relapse of chronic worry (e.g., having a plan in place for how to deal with a difficult brother's comments), or, if an unexpected situation comes up, to react mindfully to that risky situation (e.g., being mindful of one's comments and goals when being caught off guard by an accusing phone call).

SPECIAL TOPICS

PHARMACOTHERAPY

Due to their efficacy in GAD and comorbid anxiety and depressive disorders, their tolerability and safety, certain selective serotonin re-uptake inhibitors (SSRIs) should be considered the first-line of medication treatment for most patients, and the serotonin-noradrenalin re-uptake inhibitor venlafaxine (Effexor) has also been found to be effective (Baldwin & Polkinghorn, 2005). Some examples of these SSRI medications are sertraline (Zoloft), escitalopram (Lexapro), and paroxetine (Paxil). Paroxetine currently has the most empirical support (Baldwin, 2000; Baldwin, Hawley & Mellors, 2001; Rickels et al., 2003, Rocca et al., 1997), which may be primarily because it is the medication with the most clinical trials to date. Additionally, there is preliminary support for the treatment of anxiety with citalopram (Celexa), fluvoxamine (Luvox), and fluoxetine (Prozac), but GAD-specific trials are needed (Baldwin & Polkinghorn, 2005). A concern with pharmacotherapy is the duration of the therapy. There is minimal research on this topic but the available results recommend that pharmacotherapy should continue for at least six months (Baldwin & Polkinghorn, 2005). Another concern is resistant patients. The management of patients who do not respond to first-line treatment is uncertain, but some of these patients may benefit from certain tricyclic antidepressants (e.g., Adapin, Anafranil, Elavil, Endep), buspirone (Buspar), or pregabalin (Lyrica) (Baldwin & Polkinghorn, 2005).

SUMMARY AND CONCLUSIONS

To our knowledge, "relapse prevention" for GAD is not commonly described nor has it been specifically studied. However CBT, which is currently the most empirically supported GAD treatment, often includes pieces of the original relapse prevention model. In this chapter we reviewed the current CBT relapse prevention approaches (see Figure 5.1 for summary). In general, we found different versions of CBT for GAD consist of multiple overlapping strategies and interventions found to reduce pathological worry and prevent reoccurrence or relapse.

In the remainder of the chapter we introduced the application of mindfulness techniques as a specific tool that can be used to help clients prevent relapse to pathological worrying. As we described, worry can be conceptualized as a failure to focus on the present moment (i.e., a failure of mindfulness) and as such many individuals who suffer from GAD experience intense fusion with their worried thoughts and mindlessness of the current moment. A review of common CBT approaches for GAD indicated the cognitive modification component of CBT teaches evaluation of the accuracy of beliefs and worries, but does not attempt to change one's relationship to thoughts in the manner that mindfulness training does. We propose that mindfulness techniques approach worry from a different direction. Rather than changing or challenging thoughts, mindfulness can be used to recognize worry as *just* a thought, part of a long string of many thoughts. With mindfulness practice those with GAD can be taught to maintain current moment presence, even with experiencing the internal sensations and thoughts of worry. Thus, the result is a changed relationship to one's thoughts.

Currently, studies are underway to evaluate the effectiveness of mindfulness in the treatment of GAD. Although mindfulness-based interventions for GAD do not yet have the support that exists for other disorders, pilot studies are promising. Practitioners should bear in mind that empirical studies are not yet available and should orient clients to the nascent developmental stage of the integration of mindfulness and CBT for GAD. That being said, in this chapter we have argued that applying mindfulness as a foundation for skills and strategies already used in CBT for GAD may be especially helpful for individuals who are chronic worriers. Greater mindful awareness may, in particular, be an important piece of relapse prevention once a person achieves partial or full recovery from GAD. Many core relapse prevention techniques (identifying high-risk situations, recognizing the difference between a lapse and a relapse, attaining lifestyle balance) could be applied to chronic worrying, with mindful awareness, action and skills as a major focus. Mindfulness of the present moment can help one avoid or reduce the impact of high-risk situations; acknowledge worry as just thoughts and not allow them to completely take over; facilitate improved learning and practicing of general CBT skills; and manage negative affective states without inducing worry. In our clinical practice we have found these techniques to be invaluable and we hope future research will continue to test mindfulness components in the prevention of relapse to GAD and pathological worrying.

ACKNOWLEDGEMENTS

Special thanks to Jeff Milton-Hall and Blair V. Kleiber for their assistance in the collection and organization of manuscripts for this paper.

REFERENCES

Alonso, J., Angermeyer, M.C., Bernert, S., Bruffaerts, R., Brugha, T.S., Bryson, H. et al. (2004). Prevalence of mental disorders in Europe: Results from the European Study of the Epidemiology of Mental Disorders (ESEMeD) project. *Acta Psychiatrica Scandinavica* (Suppl) **16**:21–27.

Andrade, L., Walters, E.E., Gentil, V., Laurenti, R. (2002). Prevalence of ICD-10 mental disorders in a catchment area in the city of Sao Paulo, Brazil. *Social Psychiatry and Psychiatric Epidemiology* **37**:316–325.

Antony, M.M. (2002). Enhancing current treatments for anxiety disorders. *Clinical Psychology: Science and Practice* **9**:91–94.

American Psychiatric Association (1980). *Diagnostic and statistical manual of mental disorders, 3e*. Washington, DC: The Association.

American Psychiatric Association (1987). *Diagnostic and statistical manual of mental disorders, 3e, revised*. Washington, DC: The Association.

American Psychiatric Association (1994). *Diagnostic and statistical manual of mental disorders, 4e*. Washington, DC: The Association.

American Psychiatric Association (2000). *Diagnostic and statistical manual of mental disorders, 4e, revised*. Washington, DC: The Association.

Barlow, D.H. (2002). *Anxiety and its disorders: The nature and treatment of anxiety and panic, 2e*. New York: Guilford Press.

Baldwin, D.S. (2000). Clinical experience with paroxetine in social anxiety disorder. *International Clinical Psychopharmacology* **15**(Suppl 1):S19–24.

Baldwin, D.S., Hawley, C.J., Mellors, K.A. (2001). A randomized, double-blind controlled comparison of nefazodone and paroxetine in the treatment of depression: Safety, tolerability and efficacy in continuation phase treatment. *Journal of Psychopharmacology* **15**:161–165.

Baldwin, D.S., Polkinghorn, C. (2005). Evidence-based pharmacotherapy of generalized anxiety disorder. *International Journal of Neuropsychopharmacology* **8**(2):293–302.

Borkovec, T.D. (2002). Life in the future versus life in the present. *Clinical psychology: Science and practice* **9**:76–80.

Borkovec, T.D., Alcaine, O.M., Behar, E. (2004). Avoidance theory of worry and generalized anxiety disorder. In Heimberg, R.G., Turk, C.L., Mennin, D.S., eds., *Generalized anxiety disorder: Advances in research and practice*, 77–108. New York: Guilford Press.

Borkovec, T.D., Hu, S. (1990). The effect of worry on cardiovascular response to phobic imagery. *Behaviour Research and Therapy* **28**:69–73.

Borkovec, T.D., Roemer, L. (1996). Generalized anxiety disorder. In Lindemann, D.G., ed., *Handbook of the treatment of the anxiety disorders, 4e*, 81–118. Northvale, NJ: USC.

Borkovec, T.D., Ruscio, A.M. (2001). Psychotherapy for generalized anxiety disorder. *Journal of Clinical Psychiatry* **62**:37–42.

Borkovec, T.D., Shadick, R.N., Hopkins, M. (1991). The nature of normal and pathological worry. In Rapee, R.M., Barlow, D.H., eds., *Chronic anxiety: Generalized anxiety disorder and mixed anxiety–depression*, 29–51. New York: Guilford Press.

Brown, T.A., Antony, M.M., Barlow, D.H. (1995). Diagnostic comorbidity in panic disorder: Effect on treatment outcome and course of comorbid diagnoses following treatment. *Journal of Consulting and Clinical Psychology* **63**(3):408–418.

Brown, Y.A., Barlow, D.H., Liebowitz, M.R. (1994). The empirical basis of generalized anxiety disorder. *American Journal of Psychiatry* **151**:1272–1280.

Brown, T.A., Di Nardo, P.A., Barlow, D.H. (1993). *Anxiety Disorders Interview Schedule (ADIS-IV) Specimen Set:* Includes Clinician Manual and One ADIS-IV Client Interview Schedule (Treatments That Work, Paperback). Oxford University Press: New York.

Brown, T.A., Di Nardo, P.A., Barlow, D.H. (1994). *Anxiety Disorders Interview Schedule for DSM-IV (ADIS-IV)*. San Antonio, TX: Psychological Corporation/Graywind Publications Incorporated.

Chambless, D.L., Gillis, M.M. (1993). Cognitive therapy of anxiety disorders. *Journal of Consulting and Clinical Psychology* **61**:248–260.

Costello, E.J., Egger, H.L., Angold, A. (2004). Developmental epidemiology of anxiety disorders. In Ollendick, T.H., March, J.S., eds., *Phobic and anxiety disorders in children and adolescents: A clinician's guide to effective psychosocial and pharmacological interventions*, 61–91. London: Oxford Press.

Dadds, M.R., Spence, S.H., Holland, D.E., Barrett, P.M., Laurens, K.R. (1997). Prevention and early intervention for anxiety disorders: A controlled trial. *Journal of Consulting and Clinical Psychology* **65**(4):627–635.

Davey, G.C.L., Tallis, F., Capuzzo, N. (1996). Beliefs about the consequences of worrying. *Cognitive Therapy and Research* **20**:499–520.

Davidson, R.J., Kabat-Zinn, J., Schumacher, J., Rosenkrantz, M., Muller, D., Santorelli, S.F. et al. (2003). Alterations in brain and immune function produced by mindfulness meditation. *Psychosomatic Medicine* **65**:564–570.

Dozois, D.J.A., Westra, H.A. (2004). The nature of anxiety and depression: Implications for prevention. In Dozois, D.J.A., Dobson, K.S., eds., *The prevention of anxiety & depression: Theory, research and practice*, 9–41. Washington, DC: American Psychological Association.

Dugas, M.J., Rodomsky, A.S., Brillon, P. (2004). Tertiary intervention for anxiety and prevention of relapse. In Dozois, D.J.A., Dobson, K.S., eds., *The prevention of anxiety and depression: Theory, research, and practice*, 161–184. Washington, DC: American Psychological Association.

Durham, R., Chambers, J., MacDonald, R., Power, K.G., Major, K. (2003). Does cognitive behavioural therapy influence the course of generalised anxiety disorder? 10–14 year follow-up of two clinical trials. *Psychological Medicine* **33**:499–509.

Durham, R.C., Allan, T., Hackett, C.A. (1997). On predicting improvement and relapse in generalized anxiety disorder following psychotherapy. *British Journal of Clinical Psychology* **36**:101–119.

Fifer, S.K., Mathias, S.D., Patrick, D.L., Mazonson, P.D., Lubeck, D.P., Buesching, D.P. (1994). Untreated anxiety among adult primary care patients in a Health Maintenance Organization. *Archives of General Psychiatry* **51**(9):740–750.

First, M.B., Spitzer, R.L., Gibbon, M., Williams, J.B.W. (2002). *Structured clinical interview for DSM-IV-TR axis I disorders, research version, patient edition (SCID-I/P)*. New York: Biometrics Research, New York State Psychiatric Institute.

Freeston, M.H., Rheaume, J., Letarte, H., Dugas, M.J., Ladouceur, R. (1994). Why do people worry? *Personality and Individual Differences* 17:791–802.

Gorski, T.F., Miller, M. (1982). *Counseling for relapse prevention*. Independence, MO: Herald House—Independence Press.

Gould, R.A., Otto, M.W. (1996). Cognitive-behavioral treatment of social phobia and generalized anxiety disorder. In Pollack, M.H., Otto, M.W., Rosenbaum, J.F., eds., *Challenges in clinical practice: Pharmacologic and psychosocial strategies*, 171–200. New York: The Guilford Press.

Gould, R.A., Otto, M.W., Pollack, M.H., Yap, L. (1997). Cognitive behavioral and pharmacological treatment of generalized anxiety disorder: A preliminary meta-analysis. *Behavior Therapy* 28:285–305.

Grant, B.F., Hasin, D.S., Stinson, F.S., Dawson, D.A., Ruan, W.J., Goldstein, R.B. et al. (2005). Prevalence, correlates, co-morbidity, and comparative disability of DSM-IV generalized anxiety disorder in the USA: Results from the National Epidemiologic Survey on Alcohol and Related Conditions. *Psychological Medicine* 35(12):1747–1759.

Hayes, S.C., Strosahl, K., Wilson, K.G. (1999). *Acceptance and commitment therapy: An experimental approach to behavior change*. New York: Guilford Press.

Hoehn-Saric, R., McLeod, D.R. (2000). Anxiety and arousal: Physiological changes and their perception. *Journal of Affective Disorders* 61:217–224.

Hofmann, S.G., Moscovitch, D.A., Litz, B.T., Kim, H., Davis, L.L., Pizzagalli, D.A. (2005). The worried mind: Autonomic and prefrontal activation during worrying. *Emotion* 5:464–475.

ICD-10. (1992). *International Statistical Classification of Diseases and Related Health Problems: Tenth revision*, 2e. Geneva: World Health Organization (WHO)

Joormann, J., Stober, J. (1999). Somatic symptoms of generalized anxiety disorder from the DSM-IV: Associations with pathological worry and depression symptoms in a nonclinical sample. *Journal of Anxiety Disorders* 13(5):491–503.

Kabat-Zinn, J. (1994). *Wherever you go, there are you: Mindfulness meditation in everyday life*. New York: Hyperion.

Kendall, P.C., Pimentel, S., Rynn, M.A., Angelosante, A., Webb, A. (2004). Generalized anxiety disorder. In Ollendick, T.H., March, J.S., eds., *Phobic and anxiety disorders in children and adolescents: A clinician's guide to effective psychosocial and pharmacological interventions*, 334–380. London: Oxford University Press.

Kessler, R.C., Chiu, W.T., Demler, O., Walters, E.E. (2005). Prevalence, severity, and comorbidity of twelve-month DSM-IV disorders in the National Comorbidity Survey Replication (NCS-R). *Archives of General Psychiatry* 62(6):617–627.

Kessler, R.C., Wittchen, H.-U. (2002). Patterns and correlates of generalized anxiety disorder in community samples. *Journal of Clinical Psychiatry* 63(Suppl 8):4–10.

Ladouceur, R., Blais, F., Freeston, M.H., Dugas, M.J. (1998). Problem solving and problem orientation in generalized anxiety disorder. *Journal of Anxiety Disorders* 12:139–152.

Ladouceur, R., Talbot, F., Dugas, M.J. (1997). Behavioural expressions of intolerance of uncertainty in worry. *Behaviour Modification* 21:233–371.

Leger, E., Ladouceur, R., Dugas, M.J., Freeston, M.H. (2003). Cognitive-behavioral treatment of generalized anxiety disorder among adolescent: A case series. *Journal of the American Academy of Child & Adolescent Psychiatry* 42(3):327–330.

Linehan, M.M. (1993a). *Cognitive-behavioral treatment of borderline personality disorder*. New York: The Guilford Press.

Linehan, M.M. (1993b). *Skills training manual for treating borderline personality disorder*. New York: The Guilford Press.

Lyonfields, J.D., Borkovec, T.D., Thayer, J.F. (1995). Vagal tone in generalized anxiety disorder and the effects of aversive imagery and worrisome thinking. *Behavior Therapy* 24:457–466.

Maier, W., Gansicke, M., Freyberger, H.J., Linz, M., Heun, R., Lecrubier, Y. (2000). Generalized anxiety disorder (ICD-10) in primary care from a cross-cultural perspective: A valid diagnostic entity? *Acta Psychiatrica Scandinavica* **101**:29–36.

Marlatt, G.A., Gordon, J.R. (Eds.) (1985). *Relapse prevention: Maintenance strategies in the treatment of addictive behaviors, 1e.* New York: Guilford Press.

Mathews, A. (1990). Why worry? The cognitive function of anxiety. *Behaviour Research and Therapy* **28**:455–468.

Mendlowicz, M.V., Stein, M.B. (2000). Quality of life in individuals with anxiety disorders. *American Journal of Psychiatry* **157**(5):669–682.

Mennin, D.S. (2004). Emotion regulation therapy for generalized anxiety disorder. *Clinical Psychology and Psychotherapy* **11**:17–29.

Mennin, D.S., Heimberg, R.G., Turk, C.L., Fresco, D.M. (2002). Commentary on Roemer and Orsillo: Applying an emotion regulation framework to integrative approaches to generalized anxiety disorder. *Clinical Psychology: Science and Practice* **9**:85–90.

Meyer, T.J., Miller, M.L., Metzger, R.L., Borkovec, T.D. (1990). Development and validation of the Penn State Worry Questionnaire. *Behaviour Research and Therapy* **28**:487–495.

Newman, M.G., Zuellig, A.R., Kachin, K.E., Constantino, M.J. (2002). The reliability and validity of the GAD-Q-IV: A revised self-report measure of generalized anxiety disorder. *Behavior Therapy* **33**:215–233.

Noyes Jr., R., Woodman, C., Garvey, M.J., Cook, B.L., Suelzer, M., Clancy, J. et al. (1992). Generalized anxiety disorder vs. panic disorder: Distinguishing characteristics and patterns of comorbidity. *Journal of Nervous and Mental Disorders* **180**(11):737–738.

Overholser, J.C., Nasser, E.H. (2000). Cognitive-behavioral treatment for generalized anxiety disorder. *Journal of Contemporary Psychotherapy* **30**(2):149–161.

Orsillo, S.M., Roemer, L., Lerner, J.B., Tull, M.T. (2004). Acceptance, mindfulness, and cognitive-behavioral therapy: Comparisons, contrasts, and application to anxiety. In Hayes, S.C., Follette, V.M., Linehan, M.M., eds., *Mindfulness and acceptance: Expanding the cognitive-behavioral tradition*, 66–95. New York: Guilford Press.

Oxford English Dictionary. (2006). London: Oxford University Press.

Reich, J., Noyes, R., Yates, W. (1988). Anxiety symptoms distinguishing social phobia from panic and generalized anxiety disorders. *Journal of Nervous and Mental Disorders* **176**(8): 510–513.

Regier, D.A., Rae, D.S., Narrow, W.E. et al. (1998). Prevalence of anxiety disorders and their comorbidity with mood and addictive disorders. *British Journal of Psychiatry Supplement* **34**:24–28.

Rickels, K., Zaninelli, R., McCafferty, J., Bellew, K., Iyengar, M., Sheehan, D. et al. (2003). Paroxetine treatment of generalized anxiety disorder: A double-blind, placebo-controlled study. *American Journal of Psychiatry* **160**:749–756.

Robins, L.N., Reiger, D.A. (Eds.) (1991). *Psychiatric disorders in America: The epidemiologic catchment area study.* New York: The Free Press.

Rocca, P., Fonzo, V., Scotta, M., Zanalda, E., Ravizza, L. (1997). Paroxetine efficacy in the treatment of generalized anxiety disorder. *Acta Psychiatrica Scandanavica* **95**:444–450.

Rodriguez, B.F., Weisberg, R.B., Pagano, M.E., Bruce, S.E., Spencer, M.A., Culpepper, L. et al. (2006). Characteristics and predictors of full and partial recovery from generalized anxiety disorder in primary care patients. *Journal of Nervous and Mental Disorders* **194**:91–97.

Roemer, L. (2001). Measures for generalized anxiety disorder. In Antony, M.M., Orsillo, S.M., Roemer, L., eds., *Practitioner's guide to empirically based measures of anxiety*. New York: Springer.

Roemer, L., Molina, S., Borkovec, T.D. (1997). An investigation of worry content among generally anxious individuals. *Journal of Nervous and Mental Disorders* **185**(5):314–319.

Roemer, L., Orsillo, S.M. (2002). Expanding our conceptualization of and treatment for generalized anxiety disorder: Integrating mindfulness/acceptance-based approaches with existing cognitive-behavioral models. *Clinical Psychology: Science and Practice* **9**:54–68.

Roemer, L., Orsillo, S.M. (2005). An acceptance-based behavior therapy for generalized anxiety disorder. In Orsillo, S.M., Roemer, L., eds., *Acceptance and mindfulness-based approaches to anxiety: Conceptualization and treatment*. New York: Springer.

Roemer, L., Orsillo, S.M., Barlow, D.H. (2002). Generalized anxiety disorder. In Barlow, D.H., ed., *Anxiety and its disorders: The nature and treatment of anxiety and panic, 2e*, 477–515. New York: Guilford Press.

Roemer, L., Salters, K., Raffa, S., Orsillo, S.M. (2005). Fear and avoidance of internal experiences: Preliminary tests of a conceptual model. *Cognitive Therapy and Research* **29**:71–88.

Rygh, J.L., Sanderson, W.C. (2004). *Treating generalized anxiety disorder: Evidence-based strategies, tools, and techniques*. New York: Guilford Press.

Sanderson, W.C., Barlow, D.H. (1990). A description of patients diagnosed with DSM-III-R generalized anxiety disorder. *Journal of Nervous and Mental Disorders* **178**:558–591.

Segal, Z.V., Williams, M.G., Teasdale, J.D. (2002). *Mindfulness-based cognitive therapy for depression : A new approach to preventing relapse*. New York: Guilford Press.

Slade, T., Andrews, G. (2001). DSM-IV and ICD-10 generalized anxiety disorder: Discrepant diagnoses and associated disability. *Social Psychiatry and Psychiatric Epidemiology* **36**:45–51.

Story, T.J., Zucker, B.G., Craske, M.G. (2004). Secondary prevention of anxiety disorders. In Dozois, D.J.A., Dobson, K.S., eds., *The prevention of anxiety and depression: Theory, research, and practice*, 131–160. Washington, DC: American Psychological Association.

Tallis, F., Eysenck, M., Mathews, A. (1992). A questionnaire for the measurement of nonpathological worry. *Personality and Individual Differences* **13**:161–168.

Thayer, J.F., Friedman, B.H., Borkovec, T.D. (1996). Autonomic characteristics of generalized anxiety disorder and worry. *Biological Psychiatry* **39**:255–266.

Wells, A., Papageorgiou, C. (1995). Worry and the incubation of intrusive images following stress. *Behaviour Research and Therapy* **33**:579–583.

Wisocki, P.A. (1988). Worry as a phenomenon relevant to the elderly. *Behavior Therapy* **19**:369–379.

Wittchen, H.-U., Zhao, S., Kessler, R.C., Eaton, W.W. (1994). DSM-III-R generalized anxiety disorder in the National Comorbidity Survey. *Archives of General Psychiatry* **51**(5):355–364.

Yonkers, K.A., Bruce, S.E., Dyck, I.R., Keller, M.B. (2003). Chronicity, relapse and illness course of panic disorder, social phobia and generalized anxiety disorder: Findings in men and women from 8 years of follow-up. *Depression and Anxiety* **17**:173–179.

Yonkers, K.A., Dyck, I.R., Warshaw, M., Keller, M. (2000). Factors predicting the clinical course of generalised anxiety disorder. *The British Journal of Psychiatry* **176**:544–549.

Yonkers, K.A., Warshaw, M., Massion, A.O., Keller, M.B. (1996). Phenomenology and course of generalised anxiety disorder. *The British Journal of Psychiatry* **168**:308–313.

Zanarini, M.C., Skodol, A.E., Bender, D., Dolan, R., Sanislow, C., Schaefer, E. et al. (2000). The collaborative longitudinal personality disorders study: Reliability of axis I and II diagnoses. *Journal of Personality Disorders* **14**(4):291–299.

RESOURCE BIBLIOGRAPHY AND A LIST OF INTERNET LINKS

RESOURCE BIBLIOGRAPHY

Adult Clients

- Burns, D.D. (1999). *The feeling good handbook, Revised Edition*. New York: Plume.

- Davis, M., Eshelman, E.R. & McKay, M. (1995). *The relaxation and stress reduction workbook, 4e.* Oakland, CA: New Harbinger Publications.
- Greenberger, D. & Padesky, C.A. (1995). *Mind over mood: A cognitive therapy treatment manual for clients.* New York: Guilford Press.
- Leahy, R.L. (2005). *The worry cure: Seven steps to stop worry from stopping you.* New York: Harmony.
- Hazlett-Stevens, H. (2005). *Women who worry too much: How to stop worry & anxiety from ruining relationships, work & fun.* Oakland: New Harbinger Publications.

Child Clients
- Wolff, F., Savitz, H.M. & LeTourneau, M. (2005). *Is a worry worrying you?* Terre Haute: Tanglewood Press.
- Huebner, D. & Matthews, B. (2005). *What to do when you worry too much: A kid's guide to overcoming anxiety.* Washington, DC: Magination Press.
- Resource Bibliography for Clinicians
- Heimberg, R.G., Turk, C.L. & Mennin, D.S. (Eds.) (2004). *Generalized anxiety disorder: Advances in research and practice.* New York: Guilford Press.
- Rygh, J.L. & Sanderson, W.C. (2004). *Treating generalized anxiety disorder: Evidence-based strategies, tools, and techniques.* New York: Guilford Press.
- Dugas, M.J. & Robichaud, M. (2006). *Cognitive-Behavioral Treatment for Generalized Anxiety Disorder, 1e.* New York: Brunner-Routledge.

INTERNET RESOURCES ON GENERALIZED ANXIETY DISORDER FOR CLINICIANS AND CLIENTS

- National Institute of Mental Health
  http://www.nimh.nih.gov/healthinformation/gadmenu.cfm
- Mayo Clinic
  http://www.mayoclinic.com/health/generalized-anxiety-disorder/DS00502
- Psych Direct: Evidence Based Mental Health Education & Information
  http://www.psychdirect.com/anxiety/gad.htm
- Anxiety Disorders Association of America (ADAA)
  http://www.adaa.org/GettingHelp/AnxietyDisorders/GAD.asp
- Anxiety Disorders Association of Canada
  http://www.anxietycanada.ca/newenglish.htm

6

RELAPSE PREVENTION FOR SCHIZOPHRENIA

DOUGLAS ZIEDONIS,
PHILIP T. YANOS, AND
STEVEN M. SILVERSTEIN

Robert Wood Johnson Medical School
Piscataway, New Jersey

INTRODUCTION

Schizophrenia is a severe and persistent mental disorder that occurs at a prevalence rate of between 1 and 1.5 percent throughout the world. A significant proportion of individuals with schizophrenia have difficulty expressing their feelings, communicating with others, perceiving and interpreting information, managing stress, and even managing basic self-care. As a result, schizophrenia substantially impairs occupational and social functioning and is both a major public health concern and a major obstacle to effectively managing life demands. It has been estimated that as many as 10 percent of all disabled persons in the United States have schizophrenia (Rupp & Keith, 1993), and the disorder accounts for 75 percent of all mental health expenditures and approximately 40 percent of all Medicaid reimbursements (Martin & Miller, 1998). Among people with the disorder, only between 10 to 30 percent are employed at any one time (Attkisson et al., 1992), and few of these people are able to maintain consistent employment (Policy Study Associates, 1989). A recent estimate of the economic cost of treating people diagnosed with schizophrenia was 62.7 billion dollars per year, including direct treatment costs and indirect costs such as lost business productivity due to patient and family caretaker work absence (Wu et al., 2005).

Schizophrenia is very heterogeneous in its clinical presentation, course, and level of functional impact. Symptoms of schizophrenia traditionally have been grouped into two broad categories of positive and negative symptoms. The positive symptoms include hallucinations (perceptions in the absence of external

117

stimuli to cause them, in the auditory, visual, tactile, and/or olfactory domains), and delusions (fixed ideas not held by others from the same cultural group that are resistant to change in the face of contradictory evidence). The negative symptoms of schizophrenia include flat affect (limited range and intensity of emotional expression), alogia (reduced speech production), anhedonia, low motivation (goal-directed behaviors), and limited social skills. In addition, the symptoms of schizophrenia may include disorganized speech (e.g., loose associations), disorganized behavior, odd movements that are not side effects of medication, and difficulties with attention or abstract thinking. Cognitive impairment is also common (Harvey, 2000; Rund, 1998) and includes difficulties with working memory, sustained attention, executive functioning, and acquiring new skills. Individuals with schizophrenia are also vulnerable to developing other psychiatric disorders such as depression, anxiety, and substance use disorders. In fact, about 50 to 85 percent of individuals with schizophrenia will develop a co-occurring substance use disorder (alcohol, tobacco, cocaine, marijuana). This common comorbidity is associated with poor medication compliance, increased fluctuations in mental status, increased general health and legal problems, and the increased likelihood for needing expensive acute care in emergency rooms and inpatient units. Substance abuse is one of the major factors explaining the disproportionately higher rates of general medical illness, increased mortality, and suicide in this population.

Given the clinical picture of schizophrenia, preventing or increasing the time period between full or partial psychotic relapses is one of the primary goals of treatment. Psychiatric medications have been effective in reducing the frequency and length of psychotic relapses and psychiatric hospitalizations. However, despite the success of antipsychotic agents in transforming the treatment of schizophrenia, there are also clear limitations to what psychopharmacologic approaches are able to accomplish with this population. About 30 to 40 percent of individuals with schizophrenia will have a psychotic relapse within one year after a hospitalization even when being prescribed antipsychotic medications (APA Schizophrenia Guidelines, 1997; Kendler et al., 1996; Ziedonis et al., 2005). Other major limitations of antipsychotic treatment include (1) the large number of persons who have poor or partial response to antipsychotics (research indicates that positive symptoms persist for up to 40% of persons with schizophrenia; Meltzer, 1992); (2) the problem of poor medication adherence (it is estimated that between 20 to 55% of individuals with major mental disorders fail to take psychiatric medications as prescribed; Cramer & Rosenheck, 1999); and (3) the limited impact of medication on social functioning and quality of life for a significant proportion of individuals (see Corrigan et al., 2003, for a review).

There is a need to improve treatment outcomes for this population by developing better pharmacotherapies as well as integrating and enhancing tailored and individualized psychosocial treatment approaches. Psychosocial treatments can help further reduce symptom severity, prevent relapses, and improve social functioning, medication compliance, and overall quality of life; however, these approaches are currently underutilized in routine care in the United States (Lehman et al., 2003). There are many reasons for this disparity, including costs, time, transportation, and staff training. Another reason is that treatment of schizophrenia has focused on a goal of suppressing symptoms and medications have been the primary form of treatment since the 1960s. The treatment field has begun to shift its orientation to a recovery orientation, including a goal to move beyond symptom suppression and toward a treatment approach wherein multiple interventions are all brought to bear on the goal of improving functioning, reducing the likelihood of relapse, and promoting consumer involvement and recovery. The interventions discussed in this chapter can form the core of such a treatment approach.

For many mental health clinicians the terms "relapse prevention" and "recovery" had been identified as concepts used in substance abuse treatment services, and they were rarely used in reference to treatment of psychosis. These words are now being integrated into the mental health field. The term "recovery" has been embraced in recent years by both mental health consumers and treatment providers and leaders in the mental health field as a whole (see Liberman & Kopelowicz, 2005, for an overview of recovery from schizophrenia, and White, Boyle & Loveland, 2005, for a comparison of recovery from addiction and recovery from mental illness). Similarly, the concept of "relapse prevention" increasingly has been seen as a valuable framework and technique for formulating an overall treatment plan for patients with schizophrenia. Perhaps the increased awareness and development of specialized psychosocial treatments for co-occurring mental illness and addiction has played a part in the mental health setting's cultural shift to a recovery orientation and framing psychosocial treatments as relapse prevention therapies.

Evidence-based psychosocial treatments that can improve treatment outcomes for individuals with schizophrenia, such as reducing the frequency of relapses, traditionally have been labeled by the techniques they employ rather than their goal (e.g., relapse prevention). Thus, for example, a treatment plan focused on reducing relapse frequency might include a variety of interventions such as cognitive behavioral therapy, social skills training, family therapy, integrated dual disorder treatment, and cognitive rehabilitation. Most of these therapy approaches include many of the concepts and strategies of traditional Relapse Prevention (Marlatt & Donovan, 2005; Marlatt & Gordon, 1985).

This chapter will review the empirical support for relapse prevention therapy for schizophrenia, viewed broadly to include psychosocial treatments that have demonstrated effectiveness in reducing psychotic relapse and those used to prevent substance abuse relapses among individuals with schizophrenia as well. All of these approaches have targeted the common causes of psychotic relapse such as medication nonadherence and external stressors (people, places, and things or substances) through education, increased awareness of these specific stressors and how to manage them; and enhancement of general coping skills, problem-solving skills, and social skills. Through functional analysis of previous full and partial relapses, individuals may better understand their early warning/prodromal symptoms prior to relapsing. Overall, medications and psychosocial treatments have primary goals to reduce or eliminate schizophrenia-related symptoms and relapses, improve the individuals' quality of life and ability to adapt and function, and support recovery and self-empowerment to manage their condition as best possible (APA Schizophrenia Guidelines, 1997).

OVERVIEW OF PSYCHOSOCIAL TREATMENT

During the past 20 years there has been a growing literature supporting the efficacy of cognitive behavioral therapies/relapse prevention therapies for the treatment of schizophrenia, including over 20 randomized controlled trials published in the literature. Much of this research has focused on further reducing symptoms of schizophrenia that are not resolved by medications; however some of the studies specifically include early intervention to reduce the likelihood of a full relapse and efforts to shorten the relapse episode. Of note, historically, psychosocial treatment of people with schizophrenia had consisted of individual psychodynamic-oriented psychotherapy; however there is little evidence to support the efficacy of unstructured, insight-oriented techniques, such as psychodynamic psychotherapy in this population (APA Schizophrenia Guidelines, 1997; Mueser & Berenbaum, 1990). For this population, clinicians do better with a more active approach, which offers concrete and tangible solutions to day-to-day problems, in addition to teaching strategies to cope with positive and negative symptoms.

As with substance use disorders, individuals with schizophrenia fluctuate in their acceptance of their diagnosis and their willingness to collaborate with treatment providers regarding medication and psychosocial treatment adherence. Cognitive-behavioral therapy/relapse prevention therapy focuses on the here and now and the therapist uses action-oriented and structured techniques to treat schizophrenia. Therapy is administered in both the group and individual treatment formats. Social skills training and family therapy approaches tend to be administered in group treatment formats to enhance the interactive learning opportunities.

Case management commonly is used to augment relapse prevention and other psychotherapy approaches to improve treatment adherence and reduce fragmentation of care. The case managers help facilitate links with the full range of services, including social, medical, and mental health with the aim of improving treatment engagement and establishing successful community reintegration. Several case management approaches have been developed for this treatment population, including the Broker Model, Assertive Community Treatment, and intensive case management. These approaches have similar components of a needs assessment, development of a comprehensive service plan, outreach and ongoing coordination of services, monitoring and assessment of service delivery, and ongoing evaluation and follow-up (Ziedonis et al., 2005).

CORE FEATURES OF CBT FOR SCHIZOPHRENIA

CBT interventions for schizophrenia tend to include some common features, including psychoeducation, enhancing coping skills, cognitive restructuring, functional analysis, problem solving, and enhancing communication skills. As applied to schizophrenia, CBT engages patients in collaboratively challenging their interpretations of events or experiences. Treatment often begins with psychoeducation which, when used properly, can increase engagement in treatment and increase hopefulness regarding the potential for recovery (Roe & Yanos, 2006). Cognitive strategies often are used to assist patients in developing more realistic alternatives to delusional and paranoid thinking. They can also be used to help patients develop less stressful attributions for hallucinations. For example, rather than believing that the voices are omnipotent, omniscient, and must be obeyed, behavioral experiments can be set up to test this hypothesis, and to replace these thoughts with more realistic ones. In many cases, the reduction in anxiety that accompanies modified attributions regarding voices actually leads to a reduced frequency and intensity of hallucinations. In the case of negative symptoms, CBT is often used to challenge anhedonic beliefs and to assist the patient in scheduling and administering self-rewards for increasingly engaging in pleasurable activities.

The use of behavioral techniques can better help engage this population in a more active learning process that includes role plays, coaching by therapists, repetition of core concepts, modeling by other patients during group therapy, and the use of feedback and homework assignments. Social skills training uses these behavioral therapy relapse prevention techniques in psychiatric symptom management, medication management, and leisure time management modules (Liberman et al., 2005).

Another common element of CBT is to help an individual increase their self-efficacy to manage specific situations by developing a realistic plan, practicing the task and developing small steps to accomplish a task. The focus on smaller behavioral changes and building self-efficacy in everyday life problems can help this population to address the low self-efficacy and self-esteem that often results in a tendency to give up after early failures.

An additional approach is to help individuals with improving communication skills since many have difficulty interpreting social cues, especially abstract cue recognition (the ability to recognize the rules, affect, or goals of a situation and make inferences) (Corrigan et al., 1996). These factors impact communication and other interpersonal skills. Improving both verbal and nonverbal communication skills through role plays is a common technique.

In short, CBT for delusions focuses on undermining the rigid conviction and distress of the delusion by creating opportunities for considering alternative points of view. CBT for auditory hallucinations focuses on helping patients with distress resulting from voices, again by helping the patient construct an alternative belief about his or her voices. Similarly, treatment of paranoia involves a Socratic process aimed at generating and considering alternative beliefs. Finally, CBT for negative symptoms focuses on behavioral self-monitoring, assertiveness training, and behavioral techniques focused on increasing activity. CBT for all of these conditions also includes social learning techniques such as role playing with feedback, viewing a model demonstrate a target behavior, *in vivo* practice, and homework. These techniques can improve self-esteem and self-efficacy, and further motivate the patient to adopt new behaviors and beliefs. All of these techniques require the patient to develop an evaluative stance toward dysfunctional interpretations, and to activate the ability to systematically consider available evidence and alternative beliefs. Thus, activation of metacognitive processes is essential to progress in CBT.

OVERALL EFFICACY OF CBT FOR SCHIZOPHRENIA

One recent meta-analysis of CBT for schizophrenia, including seven randomized controlled trials (Beck & Rector, 2005), showed that CBT produced large clinical effects on both positive and negative symptom measures. CBT as an adjunct to routine clinical care also resulted in significant additional benefits compared with routine clinical care plus supportive therapy. Another recent review of 17 clinical trials testing efficacy of CBT for schizophrenia (Dickerson, 2004) showed that CBT results in better outcomes on specific measures compared with routine care or supportive therapies in a variety of settings (e.g., day-treatment programs, long-stay inpatient programs) and across some special patient populations (e.g., relapse-vulnerable patients, older adults with schizophrenia, individuals with comorbid substance abuse or anxiety disorders). There is also preliminary evidence that these improvements translate into improved social functioning (Temple & Ho, 2005). A long-term intervention called Personal Therapy, which bears many similarities to CBT, also led to considerable improvement in social functioning across a two-year randomized controlled trial (Hogarty et al., 1997). Personal therapy is an individualized treatment model that utilizes periods between crisis management to identify personal vulnerabilities, support recognition of cues signaling affective dysregulation, and increase coping skills. The specific symptoms shown to be alleviated with adjunctive CBT include delusions, distress or delusions related to auditory hallucinations (AH), paranoia, and negative symptoms (Beck & Rector, 2005). Improvements in distress related to AH and delusions were maintained at longer-term follow-up (Turkington et al., 2004).

Until recently, almost all the research on CBT for individuals with serious mental illness was conducted in England. A recent meta-analysis of the English research (reviewed by Pilling et al., 2002) confirms its effectiveness across specific modalities and applications. Large scale NIH-funded trials in the United States are currently under way. In addition to problems uniquely associated with psychotic disorders, various forms of CBT are effective for addressing generalized anxiety, panic, social anxiety, depression, obsessive-compulsive symptoms, and substance abuse. These problems often co-occur with chronic psychotic disorders, and there is no reason to believe that CBT interventions are any less effective in treating them in people with schizophrenia than in the general population.

INTERVENTIONS TAILORED TO PREVENT RELAPSE

Although teaching skills to monitor warning signs of potential relapse is a feature of most CBT interventions for schizophrenia, some interventions have been developed with a specific focus on this issue (Herz et al., 2000; Mueser et al., 2002). These programs usually include identifying events and situations that had triggered episodes in the past and making a conscious effort to build a routine that would help the person stay away from such events and situations. The person makes a relapse prevention plan (Mueser et al., 2002) with the coordination of people he or she chooses and trusts, including what sort of help, where, and from whom they would like to receive it in case they are not in a condition to decide and choose at the time. Controlled studies have demonstrated that relapse prevention programs based on these techniques can significantly reduce relapse rates (Mueser et al., 2002). In the largest trial conducted, 82 persons with schizophrenia were randomly assigned to receive a relapse-prevention treatment or treatment as usual and were followed up for 18 months (Herz et al., 2000). Persons randomized to relapse prevention treatment had significantly fewer relapses (17% vs. 34%) and rehospitalizations (22% vs. 39%) than persons in the treatment as usual. The impact of combining relapse prevention intervention approaches with other techniques of cognitive-behavioral therapy has not yet been studied, however.

Other possible effects of interventions using cognitive-behavioral approaches for people with schizophrenia include an improvement in insight and a reduction of medication nonadherence. A recent study demonstrated the success of a psychotherapeutic intervention in improving insight (Rathod et al., 2005). This study found that, compared with treatment as usual, participation in an insight-focused cognitive-behavioral intervention was associated with modest but significant improvements in insight at a one-year follow-up. There is also evidence for the efficacy of behavior therapy in improving medication adherence. Specific treatment strategies included establishing cues for taking medications, developing medication routines, and using a self-monitoring calendar (Azrin & Teichner, 1998; Cramer & Rosenheck, 1999; Kelly & Scott, 1990). Randomized studies have confirmed that these interventions can improve medication adherence for individuals who have an existing commitment to taking medication, but have difficulties remaining adherent due to memory problems or environmental barriers.

Social skills training for schizophrenia was developed to prevent relapses and is based on the stress-vulnerability model of schizophrenia, where stress and vulnerability factors compete with coping and competence factors to determine psychotic relapse or remission, social function or dysfunction, and the overall quality of life for schizophrenics (Liberman, 1989). The individual's coping skills and ability to use these skills effectively can decrease the impact of stresses and vulnerability. Social Skills Training is a structured approach that utilizes learning principles, along with individualized and specific goal setting. It is designed to include active collaboration with the patient, compensation for cognitive deficits, and promotion of medication treatment and social supports. Social Skills Training is most helpful for schizophrenia patients who are in partial or full remission from florid psychotic symptoms and are stable on neuroleptic medications. Its goals are to increase performance competence in critical life situations and help patients improve the way they communicate their emotions, needs, and desires to others (Hersen, 1976; Liberman, 1989). Patients are taught effective problem-solving techniques and communication skills.

CO-OCCURRING ADDICTION AND MENTAL ILLNESS

Alcohol, tobacco, and other drug addiction are the most common comorbidities for individuals with schizophrenia, and substance abuse worsens the clinical picture in several key ways. Clients have heard "don't take drugs and your medications" and will often stop their psychiatric medications when they use substances, further worsening their symptoms. The substances themselves have an impact on psychiatric symptoms (increased mood lability, suicidal ideation, etc.) and also further worsen the cognitive impairments associated with schizophrenia. For example, alcohol abuse can cause further cognitive problems such as memory difficulties and worsened executive functioning; and cocaine abuse can cause reduced perceptual-motor speed and impaired attention and concentration (APA Substance Abuse Treatment Guidelines, 2006). In addition, ongoing substance use can lead to enhanced environmental stressors (violence, legal problems, family stress, homelessness from using funds for drugs, etc.).

The treatment of co-occurring disorders has been most effectively enhanced through the blending of traditional mental health and addiction psychosocial treatments. In essence, by simultaneously treating both disorders in an integrated psychosocial treatment approach the outcomes improve for both disorders and for the individual as a whole. The blending is best conceived of as a blending of two types of relapse prevention psychotherapies.

In contrast to some traditional confrontational therapy approaches, this group of individuals responds best to a supportive, consistent, nurturing, and nonjudgmental therapist attitude and approach. The style of delivering relapse prevention treatment in this population is sensitive to the different motivational levels, acknowledges the many problems to address (e.g., use of multiple substances, medication compliance), and the need for a much longer engagement period and length of treatment. The behavioral strategies are delivered in a briefer, more concrete language, more repetitions, and the need to pay particular attention to the patient's alertness and adapt the interventions according to the level of alertness. An integrated therapy approach must adapt to the individual's need for additional support since they often have limited interpersonal relationships, uninvolved or rejecting family members, unstable living arrangements, and fewer opportunities for social, recreational, and work colleague support (Ziedonis et al., 2005).

In the literature there are at least four versions of integrated psychotherapy approaches for this population, including Dual Recovery Therapy (DRT, Ziedonis & Stern, 2001), modified cognitive-behavioral therapy (Bellack et al., 2006), modified Motivational Enhancement Therapy (Carey et al., 2000), and the Substance Abuse Management Module (SAMM; Roberts, Shaner et al., 1999). These relapse prevention approaches are more similar than different and all include elements of motivational enhancement, relapse prevention, and social skills training. In addition, these approaches are pro-recovery, supportive of the use of modified 12-Step Recovery meetings (e.g., variations of Alcoholics Anonymous such as Dual Recovery Anonymous), and the concurrent use of case management. Although the literature doesn't compare these approaches directly, the literature appears to strongly support an integrated psychosocial treatment approach that emphasizes relapse prevention (APA Substance Abuse Treatment Guidelines, APA Practice Guidelines, 2006).

DUAL RECOVERY THERAPY (DRT)

DRT blends elements of traditional substance abuse relapse prevention and motivational enhancement therapy with traditional mental health treatments of social skills training/psychosis relapse prevention into a single therapy approach. Clinicians must be attentive to the psychiatric and substance abuse symptoms and help the client appreciate the interaction between the two issues. Compliance with treatment and medications is important, but fluctuations in motivational level are expected over the course of treatment. DRT integrates the use of psychiatric social skills training techniques of problem solving and communication skills to promote the development of healthy relationships and peer-group support. The integrated treatments help patients develop a specific subset of skills (e.g., dealing with craving, talking to one's doctor) in an effort to help the individual better manage their triggers to substance use and also stabilize their psychiatric symptoms. In group treatment there is an opportunity for repeated skills practice and the use of role playing. The therapist is assumed to have an active role in the role play and to help the group identify a problem to focus on in the session that could be better managed outside of the group. The four core topics during group treatment are relapse prevention skills, affect regulation skills, cognitive regulation skills, and interpersonal regulation skills (Ziedonis & Stern, 2001).

Relapse prevention skills include teaching how to identify and manage external (people, places, and things) and internal triggers (anger, depression, anxiety, loneliness, etc.) to either relapse. Peers can help encourage each other to find and develop an environment and lifestyle that is supportive of abstinence (Carey et al., 2000). Individual therapy can complement group treatment and be most helpful to enhance motivation, therapeutic alliance, and provide additional individualized focus to issues raised in group and to prepare the individual for the group treatment approach. Four techniques used in individual therapy include having the client "tell their story," the use of functional/relapse analysis, and doing a decisional balance and routine role-plays. By "telling their story" the client creates a timeline of his or her life that can more clearly link his or her substance use and psychiatric histories. Functional analyses of recent relapses and common triggers for substance use can help link medication noncompliance and psychotic symptoms to the relapse and help the clinician rationalize strategies to avoid future relapses to substances. Since motivational levels fluctuate, doing a Decisional Balance (evaluating the pros and cons of choices) helps review the individual's reasons to make changes and reinforces the short-term and long-term goals.

ASSESSMENT ISSUES

A major problem with the way group-based psychosocial treatment for schizophrenia is delivered in typical community mental health treatment settings is that all patients are assigned to available treatments without an assessment/data-driven process that determines who needs which interventions. This often is compounded by overly large numbers of patients per group, and a lack of assessment of outcomes on an ongoing basis. Fortunately, assessment tools are available to help decide which treatments are appropriate for which people. Comprehensive assessment of schizophrenia includes inquiry into at least three primary domains: symptoms, functioning, and cognition (including learning capacity). Each of these domains will be considered briefly here.

Careful description of the frequency and intensity of symptoms of schizophrenia can help guide the choice of pharmacologic and behavioral methods targeted at symptom reduction (Haddock et al., 1994; Schwarzkopf et al., 1999; Spaulding et al., 1986). It is important to note, however, that symptom response is relatively independent of response to other targets of treatment (Carpenter et al., 1976; Wallace et al., 2000). Thus, symptom assessment alone is insufficient as an assessment strategy for schizophrenia, where many other areas of potential disability (e.g., social and instrumental role functioning) will affect long-term prognosis.

The goal of functional assessment is to determine a person's ability to complete tasks in critical everyday situations (e.g., money management, social functioning, grooming, etc.). Typically, functional assessment measures are used to identify which types of skills training patients need. That is, these measures can identify which patients have social skills deficits (and need social skills training), which have trouble with personal hygiene (and need treatments such as the UCLA Grooming and Hygiene module; Liberman et al., 2005), which have trouble managing their medication (and need illness management and recovery interventions), and so on. Often, basic diagnostic information and symptom assessment can also be used to guide choice of treatment. For example, patients with comorbid schizophrenia and substance abuse can be assigned to integrated dual disorder treatment (Drake & Mueser, 2000), and patients with PTSD symptoms can receive specialized interventions for dealing with trauma sequelae. Symptom data can also be used to guide choice of treatment. For example, patients with persistent delusions, or with distress from hallucinations, can be assigned to group or individual CBT that focuses on coping with, and reduction of these symptoms (Chadwick et al., 1996; Landa et al., 2006).

After determining which skills need intervention, cognitive assessment data can be used to determine what level of treatment is appropriate, and what other interventions or supports are needed. For example, patients with skills deficits who have severe attention problems that interfere with attending to material in groups can be assigned to skills training groups that also use attention-shaping approaches (Silverstein et al., 2005) to promote attentiveness. There are also individual and group-based forms of cognitive rehabilitation that can be used to help improve patients' cognitive abilities to the point where they can more effectively engage in skills-based relapse prevention approaches. Patients with reduced learning capacity, as identified using dynamic assessment measures, can be given additional one-to-one intervention to supplement group-based approaches. In short, effective treatment planning will use symptom, functional, and cognitive assessment data to identify which skills need intervention, in addition to other interventions to remove symptom and cognitive-deficit obstacles to effectively benefit from those interventions.

SYMPTOM ASSESSMENT

A number of symptom rating scales are currently in widespread use in evaluating individuals with schizophrenia. These include the Brief Psychiatric Rating Scale (Ventura et al., 1993); Scale for the Assessment of Negative Symptoms (SANS) (Andreasen, 1984a); Scale for the Assessment of Positive Symptoms (SAPS) (Andreasen, 1984b); and the Positive and Negative Syndrome Scale (PANSS) (Kay, Fiszbein & Opler, 1987). Each of these instruments provides important information on a range of dimensions of symptoms of schizophrenia. An important consideration in assessing symptoms is that their expression may vary over time. For example, negative symptoms have been found to be more persistent than positive symptoms (Lewine, 1990). Thus, symptom ratings should be repeated on a regular basis to determine treatment response, and the interference of symptoms on other areas of functioning.

FUNCTIONAL ASSESSMENT

Recently, a number of functional assessment instruments have been developed that assess multiple domains of functioning in the same measure. One such new measure is the Client's Assessment of Strength, Interests, and Goals (CASIG; Wallace et al., 2001). The CASIG is administered as a structured interview that begins by eliciting the individual's medium-term goals in five areas of community living: housing, money/work, interpersonal relationships, health, and spiritual activities. The rest of the CASIG involves questions assessing current and past community functioning, medication compliance and side effects, quality of life, quality of treatment, symptoms, and performance of intolerable community behaviors.

Another useful measure is the Independent Living Skills Inventory (ILSI) (Menditto et al., 1999). The ILSI was developed to measure a person's ability to perform a range of skills needed for successful community living. The scale is rated along two dimensions: the degree to which the skill can be performed, and the degree of assistance required to perform the skill. This ILSI instrument and scoring method is useful in planning a rehabilitation program because it distinguishes between skills deficits and performance deficits, each requiring different forms of intervention. The ILSI consists of 11 subscales, each representing a different domain of community functioning (e.g., money management, home maintenance, cooking, etc.). A similar measure is the Independent Living Skills Survey (ILSS) (Vaccaro et al., 1992).

In general, self-report based measures such as the CASIG are most useful for outpatients, or for higher functioning inpatients and day hospital patients who are clearly able to articulate realistic goals and whose behavior approximates community standards. For other patients, where the treatment focus is on the elimination of inappropriate behaviors and the generation of independent living skills, performance-based and observational measures are the most appropriate. Two such measures are the UCSD Performance-Based Skills Assessment (UPSA) (Patterson et al., 2001) and the Maryland Assessment of Social Competence (MASC) (Bellack et al., 1994). The UPSA assesses, via role-plays, skills in the following areas: household chores, communication, finance, transportation, and planning recreational activities. The MASC is a structured behavioral assessment that measures the ability to resolve interpersonal problems through conversation. On each administration, four scenarios are used, in three-minute role plays where a confederate plays different roles (e.g., employer, landlord, etc.). Alternate forms of the MASC are available (Bellack, 2004).

An older measure that also assesses interpersonal problem solving is The Assessment of Interpersonal Problem Solving Skills (AIPSS) (Donahoe et al., 1990). The AIPSS is a videotape-based test with an examiner's administration and scoring manual. Across 13 vignettes, the test measures an examinee's ability to describe an interpersonal social problem, to derive a solution to the problem, and to enact a solution in a role-played simulation test.

COGNITIVE ASSESSMENT

The majority of patients with schizophrenia demonstrate cognitive difficulties (APA Guidelines, 1997; Palmer et al., 1997). Because of this high prevalence, and because cognitive deficits are strong predictors of community functioning and outcome in psychosocial treatment (Green, 1996), they are an important treatment target. By improving cognitive capacities, patients appear to be better able to attend to information in psychosocial treatment, to remember more material taught in treatment, and to better problem-solve in general.

A major initiative to standardized cognitive assessment is known as the Measurement and Treatment Research to Improve Cognition in Schizophrenia (MATRICS) project (Green et al., 2004). The goal of MATRICS is to develop a standardized cognitive assessment battery that can be used in clinical trials, so as to facilitate the FDA labeling specific pharmacologic agents as being indicated for use in the treatment of cognition in schizophrenia. As of this writing, the consensus battery has been developed and tested for reliability and validity. Kits for administering this battery are scheduled to be made available before the end of 2006. A similar, but larger project is based in Sydney, Australia under the name BrainNet (Williams et al., 2005).

DYNAMIC ASSESSMENT

Most traditional cognitive and functional measures can be viewed as forms of static assessment in the sense that they measure the skills a person has at any given moment, as opposed to what they are capable of learning and therefore of a person's potential ability. This issue has been faced earlier in other areas, such as intelligence testing, and has led the development of methods of "dynamic assessment" or more specifically, "learning potential assessment" (Budoff, 1987). The goal of dynamic assessment is to quantify learning potential. This is accomplished by incorporating sensitive methods for assessing the ability to improve with instructions and/or practice into the testing conditions. Some traditional neuropsychological tests, such as measures of verbal/list learning, utilize change over time as key test indices. However, degree of change typically has not been used as an index in studies of schizophrenia, even though both initial learning (immediate memory) and total amount learned have been found to be related to treatment outcome (Green, 1996, 2000; Silverstein et al., 1998).

An example of a dynamic assessment measure, called the Micro-Module Learning Test, recently has been developed by Charles Wallace and colleagues at the UCLA Clinical Research Center for Schizophrenia and Psychiatric Rehabilitation (Robert Liberman, M.D., Principal Investigator) (Silverstein et al.,

2005). The MMLT, which has seven psychometrically equivalent alternate forms, is a brief measure of responsiveness to the three core components involved in skills training (see later): verbal instruction, modeling, and role play. The MMLT was developed, in part, because there was a need for a relatively brief and accurate assessment tool that would predict a patient's performance before being placed in relapse prevention or other social skills training interventions, which often lasts from three to six months. An assumption driving the development of the MMLT was that it uses a basic structure and content that are similar to skills training procedures, and that this would achieve greater ecological and predictive validity than previously used predictor measures. In this way, clinicians can determine, before placing a patient in a group, whether they are likely to benefit from that group, or whether they initially need other interventions (e.g., cognitive rehab, etc.).

IMPLEMENTATION OF RELAPSE PREVENTION INTERVENTIONS

Given that the treatment of the majority of people with schizophrenia in the United States is funded by the public sector (e.g., Medicaid, Medicare, and the Department of Veterans Affairs) and are treated in public health care facilities that tend to be understaffed, group treatment has been considered to be the most cost-effective means of delivering treatment. Fortunately, in many cases, group treatment has been demonstrated to be effective. There is now a wealth of evidence on the effectiveness of group-based treatment approaches to improve social and illness management skills and increase time to next relapse. However, some patients will benefit more from individual forms of treatment, and some forms of treatment are meant to be delivered to a single individual at a time. For example, many patients are uncomfortable discussing their (e.g., delusional) symptoms in groups and prefer to participate in psychotherapy on an individual basis. In addition, *in vivo* sessions to promote generalization of new skills (Wallace et al., 2000) are meant to be conducted individually. Similarly, some forms of cognitive remediation are also meant to be delivered to a single person at a time (van der Gaag et al., 2002). Ideally, a treatment program will offer both group and individual-based forms of key treatment modalities (e.g., CBT, cognitive remediation, etc.), with the decision as to which are used in an individual situation being driven by patient choice, as well as level of improvement noted in past and ongoing treatments of each type.

WHO IS QUALIFIED TO PROVIDE TREATMENT?

The majority of widely used skills training techniques are standardized and manualized so that they can be delivered the same way across treatment settings. Because of this, these interventions can, and have been, delivered by people from different professional backgrounds, including psychiatry, psychology, nursing, social work, occupational therapy, and recreational therapy. They can also be delivered by B.A. level mental health workers. The most important considerations in determining who delivers the treatment are specific training and attitude. Regarding the former, anyone who will be a group leader should have a thorough understanding of the goals of the intervention, of the rationale for cognitive behavioral treatment, and of the overall format of the group. Many hospitals and agencies have a specific sequence of readings and experiences that a staff member must go through before they can lead these groups independently, including observing groups run by others, and being observed by senior group leaders (e.g., Silverstein et al., 1997). Moreover, there are fidelity checklists that can be used to determine when a staff member is delivering the intervention in accordance with established standards. Research has demonstrated that the effectiveness with which these interventions are carried out is directly related to the extent to which the practitioner adheres to these standards (Wallace et al., 1992).

Regarding attitude, it is important that leaders of cognitive behavioral interventions adopt an active, coach-like, positive attitude when running groups, and convey expectations that everyone should participate and can succeed (Liberman et al., 1989). Specific prompting procedures can be used to include all patients, to reinforce efforts at participation, to ignore minor examples of bizarre or disruptive behavior, and to facilitate peer-to-peer feedback (Silverstein et al., in press).

SESSION STRUCTURE AND
DETERMINING TERMINATION

The structure of skills training interventions is laid out in treatment manuals, which typically resemble course curricula. However, unlike typical school classes, skills training groups typically include a combination of didactic teaching, videotaped presentations, role-playing, problem-solving exercises, in vivo exercises, and assignment and review of homework. Most standardized skills training interventions also include pre- and post-tests of knowledge and skills, as well as checklists that can be used at key points in the course of the group to assess progress. In these groups, termination occurs when all the exercises in the manual have been completed by the group. However, determination of the extent of patient progress is based on the results of the assessments that are included as part of the material, in addition to those from the instruments described earlier. Patients who still exhibit significant skills deficits after a group is completed need to have further training. A determination must be made at such points regarding the reason for the lack of progress. This can be the result of the training format (e.g., the patient has been in large groups but needs 1:1 intervention), or can be the result of cognitive deficits, symptoms, and/or medication side effects interfering with learning ability. If the latter, provision of cognitive remediation or adjustment of medication can precede further attempts at skills training (Schwarzkopf et al., 1999).

CLINICAL CASE ILLUSTRATIONS

SUCCESSFUL CASE EXAMPLE

Individuals with schizophrenia often present to public sector mental health treatment programs (Community Mental Health Centers) to receive both medication and psychosocial treatments. In this case, the client was seen for psychotherapy in the context of an extended partial hospital program that he attended five days per week. The client was an African-American man in his late 50s diagnosed with schizophrenia. The client had a long history of schizophrenia that dated to his early 20s with a history of about 20 hospitalizations and periods of full remission. In addition to schizophrenia, he had a past history of childhood sexual abuse and periods of depression that met criteria for major depression. He denied any substance use for the past 15 years and his urine toxicology screen and alcohol breathalyzer were negative for substances.

The client presented with a wide range of symptoms and problems. The client experienced persistent auditory hallucinations ordering him to harm himself. The client also experienced intense depressed mood, particularly around holidays, anniversaries, and other reminders of family members' deaths. He had frequent suicidal ideation and often contemplated specific suicidal plans. He also sometimes experienced flashbacks of childhood abuse when he was reminded of it. The client could become very angry and agitated when he felt that he was being "disrespected" on not being listened to. He had very little formal education and claimed to be illiterate. On the other hand, the client presented several strengths, including his personalility, which made him known and liked by a number of people in the community, his commitment to treatment, and his extensive and varied work history. He was able to cook, clean, and perform all other self-care activities needed to live independently.

At the beginning of treatment, the client used very primitive coping skills, such as screaming and/or banging his head against a wall when he felt that the voices were becoming overwhelming. He was also a frequent user of the acute inpatient service, especially when he became agitated and others would become frightened by his demeanor. The major initial foci of treatment were therefore to help him develop better skills to cope with his psychotic symptoms and his anger, as well as develop skills for the prevention of relapse. Although the client's inability to read and write were a barrier to using self-monitoring, bibliotherapy, and other cognitive behavioral techniques, he was able to recall and describe distressing episodes that had occurred recently in vivid detail. Through analysis of these situations, treatment focused on teaching the client self-talk skills, where coping statements could be used to coach him through difficult situations. The client developed a great affinity for this coping skill and found it to be very effective in managing distress related to hallucinations and anger. He began to replace his more primitive coping techniques with these approaches. Self-talk was also used to deal with potential triggers of substance use relapse. The client was also encouraged to reach out to support persons when he felt depressed. The client developed a small support network including some people he met at the partial hospital program, some people who attended a local church, and some residents of the boarding home. He would call or visit some of these individuals when he became depressed. The client was also taught breathing retraining but found it difficult to apply successfully.

A plan also was developed to help reduce the incidence of relapses. The client agreed to call the local crisis hotline when he became acutely distressed while at home. In therapy, he developed a list of warning signs of relapse that he was encouraged to keep track of and to notify his treatment team when he noticed them occurring. A major warning sign for the client was if his hallucinations became more demanding or threatening. The client's psychiatrist would be notified if this occurred and prescribed a nonaddictive PRN medication to reduce agitation in such instances. The client would be given support when he experienced warning signs, and would be encouraged to use self-talk and take his medication.

These interventions were successful at both keeping the client out of the hospital and reducing his symptom severity over an extended period. The client's functioning began to improve and his symptoms continued to remain under better control.

This case is considered to be successful because a pattern of regular relapse and rehospitalization was interrupted for a sustained period with a client who had many limitations and problems. In addition, some improvements were made in the client's social functioning and quality of life. A major key to success in this case was not becoming overwhelmed by the client's impairments and working with his strengths to establish a repertoire of coping skills. It is important to note that working with the client's psychiatrist was essential in this case, as his stability was strongly influenced by medication.

UNSUCCESSFUL CASE EXAMPLE

The client was a 32-year-old white male with schizophrenia, cocaine dependence, marijuana dependence, alcohol abuse, and nicotine dependence. He had an early age onset of substance abuse during junior high school. His first psychotic break was at the age of 20 years old and initially there was uncertainty as to whether the active poly-drug addiction had "caused" the psychosis; however in spite of several extended periods of abstinence in year-long jail sentences his psychotic disorder symptoms persisted during the past 12 years and appeared to require antipsychotic medication to manage the symptoms. The client had reasonable social skills in the context of drug acquisition skills and pursuing women at "cocaine houses" where cocaine could be traded for sex. He had been unable to maintain gainful employment, however he volunteered at a local church.

The client had a history of participation in treatment at the local community mental health center but had periods of poor compliance with medications and treatment during substance abuse binges. This center did not offer integrated treatment for co-occurring disorders, but he was able to enter a new Intensive Outpatient Program for Co-Occurring Disorders in another hospital. This program had a focus on helping him to try to become abstinent from all substances (except for tobacco), maintain antipsychotic medication compliance, and achieve remission of psychotic symptoms. After achieving some stability with compliance with medications and treatment he began a twice per week relapse prevention program using the Dual Recovery Therapy approach. This was his first formal treatment of co-occurring disorders. He had received minimal substance abuse treatment, but had attended some Narcotics Anonymous meetings at the mental health center, but he couldn't agree with the total abstinence approach.

The initial phase of treatment focused on development of the therapeutic alliance and better understanding the client's motivation to stop specific substances and maintain his psychiatric medications. Through discussions with the client's perception of the "good things" and "not so good things" about each of the substances he used, the therapist got a sense of limited motivation to address his marijuana or tobacco use. A review of his typical 24-hour substance use cycle and difference across a seven-day period provided a sense of his use patterns and triggers for use. Through a review of his story of his life a better sense was also established of the interrelationship of his substance use, increased psychotic symptoms, disability, and periods of medication noncompliance. He participated in both individual and group treatment with the same DRT orientation and perspective. He initially made progress in developing an increased awareness of the triggers to his substance use and avoiding them for the most part. He liked the mnemonic HALT since he would tell himself to "stop," but he couldn't remember what the letters stood for. With ongoing abstinence from the cocaine and alcohol his psychiatric symptoms appeared stable; however he continued to use marijuana and tobacco. The beginning of the month was challenging for remaining abstinent due to the trigger of money from his disability check. In spite of a relapse prevention plan and preparation of doing role plays to ask his mother to help him by taking his disability check, he cashed the check and went to the "cocaine house" to relapse to cocaine. Later he said he felt overwhelmed by the desire to be with a woman when he got the check and that was the big trigger for him. He dropped out of the new treatment program, did not return to his Community Mental Health Center mental health treatment, and returned to active substance use. While actively using substances he developed increasing depression and during a cocaine withdrawal period and while intoxicated with alcohol he committed suicide.

This case was considered to be unsuccessful because although there was some initial improvement in the patient's symptoms and situation, the patient dropped out of treatment, was not engaged in case management, and ultimately relapsed to substances and committed suicide. Suicide is a serious risk factor for individuals with schizophrenia alone and substance use disorders alone and the combination places the individual at highest risk. The patient was involved in two treatment systems and he was lost between systems. Enhancing the integration of psychosocial treatments, case management linkages within the community, and increased support with money management and housing may help improve treatment outcomes; however this can be costly. Treatment providers benefit from additional training and resources for coordination.

PHARMACOTHERAPY MEDICATION MANAGEMENT OF SCHIZOPHRENIA

As discussed previously in this chapter, medications are an important component of the treatment of individuals with schizophrenia, but they also have their limitations. Antipsychotic medications can be effective at reducing both the positive and negative symptoms of schizophrenia, and this improvement/reduction of core symptoms of schizophrenia can help the individual to better engage in psychosocial treatments and community activities. The choice of which antipsychotic agent to choose requires the clinician to consider the client's preference of available options, their other medical conditions, prior medication treatment history, other medications, and possible side effects of the medications. Some side effects will be particularly bothersome to some clients and not to others (weight gain, sexual dysfunction, sedation, etc.). Clinicians must monitor and address medication side effects in an effort to enhance medication compliance.

Common side effects of antipsychotics include movement disorder symptoms, insomnia, weight gain, sexual dysfunction, sedation, anxiety/akathisia, medication-induced dysphoria, and gastrointestinal symptoms. Medication-induced (neuroleptic) dysphoria can be difficult to diagnose since it includes symptoms of fatigue, irritability, psychomotor slowing, and lack of motivation. Individuals with co-occurring substance use disorders are often either noncompliant with taking medication when they use substances or they may misuse and take higher dosages of their prescription medications. Also alcohol, tobacco, and other drugs can reduce the effectiveness of psychiatric medications, including changing medication blood levels, worsening symptoms, and causing additional side effects. Medications are almost always a required component of treatment for individuals with schizophrenia and relapse prevention/cognitive behavioral therapy approaches can help support medication compliance as well as help in other ways to improve overall functioning and well-being.

CONCLUSIONS AND FUTURE DIRECTIONS

Although outcomes for people with schizophrenia typically are considered to be poor, long-term studies (Ciompi, 1980; DeSisto et al., 1995a, 1995b; Harding et al., 1987a, 1987b; Huber et al., 1975, 1980) indicate that many patients can actually resume independent living, if they receive adequate community-based care, including the full range of rehabilitative and relapse prevention services described in this chapter. Unfortunately, this is rare, even though many effective interventions have existed, in some cases, for 30 years (e.g., Paul & Lentz, 1977). For example, only approximately 2 percent of schizophrenia patients are receiving assertive community treatment (ACT), even though this is considered an evidence-based practice (Lehman et al., 2003).

Only recently, in the field of schizophrenia treatment, has the focus of intervention shifted away from symptom suppression, and toward reducing disability, preventing relapse, and promoting recovery, wellness, and independence. This represents a paradigm shift that is founded on a change in the perception of what is possible for people diagnosed with schizophrenia. Rather than seeing them as being relegated to a life of dependency on family and treatment providers who must provide custodial and paternalistic care, the new, recovery-based view is based on the assumption that people with schizophrenia can actively construct a life that includes meaning and role functioning. This process often involves a true collaboration between treatment providers and patients, in which all available interventions and life strategies are used to promote wellness and to reduce the chance of relapse.

Adopting a relapse prevention conceptual model for schizophrenia treatment holds the promise of recognizing the complex array of factors that affect a person's level of functioning. As noted in this chapter, these include biological and psycho-physiological abnormalities (including stress and dopaminergic hyper-reactivity), skills deficits (which contribute to higher stress levels), cognitive impairments (which also contribute to stress levels and skill performance), environmental conditions (e.g., high levels of expressed emotion in family members, which has been shown to predict relapse), and comorbid conditions such as substance abuse.

A relapse prevention perspective also promotes interdisciplinary collaboration by making full use of the professional skills and assessment and treatment tools developed from within a broader range of disciplines. This is important because treatment for people with schizophrenia often is fragmented, with major problems being unaddressed, and poor communication between treatment providers across systems. Treatment outcome studies of individuals with both schizophrenia and substance abuse strongly support the need for integrated treatment with a motivational enhancement, recovery, and relapse prevention orientation. An integrated multimethod approach to help individuals suffering from a serious mental illness with additional complication that can contribute to relapse should lead to improved outcomes for more individuals struggling to overcome the many effects of schizophrenia.

REFERENCES

American Psychiatric Association. (1997). Practice guideline for the treatment of patients with schizophrenia. *Am J Psychiatry* **154**(4 Suppl):1–63.

American Psychiatric Association. (2006). *Practice guideline for the treatment of patients with substance use disorders, 2e.*

Andreasen, N.C. (1984a). *Scale for the Assessment of Negative Symptoms (SANS).* Iowa City: University of Iowa.

Andreasen, N.C. (1984b). *Scale for the Assessment of Positive Symptoms (SAPS).* Iowa City: University of Iowa.

Attkisson, R.F., Cook, J., Karno, M., Lehman, A., McGlashan, T.H., Meltzer, H.Y. et al. (1992). Clinical services research. *Schizophr Bull* **18**:561–626.

Azrin, N.H., Teichner, G. (1998). Evaluation of an instructional program for improving medication compliance for chronically mentally ill outpatients. *Behaviour Research and Therapy* **36**: 849–861.

Beck, A.T., Rector, N.A. (2005). Cognitive approaches to schizophrenia: Theory and therapy. *Annual Review of Clinical Psychology* **1**:577–606.

Bellack, A.S. (2004). Skills training for people with severe mental illness. *Psychiatr Rehabil J* **27**(4):375–391

Bellack, A.S., Bennett, M.E., Gearon, J.S., Brown, C.H., Yang, Y. (2006). A randomized clinical trial of a new behavioral treatment for drug abuse in people with severe and persistent mental illness. *Arch Gen Psychiatry* **63**(4):426–432.

Bellack, A.S., Sayers, M., Mueser, K.T., Bennett, M. (1994). Evaluation of social problem solving in schizophrenia. *J Abnorm Psychol* **103**:371–378.

Budoff, M. (1987). The validity of learning potential assessment. In Lidz, C., ed., *Dynamic assessment,* 52–81. New York: Guilford Press.

Carey, M.P., Braaten, L.S., Maisto, S.A., Gleason, J.R., Forsyth, A.D. et al. (2000). Using information, motivational enhancement, and skills training to reduce the risk of HIV infection for low-income urban women: A second randomized clinical trial. *Health Psychology* **19**:3–11.

Carpenter, W.T. Jr, Bartko, J.J., Carpenter, C.L., Strauss, J.S. (1976). Another view of schizophrenia subtypes. A report from the international pilot study of schizophrenia. *Arch Gen Psychiatry* **33**(4):508–516.

Chadwick, P., Birchwood, M., Trower, P. (1996). *Cognitive Therapy for Hallucinations, Delusions and Paranoia.* Wiley: Chichester.

Ciompi, L. (1980). Catamnestic long-term study on the course of life and aging of schizophrenics. *Schizophr Bull* **6**:606–618.

Corrigan, P.W., Buican, B., Toomey, R. (1996). Construct validity of two tests of social cognition in schizophrenia. *Psychiatry Res* **63**:77–82.

Corrigan, P.W., Reinke, R.R., Landsberger, S.A., Charate, A., Toombs, G.A. (2003). The effects of atypical antipsychotic medications on psychosocial outcomes. *Schizophr Res* **63**(1–2): 97–101.

Cramer, J.A., Rosenheck, R. (1999). Enhancing medication compliance for people with serious mental illness. *J Nerv Ment Dis* **187**:53–55.

DeSisto, M.J., Harding, C.M. et al. (1995). The Maine and Vermont three-decade studies of serious mental illness: I. Matched Comparison of Cross-Sectional Outcome. *Br J Psychiatry* **167**(3): 331–338.

DeSisto, M., Harding, C.M. et al. (1995). The Maine and Vermont three-decade studies of serious mental illness: II. Longitudinal course comparisons. *Br J Psychiatry* **167**(3):338–342.

Dickerson, F. (2004). Update on cognitive behavioral psychotherapy for schizophrenia: Review of recent studies. *Journal of Cognitive Psychotherapy: An International Quarterly* **18**:189–205.

Donahoe, C.P., Carter, M.J., Bloem, W.D., Hirsch, G.L., Laasi, N., Wallace, C.J. (1990). Assessment of interpersonal problem-solving skills. *Psychiatry* **53**:329–339.

Drake, R.E., Mueser, K.T. (2000). Psychosocial approaches to dual diagnosis. *Schizophr Bull* **26**:105–118.

Green, M.F. (1996). What are the functional consequences of neurocognitive deficits in schizophrenia? *Am J Psychiatry* **153**(3):321–330.

Green, M.F., Kern, R.S., Braff, D.L., Mintz, J. (2000). Neurocognitive deficits and functional outcome in schizophrenia: Are we measuring the "right stuff"? *Schizophr Bull* **26**(1):119–136.

Green, M.F., Nuechterlein, K.H., Gold, J.M., Barch, D.M., Cohen, J., Essock, S. et al. (2004). Approaching a consensus cognitive battery for clinical trials in schizophrenia: The NIMH-MATRICS conference to select cognitive domains and test criteria. *Biol Psychiatry* **56**: 301–307.

Haddock, G., Sellwood, W., Tarrier, N., Yusupoff, L. (1994). Developments in cognitive behaviour therapy for persistent psychotic symptoms. *Beh Change* **11**:200–214.

Harding, C.M., Brooks, G.W., Ashikaga, T., Strauss, J.S., Breier, A. (1987a). The Vermont longitudinal study of persons with severe mental illness: I. Methodology, study sample and overall status 32 years later. *Am J Psychiatry* **144**:718–726.

Harding, C.M., Brooks, G.W., Ashikaga, T., Strauss, J.S., Breier, A. (1987b). The Vermont longitudinal research project: II. Long-term outcome functioning of subjects who retrospectively met DSM-III criteria for schizophrenia. *Am J Psychiatry* **144**:727–735.

Harvey, P.D., Moriarty, P.J., Serper, M.R., Schnur, E., Lieber, D. (2000). Practice-related improvement in information processing with novel antipsychotic treatment. *Schizophr Res* **46**(2–3): 139–148.

Hersen, M., Bellack, A.S. (1976). Social skills training for chronic psychiatric patients: Rationale, research findings, and future directions. *Compr Psychiatry* **17**(4):559–580.

Herz, M.I., Lamberti, J.S., Mintz, J., Scott, R., O'Dell, S.P., McCartan, L., Nix, G. (2000). A program for relapse prevention in schizophrenia: a controlled study. *Arch Gen Psychiatry* **57**(3):277–283.

Hogarty, G.E., Greenwald, D., Ulrich, R.F., Kornblith, S.J., DiBarry, A.L., Cooley, S., Carter, M., Flesher, S. (1997). Three-year trials of personal therapy among schizophrenic patients living with or independent of family: II. Effects on adjustment of patients. *Am J Psychiatry* **154**(11):1514–1524.

Huber, G., Gross, G., Schuttler, R. (1975). Long-term follow-up study of schizophrenia. *Acta Psychiatrica Scandinavica* **53**:49–57.

Huber, G., Gross, G., Schuttler, R., Linz, M. (1980). Longitudinal studies of schizophrenic patients. *Schizophr Bull* **6**(4):592–605.

Kay, S.R., Fiszbein, A., Opler, L.A. (1987). The positive and negative syndrome scale (PANSS) for schizophrenia. *Schizophr Bull* **13**(2):261–276.

Kelly, G.R., Scott, J.E. (1990). Medication compliance and health education among outpatients with chronic mental disorders. *Medical Care* **28**:1181–1197.

Kendler, K.S., Gallagher, T.J., Abelson, J.M., Kessler, R.C. (1996). Lifetime prevalence, demographic risk factors, and diagnostic validity of nonaffective psychosis as assessed in a US community sample. The National Comorbidity Survey. *Arch Gen Psychiatry* **53**(11): 1022–1031.

Landa, Y., Silverstein, S.M., Schwartz, F., Savitz, A. (2006). Group Cognitive Behavioral therapy for delusions: Helping patients improve reality testing. *Journal of Contemporary Psychotherapy* **36**(1):9–17.

Lehman, A.F., Steinwachs, D.M. (2003). Evidence-based psychosocial treatment practices in schizophrenia: Lessons from the patient outcomes research team (PORT) project. *J Am Acad Psychoanal Dyn Psychiatry* **31**(1):141–154.

Lewine, R.R.J. (1990). A discriminant validity study of negative symptoms with a special focus on depression and antipsychotic medication. *Am J Psychiatry* **147**:1463–1466.

Liberman, R.P., DeRisi, W.J., Mueser, K.T. (1989). *Social skills training for psychiatric patients.* New York, Pergamon Press.

Liberman, R.P., Eckman, T.A. (1989). Dissemination of skills training modules to psychiatric facilities. Overcoming obstacles to the utilisation of a rehabilitation innovation. *Br J Psychiatry* Suppl. (**5**):117–122.

Liberman, R.P., Kopelowicz, A. (2005). Recovery from schizophrenia: A concept in search of research. *Psychiatr Serv* **56**(6):735–742.

Marlatt, G.A., Donovan, D.M., eds. (2005). *Relapse Prevention: Maintenance strategies in the treatment of addictive behaviors, 2e.* New York, NY: Guilford Press.

Marlatt, G.A., Gordon, J.R., eds. (1985). *Relapse Prevention: Maintenance strategies in the treatment of addictive behaviors.* New York, NY: Guilford Press.

Martin, B.C., Miller, L.S. (1998). Expenditures for treating schizophrenia: A population-based study of Georgia Medicaid recipients. *Schizophr Bull* **24**(3):479–488.

Meltzer, H.Y. (1992). Treatment of the neuroleptic-nonresponsive schizophrenic patient. *Schizophr Bull* **18**(3):515–542.

Menditto, A.A., Wallace, C.J., Liberman, R.P., Vander Wal, J., Jones, N.T., Stuve, P. (1999). Functional assessment of independent living skills. *Psychiatric Rehabilitation Skills* **3**:200–219.

Mueser, K.T., Berenbaum, H. (1990). Psychodynamic treatment of schizophrenia: Is there a future? *Psychol Med* **20**(2):253–262.

Mueser, K.T., Corrigan, P.W., Hilton, D.W., Tanzman, B., Schaub, A. et al. (2002). Illness management and recovery: A review of the research. *Psychiatr Serv* **20**:253–262.

Palmer, B.W., Heaton, R.K., Paulsen, J.S., Kuck, J., Braff, D., Harris, M.J., Zisook, S., Jeste, D.V. (1997). Is it possible to be schizophrenic yet neuropsychologically normal? *Neuropsychology* **11**:437–446.

Patterson, T.L., Goldman, S., McKibbin, C.L., Hughs, T., Jeste, D.V. (2001). UCSD Performance-Based Skills Assessment: Development of a new measure of everyday functioning for severely mentally ill adults. *Schizophr Bull* **27**(2):235–245.

Paul, G.L., Lentz, R.J. (1997). *Psychosocial treatment of chronic mental patients: Milieu versus social learning programs.* Cambridge, MA: Harvard University Press.

Pilling, S., Bebbington, P., Kuipers, E., Garety, P., Geddes, J., Orbach, G., Morgan, C. (2002). Psychological treatments in schizophrenia: I. Meta-analysis of family intervention and cognitive behaviour therapy. *Psychol Med* **32**(5):783–791.

Rathod, S., Kingdon, D., Smith, P., Turkington, D. (2005). Insight into schizophrenia: The effects of cognitive behavioural therapy on the components of insight and association with socio-demographics-data on a previously published randomized controlled trial. *Schizophr Res* **74**:211–219.

Roberts, L.J., Shaner, A., Eckman, T.A. (1999). *Overcoming addictions: Skills training for people with schizophrenia.* New York: W. W. Norton.

Roe, D., Yanos, P.T. (2006). Psychoeducation for people with psychotic symptoms: Moving beyond education and towards inspiration. *The Behavior Therapist* **29**:63–66.

Rund, B.R. (1998). A review of longitudinal studies of cognitive functions in schizophrenia patients. *Schizophr Bull* **24**(3):425–435.

Rupp, A., Keith, S.J. (1993). The costs of schizophrenia: Assessing the burden. *Psychiatr Clin N Am* **16**(2):413–422.

Schwarzkopf, S.B., Crilly, J., Silverstein, S.M. (1999). Therapeutic synergism: Optimal pharmacotherapy and rehabilitation to enhance functional outcome in schizophrenia. *Psychiatric Rehabilitation Skills* **3**:124–147.

Silverstein, S.M., Bakshi, S., Chapman, R.M., Nowlis, G. (1998). Perceptual organisation of configural and visual patterns in schizophrenia: Effects of repeated exposure. *Cognitive Neuropsychiatry* **3**(3):209–223.

Silverstein, S.M., Bowman, J., McHugh, D. (1997). Strategies for hospital-wide dissemination of psychiatric rehabilitation interventions. *Psychiatric Rehabilitation Skills* **2**:1–24.

Silverstein, S.M., Wallace, C.J., Schenkel, L.S. (2005). The micro-module learning tests: Work-sample assessments of responsiveness to skills training. *Schizophr Bull* **31**:73–83.

Silverstein, S.M., Wong, M.-H., Wilkniss, S.M., Bloch, A., Smith, T.E., Savitz, A., McCarthy, R., Terkelsen, K. (In press). Behavioral rehabilitation of the "Treatment-Refractory" schizophrenia patient: Conceptual foundations, interventions, interpersonal techniques and outcome data. *Psychological Services*.

Spaulding, W.D., Storms, L., Goodrich, V., Sullivan, M. (1986). Applications of experimental psychopathology in psychiatric rehabilitation. *Schizophr Bull* **12**(4):560–577.

Tashjian, M., Hayward, B., Stoddard, S. et al. (1989). *Best practice study of vocational rehabilitation services to severely mentally ill persons.* Washington, DC: Policy Study Associates.

Temple, S., Ho, B.C. (2005). Cognitive therapy for persistent psychosis in schizophrenia: A case-controlled clinical trial. *Schizophr Res* **74**(2–3):195–199.

Turkington, D., Dudley, R., Warman, D.M., Beck, A.T. (2004). Cognitive-behavioral therapy for schizophrenia: A review. *J Psychiatr Pract* **10**:5–16.

Vaccaro, J.V., Pitts, D.B., Wallace, C.J. (1992). Functional assessment. In Liberman, R.P., ed., *Handbook of psychiatric rehabilitation*, 78–94. Boston: Allyn & Bacon.

Van der Gaag, M., Kern, R.S., van den Bosch, R.J., Liberman, R.P. (2002). A controlled trial of cognitive remediation in schizophrenia. *Schizophr Bull* **28**(1):167–176.

Ventura, J., Leukoff, D., Neuchterlein, K.H., Liberman, R.P., Green, M.F., Shaner, A. (1993). Manual for the expanded Brief Psychiatric Rating Scale. *Int J Methods in Psychiatr Res* **3**:221–224.

Wallace, C.J., Lecomte, T., Liberman, R.P., Wilde, J.B. (2001). CASIG: A consumer-centered assessment for planning individualized treatment and evaluating program outcomes. *Schizophr Res* **50**:105–119.

Wallace, C.J., Liberman, R.P., MacKain, S.J. (1992). Effectiveness and replicability of modules to train social and instrumental skills in the severely mentally ill. *Am J Psychiatry* **149**: 654–658.

Wallace, C.J., Liberman, R.P., Tauber, R., Wallace, J. (2000). The independent living skills survey: A comprehensive measure of the community functioning of severely and persistently mentally ill individuals. *Schizophr Bull* **26**(3):631–658.

White, W., Boyle, M., Loveland, D. (2005). Recovery in mental illness: Broadening our understanding of wellness. In Ralph, R.O., Corrigan, P.W., eds., 223–258. Washington, DC: American Psychological Association.

Williams, L.M., Simms, E., Clark, C.R., Paul, R.H., Rowe, D.L., Gordon, E. (2005). The test-retest reliability of a standardized neurocognitive and neurophysiological test battery: NeuroMarker. *Int J Neurosci* **115**:1605–1630.

Wu, E.Q., Birnbaum, H.G., Shi, L., Ball, D.E., Kessler, R.C., Moulis, M., Aggarwal, J. (2005). The economic burden of schizophrenia in the United States in 2002. *J Clin Psychiatry* **66**(9): 1122–1129.

Ziedonis, D., Stern, R. (2001). Dual recovery therapy for schizophrenia and substance abuse. *Psychiatr Ann* **31**:255–264.

Ziedonis, D.M., Smelson, D., Rosenthal, R.N., Batki, S.L., Green, A.I., Henry, R.J., Montoya, I., Parks, J., Weiss, R.D. (2005). Improving the care of individuals with schizophrenia and substance use disorders: Consensus recommendations. *J Psychiatric Practice* **11**(5):315–339.

7

SEEKING SAFETY:
AN EVIDENCE-BASED
MODEL FOR SUBSTANCE
ABUSE AND TRAUMA/PTSD

LISA M. NAJAVITS

Harvard Medical School
Boston, Massachusetts

INTRODUCTION

When I was twelve I had my first drink, and I knew immediately this was my answer.
I felt relaxed for the first time in my life. I became an instant alcoholic.

Nate had been abused by both parents as far back as he can remember, with
relentless physical, sexual, and emotional abuse. By the time he was in junior
high school he had a history of repeated fights, and was abusing alcohol. In
adulthood he was dependent on heroin and marijuana. He sometimes lived in the
woods, homeless. He had several serious suicide attempts, cycled through jail
sentences and treatment programs, and was labeled antisocial. Until his mid-40s
no one had identified his posttraumatic stress disorder (PTSD).

There are innumerable client stories, many different types of trauma, substance use, and paths of survival. However, it is clear that PTSD and substance
use disorder (SUD) are closely linked for many. *Trauma*—defined by the DSM-
IV (American Psychiatric Association, 1994) as the experience, threat, or wit-
nessing of physical harm—comprises a variety of experiences. These include
combat, childhood physical or sexual abuse, serious car accident, life-threatening
illness, natural disasters such as hurricane or tornado, and manmade disasters
such as terrorist attack and chemical spill. Most people in the United States
experience one or more traumas during their lifetime, with rates at 60 percent
for men and 50 percent for women (Kessler et al., 1995). Yet, remarkably, most

people who suffer a trauma do not go on to develop PTSD. For the approximately 20 to 30 percent of people who develop PTSD after trauma (Adshead, 2000), their symptoms cluster into three categories: (1) *reexperiencing* (e.g., flashbacks and nightmares); (2) *avoidance* (e.g., detached feelings and a wish to avoid talking about the trauma); and (3) *arousal* (e.g., anger, sleep problems, and exaggerated startle response). Persistence of these symptoms for more than one month and marked decline in functioning are also required for the diagnosis.

In the United States, among men who develop PTSD, 52 percent develop alcohol use disorder and 35 percent develop drug use disorder; among women, the rates are 28 percent and 27 percent (Kessler et al., 1995; see also Breslau, Davis & Schultz, 2003; Chilcoat & Breslau, 1998; Cottler et al., 1992). In clinical settings, the rates of co-occurring PTSD and SUD are even higher (Najavits et al., 1997). Moreover, various subgroups have particularly high rates of PTSD and SUD, such as adolescents, veterans, prisoners, gay/lesbian/transgendered/ bisexual, the homeless, rescue workers such as firefighters and police, victims of domestic violence, and prostitutes (Najavits, 2006).

The clinical needs of this population are urgent and serious. Research consistently shows that those with the dual diagnosis of PTSD and SUD, compared to those with either disorder alone, have worse treatment outcomes; more positive views of substances; more Axis I and II disorders; increased legal and medical problems, HIV risk, self harm, and suicidality; lower work and social functioning; and increased rates of future trauma (Brady, Killeen, Saladin, Dansky & Becker, 1994; Cohen & Hien, 2006; Hien, Nunes, Levin & Fraser, 2000; Najavits, Gastfriend et al., 1998; Ouimette, Finney & Moos, 1999).

Historically, treatment of the dual diagnosis has been marked by a separation that only lately has begun to improve. A culture of "other" predominated, in which mental health clinicians typically believed they could not treat SUD, and many SUD clinicians believed they could not treat PTSD (Najavits, 2002c; Read et al., 2002). There is now growing awareness that a no-wrong-door approach is most likely to be helpful (Clark, 2002). Clients need attention to both disorders regardless of how they enter the treatment system. Split systems, in which a client who uses substances is turned away from mental health treatment until abstinent, or the client with mental health problems is rejected from SUD treatment until stabilized, are believed less effective than integrated or simultaneous treatment (K. T. Brady, 2001; Ouimette & Brown, 2002). Yet older messages abound, such as "Just get clean and sober first," "Go to Alcoholics Anonymous or I won't treat you," or "You're defocusing from your addiction if you talk about the past." Clinicians in many settings fail to assess for trauma, PTSD, and SUD. Indeed, underdiagnosis or misdiagnosis of both PTSD and SUD remain common (Davidson, 2001; Najavits, 2004a), and *most* SUD clients are neither assessed for PTSD nor given treatment for it (P. J. Brown et al., 1998; Dansky et al., 1997; Hyer et al., 1991; Najavits, 2004a). Clients also tend to minimize both SUD and PTSD, sometimes out of shame, guilt, or denial.

A major effort over the past few years has been the development of integrated therapies for PTSD and SUD. It is now widely recommended to work on both disorders from the start of treatment (K. T. Brady, 2001; Najavits et al., 1996; Ouimette & Brown, 2002). Clients also prefer to include treatment of PTSD in their SUD treatment (P. J. Brown et al., 1998; Najavits et al., 2004). Moreover, research indicates that integrated treatment models for PTSD and SUD show positive outcomes. Treating PTSD and SUD at the same time helps clients with addiction recovery, rather than derailing them from abstinence (e.g., K. Brady et al., 2001; Donovan et al., 2001; Hien et al., 2004; Najavits et al., 1998, 2005; Triffleman et al., 2000; Zlotnick et al., 2003).

PTSD treatment offers a depth that many SUD clients and clinicians find helpful. It honors what clients have lived through, encourages self-awareness, and may increase motivation and reduce relapse. It can reassure clients to learn that they may have used substances to cope with overwhelming emotional pain, and that this is a common pattern. Such understanding can move them beyond the revolving door of just more treatment, into different treatment. Rather than cycling back to standard treatment, it goes down a new path. As one client said, "I was relieved to find I had something with a name. I thought it was just me—I'm crazy. But I can deal with this now . . . Now I can put down the cocaine and work on what's behind it" (Najavits, 2002d).

OVERVIEW OF TREATMENT

Seeking Safety (Najavits, 2002c) was developed beginning in the early 1990s to help meet the needs of those dually diagnosed with PTSD and SUD.[1] It was the first empirically studied treatment for the dual diagnosis (Najavits et al., 1998), and remains the most empirically studied model thus far (Najavits, in press). Seeking Safety is present-focused and specifically designed for early recovery. Its central goal is to help clients attain safety from both PTSD and SUD. The treatment is available as a book (Najavits, 2002c), providing clinician guidelines and client handouts. It was designed for group and individual format, males and females, a variety of settings (e.g., outpatient, inpatient residential), and the full range of substance use disorders and types of trauma. Seeking Safety has also been used in practice with a very wide variety of clients (e.g., those with just PTSD or SUD but not both, those with a history of one or the other, and those with other disorders). It has been studied with both adults and adolescents. Seeking Safety offers 25 topics that address cognitive, behavioral, interpersonal, and case management domains. However, one does not have to use all 25 topics,

---

[1] The term "substance abuse" is sometimes used, as in the title to this chapter, as it is more common. But the model was designed for the full range of substance use disorders, from abuse to dependence.

but rather can use as few or as many as time allows. In general, the treatment was designed for a high level of flexibility—topics can be done in any order, clients can join at any point, and a wide variety of counselors can conduct it (e.g., paraprofessionals and professionals).

The treatment was first described in a paper (Najavits et al., 1996), but evolved considerably after that: from an initial focus on women to both genders; from group format to individual as well; and from outpatient to a broader array of settings. The model was developed beginning in the early 1990s under National Institute on Drug Abuse grants. Clinical and training experiences led to various versions of the manual, with the final published version in 2002. In this chapter, the treatment is described in more detail, its empirical results are reviewed, implementation and assessment considerations are offered, and it is compared to relapse prevention.

KEY ELEMENTS

SAFETY

The title of the treatment—Seeking Safety—expresses its central idea: When a person has both active substance abuse and PTSD, the most urgent clinical need is to establish safety. "Safety" is an umbrella term that signifies various elements: safety from substances; safety from dangerous relationships (including domestic violence and drug-using friends); and safety from extreme symptoms, such as dissociation and self-harm. Many of these self-destructive behaviors reenact trauma—having been harmed through trauma, clients are now harming themselves. "Seeking safety" refers to helping clients free themselves from such negative behaviors and, in so doing, to move toward freeing themselves from trauma at a deep emotional level.

Throughout the treatment, safety is addressed over and over. For example, there is the topic *Safety*, a list of over 80 *Safe Coping Skills*, a *Safe Coping Sheet* to explore recent unsafe incidents, a *Safety Plan* to identify stages of danger, a *Safety Contract*, and a report of unsafe behaviors at each session's check-in. The idea is that, no matter what happens, clients can learn to cope in safe ways—without substances and other destructive behavior.

The treatment thus fits what has been described as first-stage therapy for both PTSD and SUD. Experts within both fields have independently described an extremely similar first stage of treatment, titled safety or stabilization, that prioritizes psychoeducation, coping skills, and reducing the most destructive symptoms (Herman, 1992; Kaufman & Reoux, 1988). Later stages, again quite similar for the two disorders, are conceptualized as mourning (facing one's past by exploring the impact of trauma and substance abuse) and reconnection (attaining a healthy engagement with the world through work and relationships) (Herman, 1992). The first stage, safety, is an enormous therapeutic task for some clients, and thus the Seeking Safety model addresses only that stage.

A VARIETY OF TOPICS

The treatment provides 25 topics to help clients attain safety (see Table 7.1 for a description of each topic). The clinician can choose as few or as many topics as fits the treatment context, depending on length of stay, client need, and clinician preferences. Similarly, each topic can be done in one session or extended over several sessions. Each topic addresses both trauma/PTSD and SUD. Topics are evenly divided among cognitive, behavioral, and interpersonal domains, with a clinician guide and extensive client handouts. The seven interpersonal topics are *Asking for Help*; *Honesty*; *Setting Boundaries in Relationships*; *Healthy Relationships*; *Community Resources*; *Healing from Anger*; and *Getting Others to Support Your Recovery*. The seven behavioral topics are *Detaching from Emotional Pain: Grounding*; *Taking Good Care of Yourself*; *Red and Green Flags*; *Commitment*; *Coping with Triggers*; *Respecting Your Time*; and *Self-Nurturing*. The seven cognitive topics are *PTSD: Taking Back Your Power*; *Compassion*; *When Substances Control You*; *Recovery Thinking*; *Integrating the Split Self*; *Creating Meaning*; and *Discovery*. In addition, the four combination topics are *Introduction to Treatment/Case Management*; *Safety*; *The Life Choices Game (Review)*; and *Termination*.

PRESENT FOCUS

Seeking Safety was created as a present-focused model, given repeated concerns in the literature that SUD clients may worsen if guided to explore past trauma (e.g., telling the trauma story). Such past-focused PTSD treatment is a major treatment intervention for PTSD and goes by names such as exposure therapy (e.g., Foa & Rothbaum, 1998), eye movement desensitization and reprocessing (Shapiro, 1995), and mourning (Herman, 1992). Research shows that both present- and past focused PTSD models work, and they achieve equivalent outcomes (Najavits, in press). Thus, the clinician and client have considerable choice and may elect to do both types of treatment (perhaps in sequence or simultaneously), or may choose just present- or just past-focused therapy (Coffey et al., 2002; Najavits et al., 2005). In general, it is recommended that the clinician carefully evaluate whether the substance abuse client needs a period of stable abstinence and functionality before beginning past focused PTSD treatment, and to consider whether it is even needed or desired by the client (Chu, 1988; Keane, 1995; Ruzek et al., 1998; Solomon et al., 1992). The special consideration for SUD clients is based on concerns that they may not yet have adequate coping skills to control their impulses. Clients may use substances more, relapse (if already abstinent), or increase dangerous behaviors such as self-harm or suicidality (Keane, 1995; Ruzek et al., 1998; Solomon et al., 1992). Opening up the "Pandora's box" of trauma memories may destabilize clients when they are most in need of stabilization. Clients themselves may not feel ready for trauma processing early in SUD recovery; others may want to talk about the past but may underestimate the impact of uncovering intense emotions and disturbing memories.

Book

Najavits, L.M. (2002). *Seeking Safety: A Treatment Manual for PTSD and Substance Abuse*. New York: Guilford. Published as a book in English and Spanish. The book includes all materials needed to conduct the treatment (clinician guide and client handouts). Both the English and Spanish versions of the book can be ordered at www.seekingsafety.org (section Order); the English version can also be ordered from any online or local bookstore (e.g., amazon.com).

Web Site

The web site www.seekingsafety.org has freely downloadable materials (articles, information on training, etc.). The web site includes sections such as:
• About Seeking Safety
• Studies (results of each study of Seeking Safety completed thus far)
• Training (calendar of trainings and information on how to set up a training)
• Articles (downloadable articles on Seeking Safety, PTSD/substance abuse, and other topics)
• Assessment (the *Seeking Safety Adherence Scale*, and links to other measures)
• Sample Seeking Safety topics
• How to refer clients to local Seeking Safety treatment

Videos

A set of training videos on Seeking Safety are available (from www.seekingsafety.org, section Order). The videos were developed under a grant from the National Institute on Drug Abuse. They are:
• A two-hour training video by Lisa Najavits
• A one-hour example of a Seeking Safety session led by Lisa Najavits with real clients
• A one-hour adherence session with real clients (to learn how to use the *Seeking Safety Adherence Scale* for supervision or research purposes)
• A demonstration of teaching grounding technique
• One client's story of PTSD and substance abuse

Translation into Spanish

A Spanish translation of Seeking Safety is available (from www.seekingsafety.org, section Store). It was designed for Spanish speakers from North, South, and Central America.

Poster

A professionally produced poster of *Safe Coping Skills* is also available (from www. seekingsafety.org, section Order). It was developed to help remind clients of safe coping throughout the treatment.

Training

Training and consultation on Seeking Safety has been available since the mid-1990s. The web site www.seekingsafety.org (section Training) provides a training calendar of all upcoming trainings, their location, and contact information for registration. Also, information is provided on how to book a training or consultation.

Adherence Scale

The *Seeking Safety adherence scale* is freely downloadable (from www.seekingsafety.org, section Assessment). The scale can be used for research and/or supervision to quantify how much a clinician is conducting Seeking Safety per the manual. It offers three sections: format, content, and process, all of which are rated for both adherence and helpfulness.

Implementation Articles

Several articles expand on how to implement Seeking Safety and are freely downloadable (from www.seekingsafety.org, section Articles).

Contact

For further information on Seeking Safety, contact Lisa M. Najavits by e-mail (info@seekingsafety.org), phone (617-731-1501), or mail (12 Colbourne Crescent, Brookline, MA 02445). See also www.seekingsafety.org.

Thus, Seeking Safety focuses on trauma and PTSD directly—but only in the present. Its goal is an empathic approach that names the trauma experience, validates its connection to substance use, provides psychoeducation, and offers specific safe coping skills to manage the often overwhelming emotions of this dual diagnosis. It was designed to help explore the link between them, but without delving into details about the past that might destabilize them. If a client brings up details of trauma during a Seeking Safety session, the clinician is taught to empathically validate the importance of such material, but to remind the client that the treatment is present-focused, that description of trauma details may be overly upsetting for the client (and others if it is a group therapy), and to gently refocus the client on the present and how to cope with whatever is coming up. However, at any point in the treatment clients can share in a brief phrase the type of trauma they experienced (such as child sexual abuse, rape, combat) if they so choose.

INTEGRATED TREATMENT

Seeking Safety was designed to continually attend to both PTSD and SUD. Both are treated at the same time by the same clinician. This integrated model contrasts with a sequential model in which the client is treated for one disorder, then the other; a parallel model, in which the client receives treatment for both but by different treaters; or a single-model, in which the client receives only one type of treatment (Weiss & Najavits, 1997). Integration is, ultimately, an intrapsychic goal for clients as well as a systems goal: to "own" both disorders, to recognize the links between them, and to understand how one disorder triggers the other. The treatment helps clients discover connections between the two disorders in their lives—in what order they arose and why, how each affects healing from the other, and their origins in other life problems (such as poverty). Integration also occurs at the intervention level. Each safe coping skill in Seeking Safety can be applied to both PTSD and SUD. For example, *Asking for Help* can apply to PTSD (e.g., calling a friend when feeling upset) and to SUD (e.g., asking a partner to stop offering drugs).

A FOCUS ON IDEALS

It is difficult to imagine two mental disorders that each individually, and especially in combination, lead to such demoralization and loss of ideals. In PTSD this loss of ideals has been written about as "shattered assumptions" (Janoff-Bulman, 1992) and the "search for meaning" (Frankl, 1963). With substance abuse there is also a loss of ideals—life narrows and, in its severe form, the person "hits bottom." Seeking Safety explicitly strives to restore ideals. The title of each topic is framed as an ideal that is the opposite of some pathological characteristic of PTSD and substance abuse. For example, the topic *Honesty* combats denial, lying, and the false self. *Commitment* is the opposite of irresponsibility and impulsivity. *Taking Good Care of Yourself* is a solution for bodily self-neglect. Throughout, the language of the treatment emphasizes values such as respect, care, integration, protection, and healing. By aiming for what can be, the hope is that clients can summon the motivation for the incredibly hard work of recovery from the two disorders.

STRUCTURE

The multiple needs, impulsivity, and intense affect of PTSD/SUD clients can lead to derailed sessions if the clinician does not create clear structure. The session structure is described in Table 7.2. It includes a check-in, quotation (for

TABLE 7.2: *Seeking Safety* Treatment Topics

(1) *Introduction to Treatment/Case management*
This topic covers: (a) Introduction to the treatment; (b) Getting to know the client; and (c) Assessment of case management needs.

(2) *Safety* (combination)
Safety is described as the first stage of healing from both PTSD and substance abuse, and the key focus of the treatment. A list of over 80 *Safe Coping Skills* is provided and clients explore what safety means to them.

(3) *PTSD: Taking Back Your Power* (cognitive)
Four handouts are offered: (a) "What is PTSD?"; (b) "The Link Between PTSD and Substance Abuse"; (c) "Using Compassion to Take Back Your Power"; and (d) "Long-Term PTSD Problems." The goal is to provide information as well as a compassionate understanding of the disorder.

(4) *Detaching from Emotional Pain: Grounding* (behavioral)
A powerful strategy, *grounding* is offered to help clients detach from emotional pain. Three types of grounding are presented (mental, physical, and soothing), with an experiential exercise to demonstrate the techniques. The goal is to shift attention toward the external world, away from negative feelings.

(5) *When Substances Control You* (cognitive)
Eight handouts are provided, which can be combined or used separately: (a) "Do You Have a Substance Abuse Problem?"; (b) "How Substance Abuse Prevents Healing From PTSD"; (c) "Choose a Way to Give Up Substances"; (d) "Climbing Mount Recovery," an imaginative exercise to prepare for giving up substances; (e) "Mixed Feelings"; (f) "Self-Understanding of Substance Use"; (g) "Self-Help Groups"; and (h) "Substance Abuse and PTSD: Common Questions."

(6) *Asking for Help* (interpersonal)
Both PTSD and substance abuse lead to problems in asking for help. This topic encourages clients to become aware of their need for help and provides guidance on how to obtain it.

(7) *Taking Good Care of Yourself* (behavioral)
Clients explore how well they take care of themselves using a questionnaire listing specific behaviors (e.g., "Do you get regular medical check-ups?"). They are asked to take immediate action to improve at least one self-care problem.

TABLE 7.2: *(Continued)*

(8) *Compassion* (cognitive)
This topic encourages the use of compassion when trying to overcome problems. Compassion is the opposite of "beating oneself up," a common tendency for people with PTSD and substance abuse. Clients are taught that only a loving stance toward the self produces lasting change.

(9) *Red and Green Flags* (behavioral)
Clients explore the up-and-down nature of recovery in both PTSD and substance abuse through discussion of "red and green flags" (signs of danger and safety). A *Safety Plan* is developed to identify what to do in situations of mild, moderate, and severe relapse danger.

(10) *Honesty* (interpersonal)
Clients discuss the role of honesty in recovery and role-play specific situations. Related issues include: What is the cost of dishonesty? When is it safe to be honest? What if the other person doesn't accept honesty?

(11) *Recovery Thinking* (cognitive)
Thoughts associated with PTSD and substance abuse are contrasted with healthier "recovery thinking." Clients are guided to change their thinking using rethinking tools such as List Your Options, Create a New Story, Make a Decision, and Imagine. The power of rethinking is demonstrated through think-aloud exercises.

(12) *Integrating the Split Self* (cognitive)
Splitting is identified as a major psychic defense in both PTSD and substance abuse. Clients are guided to notice splits (e.g., different sides of the self, ambivalence, denial) and to strive for integration as a means to overcome these.

(13) *Commitment* (behavioral)
The concept of keeping promises, both to self and others, is explored. Clients are offered creative strategies for keeping commitments, as well as the opportunity to identify feelings that can get in the way.

(14) *Creating Meaning* (cognitive)
Meaning systems are discussed with a focus on assumptions specific to PTSD and substance abuse, such as Deprivation Reasoning, Actions Speak Louder Than Words, and Time Warp. Meanings that are harmful versus healing in recovery are contrasted.

(15) *Community Resources* (interpersonal)
A lengthy list of national nonprofit resources is offered to aid clients' recovery (including advocacy organizations, self-help, and newsletters). Also, guidelines are offered to help clients take a consumer approach in evaluating treatments.

(16) *Setting Boundaries in Relationships* (interpersonal)
Boundary problems are described as either too much closeness (difficulty saying "no" in relationships) or too much distance (difficulty saying "yes" in relationships). Ways to set healthy boundaries are explored, and domestic violence information is provided.

(17) *Discovery* (cognitive)
Discovery is offered as a tool to reduce the cognitive rigidity common to PTSD and substance abuse (called "staying stuck"). Discovery is a way to stay open to experience and new knowledge, using strategies such as Ask Others, Try It and See, Predict, and Act "As If." Suggestions for coping with negative feedback are provided.

(continues)

TABLE 7.2: *(Continued)*

(18) *Getting Others to Support Your Recovery* (interpersonal)
Clients are encouraged to identify which people in their lives are supportive, neutral, or destructive toward their recovery. Suggestions for eliciting support are provided, as well as a letter that they can give to others to promote understanding of PTSD and substance abuse. A safe family member or friend can be invited to attend the session.

(19) *Coping with Triggers* (behavioral)
Clients are encouraged to actively fight triggers of PTSD and substance abuse. A simple three-step model is offered: change who you are with, what you are doing, and where you are (similar to "change people, places, and things" in AA).

(20) *Respecting Your Time* (behavioral)
Time is explored as a major resource in recovery. Clients may have lost years to their disorders, but they can still make the future better than the past. They are asked to fill in schedule blanks to explore issues such as: Do they use their time well? Is recovery their highest priority? Balancing structure versus spontaneity; work versus play; and time alone versus in relationships are also addressed.

(21) *Healthy Relationships* (interpersonal)
Healthy and unhealthy relationship beliefs are contrasted. For example, the unhealthy belief "Bad relationships are all I can get" is contrasted with the healthy belief "Creating good relationships is a skill to learn." Clients are guided to notice how PTSD and substance abuse can lead to unhealthy relationships.

(22) *Self-Nurturing* (behavioral)
Safe self-nurturing is distinguished from unsafe self-nurturing (e.g., substances and other "cheap thrills"). Clients are asked to create a gift to the self by increasing safe self-nurturing and decreasing unsafe self-nurturing. Pleasure is explored as a complex issue in PTSD/substance abuse.

(23) *Healing from Anger* (interpersonal)
Anger is explored as a valid feeling that is inevitable in recovery from PTSD and substance abuse. Anger can be used constructively (as a source of knowledge and healing) or destructively (a danger when acted out against self or others). Guidelines for working with both types of anger are offered.

(24) *The Life Choices Game* (combination)
As part of termination, clients are invited to play a game as a way to review the material covered in the treatment. Clients pull from a box slips of paper that list challenging life events (e.g., "You find out your partner is having an affair"). They respond with how they would cope, using game rules that focus on constructive coping.

(25) *Termination*
Clients express their feelings about the ending of treatment, discuss what they liked and disliked about it, and finalize aftercare plans. An optional Termination Letter can be read aloud to clients to validate the work they have done.

Note: Each topic represents a "safe coping skill" relevant to both PTSD and SUD. Domains (cognitive, behavioral, interpersonal, or a combination) are listed in parentheses. Topics can be done in any order, and one can use as few or as many topics as fits the treatment context. A topic can be done over one session or more.

emotional engagement), handouts, and check-out. The structure is designed to model good use of time, appropriate containment, and setting goals and sticking to them. For clients with PTSD and SUD, who are often impulsive and overwhelmed, the predictable session structure helps them know what to expect. It offers, in its process, a mirror of the focus and careful planning that are needed for recovery from the disorders. Most of the session is devoted to the topic selected for the session (see Table 7.1), relating it to current and specific problems in clients' lives. Priority is on any unsafe behavior the client reported during the check-in.

FLEXIBILITY

Seeking Safety was developed to be broadly applicable in a wide variety of settings. It has been conducted in a variety of formats, including group and individual; open and closed groups; sessions of varying lengths (50 minutes, 1 hour, 90 minutes, and two hours); sessions of varying pacing (weekly, twice weekly, and daily); singly and co-led; outpatient, inpatient, and residential; integrated with other treatments or as a stand-alone therapy; and single-gender or mixed-gender. Each topic in Seeking Safety is independent of the others and can be conducted as a single session or over multiple sessions, depending on the client's length of stay and needs. There are no particular coping skills or topics clients must master, but rather they are offered a wide variety from which to choose. The goal is to "go where the action is"—to use the materials in a way that adapts to the client, the clinician, and the program. Some programs have conducted all 25 topics, others created two blocks of 12 sessions each; and others have allowed clients to cycle through the entire treatment multiple times. In some programs, there is not enough time to do all topics and so just a few are selected. Topics can be conducted in any order, with the order selected by clients, clinicians, or both. Extensive handouts are available, from which they can choose those that are most relevant.

The treatment is flexible to allow clients' most important concerns to be kept primary, to allow adaptation to a variety of settings, to respect clinicians' judgments, and to encourage clinicians to remain inspired and interested in the work. These concerns are believed paramount for a population such as this, where the risks of client dropout and clinician burnout are high (Najavits, 2001). Moreover, they were designed to adapt to the managed care era, in which many clients will have limited access to treatment. The therapy is also designed to be integrated with other treatments. Although it can be conducted as a stand-alone intervention, the severity of clients' needs usually suggests that they be in several treatments at the same time (e.g., 12-step groups, pharmacotherapy, individual therapy, group therapy). The model also includes an intensive case management component to help engage clients in additional treatments. Finally, as noted earlier, Seeking Safety has been implemented with a wide variety of clients, and typically PTSD and SUD diagnoses are not required.

EASE OF USE

The model was designed to be user-friendly. For each topic, the book provides:

- A brief Summary
- A Clinician Orientation, which provides background about the topic, clinical strategies for conducting the session, and discussion of countertransference issues
- A Quotation that is read aloud at the start of each session to emotionally engage clients; for example, the quotation for the topic *PTSD: Taking Back Your Power* is from Jesse Jackson, the African-American political leader: "You are not responsible for being down, but you are responsible for getting up" (Marlatt & Gordon, 1985, p. 15)
- A set of Client Handouts, which summarize the main points of the topic
- A segment on Tough Cases, to highlight treatment challenges; for example, when conducting a session on the topic *Safety*, a client may say "I don't want to stay safe. I want to die." The clinician is encouraged to rehearse possible responses to such statements.

Background chapters on the dual diagnosis and how to conduct the treatment are also provided. A variety of resources to support use of the manual have also been developed, including videos, articles that can be downloaded, and a poster of the *Safe Coping Skills* (see the resources section at the end of this chapter).

SIMPLE, ENGAGING LANGUAGE

The goal was to write the manual in simple, emotionally compelling language. It provides a respectful tone that honors clients' courage in fighting the disorders, and teaches new ways of coping that convey empathy for their experience. Words such as "safety," "respect," "honor," and "healing" are used. Scientific jargon and polysyllabic words are avoided. Because the concepts are stated simply, the model also has been implemented with clients who cannot read. For such clients, the clinician summarizes the material briefly or encourages other clients to read small segments out loud.

REHEARSAL OF SKILLS

Each Seeking Safety topic represents a new coping skill, and thus strong emphasis is placed on rehearsal of the skills during the session. A variety of methods can be used, depending on client and clinician preferences:

- *Do a walk-through*. Clients identify a situation in which the safe coping skill might help, then describe how they would use it. For example, in the topic

Asking for Help: "If you felt like using, whom could you call? What would you say?"

- *In-session experiential exercise*. The clinician guides clients through an experience rather than simply talking about it. For example, the skill of grounding is demonstrated in a 10-minute exercise during the session.
- *Role-play*. The client tries out a new way of relating to another person by practicing out loud. This is one of the most popular methods for interpersonal topics.
- *Identify role models*. Clients think of someone who already knows the skill and explore what that person does. For the topic *Commitment*: "Do you know anyone who follows through on promises?"
- *Say aloud*. Clients practice a new style of self-talk out loud. For example, on the topic *Compassion*, "When you got fired from your job this week, how could you have talked to yourself compassionately?"
- *Process perceived obstacles*. Clients anticipate what might happen if they try to implement the skill. For example, in *Setting Boundaries in Relationships*, "What might your partner say if you requested safe sex?"
- *Involve safe family/friends*. Clients are encouraged to enlist help from safe people, as in the topic, *Getting Others to Support Your Recovery*.
- *Replay the scene*. Clients identify something that went wrong and then go through it again as if they could relive it: for example, "What would you do differently this time?" A *Safe Coping Sheet* is designed for this process or it can be done more informally.
- *Discussion questions*. For every topic, ideas to generate discussion are offered.
- *Make a tape*. Create an audiotape for clients to use outside of sessions as a way to literally "change old tapes." For the topic *Compassion*, for example, kind, encouraging statements can be recorded.
- *Review key points*. Clients summarize the main points of the handout that are meaningful to them.
- *Question/Answer*. The clinician asks questions about the topic. For example, "Does anyone know what the letters 'PTSD' stand for?"

COMMITMENTS

To reinforce rehearsal of skills, at the end of each session clients are asked to select a commitment to try before the next session. Commitments are very much like cognitive behavioral homework, but the language is changed to emphasize that clients are making a promise—to themselves, to the clinician, and, in group treatment, to the group—to promote their recovery by taking at least one action step to move forward. Also, commitments do not have to be written, as clinical experience with this population suggests that some clients do not like written assignments. Examples of commitments include "Ask your partner not to offer you any more cocaine," "Read a book on parenting," and "Write a supportive letter to the young side of you that feels scared." Ideas for commitments are offered at the end of each handout, but clinicians are encouraged to customize them to best fit each client (see also Najavits, 2005).

ATTENTION TO CLINICIAN PROCESSES

add't for providers to care for themselves

Due to the challenges of working with this population, special emphasis is placed on the clinician role, such as countertransference, self-care, and secondary traumatization. (The latter refers to clinicians developing PTSD-like symptoms when exposed to traumatized clients.) Additional clinician processes in Seeking Safety include trying the treatment's coping skills in one's own life, compassion for clients' experience, giving clients control whenever possible (empowerment), heroically doing anything possible within professional bounds to help the client get better, listening to clients' behavior more than their words, and obtaining feedback from clients. The reverse of such positive clinician processes are negative processes such as harsh confrontation; sadism; neglect; power struggles; inability to hold clients accountable; becoming victim to clients' abusiveness; and, in group treatment, allowing a client to be scapegoated. As Herman (1992) suggested, clinicians who treat traumatized clients may unwittingly repeat the classic trauma roles of victim, perpetrator, rescuer, or bystander.

Attention is also directed to the *paradox of countertransference* in PTSD and substance abuse. That is, each disorder appears to evoke opposite countertransference reactions. PTSD tends to evoke identification with clients' vulnerability, which, if taken too far, can lead to excessive support at the expense of growth. Substance abuse may evoke anxiety about the client's substance use, which, if extreme, can become harsh judgment and control (e.g., "I won't treat you if you keep using"). The goal is thus to integrate support and accountability. Clinicians are encouraged to help clients seek explanations, but not excuses, for their unsafe behavior.

EMPIRICAL RESULTS

Seeking Safety is the most studied treatment thus far for the dual diagnosis, with eleven completed outcome studies: outpatient women using group modality (Najavits et al., 1998); women in prison, in group modality (Zlotnick et al., 2003); women in a community mental health setting, in group format (Holdcraft & Comtois, 2002); low-income urban women, in individual format (D. A. Hien et al., 2004); adolescent girls, in individual format (Najavits et al., 2006); men and women veterans, in group format (Cook et al., 2006); homeless women veterans in group and/or individual format (Desai & Rosenheck, 2006); women with co-occurring disorders in group format (Morrissey et al., 2005); outpatient men traumatized as children, in individual format (Najavits et al., 2005); women veterans, in group format (Weller, 2005); and women in outpatient treatment

(McNelis-Domingos, 2004). Seven studies were pilots (Cook et al., 2006; Holdcraft & Comtois, 2002; Mcnelis-Domingos, 2004; Najavits et al., 1998, 2005; Weller, 2005; Zlotnick et al., 2003), and four were controlled trials (Desai & Rosenheck, 2006; D. A. Hien et al., 2004; Morrissey et al., 2005; Najavits et al., 2006). Two were multisite trials (Desai & Rosenheck, 2006; Morrissey et al., 2005). In all the studies, the clients were severe. That is, they had symptoms of the disorders for many years, in most cases were substance dependent, had multiple traumas (often in childhood), and typically had additional co-occurring Axis I and/or Axis II disorders. Three of the studies are omitted from the summary that follows. Two were not designed to evaluate Seeking Safety *per se*, but rather included that as one model among several, and did not report differences among models (Holdcraft & Comtois, 2002; Morrissey et al., 2005). One study was an unpublished master's thesis (Mcnelis-Domingos, 2004). Nonetheless, all three of those trials showed high acceptability and satisfaction with Seeking Safety and positive outcomes on a variety of measures.

All eight studies reviewed here evidenced positive outcomes. Seven of the eight studies reported on substance use, and six of these found improvements in that domain (D. A. Hien et al., 2004; Najavits et al., 1998, 2005, 2006; Weller, 2005; Zlotnick et al., 2003). All eight studies assessed PTSD and/or trauma-related symptoms and found improvements in those areas. Improvements were also found in various other areas, including social adjustment, general psychiatric symptoms, suicidal plans and thoughts, problem solving, sense of meaning, depression, and quality of life. Treatment satisfaction and attendance were reported to be high in all eight studies. Four studies had follow-ups after treatment ended and showed that some key gains were maintained (D. A. Hien et al., 2004; Najavits et al., 1998, 2005, 2006; Zlotnick et al., 2003).

In all three controlled trials, Seeking Safety outperformed treatment-as-usual (Desai & Rosenheck, 2006; D. A. Hien et al., 2004; Najavits et al., 2006). All three allowed clients in the Seeking Safety condition to obtain unlimited amounts of treatment-as-usual in addition to Seeking Safety, and thus essentially evaluated the impact of (1) Seeking Safety plus treatment-as-usual versus (2) treatment-as-usual alone (a challenging test as clients had so much additional treatment other than Seeking Safety). In the study by Hien et al. (2004), both Seeking Safety and Relapse Prevention (an additional arm of the study) showed positive effects with no significant difference between them, and both outperformed treatment-as-usual, which was a nonrandomized control. In Najavits, Gallop et al. (2006), Seeking Safety outperformed treatment-as-usual for adolescent outpatient girls. In the Desai et al. (2006) multisite study of homeless women veterans, Seeking Safety outperformed a nonrandomized treatment-as-usual comparison condition. That study is notable for having used case managers rather than clinicians to conduct Seeking Safety. Finally, it can also be noted that one of the pilot studies (Najavits et al., 2005) combined Seeking Safety with Exposure-Therapy-Revised (ETR), an adaptation for substance abuse clients of Foa and Rothbaum's Exposure Therapy for PTSD (Foa & Rothbaum, 1998). Clients were given a choice over the number of sessions of each type and chose an average of 21 Seeking Safety sessions and nine sessions of ETR.

In sum, Seeking Safety has shown consistent evidence of high acceptability among diverse clients and clinicians, positive outcomes on a variety of measures, superiority to treatment-as-usual, comparability to a gold standard treatment (relapse prevention), and efficacy in populations typically considered challenging (e.g., the homeless, prisoners, adolescents, public sector clients, and veterans). Nonetheless, empirical work on the model is at an early stage, with a need for more randomized controlled trials, evaluation of mechanisms of action, and studies of clinician training. For a continuously updated list of studies, vist www. seekingsafety.org (section Outcomes).

IMPLEMENTATION ISSUES

CLIENT AND CLINICIAN SELECTION

In selecting clients the goal is to be as inclusive as possible, with a plan to monitor clients over time to determine whether it is helpful to them. As noted earlier, most of the empirical studies on Seeking Safety were conducted on clients formally and currently diagnosed with both disorders, but in clinical practice the range has been much broader. It has included clients with a history of trauma and/or SUD, clients with serious and persistent mental illness, clients with just one or the other disorder, and clients with other disorders (e.g., eating disorders). An important consideration is clients' own preference. Given the powerlessness in both PTSD and substance abuse, empowerment is key. It appears best to describe the treatment and then give clients a choice in whether to participate. Letting them explore the treatment by attending a few sessions, without obligation to continue, is another helpful process.

Thus far, there do not appear to be any particular readiness characteristics or contraindications that are easily identified. As the treatment is designed for safety, coping, and stabilization, it is not likely to destabilize clients and thus has been implemented quite broadly. Similarly, clients do not need to attain stabiliza-tion before starting; it was designed for use from the beginning of treatment. For clients with addictive or impulsive behavior in addition to substance abuse (e.g., binge-eating, self-mutilation, gambling), clients are encouraged to apply the safe coping skills in Seeking Safety to those behaviors, while also referring them to specialized treatment for such problems as part of the case management compo-nent. Clients are not discontinued from the treatment unless they evidence a direct threat to staff or other clients (e.g., assault, selling drugs). An open-door policy prevails; they are welcome back at any time, a position advocated in early recovery (Herman, 1992).

The key criteria for selecting clinicians to conduct Seeking Safety are positive attitudes toward this dual diagnosis population, willingness to try a treatment manual, strong empathy, a willingness to cross-train (e.g., for mental health clinicians to learn about substance abuse), and the ability to hold clients accountable and work with aggression (Najavits, 2000). In early use of Seeking Safety, various professional characteristics were sought, such as a mental health degree and particular types of training (CBT, substance abuse). It became clear over time that far more important than any such credentials are the more subtle criteria mentioned earlier (Najavits, 2000). Clinicians who genuinely enjoy these clients, often perceiving the work as a mission or calling, bring a level of commitment that no degree per se can provide. Similarly, clinicians who are open to the value of a treatment manual, viewing it as a resource to help improve the quality of the work, can make the best use of the material. As there are no strict criteria for selecting clinicians, the treatment can be implemented across the full range of clinicians, regardless of degree or training. Many substance abuse programs, for example, do not have staff with advanced degrees or formal CBT training. Because the treatment focuses on stabilization rather than trauma processing, it is comparable to relapse prevention models, and thus does not exceed the training, licensure, or ethical limits of substance abuse counselors or paraprofessionals. However, they are guided to refer out for specialized professional mental health treatment if clients exceed the parameters of their work (e.g., dissociative identity disorder). Per the manual, it is also important that if a clinician does not have any prior background in trauma, PTSD, substance abuse, or CBT, some learning and/or supervision on these should be sought.

Additional suggestions for selecting a Seeking Safety clinician are described in a protocol that can be downloaded from www.seekingsafety.org (section Training). Briefly, it suggests a try-out to determine whether the potential clinician might be a good match. The potential clinician conducts one or more audiotaped sessions using Seeking Safety with a real client, and the sessions are rated by the client as well as evaluated on the Seeking Safety adherence scale. Once hired, methods for training and implementation are described in the manual as well as related articles (Najavits, 2000, 2004b). A study exploring clinicians' views on treating these dual diagnosis clients may also be relevant (Najavits, 2002a).

Training methods for the treatment (Najavits, 2000; 2004b) emphasize these various process issues as well as observation of the clinician in action (e.g., taped sessions) and intensive training experiences (e.g., watching videotapes of good vs. poor sessions, peer supervision, role plays, knowledge tests, identifying key themes, and think-aloud modeling).

ADAPTATION

Because of the high degree of flexibility inherent the model, Seeking Safety can be adapted without going outside of its intended use. Thus, it is not only possible but desirable to customize the treatment for particular subgroups (gender, type of trauma, race, ethnicity, age, etc.). A useful framework is to think of adaptations *inside the model* versus *outside the model*. The former are recommended whereas the latter are not unless they are carefully evaluated and deemed necessary. Adaptations inside the model include using examples from clients' experience, covering the material over as many sessions as needed, creating a pace and length of sessions based on the treatment context, using creative devices (such as drawings), and allowing clients to make use of strategies and materials they find helpful, and letting go of those that they do not find helpful. Adaptations outside of the model include changing the session structure in a way that detracts from the intent of the model (e.g., spending the entire session discussing the quotation), and *a priori* narrowing the range of materials given to clients (e.g., presuming clients will not like certain topics and thus deleting them).

In general, two suggestions are paramount. First, try the model as planned when starting out, and collect feedback directly from clients. Two forms are included in the manual for this purpose: the *End of Session Questionnaire* and the *End of Treatment Questionnaire*. If clients suggest changes, make adaptations based on that. Second, make adaptations if needed due to unusual treatment contexts. For example, one day program group had 30 clients and thus it was impossible to conduct a check-in and check-out on each person. The group leader decided to focus solely on the handouts. Other programs with large groups decided to ask just a single check-in and check-out question.

Several adaptations within the model highlight the creativity that dedicated clinicians bring to their work. For example, one day program created a "grounding table" in the back of the treatment room with various small objects and soothing materials. If clients became upset during a session, they were encouraged to use the grounding table to help calm down, while the group continued. In another program, each of the safe coping skills was written on a heart-shaped cut-out and posted on the wall. Some clinicians have developed experiential exercises as well. A recent article (V. B. Brown et al., in press) describes adaptations of Seeking Safety in three community programs, with a summary of feedback and satisfaction by both clients and clinicians.

DIVERSITY (ETHNICITY, RACE, GENDER)

Before the manual was published, Seeking Safety was conducted with diverse clients, including two heavily minority samples (D. Hien et al.; Zlotnick et al., 2003), women and men, and clients with various trauma histories (e.g., child abuse, crime victimization, and combat). The examples and language in the book were written to reflect these experiences, and to mention sexism, racism, poverty, and both female and male issues. Thus far, the treatment has obtained high client satisfaction ratings in these subgroups (see, for example, Brown et al., in press; and Zlotnick et al., 2003). Rates of diversity in published trials include 77 percent minority in Hien et al. (2004), 65 percent minority in Desai and Rosenheck (2006), 35 percent minority in Zlotnick et al. (2003), and 21 percent minority in Najavits et al. (2006). However, clinicians working with particular populations may benefit from adding more examples from their lives, cultural elements relevant to them, and addressing their particular context and burdens. In treating men, for example, exploring how certain traumas violate the masculine role may be helpful (e.g., weakness and vulnerability). In treating Latinos, one can use the Spanish-language version of Seeking Safety (see www.seekingsafety.org, section Order), and provide cultural context (e.g., concepts such as *familismo* and *marianismo* and acculturation stress).

GROUP MODALITY

Seeking Safety can be conducted in individual or group modality, and the format is the same. Groups can be open or closed format, and singly or co-led. Some issues to consider when conducting the treatment in group format are as follows. First, choose the name of the group carefully. One program called their group *Trauma Group* and few clients wanted to attend. When they renamed it *Seeking Safety Group* the attendance improved. If the group title includes the term "trauma" or "PTSD," clients may fear that they will be asked to describe their traumas or will have to listen to others do so, and may not feel ready for that. A more upbeat title is reassuring. Thus, it can be *Safety Group*, *Seeking Safety*, or *Coping Skills Group* for example. Second, the number of group members should be planned carefully. Remembering that the check-in allows up to five minutes per client (but usually goes quicker), a one-hour group could easily accommodate five to seven clients. For longer sessions, more clients can be added. As noted earlier, very large groups may need to curtail or delete the check-in and check-out. Third, because Seeking Safety focuses on trauma, the tone of the group may be different than typical substance abuse groups. In the latter, confrontation may be accepted (e.g., a client may tell another that she is "in denial" or "being too self-pitying"). In Seeking Safety such statements would be seen as detracting from the emotional safety of the group. The clinician is asked to train clients to focus on their own recovery, and to interact primarily in supportive and problem-solving ways rather than confrontational ways. Fourth, single-gender groups are the most common way of implementing the treatment, as much trauma was sexual or physical in nature and clients are likely to feel more comfortable with the same gender. However, Seeking Safety has been implemented with mixed-gender groups as well, but only when none of the clients had a major history as perpetrators (which could be too triggering), and only when clients agreed to join a mixed-gender group. The clinicians, too, typically have been the same gender as the clients, although it has also been conducted with mixed gender combinations. Finally, if clients miss a session, they can be given the handouts to keep up with the group. If a client plans to join an open group once it has begun, it is suggested that the topic *PTSD: Taking Back Your Power* be first reviewed individually, to increase the client's awareness of trauma and PTSD. However, some clients join a Seeking Safety group but do not have trauma, PTSD and/or SUD, so this too is flexible.

ASSESSMENT

A recent book chapter offers practical considerations in assessing SUD and PTSD (Najavits, 2004a). It includes a list of domains within each disorder to consider for assessment, and web sites for free assessment measures (see also www.seekingsafety.org, section Assessment, for links to key sites). Specific issues discussed in the book chapter include the therapeutic benefit of accurate assessment; the importance of routine assessment of trauma and PTSD at the start of treatment (not delaying these due to clients' substance use or withdrawal); the use of brief screenings; limiting collection of trauma information early in treatment to avoid triggering the client; and the need to delay assessment if the client is intoxicated. Also discussed are issues of diagnostic overlap between the two disorders, misconceptions of SUD criteria, age-appropriate measures, secondary gain in PTSD and SUD, common misdiagnoses, memory issues, countertransference by assessors, and the needs of clinical versus research instruments.

CLINICAL CASE ILLUSTRATION

As an example of how Seeking Safety has been used by one client, the following case material is offered. It was an unsolicited e-mail sent to the author and is reprinted here unchanged and with her permission. It illustrates several typical themes, which will be highlighted at the end of this section.

> I came upon your Seeking Safety treatment program while in a Women's PTSD program. The program used a variety of different modalities for treatment and Seeking Safety was a portion of it. Unfortunately, I had only been in the PTSD program 10 days when I tried a non-safe coping skill, abusing over-the-counter sleep-aids, to try and overcome the pain of facing my trauma and was asked to leave the program. Being asked to leave the program for resorting back to some of the behaviors that got me in there was difficult. I wasn't using as much, and was learning to admit I had a problem, and to me it seemed like I was being punished for finally asking for help. I almost let that send me into a tail-spin, but I chose to help myself if they weren't willing to help me. I bought the Seeking Safety book and I read it as though I were a going to treat a patient, only that patient was me. I admit it is difficult, and potentially dangerous, to treat oneself but it seemed I was the only one who hadn't given up on me so what choice did I have. I "meet" with myself 2–3× a week and I sit in front of a mirror and conduct sessions with myself. I check in, I review "commitments," I discuss a chapter or portion of a chapter with myself and I check-out. After "session," I write in my journal patient notes. I wish I had a treatment provider willing to help me sometimes, but doing it myself is better than nothing. As this is your program, I wanted to share what my experiences so far have been:
>
>   1. It is a lot easier to provide encouragement and support to someone else, than it is to provide encouragement and support to oneself. I would never put down someone else, or judge their progress when they are really putting forth the effort. Myself, that is a different story. I have struggled a long time with negative self-talk. Since I began treating myself as a patient, I see how hard I'm working and I see how far I've come. I'm really proud of me! I've not used substances or self-harming behaviors in 50 days. I would be

at 90 days, but I had a tough experience 50 days ago and I used. I almost gave up on myself because I'd let myself down, but I wouldn't have given up on a patient and I didn't give up on me. I learned from the experience and I moved on.

2. It feels strange to carry on a conversation with myself, but I am so much more aware of where I'm at since I've started this. I realize how often I say "I can't . . ." and I realize how distorted my view of myself is. I believe being more aware has helped me be more honest with myself. It has also made me realize how much I can gain from others. I never saw how much I push people away until I stopped having someone there to push away. I wish I could get back into that PTSD program because I could use someone else's insight, but so far they say "no."

3. I took the list of safe coping skills and I put each one on an index card. I carry those cards with me most of the time because when things get tough, I want to use what works and using drugs does help in the moment and that's my first thought. Now I have all these skills to try and sometimes the first card has a skill that doesn't help me enough, but the second or the third or the fourth or whatever eventually works. If I make it through the whole pile, I might see using as the only option but I can't see that happening. I also add new skills as they come and my pile gets bigger and I get further from believing that unsafe behaviors are the only way to make it through the moment.

I could share so much more, but I think you get my point. I just really wanted to say "Thank you" because your book has helped me to help me at least until I can get someone else to help me too.

This client's account helps bring out several themes that can occur in treatment with this population. First, her experience of being rejected by a mental health treatment program for using a substance still remains quite common. Second, she perceived that she had no other treatment options and had to do the best she could on her own. She was remarkably resilient in attempting to conduct Seeking Safety with herself. Clearly, this is not the optimal strategy, as she herself notes. But it provides a poignant example of the dilemmas that clients sometimes face. Third, she very creatively came up with strategies to use the material, such as writing the safe coping skills on index cards and practicing self-talk in front of a mirror. Fourth and finally, her description offers a realistic portrayal of some of the ups and downs that can occur. Her ability to stay abstinent and to overcome a slip on her own are notable. In a follow-up e-mail, she conveyed that she was recently married and continues to try to enter a treatment program to further her recovery. She appears to have located a program that will admit her and is pursuing that.

RELATION TO RELAPSE PREVENTION

Seeking Safety and relapse prevention have both similarities and differences. These are worth outlining as an aid to training and implementation efforts. Many clinicians who are familiar with relapse prevention report that Seeking Safety feels like a comfortable fit for them because of the similarities between the two models. Yet because of Seeking Safety's intensive focus on trauma and PTSD, it usually also requires some new learning.

SIMILARITIES

Both Seeking Safety and relapse prevention are:

- Present focused
- Coping skills oriented
- Psychoeducational
- Low risk
- Manualized
- Structured
- Empirically supported
- Focused on skill rehearsal
- Designed for a wide range of clients (all types of substances, severity, genders, etc.)
- Designed for a wide range of staff (e.g., substance abuse counselors)
- Intended for all treatment contexts (outpatient, inpatient, group, individual, etc.)
- Early-stage treatment (for active users and early recovery)
- Similar in some topics (e.g., *Coping with Triggers*)

DIFFERENCES

Seeking Safety was designed for the dual diagnosis of PTSD and SUD. Thus in contrast to relapse prevention, Seeking Safety uniquely focuses on:

- Trauma and PTSD
- Safety as a core theme
- Humanistic language
- Case management
- Emotional engagement (e.g., use of quotations)
- Some different topics (e.g., Integrating the Split Self, Setting Boundaries in Relationships, Compassion)
- Ideals to restore hope
- Emergency situations
- Increased interpersonal emphasis
- Application to both mental health and substance abuse settings
- Emphasis on clinician processes (countertransference, self-care, secondary traumatization)
- Abstinence or harm reduction, depending on the client and setting
- High flexibility (topics can be done in any order; client can choose handouts, etc.)
- Empowerment

In identifying these similarities and differences, it is important to note that research is needed to address how the two modalities compare in outcome results.

For example, in the only study thus far directly comparing Seeking Safety and Relapse Prevention, both outperformed treatment-as-usual, yet did not differ from each other overall (D. A. Hien et al., 2004). This is in keeping with the general treatment outcome literature in which manual-based treatments are generally comparable to each other in outcome and superior to treatment-as-usual (e.g., Najavits, in press). Thus, clinicians and clients can choose freely among different models. For example, in Seeking Safety, clients are encouraged to "try out" the treatment for a few sessions to see whether they like it. Some clients have been through a lot of substance abuse treatment and want a change. Other clients may want both models, and yet others may prefer just one or the other.

For a description of how Seeking Safety compares to other models (e.g., dialectical behavior therapy, cognitive behavioral therapy, exposure therapy, motivational enhancement therapy) see Najavits (2002).

CONCLUSIONS AND RECOMMENDATIONS

Integrated therapies for dual diagnosis have become prominent in the past decade to help clients better overcome SUD and co occurring mental disorders. Seeking Safety is the most empirically supported model thus far for the dual diagnosis of PTSD and SUD. It has been described in detail in this chapter, including assessment and implementation considerations.

Despite advances in this area of work, there is a need for more research. Thus far, only a few randomized controlled therapy trials have been conducted, and no trials comparing integrated models versus other models (sequential or parallel) have been published. Studies of active mechanisms and how best to combine treatments have not yet occurred. There is also a need to evaluate methods for selecting and training clinicians to work with such high-severity clients. Clinically, assessment and treatment of PTSD in SUD settings is not yet widespread, and conversely, in mental health settings both PTSD and SUD may not be sufficiently addressed. Rigorous large-scale studies are rare, as are studies of long-term outcomes (one year or more). Given the often chronic course of both PTSD and SUD through the life span (e.g., Port, 2001), further support for clinical implementation and research are needed. In short, much more is unknown than known at this point. Learning from a variety of patients, clinicians, settings, and studies will be an evolving process. In closing, the quotation by Jacob (1997), from the Seeking Safety topic *Discovery*, is apt:

> Progress . . . begins with the invention of a possible world . . . which is then compared by experimentation with the real world. And it is this constant dialogue between imagination and experiment that allows . . . an increasingly fine-grained conception of what is called reality.

TABLE 7.3:   Conducting the Session

The session has four parts: check-in, quotation, relate the topic to clients' lives, and check-out.

1) Check-In
The goal of the check-in is to find out how clients are doing (up to 5 minutes per client). Clients report on five questions: "Since the last session (a) How are you feeling?; (b) What good coping have you done?; (c) Describe your substance use and any other unsafe behavior; (d) Did you complete your Commitment?; and (e) Provide a Community Resource update."

2) Quotation
The quotation is a brief device to help emotionally engage clients in the session (up to 2 minutes). A client reads the quotation out loud. The clinician asks, "What is the main point of the quotation?" and links it to the session topic.

3) Relate the Topic to Clients' Lives
The clinician and/or client selects any one of the 25 treatment topics (listed in Table 7.1) that feels most relevant. This is the heart of the session, with the goal of meaningfully connecting the topic to clients' experience (30–40 minutes). Clients look through the handout for a few minutes, which may be accompanied by the clinician summarizing key points (especially for clients who are cognitively impaired). Clients are asked what they most relate to in the material, and the rest of the time is devoted to addressing the topic in relation to specific and current examples from clients' lives. As each topic represents a safe coping skill, intensive rehearsal of the skill is strongly emphasized.

4) Check-Out
The goal is to reinforce clients' progress and give the clinician feedback (a few minutes per client). Clients answer two questions: (a) "Name one thing you got out of today's session (and any problems with it)"; and (b) "What is your new Commitment?"

AUTHOR NOTE

Adapted parts of this chapter were drawn from several previous publications on Seeking Safety (Najavits, 2002b; 2004c; 2006).

REFERENCES

Adshead, G. (2000). Psychological therapies for post-traumatic stress disorder. *British Journal of Psychiatry* **177**:144–148.

American Psychiatric Association. (1994). *Diagnostic and statistical manual of mental disorders IV.* Washington, DC: American Psychiatric Association.

Brady, K., Dansky, B., Back, S., Foa, E., Caroll, K. (2001). Exposure therapy in the treatment of PTSD among cocaine-dependent individuals: Preliminary findings. *Journal of Substance Abuse Treatment* **21**:47–54.

Brady, K.T. (2001). Comorbid posttraumatic stress disorder and substance use disorders. *Psychiatric Annals* **31**:313–319.

Breslau, N., Davis, G.C., Schultz, L.R. (2003). Posttraumatic stress disorder and the incidence of nicotine, alcohol, and other drug disorders in persons who have experienced trauma. *Archives of General Psychiatry* **60**:289–294.

Brown, P.J., Stout, R.L., Gannon-Rowley, J. (1998). Substance use disorders—PTSD comorbidity: Patients' perceptions of symptom interplay and treatment issues. *Journal of Substance Abuse Treatment* **14**:1–4.

Brown, V.B., Najavits, L.M., Cadiz, S., Finkelstein, N., Heckman, J., Rechberger, E.C. (in press). Implementing an evidence–based practice: Seeking Safety group. *Journal of Psychoactive Drugs.*

Chilcoat, H.D., Breslau, N. (1998). Posttraumatic stress disorder and drug disorders: Testing causal pathways. *Archives of General Psychiatry* **55**:913–917.

Chu, J.A. (1988). Ten traps for therapists in the treatment of trauma survivors. *Dissociation: Progress in the Dissociative Disorders* **1**:24–32.

Clark, H.W. (January 2002). *Meeting overview.* Paper presented at the Trauma and Substance Abuse Treatment Meeting, Bethesda, MD.

Coffey, S.F., Dansky, B.S., Brady, K.T. (2002). Exposure-based, trauma-focused therapy for comorbid posttraumatic stress disorder-substance use disorder. In Ouimette, P., Brown, P.J., eds., *Trauma and substance abuse: Causes, consequences, and treatment of comorbid disorders,* 209–226. Washington, DC: American Psychological Association Press.

Cohen, L.R., Hien, D.A. (2006). Treatment outcomes for women with substance abuse and PTSD who have experienced complex trauma. *Psychiatric Services* **57**(1):100–106.

Cook, J.M., Walser, R.D., Kane, V., Ruzek, J.I., Woody, G. (2006). Dissemination and feasibility of a cognitive-behavioral treatment for substance use disorders and posttraumatic stress disorder in the Veterans Administration. *Journal of Psychoactive Drugs* **38**:89–92.

Cottler, L.B. et al. (1992). Posttraumatic stress disorders among substance users from the general population. *American Journal of Psychiatry* **149**:664–670.

Dansky, B.S., Roitzsch, J.C., Brady, K.T., Saladin, M.E. (1997). Posttraumatic stress disorder and substance abuse. Use of research in a clinical setting. *Journal of Traumatic Stress* **10**: 141–148.

Davidson, J.R.T. (2001). Recognition and treatment of posttraumatic stress disorder. *Journal of the American Medical Association* **286**:584–588.

Desai, R., Rosenheck, R. (2006). *Effectiveness of treatment for homeless female veterans with psychiatric and/or substance abuse disorders: Impact of "Seeking Safety" and residential treatment on one-year clinical outcomes* (Report to Congress). West Haven, CT: VA Connecticut Health Care System.

Foa, E.B., Rothbaum, B.O. (1998). *Treating the trauma of rape: Cognitive-behavioral therapy for PTSD.* New York: Guilford.

Frankl, V.E. (1963). *Man's search for meaning.* New York: Pocket Books.

Herman, J.L. (1992). *Trauma and recovery.* New York: Basic Books.

Hien, D.A., Cohen, L.R., Miele, G.M., Litt, L.C., Capstick, C. (2004). Promising treatments for women with comorbid PTSD and substance use disorders. *American Journal of Psychiatry* **161**(8):1426–1432.

Holdcraft, L.C., Comtois, K.A. (2002). Description of and preliminary data from a women's dual diagnosis community mental health program. *Canadian Journal of Community Mental Health* **21**:91–109.

Hyer, L., Leach, P., Boudewyns, P.A., Davis, H. (1991). Hidden PTSD in substance abuse inpatients among Vietnam veterans. *Journal of Substance Abuse Treatment* **8**:213–219.

Jacob, F. (1997). *The statue within: An autobiography.* New York: Basic Books.

Janoff-Bulman, R. (1992). *Shattered assumptions: Towards a new psychology of trauma.* New York: Free Press.

Kaufman, E., Reoux, J. (1988). Guidelines for the successful psychotherapy of substance abusers. *American Journal of Drug and Alcohol Abuse* **14**:199–209.

Keane, T.M. (1995). The role of exposure therapy in the psychological treatment of PTSD. *Clinical Quarterly (National Center for Posttraumatic Stress Disorder)* **5**:1, 3–6.

Kessler, R.C., Sonnega, A., Bromet, E., Hughes, M., Nelson, C.B. (1995). Posttraumatic stress disorder in the national comorbidity survey. *Archives of General Psychiatry* **52**:1048–1060.

Marlatt, G., Gordon, J. (1985). *Relapse prevention: Maintenance strategies in the treatment of addictive behaviors.* New York: Guilford.

Mcnelis-Domingos, A. (May 2004). *Cognitve behavioral skills training for persons with co-occurring posttraumatic stress disorder and substance abuse.* Thesis submitted for the degree of Master of Social Work, Southern Connecticut State University, New Haven, Connecticut.

Morrissey, J.P., Jackson, E.W., Ellis, A.R., Amaro, H., Brown, V.B., Najavits, L.M. (2005). Twelve-month outcomes of trauma-informed interventions for women with co-occurring disorders. *Psychiatric Services* **56**:1213–1222.

Najavits, L.M. (2000). Training clinicians in the *Seeking Safety* treatment for posttraumatic stress disorder and substance abuse. *Alcoholism Treatment Quarterly* **18**:83–98.

Najavits, L.M. (2001). Early career award paper: Helping difficult patients. *Psychotherapy Research* **11**:131–152.

Najavits, L.M. (2002a). Clinicians' views on treating posttraumatic stress disorder and substance use disorder. *Journal on Substance Abuse Treatment* **22**:79–85.

Najavits, L.M. (2002b). Seeking Safety: A new psychotherapy for posttraumatic stress disorder and substance use disorder. In Ouimette, P., Brown, P.J., eds., *Trauma and substance abuse: Causes, consequences, and treatment of comorbid disorders*, 147–170. Washington, DC: American Psychological Association Press.

Najavits, L.M. (2002c). *Seeking Safety: A treatment manual for PTSD and substance abuse.* New York, NY: Guilford.

Najavits, L.M. (2002d). *A woman's addiction workbook.* Oakland, CA: New Harbinger.

Najavits, L.M. (2004a). Assessment of trauma, PTSD, and substance use disorder: A practical guide. In Wilson, J.P., Keane, T.M., eds., *Assessment of psychological trauma and PTSD*, 466–491. New York: Guilford.

Najavits, L.M. (2004b). Treatment for posttraumtic stress disorder and substance abuse: Clinical guidelines for implementing the *Seeking Safety* therapy. *Alcoholism Treatment Quarterly* **22**:43–62.

Najavits, L.M. (2004c). Treatment for the dual diagnosis of posttraumatic stress and substance use disorders (continuing education lesson). *Directions in Addiction Treatment and Prevention* **8**:1–11. Hatherleigh Company.

Najavits, L.M. (2005). Substance abuse. In Kazantzis, N., Deane, F.P., Ronan, K.R., L'Abate, L., eds., *Using homework assignments in cognitive behavior therapy.* Brunner-Routledge.

Najavits, L.M. (2006). Seeking Safety. In Follette, V., Ruzek, J.L., eds., *Cognitive-behavioral therapies for trauma, 2e*, 228–257. New York: Guilford Press.

Najavits, L.M. (In press). Psychosocial treatments for posttraumatic stress disorder. In Nathan, P.E., Gorman, J.M., eds., *A guide to treatments that work, 3e.* New York: Oxford.

Najavits, L.M., Gallop, R.J., Weiss, R.D. (2006). Seeking Safety therapy for adolescent girls with PTSD and substance use disorder: A randomized controlled trial. *Journal of Behavioral Health Services and Research* **33**:453–463.

Najavits, L.M., Schmitz, M., Gotthardt, S., Weiss, R.D. (2005). Seeking Safety plus exposure therapy: An outcome study on dual diagnosis men. *Journal of Psychoactive Drugs* **37**:425–435.

Najavits, L.M., Sullivan, T.P., Schmitz, M., Weiss, R.D., Lee, C.S.N. (2004). Treatment utilization of women with PTSD and substance dependence. *American Journal on Addictions* **13**:215–224.

Najavits, L.M., Weiss, R.D., Liese, B.S. (1996). Group cognitive-behavioral therapy for women with PTSD and substance use disorder. *Journal of Substance Abuse Treatment* **13**:13–22.

Najavits, L.M., Weiss, R.D., Shaw, S.R. (1997). The link between substance abuse and posttraumatic stress disorder in women: A research review. *American Journal on Addictions* **6**:273–283.

Najavits, L.M., Weiss, R.D., Shaw, S.R., Muenz, L.R. (1998). "Seeking Safety": Outcome of a new cognitive-behavioral psychotherapy for women with posttraumatic stress disorder and substance dependence. *Journal of Traumatic Stress* **11**:437–456.

Ouimette, P., Brown, P.J. (2002). *Trauma and substance abuse: Causes, consequences, and treatment of comorbid disorders*. Washington, DC: American Psychological Association Press.

Port, C.L. (2001). New research on the course of PTSD. *Amercican Journal of Psychiatry* **158**: 1474–1479.

Read, J.P., Bollinger, A.R., Sharansky, E. (2002). Assessment of comorbid substance use disorder and posttraumatic stress disorder. In Ouimette, P., Brown, P.J., eds., *Trauma and substance abuse: Causes, consequences, and treatment of comorbid disorders*, 111–125. Washington, DC: American Psychological Association Press.

Ruzek, J.I., Polusny, M.A., Abueg, F.R. (1998). Assessment and treatment of concurrent posttraumatic stress disorder and substance abuse. In Follette, V.M., Ruzek, J.I., Abueg, F.R., eds., *Cognitive-behavioral therapies for trauma*, 226–255. New York: Guilford.

Shapiro, F. (1995). *Eye movement desensitization and reprocessing: Basic principles, protocols, and procedures*. New York: Guilford.

Solomon, S.D., Gerrity, E.T., Muff, A.M. (1992). Efficacy of treatments for posttraumatic stress disorder. *Journal of the American Medical Association* **268**:633–638.

Weiss, R.D., Najavits, L.M. (1997). Overview of treatment modalities for dual diagnosis patients: Pharmacotherapy, psychotherapy, and twelve-step programs. In Kranzler, H.R., Rounsaville, B.J., eds., *Dual diagnosis: Substance abuse and comorbid medical and psychiatric disorders*, 87–105. New York, NY: Marcel Dekker.

Weller, L.A. (2005). Group therapy to treat substance use and traumatic symptoms in female veterans. *Federal Practitioner* **22**:27–38.

Zlotnick, C., Najavits, L.M., Rohsenow, D.J. (2003). A cognitive-behavioral treatment for incarcerated women with substance use disorder and posttraumatic stress disorder: Findings from a pilot study. *Journal of Substance Abuse Treatment* **25**:99–105.

8

RELAPSE PREVENTION FOR EATING DISORDERS

TANYA R. SCHLAM AND
G. TERENCE WILSON

Rutgers University
Psychology Department
Piscataway, New Jersey

INTRODUCTION

The *Diagnostic and Statistical Manual of Mental Disorders* (*DSM-IV-TR*; American Psychiatric Association, 2000) describes two main types of eating disorders: anorexia nervosa (AN) and bulimia nervosa (BN). The *DSM-IV* also describes a third residual category, eating disorder not otherwise specified (EDNOS).

Patients with AN are severely underweight, but fear gaining weight and refuse to do so. Patients with AN are classified as belonging to either the binge-eating/purging subtype or the restricting subtype, who do not binge and purge. A binge is defined as eating an objectively large amount of food while feeling a loss of control.

Patients with BN binge on average at least twice a week and subsequently engage in compensatory behaviors by purging (e.g., vomiting or misusing laxatives), fasting, or exercising excessively. The EDNOS category includes patients who have a clinically significant eating disorder but who do not meet full criteria for either AN or BN. The EDNOS category also includes binge eating disorder (BED), a provisional diagnosis that has begun to receive more study. BED patients binge at least two days a week, do not practice compensatory behaviors, and are typically overweight.

EMPIRICALLY SUPPORTED TREATMENTS

Theory-driven, manual-based cognitive behavioral therapy (CBT) is the treatment of choice for both BN and BED (National Institute for Clinical Excellence, 2004; Wilson, 2005). CBT is also used to treat AN, and articles have described the approach (e.g., Pike, Loeb & Vitousek, 1996), but there is no published, accepted manual. Due in part to the rarity of the disorder and patients' resistance to therapy, there has been little research on treatment for AN (Agras et al., 2004). There is some evidence to support the use of a specific form of family therapy for adolescents with AN, but the empirical basis for this so-called Maudsley approach is very limited (Fairburn, 2005). This chapter therefore will focus primarily on the research and practice of CBT and relapse prevention (RP) for BN and BED, although much of the discussion will be relevant to AN as well. This chapter will conclude with case examples of a woman with BN and a man with BED.

The National Institute for Clinical Excellence (NICE, 2004) in the United Kingdom has designated CBT as the preferred treatment for adults with BN. The institute based this decision on a rigorous review of the literature, which included multiple randomized controlled trials (RCTs) showing that CBT for BN is superior to psychotropic medication and to other forms of psychological treatment, such as interpersonal therapy (IPT). The NICE guidelines had never before recommended a psychological treatment as the preferred treatment for a mental disorder (Wilson & Shafran, 2005).

NICE (2004) also recommended CBT as the preferred treatment for adults with BED based on the strength of the evidence, although CBT is not the only effective treatment. CBT has been shown to be superior to medication in the treatment of BED (Grilo, Masheb & Wilson, 2005; Ricca et al., 2001), but it has not been shown to be superior to IPT (Wilfley et al., 2002).

OVERVIEW OF COGNITIVE BEHAVIOR THERAPY FOR BULIMIA NERVOSA AND BINGE EATING DISORDER

In 1981, Fairburn published the original treatment manual for CBT for BN. An updated version was published in 1993 (Fairburn, Marcus & Wilson, 1993), followed by a supplement in 1997 (Wilson, Fairburn & Agras, 1997). Fairburn (1995) also published a book, *Overcoming Binge Eating*, directed at a lay audience, which included a self-help manual based on CBT. The 1993 manual, the supplement, and the Fairburn book all address the treatment of binge eating as well as BN. RP has been included in manual-based CBT in an explicit effort to address the problem of relapse, and RP is a key component of treatment. Although RP is formally taught toward the end of treatment, the earlier stages of treatment also teach techniques necessary to maintain change and resist relapse.

CBT for BN and BED generally consists of approximately 20 weekly sessions (Fairburn, Marcus et al., 1993). The final few sessions, however, may occur every other week or even once a month to allow patients the chance to practice what they have learned and become "their own therapists" (Wilson et al., 1997, p. 85). Patients sometimes experience lapses during these breaks; this gives them the chance to practice preventing lapses from becoming relapses while still in therapy.

The core elements of CBT for BN and BED include (1) creating a written self-monitoring record of all food consumed including during binges; (2) weighing weekly; (3) planning meal times so as to consume three meals and two to three snacks, separated by no more than three to four hours; (4) ceasing any compensatory behaviors such as vomiting; (5) practicing stimulus control around food; (6) engaging in alternative pleasurable activities instead of binge eating; (7) employing problem solving as needed; (8) consuming enough calories at meals and snacks; (9) eating formerly forbidden foods; (10) decreasing overconcern with shape and weight through eliminating body checking and body avoidance, and through cognitive restructuring; and last but not least (11) developing a maintenance plan to prevent relapse (Fairburn, Marcus et al., 1993). Patients are also asked to read the Fairburn (1995) book *Overcoming Binge Eating*. If patients have difficulty making any of the behavior changes just listed, the therapist works with them to increase their motivation (Wilson & Schlam, 2004) by, for example, collaboratively examining the pros and cons of making that change (Wilson et al., 1997).

RELAPSE PREVENTION FOR EATING DISORDERS

RP for eating disorders is based on Marlatt and Gordon's (1985) RP theory and interventions (originally designed for the treatment of addictions), including (1) learning to distinguish a lapse from a relapse; (2) defusing the abstinence violation effect (AVE), (3) preparing to handle high-risk situations that in the past might have led to relapse, and (4) developing a plan to handle any lapses that do occur (Marlatt & Witkiewitz, 2005). The formal RP instruction in CBT for BN or BED typically occurs during the final three treatment sessions. At this point, the therapist explains to patients that to help prevent relapse they should continue following the guidelines they have learned in treatment, and they should particularly focus on the strategies that have worked best for them. The therapist and patient discuss which strategies these are. (Patients often mention monitoring, eating every 3 to 4 hours, using alternative activities, and keeping binge foods out of the house.) Patients are informed that they can stop monitoring their food intake when it seems no longer necessary, but that if they encounter problems they should resume monitoring. Patients are encouraged to schedule regular review sessions with themselves every two weeks to check on their progress and to determine if they need to make any changes (Fairburn, 1995).

Patients are asked whether they expect to never binge or purge again, after which they are informed that it is important to have realistic expectations. They may well binge or purge again, but their cognitive appraisal of such setbacks helps determine whether it becomes a problem. Patients are taught to distinguish between a lapse and a relapse (Fairburn, Marcus et al., 1993). They are told that if they experience a lapse it is important to get back on track as soon as possible, and not to let one slip destroy the healthy changes they have made. They are also given some strategies for preventing a lapse from becoming a relapse including (1) catching the problem early before it becomes a big problem; (2) restarting the program they learned in therapy, including monitoring their food intake; and (3) determining sources of stress and using problem solving to lessen the stress (Fairburn, 1995, p. 201).

The therapist discusses with patients any situations they anticipate might make them vulnerable to relapse, and together they problem-solve to come up with ways to cope with these situations. For homework, patients are asked to develop a written RP plan (Fairburn, Marcus et al., 1993). RP plans generally state that, if needed, patients should reread the Fairburn (1995) book and start following the self-help program in the back of the book. The therapist goes over the RP plan with patients and makes suggestions before patients prepare a final version.

In a sense, RP is prepared for throughout CBT since, while striving for abstinence from binge eating, patients often succumb and binge, and thus have the chance to practice coping with a lapse. Binges frequently are triggered by the AVE. For example, patients may binge if they break a dietary rule and eat a food they consider forbidden, such as ice cream. Similarly, if patients have one binge they may decide the whole day is ruined and they might as well binge for the rest of the day. Therapists tell patients that if they do binge, they should write down what they consumed and return to monitoring and eating planned meals and snacks as soon as possible. Patients are also informed that having rigidly forbidden foods or dieting strictly may set them up for the AVE, binge eating, and subsequent relapse.

Lapses are common even when patients have had an excellent response to treatment. Olmsted and colleagues (Olmsted, Kaplan & Rockert, 2005) found in a 19-month follow-up study that even BN patients who were abstinent from bingeing and purging when treatment ended, at follow-up often reported a month in which they binged and purged. For these patients, however, a one-month lapse did not necessarily turn into a three-month relapse.

EVIDENCE ON RELAPSE PREVENTION FOR EATING DISORDERS

How effective CBT for BN and BED would be without a module on RP has not been determined. In a sense, the question is impossible to answer, since RP training is integrated throughout the treatment and is not just limited to the official module on RP towards the end of treatment.

One study (Mitchell et al., 2004) offered an intervention to prevent relapse to a portion of successful completers of CBT for BN. These patients were told to try to catch any problems early and to contact their therapist for booster sessions at no charge if they thought they were in danger of relapse. Patients would then be offered two to three booster sessions and would be allowed up to eight visits over the 17-week follow-up. Although some of the patients had problems and some relapsed during the 17 weeks after treatment, none of them contacted the clinic for booster sessions.

The authors suggest that more structured approaches to preventing relapse post-treatment, such as periodic phone contact or therapy sessions, may be more effective, although they do not suggest a time frame. In BN treatment, it may be most helpful to schedule such support in the first four months following complete symptom remission, since one study found that was the period where relapse was most likely (Kordy et al., 2002). That study also found that, six months following symptom remission, relapse rates became low and remained at that level.

Although there are few studies on the treatment of AN, there is one study suggesting that CBT is helpful in the prevention of relapse for this population. This study (Pike, Walsh, Vitousek, Wilson & Bauer, 2003) assigned AN patients after hospitalization to a year of either outpatient CBT or nutritional counseling. CBT was significantly more effective than nutritional counseling (22% versus 53% of patients relapsed), and those receiving nutritional counseling relapsed earlier. This finding is particularly important because AN is difficult to treat and relapse is common (Eckert, Halmi, Marchi, Grove & Crosby, 1995).

DEFINING RELAPSE

Definitions of relapse in eating disorders vary and have yet to be standardized. One study (Olmsted et al., 2005) compared the relapse rate in their study with the relapse rates reported in other studies of patients treated for BN. They found that as long as both studies defined relapse in the same way, the relapse rates were fairly similar. To facilitate future comparisons, Olmsted et al. (2005) recommend defining relapse as meeting full diagnostic criteria for BN (having two bulimic episodes a week on average for three months). They then suggest defining partial remission as having some symptoms but no more than two bulimic episodes a month for two months. Finally, they note that most studies consider remission to be complete abstinence from bingeing and compensatory behaviors for either one or two months.

Kordy et al. (2002) proposed the same definition of relapse for BN, but somewhat different definitions of partial remission (no more than one bulimic episode a week for a month) and full remission (abstinence for four months with no extreme shape and weight concerns). Kordy et al. (2002) define an additional term, recovery, to mean abstinence for a year with no extreme shape and weight concerns. The inclusion of shape and weight concerns in their definitions of remission and recovery is important. Olmsted et al. (2005) note that the majority of published studies have defined remission as abstinence for either one or two months. This behavioral definition of remission overlooks cognitive shape and weight concerns. However, lingering shape and weight concerns seem to increase vulnerability to relapse (Fairburn, Peveler, Jones, Hope & Doll, 1993; Keel, Dorer, Franko, Jackson & Herzog, 2005) and probably need to be addressed before treatment can be considered entirely successful. CBT, particularly the most recent versions, does attempt to decrease shape and weight concerns.

Although both Kordy et al. (2002) and Olmsted et al. (2005) recommend defining relapse for BN as meeting diagnostic criteria, this practice is not yet standard. For example, Halmi et al. (2002) defined relapse as bingeing or purging even once in the past month, an approach that could be criticized for viewing a mere lapse as a relapse. Using this approach, Halmi et al. (2002) reported that 44% of BN patients successfully treated with CBT had relapsed within 4 months after treatment. Fairburn and Cooper (2003) pointed out that this relapse rate was high for CBT for BN and questioned how relapse had been defined in the study. In fact, after 4 months only 25% were considered to have relapsed when relapse was defined as meeting criteria for an eating disorder (Halmi, Agras, Mitchell, Wilson & Crow, 2003).

PREDICTORS OF RELAPSE

Identifying the predictors of relapse can help researchers determine what elements to target to prevent relapse more effectively. Halmi et al. (2002) examined the predictors of relapse in patients with BN who were successfully treated with CBT. Predictors of relapse in this study included a shorter number of weeks abstinent from binge eating and purging at the conclusion of treatment, more restrained eating, "a higher level of preoccupation and ritualization of eating and less motivation for change" (Halmi et al., 2002, p. 1105). Another study (Fairburn, Peveler et al., 1993) found that for BN patients who had a good response to one of three treatments (CBT, IPT, or behavior therapy), the extent the patients had overvalued ideas regarding the importance of their shape and weight predicted relapse. A third study (Keel et al., 2005) similarly found that, for patients with BN who had achieved full remission, excessive concern about their shape or weight predicted relapse. Poor psychosocial functioning also predicted relapse in this sample.

These studies suggest important targets of RP including helping patients develop a healthier body image (Keel et al., 2005), helping patients improve their psychosocial functioning, and encouraging patients to decrease restrained eating by consuming enough calories. Patients should also be encouraged to remain completely abstinent from bingeing and purging if possible. In one sample, patients with BN who remained symptom free for four months had a fairly low risk of relapse (Kordy et al., 2002). A higher frequency of vomiting at the end of treatment is also associated with a higher risk of relapse (Olmsted, Kaplan & Rockert, 1994). Thus, it should also help prevent relapse if patients can at least decrease, if not eliminate, vomiting during treatment. Halmi et al. (2002) suggest that it may decrease relapse if CBT treatment is lengthened for patients who arrive at the allotted number of therapy sessions having achieved only a short period of abstinence.

INNOVATIONS IN RELAPSE PREVENTION FOR EATING DISORDERS

Approximately 30 to 50 percent of patients with BN respond to CBT with complete abstinence. Many others improve substantially, but some do not respond to treatment or drop out. One study (Halmi et al., 2003) found that, among those patients who responded with abstinence to CBT for BN, 25 percent had relapsed after four months and once again met criteria for an eating disorder. Researchers are actively pursuing ways to increase the efficacy of CBT and to decrease relapse, including (a) evaluating a more individualized, transdiagnostic CBT approach; (b) including a focus on acceptance; (c) incorporating mindfulness techniques; and (d) refining interventions based on a greater understanding of relapse.

ENHANCED COGNITIVE BEHAVIOR THERAPY

Fairburn, Cooper, and Shafran (2003) recently proposed an extension of manual-based CBT for BN. They call this enhanced version transdiagnostic because it ignores traditional diagnoses and is intended for any eating disorder appropriate for outpatient therapy. The basic treatment remains 20 weeks, but there is an extended 40-week version for patients who are underweight.

The treatment includes four optional modules on interpersonal issues, extreme perfectionism, mood intolerance, and poor self-esteem. There is some evidence that problems in these areas contribute to the maintenance of eating disorders in some patients. For example, as mentioned earlier, Keel et al. (2005) found that poor psychosocial functioning helped predict relapse.

Addressing these four areas should improve outcome and help prevent relapse. Therapists decide which modules to include by assessing patients' progress after the first four weeks of treatment (Fairburn et al., 2003). The treatment, in many ways, still resembles CBT for BN as described earlier; however, the four additional modules are added to treatment as needed. This more individualized approach should more fully treat the mechanisms that maintain the disorder, thus improving treatment outcome and more effectively preventing relapse. This innovative transdiagnostic approach is currently being evaluated.

A FOCUS ON ACCEPTANCE

In developing dialectical behavior therapy (DBT), Linehan (1993) hypothesized that the relentless emphasis on change in CBT might be more effective if it were tempered by a complementary emphasis on acceptance. DBT has had a profound influence on psychological treatment. In 1996, Wilson suggested that eating disorders treatment could benefit from Linehan's concept of a dialectic between acceptance and change. More specifically, Wilson proposed that once eating disorder patients have made lifestyle changes so that they are eating and exercising in a moderate, healthy way, they need to accept their shape and weight or remain vulnerable to relapse. RP for eating disorders therefore has evolved to include an emphasis on acceptance. Patients need to accept that rigid dieting makes them vulnerable to relapse, that food may remain a loaded issue, that their body shape and weight are not readily malleable, and that vigilance may be required to avoid relapse.

One way therapists can help patients move toward acceptance is by asking them to generate lists of the short- and long-term pros and cons of change (Wilson et al., 1997). For example, a patient can create a list of the pros and cons of dieting versus accepting her current weight. Although in some ways a focus on acceptance in CBT is fairly new, analyzing the pros and cons is derived from a strategy that Marlatt (1985) had earlier described as "the decision matrix," which in turn was based on decision-making research by Janis and Mann (1977).

Another way therapists can incorporate a focus on acceptance, as well as mindfulness and emotion regulation, into CBT treatment is by including modules from the DBT skills training manual (Linehan, 1993). These modules integrate easily into CBT because DBT is conceptually compatible with CBT. DBT has also been adapted as a stand-alone treatment for BN and BED focused on affect regulation, and results thus far have been promising (Safer, Telch & Agras, 2001; Telch, Agras & Linehan, 2001).

MINDFULNESS

There is considerable interest in incorporating mindfulness techniques into CBT for eating disorders. Mindfulness could potentially help patients with stress management, eating with greater awareness and satisfaction, and coping with negative affect and urges to binge. One technique, called "urge surfing," involves mindfully observing but not acting upon an urge to binge. This technique is adapted from substance abuse treatment (e.g., Marlatt & Witkiewitz, 2005, p. 15).

Mindfulness and acceptance seem particularly suited to decreasing patients' concerns about their body shape and weight (Wilson, 2004), concerns that have been shown to predict relapse (Fairburn, Peveler et al., 1993; Keel et al., 2005). Mindfulness can help patients to develop metacognitive awareness and thus distance themselves from their negative thoughts about their shape and weight. Through mindfulness, patients can learn to see these negative thoughts as events in their mind that come and go and may not reflect reality (Segal, Williams & Teasdale, 2002, p. 38). Building on Teasdale and colleagues' (Teasdale, Segal & Williams, 1995) observations on coping with depressive thoughts, therapists can help patients learn to say to themselves: "Now I am in the state where I feel like I'm fat and disgusting but this feeling will pass" rather than "I am fat and disgusting and that is reality." Ideally, then, patients can mindfully observe their negative thoughts without immediately locking into their former eating disordered mindset—a mindset in which their shape and weight are of overriding importance and worth such sacrifices as skipping meals and purging.

Mindfulness-based cognitive therapy decreases the incidence of relapse in patients who have had three or more episodes of depression (Ma & Teasdale, 2004; Teasdale et al., 2000). It is theorized that mindfulness training works, at least in part, because it stops patients from automatically sinking into their former familiar depressogenic mind-set. Perhaps training in mindfulness can similarly decrease relapse rates in eating disorder patients by preventing them from fully reactivating their dysfunctional overconcern with their shape and weight.

Another way mindfulness may be used to address body dissatisfaction is through mirror exposure, a procedure that involves patients standing in front of a three-way mirror and mindfully and nonjudgmentally describing their body from head to toe. Many patients with eating disorders avoid mirrors and this exercise can help them overcome their fear and develop a more realistic and accepting attitude toward their bodies. There is some evidence (Delinsky & Wilson, 2006) of the effectiveness of mirror exposure when combined with behavioral exercises to stop body checking (e.g., pinching or measuring certain parts) and body avoidance (e.g., wearing baggy clothes), at least in an analogue sample of college women high in shape and weight concerns.

A NEW THEORY OF RELAPSE

Recent changes in our understanding of learning and extinction have the potential to help therapists prevent relapse more effectively. For example, Bouton (2000) has developed a contextual theory of why relapse occurs even after a behavior has been extinguished. Bouton and Swartzentruber (1991) found that "... extinction does not erase the original learning, but rather makes behavior especially sensitive to the background, or context, in which it occurs" (p. 123). Extinction also seems to be more vulnerable to contextual effects than acquisition. Therefore, therapy can successfully extinguish a behavior in one context, but the maladaptive behavior can reappear when the context changes. An example of this phenomenon in eating disorders is a patient who drove past a bakery where she used to buy chocolate éclairs and then return to her car and binge on them. The patient had been abstinent from bingeing and purging for over a month, but the context of the bakery elicited her old behavior and she, once again, binged on éclairs in the car.

Bouton (2000) lists a number of contexts in which patients may revert to previously extinguished behaviors including specific physical places, moods, or after time has passed. To prevent relapse, therapists and patients need to determine the contexts in which patients previously engaged in the maladaptive behavior. Bouton (2000) suggests that patients can then practice their adaptive behaviors in the difficult contexts they encounter most frequently (such as eating from a buffet or eating dinner alone). Patients can also learn to avoid, as much as possible, contexts in which they are particularly vulnerable to relapse (such as not eating for 6 hours and then buying a whole pizza with the unrealized intention of having leftovers).

Bjork and Bjork (1992) developed a "new theory of disuse," a theory compatible with Bouton's (2000) approach, that helps explain relapse. Lang, Craske, and Bjork (1999) used Bjork and Bjork's (1992) theory to suggest ways to improve CBT. Bjork and Bjork's (1992) new theory of disuse proposes that any learning possesses a certain retrieval strength (how easily accessible the memory is at a given moment) and a certain storage strength (how strong the memory is more permanently). Lang, Craske, and Bjork (1999) argue that at the completion of effective psychological treatment, the recent adaptive learning's retrieval strength will be stronger than the old maladaptive learning's retrieval strength. The old maladaptive learning probably has greater storage strength, however, since it has been practiced over a longer period of time. Without practice, over time both the old and new learning lose retrieval strength, but the old learning loses less because of its greater storage strength. The old maladaptive learning therefore returns leading to relapse. Lang et al. (1999) believe therapy must maximize any new learning's storage strength, and not just its retrieval strength, to increase the likelihood that in the future patients still will engage in the new, rather than the old, behaviors.

Lang and colleagues (1999) recommend strategies designed to prevent relapse by enhancing the storage and retrieval strength of new, adaptive learning. They suggest that patients must develop adaptive behaviors in response to cues that formerly evoked only maladaptive behaviors. To stop the reappearance of maladaptive behaviors and to strengthen adaptive learning Lang et al. (1999) make a number of recommendations, some of which we have tailored to fit the treatment of eating disorders:

(1) Therapists should schedule sessions close together at first and then gradually farther and farther apart. Patients thus have time to partly forget the adaptive behaviors they have learned. When they then successfully recall these behaviors, it strengthens their memories for the behaviors and increases the likelihood they will remember to perform them in the future.

(2) Patients should practice the new healthy behaviors they learn in therapy in a variety of challenging contexts, and while feeling different moods, to increase the likelihood that in any given context (be it a location or an emotional state) they will retrieve their adaptive rather than their maladaptive behaviors. This recommendation resembles Bouton's (2000) recommendation that patients practice their adaptive behavior in the challenging contexts where they are most likely to need it. For example, some patients always

purge if they feel "uncomfortably full" after they eat. These patients need to practice tolerating the feeling of being full in a variety of situations (e.g., in a restaurant, alone at home) and moods in which they previously would have purged. With practice, they can learn to tolerate the discomfort and resist the urge to purge regardless of the circumstances.

(3) It is important that patients continue to practice and use the techniques they have learned in therapy so that they do not start to forget them. Öst (1989) evaluated an intervention intended to help patients remember what they learned in therapy and prevent relapse. If his intervention were adapted and updated for eating disorder patients, it might work as follows. After the end of treatment, therapists would e-mail their patients first every two weeks and then once a month for at least the first four months. The e-mail would contain a form to complete and return similar to the review checklist Fairburn (1995) included in the self-help manual. The questions on the Fairburn (1995) review checklist that patients are supposed to ask themselves include: "Are the gaps between my meals and snacks no longer than three to four hours? . . . When the opportunity arises, am I using my list of alternative activities?" (p. 196). After therapists received the return e-mail, they would briefly follow up with patients by telephone.

A pilot study (Robinson et al., in press) explored using text messaging via cell phones as a way to help prevent relapse in BN patients following treatment. There was no comparison group and patients did not use the text messaging extensively, but patients appeared to maintain their treatment gains and, as the authors point out, text messaging may help identify early signs of relapse.

Another technique that may help prevent relapse is to encourage patients, while they are still doing well, to rehearse how much better off they are now than they were prior to treatment. For example, it may be helpful for patients with BN to actively think about how much happier they are now than when they were dieting and bingeing. Otherwise patients tend to forget how difficult things were, and they are tempted to try to diet again. New learning is fragile and easily forgotten, and it needs to be strengthened. Rehearsing how well the treatment has worked should enhance the retrieval of therapy-induced learning when patients need it during lapses.

OTHER APPROACHES TO TREATING EATING DISORDERS

While innovations within CBT are evaluated, CBT that follows the current manuals (Fairburn et al., 1993; Wilson et al., 1997) remains the treatment of choice for BN and BED. There are also other treatments, however, that have received some empirical support, namely IPT and antidepressant medication. These approaches may be effective for patients who do not want CBT, do not respond to CBT, or do not have access to it.

INTERPERSONAL THERAPY

IPT has been used to treat both BN and BED. In the treatment of BN, one study found CBT to be faster and more effective than IPT immediately following treatment, but at the one-year follow-up the two treatment conditions were equivalent (Agras, Walsh, Fairburn, Wilson & Kraemer, 2000). In the treatment of BED, studies have found that CBT and IPT produce similar outcomes (Wilfley et al., 1993, 2002). A manual is published on IPT for BN (Fairburn, 1997), and group IPT for BED is closely derived from this manual (Wilfley, Frank, Welch, Spurrell & Rounsaville, 1998; Wilfley, MacKenzie, Welch, Ayres & Weissman, 2000). IPT does not focus on the patient's eating the way CBT does. Instead the patient identifies a few specific interpersonal problems, sets goals related to those problems, and works to achieve them. As the theory of RP suggests, if a patient's interpersonal life is satisfactory, the patient should be less vulnerable to relapse. Although it is not extensively addressed in treatment manuals for BN, properly done CBT can also effectively address interpersonal issues through such techniques as problem solving and assertiveness training.

MEDICATION

CBT has been shown to be more effective than antidepressant medication in the treatment of BN (Whittal, Agras & Gould, 1999). Nevertheless, antidepressant medication is more effective than placebo for BN. Pharmacotherapy has also been studied as a way to prevent relapse in BN patients following initial treatment with medication. Although pharmacotherapy does reduce relapse rates, many patients stop taking the medication (for a review see Mitchell et al., 2004). CBT is also more effective than antidepressant medication in the treatment of BED (Grilo et al., 2005; Ricca et al., 2001). The findings are mixed as to whether antidepressant medication is more effective than placebo for patients with BED. A recent study (Grilo et al., 2005) found that fluoxetine was not more effective than placebo in the treatment of BED.

ASSESSMENT

Before considering two case studies in detail, we will review assessment instruments and some challenges therapists frequently face when implementing CBT for eating disorders.

In clinical trials, the Eating Disorder Examination (EDE; Fairburn & Cooper, 1993) is the generally used pretreatment to determine eligibility and post-treatment to assess outcome. The EDE, a semi-structured clinical interview, is considered the gold standard for diagnosing an eating disorder and determining its severity. The EDE has well-documented reliability and validity (Cooper, Cooper & Fairburn, 1989; Guest, 2000). There is also a pencil-and-paper version, the Eating Disorder Examination-Self-Report Questionnaire Version (EDE-Q; Fairburn & Beglin, 1994), which has demonstrated adequate reliability and validity for the assessment of BN and BED (Black & Wilson, 1996; Grilo, Masheb & Wilson, 2001; Sysko, Walsh & Fairburn, 2005). The Eating Disorder Diagnostic Scale (Stice, Telch & Rizvi, 2000) is a more recent self-report questionnaire that can be used diagnostically. Diagnoses using this scale show test-retest reliability and good criterion validity with diagnoses using structured interviews. Finally, the Body Shape Questionnaire (BSQ; Cooper, Taylor, Cooper & Fairburn, 1987) is a valid and reliable self-report questionnaire that assesses body image dissatisfaction (Rosen, Jones, Ramirez & Waxman, 1996).

IMPLEMENTING CBT

CBT for BN generally is administered individually, and CBT for BED is administered either individually or in a group. Psychologists are probably the most likely to be trained to conduct CBT for eating disorders, but some psychiatrists and social workers also have received training and conduct the treatment. To implement the treatment effectively, it is not enough to understand how to carry out the various interventions described in the manual. Therapists must also understand the cognitive behavioral model of what maintains the disorder that is detailed in the manual. This model, together with more general cognitive behavioral principles, guides therapists when unique situations arise with a patient and the manual provides little or no direction.

The session structure in CBT for BN or BED is generally as follows. All sessions except the first begin with a brief review of the patient's food monitoring records and other homework. The therapist, with the patient's input, then sets an agenda for the session, and the therapist and patient discuss the topics and interventions agreed upon. The therapist then gives a brief summary of the session and assigns homework. Treatment typically involves between 16 and 20 sessions.

At the end of treatment, patients ideally will be eating moderately and regularly, and will have ceased any binge eating or compensatory behaviors for at least two months. In addition, patients' negative body image ideally will have improved at least to the point where they have no more "normative discontent" with their bodies than the majority of women in this culture do (Striegel-Moore, Silberstein & Rodin, 1986).

There are a number of difficulties typically encountered while conducting CBT for BN or BED. We will review four. One primary difficulty is that patients fear weight gain. This fear means they may be reluctant to give up dieting and engaging in compensatory behaviors. They also may be afraid to weigh themselves only once a week. Patients can be informed that most people do not gain weight while in this treatment. Indeed, in the case of BED, eliminating binge eating can stop additional weight gain (Wilfley, Wilson & Agras, 2003). Ultimately, however, the therapist must encourage patients to conduct a behavioral experiment by changing their behavior and seeing if they gain weight. Patients generally do not gain weight when, for example, they replace skipping meals and bingeing with eating regular meals and snacks. It is this experience that helps patients to overcome their fear.

A second related difficulty that therapists encounter is how to address BN patients' body dissatisfaction effectively. BN patients do not want to hear that after they have developed healthy moderate eating and exercise habits, they must accept their weight even if it is heavier than they like. Patients need to accept what they can and cannot change, but this is a hard lesson for many (Wilson, 1996). Asking BN patients to list the pros and cons of continuing to pursue the thin ideal is often a good place to start. Perhaps a reachable outcome for many BN patients is to recognize that, as Orimoto and Vitousek (1992) state: "the thin ideal is unattainable for them, and that its pursuit exacts an unacceptable toll in personal suffering and is incompatible with the achievement of other important goals" (p. 117). Unfortunately, as Orimoto and Vitousek (1992) also note, patients' acceptance of the situation may fade with time and exposure to their culture, family, and friends' emphasis on the thin ideal. Body dissatisfaction and desire for weight loss remain an Achilles' heel for many BN patients, and they are prone to resume dieting believing they have recovered. Too often, rigid food restriction leads back to the diet-binge cycle and to relapse.

A third difficulty therapists may encounter is that, although BN and BED patients are assigned homework to develop a written RP plan, a number of patients do not complete it the first time it is assigned. An RP plan can be developed in session with the therapist, but it is better if patients take ownership of the plan and develop a draft at home. Then the therapist can help patients in session to revise the plan. There are a number of techniques to encourage homework completion when treating eating disorders (Schlam and Wilson, in press), and these can be used to help patients complete an RP plan.

A final practical difficulty is that with only approximately 20 sessions, there is not much time to focus on RP. Sessions 18 through 20 are intended to be devoted to RP, and for patients who respond early to treatment this schedule works well. Some patients progress through the treatment more slowly, however, and will still be struggling with binge eating and/or purging at session 18. Rapid response to treatment is associated with good outcome in CBT for BN (Wilson, Fairburn, Agras, Walsh & Kraemer, 2002) and BED (Grilo, Masheb & Wilson, in press). The prognosis for patients who do not respond rapidly to CBT is not as good. Nevertheless, it may make sense to extend treatment somewhat for these patients rather than rush through RP training. In the treatment of BED, there is some evidence that extending CBT treatment for nonresponders can improve outcome (Eldredge et al., 1997).

CLINICAL CASE ILLUSTRATIONS

We will now present two case examples: one successful and one less so. Details of these cases have been changed to protect confidentiality.

Lisa was a 19-year-old who had struggled with BN for six years. Lisa had a body mass index (BMI) of 23, in the normal range, but was convinced that she was fat. She binged and then vomited approximately four times a week. At the end of the first session, Lisa's therapist encouraged her to begin, as soon as she got home, writing down the food she ate immediately after she ate it and to record any purges.

When Lisa returned for session 2, she brought in her completed monitoring records. Her therapist praised her hard work, and together they examined the records in detail. Her therapist observed that on the two days that Lisa had binged and purged, she had not written down what she ate during the binge and she had stopped monitoring for the rest of the day. Her therapist pointed out this example of all-or-nothing thinking and encouraged Lisa to get back on track with monitoring as soon as possible after a binge and, indeed, to monitor the binge itself. This example provided Lisa with some early experience with the idea that after a lapse it is possible, and important, to limit the damage and to get back on track.

Lisa's next homework assignment was to plan daily the times she would eat three meals and two to three snacks. Lisa was not accustomed to eating so frequently. She tended to skip breakfast and sometimes skipped lunch. On evenings when she did not binge, she typically ate a small salad with grilled chicken for dinner. Lisa was extremely worried about gaining weight if she ate so frequently. Her therapist reassured her that, in general, when patients with BN start eating regularly they do not tend to gain weight because the meals replace the binge eating. Her therapist also suggested she experiment with eating regularly since she could always return to her previous behavior.

Lisa did begin to eat regularly. She also developed a useful list of alternative activities to use when she felt like binge eating, including going for a walk with a friend and taking a bubble bath by candlelight. The combination of eating regularly and using alternative activities helped Lisa to stop binge eating entirely, which eliminated her desire to purge.

In session 10, however, Lisa appeared quite distraught. She had gained four pounds, she said, adding that after she had weighed herself that week, she had binged on chocolate chip cookies and subsequently purged. She had then decided that she needed to diet more strictly and had begun to count calories using her monitoring forms. Lisa's therapist identified her behavior as an example of the AVE since Lisa had broken a personal rule that she must not gain weight and subsequently binged and purged. Her therapist also pointed out that counting calories and having a strict calorie limit would leave Lisa vulnerable to the AVE and to staying obsessed with food. Lisa's therapist then went over with her the information in the Fairburn (1995) book Lisa had been asked to read. The book encourages patients not to overreact to small fluctuations in weight, but to look at trends over several weeks; patients need to accept a weight range for themselves rather than insisting on weighing a specific number. Her therapist also pointed out that even after gaining four pounds Lisa was still well within the normal BMI range.

Lisa said that intellectually she understood that scientists might consider her weight normal, but that for her it was completely unacceptable. Her therapist then realized that perhaps she had been lecturing Lisa too much. They spent the remainder of that session and the next exploring the pros and cons for Lisa of dieting versus accepting her current weight.

Lisa's therapist pointed out that dieting would keep Lisa focused on her appearance. Her therapist said: "It's like if you keep picking at a sore, then it never heals. You can be happy even if you're not as thin as you'd like to be. It would be ideal if you could get to the point where you can say, 'I'd like it better if I lost a little weight, but it's not a catastrophe if I don't.'" Lisa continued to restrict her food somewhat, but she was able to stop counting calories. Since Lisa was no longer binge eating, her therapist eventually let the matter drop. They focused on helping Lisa to improve her body image through decreasing avoidance and body checking. Lisa had always avoided wearing tank tops and shorts because she felt her arms and legs were too fat, but now she began to wear them. Lisa also succeeded in eliminating some of the body checking she engaged in, such as pinching her arms and stomach before going to bed at night.

The last few sessions of treatment were focused on RP. Lisa agreed to donate to charity her clothes that she had worn when she was younger and that were now too small for her. She also got rid of a specific pair of tight jeans that she utilized to determine whether, in her view, she weighed too much. Lisa wrote up a detailed RP plan and revised it with the help of her therapist. The plan included her intention to restart monitoring if she noticed any problems and to reread the book *Overcoming Binge Eating* and, if necessary, to follow the self-help plan in the book. The plan also stated explicitly that it was a bad idea to go back to strict dieting since restriction would put her at risk of binge eating. In addition, the therapist and Lisa discussed how in the past when Lisa had dieted strictly it had led to binge eating.

For the first month after treatment Lisa succeeded in not binge eating or purging. She remained dissatisfied with her weight, however, and a friend told her about The Zone diet. Her friend had lost 25 pounds on the diet, and Lisa decided that since she was doing so well with not binge eating or purging she would try the diet. Lisa lost some weight on the diet too and felt great but one night, after a fight with her mother, Lisa ended up bingeing on a gallon of chocolate chip cookie dough ice cream. After that night, Lisa began to binge and purge more regularly and regained the weight she had lost.

During this time it did not occur to Lisa to look at or follow her RP plan. When things became bad enough, however, she did call her therapist and her therapist then suggested that Lisa return for several sessions and in the meantime follow her RP plan. In session, her therapist pointed out to Lisa what it says in the Fairburn (1995) book: ". . . strict dieting puts people at risk of bingeing, the return of which will run counter to any weight loss efforts" (p. 200). Lisa's dissatisfaction with her shape and weight was so intense that, although for the next two years for the most part she was able to refrain from binge eating and purging, she continued to periodically diet which led to lapses. Although Lisa was much improved, she had not yet fully overcome her eating disorder.

The second case involved a 32-year-old man named Rob with BED. Rob's BMI of 31 indicated that he was obese. In addition to binge eating nearly every day, primarily on potato chips, pizza, and fried chicken, Rob almost met criteria for alcohol abuse. In the first session, Rob's therapist suggested he monitor both what he ate and what he drank.

In the second session, Rob and his therapist examined his records together closely and noticed Rob's pattern of drinking too much at restaurants and parties and then binge eating either at the time or when he returned home. At one restaurant, however, where Rob had only two drinks, he did not binge. His therapist pointed out the section in the Fairburn (1995) book that explains that drinking too much alcohol will negatively affect self-control (p. 164). Rob's therapist suggested that he experiment with setting himself a two-drink limit and seeing whether this affected his binge eating. His therapist also recommended that Rob plan his alcohol consumption, explaining that if he is taken by surprise, then he would do what is automatic.

Rob's therapist also noted that, like many patients with BN or BED, Rob tended to eat little during the day and then binge in the late afternoon or early evening, particularly if he felt upset and tired after a stressful day. On those days, Rob would draw a big X through the rest of the day on his monitoring sheet and decide he could binge on whatever he wanted since that day was already ruined. Rob's therapist identified this as an example of the AVE and encouraged Rob to write down what he ate in the binge as soon as possible after it happened and then to continue to monitor for the rest of the day. By avoiding monitoring, Rob was giving up a technique that could help him control his eating.

Limiting his alcohol consumption and eating regularly throughout the day helped Rob to stop binge eating entirely. Toward the end of treatment, Rob mentioned that he was going to Atlantic City for a bachelor party and was concerned that while he was there he might end up drinking too much and binge eating. Rob and his therapist problem-solved together regarding the trip. Rob decided that he would stick to his two-drink limit and that he would look over the buffet, decide what to eat, and only return for seconds once. His therapist recommended that Rob take a snack for the trip there to make sure he ate every three to four hours. Rob, however, did not like that idea since he wanted to save all his calories for eating from the buffet, but he said he would think about it. His therapist also suggested that Rob give himself permission to eat more than usual while avoiding bingeing, explaining that it would help him resist bingeing if he were enjoying himself and not feeling deprived.

Rob had an enjoyable trip to Atlantic City, made a little money playing blackjack, and did not binge. He said that he had "gambled" a bit by not taking a snack or monitoring what he ate, but he had kept to his two-drink limit and he had looked over the buffet and planned what he wanted to eat. One year following treatment, Rob remained binge free and able to stick to his two-drink limit. He did not lose any weight, but he succeeded in maintaining his weight whereas before he had been steadily gaining weight.

SUMMARY AND CONCLUSIONS

CBT is an effective treatment for both BN and BED, and efforts are under way to make CBT even more effective. Part of that effort should involve examining how best to prevent relapse. Research is needed to identify more of the mechanisms that maintain eating disorders and the most effective ways of influencing those mechanisms. Such research should help more patients to "break the back" of their eating disorder and achieve lasting recovery.

REFERENCES

Agras, W.S., Brandt, H.A., Bulik, C.M., Dolan-Sewell, R., Fairburn, C.G., Halmi, K.A. et al. (2004). Report of the National Institutes of Health workshop on overcoming barriers to treatment research in anorexia nervosa. *International Journal of Eating Disorders* **35**:509–521.

Agras, W.S., Walsh, B.T., Fairburn, C.G., Wilson, G.T., Kraemer, H.C. (2000). A multicenter comparison of cognitive-behavioral therapy and interpersonal psychotherapy for bulimia nervosa. *Archives of General Psychiatry* **57**:459–466.

American Psychiatric Association. (2000). *Diagnostic and Statistical Manual of Mental Disorders, 4e* (text revision). Washington, DC: Author.

Bjork, R.A., Bjork, E.L. (1992). A new theory of disuse and an old theory of stimulus fluctuation. In Healy, A.F., Kosslyn, S.M., Shiffrin, R.M., eds., *From learning processes to cognitive processes: Essays in honor of William K. Estes*, Vol. 2, 35–67. Hillsdale, NJ: Erlbaum.

Black, C.M.D., Wilson, G.T. (1996). Assessment of eating disorders: Interview versus questionnaire. *International Journal of Eating Disorders* **20**:43–50.

Bouton, M.E. (2000). A learning theory perspective on lapse, relapse, and the maintenance of behavior change. *Health Psychology* **19**:57–63.

Bouton, M.E., Swartzentruber, D. (1991). Sources of relapse after extinction in Pavlovian and instrumental learning. *Clinical Psychology Review* **11**:123–140.

Cooper, P.J., Taylor, M.J., Cooper, Z., Fairburn, C.G. (1987). The development and validation of the Body Shape Questionnaire. *International Journal of Eating Disorders* **6**:485–494.

Cooper, Z., Cooper, P.J., Fairburn, C.G. (1989). The validity of the Eating Disorder Examination and its subscales. *British Journal of Psychiatry* **154**:807–812.

Delinsky, S.S., Wilson, G.T. (2006). Mirror exposure for the treatment of body image disturbance. *International Journal of Eating Disorders* **39**:108–116.

Eckert, E.D., Halmi, K.A., Marchi, P., Grove, W., Crosby, R. (1995). Ten-year follow-up of anorexia nervosa: Clinical course and outcome. *Psychological Medicine* **25**:143–156.

Eldredge, K.L., Agras, W.S., Arnow, B., Telch, C.F., Bell, S., Castonguay, L. et al. (1997). The effects of extending cognitive-behavioral therapy for binge eating disorder among initial treatment nonresponders. *International Journal of Eating Disorders* **21**:347–352.

Fairburn, C.G. (1981). A cognitive-behavioral approach to the management of bulimia. *Psychological Medicine* **11**:707–711.

Fairburn, C.G. (1995). *Overcoming binge eating.* New York: Guilford Press.

Fairburn, C.G. (1997). Interpersonal psychotherapy for bulimia nervosa. In Garner, D.M., Garfinkel, P., eds., *Handbook of treatment for eating disorders*, 278–294. New York: Guilford Press.

Fairburn, C.G. (2005). Evidence-based treatment of anorexia nervosa. *International Journal of Eating Disorders* **37**:S26–S30.

Fairburn, C.G., Beglin, S.J. (1994). Assessment of eating disorders: Interview or self-report questionnaire? *International Journal of Eating Disorders* **16**:363–370.

Fairburn, C.G., Cooper, Z. (1993). The eating disorder examination, 12e. In Fairburn, C.G., Wilson, G.T., eds., *Binge eating: Nature, assessment and treatment*, 317–360. New York: Guilford Press.

Fairburn, C.G., Cooper, Z. (2003). Relapse in Bulimia Nervosa. *Archives of General Psychiatry* **60**:850.

Fairburn, C.G., Cooper, Z., Shafran, R. (2003). Cognitive behaviour therapy for eating disorders: A "transdiagnostic" theory and treatment. *Behaviour Research and Therapy* **41**:509–528.

Fairburn, C.G., Marcus, M.D., Wilson, G.T. (1993). Cognitive-behavioral therapy for binge eating and bulimia nervosa: A comprehensive treatment manual. In Fairburn, C.G., Wilson, G.T., eds., *Binge eating: Nature, assessment and treatment*, 361–404. New York: Guilford Press.

Fairburn, C.G., Peveler, R.C., Jones, R., Hope, R.A., Doll, H.A. (1993). Predictors of 12-month outcome in bulimia nervosa and the influence of attitudes to shape and weight. *Journal of Consulting and Clinical Psychology* **61**:696–698.

Grilo, C.M., Masheb, R.M., Wilson, G.T. (2001). A comparison of different methods for assessing the features of eating disorders in patients with binge eating disorder. *Journal of Consulting and Clinical Psychology* **69**:317–322.

Grilo, C.M., Masheb, R.M., Wilson, G.T. (2005). Efficacy of cognitive behavioral therapy and fluoxetine for the treatment of Binge Eating Disorder: A randomized double-blind placebo-controlled comparison. *Biological Psychiatry* **57**:301–309.

Grilo, C.M., Masheb, R.M., Wilson, G.T. (In press). Rapid response to treatment for binge eating disorder. *Journal of Consulting and Clinical Psychology.*

Guest, T. (2000). Using the Eating Disorder Examination in the assessment of bulimia and anorexia: Issues of reliability and validity. *Social Work in Health Care* **31**:71–83.

Halmi, K., Agras, S., Mitchell, J., Wilson, T., Crow, S. (2003). Relapse in Bulimia Nervosa—Reply. *Archives of General Psychiatry* **60**:850–851.

Halmi, K.A., Agras, W.S., Mitchell, J., Wilson, G.T., Crow, S., Bryson, S.W. et al. (2002). Relapse predictors of patients with bulimia nervosa who achieved abstinence through cognitive behavioral therapy. *Archives of General Psychiatry* **59**:1105–1109.

Janis, I., Mann, L. (1977). *Decision-making.* New York: The Free Press.

Keel, P.K., Dorer, D.J., Franko, D.L., Jackson, S.C., Herzog, D.B. (2005). Postremission predictors of relapse in women with eating disorders. *The American Journal of Psychiatry* **162**:2263–2268.

Kordy, H., Kramer, B., Palmer, R.L., Papezova, H., Pellet, J., Richard, M. et al. (2002). Remission, recovery, relapse, and recurrence in eating disorders: Conceptualization and illustration of a validation strategy. *Journal of Clinical Psychology* **58**:833–846.

Lang, A.J., Craske, M.G., Bjork, R.A. (1999). Implications of a new theory of disuse for the treatment of emotional disorders. *Clinical Psychology: Science and Practice* **6**:80–94.

Linehan, M.M. (1993). *Skills training manual for treating borderline personality disorder.* New York: Guilford Press.

Ma, S.H., Teasdale, J.D. (2004). Mindfulness-based cognitive therapy for depression: Replication and exploration of differential relapse prevention effects. *Journal of Consulting and Clinical Psychology* **72**:31–40.

Marlatt, G.A. (1985). Cognitive assessment and intervention procedures for relapse prevention. In Marlatt, G.A., Gordon, J.R., eds., *Relapse prevention: Maintenance strategies in the treatment of addictive behaviors, 1e*, 201–279. New York: Guilford Press.

Marlatt, G.A., Gordon, J.R., eds. (1985). *Relapse prevention: Maintenance strategies in the treatment of addictive behaviors, 1e*. New York: Guilford Press.

Marlatt, G.A., Witkiewitz, K. (2005). Relapse prevention for alcohol and drug problems. In Marlatt, G.A., Donovan, D.M., eds., *Relapse prevention: Maintenance strategies in the treatment of addictive behaviors, 2e*, 1–44. New York: Guilford Press.

Mitchell, J.E., Agras, W.S., Wilson, G.T., Halmi, K., Kraemer, H., Crow, S. (2004). A trial of a relapse prevention strategy in women with bulimia nervosa who respond to cognitive-behavior therapy. *International Journal of Eating Disorders* **35**:549–555.

National Institute for Clinical Excellence. (2004). *Eating disorders—Core interventions in the treatment and management of anorexia nervosa, bulimia nervosa and related eating disorders.* NICE Clinical Guideline No. 9. London: NICE. Retrieved January 28, 2004, from http://www.nice.org.uk.

Olmsted, M.P., Kaplan, A.S., Rockert, W. (1994). Rate and prediction of relapse in bulimia nervosa. *American Journal of Psychiatry* **151**:738–743.

Olmsted, M.P., Kaplan, A.S., Rockert, W. (2005). Defining remission and relapse in bulimia nervosa. *International Journal of Eating Disorders* **38**:1–6.

Orimoto, L., Vitousek, K.B. (1992). Anorexia nervosa and bulimia nervosa. In Wilson, P.H., ed., *Principles and practice of relapse prevention*, 85–127. New York: Guilford Press.

Öst, L. (1989). A maintenance program for behavioral treatment of anxiety disorders. *Behaviour Research and Therapy* **27**:123–130.

Pike, K.M., Loeb, K.L., Vitousek, K. (1996). Cognitive-behavioral therapy for anorexia nervosa and bulimia nervosa. In Thompson, J.K., ed., *Body image, eating disorders, and obesity: An integrative guide for assessment and treatment*, 253–302. Washington, DC: American Psychological Association Press.

Pike, K.M., Walsh, B.T., Vitousek, K., Wilson, G.T., Bauer, J. (2003). Cognitive behavior therapy in the posthospitalization treatment of anorexia nervosa. *American Journal of Psychiatry* **160**:2046–2049.

Ricca, V., Mannucci, E., Mezzani, B., Moretti, S., Di Bernardo, M., Bertelli, M. et al. (2001). Fluoxetine and fluvoxamine combined with individual cognitive-behaviour therapy in binge eating disorder: A one-year follow-up study. *Psychotherapy and Psychosomatics* **70**:298–306.

Robinson, S., Perkins, S., Bauer, S., Hammond, N., Treasure, J., Schmidt, U. (In press). Relapse prevention through text messaging. *International Journal of Eating Disorders.*

Rosen, J.C., Jones, A., Ramirez, E., Waxman, S. (1996). Body Shape Questionnaire: Studies of validity and reliability. *International Journal of Eating Disorders* **20**:315–319.

Safer, D.L., Telch, C.F., Agras, W.S. (2001). Dialectical behavior therapy for bulimia nervosa. *American Journal of Psychiatry* **158**:632–634.

Schlam, T.R., Wilson, G.T. (In press). Strategies to enhance homework completion in cognitive behavioral therapy for eating disorders. In Kazantzis, N., L'Abate, L., eds., *Handbook of homework assignments in psychotherapy: Research, practice, and prevention.* New York: Springer/Verlag.

Segal, Z.V., Williams, J.M.G., Teasdale, J.D. (2002). *Mindfulness-based cognitive therapy for depression: A new approach to preventing relapse.* New York: Guilford Press.

Stice, E., Telch, C.F., Rizvi, S.L. (2000). Development and validation of the eating disorder diagnostic scale: A brief self-report measure of anorexia, bulimia, and binge-eating disorder. *Psychological Assessment* **12**:123–131.

Striegel-Moore, R.H., Silberstein, L.R., Rodin, J. (1986). Toward an understanding of risk factors for bulimia. *American Psychologist* **41**:246–263.

Sysko, R., Walsh, B.T., Fairburn, C.G. (2005). Eating Disorder Examination-Questionnaire as a measure of change in patients with bulimia nervosa. *International Journal of Eating Disorders* 37:100–106.

Teasdale, J.D., Segal, Z.V., Williams, J.M.G. (1995). How does cognitive therapy prevent depressive relapse and why should attentional control (mindfulness) training help? *Behaviour Research and Therapy* 33:25–39.

Teasdale, J.T., Segal, Z.V., Williams, J.M.G., Ridgeway, V.A., Soulsby, J.M., Lau, M.A. (2000). Prevention of relapse/recurrence in major depression by mindfulness-based cognitive therapy. *Journal of Consulting and Clinical Psychology* 68:615–623.

Telch, C.F., Agras, W.S., Linehan, M.M. (2001). Dialectical behavior therapy for binge eating disorder. *Journal of Consulting and Clinical Psychology* 69.1061–1065.

Whittal, M.L., Agras, W.S., Gould, R.A. (1999). Bulimia nervosa: A meta-analysis of psychosocial and pharmacological treatments. *Behavior Therapy* 30:117–135.

Wilfley, D.E., Agras, W.S., Telch, C.F., Rossiter, E.M., Schneider, J.A., Cole, A.G. et al. (1993). Group cognitive-behavioral therapy and group interpersonal psychotherapy for the nonpurging bulimic individual: A controlled comparison. *Journal of Consulting and Clinical Psychology* 61:296–305.

Wilfley, D.E., Frank, M.A., Welch, R., Spurrell, E.B., Rounsaville, B.J. (1998). Adapting interpersonal psychotherapy to a group format (IPT-G) for binge eating disorder: Toward a model for adapting empirically supported treatments. *Psychotherapy Research* 8:379–391.

Wilfley, D.E., MacKenzie, K.R., Welch, R.R., Ayres, V.E., Weissman, M.M. (2000). *Interpersonal psychotherapy for group*. New York: Basic Books.

Wilfley, D.E., Welch, R.R., Stein, R.I., Spurrell, E.B., Cohen, L.R., Saelens, B.E. et al. (2002). A randomized comparison of group cognitive-behavioral therapy and group interpersonal psychotherapy for the treatment of overweight individuals with binge-eating disorder. *Archives of General Psychiatry* 59:713–721.

Wilfley, D.E., Wilson, G.T., Agras, W.S. (2003). The clinical significance of binge eating disorder. *International Journal of Eating Disorders* 34:S96–S106.

Wilson, G.T. (1996). Acceptance and change in the treatment of eating disorders and obesity. *Behavior Therapy* 27:417–439.

Wilson, G.T. (2004). Acceptance and change in the treatment of eating disorders: The evolution of manual-based cognitive-behavioral therapy In Hayes, S.C., Follette, V.M., Linehan, M.M., eds., *Mindfulness and acceptance: Expanding the cognitive-behavioral tradition*, 243–260. New York: Guilford Press.

Wilson, G.T. (2005). Psychological treatment of eating disorders. *Annual Review of Clinical Psychology* 1:439–465.

Wilson, G.T., Fairburn, C.G., Agras, W.S. (1997). Cognitive-behavioral therapy for bulimia nervosa. In Garner, D.M., Garfinkel, P., eds., *Handbook of treatment for eating disorders*, 67–93. New York: Guilford Press.

Wilson, G.T., Fairburn, C.G., Agras, W.S., Walsh, B.T., Kraemer, H. (2002). Cognitive-behavioral therapy for bulimia nervosa: Time course and mechanisms of change. *Journal of Consulting and Clinical Psychology* 70:267–274.

Wilson, G.T., Schlam, T.R. (2004). The transtheoretical model and motivational interviewing in the treatment of eating and weight disorders. *Clinical Psychology Review* 24:361–378.

Wilson, G.T., Shafran, R. (2005). Eating disorders guidelines from NICE. *Lancet* 365:79–81.

INTERNET RESOURCES

- http://www.aedweb.org/
  The Academy for Eating Disorders is a multidisciplinary organization for professionals who specialize in eating disorders.
- http://www.anred.com/relpr.html
  The web site of Anorexia Nervosa and Related Disorders, Inc. includes a page on RP.
- http://www.myselfhelp.com/
  This site provides web-based self-help programs for BN, binge eating, and other psychological disorders for a small monthly fee. The programs include strategies for preventing relapse.

9

STOPPING SELF-HARM ONCE AND FOR ALL: RELAPSE PREVENTION IN DIALECTICAL BEHAVIOR THERAPY

MILTON Z. BROWN

Alliant International University
San Diego, California

ALEX L. CHAPMAN

Simon Fraser University
Burnaby, British Columbia

Behaviors that involve direct, deliberate self-harm recently have received increasing attention in the media and in research studies. Deliberate self-harm (DSH) involves the direct and intentional destruction or alteration of one's bodily tissue without the intent to die (Chapman, Gratz & Brown, 2006). Although previously considered a phenomenal characteristic only of particular subgroups of individuals (e.g., female adolescents, persons with cognitive or developmental disabilities; psychotic individuals; persons with borderline personality disorder), emerging research demonstrates a high prevalence of DSH in a variety of populations (in particular, female prisoners, college undergraduates, and high school students; see Chapman, Specht & Cellucci, 2005; Gratz, 2001; Zoroglu et al., 2003, respectively). However, rarely is DSH seen with the prevalence and frequency with which it occurs among individuals with borderline personality disorder (BPD).

Therapist's Guide to Evidence-Based
Relapse Prevention

191

BPD is characterized by ". . . a pervasive pattern of instability of interpersonal relationships, self-image, and affects, and marked impulsivity beginning by early adulthood and present in a variety of contexts" (American Psychiatric Association, p. 650). Defining features involve instability in a variety of life domains, including interpersonal functioning, mood, identity, and cognition (APA, 1994). Although the prevalence of BPD is approximately 1 to 2 percent (Torgersen, Kringlen & Cramer, 2001), it is estimated that between 9 and 40 percent of high inpatient services utilizers have a diagnosis of BPD (Surber et al., 1987; Swigar, Astrachan, Levine, Mayfield & Radovich, 1991). This disproportionately high rate of mental healthcare utilization likely is due to an exceedingly high prevalence of suicide attempts and DSH.

Although relapse prevention generally is discussed with regard to addictive behaviors and substance abuse/dependence (Irvin et al., 1999), preventing relapse also is quite relevant to DSH and other related behaviors. Similar to addictive behaviors, emerging research (Haines et al., 1995; Shaw-Welch et al., 2003), and theories (e.g., Chapman, Gratz & Brown, 2006) on DSH suggest that this behavior reduces or eliminates unwanted or intolerable emotions, particularly among persons with BPD (Chapman and Dixon-Gordon, in press). Clinically, we have observed that persons who engage in DSH have many of the experiences commonly encountered by individuals who abuse alcohol or drugs, including (1) a build-up of cravings and urges to engage in DSH over time; (2) the presence of distressing emotions as triggers for DSH (see also Chapman & Dixon-Gordon, 2005 for research on the emotions that may trigger DSH); (3) idiosyncratic "high-risk situations" (Carroll, 1996; Witkiewitz & Marlatt, 2005) consisting of people, places, and events that make it difficult for the individual to refrain from DSH; and (4) an increased probability of "relapse" following DSH.

This chapter provides an overview of the issues and strategies associated with *preventing* the relapse of deliberate self-harm. We focus on treatment of DSH among persons with BPD because there is currently little empirical evidence on treatments for DSH in other clinical populations (evidence is reviewed later). To date, Dialectical Behavior Therapy (DBT; Linehan, 1993) is the only psychosocial treatment for BPD that may be considered well-established, or *efficacious and specific* (Chambless & Ollendick, 2001). DBT consists of many interventions that aim to reduce DSH and other self-destructive behaviors, and to prevent the recurrence or relapse of these behaviors. As such, this chapter focuses on interventions in DBT that prevent relapse, providing a mix of research findings and practical clinical examples.

THE PROBLEM OF DELIBERATE SELF-HARM IN BORDERLINE PERSONALITY DISORDER

As defined in this chapter, and by others (e.g., Chapman et al., 2006; Gratz, 2001), DSH involves direct destruction or alteration of one's body tissue with the intent to cause harm, but without conscious intent to die. As such, DSH does not include suicide attempts, which involve the intent to die or other forms of behaviors that may cause harm, but are not intended directly to cause harm, such as most forms of tattooing or body piercing (when the intent is not to inflict harm), or excessive drug or alcohol use or cigarette smoking. DSH commonly involves behavior such as cutting or burning, banging or hitting oneself, but also may involve drug overdoses, self-poisoning, or other such behaviors, as long as there is direct intent to cause harm, but no intent to die.

DSH falls under the broader category of *parasuicide* (Kreitman, 1977), which involves any deliberate destruction of bodily tissue, with or without intent to die; hence, parasuicide may include DSH and/or suicide attempts. It is important to note that not everyone who engages in DSH is suicidal or has attempted suicide (Kessler, Borges & Walters, 1999; Velamoor & Cernovsky, 1992). In addition, emerging research has suggested important differences between DSH and suicide attempts (e.g., Brown, Comtois & Linehan, 2002; Chapman & Dixon-Gordon, 2006). Nonetheless, many individuals who engage in DSH also have concurrent suicide ideation and a history of suicidal behavior (Kessler et al., 1999; Velamoor & Cernovsky, 1992).

DSH is prevalent and chronic among persons with BPD. Although other diagnostic groups have comparable suicide rates, a larger proportion of persons with BPD *attempt* suicide, engage in DSH, and have repeated episodes over time (Langbehn & Pfohl, 1993; Linehan & Heard, 1997; Tanney, 1992). Lifetime prevalence rates of suicide attempts (75%), suicide completion (10%), and, in particular, DSH (69–80%) are exceptionally high (Clarkin, Widiger, Frances, Hurt & Gilmore, 1983; Stone, Hurt & Stone, 1987), compared with most clinical groups. This is hardly surprising, as parasuicidal behavior is a diagnostic criterion for BPD. However, BPD is associated with an elevated parasuicide risk even when the diagnosis is determined without the parasuicide criterion (Corbitt, Malone, Haas & Mann, 1996; Friedman, Aronoff, Clarkin, Corn & Hurt, 1983; Schaffer, Carroll & Abramowitz, 1982). Therefore, the question remains as to why persons with BPD tend to engage in DSH so frequently.

A couple of evidence-based theories have been proposed to explain DSH generally (the Experiential Avoidance Model, or EAM; Chapman, Gratz & Brown, 2006), and DSH as it specifically occurs in persons with BPD (Linehan, 1993). Linehan's *biosocial theory* proposes that the central underlying feature of BPD is pervasive "emotion dysregulation," which results from a combination of emotion vulnerability and difficulty regulating emotional experiences. According to the biosocial theory, emotion dysregulation in BPD develops from a transaction between an *invalidating rearing environment* and a biologically based vulnerability to quick, strong, and long-lasting emotional reactions (*emotion vulnerability*).

According to Linehan (1993), the individual with BPD is intensely emotional, but grows up in an environment in which he or she does not learn the skills required to regulate emotions. In addition, the invalidating environment often involves various forms of abuse, or harsh criticism, punishment, or other dysfunctional reactions to the emotional child. Consequently, persons with BPD lack adaptive skills for regulating emotions, and end up with frequent and intense emotional experiences. Sometimes DSH functions to escape negative emotions, and at other times this behavior is an automatic mood-dependent response to emotions.

According to the Experiential Avoidance Model (EAM), DSH is maintained by negative reinforcement in the form of escape or avoidance of unwanted or intolerable experiences such as distressing thoughts or emotions. In particular, DSH appears to reduce emotional arousal, and persons who engage in DSH often report that they do so in order to escape emotions (for a review, see Chapman et al., 2006). As a result, the person with BPD is caught in a vicious cycle of intense emotions and self-destructive behavior, both of which are maintained by relief or escape from emotions. Based on this conceptualization of DSH and related problems in BPD, treatments tend to focus on ways to improve emotion regulation in BPD patients.

TREATMENT FOR DELIBERATE SELF-HARM: DIALECTICAL BEHAVIOR THERAPY

Dialectical behavior therapy (DBT) originally represented an attempt to apply established behavioral and cognitive therapy techniques to the treatment of individuals with chronic suicidal behaviors and self-injury (Linehan, 1993). Over time, Dr. Marsha Linehan discovered that many of the change-oriented CBT approaches that had garnered considerable empirical evidence in the treatment of other disorders were not acceptable to multiproblem, self-injurious BPD patients. Due to an almost exclusive focus on *changing* thoughts and behaviors, patients often felt invalidated and failed to comply with CBT. As a result, Linehan incorporated into DBT acceptance-based strategies from a variety of sources, including client-centered therapies and Zen practice, aimed at conveying acceptance of the patient, as well as helping the patient learn acceptance. With its focus on both accepting the patient and helping the patient to change self-destructive behaviors (such as DSH) and work toward a fulfilling life (i.e., a "life worth living"), DBT came to rest on a theoretical foundation of *dialectical philosophy.*

Dialectical philosophy views reality as consisting of a continual interplay of opposing forces (e.g., thesis and antithesis). According to the dialectical worldview, many positions (thesis) naturally pull for an opposite position (antithesis). Thesis and antithesis exist in a "dialectical tension" until they are brought together and synthesized into a more complete whole. For instance, the tendency of therapists to push their BPD patients to *change* their destructive behavior (thesis) often elicits an opposing force; namely, patients often insist that their therapists *accept* and understand them (antithesis). In contrast, when therapists rely solely on understanding and acceptance, BPD patients often increase their demands for help (i.e., change). Either position, on its own, is incomplete—focusing only on acceptance is unlikely to stop DSH, and too much pushing for change could push the patient right out of therapy. Within this framework, DBT therapists balance a variety of interventions focused on acceptance (e.g., mindfulness skills, radical acceptance, and validation) and change (problem solving, exposure therapy, skills training, contingency management, and cognitive restructuring).

The acceptance and change-based interventions in DBT are the building blocks of a comprehensive treatment that aims to address several key functions. First, DBT involves a skills training (often delivered in a group format) designed to increase the skills and capabilities of patients with BPD. Second, standard DBT consists of weekly individual therapy sessions that focus on solving problems, improving the patient's motivation, reducing emotional reactivity, developing a life worth living, managing crises, and generalizing the patient's treatment gains to the natural environment. Third, DBT involves a treatment team (the DBT Consultation Team) that meets regularly to provide support and maintain therapists' skill and motivation, and to help structure the treatment in an effective manner. In addition, DBT may involve pharmacotherapy, case management and/ or inpatient psychiatric treatment.

RESEARCH ON TREATMENTS FOR DELIBERATE SELF-HARM

Several well-controlled studies have indicated that DBT and other similar approaches reduce DSH and prevent relapse following treatment. In the first randomized controlled trial (RCT) of DBT for BPD (Linehan et al., 1987), more patients in DBT abstained from *parasuicide* during the one-year follow-up period, compared with patients in a control condition (74% vs. 40%) that involved treatment as it normally is conducted in the community (treatment-as-usual, or TAU). Although DSH outcomes were not analyzed separately from suicide attempts in this first study, a second study did make this distinction.

In the second study of DBT for BPD (Linehan et al., in press), most patients receiving either DBT (60%) or nonbehavioral treatment by experts (58%) abstained from DSH during the one-year follow-up, in contrast with the pretreatment year (12% vs. 18%, respectively). In addition, in three other RCTs, DBT was more effective than TAU at reducing DSH (Bohus, 2004; van den Bosch, 2005; Verheul et al., 2003) and parasuicide (Koons et al., 2001) in BPD. However, none of these studies reported long-term relapse rates following treatment termination.

Additionally, there is evidence that other similar treatment approaches reduce DSH among BPD patients. For example, Dr. Kim Gratz developed a 14-week group treatment that involves strategies to improve emotion regulation and emotional acceptance/experiencing, increase behavioral activation, and block experiential avoidance behaviors (Gratz, in press). In a small clinical trial, this intervention resulted in greater reductions in DSH, compared with a treatment-as-usual condition, but thus far, no follow-up data are available.

Although all the aforementioned studies evaluated DBT or similar treatments for DSH in persons with BPD, we believe that DBT-based interventions also may be efficacious for preventing the *relapse* of DSH in patients without BPD (e.g., those with post-traumatic stress disorder or dissociative disorders). However, we know of no published studies that have examined the efficacy of DBT for reducing DSH in populations other than BPD. Several other RCTs have shown that problem-solving therapies reduce *parasuicidal acts* more than nonproblem-solving treatments or no treatment controls, but these studies have not examined DSH outcomes in particular (versus suicide attempts), and follow-up data are not yet available (Hawton et al., 1998; Turner et al., 2000).

In sum, there is some evidence that DBT and similar treatments reduce DSH and may have lasting effects (i.e., in preventing relapse); however, more research is needed to examine the long-term effects of DBT and DBT-oriented interventions for preventing relapse in persons with BPD as well as those with other clinical problems. In addition, further work is needed to identify predictors of relapse and the best ways to prevent relapse. In the next section, we highlight several potentially important factors that may contribute to relapse in self-harming individuals with BPD.

CHARACTERISTICS OF BORDERLINE PERSONALITY DISORDER THAT CONTRIBUTE TO DSH RELAPSE

Current data suggest that about half of BPD individuals treated for DSH engage in at least one additional DSH act after treatment ends (Linehan et al., in press). From the perspective of Linehan's (1993) biosocial theory, several key characteristics, behaviors, and environmental events typical of persons with BPD may contribute to relapse of DSH. Although numerous factors contribute to relapse, in this section we focus primarily on those factors related to BPD, based on the *biosocial theory* of BPD and the *experiential avoidance model* of DSH. These factors include emotion vulnerability, chaotic and adverse life events, and crisis-generating behaviors.

EMOTION VULNERABILITY AND AVOIDANCE

According to the biosocial theory, persons with BPD are characterized by a vulnerability to emotional reactions that are easily elicited (i.e., do not require intense stimuli), intense, and long-lasting. This emotional reactivity is also pervasive in that a broad range of stimuli and situations elicit a broad range of emotions. Emerging evidence from brain imaging research (Herpertz et al., 2001) and self-report studies (Stiglmayr, Grathwol, Linehan, Ihorst, Fahrenberg & Bohus, 2005) suggests that persons with BPD are emotionally vulnerable.

On the other hand, the biosocial theory states that BPD individuals also have the tendency to inhibit and avoid the experience and expression of emotions (which Linehan terms "inhibited grieving" and "apparent competence"). Indeed, studies of BPD have failed to consistently demonstrate excessive physiological responses to emotional stimuli (e.g., Herpertz et al., 1999, 2000). Similarly, individuals who engage in DSH tend to experience dissociative states during episodes of emotional arousal (Bohus et al., 2000; Russ et al., 1993), and BPD features are related to the tendency to avoid and escape unwanted emotions or thoughts (Chapman et al., 2005).

Although many DBT interventions target emotion vulnerability and regulation, vulnerability to emotions may persist beyond the end of treatment and continue to place persons with BPD at risk for relapse. According to the biosocial theory, emotion vulnerability is partly a biologically "hard-wired" temperament feature, and therefore, reactivity to certain stimuli may be particularly difficult to change. Furthermore, the inhibition, suppression, and escape from emotions likely interfere with the emotional processing that is necessary for therapy to reduce emotional reactivity (Foa & Kozak, 1986). Dissociation may have a similar detrimental effect.

Research suggests that negative emotion is one of the key factors contributing to relapse for both substance abuse (Greeley & Oei, 1999) and DSH (Brown, 2002). Several studies have suggested that people tend to engage in DSH when they are emotionally distressed (Brown, Comtois & Linehan, 2002; Chapman & Dixon-Gordon, 2006), and with the intent to escape or modify their emotional experiences (Brown et al., 2002). Thus, even after successfully reducing DSH, persons with BPD may be vulnerable to relapse due to the continued experience of intense negative emotions.

CHAOTIC AND ADVERSE LIFE EVENTS

Additionally, the tendency of persons with BPD to encounter stressful life events (Linehan, 1993) may further increase relapse risk. In treating self-harming patients with BPD, the authors have observed an overwhelmingly large number of unpleasant, stressful, and adverse events and daily hassles in the lives of these individuals. It is not uncommon to see a BPD patient, who, in the space of one week, has quit his or her job, experienced a death in the family, gotten into a serious car accident, been abandoned by an intimate partner, tripped and fallen down the stairs, experienced public humiliation, and so on. In particular, interpersonal conflict is common among persons with BPD, and is one of the most common triggers of DSH and chronic suicidal behavior (Welch & Linehan, 2002). Linehan's (1993) term for this tendency to encounter frequent stressors is *unrelenting crisis*, related to a variety of factors, including adverse environments, poor judgment, and *crisis-generating behaviors*, which we emphasize in this section.

CRISIS-GENERATING BEHAVIORS

Many of the frequent adverse events result from behaviors of the BPD individual, a pattern that Linehan terms crisis-generating behavior (Linehan, 1993). Persons with BPD tend to engage in two different types of crisis-generating behaviors: crisis-generating interpersonal behaviors and avoidant problem solving.

Persons with BPD engage in a variety of interpersonal behaviors that frustrate or burn out friends, family members, or therapists (cf. Potthoff, Holahan & Joiner, 1995). For instance, people who engage in DSH often lack interpersonal problem-solving skills and tend to use passive strategies to solve their problems (Kehrer & Linehan, 1996; Linehan et al., 1987). At the same time, they can be quite active in getting others to solve their problems, a phenomenon referred to as *active passivity* (Linehan, 1993). In addition, other individuals may actually reinforce DSH by increasing support or practical assistance. Over the long-term, however, active passivity and other dysfunctional interpersonal behaviors lead to conflict, crisis, and abandonment, which often are potent triggers for DSH.

As described by Linehan (1993), self-harming individuals with BPD also tend to use *avoidant* problem-solving strategies, which ultimately backfire and result in increased environmental stressors. Similarly, the *experiential avoidance model* (EAM; Chapman et al., 2006) proposes that persons who engage in DSH tend to engage in a variety of behaviors that help them avoid or escape from unwanted emotions, thoughts, or problems. For example, a patient expecting a difficult day at work may fail to show up for work, or a patient feeling overwhelmed by financial problems may fail to open his or her mail. These avoidance behaviors may allow the individual to avoid stress in the short term, but ultimately perpetuate long-term stressful events (cf. Jacobson, Martell & Dimidjian, 2001). Long after BPD patients stop self-harm, they may still face negative events that result from previous maladaptive behaviors (e.g., large financial debts or arrests for prior crimes) and could trigger further DSH.

TRANSACTIONAL MODEL OF RELAPSE

The enduring tendencies of BPD individuals to encounter stressful life events, experience heightened negative emotionality, and engage in crisis-generating and avoidant behaviors, are interrelated processes that increase risk of relapse following periods of abstinence from DSH. The tendency to encounter and generate stressors leads to a potent mix of diverse triggers for DSH. Once a patient with BPD experiences emotional arousal, he or she may act in ways that further exacerbate an already stressful situation. Although some crisis-generating behaviors, such as avoidance behaviors, may produce short-term relief, they often worsen stressful events. Furthermore, forcefully suppressing unwanted thoughts and feelings can paradoxically increase their recurrence (Purdon, 1999). This confluence of factors can result in a broad array of internal (emotions) and external triggers for urges to engage in DSH, perhaps a greater variety than in less severe patients.

As an example, one of the authors had a patient ("Wendy"), who frequently struggled with strong urges to engage in DSH, even though she had stopped harming herself several months ago. This particular patient struggled with obesity and chronic knee and back pain, which flared up episodically in concert with increased physical activity at work. During a particularly difficult week, she was experiencing intense, prolonged pain in her knees and a related increase in her feelings of agitation and frustration (emotion vulnerability) in response to stressful interactions with a coworker (stressful, adverse events).

Instead of actively seeking to solve the problem with the coworker, she avoided this individual and vacillated between ruminating about the situation and suppressing her emotions. Eventually, she was so distressed about the work situation that she took three days off, but when she returned, she was overwhelmed with work that had piled up during her absence, and the situation with the coworker remained unresolved (crisis-generating behaviors). She became increasingly hostile toward the coworker and others (crisis-generating behaviors), and eventually, her supervisor provided some critical feedback about her behavior. In response, she felt intense shame, along with urges to cut herself. Unfortunately, the patient acted on these urges and cut herself. The interplay between these key factors (emotion vulnerability, adverse/stressful events, emotion suppression, and crisis-generating behaviors) produced intense shame, which was a key internal conditioned stimulus (CS) for urges to engage in DSH for this patient.

CHARACTERISTICS OF TREATMENT THAT CONTRIBUTE TO RELAPSE OF DSH

There are many reasons why therapy might fail to prevent DSH relapse. For instance, therapy sometimes fails to change some key factors leading to DSH. For example, we believe that many therapists get DSH to stop by getting the patient to commit to not engaging in self-harm and helping the patient reduce stressful events and DSH triggers and opportunities. It is likely that such a patient would still be highly emotionally reactive and unprepared to effectively handle triggering events that would eventually occur despite his or her best problem solving. An additional key treatment component, therefore, is teaching patients skills for regulating emotions triggered by high-risk situations. Although reducing emotional arousal is an essential skill, these patients sometimes have great difficulty reducing arousal in exceptionally challenging situations, particularly when emotional arousal quickly becomes intense and intolerable. Therefore, when therapy focuses solely on regulating emotions, the therapist might fail to help the patient reduce reactivity to, or increase tolerance of, overwhelming emotions and emotion triggers.

A second treatment failure occurs when treatment gains fail to generalize to new contexts. To the extent that the therapy context is different from the patient's normal life, therapy gains may not generalize to the natural environment. Also, new emotional responses to conditioned stimuli may be strongly evident in some settings, but then the new learning often does not extend to new contexts or even to the same context at a different time (e.g., Bouton, 1988, 2002).

In considering the relapse of the patient "Wendy," it was clear that during her abstinence, she generally did not experience intense shame, but the occurrence of the previous shame triggers in a novel context (at work while interacting with the supervisor) resulted in a *renewal* of intense shame and DSH urges. The following is an extended case example designed to illustrate the phenomenon of DSH in BPD and the factors that might contribute to relapse.

CLINICAL CASE ILLUSTRATION

This case illustration depicts some of the key factors that might contribute to relapse of DSH in persons with BPD. We note that this is not a specific case, but rather, a hypothetical amalgam of typical BPD cases designed to represent treatment with a self-harming BPD patient.

PATIENT PRESENTATION

Jody was a 29-year-old single, Caucasian female who initially presented for help after having spent a few days in an inpatient psychiatric clinic (following a serious episode of self-injury) and being referred to our DBT treatment program. Jody noted that she would like to "get her life together" and stop harming herself. Jody presented as a warm, congenial individual, but also frequently switched topics during her initial interview and, on several occasions, expressed intense sadness and anger.

ASSESSMENT

Throughout the initial diagnostic and psychosocial assessment, it was apparent that Jody met criteria for BPD. For instance, on both the Structured Clinical Interview for DSM-IV Personality Disorders (First, Spitzer, Gibbons, Williams & Benjamin, 1996) and the Personality Disorder Examination (Loranger, 1995), Jody met six out of the nine BPD criteria; five criteria are required for the diagnosis. Her most notable difficulties included (1) intense interpersonal discord and chaos, characterized by repeated conflicts with intimate others and friends; (2) impulsive, self-damaging behavior, in the form of periodic mood-driven binge eating, reckless driving, and binge drinking; (3) chronic feelings of emptiness and an unstable sense of direction in life (she would jump from job to job, often changing career directions and interests); and (4) repeated deliberate self-harm (DSH), along with a history of two serious suicide attempts, both of which occurred more than five years ago.

To assess Jody's suicide attempts and DSH episodes, her therapist administered the Suicide Attempt and Self-Injury Interview, which collects information on topography, intent, medical severity, social context, high risk situations, and function (Linehan, Comtois, Brown, Heard & Wagner, 2006).

CASE CONCEPTUALIZATION

With regard to DSH, Jody reported that she began burning herself when she was 15 years old, initially as a "dare" by friends, but she noticed that the burning tended to "release steam," and led to a sense of calmness. She continued burning periodically (twice a week), most often following interpersonal conflicts or when she was overwhelmed with work or other obligations. Typically, she burned herself with cigarettes, but after she quit smoking, she cut herself with razors. Eventually, the cutting behavior increased in frequency (3–4 times per week), with periodic flare-ups (6–7 times per week) following break-ups with boyfriends or difficult interactions with others at work. Jody most commonly cut herself when she experienced shame or intense anger, and she reported that she "doesn't know what else to do to get rid of the feelings."

In terms of *emotion vulnerability*, Jody reported intense, rapidly shifting emotional states throughout the day, along with difficulty regulating her emotional reactions. Specifically, she reported intense shame, both about being a person who engages in DSH, and about many of the crisis-generating behaviors that have alienated her from her family and friends (e.g., stealing, verbal abuse). She also reported frequent sadness and anger, and indicated that these emotions tend to occur very quickly, become unmanageably intense, and take several hours to diminish. Having considerable difficulty regulating her emotions, Jody tended to "freeze" and was unable to problem-solve or think about adaptive coping strategies, and she often ruminated about upsetting events, which served to continually rekindle her distress.

As a result of her difficulty thinking and regulating her behavior when she was upset, Jody often engaged in crisis-generating behaviors that burned out her social network and exacerbated her already stressful life. For instance, when her boyfriend (with whom she lived) suggested that she get a job, she felt intense shame about her lack of employment, and instead of communicating effectively with him, she would become angry and critical. Her boyfriend would criticize her in return. These conflicts often ended with Jody cutting herself, followed by her boyfriend making up with her and/or being more supportive (i.e., *reinforcement* for self-harm). Jody's difficulty regulating her emotion vulnerability also led to stress at work, as she often would avoid stressful tasks and procrastinate to the point that she was faced with overwhelming deadlines. This interplay between emotion vulnerability, crisis-generating behaviors, and adverse, stressful life events led to a variety of triggers and cues for the very emotions related to DSH urges (e.g., shame and anger, particularly).

TREATMENT: DIALECTICAL BEHAVIOR THERAPY

Treatment with Jody involved 12 months of standard outpatient Dialectical Behavior Therapy (DBT). Jody attended a weekly individual therapy session, as well as a group skills training session. Individual therapy initially focused on reducing life threatening and out-of-control behaviors, such as DSH and suicidal ideation. One of the hallmarks of DBT is its use of a target hierarchy to guide the therapist's prioritization of treatment targets in each session. The most important item on the hierarchy is life-threatening behavior, which consists of behaviors such as suicidal crises, suicide attempts, serious suicidal ideation, self-harm ideation and urges, and self-harm, among other behaviors that imminently threaten the patient's life. As such, many of the first several sessions focused largely on repeated DSH, as Jody's suicidal ideation tended to be episodic, mild, and not linked with strong intent or a plan to attempt suicide. The following section illustrates the aspects of DBT that specifically work to prevent relapse, and we provide examples of how these interventions were used in the case of Jody.

STOPPING SELF-HARM ONCE AND FOR ALL: RELAPSE PREVENTION IN DBT

Although many DBT strategies may help patients to stop engaging in DSH during therapy, several strategies are particularly important in preventing the *relapse* of DSH, either following a period of abstinence during therapy, or following the termination of therapy. Largely, these strategies target the key factors highlighted earlier as contributing to relapse (emotion vulnerability, adverse life events, crisis-generating behaviors, and failure to generalize treatment gains). As such, these interventions include the following: (1) strategies to reduce emotional sensitivity and reactivity, (2) strategies to prevent or modify high-risk situations, (3) strategies to reduce dysfunctional or crisis-generating behaviors, and (4) strategies to promote the generalization of treatment gains.

REDUCING VULNERABILITY TO HIGH-RISK SITUATIONS THROUGH EXPOSURE-BASED INTERVENTIONS

To reduce the probability of DSH relapse, DBT involves specific strategies to reduce the likelihood that environmental events will trigger problematic emotions. Thus, one major goal is to change conditioned associations of environmental cues with intense, intolerable emotional responses. Because many aspects of emotion vulnerability in BPD may be based on temperament and long-standing biology, persons with BPD may always be more emotionally intense than others, but we would argue that some strategies can decrease reactivity to many high-risk environmental events. These strategies include exposure and response prevention and opposite action.

EXPOSURE AND RESPONSE PREVENTION

Exposure and response prevention primarily is used to decrease the likelihood that particular environmental cues will trigger unwanted or dysfunctional emotional responses. Exposure-based treatments have proven effective for a wide range of anxiety disorders, such as post-traumatic stress disorder (Foa & Kozak, 1986), obsessive-compulsive disorder (Franklin, Abramowitz, Kozak, Levitt & Foa, 2000), and panic disorder (Barlow, 1988). Similarly, some research suggests that exposure therapy is effective for other emotions, such as anger (Grodnitzky & Tafrate, 2000; Tafrate & Kassinove, 1998).

The basic procedure of exposure and response-prevention involves exposing the patient to stimuli that elicit emotional responses and blocking behaviors that function to escape from those stimuli. For example, Jody's therapist employed exposure and response prevention to reduce her fear of social performance situations. Exposure and response prevention initially involved *imaginal exposure*, by having Jody imagine anxiety-provoking performance situations, while blocking any avoidance behaviors, such as self-harm (or related, less severe behaviors, such as picking her skin), distraction, or escape. As treatment progressed, the therapist had Jody try *in vivo exposure* assignments, involving exposing herself to actual performance situations in real life, while blocking all avoidance or escape behaviors.

The theory behind exposure and response prevention is that exposure to a conditioned stimulus (CS) that elicits a conditioned emotional response (CR) will eventually result in the extinction of the emotion, as long as the feared event (in Jody's case, being publicly ridiculed) never occurs. In Jody's case, after several trials of exposure and response prevention, her fear about social performance situations reduced from 80/100 (where 100 = maximum fear) to about 30/100, a more tolerable level of fear that did not trigger urges to engage in DSH.

DBT also involves a variety of interventions that encourage *interoceptive exposure* to avoided or feared internal experiences. The experiential avoidance model (Chapman et al., 2006) suggests that DSH is often an escape from intolerable emotions and thoughts. Similarly, Linehan (1993) has described BPD patients as "emotion phobic" in the sense that they tend to react to their emotions with fear, shame, and anger (secondary reactions). Thus, interoceptive exposure involves exposure to the physical sensations of emotion as well as to unwanted thoughts and images, without struggling with or escaping these experiences. The therapist does this by eliciting feared internal experiences in sessions, or by encouraging patients to observe their thoughts and emotional experiences without acting on them or getting rid of them (i.e., mindfulness).

To help Jody reduce her fear of social performance situations, her therapist had her repeatedly imagine others rejecting her for performing poorly. Jody ended up feeling more confident that she could effectively deal with rejection if it were to occur. Also, when Jody reported that she felt ashamed of feeling sad, the therapist had her practice mindfully experiencing sadness rather than avoiding it. By repeatedly talking in detail about what made her feel sad, her shame response diminished considerably. Over time, Jody's reactivity to these unwanted internal experiences diminished, and her urge to engage in DSH extinguished.

Certainly, in any type of exposure with self-harming BPD patients, it is absolutely essential to block self-harm behavior. There is clear evidence that DSH effectively relieves unpleasant emotions such as fear and anger. Thus, if the patient escaped emotional reactions by engaging in DSH, the conditioned emotional responses would never weaken. DBT therapists teach patients several practical ways to block and prevent DSH, such as reviewing negative consequences of DSH, reducing the availability of self-harm implements, and distress tolerance skills, among other strategies (Linehan, 1993a, 1993b).

OPPOSITE ACTION

Opposite action is another exposure-oriented intervention in DBT. In contrast with standard applications of exposure and response prevention, which tend to focus primarily on *fear*, opposite action in DBT applies to the whole gamut of emotional experiences. In addition, opposite action involves not only the extinction of certain emotional responses, but also the active learning of more effective responses to emotions.

When using opposite action, the therapist exposes the patient (or ideally, has the patient do this him- or herself) to the situation that elicits the emotion, blocks any actions that are consistent with the action-urge associated with the emotion, and has the patient engage in behaviors that are *opposite* to the action urge associated with the emotion. The theory is that acting in a manner that is congruent with the action urge/emotion will strengthen the emotion. In contrast, acting opposite to the action urge/emotion will weaken the emotional response and strengthen more effective responses to the situation (e.g., acting nonfearful in safe situations). As with standard exposure and response prevention, it is essential that the exposure be *nonreinforced*; that is, the feared event or "catastrophe" (e.g., public humiliation in the case of Jody's social anxiety; being assaulted in the case of PTSD; being attacked in the case of someone who feels intense anger; being ostracized in the case of someone who experiences intense shame) must not occur.

For Jody, one of the key emotional triggers for DSH was intense shame and an urge to punish herself. Her shame, however, often was out of proportion to the situation, in that people were unlikely to reject or ostracize her for the personal characteristics or behaviors of which she felt ashamed. For example, she often felt intense shame about her appearance, yet, she actually was moderately attractive. Often, when she felt ashamed of her appearance, Jody would feel the urge to hide her body with unflattering clothing, or to avoid social situations. Many of Jody's normal behaviors (including thinking about her behaviors) frequently elicited shame, thinking that she was "bad" and deserving of pain and punishment; this reaction was even more intense when others communicated even slight disapproval, which led to her incorrectly assume they were angry and judgmental of her. Her urges were to punish herself by inflicting pain in various ways and to deprive herself of pleasurable activities.

Opposite action involved having Jody actively enter into social situations without avoiding, escaping, or hiding her body. In fact, as treatment progressed, Jody's therapist encouraged her to seek out situations in which she could publicly reveal (clothed, of course) aspects of appearance of which she felt ashamed (called "all-the-way" opposite action). Other opposite action strategies involved repeatedly acting contrary to her shame by doing many nice things for herself despite thinking she "deserves" to suffer. In addition, when Jody experienced unjustified shame in therapy sessions, her therapist would identify the trigger, and repeat it until the emotion diminished, encouraging Jody to act in ways that are inconsistent with shame (e.g., direct eye contact while nonjudgmentally describing, in a confident voice, the facts about her perceived bad qualities and behaviors).

REDUCING EMOTION VULNERABILITY THROUGH SELF-CARE AND POSITIVE ACTIVITIES

Another way to reduce the likelihood that high-risk situations will trigger negative emotions is to enhance self-care and increase the frequency of positive life events. DBT skills training involves teaching patients ways to improve sleep, physical exercise, and nutrition, as well to as avoid mood-altering drugs and alcohol, and take care of physical illnesses. Similar to cognitive therapy for depression (Young, Weinberger & Beck, 2001), treatment involves accumulating positive life events and getting involved in activities that trigger positive emotions and a sense of competence and mastery. For example, Jody's therapist noticed that she was taking her prescribed antidepressants irregularly, and that she had frequent insomnia and was not eating consistently. Any one of these factors may have made her more vulnerable to negative emotions. As a result, he taught Jody sleep hygiene and stimulus control strategies to improve sleep; helped her monitor and keep her medication regimen more regular; and assisted her in developing healthier eating habits.

PROBLEM SOLVING TO PREVENT AND
MODIFY HIGH-RISK SITUATIONS

DBT fundamentally is a problem-solving based treatment, and as such, there are several interventions aimed at avoiding, preventing, or modifying high-risk situations. For many patients, their environments need a major overhaul in order to reduce chaos and stressful events. In doing so, DBT therapists commonly employ standard problem-solving procedures, such as (1) identifying the problem, (2) identifying a goal for the situation, (3) brainstorming possible solutions, (4) entertaining the pros and cons of each solution, (5) implementing the solution, and (6) evaluating the effectiveness of the solution (Goldfried & Davison, 1994). In addition, the therapist often models effective coping or problem solving by disclosing ways in which he or she prevented or modified problems in life.

A common obstacle to problem solving is that BPD patients often avoid talking about or working on their problems, due to intense shame or feeling overwhelmed. Jody illustrates this problem well. She was extremely reluctant to talk about her problems. Whenever problem solving came up, she felt intense shame and often diverted her attention, shut down the conversation, or left the room. The therapist prompted Jody to "act opposite" by actively engaging in problem discussions.

The hope is that, with practice, the patient will develop the ability to employ problem-solving strategies ahead of time to prevent high-risk situations, and thus, to prevent the relapse of DSH. Therefore, DBT therapists help their patients "cope ahead" by coming up with effective plans to cope with, modify, or avoid future stressors. Along these lines, one useful strategy is imaginal practice. For instance, Jody's therapist often guided her through imaginal scenes in which she must speak in front of others at work, or cope with insulting comments from her boyfriend, and coached her through effective problem solving or emotion regulation coping strategies. This approach is similar to *stress inoculation training*, described by Meichenbaum and Jaremko (1983). In terms of relapse prevention, it is essential that coping ahead involves a large variety of situations, in order to promote the generalization of skillful behavior to the plethora of life situations related to self-harm.

REDUCING CRISIS-GENERATING BEHAVIORS
AND SELF-HARM THROUGH
EMOTION REGULATION

Because DSH and other crisis-generating behaviors are usually dysfunctional responses to emotional distress, teaching patients alternative ways to alter or respond to their emotional experiences can prevent these behaviors. DBT involves a variety of emotion regulation skills that patients can use in high-risk situations to reduce their emotional arousal and to control their behavior when emotionally aroused.

Consistent with the focus on balancing acceptance and change in DBT, some of the emotion regulation strategies involve changing emotions, and others involve accepting and experiencing emotions as they are. The acronym TIP describes the newest skills for reducing emotional arousal. The TIP skills involve activities that reduce emotional arousal by changing body physiology through changing temperature (T), intense exercise (I), and progressive muscle relaxation (P). One such skill that was particularly effective for Jody involved immersing her face for 30 seconds in a bowl of ice water. Studies have suggested that doing so activates the "dive reflex" and stimulates the parasympathetic nervous system to reduce aspects of emotional arousal (e.g., heart rate) (Marsh et al., 1995).

In terms of acceptance-based emotion regulation skills, mindfulness is a way to accept and observe current internal experiences to prevent dysfunctional emotion avoidance behaviors. Thus, a goal of mindfulness training in DBT is to reduce reactivity to emotional arousal and emotional thinking. Patients are taught to step back, observe, and get "unstuck" from ruminative thinking, emotions, and urges, without having to change or act upon them, which interrupts patients' habitual and automatic responses to distress. Accepting and tolerating emotions also promotes emotion regulation by preventing the usual paradoxical rebound effects that occur when people forcefully suppress unwanted thoughts and feelings (Purdon, 1999). This mindfulness strategy resembles the "urge surfing" skill taught to prevent alcohol and drug relapse (Witkiewitz, Marlatt & Walker, 2005). In Jody's case, the therapist targeted shame and urges to self-harm by teaching her to step back and observe her shame-related thoughts (such as "I'm bad"), nonjudgmentally describe the relevant facts, not take certain thoughts literally (e.g., "I deserve to be punished"), and to step back and observe the urge to punish and harm herself.

INTERVENTIONS TO PREVENT RELAPSE BY IMPROVING GENERALIZATION

Many patients, we believe, stop DSH by reducing their emotion vulnerability and improving their abilities to solve problems and regulate their emotions. Relapse can occur when these improvements do not generalize to the variety of situations that occur in their natural environments. We believe that generalization failures occur when new learning has not occurred in enough relevant contexts. There is considerable evidence that both respondent extinction and skills acquisition are quite context-specific (Bouton, 1988, 2002). New learning may be strongly evident in a particular setting, but then the new learning often does not extend to new contexts or even to the same context at a different time (Bouton, 1988, 2002). A patient can have all the relapse prevention skills in the world but still not use them in critical situations.

GENERALIZATION OF SKILLS

DBT therapists have several methods to ensure that patients can effectively implement skillful responses learned in therapy when they face high-risk situations in their natural environments without the help of a therapist. For instance, one strategy involves conducting a chain analysis after each occurrence of the problem behavior (in this case, DSH). Essentially, a chain analysis is a micro-level, moment-to-moment examination of the events that led up to DSH, the instance of DSH itself, and the consequences and events that followed DSH. Over time, these chain analyses may actually increase the likelihood that patients will remember skillful responses when confronted with high-risk situations (Lynch et al., 2006).

Another strategy involves having patients practice their skills frequently and in a variety of contexts. In therapy sessions, DBT therapists "drag out" and reinforce skillful behaviors through role-plays and other activities. Most importantly, the therapist looks for dysfunctional behaviors in-session that resemble the problems patients experience in their daily lives (e.g., sensitivity to criticism) and has the patient actively practice skills. Skillful behavior practiced during naturalistic therapy situations is more likely to generalize to patients' daily lives than contrived role-play practice.

Additionally, if therapy elicits problematic emotions that occur in the patient's natural environment, and the patient learns to respond skillfully while emotionally aroused, then the skillful responses are more likely to generalize to similar high-risk situations (Samoilov & Goldfried, 2000). The principles of state-dependent learning, whereby a person is more likely to exhibit learned behavior in states that are similar to those in which he or she learned the behavior, may explain this generalization effect (Matt, Vasquez & Campbell, 1992). Thus, the therapist may elicit negative emotions by simulating a problem situation (i.e., using imaginal or *in vivo* exposure) and then have the patient practice implementing skillful behavior.

Relapse can occur when neither the therapist nor the patient have anticipated certain situations in which skills are needed. Thus, the therapist encourages the patient to practice new skills frequently and in as many contexts as possible, in order to maintain abstinence from DSH even when he or she faces new and challenging situations. The therapist also provides telephone skills coaching to help guide the patient through difficult, high-risk situations. In this way, the therapist reduces relapse risk by bringing therapy (and quite literally, him or herself) into the patient's natural environment (Lynch et al., 2006). In order to maintain abstinence even after therapy termination, the therapist may reduce the frequency or length of telephone calls in order to encourage the patient to continue skillful behavior in the absence of the therapist.

In the situation with her boss described earlier, Jody had been through the DBT emotion regulation skills twice and was even coaching and helping some of the other patients with the skills. However, her emotions were so overwhelming that she could not even think about which skills to use at that time. In order to prevent further relapses, therapy with Jody involved coping ahead and imagining using emotion regulation skills in very difficult or overwhelming situations, and stimulus control strategies, involving having Jody carry around a "coping card" that reminded her of important skills to use when she is emotionally overwhelmed.

GENERALIZATION OF EXTINCTION

Both respondent and operant extinction effects are context specific, that is, extinction does not generalize well to new settings. Therefore, DBT therapists try to help the patient get exposure to emotion triggers across multiple contexts, and maximize the match between therapy exposure contexts and naturalistic settings. One way to do this is to encourage the patient to implement exposure homework assignments in her natural environment via audiotapes of sessions, or to provide *in vivo* coaching over the telephone.

The use of extinction reminders is another method to maximize the match between therapy exposure contexts and naturalistic settings. Extinction is more likely to generalize to new contexts when a cue that was present during extinction is presented again later (Bouton, 1988; Brooks & Bouton, 1993). The therapist's voice (via phone calls or audio recordings) and reminder cards may serve as extinction reminders.

To promote generalization of extinction, Jody's therapist implemented exposure strategies in naturalistic therapy situations. Specifically, he did not treat her as fragile by avoiding sensitive topics or direct feedback about problematic behaviors (including those that occur in sessions) even though she often responded with shame or anger. When these problematic emotions got elicited in session her therapist tried, in a collaborative manner, to identify the precise triggers and repeat them until the emotion diminished, while prompting the patient to engage in opposite action. Her therapist also avoided reinforcing behaviors consistent with shame (such as self-criticism and hiding) or anger (such as yelling or insults) by compassionately plowing forward with therapy and not backing off when these behaviors occurred.

SUMMARY AND CONCLUSION

Although relapse prevention normally is discussed with regard to substance use behaviors (e.g., Marlatt & Gordon, 1985; Witkiewitz & Marlatt, 2004), preventing relapse is a key feature in the treatment of deliberate self-harm (DSH) and other dysfunctional emotion regulation behaviors. Thus far, the treatment with the most empirical support for reducing DSH is DBT (Linehan, 1993), typically applied to patients with borderline personality disorder (BPD).

Based on the difficulties encountered by BPD patients, we have proposed a model of relapse that involves the interplay between emotion vulnerability, high-risk situations, and crisis-generating behaviors. As a relatively static factor that increases vulnerability to high-risk situations, *emotion vulnerability* is similar to the "tonic" risk factors proposed by Witkiewitz and Marlatt (2004) for alcohol relapse. In contrast, crisis-generating behaviors are similar to the phasic factors (factors that led to sudden changes in the likelihood of DSH) proposed by Witkiewitz and Marlatt (2004). Whereas emotion vulnerability and high-risk situations may bring the patient to the edge of the cliff, crisis-generating behaviors and failure to regulate emotions get the patient to jump.

Treatment in DBT has many features that target these processes. For instance, exposure-based methods aim to reduce emotional reactivity to high-risk situations, when that reactivity is unwarranted by the situation (as in the case of feeling ashamed in the absence of risk for rejection). Problem-solving involves changing or avoiding high-risk situations. In addition, both emotion-regulation skills and problem-solving skills reduce the likelihood of crisis-generating behaviors. As we propose that relapse largely represents a failure to generalize treatment gains, a variety of strategies in DBT encourage the patient to transfer new skills from therapy to his or her natural environment. Although many of these relapse issues pertain to BPD, we believe the relapse prevention strategies discussed here apply to other clinical populations who engage in DSH, as well as to other disorders involving difficulties with emotion regulation.

REFERENCES

Bohus, M., Haaf, B., Simms, T., Limberger, M., Schmahl, C., Unckel, C. et al. (2004). Effectiveness of inpatient dialectical behavioral therapy for borderline personality disorder: A controlled trial. *Behaviour Research & Therapy* 42:487–499.

Bohus, M., Limberger, M., Ebner, U., Glocker, F., Schwarz, B., Wernz, M., Lieb, K. (2000). Pain perception during self-reported distress and calmness in patients with borderline personality disorder and self-mutilating behavior. *Psychiatry Research* 95:251–260.

Bouton, M. (1988). Context and ambiguity in the extinction of emotional learning: Implications for exposure therapy. *Behaviour Research & Therapy* 26(2):137–149.

Bouton, M. (2002). Context, ambiguity, and unlearning: Sources of relapse after behavioral extinction. *Biological Psychiatry* 52:976–986.

Brooks, D., Bouton, M. (1993). A retrieval cue for extinction attenuates spontaneous recovery. *Journal of Experimental Psychology: Animal Behavior Processes* 19:77–89.

Brown, M., Comtois, K., Linehan, M. (2002). Reasons for suicide attempts and nonsuicidal self-injury in women with borderline personality disorder. *Journal of Abnormal Psychology* 111(1):198–202.

Chambless, D., Ollendick, T. (2001). Empirically supported psychological interventions: Controversies and evidence. *Annual Review of Psychology* 52:685–716.

Chapman, A., Dixon-Gordon, K. (in press). Emotional Antecedents and Consequences of deliberate self–harm and suicidal attempts. *Suicide & Life Threatening Behaviour*.

Chapman, A., Gratz, K., Brown, M. (2006). Solving the puzzle of deliberate self-harm: The experiential avoidance model. *Behaviour Research & Therapy* 44:371–394.

Chapman, A., Specht, M., Cellucci, T. (2005). Factors associated with suicide attempts in female inmates: The hegemony of hopelessness. *Suicide and Life-Threatening Behavior* 35:558–569.

Clarkin, J., Widiger, T., Frances, A., Hurt, S., Gilmore, M. (1983). Prototypic typology and the borderline personality disorder. *Journal of Abnormal Psychology* **92**:263–275.

Corbitt, E., Malone, K., Haas, G., Mann, J. (1996). Suicidal behavior in patients with major depression and comorbid personality disorders. *Journal of Affective Disorders* **39**:61–72.

Goldfried, M., Davison, G. (1995). *Clinical Behavior Therapy.* New York: John Wiley & Sons.

Gratz, K. (2001). Measurement of deliberate self-harm: Preliminary data on the deliberate self-harm inventory. *Journal of Psychopathology & Behavioral Assessment* **23**(4):253–263.

Gratz, K., Gunderson, J.G. (2006). Preliminary data on an acceptance-based emotion regulation group intervention for deliberate self-harm among women with borderline personality disorder. *Behavior Therapy* **37**:25–35.

Greeley, J., Oei, T. (1999). Alcohol and tension reduction. In Leonard, K., Blane, H., eds., *Psychological theories of drinking and alcoholism, 2e.* New York: Guilford Press.

Grodnitzky, G., Tafrate, R. (2000). Imaginal exposure for anger reduction in adult outpatients: A pilot study. *Journal of Behavior Therapy & Experimental Psychiatry* **31**(3–4):259–279.

First, M.B., Spitzer, R.L., Gibbons, M., Williams, J.B.W., Benjamin, L. (1996). *User's Guide for the Structured Clinical Interview for DSM-IV Axis II Personality Disorders (SCID-II).* New York: Biometrics Research Department, New York State Psychiatric Institute.

Foa, E.B., Riggs, D.S., Massie, E.D., Yarczower, M. (1995). The impact of fear activation and anger on the efficacy of exposure treatment for posttraumatic stress disorder. *Behavior Therapy* **26**:487–499.

Friedman, R., Aronoff, M., Clarkin, J., Corn, R., Hurt, S. (1983). History of suicidal behavior in depressed borderline personality disorder inpatients. *American Journal of Psychiatry* **140**:1023–1026.

Haines, J. et al. (1995). The psychophysiology of self-mutilation. *Journal of Abnormal Psychology* **104**:471–489.

Hawton, K., Arensman, E., Townsend, E., Bremner, S., Feldman, E., Goldney, R. et al. (1998). Deliberate self-harm: Systematic review of efficacy of psychosocial and pharmacological treatments in preventing repetition. *British Medical Journal* **317**:441–447.

Herpertz, S., Kunert, H., Schwenger, U., Sass, H. (1999). Affective responsiveness in borderline personality disorder: A psychophysiological approach. *American Journal of Psychiatry* **156**:1550–1556.

Herpertz, S.C., Dietrich, T.M., Wenning, B., Krings, T., Erberich, S.G., Willmes, K. et al. (2001). Evidence of abnormal amygdala functioning in borderline personality disorder: A functional MRI study. *Biological Psychiatry* **50**:292–298.

Herpertz, S.C., Schwenger, U., Kunert, H., Lukas, G., Gretzer, U., Nutzmann, J. et al. (2000). Emotional responses in patients with borderline as compared with avoidant personality disorder. *Journal of Personality Disorders* **14**(4):339–351.

Irvin, J., Bowers, C., Dunn, M., Wang, M. (1999). Efficacy of relapse prevention: A metaanalytic review. *Journal of Consulting and Clinical Psychology* **67**:563–570.

Jacobson, N., Martell, C., Dimidjian, S. (2001). Behavioral activation treatment for depression: Returning to contextual roots. *Clinical Psychology: Science and Practice* **8**:255–270.

Kehrer, C., Linehan, M. (1996). Interpersonal and emotional problem solving skills and parasuicide among women with borderline personality disorder. *Journal of Personality Disorders* **10**:153–163.

Kessler, R., Borges, G., Walters, E. (1999). Prevalence of and risk factors for lifetime suicide attempts in the national comorbidity survey. *Archives of General Psychiatry* **56**:617–626.

Koons, C., Robins, C., Tweed, J., Lynch, R., Gonzalez, M., Morse, Q. et al. (2001). Efficacy of dialectical behavior therapy in women veterans with borderline personality disorder. *Behavior Therapy* **32**(2):371–390.

Langbehn, D., Pfohl, B. (1993). Clinical correlates of self-mutilation among psychiatric inpatients. *Annals of Clinical Psychiatry* **5**:45–51.

Linehan, M. (1993). *Cognitive-behavioral treatment of borderline personality disorder.* New York: Guilford Press.

Linehan, M., Armstrong, H., Suarez, A., Allmon, D., Heard, H. (1991). Cognitive-behavioral treatment of chronically parasuicidal borderline patients. *Archives of General Psychiatry* **48**:1060–1064.

Linehan, M., Camper, P., Chiles, J., Strosahl, K., Shearin, E. (1987). Interpersonal problem solving and parasuicide. *Cognitive Therapy and Research* **11**:1–12.

Linehan, M., Comtois, K.A., Brown, M.Z., Heard, H.L., Wagner, A. (2006). Suicide Attempt Self-Injury Interview (SASII): Development, reliability, and validity of a scale to assess suicide attempts and intentional self-injury. *Psychological Assessment.*

Linehan, M., Comtois, K., Murray, A., Brown, M., Gallop, R.J., Heard, H. et al. (2006). Two-year randomized trial + follow-up of dialectical behavior therapy vs. therapy by experts for suicidal behaviors and borderline personality disorder. *Archives of General Psychiatry* **18**(3):303–312.

Linehan, M., Heard, H. (1997). Borderline personality disorder: Costs, course, and treatment outcomes. In Anonymous, *The Cost-Effectiveness of Psychotherapy: A Guide for Practitioners, Researchers and Policy-Makers.* New York: Oxford University Press.

Loranger, A.W. (1995). *International personality disorder examination (IPDE) manual.* White Plains, NY: Cornell Medical Center.

Marsh, N., Askew, D., Beer, K., Gerke, M., Muller, D., Reichman, C. (1995). Relative contributions of voluntary apnea, exposure to cold and face immersion in water to diving bradycardia in humans. *Clinical and Experimental Pharmacology & Physiology* **22**:886–887.

Matt, G., Vasquez, C., Campbell, W. (1992). Mood congruent recall of affectively toned stimuli: A meta-analytic review. *Clinical Psychology Review* **12**:227–255.

Meichenbaum, D., Jaremko, M. (1983). *Stress prevention and management: A cognitive-behavioral approach.* New York: Plenum Press.

Potthoff, J., Holahan, C., Joiner, T. (1995). Reassurance seeking, stress generation, and depressive symptoms: An integrative model. *Journal of Personality & Social Psychology* **68**:664–670.

Purdon, C. (1999). Thought suppression and psychopathology. *Behaviour Research & Therapy* **37**:1029–1054.

Russ, M., Shearin, E., Clarkin, J., Harrison, K., Hull, J. (1993). Subtypes of self-injurious patients with borderline personality disorder. *American Journal of Psychiatry* **150**(12):1869–1871.

Samoilov, A., Goldfried, M. (2000). Role of emotion in cognitive-behavior therapy. *Clinical Psychology: Science and Practice* **7**(4):373–385.

Schaffer, C., Carroll, J., Abramowitz, S. (1982). Self-mutilation and the borderline personality. *Journal of Nervous and Mental Disease* **170**:468–473.

Segal, Z.V., Williams, J.M.G., Teasdale, J.D. (2001). *Mindfulness-based cognitive therapy for depression: A new approach to preventing relapse.* New York: Guilford Press.

Shaw-Welch, S., Kuo, J., Sylvers, P., Chittams, J., Linehan, M. (2003). *Correlates of parasuicidal behaviors in women meeting criteria for borderline personality disorder.* Poster session presented at the 37th annual meeting of the Association for the Advancement of Behavior Therapy, Boston, MA.

Stiglmayr, C., Grathwol, T., Linehan, M., Ihorst, G., Fahrenberg, J., Bohus, M. (2005). Aversive tension in patients with borderline personality disorder: A computer-based controlled field study. *Acta Psychiatrica Scandinavica* **111**(5):372–379.

Stone, M., Hurt, S., Stone, D. (1987). The PI 500: Long-term follow-up of borderline inpatients meeting DSM-III criteria. I: Global outcome. *Journal of Personality Disorders* **1**:291–298.

Surber, R.W., Winkler, E.L., Monteleone, M., Havassy, B.E., Goldfinger, Hopkin (1987). Characteristics of high users of acute psychiatric inpatient services. *Hospital and Community Psychiatry* **38**:1112–1114.

Swigar, M.E., Astrachan, B., Levine, M.A., Mayfield, V., Radovich (1991). Single and repeated admissions to a mental health center: Demographic, clinical and use of service characteristics. *International Journal of Social Psychiatry* **37**:259–266.

Tafrate, R., Kassinove, H. (1998). Anger control in men: Barb exposure with rational, irrational, and irrelevant self-statements. *Journal of Cognitive Psychotherapy* **12**(3):187–211.

Tanney, B. (1992). Mental disorders, psychiatric patients, and suicide. In Maris, R.W., Berman, A.L., Maltsberger, J.T., eds., *Assessment and prediction of suicide*, 277–320. New York: Guilford.

Torgersen, S., Kringlen, E., Cramer, V. (2001). The prevalence of personality disorders in a community sample. *Archives of General Psychiatry* **58**:590–596.

Turner, R. (2000). Naturalistic evaluation of dialectical behavioral therapy-oriented treatment for borderline personality disorder. *Cognitive and Behavioral Practice* **7**:413–419.

van den Bosch, L., Koeter, M., Stijnen, T., Verheul, R., van den Brink, W. (2005). Sustained efficacy of dialectical behaviour therapy for women with borderline personality disorder. *Behaviour Research & Therapy* **43**:1231–1241.

Verheul, R., van den Bosch, L., Koeter, M., de Ridder, M., Stijnen, T., van den Brink, W. (2003). Dialectical behaviour therapy for women with borderline personality disorder: 12-month, randomised clinical trial in The Netherlands. *British Journal of Psychiatry* **182**:135–140.

Witkiewitz, K., Marlatt, G.A., Walker, D. (2005). Mindfulness-based relapse prevention for alcohol and substance use disorders. *Journal of Cognitive Psychotherapy: An International Quarterly* **19**(3):211–228.

Zoroglu, S., Tuzun, U., Sar, V., Tutkun, H., Savas, H., Ozturk, M. et al. (2003). Suicide attempt and self-mutilation among Turkish high school students in relation with abuse, neglect, and dissociation. *Psychiatry & Clinical Neurosciences* **57**:119–126.

INTERNET RESOURCES ON DIALECTICAL BEHAVIOR THERAPY AND BORDERLINE PERSONALITY DISORDER

- http://www.brtc.psych.washington.edu
  Research web page of Marsha Linehan
- http://faculty.washington.edu/linehan
  Faculty web page of Marsha Linehan
- http://www.behavioraltech.com
  Behavioral Tech
- http://www.tara4bpd.org
  National Education Alliance for Borderline Personality Disorder
- http://www.borderlinepersonalitydisorder.com
  Treatment and Research Advancements Association for Personality Disorder (TARA)

10

TREATMENT OF SEXUAL OFFENDERS: RELAPSE PREVENTION AND BEYOND

PAMELA M. YATES

Cabot Consulting and Research Services
Ottawa, Ontario

TONY WARD

School of Psychology
University of Wellington
Wellington, New Zealand

INTRODUCTION

It has long been well established that sexual offenders are a heterogeneous group of individuals who commit a variety of offenses for diverse reasons and who present with varying degrees of risk to reoffend and treatment needs (Marshall, 1999; Polaschek, 2003). In fact, perhaps the only commonality among this group as a whole lies in the fact that they have engaged in illegal activity that is sexual in nature. Sexual offenders commit crimes against male and female adults and children, victims known or unknown to them, related or unrelated, in public, private, and institutional settings. They may be paraphilic, meeting diagnostic criteria such as those contained within the DSM-IV-TR (American Psychiatric Association, 2000), or they may not, and they may or may not present with comorbid disorders, such as personality disorder, substance abuse, and mental illness. They come from all classes and walks of life, and may or may not be motivated to change their behavior. They are driven by a variety of motivations to commit sexual crimes, including deviant sexual interests or preference; a desire to establish relationships in order to meet intimacy or sexual needs; a need for personal power, control, and domination; a desire to injure or humiliate others; retaliation for real or perceived wrongs or injustices committed against them; hostility or anger toward a specific group of people; problems with emotional regulation; or simply because they have learned throughout their lives that sexual abuse of others is acceptable.

Much research on sexual offenders has been conducted, most notably over the past 30 years, in order to understand the motivations and dynamics of offending behavior so the recurrence of these harmful and destructive acts can be prevented. Simultaneously, various treatment intervention models have been developed and implemented with this group of offenders in order to reduce the risk of revictimization. This chapter reviews treatment approaches utilized historically and presently with this population, with a focus on recent adaptations to the relapse prevention (RP) model that have been applied to the treatment of sexual offenders.

TREATMENT OF SEXUAL OFFENDERS

The variety of treatment interventions that have been implemented with sexual offenders include general psychotherapy, surgery, hormonal therapy, behavioral reconditioning, cognitive-behavioral intervention, and relapse prevention (e.g., Abel et al., 1984; Barbaree & Seto, 1997; Grossman, Martis & Fichtner, 1999; Hansen & Lykke-Olesen, 1997; Maletzky, 1991; Marshall, 1996; Marshall, Jones, Ward, Johnson & Barbaree, 1991; Robinson & Valcour, 1995; Yates, 2002). Earlier treatment approaches assumed that sexual offending was caused by a single factor, such as anger or deviant sexual arousal (Becker & Murphy, 1998; Marshall, 1996). Over time, the multidimensional nature of sexual offending came to be recognized, and treatment approaches incorporated a variety of elements designed to address these multiple criminogenic needs (Marshall, Anderson & Fernandez, 1999; Yates et al., 2000).

The treatment of choice for sexual offenders at present adheres to the principles of effective correctional intervention (Andrews & Bonta, 1998), in which treatment is matched to the risk posed by individual offenders (*risk principle*), specifically targets their criminogenic needs (*need principle*), and is tailored to the individual learning styles and abilities of offenders (*responsivity principle*). Effective treatment also follows the cognitive-behavioral model, which demonstrates the greatest impact on reoffense rates of sexual offenders (Hanson, Gordon, Harris, Marques, Murphy, Quinsey & Seto, 2002).

Generally, cognitive-behavioral interventions are based on the premise that cognition, emotion, and behavior are linked and that each influences the other in the development, shaping, and maintenance of behavior (Yates, 2003). Treatment based on this model traditionally attempts to replace offenders' maladaptive and deviant responses and attitudes with "adaptive" beliefs and behavior by focusing on eliminating deficiencies and improving a variety of skills via reflection, cognitive restructuring, and behavioral rehearsal. Common methods of intervention include identifying high risk situations, identifying coping and other skills deficits, challenging cognitive distortions utilized by offenders in the commission of their offenses, developing empathy (either in general or toward the victims of sexual crimes), coping with negative emotional states, enhancing social and intimate relationships, reconditioning deviant sexual arousal, and developing effective problem-solving strategies (Marshall et al., 1999; Yates et al., 2000).

There have been several problems with the treatment of sexual offenders to date. First is the application of the cognitive-behavioral model to the treatment of sexual offenders in the absence of a coherent overarching theory that serves to unify its various elements and to guide practice. Another problem with treatment models to date has been the assumption that offenders have responded to their life circumstances in a maladaptive manner. It is suggested, however, that some offenders have responded adaptively to the circumstances they encounter, including their own experiences of abuse and the humiliation of being the social pariah known as the sexual offender (Marshall et al., 1999). This assumption has led to treatment methods that are problem-focused and that seek to eliminate offenders' deficits and to overcome their various deficiencies. Until recently, treatment methods have ignored offenders' strengths, goals, and aspirations, and have failed to incorporate positive psychology (Aspinwall & Staudinger, 2003; Linley & Joseph, 2004; Ward & Gannon, 2006; Ward & Stewart, 2003) or to situate their offending behavior and risk management in the context of their lives (Ward, Vess, Collie & Gannon, in press; Ward, Yates & Long, 2006).

As described in the next section, the application of the RP model to sexual offending has contributed to the problems inherent in the treatment of sexual offenders. In the section following, recent revisions to cognitive-behavioral intervention with sexual offenders, which incorporate and expand upon RP and situate intervention within an overarching theory of rehabilitation, are described.

RELAPSE PREVENTION APPLIED TO THE TREATMENT OF SEXUAL OFFENDERS

As indicated earlier, treatment of sexual offenders in many jurisdictions purports to follow the cognitive-behavioral model. Adherence to the principles of this model may vary considerably, but a consistent trend among treatment programs is the inclusion of the RP approach to treatment (Freeman-Longo, Bird, Stevenson & Fiske, 1994; Laws, Hudson & Ward, 2000; Polaschek, 2003). What is clear, however, based on reviews of treatment programs and discussions with clinicians and agencies, is that none of these programs actually apply either the original Marlatt (Marlatt, 1982, 1985; Marlatt & Gordon, 1985) model of RP, nor its later adaptations to sexual offenders (Laws, 1989; Pithers, 1990; Pithers, Kashima, Cumming & Beal, 1988; Pithers, Marques, Gibat & Marlatt, 1983). It has been suggested (Ward & Hudson, 1998, 2000; Yates, 2005; Yates & Kingston, 2005) that this has resulted from the inability of this model to account for the diversity evident among sexual offenders and their unique pathways to offending, which has resulted in clinicians having to adapt the model on an *ad hoc* basis in the absence of theory, as client needs present in treatment.

Based on these adaptations, the goal of treatment for sexual offenders using RP was to assist them to identify and anticipate problems that could lead to *relapse* (i.e., a return to sexual offending behavior) and to teach them a variety of cognitive and behavioral skills to cope with these problems when they arose (Laws & Ward, 2006; Marques et al., 1992; Pithers, 1990, 1991). Sexual offending behavior was viewed as a cycle or sequence of events that could be interrupted by the individual, thus preventing reoffending, when the individual became aware of the cycle and developed the ability to intervene in the sequence. Sexual offenders following RP-based programs were taught to identify high-risk situations that would place them at risk for a *lapse*, originally defined (Marlatt, 1982) as a return to the problematic behavior (i.e., substance abuse) and redefined in sexual offender treatment as behavior approximating or preceding sexual offending, such as the reemergence of deviant sexual fantasy or the use of pornography (Ward et al., 2006). In encountering high-risk situations, individuals were purported to make a series of seemingly irrelevant decisions, embarking on a course of action that, while appearing innocuous, was in reality subconsciously purposive and would lead to offending behavior. Once in the situation, it was then that offenders would experience the problem of immediate gratification, essentially being unable to resist offending due to anticipation of its positive rewards. When a lapse occurred, the individual would then experience the *abstinence violation effect*, a series of negative emotions, expectations of failure, and ultimately, abandonment of the abstinence goal and an increased risk to reoffend. In treatment using RP, the individual would be taught a variety of skills in order to implement adaptive coping responses at various points in the sequence, which would function to further increase self-efficacy and positive outcome expectancies, and reduce risk via a return to abstinence behavior.

The RP model as applied to sexual offenders has been widely accepted as a method of treatment for sexual offenders, despite a lack of empirical research supporting its use with this population (Hanson, 1996, 2000; Laws, 2003; Laws & Ward, 2006; Yates, 2005; Yates & Kingston, 2005) and problems with the theoretical model (Ward et al., 2006; Yates, 2005). In addition to problems with the theoretical model (for a detailed discussion of these problems, see Laws, Hudson, and Ward, 2000 and Ward et al., 2006), the application of RP to the treatment of sexual offenders has been problematic in practice (Yates, 2005; Yates & Kingston, 2005; Yates et al., 2000; Ward et al., 2006). To begin, the RP model is viewed as insufficient to account for the heterogeneity evident among sexual offenders and their multiple motivations for engaging in sexually offensive behavior. In addition, the RP model assumes that these individuals are motivated to change their behavior and to abstain from sexual offending (Laws, 2000; Thornton, 1997). As any clinician will note, sexual offenders are not infrequently disinclined to cease offending. It can be argued that RP-based treatment is simply inappropriate for individuals who are unmotivated to change at the start of treatment. In addition, the construct of abstinence as applied to sexual offenders is, in itself, problematic, as the ultimate outcome of treatment is not to ensure abstinence from sexual behavior, but to ensure cessation of sexually *offensive* behavior. Furthermore, that which an individual seeks via sexual offending behavior (e.g., intimacy, sexual gratification) can be viewed as an essential human goal that the sexual offender obtains via unacceptable means (Ward & Gannon, 2006; Ward & Stewart, 2003) and which he or she should continue to pursue, although via acceptable means.

Another problem with the RP model as it has been applied to sexual offenders is its reliance on predominantly negative affect as a motivating factor for offending behavior (Ward & Hudson, 1998; Yates, 2005). Although negative emotional states certainly play a role in offending for some individuals, others are motivated by positive affect, such as anticipation of offending, sexual gratification, successfully achieving revenge or causing harm, and achieving "intimacy." Such individuals are unlikely to experience an abstinence violation effect, as their offending behavior indicates successful progression toward a desired end.

The RP model as applied to sexual offending also fails to account adequately for variations in the degree of planning of sexual offending which, for some individuals, is quite extensive and explicit. As such, whereas those individuals who desire to avoid offending may progress to offending via engaging in seemingly irrelevant decisions, those who do not so desire are unlikely to experience this process, thus rendering inapplicable this essential aspect of the RP model to these particular individuals. In fact, if the offender is working toward a desired end, the applicability of the construct of seemingly irrelevant decisions is itself questionable—that is, the decisions they make may in fact be quite relevant to the achievement of the desired end resulting from sexual offending.

Another problem with the application of RP to the treatment of sexual offenders lies in its overemphasis on avoidance strategies for reducing risk to reoffend. Although RP in the field of substance abuse and its treatment has been refined, and over the years incorporated multiple influences on behavior (Buhringer, 2000; Donovan, 1996; Marlatt, 1996; Shiffman, 1989; Witkiewitz & Marlatt, 2004), the model has remained essentially unchanged over the past 15 years in the treatment of sexual offenders. Furthermore, the consideration of approach goals, which are easier to achieve over the long term than are avoidance goals (Mann, 2000; Mann, Webster, Schofield & Marshall, 2004), appears to have changed very little in the field of sexual offending. That is, many treatment programs continue to rely on ensuring that offenders adequately identify situations that are likely to place them at risk, for which the predominant coping strategy is to avoid these situations. It is acknowledged that there are clearly some situations that offenders should avoid, at least in the early stages of treatment (e.g., victim access—an empirically demonstrated risk factor for recidivism; Hanson & Harris, 1998, 2000) and that avoidance can be essential to ensuring public safety and managing risk to reoffend. However, many of the circumstances that place sexual offenders at risk are *unavoidable* in the sense that they represent internal conditions, rather than external circumstances. In addition, if it is accepted that the ultimate goals that offenders seek via offending are legitimate (e.g., achievement of intimacy, establishment of relationships, sexual gratification), then it is obvious that it is more appropriate to assist them in treatment to achieve these in acceptable, legal, and nonharmful ways, rather than to avoid attempting to achieve these altogether.

BEYOND RELAPSE PREVENTION: THE SELF-REGULATION MODEL

Recent research suggests that, whereas some sexual offenders commit their offenses as a result of self-regulatory failure, others do so via careful and systematic planning (Laws et al., 2000; Ward, Louden, Hudson & Marshall, 1995; see later). As a result of this research and the problems with RP identified earlier, Ward and Hudson (1998, 2000) developed an alternative approach to the treatment of sexual offenders, based on self-regulation theory (Baumeister & Heatherton, 1996; Karoly, 1993; Thompson, 1994). The self-regulation model of offending was explicitly developed to account for the variety of offense pathways evident in sexual offenders and to provide therapists with a more comprehensive treatment model (Ward et al., 2004). Consistent with research on best practice in correctional and sexual offender therapy, the model follows a cognitive-behavioral orientation (Hanson et al., 2002), utilizes a skills-based approach (Hanson & Yates, 2004), is designed to assist offenders to work toward positive (approach) goals (Mann, 2000; Mann et al., 2004) and to gain a sense of agency (Ward et al., in press), and encour-ages the use of effective therapeutic techniques (Fernandez, 2006; Marshall et al., 1999).

NINE-PHASE SELF-REGULATION MODEL OF OFFENDING

The Self-Regulation Model (SRM) posits nine phases in the offense progression and four distinct pathways that lead to sexual offending. The nine phases of offending are illustrated in Figure 10.1 and are briefly described next. A comprehensive description of the nine phases and four pathways can be found in Ward and Hudson (1998, 2000) and in Ward et al. (2004).

In Phase 1 of the SRM, the individual experiences a life event that triggers an appraisal of the event based on existing cognitive schema, goals, needs, and implicit theories. This appraisal occurs relatively automatically, influences the information to which the individual attends, and activates entrenched cognitive and behavioral scripts and emotional states (positive or negative) developed

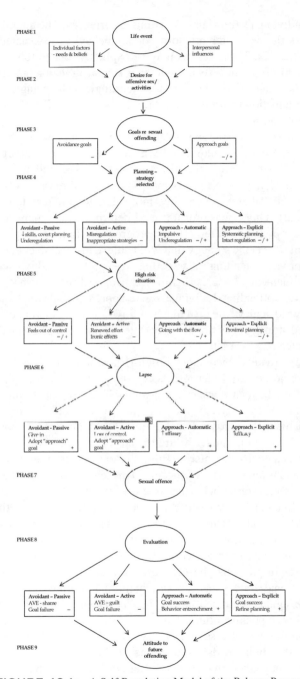

FIGURE 10.1: A Self-Regulation Model of the Relapse Process

during the individual's life via his learning experiences. The appraisal of the life event triggers the desire for offending or for behaviors associated with sexual offending (Phase 2). These desires may be explicitly related to sexual offending (direct route to offending), such as deviant sexual urges or fantasy, or may be related to other states (indirect route to offending), such as anger, hostility, suspicion, or anticipation that are associated in the individual's offense progression with sexual offending.

After the desire to offend is triggered, the individual establishes an offense-related goal (Phase 3). The individual evaluates the acceptability of this goal and his or her ability to tolerate the affective states associated with the desire to offend. Specifically, some offenders may be motivated to refrain from offending (avoidance goal), whereas others are motivated to progress toward offending (approach goal). This offense-related goal determines the manner in which the individual next proceeds in the offense progression. In the next phase (Phase 4), the individual selects the strategy that will achieve his goal to either avoid offending or to approach offending. In selecting strategies, individuals with avoidance goals will implement strategies that they expect will reestablish self-control and that will prevent offending. Individuals with approach goals implement strategies that will serve to achieve the goal of offending. The combination of offense goals (Phase 3) and strategy selection (Phase 4) determines the pathway the individual follows to offending (see later).

When the individual encounters a high-risk situation (Phase 5), he or she has gained access to potential victims. Access may result from implicit or explicit planning or from happenstance or opportunity. The individual evaluates this situation in light of offense-related goals and the expected effectiveness of strategies selected to achieve these goals. For individuals with an avoidant goal, encountering a high-risk situation signals failure to control behavior, whereas for offenders with an approach goal, encountering this situation signals progress toward achieving the goal and is an indicator of success. This leads to a lapse (Phase 6), defined in the SRM as preoffense behaviors that are likely to lead to sexual offending. Once the individual has reached this phase, it is hypothesized that he or she intends to offend and that individuals following avoidance pathways switch to approach pathways, at least temporarily, attributing the lapse to personal failure and the inability to exercise self-control. If the offender has experienced negative affective states in previous phases, these may be replaced or supplemented by positive emotional states, such as anticipation; for offenders having approach goals, a lapse signals continued success in achieving the desired end and typically is associated with positive affect.

In the commission of a sexual offense (Phase 7), the SRM suggests (Ward et al., 1995) that individuals' perceptions of the victims of their offenses are related to distinct goals with respect to offending. Specifically, in committing the offense, different offenders will have a *self focus* (in which their own needs were paramount), a *victim focus* (in which they view the offense as justifiable based on a "caring" perspective toward the victim), or a *mutual focus* (in which the offender views the offense as constituting a "relationship" with the victim). These foci are hypothesized to be associated with differences in the duration and intrusiveness of the offense (Ward et al., 1995), and clearly reflect different offense goals and the individuals' cognitive construction of the offense.

One innovation in the SRM is the addition of two post-offense phases, in which individuals evaluate their behavior immediately following the offense (Phase 8) and develop intentions and expectations with respect to future offending (Phase 9). Following the commission of the offense, individuals following having an avoidant goal are likely to experience guilt, shame, a sense of failure, cognitive deconstruction, and cognitive dissonance associated with the contrast between their behavior and their goal of avoiding offending. They are likely to attribute the cause of offending to internal factors that are uncontrollable and stable and to engage in cognitive distortions that justify their offending behavior based on these causes (e.g., "I don't know what happened to me," "I tried to stop, but I couldn't"). Conversely, individuals with an approach goal are likely to attribute their offending behavior to external causes and to engage in cognitive distortions that focus outside themselves, such as blaming the victim. In the final phase, the SRM posits that offenders with avoidant goals may resolve not to offend again in future, or, alternatively, they may conclude that they lack the requisite skills to prevent offending and so adopt an approach goal with respect to future offending. Offenders with approach goals are reinforced for their "success" in achieving their offense goals, and may use the offense experience to refine their offense strategies in the future. For all individuals, the offense experience is assimilated into their existing implicit theories and cognitive schema and influence their attitude toward offending and the interpretation and appraisal of future offense-related events.

FOUR SELF-REGULATION PATHWAYS

In brief, the SRM contains a number of pathways, representing different combinations of offense-related goals (i.e., the aim to approach or avoid the sexual offense), and the use of distinct regulation styles in relation to sexually offensive contact (underregulation, misregulation, and effective regulation). Each pathway is then further divided into implicit and explicit subpathways according to the varying degrees of awareness associated with offending. These pathways are reviewed briefly here and are summarized in Table 10.1. For additional information, refer to Ward and Hudson (1998, 2000), Ward et al. (2004), and Yates and Kingston (2005).

The *avoidant-passive* pathway is characterized by the desire to avoid sexual offending but the person lacks the coping skills to prevent it from happening (i.e., underregulation). The *avoidant-active* pathway is characterized by misregulation. There is a direct attempt to control deviant thoughts and fantasies but use of ineffective or counterproductive strategies. The *approach-automatic* pathway is characterized by underregulation, the desire to offend sexually, and impulsive

TABLE 10.1:   Summary of the Four Pathways Proposed by the Self-Regulation Model

Pathway	Self-Regulatory Style	Description
Avoidant-passive	Underregulation	Desire to avoid sexual offending but lacking the coping skills to prevent it from happening
Avoidant-active	Misregulation	Direct attempt to control deviant thoughts and fantasies but use of ineffective or counterproductive strategies
Approach-automatic	Underregulation	Overlearned sexual scripts for offending, impulsive, and poorly planned behavior
Approach-explicit	Effective regulation	Desire to sexually offend and the use of careful planning to execute offenses; harmful goals concerning sexual offending

and poorly planned behavior. Finally, the *approach-explicit* pathway is characterized by the desire to offend sexually, the use of careful planning to execute offenses, and the presence of harmful goals concerning sexual offending.

EMPIRICAL SUPPORT FOR THE
SELF-REGULATION MODEL OF OFFENDING

Because the SRM has been developed relatively recently, there has been little opportunity to evaluate its practical application. Although implemented as the model of treatment in several jurisdictions (Yates, 2005), data on treatment effectiveness and impact on recidivism are not yet available. However, several empirical studies have been conducted to validate the theoretical constructs of the model. This research is summarized here. For a more detailed review of this research, refer to Ward et al. (2004) and Yates and Kingston (2005).

In an initial qualitative analysis of the self-regulation model that yielded the nine-stage model of offending described above, Ward et al. (1995) found that the model was able to accommodate two distinct types of child molesters. Specifically, the first type of child molester (n = 5) fit the profile of a typical pedophile (i.e., preferential), whose offense progression incorporated explicit planning, high levels of positive emotion during offending, and an explicit desire to offend (i.e., an approach-type pathway). The second group of child molesters (n = 6) was characterized by high levels of anxiety and negative affect, implicit rather than explicit planning of offenses, and a desire to avoid offending (i.e., an avoidant-type pathway). This pathway was consistent with child molesters who are situational rather than preferential.

Proulx, Perreault, and Ouimet (1999) found evidence of two offense pathways, which they termed *coercive* and *noncoercive*. In a study of untreated extrafamilial child molesters (n = 44), the coercive pathway (68%) was associated with unplanned offending against a female victim who was well known to the offender and whom the offender did not perceive as vulnerable. By contrast, the noncoercive pathway (31%) was associated with planned offenses against unfamiliar male victims whom the offender perceived as vulnerable, significantly more deviant sexual fantasies, significantly greater use of pornography, and greater use of psychoactive substances.

In a study of male child molesters (n = 87) participating in a community-based residential treatment program, Bickley and Beech (2002) found that offenders following an approach pathway were significantly more likely to have offended against either extrafamilial victims or against both extrafamilial and intrafamilial victims, against boy victims or both boy and girl victims' and to have previous convictions for sexual offenses. They were less likely to be involved in a long-term marital relationship, demonstrated significantly higher levels of cognitive distortions and significantly higher levels of emotional congruence with children, and experienced positive emotional states during the offence progression than offenders following an avoidant pathway. This study also found that offenders using passive strategies were more likely than offenders using active strategies to blame external factors for their offending behavior, were more likely to have a prior conviction for a sexual offense, and were less likely to be involved in a long-term relationship.

In a study of treated intrafamilial and extrafamilial child molesters (n = 59), Bickley and Beech (2003) found that offenders could be reliably classified as following an approach (n = 44) or avoidant (n = 15) pathway. As compared to offenders following an avoidant pathway, offenders following an approach pathway were less likely to be involved in a stable marital or long-term relationship, were more likely to have offended against either extrafamilial or both intrafamilial and extrafamilial victims, and were more likely to have had offended against boys or against both boys and girls. This study also found differences between offenders following different pathways with respect to pre/post change on treatment targets, with offenders following an approach pathway demonstrating significantly greater improvements in cognitive distortions and victim empathy.

Webster (2005) examined the offense pathways of sexual recidivists (n = 25) who had participated in sex offender treatment. This study found coping and planning strategies were different for offenders following different pathways. Specifically, recidivists following an avoidant-active pathway were characterized by substance use and pornography to cope with deviant thoughts. Offenders following an approach-automatic pathway demonstrated a tendency to respond rapidly to situational cues and to hold offense-supportive cognitions activated upon meeting the victim. Offenders following an approach-explicit pathway were characterized by deviant behavior that was carefully planned. In addition, recidivists with approach goals expressed a desire to offend sexually.

In a study designed to evaluate the relationship between risk to reoffend sexually and offense pathways, Yates, Kingston, and Hall (2003) found significant differences in offense pathways among various types of treated incarcerated sexual offenders (n = 80). Rapists were more likely to follow either an approach-automatic (58%) or approach-explicit (36%) pathway than an avoidant pathway, whereas child molesters with male victims were most likely to follow an approach-explicit pathway (83%). Child molesters with female victims were equally likely to follow either an approach-automatic or approach-explicit pathway (43%). Finally, although half of intrafamilial (incest) offenders followed an approach-explicit pathway, a considerable number of these offenders also followed an avoidant-passive pathway to offending (38%). This study also found that offenders following an approach-automatic pathway were at significantly higher risk to re-offend than offenders following any of the other pathways, as measured by the Static-99 (Hanson & Thornton, 1999). Between 60 and 70 percent of offenders classified as medium-high or high risk on the Static-99 fell into the two approach pathways.

In a follow-up analysis, Yates & Kingston (2006) examined differences in static and dynamic risk levels and factors among offenders following the four self-regulation pathways. Offenders following an avoidant-passive pathway scored significantly lower on the Static-99 than did offenders following either an approach-automatic or approach-explicit pathway. Dynamic risk was assessed using the Violence Risk Scale: Sex Offender Version (Gordon, Nicholaichuk, Olver & Wong, 2000), which yields three dynamic risk factors, including sexual deviance (reflecting such processes as a sexually compulsive lifestyle and deviant sexual preference), criminality (reflecting nonsexual criminal behavior and criminal personality), and treatment responsivity (reflecting amenability to, and compliance with, treatment and supervision). Offenders following the approach-automatic or approach-explicit pathway scored significantly higher on the dynamic risk factor, criminality, than offenders following an avoidant-passive pathway. Criminality scores were significantly higher for the approach-automatic path way as compared to the approach-explicit pathway. Finally, higher static risk significantly predicted membership in the approach pathways, and there was a non-significant tendency for higher criminality scores to be predictive of membership in the approach pathways.

DEVELOPMENT OF THE SRM

One strength of the SRM is its attention to the roles of agency and self-regulation in the offense process. The notion that offenders are seeking to achieve specific, legitimate goals suggests that they respond to the meaning of particular events in light of their values and knowledge. They intervene in the world on the basis of their interpretations of personal and social events in striving to achieve these life goals. Though it is true that individuals following pathways characterized by *implicit* goals and plans are less aware of the implications of these underlying goals, within the SRM, they are still psychological agents capable of engaging in meaningful actions. A second strength of the SRM is its dynamic nature and its assumption that the offense process can only be adequately understood in light of the interaction between individuals, their goals, and their relevant life circumstances. As such, there is a strong contextual element in the SRM in the determination of offending and relapse behavior. Third, it has received empirical support by a number of independent studies (see earlier) indicating its content and construct validity.

Alongside these strengths are some areas of weakness. Perhaps the greatest weakness of the SRM resides in its privileging of goals relating to behavioral control (i.e., purely offense-related goals concerning deviant sexual activity) and subsequent failure to explicitly document the manner in which human goods and their pursuit are causally related to sexually offending. From the perspective of self-regulation theory, sexual offending is likely to reflect the influence of a multitude of goals and their related human goods. One of the assumptions of our recent theory of rehabilitation, the Good Lives Model (GLM; Ward & Gannon, 2006; Ward & Stewart, 2003; Ward, Vess et al., in press; Ward et al., 2006), is that offenders are psychological agents who are seeking to live meaningful, satisfactory, and worthwhile lives. The fact that they fail to do this suggests there are problems in the ways they are seeking human goods; problems embodying a number of flaws in their good lives plans (i.e., inappropriate means, lack of scope, incoherence or conflict, and lack of capacity). Thus, an important level of analysis when working with sexual offenders revolves around their sense of personal identity and the value commitments and aspirations that comprise this important psychological factor.

We do not have the space to describe the embedding of the SRM with the larger rehabilitative framework of the GLM in this chapter and refer interested readers to the publications cited earlier. However, in brief we have broadened the range of approach goals likely to be directly or indirectly associated with both the initial offense and subsequent relapse. For example, individuals may be seeking intimacy, emotional relief, retribution, pleasure, or a sense of agency (i.e., via dominating or controlling another person) through the commission of a sexual offense. Thus, treatment within the GLM/SRM focuses not only on self-regulation deficits, problem areas, and risk factors, but also on individuals' strengths and the goals they seek to achieve in life, with the aim of working toward the achievement of these goals in prosocial, nonoffending ways.

CLINICAL CASE ILLUSTRATION

We will now briefly illustrate the application of the SRM to the treatment of sex offenders by way of two case examples. The two cases represent composites of a number of individuals from each pathway, and we have set out to capture the particular treatment challenges and issues associated with each type of offender.

CASE EXAMPLE: MR. A

Mr. A has been convicted of two sexual offenses against boys under the age of 10 years. All offenses, which Mr. A committed between the ages of 15 and 23 years, involved fondling and fellatio. Mr. A received a fine and a period of probation for the first offense and a prison term for the second offense. Mr. A has no other criminal history.

Mr. A has never attained a long-term intimate relationship with an adult partner and reports never having engaged in sexual intercourse with an age-appropriate female and that he is not sexually attracted to adult males. He indicates that he is shy and reluctant to attempt establishing age-appropriate relationships.

Mr. A's offenses are based in a variety of skills deficits, including intimacy and social relationships, and sexual arousal to boys. The first two incidents of offending were similar in that he made contact with an unknown prepubescent male whom he manipulated to go to a park and whom he fondled and fellated. The second involved "cruising" his neighborhood to find a victim. He reported that, at the time, he had been unable to find employment and felt worthless. The index offense was committed against a neighbor's child whom he had agreed to baby-sit.

Prior to offending, at the age of twelve, Mr. A began to masturbate to fantasies of boys, although he attempted to think about age-appropriate females while doing so. This strategy ultimately failed, and he felt guilty about his sexual attraction to boys. He spoke to a school counselor following his first offense but reported no impact of this intervention, after which he "just wanted to forget" about the incident. His sexual attraction to boys was preferential. He had not previously participated in treatment for sexual offending.

Mr. A was allocated to the avoidant-passive pathway due to his desire to avoid offending (e.g., feeling guilty after the offenses). Although he had attempted on occasion to intervene, which would be indicative of an avoidant-active pathway, he generally tended to ignore high-risk situations, to view his actions as beyond his control, to feel helpless and inadequate, and to avoid acting to address his problems, and was thus assessed as predominantly following an avoidant-passive pathway. His early strategies as an adolescent, prior to offending (i.e., avoidance, switching the object of his masturbatory fantasizes from boys to age-appropriate females), failed. It was noted that Mr. A may have been moving toward an approach pathway as indicated in his third offense, in which he actively sought out a victim.

Mr. A was assessed as demonstrating several risk factors that indicated he sought to achieve intimacy, agency, emotional control, and social acceptance via offending. His dynamic risk factors included intimacy deficits, social rejection, emotional identification or congruence with children (provisional), problems with general self-regulation (problem solving, coping with negative emotionality), use of sex as a coping mechanism (provisional), deviant sexual interests, and attitudes supportive of sexual activity with children.

Based on assessment and matching of static and dynamic risk factors (risk level moderate-high), Mr. A completed a high intensity sexual offender treatment program (approximately 9 to 12 months), followed by maintenance programming. This intensity level reflected the presence of multiple static and dynamic risk factors and, particularly, the need in treatment to adequately assess and modify deviant sexual interest or preference. Treatment focused on the development of skills to modify the dynamic risk factors listed earlier, and to secure important personal goals (e.g., intimacy, emotional control) in prosocial and adaptive ways. Treatment proceeded well and Mr. A acquired both risk-management skills and was able to start to pursue his personal goals satisfactorily without offending.

UNSUCCESSFUL CASE EXAMPLE: MR. B

Mr. B was a 40-year-old man convicted of six counts of sexual assault for offenses committed over a period of eight years against one victim, a boy between the ages of 10 and 18 years. He pled guilty to these offenses. Mr. B had met the victim of his offenses when he was working as a handyman for the boy's family and offended against him progressively via fondling, having the boy masturbate him and perform fellatio on him, and forcing anal sexual intercourse. He was able to maintain the abuse via threats that the boy would not be believed if he reported the assaults. Mr. B had been previously arrested on two occasions for sexual assault of teenaged boys, when Mr. B was 19 years old and again when he was 26 years old. He participated in prison-based treatment and was released at the age of 32. While in prison, Mr. B coerced sexual activity from other inmates in exchange for helping them in prison, as well as against other boys when he was young and in school.

Mr. B was allocated to the approach-explicit pathway, due to his approach goal to offending and his explicit and planned behavior to achieve this goal. He did not attempt to refrain from offending and sought out his victims via his employment, choosing to work in settings in which he knew he would have access to children and would be alone with them. He specifically targeted vulnerable children, whom he described as "misfits, the lonely ones who would spend time around me," and whose trust he believed he could easily gain. Mr. B had also targeted boys in the residential school he attended as a boy, where he was also sexually abused by the priests running the school. He reported a sense of power associated with abusing the other boys, which he regarded as "teaching them about life." During his first prison term, Mr. B was similarly sexually assaulted by an older inmate, whom he regarded as a "protector," and later began to target younger inmates in order to "educate them about prison life," charging them his rightful "fee" for their protection. He regarded these activities as consensual. He does not regard his sexual abuse of boys and men throughout his life as harmful or abusive. In fact, he believes that he provides them a service or legitimately obtains what is rightfully his. Mr. B had completed sexual offender treatment during his prison term, after which he reoffended.

Mr. B was assessed as demonstrating several risk factors that indicated he sought to achieve a sense of agency and personal power and control via offending, and that he held a hostile and suspicious worldview. His dynamic risk factors included intimacy deficits, lack of concern for others, attitudes supportive of sexual offending, cognitive distortions, deviant sexual interests, and a lack of positive social influences.

Based on assessment and matching of static and dynamic risk factors (assessed as high risk), Mr. B required intensive treatment and supervision, including a high intensity sexual offender treatment program (approximately 12 to 24 months), followed by follow-up maintenance programming and intensive supervision in the community. This intensity level reflected Mr. B's high risk to reoffend, relative to other sexual offenders, and the nature and persistence of dynamic risk factors with which he presented.

The key in treatment with Mr. B was to invoke change with respect to both his attitudes that support sexual offending and his view of the world. If Mr. B did not come to regard sexual offending as inappropriate or did not change his worldview, treatment likely would be ineffective. It is likely that the previous treatment program in which he participated was unsuccessful in preventing reoffending because it was not able to assist Mr. B to challenge and change his core belief systems or to provide him with a sense of optimism, efficacy, and options to achieve goals, such as agency or personal power, and to change his life in a positive manner. Once amenability to explore alternatives was created, the dynamic risk factors indicated earlier were targeted, and strategies later developed when Mr. B had begun to consider adopting an avoidance goal with respect to sexual offending and positive life goals toward which he needs to continue to work.

Treatment with Mr. B proved to be very difficult due to the entrenched nature of his pedophilic beliefs and also his high level of offense-related expertise. He expressed considerable pride in his ability to effectively establish relationships with children and to identify their "emotional needs." At present Mr. B is being considered for further, more intensive treatment specifically focused on his schemata involving children and adults.

CONCLUSIONS AND FUTURE DIRECTIONS

In this chapter we have described the formulation and development of the self-regulation model of the offense and relapse process. In our view, this model works because of its ability to accommodate three very simple but important insights into sexual offending: (1) individuals seek a variety of goals through sexual offending, and utilize various strategies to achieve them; (2) there are different offense trajectories reflecting the fact that these goals are indirectly or directly associated with offending; and (3) treatment therefore needs to equip offenders with the capabilities to achieve their goals based on these differences in goals and strategies in certain environments.

It is our expectation that future empirical and theoretical work will continue to evaluate and refine the SRM. One message is clear: one size does not fit all and the SRM by virtue of its inclusion of multiple pathways and goals, is able to deal with the heterogeneity of offenders and the variations in risk to offend with which they present. It is an integrated, comprehensive, and relatively simple model that is consistent with what we know, at this stage, to be the essential features of effective intervention with sex offenders.

REFERENCES

Abel, G.G., Becker, J.V., Cunningham-Rathner, J., Rouleau, J., Kaplan, M., Reich, J. (1984). *The treatment of child molesters.* Atlanta, GA: Behavioral Medicine Laboratory, Emory University.

Abel, G.G., Blanchard, E.B. (1974). The role of fantasy treatment of deviation. *Archives of General Psychiatry* 30:467–475.

American Psychiatric Association (2000). *Diagnostic and statistical manual of mental disorders* (Fourth Edition; DSM-IV-TR). Arlington, VA: American Psychiatric Publishing, Inc.

Andrews, D.A., Bonta, J. (1998). *The psychology of criminal conduct.* Cincinnati, OH: Anderson Publishing Co.

Aspinwall, L.G., Staudinger, U.M. (Eds.) (2003). *A psychology of human strengths: Fundamental questions and future directions for a positive psychology.* Washington, DC: American Psychological Association.

Barbaree, H.E., Seto, M.C. (1997). Pedophilia: Assessment and treatment. In Laws, D.R., O'Donohue, W.T., eds., *Sexual deviance: Theory, assessment, and treatment*, 175–193. New York: The Guilford Press.

Baumeister, R.F., Heatherton, T.F. (1996). Self-regulation failure: An overview. *Psychological Inquiry* 7:1–15.

Becker, J.V., Murphy, W.D. (1998). What we know and do not know about assessing and treating sex offenders. *Psychology, Public Policy, Law* 4:116–137.

Bickley, J.A., Beech, R. (2002). An empirical investigation of the Ward and Hudson self-regulation model of the sexual offence process with child abusers. *Journal of Interpersonal Violence* 17:371–393.

Bickley, J.A., Beech, R. (2003). Implications for treatment of sexual offenders of the Ward and Hudson model of relapse. *Sexual Abuse: A Journal of Research and Treatment* 15(2):121–134.

Buhringer, G. (2000). Testing CBT mechanisms of action: Humans behave in a more complex way than our treatment studies would predict. *Addiction* 95:1715–1716.

Donovan, D.M. (1996). Marlatt's classification of relapse precipitants: Is the Emperor still wearing clothes? *Addiction* 91:131–137.

Fernandez, Y.M. (2006). Focusing on the positive and avoiding the negative in sexual offender treatment. In Marshall, W.L., Fernandez, Y.M., Marshall, L.E., Serran, G.A., eds., *Sexual offender treatment: Controversial issues*, 187–197. New Jersey: John Wiley, Sons.

Freeman-Longo, R.E., Bird, S.L., Stevenson, W.F., Fiske, J.A. (1994). *1994 nationwide survey of sexual offender treatment and models*. Brandon, VT: Safer Society Press.

Gordon, A., Nicholaichuk, T., Olver, M., Wong, S. (2000). *Violence risk scale: Sexual offender version*. Saskatchewan: Correctional Service of Canada.

Grossman, L.S., Martis, B., Fichtner, C.G. (1999). Are sex offenders treatable? A research review. *Psychiatric Services* **50**:349–361.

Hanson, R.K. (1996). Evaluating the contribution of relapse prevention theory to the treatment of sexual offenders. *Sexual Abuse: A Journal of Research and Treatment* **8**:201–208.

Hanson, R.K. (2000). What is so special about relapse prevention? In Laws, D.R., Hudson, S.M., Ward, T., eds., *Remaking relapse prevention: A sourcebook*, 27–38. Thousand Oaks, CA: Sage.

Hanson, R.K., Gordon, A., Harris, A.J.R., Marques, J.K., Murphy, W., Quinsey, V.L., Seto, M.C. (2002). First report of the collaborative outcome data project on the effectiveness of psychological treatment for sex offenders. *Sexual Abuse: A Journal of Research and Treatment* **14**:169–194.

Hanson, R.K., Harris, A. (1998). *Dynamic predictors of sexual recidivism*. (User Report No. 1998-01). Ottawa: Department of the Solicitor General of Canada.

Hanson, R.K., Harris, A. (2000). Where should we intervene? Dynamic predictors of sexual offence recidivism. *Criminal Justice and Behavior* **27**:6–35.

Hanson, R.K., Thornton, D. (1999). *Static-99: Improving actuarial risk assessment for sex offenders*. Ottawa: Department of the Solicitor General of Canada.

Hanson, R.K., Yates, P.M. (2004). Sexual violence: Risk factors and treatment. In Eliasson, M., ed., *Anthology on interventions against violent men*, 151–166. Acta Universitatis Upsaliensis, Uppsalla Women's Studies B: Women in the Humanities: 3. Uppsala, Sweden: Uppsala Universitet.

Karoly, P. (1993). Mechanisms of self-regulation: A systems view. *Annual Review of Psychology* **44**:23–52.

Langevin, R. (1983). *Sexual strands*. Hillsdale, NJ: Earlbaum.

Laws, D.R. (Ed.) (1989). *Relapse prevention with sex offenders*. New York, NY: Guilford Press.

Laws, D.R. (2000). Relapse prevention: Reconceptualization and revision. In Hollin, C.R., ed., *Handbook of offender assessment and treatment*, 297–307. Chichester, UK: Wiley.

Laws, D.R. (2003). The rise and fall of relapse prevention. *Australian Psychologist* **38**:22–30.

Laws, D.R., Hudson, S.M., Ward, T. (2000). *Remaking relapse prevention with sex offenders: A sourcebook*. Thousand Oaks, CA: Sage Publication, Inc.

Laws, D.R., Marshall, W.L. (1990). A conditioning theory of the etiology and maintenance of deviant sexual preference and behavior. In Marshall, W.L., Barbaree, H.E., eds., *Handbook of sexual assault: Issues, theories, and treatment of offenders*, 103–113. New York: Plenum Press.

Laws, D.R., Ward, T. (2006). When one size doesn't fit all: The reformulation of relapse prevention. In Marshall, W.L., Fernandez, Y.M., Marshall, L.E., Serran, G.A., eds., *Sexual offender treatment: Controversial issues*, 241–254. New Jersey: John Wiley, Sons.

Linley, P.A., Joseph, S. (2004). Applied positive psychology: A new perspective for professional practice. In Linley, P.A., Joseph, S., eds., *Positive psychology in practice*, 3–12. New Jersey: John Wiley, Sons.

Maletzky, B.M. (1991). *Treating the sexual offender*. Newbury Park: Sage Publications.

Mann, R.E. (2000). Managing resistance and rebellion in relapse prevention intervention. In Laws, D.R., Hudson, S.M., Ward, T., eds., *Remaking relapse prevention with sex offenders: A sourcebook*, 197–200. Thousand Oaks, CA: Sage.

Mann, R.E., Webster, S.D., Schofield, C., Marshall, W.L. (2004). Approach versus avoidance goals in relapse prevention with sexual offenders. *Sexual Abuse: A Journal of Research and Treatment* **16**:65–75.

Marlatt, G.A. (1982). Relapse prevention: A self-control program for the treatment of addictive behaviours. In Stuart, R.B., ed., *Adherence, compliance and generalization in behavioural medicine*, 329–378. New York: Brunner/Mazel.

Marlatt, G.A. (1985). Relapse prevention: Theoretical rationale and overview of the model. In Marlatt, G.A., Gordon, J.R., eds., *Relapse prevention: Maintenance strategies in the treatment of addictive behaviors*, 3–70. New York, NY: Guilford Press.

Marlatt, G.A. (1996). Lest taxonomy become taxidermy: A comment on the relapse replication and extension project. *Addiction* **91**:147–153.

Marlatt, G.A., Gordon, J.R. (1985). *Relapse prevention: Maintenance strategies in the treatment of addictive behaviours*. New York: Guilford.

Marques, J.K., Day, D.M., Nelson, C. (1992). *Findings and recommendations from California's experimental treatment program*. Unpublished manuscript, Sex Offender Treatment and Evaluation Project, Atascadero State Hospital, California.

Marshall, W.L. (1996). Assessment, treatment and theorizing about sex offenders: Developments during the past twenty years and future directions. *Criminal Justice and Behavior* **23**:162–199.

Marshall, W.L. (1999). Current status of North American assessment and treatment programs for sexual offenders. *Journal of Interpersonal Violence* **14**:221–239.

Marshall, W.L., Anderson, D., Fernandez, Y.M. (1999). *Cognitive behavioural treatment of sexual offenders*. Toronto, ON: John Wiley, Sons.

Marshall, W.L., Jones, R., Ward, T., Johnson, P., Barbaree, H.E. (1991). Treatment outcome with sex offenders. *Clinical Psychology Review* **11**:465–485.

Meyer, W.J., Cole, C., Emory, E. (1992). Depo provera treatment for sex offending behavior: An evaluation of outcome. *Bulletin of the American Academy of Psychiatry and Law* **20**:249–259.

Pithers, W.D. (1990). Relapse prevention with sexual aggressors: A method for maintaining therapeutic gain and enhancing external supervision. In Marshall, W.L., Laws, D.R., Barbaree, H.E., eds., *Handbook of sexual assault*, 343–361. New York, NY: Plenum Publishing.

Pithers, W.D., Kashima, K.M., Cumming, G.F., Beal, L.S. (1988). Relapse prevention. A method of enhancing maintenance of change in sex offenders. In Salter, A.C., ed., *Treating child sex offenders and victims: A practical guide*, 131–170. Newbury Park, CA: Sage.

Pithers, W.D., Marques, J.K., Gibat, C.C., Marlatt, G.A. (1983). Relapse prevention: A self-control model of treatment and maintenance of change for sexual aggressives. In Greer, J., Stuart, I., eds., *The sexual aggressor*, 214–239. New York, NY: Van Nostrand Reihold.

Polaschek, D.L.L. (2003). Relapse prevention, offence process models, and the treatment of sexual offenders. *Professional psychology: Research and practice* **34**:361–367.

Proulx, J., Perreault, C., Ouimet, M. (1999). Pathways in the offending process of extra-familial sexual child molesters. *Sexual Abuse: A Journal of Research and Treatment* **11**(2):117–129.

Quinsey, V.L., Chaplin, T.C., Carrigan, W.F. (1980). Biofeedback and signalled punishment in the modification of inappropriate sexual age preferences. *Behavior Therapy* **11**:567–576.

Rice, M.E., Harris, G.T. (2003). The size and sign of treatment effects in sex offenders therapy. *Annals of the New York Academy of Sciences* **989**:428–440.

Robinson, T., Valcour, F. (1995). The use of depo-provera in the treatment of child molesters and sexually compulsive males. *Sexual Addictions, Compulsivity* **2**:277–294.

Shiffman, S. (1989). Conceptual issues in the study of relapse. In Gossop, M., ed., *Relapse and addictive behavior*, 149–179. London: Routledge.

Schweitzer, R., Dwyer, J. (2003). Sex crime recidivism: Evaluation of a sexual offender treatment program. *Journal of Interpersonal Violence* **18**:1292–1310.

Thompson, R.A. (1994). Emotional regulation: A theme in search of definition. In Fox, N.A., ed., *The development of emotion regulation: Biological and behavioral considerations*, 25–52. Monographs of the Society for Research in Child Development, Vol. 59, Serial No. 240.

Thornton, D. (1997). *Is relapse prevention really necessary?* Paper presented at the meeting of the Association for Sexual Abusers, Arlington, VA, October.

Ward, T., Bickley, J., Webster, S.D., Fisher, D., Beech, A., Eldridge, H. (2004). *The self-regulation model of the offense and relapse process: A manual: Volume I: Assessment.* Victoria, BC: Pacific Psychological Assessment Corporation.

Ward, T., Gannon, T. (2006). Rehabilitation, etiology, and self-regulation: The Good Lives model of sexual offender treatment. *Aggression and Violent Behavior* **11**:77–94.

Ward, T., Hudson, S.M. (1998). The construction and development of theory in the sexual offending area: A metatheoretical framework. *Sexual Abuse: A Journal of Research and Treatment* **10**:47–63.

Ward, T., Hudson, S.M. (2000). A self-regulation model of relapse prevention. In Laws, D.R., Hudson, S.M., Ward, T., eds., *Remaking relapse prevention with sex offenders: A sourcebook,* 79–101. Thousand Oaks, CA: Sage.

Ward, T., Louden, K., Hudson, S.M., Marshall, W.L. (1995). A descriptive model of the offence chain for child molesters. *Journal of Interpersonal Violence* **10**:452–472.

Ward, T., Polaschek, D.L.L., Beech, A.R. (2006). *Theories of sexual offending.* New Jersey: John Wiley, Sons.

Ward, T., Stewart, C.A. (2003). The treatment of sex offenders: Risk management and good lives. *Professional Psychology: Research and Practice* **34**:353–360.

Ward, T., Vess, J., Gannon, T., Collie, R. (2006). Risk management or goods promotion: The relationship between approach and avoidance goal in the treatment of sex offenders. *Aggression and Violent Behavior.*

Ward, T., Yates, P.M., Long, C.A. (2006). *The self-regulation model of the offence and re-offence process, Volume II: Treatment.* Victoria, BC: Pacific Psychological Assessment Corporation.

Webster, S.D. (2005). Pathways to sexual offense recidivism following treatment: An examination of the Ward and Hudson self-regulation model of relapse. *Journal of Interpersonal Violence* **20**:1175–1196.

Witkiewitz, K., Marlatt, G.A. (2004). Relapse prevention for alcohol and drug problems: That was Zen, this is Tao. *American Psychologist* **59**:224–235.

Yates, P.M. (2002). What works: Effective intervention with sex offenders. In Allen, H.E., ed., *What works: Risk reduction: Interventions for special needs offenders.* Lanham, MD: American Correctional Association.

Yates, P.M. (2003). Treatment of adult sexual offenders: A therapeutic cognitive-behavioral model of intervention. *Journal of Child Sexual Abuse* **12**:195–232.

Yates, P.M. (2005). Pathways to the treatment of sexual offenders: Rethinking intervention. *Forum, Summer.* Beaverton OR: Association for the Treatment of Sexual Abusers, 1–9.

Yates, P.M., Goguen, B.C., Nicholaichuk, T.P., Williams, S.M., Long, C.A., Jeglic, E., Martin, G. (2000). *National sex offender programs (moderate, low, and maintenance intensity levels).* Ottawa: Correctional Service of Canada.

Yates, P.M., Kingston, D. (2005). Pathways to sexual offending. In Schwartz, B.K., Cellini, H.R., eds., *The sex offender (Volume V)* **3**:1–15. Kingston, NJ: Civic Research Institute.

Yates, P.M., Kingston, D. (2006). Pathways to sexual offending: relationship to static and dynamic risk among treated sexual offenders. *Sexual Abuse: A Journal of Research and Treatment* **18**:259–270.

Yates, P.M., Kingston, D., Hall, K. (2003). *Pathways to sexual offending: Validity of Hudson and Ward's (1998) self-regulation model and relationship to static and dynamic risk among treated high risk sexual offenders.* Presented at the 22nd Annual Research and Treatment Conference of the Association for the Treatment of Sexual Abusers (ATSA). St. Louis, Missouri: October 2003.

SPECIFIC POPULATIONS AND TREATMENT SETTINGS

11

FOCUS ON FAMILIES: INTEGRATION OF RELAPSE PREVENTION AND CHILD DRUG ABUSE PREVENTION TRAINING WITH PARENTS IN METHADONE TREATMENT

RICHARD F. CATALANO,
KEVIN P. HAGGERTY,
CHARLES B. FLEMING, AND
MARTIE L. SKINNER

Social Development Research Group
School of Social Work
University of Washington
Seattle, Washington

INTRODUCTION

The Focus on Families (FOF) program works with men and women who are parents of young children and are in methadone treatment for opiate addiction. A primary goal of FOF is to reduce parents' illicit drug use by teaching them relapse prevention and coping skills. Parents also are taught how to manage their families better, with the goal of preventing drug abuse among their children. The program integrates strategies to address risk factors for parents' relapse, family-related risk factors for children's substance abuse, and the enhancement of family-related protective factors. Focus on Families uses a combination of group skills instruction to parents and their children and individualized, home-based case management. Improvements in family function have a positive impact on the developmental environment for children, and affect family factors that influence parents' relapse. Focus on Families is unique in that it integrates prevention of drug use relapse among parents with the prevention of youth drug use among their children.

Methadone treatment is a tested, effective strategy for reducing illicit drug use among long-term opiate addicts (Farrell et al., 1994). It has been shown to reduce illicit drug use, involvement in criminality, and HIV risk behaviors (National Consensus Development Panel on Effective Medical Treatment of Opiate Addiction, 1998; Sechrest, 1979; Ward, Mattick & Hall, 1998). However, many patients in methadone treatment relapse into abuse of illicit drugs or alcohol (National Consensus Development Panel on Effective Medical Treatment of Opiate Addiction, 1998).

Children of methadone patients are an important target of prevention programs because of the risky environments in which they live. Substance-abusing parents expose their children to numerous risk factors for drug abuse and other problem behaviors (Barnard & McKeganey, 2004; Catalano, Haggerty & Gainey, 2003; Chassin, Pillow, Curran & Molina, 1993; Goodwin, 1985; Sher, 1991). Children living in these families face social isolation and multiple entrapments of parents in extreme poverty, poor living conditions, and low-status occupations (Kumpfer, 1987; Suchman & Luthar, 2000). Difficult life circumstances, such as trouble with the law, frequent moves, frequent arguments, illness, drug and alcohol use by household members, and abusive relationships make parenting more difficult (Jester, Jacobson, Sokol, Tuttle & Jacobson, 2000; Kolar, Brown, Haertzen & Michaelson, 1994; Mercer, 1990; Roosa, Beals, Sandler & Pillow, 1990; Spieker & Booth, 1988). Substance-abusing parents spend fewer hours per week with their children than nonabusers, have poorer parenting practices, and have more problems in many areas of their lives (Bauman & Levine, 1986; Kolar et al., 1994; Sowder & Burt, 1980). These circumstances produce families that are generally disorganized, have few family management skills, have low family cohesion, have high stress, and suffer financial troubles (Kumpfer, 1987; Kumpfer & DeMarsh, 1985). Discipline problems are likely to be elevated in these families due to parents' use of substances (Tarter, Blackson, Martin, Loeber et al., 1993).

The following case note from a Focus on Families case manager offers a glimpse into the chaotic world of methadone patients who are raising children.

> *My first trip to the mother's house was in the evening so that I could have a chance to meet her two sons, ages fourteen and eleven. When I arrived, I saw a woman sitting in a wheelchair about two feet from a large television screen. It was the grandmother and it was evident that the mother was responsible for taking care of her. The grandmother is nearly blind and confined to the house. The house was dimly lit, very cluttered, with things piled on top of every surface.*

> *The mother is unemployed and reports that she spends the majority of her time sleeping. She wanted to get into Focus on Families because she and her kids were "arguing all the time."*
> *The older son, already involved with the juvenile justice system for assaulting his mom and younger brother, has again assaulted his younger brother, and has another referral. This time the older brother wrapped a bathrobe belt around his brother's neck, causing a burn serious enough to warrant reports to CPS by the school psychiatrist. The younger son is developmentally disabled.*
> *The mother's ex-husband is an unemployed house painter who hangs around a lot. He injured his shoulder and is having surgery soon. The mother warned me that the ex-husband is an alcoholic "but I don't let him drink at our house anymore." However, at one meeting I had with the family, he had recently reappeared after being away for a few days and he smelled of alcohol and his speech was slurred.*

This case narrative is an example of the chaotic circumstances of many methadone clients, and of the high-risk environments in which their children are raised.

Studies have identified family factors that contribute to relapse after treatment, including family conflict, lack of family support, drug use among other family and network members, skill deficits, and high life stress (Breese et al., 2005; Brewer et al., 1998; ElGeili & Bashir, 2005; Goehl, Nunes, Quitkin & Hilton, 1993; Havassy, Hall & Wasserman, 1991; Marlatt & Gordon, 1985; Surgeon General, 1988). These malleable relapse factors overlap with family risk factors for children's substance use. These risk factors include poor family management practices, family conflict, favorable parental attitudes toward drug use, and parents involving their children in their drug use. Family characteristics that protect or buffer children from risk include parent-child attachment and warmth, parent support of child competencies, and positive parent-child interaction and communication (Arthur, Hawkins, Pollard, Catalano & Baglioni, 2002; Beyers, Toumbourou, Catalano, Arthur & Hawkins, 2004; Hawkins, Catalano & Miller, 1992; Mrazek & Haggerty, 1994). This overlap in relapse and risk factors in families suggests that the integration of strategies addressing both risk factors for post-treatment relapse and risk and protective factors for adolescent drug use may have a synergistic effect in preventing relapse, as well as children's substance use, in families with parents in substance abuse treatment.

To evaluate this potential synergy, a randomized experimental evaluation of this combined approach was conducted between 1990 and 1997. The Focus on Families program was developed and funded by the National Institute on Drug Abuse. One hundred and thirty families were randomly assigned to program or control conditions and were followed over two and a half years. In these families, 144 parents and 178 children (ages 3 to 14) were enrolled in the study. Three published research reports provide empirical support for the Focus on Families program's effects on relapse outcomes. For the first study (Catalano, Haggerty, Gainey & Hoppe, 1997), parent data were collected immediately after the program ended, and analyses revealed improved relapse coping skills and reduced heroin use among program parents compared to controls. The second (Catalano,

Gainey, Fleming, Haggerty & Johnson, 1999) used data from parent and child surveys six and 12 months after the program and again found significant differences in relapse coping skills and drug use, favoring parents in the experimental group. The third (Catalano et al., 2003) found significant differences in relapse skills, favoring parents in the experimental group at 24-month follow-up and children's report of drug use and antisocial behavior continued to be in the favored direction. The results of these studies are discussed in more detail later. Based on the promising outcomes of this experimental evaluation, Focus on Families has been identified by the National Institute on Drug Abuse and the Substance Abuse and Mental Health Services Administration as a promising program for preventing drug abuse. It is currently being implemented at multiple sites across the United States.

THE PROGRAM

The goals of the Focus on Families program are to (1) reduce the risk of illicit drug use relapse among methadone-treated parents, (2) reduce the risk of drug abuse by children of methadone-treated parents, and (3) increase protective factors against drug abuse among children of methadone-treated parents. The program seeks to create conditions for bonding within the family as well as bonding to prosocial others outside the family by enhancing opportunities, skills, and recognition for involvement, and encouraging families to set clear family policies on drug use (Catalano & Hawkins, 1996). The program accomplishes these goals by using a combination of group-administered parent and child skills training and individualized home-based case management. The Focus on Families program is of long duration, pays particular attention to recruitment and retention mechanisms, and offers other supportive services. The Focus on Families program lasts nine months (4 months of parent-training groups, 9 months of home-based case management services).

PARENT AND CHILD SKILL TRAINING

The Focus on Families parent and child skills training curriculum consists of one five-hour family retreat, 32 1.5-hour parent training sessions, and a home-based case management component. This retreat and parent training are group-administered, with optimal group sizes between six and eight families. Sessions are conducted twice a week over a 16-week period. Children attend 12 of the sessions to practice developmentally appropriate skills with their parents. Parent-only sessions are held in the morning; the sessions children attend generally are conducted in the evening when the children are not in school. Training sessions are co-led by a two-person team to allow for effective demonstration of the skills being taught. Group leaders are master's-level clinicians with extensive backgrounds in parenting, addiction, and mental health issues.

The parent training format combines a peer support and skill training model. The training curriculum teaches skills using "guided participant modeling" (Rosenthal & Bandura, 1978), in which skills are modeled by trainers and other group members, discussed by participants, and then practiced. Videotaping is used frequently in modeling the skills or giving feedback after skill practice. To maximize effectiveness, the training focuses on affective and cognitive as well as behavioral aspects of performance (W.T. Grant Consortium on the School-Based Promotion of Social Competence, 1992). Each session is manualized.

The Focus on Families curriculum allows parents the flexibility to practice skills learned in the program in situations they currently face with their own children. Parents complete home extension exercises after each session to generalize the skills from the training to the home setting (Goldstein & Kanfer, 1979). After parents learn and practice skills, parents and children practice using their new skills together in family training sessions. Following graduation from the parent-training group, families are invited to a monthly potluck. The potlucks serve as a booster sessions for families to help them maintain skills and behavior changes learned or achieved through parent-training sessions. At each potluck, families review their progress toward their goals, go over skill steps, and discuss their use of skills at home.

Session topics are targeted at specific developmental risk and protective factors including the following.

FAMILY GOAL SETTING

The five-hour kickoff retreat focuses on goal setting, bringing families together to share a common, trust-building experience. This session empowers families to work together to develop goals for their participation in the family sessions. Case managers later work with individual families to identify the small steps they need to take in order to reach their identified goals.

RELAPSE PREVENTION

The first four sessions include (1) identification of relapse signals or triggers, (2) anger and stress control, and (3) creating and practicing a plan to follow if relapse occurs. The impact of relapse on the participant's children is emphasized as a motivational tool, and skills are taught to cope with relapse and to prevent relapse-inducing situations. Parents are taught to identify the cognitive, behavioral, and situational antecedents of relapse, and to use self-talk to anticipate the consequences of their drug-using behavior (Hawkins, Catalano & Wells, 1986). In addition to self-talk, parents are taught to use "urge surfing" and distractions as preventive measures against relapse (Marlatt & Gordon, 1985).

FAMILY COMMUNICATION SKILLS

The skills of paraphrasing, open questions, and "I" messages are taught during these sessions. Families practice using the skills during two practice sessions. Families then use these skills to develop family expectations, to conduct regular family meetings, and to make family play and fun time successful.

FAMILY MANAGEMENT SKILLS

Parents learn and practice setting clear and specific expectations, monitoring expectations, rewarding, and providing appropriate negative consequences. They chart both their own behavior consistency and their children's behavior to aid in recognizing and reinforcing the desired behaviors. Parents are taught appropriate consequences for negative behaviors. Parents practice implementing "the law of least intervention," using the smallest intervention to get the desired behavior from their child. A variety of discipline skills are learned and practiced by parents, including praising, ignoring, expressing feelings, using "if-then" messages, using time-outs, and restricting privileges. The pros and cons of using spanking as a discipline technique are discussed and parents review tips for reducing spanking. In addition, parents target one behavior to work on with each of their children. Parents are referred to outside resources for children's behavioral problems if needed.

CREATING FAMILY EXPECTATIONS ABOUT DRUGS AND ALCOHOL

Families work together to define and clarify expectations about drugs and alcohol in their families. Parents are taught how to involve their children in creating clear and specific expectations, how to monitor, and how to provide appropriate consequences for violations of the expectations. Families work together to establish written policies for tobacco, alcohol, and other drug use. They then use previously learned skills of family involvement, communication, and family management to develop and implement the policy.

TEACHING CHILDREN SKILLS

Parents learn how to teach their children two important types of skills—refusal skills and problem-solving skills—using a five-step process:

(1) *Sell/Tell*—Sell the skill to your children and tell them the steps.
(2) *Show*—Model the skill steps for your child.
(3) *Do*—Provide guided practice steps for the child.
(4) *Feedback*—Provide feedback, accentuating the strengths.
(5) *Application*—Plan application to real-life situations.

Parents teach and practice the skills with their children during program sessions so that trainers can guide parent teaching practices.

HELPING CHILDREN SUCCEED IN SCHOOL

Parents build on the previously learned skills to create, monitor, and provide appropriate consequences for their children's home learning routine. Parents identify time, place, and consequences for homework completion. Strategies to assist children with homework are taught and practiced. Parents review communication skills and practice using the skills to communicate with school personnel.

PARENT-CHILD SESSIONS

The parent and child sessions are designed to be interactive and provide parents with many opportunities to practice new skills with other parents and with their own children. Here is one parent's reflection on the Focus on Families parent and child sessions.

> *Upon entering I thought I was in another lecturing parenting class that just brushed the surface. This class was different than others. It was informative and pushed me to do better. I really learned a lot of tools that work. Also, in this class I have learned valuable life skills. There's no handbook on how to be a parent, but this class comes pretty close. Focus on Families has considerably changed my life.*

HOME-BASED CASE MANAGEMENT

The complex nature of many families in treatment and the multiple risks facing the children in these families make it necessary to combine the resources of community, school, positive peer network, and positive extended family in order to achieve a level of support adequate to assure recovery, reduce risks, and increase protective factors. Increasingly, case management is used as an intervention strategy for those with multiple problems, including having children with emotional disturbances and delinquency (Haggerty, Wells, Jenson, Catalano & Hawkins, 1989) and drug abusers (Grant, Ernst & Streissguth, 1999; Rapp, Siegal & Fisher, 1992; Ridgely, 1994).

The Focus on Families definition of case management focuses on habilitation, the process of developing an empowering relationship with families to reduce risk and at the same time enhance family strengths, integrate skills into the family, strengthen family bonds, and create and reinforce clear norms opposed to drug use.

Case managers facilitate participation in parenting groups by contacting clients before each session to make sure they are planning to attend, and by reducing barriers to participation such as transportation or child care needs.

When clients miss a group session, case managers conduct home visits in which they summarize the session's content, practice worksheets, and provide opportunities for practicing skills before the next group session. Case managers work with families to define specific goals for the family as a whole and for individual family members. Case managers also facilitate access to needed services and linkages to other agencies. Initially, case managers assist families in solving their problems, and then gradually teach them a process they can use to solve their own problems. Weekly clinical meetings review case management practices and highlight the week's action plans for each family receiving services. The case management system uses a six-step model.

STEP 1: JOINING AND ENGAGING WITH FAMILIES

Case managers seek to build a trusting relationship not only with the addicted parent but with all family members. Although initially, the addicted parent is the client, after the first meeting the case manager shifts the focus from the client as addict to the client as parent, and then from the parent as client to the family as identified client. Frequent visits build trust. Clients are initially met at the methadone clinic, often informally, and an invitation is extended to go for a cup of coffee. This provides a neutral setting to conduct an informal assessment of the family, meet the parent, and develop a plan to meet the rest of the family. Soon afterward, case managers visit the home, where they meet the rest of the family and begin the assessment process. Case managers engage in fun, nonthreatening activities with the children, such as games, sports, or walks, in order to establish themselves as caring and competent adults who can help the family. They may establish themselves immediately as family advocates by assisting in problem-solving critical issues (housing, child care, treatment issues, etc.) and by providing concrete services to clients when needed, such as assistance with power bills, diapers, transportation, and such. The main goal of this relationship-building period is to create a strong bond with the family so that the family will want to attend the parent training sessions.

STEP 2: RISK AND RELAPSE ASSESSMENT

An assessment form is used to identify families' strengths and their risk potential. Assessments are organized into seven sections:

(1) Parenting Skills
(2) Social Skills/Relationships
(3) Community Services
(4) Employment/Education
(5) Recreation/Leisure
(6) Family Support (e.g., children's academic success)
(7) Life Support (e.g., health services, housing, employment, etc.).

The case manager conducts this assessment with the family and uses it to develop a service plan.

STEP 3: SERVICE PLAN AGREEMENT

Case managers work with families to identify potential risk areas and jointly develop goals with the family for priority areas identified in the assessment. Families are encouraged to develop goals for their family, and these goals become the center of the case management service plan. In the treatment service agreement, case managers identify the target behaviors to be changed, graduated steps to these behavior changes, and strategies to reach them.

STEP 4: SERVICE PLAN IMPLEMENTATION

Given the broad variety of assessment and client goal areas, case managers need to have the knowledge and ability to apply a variety of therapeutic interventions. These may include couples therapy, strategic family therapy, skills training, problem solving, and crisis intervention. Effective home visits require that case managers respect their clients and utilize some fundamental helping skills, such as active listening and open-ended questions (see Wasik, Bryant & Lyons, 1990) and skills to motivate and encourage steps toward recovery (see Miller & Rollnick, 1991). Case managers empower families by providing opportunities for practicing and utilizing the skills learned in the parent training and by implementing the service plan in ways that are consistent with the family's goals.

Case managers also need to possess supportive confrontation skills since case management with drug-affected families requires that family members be confronted with the reality of their behaviors. For example, a parent who wants his five-year-old to stop swearing, yet swears continually himself, needs to be confronted directly on his behavior. Likewise, a parent who is concerned about her daughter's use of alcohol, yet is smoking marijuana in front of her children, needs to examine her own behavior. Focus on Families works under the assumption that no parent intends or wants his or her child to become addicted. Consequently, behaviors increasing the risk of the child's drug abuse are pointed out to parents clearly and specifically, focusing on the behavior rather than on the person.

In the experimental test of the Focus on Families program, a discretionary fund of $150.00 was available for leisure activities, crisis intervention, and services. For example, one client established a goal of controlling her anger, and funds were made available to pay for her intake interview at an anger management program. In other cases, funds were used to pay fees for critically needed services or for part of a family leisure activity such as summer camp or membership in an organization such as Boys and Girls Clubs.

STEP 5: MONITORING, EVALUATING,
AND REVISING SERVICE PLANS

Each month, case managers review with clients the progress toward their goals. Regular monitoring of the service plan serves two purposes: (1) it helps clients know where they are and where they are headed with regard to their goals, and (2) it provides focus and accountability for services from case managers. Service plans are revised if planned goal steps are unrealistic. New goals are added if clients have achieved targeted goals. The following case notes illustrate how a parent revised her relapse plan.

> *The client identified a fear that once her baby was born she might be tempted to use again. She had not had positive UA's while I was working with her and seemed genuinely concerned about the baby's health while she was pregnant. We reviewed relapse prevention strategies such as identifying and avoiding high-risk situations, strategies to cope with high-risk situations, and focusing on the "big picture" of parenting. I visited the client while she was in the hospital after her baby was born, and we reviewed her plan to avoid relapse. Together, we updated her relapse plan while she was in the hospital with her baby to include new relapse signals. At termination, she had not reported any relapse to drug use.*

STEP 6: TERMINATING WITH CLIENTS

Before the end of eight months of services, the case managers work with their clients proactively to terminate services. Termination includes providing clients with alternate resources they can access on their own, assisting them in developing at least one strong healthy prosocial relationship, and modeling terminating a relationship in a healthy, nonaggressive manner.

One home-based service provider made the following notes about a client:

> *Given the mother's history of destroying relationships before they could terminate successfully, we set successful termination with the case management services as a goal. I discussed this with the mother two months prior to our termination date, and we worked toward it consistently. She took an active role in identifying and seeking out new supports for herself, including ACOA (Adult Children of Alcoholics) and NA (Narcotics Anonymous) groups. Our final meeting was a success.*

At termination, case managers evaluate minimum outcomes expected with each family. These include: parents refraining from using illegal drugs in front of their children; no physical abuse in the family; the family carrying out one successful family meeting without case managers present; the family making a written family drug policy; all school-age youth regularly attending school; families having an established home learning routine; families using communication skills of "I" messages, paraphrasing, and open questions; each family having one new resource in their network; and each family attending at least two follow-up booster sessions.

FOCUS ON FAMILIES EVALUATION

The average age of participating parents in the evaluation was 35 years, and 75 percent were female. Seventy-seven percent of the parents were European-American, 18 percent were African-American, and 5 percent were of other ethnic backgrounds. The average age of first heroin use by parents was 19.14 years. Although subjects were receiving methadone treatment at baseline, 54 percent engaged in illicit drug use in the month prior to enrolling in the Focus on Families project.

Parents were randomly assigned to receive the Focus on Families intervention in addition to regular methadone services or to receive only methadone services. Parents in both conditions were interviewed in person prior to the program, immediately after the end of the parent training component, and at six, 12, and 24 months following parent training. Children under age six but over age three were assessed by parent report. Children age six and older were assessed by parents and interviewed at baseline and at six-, 12-, and 24-month follow-up. For children, three different developmentally appropriate interviews were used for the age groups six to eight, nine to 10, and 11 and older. The interviews for older children included more items and gave respondents extended response options.

All measures were based on responses to survey questions with the exception of the two measures of parent problem-solving skills. The skills measures were derived from the Problem Situation Inventory (PSI) (Hall et al., 1983), an audio-taped role-play instrument. The PSI has demonstrated reliability and validity, and discrimination of program-related changes in general, in drug refusal, and in relapse-prevention skills (Hawkins, Catalano, Gillmore & Wells, 1989; Hawkins et al., 1986; Wells, Hawkins & Catalano, 1988a, 1988b).

In order to examine and enhance the validity of parent self-reported drug use, all participants were informed that a different 25 percent random sample of participants at each data collection point would be asked for a urine sample. Clients selected to provide a urine sample were also asked to answer a set of questions concerning drug use during time frames corresponding to detection periods covered by the toxicology screens.

Overall, few false negatives were found across substances (from 4.5% to 6.1% depending on the substance) and no statistical differences were found in false negatives across the experimental and control groups. This suggests that self-reports are largely valid, with no difference in reporting veracity by condition.

RELAPSE AND DRUG USE OUTCOMES FOR PARENTS

Analysis of covariance and logistic regression were used to assess differences between the experimental and control group at follow-up time points. For analyses of parent outcomes, a baseline measure corresponding to the given outcome measure was included as a control variable. Differences consistently favored the

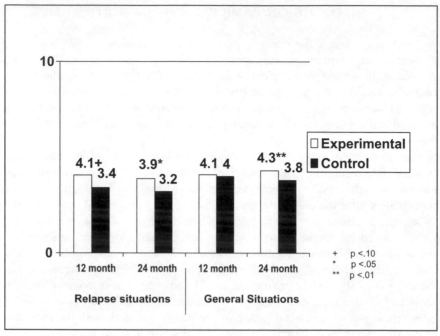

FIGURE 11.1:   Parents Problem-Solving Skills, 12- and 24-Month Follow-up

experimental group for key parent outcomes. Experimental parents demonstrated more skillful behavior on both general and drug-related PSI situations at all time points (see Figure 11.1). Differences did not diminish over time and were statistically significant at the 24-month follow-up. Few statistically significant differences between experimental and control parents were found in parent reports of family involvement, management, conflict, and bonding until later follow-up periods.

Overall, experimental parents reported less drug use than control parents (see Figure 11.2). Experimental parents used significantly less heroin at the end of the parent training and at the 12-month follow-up, and less cocaine at the 12-month follow-up. No significant differences were found at the 24-month follow-up. At the 12-month follow-up, there was a trend level difference indicating that experimental participants had fewer deviant peers than controls. Although the difference on this measure favored experimental participants at 24-month follow-up, it was not statistically significant.

DRUG USE OUTCOMES FOR CHILDREN

Results of analyses comparing experimental and control children for drug use outcomes at 12 and 24 months are presented in Figure 11.3. There were few

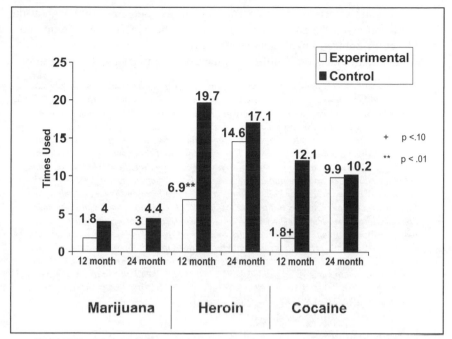

FIGURE 11.2:   Parental Drug Use in Last 30 Days, 12- and 24-Month Follow-up

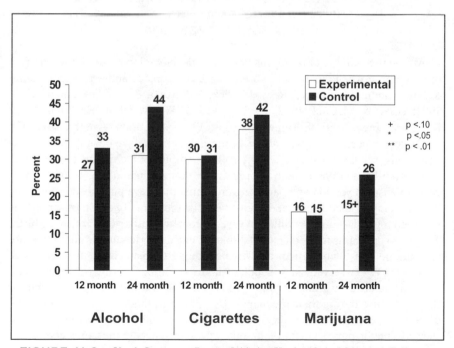

FIGURE 11.3:   Youth Outcomes: Percent Initiating Use by 12- and 24-month Follow-up

significant main effects of the program on drug use outcomes, although at the 24-month follow-up the pattern of effects favors the experimental group and a trend level difference in marijuana use (p < .10).

A graduate of Focus on Families summarized the impact of the program:

> *In Focus on Families I learned to take back the "control" in my home. The habits our children fall into now are generally what stays with them throughout their lives. It's our responsibility as parents to instill good work habits, study habits, manners, and communication skills. It's also our job to set rules. Also, it's our job to establish goals and work with our family to achieve them. It's important for us to use open questions and know and understand the challenges and peer pressure that they come into contact with everyday. We must be aware of our children's friends, monitor their schoolwork, and get children to open up more about things we think they may be having problems with at school. We must praise our kids for good, and not just harp on the bad that they do. I also learned that relapse is not the end of the world. Guilting myself will only make the situation worse. The quicker we pull ourselves out, the better off we will be. Guilt only causes more relapse. I must recognize "why" I relapsed, make a plan—stop, think, question—and apply myself to the plan and then reward myself. Then communicate with my family and tell them how I feel. Our kids will only respect us when we respect ourselves. I learned to make goals with my boys. Most of all, when I make promises or plan activities, STICK TO THEM! BE CONSISTENT! COMMUNICATE! PRAISE, LOVE, and most of all . . . HAVE FUN!*

COMPARISON WITH OTHER APPROACHES INTEGRATING FAMILY-FOCUSED RELAPSE PREVENTION

Although a number of programs have been developed to reduce children's risk of drug abuse when one or both parents have a substance abuse problem (Camp & Finkelstein, 1997; Dawe, Rees, Mattick, Sitharthan & Heather, 2002; Falco, 1992; Gross & McCaul, 1992; Haskett, Miller, Whitworth & Huffman, 1992; Russell & Free, 1991; Springer, Phillips, Phillips, Cannady & Derst-Harris, 1992), few experimental evaluations of these programs have been published (for exceptions, see Catalano et al., 1997, 2003; Kumpfer & DeMarsh, 1985). Fewer still explicitly incorporate both relapse prevention and parenting. To our knowledge, relapse prevention and parenting programs that have published evaluations were developed specifically and exclusively for mothers. Two notable programs recruited high-risk mothers while they were pregnant or shortly after giving birth. These two programs focus on parents' roles in caring for newborns and on relapse prevention. The Seattle Birth to Three program (Ernst, Grant, Streissguth & Sampson, 1999) served as a supplement to traditional drug treatment, and, through maternity wards, recruited women who had a high level of alcohol or illicit drug use during their pregnancy. Compared to randomly assigned control cases (n = 25), the clients receiving paraprofessional home visitors (n = 60) showed greater improvement on an outcome summarizing measures across five domains, including abstinence from drug and alcohol use. The second program targeted polydrug-using adolescent mothers (Field et al., 1998) and provided treatment in school that was a combination of parenting skills for newborns and relapse prevention. Intervention participants were compared to age- and race-matched drug-using and non-drug-using controls. The adolescent mothers in the treatment program demonstrated a lower incidence of continued drug use and scored higher on a measure of well-being of the child (had a regular doctor, had well child visits and immunizations) compared to drug-using controls. The total sample size was 128 adolescent girls, but no information was provided concerning how many were in each of the three groups.

Three programs reported in the literature specifically address parenting in the context of drug treatment and/or relapse prevention. CASAWORKS (McLellan et al., 2003; Morgenstern et al., 2003) is a comprehensive case management program for substance-using recipients of Temporary Assistance for Needy Families (TANF), providing services in multiple areas, one of which is parenting. To date, only repeated measures on recipients in the 10-site field test have been reported, although a controlled comparison is currently under way. The within-subject comparisons between baseline and 12-month follow-up (n = 529) showed improvements in multiple domains including reduced substance use and substance use problems, increased employment, and increased liklihood of having appropriate child care. No other information on the welfare of the children of the women in the study has been published. Parenting Under Pressure (Dawe, Harnett, Rendalls & Staiger, 2003; Dawe, Harnett, Staiger & Dadds, 2000) is an individually delivered treatment program designed to reduce parent psychopathology and improve parenting and relapse prevention skills among mothers in methadone treatment. Only eight subjects were exposed to the intervention and it was evaluated with pre-post test data and no comparison group. Subjects did demonstrate significantly improved parent-child relationships, reduced substance use, and improved overall parental functioning. The Relational Psychotherapy Mothers' Group (RPMG; Luthar & Suchman, 2000), a women-only group therapy program for heroin-addicted mothers in methadone treatment, devotes a large portion of program sessions to insight-oriented, nondirective parenting skill facilitation. The participants (n = 32) demonstrated reduced risk for maltreatment of their children and improved affective interactions when compared to randomly assigned controls (n = 20) who received only methadone treatment. These effects persisted six months after treatment. Participants in the intervention also decreased their opiate use whereas methadone-treatment-only controls increased their use. Additionally, Ashley, Marsden & Brady (2003) report that many drug treatment programs for women focus on parenting issues in the context of recovery and relapse prevention. They found that programs offering child care, prenatal care, women-only programming, and workshops that address women-focused topics (such as parenting), mental health programming, and comprehensive programming (such as housing and employment assistance) were associated with improved treatment outcomes for both the mother and her children.

Though addressing relapse in the context of parenting has not become widely accepted or implemented, this approach appears promising. Focus on Families is unique in that it works with both mothers and fathers and combines case management/home visits with a structured curriculum that includes both parent training and relapse prevention skills training. Further, it is designed to work with families that have children from preschool age to adolescence and has demonstrated promise through experimental evaluation.

CHALLENGES

A major challenge to successful implementation of programs such as the Focus on Families program is the difficulty of recruitment and retention (Dawe et al., 2000; Grady, Gersick & Boratynski, 1985; Hawkins, Catalano, Jones & Fine, 1987). Parents in methadone treatment are good candidates for such a program because they have already made a commitment to examine their drug use and have begun to work on making changes in their lives. Their regular attendance at the clinic provides ready availability for parent training sessions. Another challenge is relapse into drug use among parents. Because of this, it is essential that relapse prevention and coping skills be an integral part of parenting programs for parents in treatment for drug abuse. The following case notes from a case manager exemplify the challenges of integrating relapse prevention with drug abuse prevention for children:

> The stated family goals were to prevent mother's relapse and develop a home learning routine and chore routine for the girls. Much of my time went to supporting mother's staying clean. The mother's urine tests at the methadone clinic tested positive for Klonopin, a benzodiazepine. We developed a relapse prevention strategy. The strategies were to meet with me and the methadone counselor to contract for daily checks and coaching on relapse skills along with random urine tests. Her methadone counselor contracted with her for attending daily 12-step or relapse groups at the clinic. We located and I attended several NA meetings with the mom and debriefed with her afterwards. She eventually attended several meetings on her own and reported "she got a lot out of it." At the time of termination, the mother reported interest in attending NA (in particular a women's NA group) and I provided her a listing of times and places of NA meetings.
>
> Although mother has made progress in some areas, she still isolates herself and has no drug-free friends. She is ambivalent about participating in support groups, even though she states an interest. Her husband is a negative influence and has expressed no commitment to recovery, hers or his. He has detracted from her participation in the Focus on Families program and NA. I have provided her with resources for couples therapy that is coordinated with her husband's treatment program. She was markedly ambivalent about this and her husband has refused to consider it.
>
> The other goals of developing homework and chore routines met with some success. Chore behaviors focused on cleaning the family's living space in the basement of the mother's parent's home. I facilitated the family's choice of a time (after school) for the mother to join with the girls to work together to clean the area. The family decided on no Nintendo until the area was clean to the mother's satisfaction. Grandmother was

enlisted to assist in monitoring and supporting this goal. The family had a difficult time getting started with this goal as mother initiated the project inconsistently. Despite this, at time of termination, the family reported they were accomplishing the tasks with some regularity.

The development of a home learning routine went similarly. The family identified a time, place and support for homework. Initially, mother had a difficult time following through with monitoring. The family showed improvement, particularly in following through with rewards when the girls accomplished expected tasks. The rewards usually included going to the park or out for ice cream.

The current living situation at the grandparents offers stability that otherwise would not exist. The threat of relapse will increase dramatically if the current living situation changes.

CONCLUSIONS

Focus on Families assists drug-addicted parents in strengthening their families and attending to their own relapse risks and parenting behaviors. The program incorporates relapse prevention and coping within the motivational context of substance-abusing parents reducing their children's risk for developing abusive patterns of substance use. It addresses predictors of relapse for parents and risk factors for substance abuse among their children. As a result, parents have less risk for relapse, are better skilled to cope with relapse incidents without progressing into a full-blown relapse, and ultimately have decreased drug use. In addition, parents develop better family management skills (reduction in family conflict and increases in family rules) and better social and problem-solving skills, as well as relapse prevention and coping skills. Parents in the program condition reported 30 day heroin use at about one third the rate of those in the control condition and reported 30-day cocaine use as six times less in the experimental condition than in the control condition. Although differences in drug use were no longer significant at the 24-month follow-up, parents in the experimental condition continued to demonstrate significantly stronger relapse prevention, coping, and general problem-solving skills than parents in the control condition, and lower drug use overall.

These results show the promise of integrating a relapse prevention skills training with family-focused prevention programming among parents in methadone treatment. We are currently conducting 12-year follow-up interviews with parents and children enrolled in the experimental condition to see if the promising impact of the program at two-year follow-up is maintained. Additional experimental tests of such programs may be an important direction for future research.

ACKNOWLEDGEMENTS

Preparation of this report was supported by NIDA grant # RO1 DA17908-01. Focus on Families was conducted by the Social Development Research Group, University of Washington, in cooperation with Therapeutic Health Services of Seattle, WA. The authors gratefully acknowledge the assistance of Norman O. Johnson, Executive Director, and all the staff of Therapeutic Health Services.

REFERENCES

Arthur, M.W., Hawkins, J.D., Pollard, J.A., Catalano, R.F., Baglioni, A.J., Jr. (2002). Measuring risk and protective factors for substance use, delinquency, and other adolescent problem behaviors: The communities that care youth survey. *Evaluation Review* **26**:575–601.

Ashley, O.S., Marsden, M.E., Brady, T.M. (2003). Effectiveness of substance abuse treatment programming for women: A review. *American Journal of Drug and Alcohol Abuse* **29**:19–53.

Barnard, M., McKeganey, N. (2004). The impact of parental problem drug use on children: What is the problem and what can be done to help? *Addiction* **99**:552–559.

Bauman, P.S., Levine, S.A. (1986). The development of children of drug addicts. *International Journal of the Addictions* **21**:849–863.

Beyers, J.M., Toumbourou, J.W., Catalano, R.F., Arthur, M.W., Hawkins, J. (2004). A cross-national comparison of school drug policy environments in Washington State, United States, and Victoria, Australia. *Journal of Adolescent Health* **35**:3–16.

Breese, G.R., Chu, K., Dayas, C.V., Funk, D., Knapp, D.J., Koob, G.F. et al. (2005). Stress enhancement of craving during sobriety: A risk for relapse. *Alcoholism: Clinical and Experimental Research* **29**:185–195.

Brewer, D.D., Catalano, R.F., Haggerty, K., Gainey, R.R., Fleming, C.B. (1998). A meta-analysis of predictors of continued drug use during and after treatment for opiate addiction. *Addiction* **93**(1):73–92.

Camp, J.M., Finkelstein, N. (1997). Parenting training for women in residential substance abuse treatment: Results of a demonstration project. *Journal of Substance Abuse Treatment* **14**:411–422.

Catalano, R.F., Gainey, R.R., Fleming, C.B., Haggerty, K.P., Johnson, N.O. (1999). An experimental intervention with families of substance abusers: One-year follow-up of the Focus on Families project. *Addiction* **94**:241–254.

Catalano, R.F., Haggerty, K.P., Gainey, R.R. (2003). Prevention approaches in methadone treatment settings: Children of drug abuse treatment clients. In Bukoski, W.J., Sloboda, Z., eds., *Handbook of drug abuse prevention. Theory, science and practice*, 173–196. New York: Kluwer Academic/Plenum Publishers.

Catalano, R.F., Haggerty, K.P., Gainey, R.R., Hoppe, M.J. (1997). Reducing parental risk factors for children's substance misuse: Preliminary outcomes with opiate-addicted parents. *Substance Use and Misuse* **32**:699–721.

Catalano, R.F., Hawkins, J.D. (1996). The social development model: A theory of antisocial behavior. In Hawkins, J.D., ed., *Delinquency and crime: Current theories*, 149–197. New York: Cambridge University Press.

Chassin, L., Pillow, D.R., Curran, P.J., Molina, B.S. (1993). Relation of parental alcoholism to early adolescent substance use: A test of three mediating mechanisms. *Journal of Abnormal Psychology* **102**:3–19.

Dawe, S., Harnett, P.H., Rendalls, V., Staiger, P. (2003). Improving family functioning and child outcome in methadone maintained families: The Parents Under Pressure programme. *Drug and Alcohol Review* **22**:299–307.

Dawe, S., Harnett, P.H., Staiger, P., Dadds, M.R. (2000). Parent training skills and methadone maintenance: Clinical opportunities and challenges. *Drug and Alcohol Dependence* **60**:1–11.

Dawe, S., Rees, V.W., Mattick, R., Sitharthan, T., Heather, N. (2002). Efficacy of moderation-oriented cue exposure for problem drinkers: A randomized controlled trial. *Journal of Consulting and Clinical Psychology* **70**:1045–1050.

ElGeili, E.S.S., Bashir, T.Z. (2005). Precipitants of relapse among heroin addicts. *Addictive Disorders & Their Treatment* **4**:29–38.

Ernst, C.C., Grant, T.M., Streissguth, A.P., Sampson, P.D. (1999). Intervention with high-risk alcohol and drug-abusing mothers: II. Three-year findings from the Seattle model of paraprofessional advocacy. *Journal of Community Psychology* **27**:19–38.

Falco, M. (1992). *The making of a drug-free America: Programs that work.* New York: Times Books.

Farrell, M., Ward, J., Mattick, R., Hall, W., Stimson, G.V., des Jarlais, D. et al. (1994). Fortnightly review: Methadone maintenance treatment in opiate dependence: A review. *British Journal of Medicine* **309**:997–1001.

Field, T.M., Scafidi, F., Pickens, J., Prodromidis, M., Pelaez-Nogueras, M., Torquati, J. et al. (1998). Polydrug-using adolescent mothers and their infants receiving early intervention. *Adolescence* **33**:117–143.

Goehl, L., Nunes, E., Quitkin, F., Hilton, I. (1993). Social networks and methadone treatment outcome: The costs and benefits of social ties. *American Journal of Drug and Alcohol Abuse* **19**:251–262.

Goldstein, A.P., Kanfer, F.H. (1979). *Maximizing treatment gains: Transfer enhancement in psychotherapy.* Oxford, England: Academic Press.

Goodwin, D.W. (1985). Alcoholism and genetics: The sins of the fathers. *Archives of General Psychiatry* **42**:171–174.

Grady, K., Gersick, K.E., Boratynski, M. (1985). Preparing parents for teenagers: A step in the prevention of adolescent substance abuse. *Family Relations: Journal of Applied Family & Child Studies* **34**:541–549.

Grant, T.M., Ernst, C.C., Streissguth, A.P. (1999). Intervention with high-risk alcohol and drug-abusing mothers: I. Administrative strategies of the Seattle model of paraprofessional advocacy. *Journal of Community Psychology* **27**:1–18.

Gross, J., McCaul, M.E. (1992). An evaluation of a psychoeducational and substance abuse risk reduction intervention for children of substance abusers. *Journal of Community Psychology, Special Issue. Programs for change: Office for Substance Abuse Prevention demonstration models,* 75–87.

Haggerty, K.P., Wells, E.A., Jenson, J.M., Catalano, R.F., Hawkins, J.D. (1989). Delinquents and drug use: A model program for community reintegration. *Adolescence* **24**:439–456.

Hall, J.A., Vaughan, J.E., Gross, G., Catalano, R.F., Hawkins, J.D., Farber, J. (1983). *Project skills problem situation inventory.* Seattle, WA: University of Washington, Social Development Research Group.

Haskett, M.E., Miller, J.W., Whitworth, J.M., Huffman, J.M. (1992). Intervention with cocaine-abusing mothers. *Families in Society* **73**:451–461.

Havassy, B.E., Hall, S.M., Wasserman, D.A. (1991). Social support and relapse: Commonalities among alcoholics, opiate users, and cigarette smokers. *Addictive Behaviors* **16**:235–246.

Hawkins, J.D., Catalano, R.F., Jr., Gillmore, M.R., Wells, E.A. (1989). Skills training for drug abusers: Generalization, maintenance, and effects on drug use. *Journal of Consulting and Clinical Psychology* **57**:559–563.

Hawkins, J.D., Catalano, R.F., Jones, G., Fine, D.N. (1987). Delinquency prevention through parent training: Results and issues from work in progress. In Wilson, J.Q., Loury, G.C., eds., *From children to citizens: Vol. III. Families, schools, and delinquency prevention,* 186–204. New York: Springer-Verlag.

Hawkins, J.D., Catalano, R.F., Miller, J.Y. (1992). Risk and protective factors for alcohol and other drug problems in adolescence and early adulthood: Implications for substance-abuse prevention. *Psychological Bulletin* **112**:64–105.

Hawkins, J.D., Catalano, R.F., Wells, E.A. (1986). Measuring effects of a skills training intervention for drug abusers. *Journal of Consulting and Clinical Psychology* **54**:661–664.

Jester, J.M., Jacobson, S.W., Sokol, R.J., Tuttle, B.S., Jacobson, J.L. (2000). The influence of maternal drinking and drug use on the quality of the home environment of school-aged children. *Alcoholism: Clinical and Experimental Research* 24:1187–1197.

Kolar, A.F., Brown, B.S., Haertzen, C.A., Michaelson, B.S. (1994). Children of substance abusers: The life experiences of children of opiate addicts in methadone maintenance. *American Journal of Drug and Alcohol Abuse* 20:159–171.

Kumpfer, K.L. (1987). Special populations: Etiology and prevention of vulnerability to chemical dependency in children of substance abusers. In Brown, B.S., Mills, A.R., eds., *Youth at high risk for substance abuse*, 1–72. Rockville, MD: National Institute on Drug Abuse.

Kumpfer, K.L., DeMarsh, J. (1985). Family environmental and genetic influences on children's future chemical dependency. *Journal of Children in Contemporary Society* 18:49–91.

Luthar, S.S., Suchman, N.E. (2000). Relational Psychotherapy Mothers' Group: A developmentally informed intervention for at-risk mothers. *Development and Psychopathology* 12:235–253.

Marlatt, G.A., Gordon, J.R. (1985). *Relapse prevention: Maintenance strategies in the treatment of addictive behaviors*. New York: Guilford.

McLellan, A., Gutman, M., Lynch, K., McKay, J.R., Ketterlinus, R., Morgenstern, J. et al. (2003). One-year outcomes from the CASAWORKS for Families intervention for substance-abusing women on welfare. *Evaluation Review* 27:656–680.

Mercer, R.T. (1990). *Parents at risk*. New York: Springer.

Miller, W.R., Rollnick, S. (1991). *Motivational interviewing: Preparing people to change addictive behavior*. New York: The Guilford Press.

Morgenstern, J., Nakashian, M., Woolis, D.D., Gibson, F.M., Bloom, N.L., Kaulback, B.G. (2003). CASAWORKS for Families: A new treatment model for substance-abusing parenting women on welfare. *Evaluation Review* 27:583–596.

Mrazek, P.J., Haggerty, R.J. (Eds.), Committee on Prevention of Mental Disorders, Institute of Medicine. (1994). *Reducing risks for mental disorders: Frontiers for prevention intervention research*. Washington, DC: National Academy Press.

National Consensus Development Panel on Effective Medical Treatment of Opiate Addiction. (1998). Effective medical treatment of opiate addiction. *Journal of the American Medical Association* 280:1936–1943.

Rapp, R.C., Siegal, H.A., Fisher, J.H. (1992). A strengths-based model of case management/advocacy: Adapting a mental health model to practice work with persons who have substance abuse problems. In Ashety, R.S., ed., *NIDA Research Monograph: Vol. 127. Progress and issues in case management*, 79–91. Rockville, MD: National Institute on Drug Abuse.

Ridgely, E. (1994). The self of the consultant: "In" or "out?" In Andolf, M. and Huber, R. eds., *Please help me with this family: Using consultants as resources in family therapy*, 53–65. Philadelphia, PA: Brunner/Mazel, Inc.

Roosa, M.W., Beals, J., Sandler, I.N., Pillow, D.R. (1990). The role of risk and protective factors in predicting symptomatology in adolescent self-identified children of alcoholic parents. *American Journal of Community Psychology* 18:725–741.

Rosenthal, T., Bandura, A. (1978). Psychological modeling: Theory and practice. In Garfield S.L., Bergin, A.E., eds., *Handbook of psychotherapy and behavior change: An empirical analysis*, 621–658. New York: Wiley.

Russell, F.F., Free, T.A. (1991). Early intervention for infants and toddlers with prenatal drug exposure. *Infants and Young Children* 3:78–85.

Sechrest, D.K. (1979). Methadone programs and crime reduction: A comparison of New York and California addicts. *The International Journal of the Addictions* 14:377–400.

Sher, K.J. (1991). *Children of alcoholics: A critical appraisal of theory and research*. The John D and Catherine T MacArthur Foundation series on mental health and development. Chicago, IL: University of Chicago Press.

Sowder, B.J., Burt, M.R. (1980). *Children of heroin addicts: An assessment of health, learning, behavioral, and adjustment problems*. New York: Praeger.

Spieker, S.J., Booth, C.L. (1988). Maternal antecedents of attachment quality. In Belsky, J., Nezworski, T., eds., *Clinical implications of attachment*, 95–135. Hillsdale, NJ: Erlbaum.

Springer, J.F., Phillips, J.L., Phillips, L., Cannady, L.P., Derst-Harris, E. (1992). CODA: A creative therapy program for children in families affected by abuse of alcohol or other drugs. *Journal of Community Psychology, Special Issue: Programs for change: Office for Substance Abuse Prevention demonstration models*, 55–74.

Suchman, N.E., Luthar, S.S. (2000). Maternal addiction, child maladjustment and socio-demographic risks: Implications for parenting behaviors. *Addiction* **95**:1417–1428.

Surgeon General. (1988). *The health consequences of smoking: Nicotine addiction: A report of the Surgeon General*. Rockville, MD: U.S. Department of Health and Human Services.

Tarter, R.E., Blackson, T.C., Martin, C.S., Loeber, R., Moss, H.B. (1993). Characteristics and correlates of child discipline practices in substance abuse and normal families. *American Journal on Addictions* **2**:18–25.

Grant, W.T. (1992). Consortium on the School-Based Promotion of Social Competence. Drug and alcohol prevention curricula. In Hawkins, J.D., Catalano, Jr., R.F., and Associates, eds., *Communities That Care. Action for drug abuse prevention*, 129–148. San Francisco: Jossey-Bass.

Ward, J., Mattick, R.P., Hall, W. (1998). *Methadone maintenance treatment and other opioid replacement therapies*. Amsterdam, Netherlands: Harwood Academic.

Wasik, B.H., Bryant, D.M., Lyons, C.M. (1990). *Home visiting: Procedures for helping families*. Thousand Oaks, CA: Sage Publications, Inc.

Wells, E.A., Hawkins, J.D., Catalano, R.F., Jr. (1988a). Choosing drug use measures for treatment outcome studies. I. The influence of measurement approach on treatment results. *International Journal of the Addictions* **23**:851–873.

Wells, E.A., Hawkins, J.D., Catalano, R.F., Jr. (1988b). Choosing drug use measures for treatment outcome studies. II. Timing baseline and follow-up measurement. *International Journal of the Addictions* **23**:875–885.

12

RELAPSE PREVENTION WITH HISPANIC AND OTHER RACIAL/ETHNIC POPULATIONS: CAN CULTURAL RESILIENCE PROMOTE RELAPSE PREVENTION?

FELIPE GONZÁLEZ CASTRO,
ERICA NICHOLS, AND KARISSA KATER

Department of Psychology
Arizona State University
Tempe, Arizona

INTRODUCTION: ISSUES IN RELAPSE PREVENTION WITH HISPANIC AND OTHER RACIAL/ETHNIC POPULATIONS

RACIAL AND ETHNIC FACTORS IN TREATMENT AND RELAPSE PREVENTION

Today, the population of clients entering drug abuse treatment programs in the United States is diverse on many dimensions, including their racial/ethnic heritage and identity. Sources of this cultural diversity include language, religious background, and socio-political beliefs and attitudes (Locke, 1998). This diversity introduces significant challenges to the delivery of effective drug abuse treatments. Moreover, as the two largest racial/ethnic minority groups in the United States, Hispanics/Latinos(as) and African-Americans are disproportionately represented in the population of clients referred to drug and alcohol abuse treatment programs (Kandel, 1995). Understanding the socio-cultural and political reasons for this and other health-related disparities is important (Shulz & Mullings, 2006) for the delivery of effective drug abuse treatments and for effective relapse prevention.

The Hispanic/Latino population of the United States numbered 41.32 million as of July 1, 2004, constituting 14.07 percent of the U.S. population, making Hispanics/Latinos(as) the largest racial/ethnic population within the United States (U.S. Census Bureau, 2005). In this chapter, we will use the terms "Latinos" and "Hispanics" interchangeably, based on the dual usage that occurs within the contemporary literature. The terms "Hispanic" and "Latino" are generic labels that refer to people living in the United States, primarily Mexican-Americans, who live in the Southwestern United States; Puerto Ricans (both from the Island of Puerto Rico and from the U.S. mainland); Cubans; as well as other Hispanics/Latinos including Colombians, Guatemalans, Nicaraguans, and other immigrants and naturalized persons from Central America and South America.

Regarding the major racial/ethnic groups in the United States, U.S. Census population estimates for July 1, 2005 report a total U.S. population of 296.41 million, and of these, 237.85 million (80.24%) were White Americans/Euro-Americans (U.S. Census Bureau, 2006). And among other U.S. population racial groups, in terms of counts of single-race identifiers, 37.91 million (12.79%) were Blacks/African-Americans; 12.69 million (4.28%) were Asians (Chinese, Koreans, Japanese, Filipinos, East Indians, etc.); 2.86 million (0.96%) were American Indians or Alaskan Natives; and 516,612 (0.17%) were Native Hawaiians and other Pacific Islanders. For July 1, 2005, the Hispanic/Latino population of the United States, which is a multiracial population, was estimated to be 42.69 million (14.40%). And for July of 2005, the racial composition of this Hispanic/Latino population consisted of 39.48 million (92.50%) who were of the White race (Caucasians), and 1.58 million (3.7%) who were of the Black race.

CULTURAL FACTORS NOT EXAMINED IN NIDA PRINCIPLES OF DRUG ADDICTION TREATMENT

The National Institute on Drug Abuse has developed a research-based guide that presents 13 principles and related issues for effective drug abuse treatment (National Institute on Drug Abuse, 1999). These principles are the following:

(1) No single treatment is appropriate for all individuals.
(2) Treatment needs to be readily available.
(3) Effective treatment attends to the client's multiple needs and not just to drug abuse.
(4) Continual assessment and modification of the treatment plan is necessary.

(5) Remaining in treatment is crucial to treatment effectiveness.
(6) Behavioral treatments are essential for effective outcomes.
(7) Medications, especially in combination with counseling, are important for many patients.
(8) For patients with coexisting mental and drug abuse disorders, both disorders should be treated.
(9) Medical detoxification is only a first step in a full treatment.
(10) Treatment does not need to be voluntary to be effective.
(11) Possible drug use during treatment must be monitored continuously.
(12) Patient behaviors that risk infectious diseases such as HIV/AIDS should be addressed in treatment.
(13) Recovery often involves multiple episodes of treatment; that is, relapse is a frequent outcome.

It is noteworthy that among these principles, none addresses cultural factors as important for effective treatment of racial/ethnic clients. Today, much work is needed to clarify the influence of various cultural factors, including race/ethnicity, as they relate to effective drug abuse treatment outcomes including relapse prevention.

CONTEXT OF RACE/ETHNICITY IN HEALTH DISPARITIES AND TREATMENT NEEDS

In 2001, the Surgeon General of the United States, Dr. David Satcher, introduced a major report on issues affecting the health and mental health of racial/ethnic populations of the United States. In this report, the Surgeon General proclaimed that "culture counts," and should not be ignored in addressing the health needs of Americans (U.S. Dept. of Health and Human Services, 2001; David Satcher, 2001). This and other recent reports have emphasized the importance of developing a clear understanding of socio-cultural factors in conducting effective assessments, treatments, and research with racial/ethnic populations (Castro, 1998).

In particular, effective drug abuse treatment must recognize the deeper influences of psychological, psychiatric, legal, familial, and other factors on recovery from drug abuse and dependence (Resnicow, Soler & Braithwaite, 2000). For ethnic clients, effective drug abuse treatment must recognize the effects of early life and current socio-cultural or environmental situations as these operate as triggers for high-risk behavior. In this regard, to make "culture count" in effective drug abuse treatment with racial/ethnic clients, the counselor or therapist must also develop *cultural competence*. Given the growing ethnic diversity within the United States it should be recognized that a client's *ethnic label*, that is, the identifier label of being Hispanic, typically does not provide sufficient information to fully understand an ethnic client's needs and risks of relapse. This does not mean that culture and ethnicity are unimportant. To the contrary, ethnic identity and other cultural factors, when examined in depth, aid in understanding the influence of early life experiences and current ways of thinking that can influence current and future risks of relapse. In other words, an identifying ethnic label is not synonymous with the client's rich cultural heritage, developmental history, and cultural life ways that in turn influence risks and protection toward the use of illegal drugs.

Despite this perspective, today few drug abuse treatment programs attend to cultural factors as integral components of their program. For example, among less-acculturated (low-acculturated and bicultural) Latinos, cultural issues such as *familism*—close family relations and expectations (Sabogal, Marin, & Otero-Sabogal, 1987), the role of *ethnic identity* formation in recovery, and culturally relevant ways of coping constitute cultural areas worthy of attention in treatment to facilitate recovery and aid in avoiding relapse. Similarly, recognizing the cultural value of harmonious *social relations* observed among Latinos, that is, *simpatia* (Marin & Marin, 1991), may aid in building culturally relevant skills to help Hispanic clients avoid relapse. Furthermore, these core cultural values must be examined within the context of each individual Hispanic client's orientation toward cultural norms and traditions. For example, highly assimilated Mexican-Americans may not adhere to Mexican cultural traditions, and may dismiss the need for attention to these cultural factors in treatment. By contrast, many bilingual/bicultural and low-acculturated Latinos may prefer, seek out, and find comfort in such traditional cultural approaches, and they may benefit from a culturally relevant intervention that explicitly addresses cultural perspectives in recovery and in promoting relapse prevention.

LATINOS AND FAMILY SYSTEMS

Among bilingual/ bicultural Hispanics and among low-acculturated Hispanics (those who are primarily Spanish-speaking and/or who are actively involved in their culture), cultural modules may be added to a standard treatment program to make that program culturally relevant (Hanson, 1992). Generally, within certain Hispanic families, *traditionalism*, conservative cultural expectations, values, and attitudes, may influence the family system's responsiveness to a family member's problems with drug use. Moore (1990) notes that Mexican-American families whose members have used drugs across multiple generations often develop ways to support their recovering drug-using family member. By contrast, for young Latinos and Latinas from conservative traditional families who have never before faced drug abuse problems, their young adults may experience a lack of support from members of their family (Moore, 1990). Such traditional families may condemn illegal drug use, and may be unprepared or unwilling to provide needed social support based on a perceived violation of social norms and the embarrassment to the family represented by the use of illegal drugs.

Most recovering substance users feel stigmatized regarding their addiction and are sensitive to rejection from society and their family. Thus, a return to an enmeshed, nonsupportive, rejecting, guilt-inducing family system (Szapocznik & Kurtines, 1989) will likely promote failure in recovery and relapse. By contrast, a permissive family system may also promote relapse by failing to set appropriate limits and a sense of responsibility. In a culturally oriented study of Mexican-American heroin addicts, Jorquez (1984) found that many felt alienated from conventional treatment. Jorquez suggests that the treatment of Mexican-American opiate addicts should include a discussion of the likelihood of multiple relapses, and social support to avoid client feelings of discouragement from a perceived lack of progress in recovery from addiction.

EMERGING TRENDS IN THEORY DEVELOPMENT

Many theoretical models have been developed to describe and understand the etiology, course, and maintenance of drug use (e.g., Lettieri, Sayers & Pearson, 1984; Pandina & Johnson, 1999; Petraitis, Flay & Miller, 1995). As indicated earlier, some theories are relevant for Hispanic populations, although most of these theories have lacked specific reference to cultural factors that describe important aspects of Hispanic cultural identity and lifestyle (Castro and Hernandez-Alarcon, 2002; Oetting & Bearvais, 1987, 1990; Oetting, Donnermeyer, Trimble & Bearvais, 1998).

Structural Ecosystems Theory (SET) (Szapocznik & Coatsworth, 1999; Szapocznik & Williams, 2000) has been introduced recently within a multisystemic Ecodevelopmental Model to aid in understanding risk and protective factors that are relevant to the life experiences of racial/ethnic people. This multiple systems perspective describes a series of social ecological domains under a proximal-distal continuum. These domains include the *microsystems*, *mesosystems*, *exosystems*, and *macrosystems* (Szapocznik & Coatsworth, 1999). During youth development complex influences emerge over time within and among these ecosystems. Locke, Newcomb, and Goodyear (2005) conducted one of the first studies to examine this Ecodevelopmental Model in a rigorous manner using structural equation modeling. Locke and colleagues observed that *traditional* gender role identities were related to increased risks of engaging in HIV-risk behaviors, whereas sexual identification and cultural pride were unrelated to high-risk sexual behaviors. This study illustrates how the ecodevelopmental perspective, as a multilevel model, provides a viable framework for conceptualizing and examining the complex social and cultural factors that influence HIV risks among Hispanics.

A recurring issue in the analysis of illegal drug use among Hispanics and other ethnic populations is whether conventional risk factors for drug use and for relapse exert similar or differential effects among members of various Hispanic subpopulations; for example, low-acculturated immigrant Hispanic adolescents versus their highly acculturated Hispanic peers (Castro, Maddahian, Newcomb & Bentler, 1987; Galaif & Newcomb, 1999). In a study of cultural risk and protective factors among Hispanic adolescents, Gil, Wagner, and Vega (2000) examined culturally common (conventional) and culturally specific risk factors (e.g., *respeto*) and found that greater *familism* (strong Hispanic family bonds) predicted a lower disposition toward deviance one year later, and that greater *respeto* (youth respect for their parents and elders), also predicted a lower disposition toward deviance among U.S.-born Latino adolescents. Greater *respeto* also predicted less alcohol involvement one year later. In a study of Mexican-American high school students, McQueen and collaborators found that *emotional attachment* and *separation from parents* were salient risk factors for substance use (McQueen, Getz & Bray, 2003). These studies suggest that certain cultural constructs, such as *familism*, *respeto*, emotional attachment, and separation from parents, exert remarkable culturally specific effects as risk or protective factors among Hispanic youth (Felix-Ortiz & Newcomb, 1999).

RELAPSE ISSUES WITH ADULT DRUG USERS

In the treatment of adult cocaine and heroin-addicted clients, one goal of relapse prevention is to teach skills for recognizing, avoiding, and exerting control over events that produce relapse (Brownell, Marlatt, Lichtenstein & Wilson, 1986; Marlatt & Gordon, 1985). It has been noted that a comprehensive program for relapse prevention delivered within a clinical setting should address at least seven thematic areas: (1) reducing client ambivalence in treatment motivation, (2) reducing cocaine and other drug availability, (3) coping with high risk situations, (4) overcoming cravings prompted by conditioned cues, (5) avoiding "Apparently Irrelevant Decisions," (6) making lifestyle changes toward healthier behaviors, and (7) coping with the Abstinence Violation Effect (Carroll, Rounseville & Keller, 1991).

For adults addicted to cocaine, relapse prevention education and training has focused on the identification of triggers, events or situations (i.e., cues) that prompt or initiate a return to drug use. Moreover, adult cocaine users suffering from a coexisting Axis I or Axis II psychiatric disorder (such as depression or antisocial personality disorder) experience compromised capabilities for coping with the stressors that prompt relapse. However, to date, little research has been conducted on ways in which the principles of Relapse Prevention Treatment (RPT) when coupled with complications of coexisting psychiatric disorder may influence the occurrence of relapse among various Hispanic clients. Hispanics in recovery from drug dependence will typically face various conventional triggers for relapse, although they may also face certain culturally specific triggers. Cultural factors that might promote relapse among Hispanics may include certain cultural expectations or pressures imposed by the cultural values of *personalismo*, personalized expectations that demand sensitivity toward others, and *familism*, strong affective bonds and mutual expectations held between members of a family (Marin & Marin, 1991). Regarding conventional aspects of relapse, as described by Relapse Prevention Theory (RPT) (Marlatt & Gordon, 1985), the two concepts central to RPT: (1) *Apparently Irrelevant Decisions*, and (2) the

Abstinence Violation Effect, have not been examined previously as these may influence the behavior of Hispanic drug-using clients. Such research may help understand how various subgroups of Hispanics may differ from non-Hispanics in their thoughts and behaviors, that may produce lapses on a full-blown relapse. Are the attributional processes of certain Hispanics different in response to specific triggers, and in their likelihood of experiencing a lapse (i.e., reactions to the Abstinence Violation Effect), as these attributions may then lead to a full-blown relapse (Walton, Castro & Barrington, 1994)?

DEFINITIONS OF CONSTRUCTS SPECIFIC FOR EXPLORING GROUP DIFFERENCES

ACCULTURATION, TRADITIONALISM, FAMILISM, AND OTHER CULTURAL VARIABLES

Three important factors that describe the within-group variability (diversity) observed among Hispanic clients are: (1) level of acculturation (Berry, 1980), (2) traditionalism (Buriel, Calzada & Vasquez, 1983; Ramirez, 1999), and (3) socio-economic status. *Acculturation* refers to a process of social learning, change, and adaptation that in part involves the acquisition of the normative values, belief, and behaviors from a new cultural environment (e.g., the culture of the mainstream or dominant society) (Trimble, 2003). In general, *acculturative change* refers to socio-cultural processes that require progressively greater levels of adaptive change in adjusting to a new environment, especially when large cultural differences exist between the immigrant's native cultural values, beliefs, and traditions, and those of the new cultural environment. However, the acculturation literature remains unclear regarding beneficial factors that can ease cultural adaptation, as contrasted with detrimental factors that pose barriers and introduce stress and distress during cultural adaptation. Given the complexity and the ambiguities present today in the conceptualization and measurement of acculturation, some scholars have argued that further research on acculturation should be eschewed (Hunt, Schneider & Comer, 2004). Despite these views, the process of acculturative change is ubiquitous, as the process of migration, social mobility, and the challenges requiring adaptation among migrating populations occur daily and worldwide. In this regard, acculturative change does not occur solely in cases of cross-national migration, but also in cases of migration within a nation's geographic boundaries, such as in migration from rural to urban environments (Castro & Gutierres, 1997; Portes & Rumbaut, 1996). Generally, for Hispanics/Latinos, acculturative change toward the mainstream American culture has been associated with increased risks for drug abuse (Carvajal, Photiades, Evans & Nash, 1997; Rebhun, 1998).

Traditionalism refers to adherence to conservative "old culture," familial and other life norms and values, and for Hispanics this involves adherence to old-time cultural norms and values observed within the migrant's native Latin American country (Castro & Gutierres, 1997; Ramirez, 1999). And, *socioeconomic status* serves as an index of educational, occupational, and socio-cultural position. However, when examining social resources and standards of living, a middle-class status within Mexico and other Latin American countries may be equivalent to a lower-middle socioeconomic status within the United States (Castro, Balcazar & Krull, 1995).

Many investigators have written about the process of acculturation, although few studies have truly examined the *process of acculturative change* across time. In early acculturation research, the concept of acculturation as measured under a unidimensional continuum (Cuellar, Harris & Jasso, 1980) implied a loss of Mexican or other Hispanic cultural identity with increasing acculturation toward mainstream American culture. However, more recently an orthogonal acculturation model has been developed, which also describes variations in cultural identity within mainstream American culture. Under this orthogonal model, certain variations in cultural identities can occur including a full bicultural/bilingual identity (Berry, 1980; Cuellar, Arnold & Maldonado, 1995; Marin & Gamboa, 1996; Zane & Mak, 2003) (see Figure 12.2).

ACCULTURATION AND DRUG USE

Epidemiologic studies have implicated increases in acculturation as an important factor associated with increasing drug use (Amaro, Whiteker, Coffman & Heeren, 1990). Data from the HHANES (the Hispanic Health and Nutrition Examination Study) has shown that Mexican Americans who were highly acculturated and low in level of education are the subgroup of Hispanics most likely to use marijuana and cocaine (Amaro, Whittaker, Coffman & Heeren, 1990). Vega and collaborators recently also have concluded that acculturation is more strongly associated with drug use among Mexican-American women as compared with Mexican-American men, an instance of effect modification (moderation) by gender (Vega, Alderate, Kolody & Aguilar-Gaxiola, 2003). In other words, the process of acculturative change, as a factor that prompts greater illicit drug use, appears to exert a stronger effect among Mexican-American females as compared with Mexican-American males. Besides this effect of gender, recent studies also indicate a combined gender and cohort effect that involves changing patterns of illicit drug use among younger cohorts of Hispanics such that increases in acculturation are producing a convergence in lifetime rates of drug use between Hispanic females and males, thus creating gender parity in absolute rates of drug use (Vega, Alderate, Kolody & Aguilar-Gaxiola, 2003).

ACCULTURATIVE STRESS

Acculturative stress is the stress associated with the process of acculturative change, particularly among Hispanic immigrants (Cervantes, Padilla & Salgado de Snyder, 1991). In one study, Vega, Gil, Warheit, Zimmerman, and Apospori (1993) found that acculturative strain (chronic stress) was associated with youth problem behaviors, but only in the presence of family-related difficulties and vulnerabilities. Youth perceptions of discrimination also have been associated with drug use (Félix-Ortiz, Newcomb & Myers, 1994; Vega, Zimmerman, Warheit, Apospori & Gil, 1993). Regarding these effects, acculturation is best conceptualized as an effect modifier (a moderator) rather than as a causal factor of drug use (Castro & Hernandez-Alarcon, 2002). Understanding these complex conditional effects prompts the need for well-conceptualized and theory-driven analyses. Such analyses should examine models that include moderator and mediator effects produced by acculturation and other cultural variables, as these may promote drug use and its progression to abuse and dependence (e.g., Brook, Finch, Whiteman & Brook, 2002; McQueen, Getz & Bray, 2003; Newcomb & Locke, 2005). Finally, the significant acculturative heterogeneity observed among various Hispanics prompts the need to disaggregate Hispanics as a generic population into more homogeneous subgroups; that is, it requires *population segmentation* to identify more specific and well-defined subgroups by levels of acculturation or other cultural variables, subgroups that may also differ in their risks for drug use and abuse.

GENDER ROLES AND EXPECTATIONS

A second culturally related issue for Mexican-Americans and other Hispanics involves within-group variation by gender. Within conservative and traditional Hispanic communities and families, illicit drug use is typically rebuked, although heavy alcohol use has been tolerated among men, but forbidden among women. The traditional Hispanic gender constructs of *machismo* and *marianismo* embody these traditional Hispanic/Latino gender roles and their related norms that define appropriate or normative gender role behaviors. *Machismo* refers to exaggerated masculine norms involving male privilege and an ascribed superiority over women (Casas, Wagenheim, Branchero & Mendoza-Romero, 1994; Fragoso & Kashubeck, 2000). *Machismo* is a complex construct that originated in Spain and was introduced into Mexico and other Latin American countries in the 1500s by the conquistadors as one means of subduing indigenous people and destroying their cultural and family norms (Lafayette de Mente, 1996). Despite its negative characteristics, other aspects of *machismo* have been recognized that involve positive attributes including nobility, family responsibility, and courtesy toward others (Gutmann, 1996; Mirande, 1997). *Machismo* in its negative form has been implicated as a risk factor for stress, depression, and alcohol abuse among Hispanic males (Fragoso & Kashubeck, 2000; Jung, 2001).

Negative *machismo* is contrasted with the Latina gender identity construct of *Marianismo. Marianismo* refers to the beliefs and behavior of the idyllic Latina who is selfless, submissive, and maintains her virginity until marriage (Gil & Vazquez, 1996; Torres, 1998). These prototypical gender roles and the traditional social norms and expectations that accompany them may operate in daily life as potent cultural scripts (personalized cultural norms) that establish rules of acceptable conduct based on gender. These include the acceptable use of alcohol, tobacco, and drugs, or their avoidance, based also on the person's acceptance of and adherence to these traditional gender role norms and expectations.

EGO DEVELOPMENT, ETHNIC IDENTITY, AND RESILIENCE

Regarding ethnic identity, it has been hypothesized that Hispanic youth who develop a mature (achieved) ethnic identity (Phinney, 1990) that includes *ethnic pride* and/or *bicultural competence* (Castro, Boyer & Balcazar, 2000; LaFromboise, Coleman & Gerton, 1993; Trimble, 1995) would have greater resilience against substance use, relative to other less culturally mature Hispanic youth. Several studies have examined the possible effects of a bilingual/bicultural identity as a form of resilience that is protective against substance abuse (Brook, Whiteman, Balka, Win & Grusen, 1998; Felix-Ortiz, Newcomb & Myers, 1994; Felix-Ortiz & Newcomb, 1995; Marsiglia, Kulis, Hecht & Sills, 2004).

Resilience is a set of personal attitudes and skills that afford a capacity to recover from adversity despite exposure to serious threats to adaptation or development (Masten, 2001). Klohnen (1996) examined the major dimensions of *ego-resilience*, and identified four important dimensions: (1) confident optimism, (2) productive activity, (3) insight and warmth, and (4) skilled expressiveness. Ego-resilient individuals exhibit a sense of *active and meaningful engagement in the world*, and an energetic approach toward life involving confident, autonomous, and competent functioning and a *sense of mastery*. Ego-resiliency is seen as a capacity to adapt in response to changing environmental contingencies and for successfully attaining goals and desires (Klohnen, 1996). These actions reflect adaptive *self-regulation* of affect and behavior, which allows the person to successfully negotiate the many challenges of adaptation including acculturative change.

Resiliency has also been associated with characteristics observed among leaders, wherein four of the five traits from the Big Five Model of personality structure have been associated with ratings of leadership effectiveness: surgency, emotional stability, conscientiousness, and agreeableness (Hogan, Curphy & Hogan, 1994). In summary, resilience is a complex construct, which may be defined by the following elements: (1) personal control, (2) optimism, (3) goal orientation, (4) life purpose, (5) persistence, (6) a positive self-esteem and self-concept. For certain persons, resilience may also be associated with (7) high spirituality, and (8) strong cultural involvement. An emerging question regarding the influence of resilience on health outcomes is, "Can a resilience-building intervention be developed to fortify less resilient individuals by enhancing their skills and capacities for resilience?"

CULTURAL RESILIENCE AS PROTECTION
AGAINST RELAPSE

Can certain traditional (conservative) cultural norms and practices that embody cultural strengths promote resilience and healthy outcomes including the capacity to avoid relapse? Conversely, will a loss of these traditions and norms elevate risks for disease, disorders, and relapse? A *Hispanic Paradox* recently has emerged within the literature on Hispanic health in three areas: (1) the perinatal health of Hispanic/Latina women, (2) mortality rates from cardiovascular disease, and (3) rates of psychiatric disorder. In a series of community-based studies of diagnosed psychiatric disorders, Mexican migrant farmworkers, when compared with native-born Mexican-Americans and with non-Hispanic whites, exhibited *lower* rates of psychiatric disorder (Alderete, Vega, Kolody & Aguilar-Gaxiola, 2000). Although this and other related studies have been solely cross-sectional in design, their results suggest the presence of traditional cultural strengths that seem to safeguard against disease and psychiatric disorder despite the challenges of *acculturative change.*

Similarly, among Asian-Americans certain traditional cultural patterns, the *Pan-Asian Ideals,* have been described (Shon & Ja, 1982) as traditional social norms that promote self-regulation that is consistent with resilience. These *Pan-Asian Ideals* capture the value orientations of three philosophical/religious traditions: (1) *Confucianism,* which emphasizes proper balance and regulation in life; (2) *Buddhism,* which emphasizes avoiding worldly activities in favor of an ascetic lifestyle, a view that life involves suffering; and (3) *Taoism,* which emphasizes harmony between human beings and nature, and the need to avoid confrontation. Adherence to these ideals include (1) discipline and self-directedness, "listening from within"; (2) observing social hierarchies, propriety in relationships including respect and deference toward authority; (3) restraint, long-suffering, suppression of overt expression of emotions; and (4) the role of *shame* in motivating correct action, which motivates the avoidance of antisocial conduct that brings shame to self and family, and thus a motive to avoid suffering a *loss of face* (Shon & Ja, 1982). This pattern of self-regulatory behavior is opposite to the narcissistic, impulsive, self-indulgent, and often antisocial behaviors often observed among many illegal drug users. This "traditional idealism," and its related social norms for self-directed behavior and harmonious social interactions may promote self-regulation that guides prosocial behavior, avoids risk taking, and may aid in relapse prevention. Future research may examine how these ideals might promote resilience, self-regulation, and an enhanced capacity to avoid relapse among drug-dependent clients, especially among racial/ethnic minority clients.

ASSESSMENT, TREATMENT, AND
RELAPSE PREVENTION

ASSESSMENT: CULTURAL SENSITIVITY AND BEYOND

Cultural Competence in Assessment

Culture is a complex entity; and as noted previously, racial/ethnic minority cultures within the United States are not homogeneous. For substance abuse counselors and therapists who work with ethnic clients, *cultural competence* consists of the capacity: (1) to conduct accurate assessments (devoid of stereotypes and misconceptions) and (2) to conduct efficacious interventions that address complex real-world issues (Sue et al., 1998). In treatment for drug dependence, such interventions involve understanding the effects of historical, social, and cultural factors as contexts that influence personality, familial, and other relationships (Paniagua, 1998). A culturally relevant assessment can uncover several culturally specific life themes when conducting a life history analysis that examines important life areas: (1) early childhood and developmental histories, (2) linguistic preferences and skills, (3) the process of acculturation and its acculturative stressors, and (4) the client's cultural orientation as indicated by level of acculturation, traditional norms, values, beliefs, and related behaviors (Ramirez, 1998, 1999).

The Cultural Capacity Continuum

Cultural competence has been defined as: A set of attitudes, skills, behaviors, and policies that aid in understanding and appreciating cultural differences and similarities, and in working effectively in cross-cultural situations. This involves a willingness and ability to draw on community-based values, traditions, and customs. It also involves the ability to work with knowledgeable persons from the community (Orlandi, Weston & Epstein, 1992).

The Cultural Competence Continuum (Cross, Bazeon, Dennis & Isaac, 1989) illustrates the existence of progressive levels of cultural capacity ranging from the most negative, Cultural Destructiveness (−3), to the most positive, Cultural Proficiency (+3) (see Figure 12.1). It also suggests that total capacity development involves a process of personal growth that requires time and commitment to the task of cultural skills development. It also indicates that ignoring differences (Cultural Blindness (−1)) under the guise of "equality for all," actually discriminates against those who are disadvantaged physically, psychologically, or economically. It also emphasizes that Cultural Sensitivity is a positive state (+1), although it solely constitutes an initial stage of cultural capacity in which positive attitudes toward diversity coupled with a limited knowledge of diversity produces sympathetic responses, albeit stereotypical ones. With progressively greater knowledge and experience, one can develop Cultural Competence (+2), a more complete capacity to understand *cultural nuances*, and with further competence

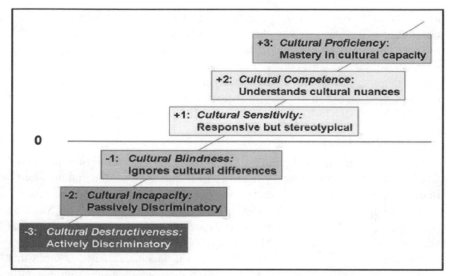

FIGURE 12.1: The Cultural Capacity Continuum

training, one can attain Cultural Proficiency, a level of mastery in cultural capacity (Castro, 1998; Castro & Garfinkle, 2003).

Universal vs. Culturally Specific Aspects in Assessment

A challenge in the delivery of drug abuse treatment to Hispanic and other racial/ethnic minority clients involves skills for conducting effective assessments for accurate problem definition, conceptualization, and treatment. A recurring challenge in assessment involves the appropriate use of standardized assessment instruments with various racial/ethnic minority clients. Here, the reliability and validity of any assessment is a *matter of degree*. No instrument is totally reliable and valid for all populations, nor is an instrument that has been validated for one population automatically invalid when used with a new population. Conceptually, the closer the profile of *match* between the validating and current population, the greater the expected reliability and validity of an assessment instrument when applied with the current population. Conversely, the greater the profile of *mismatch*, the greater the likelihood of nonfit, which can erode the instrument's reliability and validity.

A second important distinction in culturally relevant assessment is the distinction between *culturally common* (universal) constructs and *culturally specific* constructs. Certain culturally specific constructs are difficult to translate cross-culturally. Examples of universal constructs when examined broadly are depression, anxiety, anger, fear, given that these core emotions exist across most or all cultures worldwide. However, for these emotions there may exist culturally specific forms of expression, for example, somatization of depression that is reported as bodily pain. Based on their approach to assessment that includes Western assumptions, Western instruments may lack certain culturally specific items that measure certain forms of emotional expression, thus limiting their reliability and validity in their use with clients from a different cultural groups. For example, unique factors in the expression of anxiety among Asian populations may not be captured by established Western instruments that measure anxiety, such as the State–Trait Anxiety Index (Leong, Okazaki & Tak, 2003).

Assessment of Acculturation

For work with various Latino populations, level of acculturation has served as an indicator of within-group variability in cultural orientation and integration into mainstream American society. An early and often-used unidimensional acculturation scale has been the 20-item Acculturation Rating Scale for Mexican Americans (ARSMA) (Cuellar, Harris & Jasso, 1980). However, as noted, several year later, Rogler, Cortés, and Malgady (1991) criticized the use of this single-continuum model as being a "zero sum" model, which implicitly assumes that increases in acculturation toward the Euro-American culture automatically decrease identification with the native culture. Rogler and colleagues argued that a person's rating on one cultural dimension is independent of their rating on a second cultural dimension, thus prompting the need for an orthogonal (independent factors) model. As one outcome in cultural orientation, identifying strongly with the mainstream Euro-American culture (an American Orientation), while also identifying strongly with one's own ethnic culture (e.g., Latino Orientation), would characterize the person as having a bilingual/bicultural identity (LaFromboise, Coleman & Gerton, 1993) (see Figure 12.2). From this perspective, Oetting and Beauvais (1990) introduced an orthogonal model and a measurement of cultural identification for adolescents as related to alcohol, tobacco, and illegal drug use. It has been hypothesized that a bicultural identity (LaFromboise, Trimble & Mohatt, 1990) can confer protective effects against substance use and abuse. Currently, available evidence presents mixed results regarding the advantages of a bicultural identity as protective against substance abuse (Felix-Ortiz & Newcomb, 1995).

This orthogonal model, when used with adult drug users, indicates that within the United States ethnic persons who exhibit a bicultural identity are those who identify strongly with their ethnic culture (i.e., Latino Orientation; see Figure 12.2; or Mexican lifeways), and also identify strongly with the mainstream American culture, an American Orientation (see Figure 12.2). Figure 12.2 pre-sents a scatterplot for the Orthogonal Cultural Identification Model with Latino cases (light dots) and White American cases (dark dots), as plotted by scaled values of American Orientation and by scaled values of Latino Orientation. Cut points that segment each distribution at about the 33rd and 66 percentiles aid in the identification of seven specific cultural identities: Separatist, Traditional, Bicultural, Acculturated, Assimilated, Partly Bicultural, and Marginalized. Occasionally, a White American client may exhibit a Bicultural or Traditional identity, as do several Latino clients, although most White Americans exhibit a strong or moderate

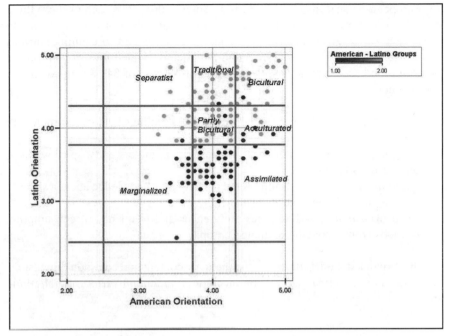

FIGURE 12.2: Orthogonal Model of Cultural Orientation

American Orientation. For White Americans this form of identification does not constitute Assimilation, but rather a full or partial Integration into their American native-born culture. For this client sample, no Latinos (light dots) were classified as Assimilated although a few were classified as Acculturated. The Marginalized identity that involves a weak orientation to both cultures is relevant for American and Latino clients, and shows a cultural detachment from both societies. It may be hypothesized that these Marginalized clients are disenfranchised and thus are at greatest risk for relapse, as they may lack the requisite emotional bonding and social supports that may otherwise aid in relapse prevention.

From a similar acculturative perspective, Kolonoff and Landrine (2000) developed a scale to measure aspects of acculturation that are specific to the life experiences of African-Americans. The thematic item content, as described by various scale factors, reveals several salient cultural issues for African-Americans. The three most prominent factors generated from this scale's item content were: (1) religious and spiritual beliefs, (2) preferences for African-American music and media, and (3) interracial attitudes including social distrust and concerns about racism and discrimination.

Asian-American Acculturative Assessment

An expanded model of acculturation-related identities for Asian-Americans has been proposed, which examines cultural orientation and identification toward three reference groups: (1) Culture of Origin, (2) Asian-Americans, and

(3) European-Americans (Chung, Kim & Abreu, 2004). For each of these three dimensions, item responses are measured on a dimension of (1) = *not very* to (6) = *very much*. A factor analysis of 15 items developed to examine various aspects of cultural orientation for Asian-Americans yielded four dimensions of acculturation based on responses examined for a group of 342 Asian-American young adults:

(1) *Cultural Identity*—Examines the participant's feelings held in common with people from a specific reference group.
(2) *Language*—Examines how well the participant understands, speaks, reads, and writes a language.
(3) *Cultural Knowledge*—Examines the participant's knowledge about a specific culture, its traditions and its history.
(4) *Food Consumption*—Examines preferences and frequency of consumption of foods from a specific reference group.

This expanded model illustrates the thematic content and common dimensions used currently to define and measure acculturation among various racial/ethnic groups.

IMPLEMENTATION: EVIDENCE-BASED TREATMENTS

Incorporating Cultural Variables into Treatment

A contemporary imperative for Hispanic and other racial/ethnic minority populations is to make drug abuse treatment culturally relevant, to obtain improved treatment outcomes relative to a standard (culturally neutral) treatment (Pantin, Coatsworth, Feaster, Newman, Briones, Prado, Schwartz & Szapocznik, 2003). Ideally, a culturally sensitive treatment program will yield better outcomes as measured by lower rates and severity of relapse, higher life satisfaction, higher rates of return to work, an improved life situation (legal, familial, social, medical, psychiatric), and so on (Castro & Garfinkle, 2003). Although this "cultural enhancement hypothesis" is tenable and logically coherent, currently further evidence is needed either to support or refute it.

The limited empirical evidence currently available reflects the regency of interest in the role of cultural factors in enhancing treatment outcomes. In the past, rudimentary and superficial conceptions of race and ethnicity involved their conceptualizations solely as demographic or group variables used to conduct group comparisons (Ja & Aoki, 1993; Terrell, 1993). More recently, ethnicity has been conceptualized in greater depth and complexity in the forms of ethnic identity, ethnic involvement, and ethnic pride (Keefe, 1992; Meyerowitz, Richardson, Hudson & Leedham, 1998; Schwartz, Montgomery & Briones, 2006). This greater depth of conceptualization has prompted new considerations of how ethnic factors may influence drug abuse treatment outcomes (Castro &

Hernandez-Alarcon, 2002), including levels and patterns of relapse. The emerging question for ethnic clients in treatment is, "Can promoting ethnic identity development, ethnic involvement, and/or ethnic pride exert significant treatment effects that enhance treatment effectiveness for certain ethnic clients?" (Castro, Obert, Rawson, Valdez & Denne, 2002).

Typical Difficulties or Roadblocks

Culturally sensitive relapse prevention must address issues of family support as these can influence treatment progress among recovering drug users. The preparedness of family to help their recovering family member avoid relapse may serve as a major determinant of success in drug abuse treatment, especially for Hispanics and other ethnic clients who were raised with strong family ties (i.e., *familism*) that have been severed by their use of illegal drugs. Moreover, for Latino drug users in recovery, a comprehensive and culturally relevant program may require a treatment offered in the client's preferred language (e.g., in Spanish) (Castro & Tafoya-Barraza, 1997). A culturally enhanced treatment may include cultural activities, such as spirituality, especially for Hispanic clients who were raised within strong Catholic or other religious family traditions, but who have abandoned these when turning to the use of illegal drugs. The act of rediscovering or recapturing abandoned familial and cultural traditions during the process of recovery may serve as a therapeutic cultural thread that can serve as a potent foundation for a full recovery and relapse prevention.

As a cost-effective approach to treatment enhancement, specific *treatment components* that address such relevant socio-cultural issues can be introduced in the form of *supplemental modules*. Another important approach is to increase the *cultural competence* of treatment staff (Szapocznik, Santisteban, Rio, Perez-Vidal et al., 1989). The professional skills of the "messenger" (i.e., program delivery staff) often serve as an important source of effect that determine treatment-related outcomes (Durantini, Albarracin, Mitchell, Earl & Gillette, 2006).

Controversy Over Evidence-Based Treatments

Today, some drug abuse treatment programs and prevention interventions are delivered in a standardized manner using scripted or manualized programming guidelines and activities (Morganstern, Morgan, McCrady, Keller & Carroll, 2001). This contrasts with the old-style delivery of individualized drug abuse treatments in which the clinician addressed treatment issues based primarily on clinical judgment. Here a distinction should be made between adherence to a manualized protocol as required for clinical research studies, and the provision of drug abuse treatment services that are offered within a conventional clinical setting (Obert, McCann, Marinelli-Casey, Weiner, Minsky, Brethen & Rawson, 2000). Whereas randomized controlled clinical trials require detailed screening for admission into a scientific study, within the clinical setting, client screening often is conducted on the basis of program eligibility. Accordingly, within the clinical setting clients are typically more diverse. Thus within a community-based treatment setting it becomes more difficult for clinicians to adhere with high fidelity to a narrowly constructed manualized treatment protocol (Norcross, Beutler & Levant, 2006). Within environments that have a heterogeneous con-stituency of clients, the challenge to presenting Relapse Prevention Training as a fixed package based on a strictly defined manualized intervention is that this approach may underestimate the unique or atypical cultural variations observed within that local treatment setting. The need arises to balance standardization of program activities with flexibility to allow clinical responsiveness in serving clients' unique needs and best interests. Accordingly, manualized protocols deliv-erable within community settings should build in flexibility that offers therapists some discretion in clinical decision making. This also calls for therapist training in cultural competency to expand their capacity to exercise culturally relevant clinical judgment. Initial client-treatment matching may also help to apply relapse prevention in more direct correspondence between client needs and treatment program characteristics (Marlatt, 1996).

ISSUES IN PROGRAM ADAPTATION

Fidelity Adaptation Controversies

A fidelity-adaptation controversy has emerged recently as a significant theo-retical and practical issue within the prevention and treatment fields (Schinke, Brounstein & Gardner, 2003). Recently, lists of tested-and-effective programs have been compiled that identify "model programs," which are shown to yield effective outcomes when tested using randomized control studies. These programs are then manualized to present specific content and the conditions necessary for a sound delivery of the scientifically proven intervention. The imple-mentation of such tested-and-effective model programs as a manualized interven-tion protocol (for prevention or for treatment) and with high fidelity (strong adherence to the established protocol) is typically vital to the delivery of a science-based program that yields specific intervention-related outcomes. However, when such model programs, which have been tested with mainstream (nonminority) populations, are delivered to ethnic minority populations, certain assumptions and program activities have lacked relevance or fit, thus prompting the need for program adaptations. Opponents of program adaptation have argued that deviating from the tested and established intervention protocol (low fidelity of implementation) erodes the program's capacity to attain the specific outcomes that it was designed to produce (Elliot & Mihalic, 2004).

By contrast, a lack of program cultural relevance to the needs of a local popu-lation argues against a blind implementation with fidelity, when a program exhib-its known flaws and a lack of relevance or fit for members of the local population. Clearly program adaptation is necessary to make the program culturally relevant to the needs of the local population. Translation from the program's original language (e.g., from English) to the new language needed, is one obvious form of program adaptation that is essential for program delivery with members of a local population. More challenging is the adaptation of the model program to address fundamental cognitive, affective, and ecological sources of nonfit (Castro, Barrera & Martinez, 2004).

An Approach to Adaptation-Hybrid Programs

One approach to this fidelity-adaptation dilemma is to design and implement *hybrid treatment programs* (Castro, Barrera & Martinez, 2004). This approach consists of modifications to an existing model program that incorporate local cultural relevance. This approach may be conducted in three sequential stages: (1) Stage 1: local adaptation; (2) Stage 2: a pilot adaptation testing phase; and (3) Stage 3: implementation with fidelity. First, this approach aims to "ground" the current program to fit the needs of local client constituencies, thus increasing program relevance and fit. Effective local adaptation incorporates culturally relevant treatment content or program activities in a manner that does not conflict, but instead complements and enhances the *core science-based content* offered by the original treatment program (Kumpfer, Alvarado, Smith & Bellamy, 2002). Such localized cultural adaptation does *not* consist of *haphazardly* eliminating certain program sessions or activities based on the counselor's personal preferences. That haphazard activity constitutes *misadaptation*, not genuine and proper treatment adaptation (Castro, Barrera & Martinez, 2004).

Then in Stage 2, the culturally enhanced intervention would be implemented in small-scale, for example, as a pilot program. A formative evaluation approach would be used to evaluate the appeal and initial effectiveness of this localized and culturally enhanced manualized treatment program (Morganstern, Morgan, McCrady, Keller & Carroll, 2001). Thus, this second stage serves as an adjustment and validation stage to examine and fine tune this locally adapted program, and to evaluate the efficacy of innovative content. Finally, Stage 3 would require treatment program implementation now with an emphasis on high fidelity, which would involve a strict adherence to the locally adapted manualized treatment program.

In relating issues of program adaptation to relapse prevention with racial/ ethnic clients, core aspects of conventional relapse prevention should be examined. Important factors identified as determinants of relapse prevention include the identification of high risk events that constitute "triggers" for relapse, motivation and preparedness for treatment involvement, and enhanced coping in the form of self-regulation and effective self-management. Conversely, the presence of negative affect and low levels of social support have been associated with the occurrence of lapses. *Self-regulation* and a related construct *self-reliance* also appear as important factors associated with effective coping and lowered risks of relapse. A Dynamic Model of Relapse has been proposed recently that emphasizes the importance of a dynamic feedback process that considers the effects of contextual factors, the timing of events, as well as distal and proximal classes of risk factors, all operating as multiple ecological factors that influence the probability of relapse (Witkiewitz & Marlatt, 2004). Thus, the local adaptation of a standard relapse prevention program for use within a local ethnic community may consider the hybrid program development approach as described here.

A Logic Model and Analysis of Cultural Treatment Enhancement

Figure 12.3 presents a structural and logic model of the effects of a Culturally Enhanced Treatment (F_5) on mediators of treatment-related Cognitions (F_6) and Skills (F_7), as these would yield effective treatment outcomes as measured by Relapse Avoidance (F_9) and other desirable Treatment Outcomes (F_{10}). Pretreatment baseline conditions are pretreatment Cognitions (F_1) and Skills (F_2), which must be addressed in treatment to effect psychological changes that promote effective recovery. Ethnic Identification is a special factor that in the past has not been addressed within conventional (standard) drug treatment programs. Thus, a structural model that describes a standard program of drug abuse treatment would consist of the portion of this model, in Figure 12.3, that excludes the Ethnic Identification factors (F_4) and (F_8). Conversely, a culturally enhanced treatment program would explicitly address issues involving the development of Ethnic Identification that may then contribute toward improving the client's capacity for Relapse Avoidance (+ b_{89}) and Other Outcomes (+ $b_{8\,10}$).

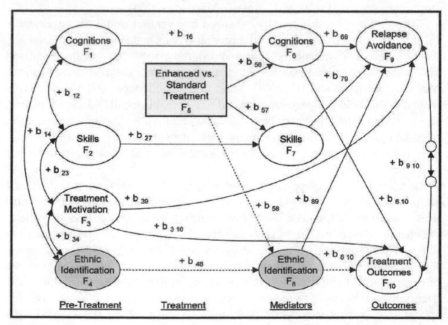

FIGURE 12.3: Structural and Logic Model of Culturally Enhanced Treatment on Relapse Outcomes

Given the presence of requisite levels of Treatment Motivation (F_3), perhaps aided by a pretreatment regimen of Motivational Interviewing (Miller & Rollnick, 1991), the Enhanced Treatment as compared with the original treatment (F_3), is hypothesized to change treatment-related Cognitions (F_6) (beliefs, attitudes, expectations, such as those that involve the Abstinence Violation Effect), and treatment-related Skills (F_7) (skills in identifying triggers to relapse, situational avoidance skills, emotional self-management, coping with cravings), to produce effective increases in client capacities for Relapse Avoidance (F_9) (as measured by self-efficacy in avoiding relapse, avoidance of the primary drug, avoidance of other drugs) and other effective Treatment Outcomes (F_{10}), such as problem improvement in several life areas: legal, medical, psychiatric, familiar, and so on.

Aiken, Stein, and Bentler (1994) conducted a study using structural equation modeling to examine the effects of drug abuse treatment on several indicators of treatment outcome by comparing treatment effects on pretreatment to post-treatment outcomes. Aiken and colleagues used structured means analyses within a structural equation model to compare the health-related daily life behaviors of drug users in a methadone maintenance (MM) program, with those within an outpatient counseling (OC) program. These investigators examined the effect of these two treatment modalities, controlling for group differences at baseline, and controlling for rates of retention in treatment. Among several findings, these investigators observed that when measured in terms of standardized effect size indices, a small effect size was observed in favor of the methadone maintenance group as compared with the outpatient counseling group, on the outcome measures of more leisure activities, and less drug and criminal involvement. Regarding the use of SEM in studies of comparative treatment outcomes, these investigators cautioned that SEM can correct but cannot entirely eliminate biases or ambiguities in sample selection and in related model misspecification. Other challenges also exist in obtaining stable estimates of model fit. Nonetheless, and despite these challenges, Aiken and colleagues encourage the use of SEM in conducting such comparative treatment outcomes research.

As shown in Figure 12.3, the conventional (standard) treatment consists of the portion of this overall model that is devoid of the Ethnic Identification factors (F_4 and F_8). Here, the Culturally Enhanced Treatment (F_5) would include content and activities that build on the original cognitive and skills factors, with the addition of culturally relevant content. This content would promote clients' cultural sensitivity in cognitions and skills; for example, improving family relations and available social support, reducing negative *machismo* and increasing positive *machismo*, enhancing relapse avoidance skills. In addition, this culturally enhanced program explicitly would address specific aspects of Ethnic Identification—ethnic identity development, ethnic involvement, and ethnic pride—as culturally relevant approaches to promote more favorable treatment-related outcomes (Castro, Sharp, Barrington, Walton & Rawson, 1991). Table 12.1 presents

TABLE 12.1:   Measured Variables and Latent Factors for a Culturally Enhanced
Treatment Model

Latent Factor and Measured Indicators	Description and Comments
1. Cognitions (F_1) and (F_6)	
Beliefs	* Beliefs about relapse, e.g., about the Abstinence Violation Effect
Attitudes	* Positive attitudes toward treatment and recovery
Expectations—Self-Efficacy	* Self-efficacy in expectations for improved outcomes; relapse avoidance
2. Skills (F_2) and (F_7)	
Situational Avoidance	* Skills in recognizing Apparently Irrelevant decisions
Emotional Self-Management	* Skills in coping with negative affect: anger, anxiety, depression
Coping with Cravings	* Self-control and management over cravings
3. Treatment Motivation (F_3)	* Preparedness for treatment or pretreatment exposure to Motivational Interviewing
4. Ethnic Identification (F_4) and (F_8)	
Ethnic Identity Development	* Stage of ethnic self-concept
Ethnic Involvement	* Involvement in ethnic issues and activities
Ethnic Pride	* Feelings of pride and belonging
5. Treatment (Culturally Enhanced vs. Standard) (F_5)	* Enhanced treatment involving original (standard) treatment with addition of culturally relevant content and activities
6. Relapse Avoidance (F_9)	
Self-Efficacy in Avoiding Relapse	* Increased confidence in ability to avoid relapse
Avoiding Apparently Irrelevant Decisions	* New skills for avoiding triggers and high-risk situations
Abstinence Violation Coping Skills	* New skills self-management against abstinence violation effects
7. Treatment Outcomes (F_{10})	
Abstinence from Primary Drug	* Complete abstinence from primary drug
Abstinence from Other Drugs	* Complete abstinence from other drugs
Family Relations	* Improved family relations
Occupational Situation	* Improved employment or occupational status
Health and Well Being	* Enhanced health and psychological well-being; improved quality of life

a set of variables and the latent factors they define, to illustrate relevant measured indicators for testing such a model.

Among persons recovering from addiction to drugs or alcohol, relapse prevention that fosters skills for Relapse Avoidance would aim to prevent the "revolving door syndrome," that involves a series of treatment episodes followed by relapses. By helping clients identify high-risk situations that trigger relapse, and by building relapse prevention skills, it is possible to reduce the level and extent of relapse (Dailey, 1986; Gorski & Miller, 1982; Marlatt & Gordon, 1985). Here, an important goal in Relapse Prevention Training is the development of generalizable coping skills for coping with high-risk situations that trigger relapse-related emotions and behaviors (Marlatt, 1996; McKay, Rutherford, Alterman, Cacciola & Kaplan, 1995). For racial/ethnic clients, culturally based skills may aid in coping with ethnically related familial and socio-cultural conflicts in a manner that is congruent with local community or cultural norms. In other words, the aim is to identify and inculcate self-management skills that are culturally appropriate within the context of the ethnic person's family and ethnic community.

CLINICAL CASE ILLUSTRATION

CONTRASTED CASES: SUCCESSFUL AND UNSUCCESSFUL RECOVERIES FROM ILLEGAL DRUG USE

Armando and Juan are two adults in their 50s who used illegal drugs during their early adult years. Armando, however, exhibits a life trajectory that led to becoming a prominent Hispanic leader, in contrast with Juan who has remained a drug user into his early 50s. This section compares and contrasts these actual cases to highlight important differences that relate to resilience, relapse prevention, and to a successful recovery from the use of illegal drugs.

Case of Armando

Armando is a 57-year-old Hispanic male who has a high school education, and who has advanced professionally to the position of vice president of a large community-based health and human service agency. Regarding his history of drug use, Armando used heroin in late adolescence and went to prison in part as the result of his heroin use.

In structured clinical interview ratings of client *memory*, this leader was rated as having an "excellent" memory (5 on a scale of 1 to 6). In terms of *cognitive complexity*, the ability to give detailed and integrative responses to issues, thus reflecting a deep understanding of life events and their implications, Armando was rated as "very high" (4 on a scale ranging from 1 to 4). Also, on clinically rated level of *resilience*, he was rated as "exceptional" in his resilience (a 6 on a scale ranging from 1 to 6). Regarding responses on items from a Life Satisfaction scale, Armando reported being "very much satisfied" with social aspects of his life (e.g., a sense of trust with persons important to him), and with personal aspects of his life (e.g., his ability to overcome life's problems). Regarding specific aspects of *resilience*, Armando responded to resilience scale items as being "true for him" on the following items: (1) having a strong sense of purpose in life, (2) feeling in control of his life, (3) enjoying life challenges, (4) having the ability to remain focused under pressure, and (5) developing new capabilities when facing challenges to cope with stress.

Case of Juan

Juan is a 50-year-old Hispanic male who has a high school education and also reports completing "some college." Regarding his history of drug use, Juan has used cocaine in the past at a level of "several times a week." He has also used heroin at levels of "once a day," and has been on methadone maintenance during the past year. His use of illegal drugs has included injection drug use and sharing needles, two high-risk behaviors for HIV infection. Juan has been working full time on a job classified as "unskilled labor." Although Juan has been able to maintain a regular job, his ongoing drug use has led to a divorce, problems with child custody, and other major family conflicts.

From structured clinical interview ratings, Juan's *memory* was rated as "excellent," (5 on a scale of 1 to 6). Regarding his *cognitive complexity*, as defined earlier, he was rated as "high," (3 on a scale ranging from 1 to 4). And regarding clinical ratings of his *resilience*, he was rated as responding "well to life problems," (3 on a scale ranging from 1 to 6), thus indicating a mediocre level or resilience. Regarding his responses to items on a Life Satisfaction scale, Juan reported being "somewhat satisfied" (3 on a scale ranging from 1 = *not at all satisfied* to 5 = *extremely satisfied*) for most life areas that are examined by this scale. However, he indicated having only "a little" satisfaction with his ability to overcome life's problems. And, on resilience scale items (with response choices ranging from 1 = *not true* to 5 = *true* almost all the time) for most scale items Juan gave mid-range scores of 3 = "sometimes true" for him, while expressing low self-report ratings of resilience (1 = *not true* or 2 = *rarely true* for him) regarding (1) his ability to see the humorous side of things, (2) making unpopular decisions or acting on a hunch, and (3) facing challenges to cope makes him a stronger person. Also, he indicated, (4) that it is "not at all true" that he is "in control of his life." Juan also indicated that it is only "sometimes true" for him that he: (1) can bounce back from adversity, (2) can remain focused on tasks, (3) refuses to give up, (4) has a purpose in life, (5) likes life challenges, and (6) is able to attain his life goals.

Analysis of Similarities and Differences

Both the former drug-using leader, Armando, and the current drug-using nonleader, Juan, experienced life difficulties as a consequence of their use of illegal drugs during their adolescence and early adulthood. However in contrast to Juan who remains a drug user today, Armando stopped using drugs in his early 20s after being released from prison. Given that resiliency involves the ability to "bounce back" from adversity, there exist remarkable differences between these two middle-aged Hispanic males in their profile of resiliency-related cognitions and behaviors. Armando reports that coping with stress makes him stronger and this contention is supported by the positive life changes that he took after being released from prison. While in prison he was inspired by a positive role model to avoid drug use and to "give back to the Hispanic community." Accordingly,

Armando adopted this leadership role and focused on helping the Hispanic community. Moreover, Armando exhibited persistence in pursuing his dreams and life goals, while also acknowledging that he needs the support of other people in order to be successful. Additionally, Armando reports taking personal responsibility for his choices, and believes that he has the power to make positive decisions.

By comparison, Juan was rated as having an excellent memory and his cognitive complexity scores were good although a bit lower than those of Armando. Thus, Juan appears to be a bright and capable individual based on the clinical interview ratings of his cognitive capabilities. However, Juan's life trajectory involved a continued and heavy use of cocaine and heroin for several years and up to his current age of 50. This use also involved needle sharing, which exposed him and others to HIV/AIDS and to other communicable diseases. Currently Juan feels out of control of his life, and he is dissatisfied with his ability to overcome life's problems. He also expresses only moderate levels of resilience, as indicated by his various responses to resilience scale items and by his general inability to persist in the pursuit of important life goals.

In summary, as resiliency involves the capacity to respond actively to life situations, Armando has exhibited a life trajectory that involves strategic planning and active decision making that constitute actions congruent with resilience and successful goal attainment. Armando takes personal responsibility for his actions and expresses confidence in his abilities. In this regard, Armando reports having a strong sense of self-efficacy and some sense of control over various aspects of his life. Armando's capacity for careful thinking and planning, and subsequent self-regulation reflect core aspects of resiliency: (1) identifying and establishing goals and a direction in life, and (2) maintaining persistence in pursuing life goals. As indicated in one empirical study, successful goal attainment also adds to Armando's satisfaction with life, and it builds his sense of confidence and sense of self-efficacy (Griffin, Scheirer, Botvin & Diaz, 2001).

Despite his intelligence, and in contrast to Armando, Juan continued for many years in a life trajectory involving heavy drug use. Perhaps aided by his intelligence, Juan has been able to survive adequately despite his drug use, and has been employed full-time. However, his constant use of heroin and cocaine has compromised achievement to his full potential, and also resulted in time in prison, a divorce, and various family conflicts. Had Juan pursued a life trajectory early in life that avoided drug use, as did Armando, Juan may have been able to attain greater occupational success and a higher standing within the community, and perhaps he could have avoided the multiple family problems that he now must resolve, in addition to his recovery from drug abuse and dependence.

A CASE OF RELAPSE: JAMAL, AN AFRICAN-AMERICAN

Jamal is a 36-year-old African-American male who was born and raised within an urban community in the Midwest. Jamal attended a community-based drug treatment program and after one month of treatment was discharged with optimistic hopes that he could sustain his recovery and avoid relapse. However, a few months after his discharge, Jamal reentered the same program on a voluntarily basis. Jamal hardly knew his father, and as a child lived with his mother and grandmother, although he was raised primarily by his grandmother. Jamal described his relationship with his mother as "good," but not especially close. He described his limited relationship with his father as "OK or neutral." Jamal is the oldest of two half-brothers and one half-sister. Jamal characterized his family system as one in which there was "lots of bickering." A significant early life event occurred when Jamal was 13 years of age, which is when his grandmother died. In session, Jamal cried as he recalled this loss.

Given the ongoing tension within his family, Jamal was relieved to leave the family to attend college on a football scholarship. However, he compromised his college studies by getting a girl pregnant, and also by being arrested for theft. In retrospect, Jamal regards his college experience as "a big failure." Jamal reports having two ex-wives, having fathered two children with each, and currently lives with a third female with whom he has a young daughter.

Regarding his drug use and prior to entering treatment, Jamal has used both marijuana and cocaine at frequencies of "more than once a day." Thus, he experienced a "major relapse" (Walton, Castro & Barrington, 1994), returning to high levels of use that are similar to those prior to his entry into treatment. His severe relapse was prompted in part by his inability to control negative affect (anger, fear, sadness) and also by a low sense of control over his life situation. This pattern of relapse is consistent with the detrimental effects of an inability to manage negative affect, which often serves as a trigger for relapse (McKay, Rutherford, Alterman, Cacciola & Kaplan, 1995).

In response to items from a Life Satisfaction scale, Jamal indicates that he currently is "somewhat satisfied" with several social life situations, and "a little satisfied" with several personal life situations. Jamal's responses to items from a resilience scale yielded a resilience score that indicates that he nonetheless sees himself as being "resilient." In addition, his score on a scale of Self-Efficacy for Avoiding Relapse indicates that he remains "almost entirely," confident that he can avoid relapse during a period of two weeks following his discharge from treatment. This high Self-Efficacy scale score may reflect the social support and renewed confidence that Jamal has enjoyed from attending the treatment program. However, his perceived ability to avoid relapse may lessen as Jamal again faces challenging life situations outside of treatment. From this treatment episode, Jamal is once again confident that "this time" he can avoid relapse. Given that Jamal felt this way at the completion of his prior treatment episode, it remains unclear whether this newly established optimism about his capacity for avoiding relapse is entirely accurate; a degree of guarded optimism remains about Jamal's chances of being successful in avoiding another "full-blown relapse" and a return to treatment.

CONCLUSIONS AND FUTURE DIRECTIONS

The field of relapse prevention with racial/ethnic clients is new and much research is needed to establish a more solid base of evidence to guide relevant treatment planning and interventions. Needed now are empirical studies, such as randomized controlled trials, that can compare treatment effects and post-treatment relapse outcomes in clients who receive a culturally enhanced version of Relapse Prevention Training (E_2), as compared with an original Relapse Prevention Training program (E_1), and ideally when compared with a Treatment-as-Usual comparison group that excludes Relapse Prevention Training (C). Ideally, the culturally enhanced Relapse Prevention Training would be more effective or at least as effective, when compared with the original Relapse Prevention Training. Within the field of drug abuse prevention a few studies conducted with Hispanic populations have observed comparable outcomes when comparing the effectiveness of a culturally enhanced intervention program relative to the original prevention intervention program (Botvin, Schinke, Epstein & Diaz, 1994; Castro, Barrera, Pantin, Martinez, Felix-Ortiz, Rios, Lopez & Lopez, 2006). Sufficient evidence of *significantly better* outcomes for culturally enhanced interventions has not yet accrued, although improved culturally enhanced interventions might offer a stronger test of the putative benefits of such culturally enhanced interventions. Model analyses of relapse that examine the life trajectories of ethnic clients may utilize latent curve models (Bollen & Curran, 2006) in the analysis of specific structural models (see Figure 12.3) to understand the complex effects exerted by specific cultural variables on relapse outcomes (Byrne, 2006) (see Chapter 2).

Some evidence exists that the effectiveness of relapse prevention programs can vary by substance of abuse (Witkiewitz & Marlatt, 2004). This issue may also be examined as related to treatment specificity by race/ethnicity or by other cultural factors. For example, a marijuana-specific relapse prevention intervention has been developed that differs from the original relapse prevention approach that is reported to be the most effective with alcohol users (Roffman, Stephens, Simpson & Whittaker, 1990). Similarly, a variant of the original Relapse Prevention Training might be developed to address the cultural needs of certain racial/ethnic minority clients within an expanded and culturally oriented version of the original relapse prevention program.

As illustrated by the cases of Juan and Jamal, certain ethnic clients face remarkable culturally related personal or social conditions that may merit the development of culturally focused relapse prevention interventions, either as complete programs or as supplemental modules to an existing relapse prevention program. A family-orientation module offering culturally relevant skills in providing effective social support may be helpful for reestablishing a supportive family system that aids in preventing relapse. Similarly for clients like Jamal, culturally focused intervention activities could address issues such as coping with actual or perceived racial discrimination, to foster effective coping that avoids drug use as a response to anger, or to other forms of negative affect. Culturally relevant strategies that incorporate a cognitive restructuring approach to address perceived racial discrimination and that prompt constructive social action may be used to avoid angry acting out, thus serving as culturally relevant and useful relapse prevention interventions for Jamal and for similar African-American clients.

Finally, this chapter has presented several fundamental concepts and approaches for designing and conducting culturally relevant relapse prevention interventions with Hispanic and other racial/ethnic clients in treatment for the abuse of illegal drugs. A critical mass of specific knowledge, theories, and models has accumulated that offers initial tools for adapting standard relapse prevention programs for use with various racial/ethnic clients. Further research that is guided by culturally relevant theory and models is still needed to test the efficacy of newly developed and culturally enhanced relapse prevention programs. Such research will help refine our current knowledge and to improve our capacity to prevent relapse among various ethnic clients by using more effective relapse prevention programs that are both scientifically rigorous and culturally relevant.

ACKNOWLEDGEMENTS

Work on this chapter was supported by grant P01 DA 1070 from the National Institute on Drug Abuse, P. M. Bentler, Principal Investigator, and by R24 DA 013937 from the National Institute on Drug Abuse, Flavio Marsiglia, Principal Investigator.

REFERENCES

Aiken, L.S., Stein, J.A., Bentler, P.M. (1994). Structural equation analysis of clinical subpopulation differences and comparative treatment outcomes: Characterizing the daily lives of drug addicts. *Journal of Consulting and Clinical Psychology* **62**:488–499.

Alderete, E., Vega, W.A., Kolody, B., Aguilar-Gaxiola, S. (2000). Lifetime prevalence of and risk factors for psychiatric disorders among Mexican migrant farmworkers in California. *American Journal of Public Health* **90**:608–614.

Amaro, H., Whitaker, R., Coffman, G., Heeren, T. (1990). Acculturation and marijuana and cocaine use: Finding from HHANES 1982–1984. *American Journal of Public Health, Supplement* **80**:54–60.

Berry, J.W. (1980). Acculturation as varieties of adaptation. In Padilla, A.M., ed., *Acculturation: Theory, models and some new findings*. Boulder, CO: Westview Press.

Bollen, K.A., Curran, P.J. (2006). *Latent curve models: A structural equation perspective*. Hoboken, NJ: Wiley.

Botvin, G.J., Schinke, S.P., Epstein, J.A., Diaz, T. (1994). Effectiveness of culturally-focused and generic skills training approaches to alcohol and drug abuse prevention among minority youths. *Psychology of Addictive Behaviors* **8**:116–127.

Brownell, K.D., Marlatt, G.A., Lichtenstein, E., Wilson, G.T. (1986). Understanding and prevention relapse. *American Psychologist* **41**:765–782.

Brook, J.S., Finch, S.J., Whiteman, M., Brook, D.W. (2002). Drug use and neurobehavioral, respiratory, and cognitive problems: Precursors and mediators. *Journal of Adolescent Health* **30**: 433–441.

Brook, J.S., Whiteman, M., Balka, E.B., Win, P.T., Grusen, M.D. (1998). Similar and different precursors of drug use and delinquency among African Americans and Puerto Ricans. *Journal of Genetic Psychology* **159**:13–29.

Buriel, R., Calzada, S., Vasquez, R. (1983). The relationship of traditional Mexican American culture to adjustment and delinquency among three generations of Mexican American male adolescents. *Hispanic Journal of Behavioral Sciences* **4**:41–55.

Byrne, B.M. (2006). *Structural equation modeling with EQS: Basic concepts, applications, and programming, 2e.* Mahwah, NJ: Lawrence Erlbaum.

Carroll, K.M., Rounseville, B.J., Keller, D.S. (1991). Relapse prevention strategies for the treatment of cocaine abuse. *American Journal of Drug and Alcohol Dependence* **17**:249–265.

Carvajal, S.C., Photiades, J.R., Evans, R.I., Nash, S.G. (1997). Relating a social influence model to the role of acculturation in substance use among Latino adolescents. *Journal of Applied Social Psychology* **27**(18):1617–1628.

Casas, J.M., Wagenheim, B.R., Branchero, R., Mendoza-Romero, J. (1994). Hispanic masculinity: Myth or psychological schema meriting clinical considerations. *Hispanic Journal of Behavioral Sciences* **16**:315–331.

Castro, F.G. (1998). Cultural competence training in clinical psychology. Assessment, clinical intervention, and research. In Bellack, A.S., Hersen, M., eds., *Comprehensive clinical psychology: Sociocultural and individual differences* (Vol 10), 127–140. Oxford: Pergamon.

Castro, F.G., Barrera, M., Martinez, C. (2004). The cultural adaptation of prevention interventions: Resolving tensions between fidelity and fit. *Prevention Science* **5**:41–45.

Castro, F.G., Barrera, M., Pantin, H., Martinez, C., Felix-Ortiz, M., Rios, R., Lopez, V.A., Lopez, C. (2006). Substance abuse prevention research with Hispanic populations. *Drug and Alcohol Abuse* **84S**:S29–S42.

Castro, F.G., Balcazar, H.G., Krull, J. (1995). Cancer risk reduction in Mexican American women: The role of acculturation, education, and health risk factors. *Health Education Quarterly* **22**:61–84.

Castro, F.G., Boyer, G.R., Balcazar, H.G. (2000). Healthy adjustment in Mexican American and other Hispanic adolescents. In Montemayor, R., Adams, G.R., Gullotta, T.P., eds., *Adolescent diversity in ethnic, economic and cultural contexts*, 141–178. Thousand Oaks, CA: Sage.

Castro, F.G., Garfinkle, J. (2003). Critical issues in the development of culturally-relevant substance abuse treatments for specific minority groups. *Alcoholism: Clinical and Experimental Research* **27**:1–8.

Castro, F.G., Gutierres, S. (1997). Drug and alcohol use among rural Mexican Americans. In Robertson, E.R., Sloboda, Z., Boyd, G.M., Beatty, L., Kozel, N.J., eds., *Rural substance abuse: State of knowledge and issues.* NIDA Research Monograph No. 168, 499–533. Rockville, MD: National Institute on Drug Abuse.

Castro, F.G., Hernandez-Alarcon, E. (2002). Integrating cultural variables into drug abuse prevention and treatment with racial/ethnic minorities. *Journal of Drug Issues* **32**:783–810.

Castro, F.G., Maddahian, E., Newcomb, M.D., Bentler, P.M. (1987). A multivariate model of the determinants of cigarette smoking among adolescents. *Journal of Health and Social Behavior* **28**:273–289.

Castro, F.G., Obert, J.L., Rawson, R., Valdez, C., Denne, R. (2002). Drug abuse treatments with racial/ethnic clients: Towards the development of culturally competent treatments. In Bernal, G., Trimble, J., Burlow, A.K., Leong, F.T., eds., *Handbook of Racial and Ethnic Minority Psychology*, 539–560. Washington, DC: American Psychological Association.

Castro, F.G., Sharp, E.V., Barrington, E.H., Walton, M., Rawson, R. (1991). Drug abuse identity in Mexican Americans: Theoretical and empirical considerations. *Hispanic Journal of Behavior Sciences* **13**:209–225.

Castro, F.G., Tafoya-Barraza, H.M. (1997). Treatment issues with Latinos addicted to cocaine and heroin. In Garcia, J., Zea, M.C., eds., *Psychological interventions and research with Latino populations*, 191–216. Boston, MA: Allyn & Bacon.

Cervantes, R.C., Padilla, A.M., Salgado de Snyder, N. (1991). The Hispanic Stress Inventory: A culturally relevant approach to psychosocial assessment. *Psychological Assessment* **3**:438–447.

Chung, R.H.G., Kim, B.S.K., Abreu, J.M. (2004). Asian American Multidimensional Acculturation Scale: Development, factor analysis, reliability and validity. *Cultural Diversity and Ethnic Minority Psychology* **10**:66–80.

Cross, T.L., Bazeon, K.W., Dennis, K.W., Isaacs, M.R. (1989). *The cultural competence continuum: Towards a culturally-competent system of care.* Washington, DC: Georgetown University.

Cuellar, I., Arnold, B., Maldonado, R. (1995). Acculturation Raging Scale for Mexican Americans II: A revision of the original ARSMA scale. *Hispanic Journal of Behavioral Sciences* **17**:275–304.

Cuellar, I., Harris, L.C., Jasso, R. (1980). An acculturation scale for Mexican American normal and clinical populations. *Hispanic Journal of Behavioral Sciences* **2**:199–217.

Dailey, D.C. (1986). *Relapse prevention workbook for recovering alcoholics and drug dependent persons.* Holmes Beach, FL: Learning Publishers.

Durantini, M.R., Albarracin, D., Mitchell, A.L., Earl, A.N., Gillette, J.C. (2006). A meta-analysis of the effectiveness of HIV-prevention interventionists for different groups. *Psychological Bulletin* **132**:212–248.

Elliot, D.S., Mihalic, S. (2004). Issues in disseminating and replicating effective prevention programs. *Prevention Science* **5**:47–53.

Félix-Ortiz, M., Newcomb, M.D. (1995). Cultural identity and drug use among Latino and Latina adolescents. In Botvin, G.J., Schinke, S., Orlandi, M.A., eds., *Drug abuse prevention with multiethnic youth*, 147–165. Thousand Oaks, CA: Sage.

Félix-Ortiz, M., Newcomb, M.D., Myers, H. (1994). A multidimensional scale of cultural identity for Latino and Latina adolescents. *Hispanic Journal of Behavioral Sciences* **16**:99–115.

Fragoso, J.M., Kashubeck, S. (2000). Machismo, gender role conflict, and mental health in Mexican American men. *Psychology of Men & Masculinity* **1**:87–97.

Galaif, E.R., Newcomb, M.D. (1999). Predictors of polydrug use among four ethnic groups: A 12-year longitudinal study. *Addictive Behaviors* **24**:607–631.

Gil, R.M., Vazquez, C.I. (1996). *The Maria paradox: How Latinas can merge old world traditions with new world self-esteem.* New York: The Berkeley Publishing Group.

Gil, A., Wagner, E., Vega, W. (2000). Acculturation, familism and alcohol use among Latino adolescent males: Longitudinal relations. *Journal of Community Psychology* **28**:443–458.

Gorski, T.T., Miller, M. (1982). *Counseling for relapse prevention.* Independence, MO: Harald House—Independent Press.

Gould, J.B., Madan, A., Qin, C., Chavez, G. (2003). Perinatal outcomes in two dissimilar immigrant populations in the United States: A dual epidemiologic paradox. *Pediatrics* **111**: 676–682.

Griffin, K.W., Scheier, L.M., Botvin, G.J., Diaz, T. (2001). Protective role of personal competence skills in adolescent substance use: Psychological well being as a mediating factor. *Psychology of Addictive Behaviors* **15**:194–203.

Gutmann, M.C. (1996). *The meanings of macho: Being a man in Mexico City.* Berkeley, CA: University of California Press.

Hanson, W.B. (1992). School-based substance abuse prevention: A review of the state of the art curriculum, 1980–1990. *Health Education Research: Theory & Practice* **7**:403–430.

Hogan, R., Curphy, G.J., Hogan, J. (1994). What we know about leadership: Effectiveness and personality. *American Psychologist* **49**:493–504.

Hunt, L.M., Schneider, S., Comer, B. (2004). Should "acculturation" be a variable in health research? A critical review of research with U.S. Hispanics. *Social Science & Medicine* **59**:973–986.

Ja, D., Aoki, B. (1993). Substance abuse treatment: Cultural barriers in the Asian American community. *Journal of Psychoactive Drugs* **25**:61–71.

Jorquez, J.S. (1984). Heroin use in the barrio: Solving the problem of relapse or keeping the Tecato Gusano asleep. *American Journal of Drug and Alcohol Abuse* **10**:63–75.

Jung, J. (2001). *Psychology of Alcohol and Other Drugs*. Newbury Park, CA: Sage Publications.

Kandel, D. (1995). Ethnic differences in drug use: Patterns and paradoxes. In Botvin, G.J., Schinke, S., Orlandi, M.A., eds., *Drug abuse prevention with multiethnic youth*, 81–104. Thousand Oaks, CA: Sage.

Keefe, S.E. (1992). Ethnic identity: The domain of perceptions of and attachment to ethnic groups and cultures. *Human Organization* **51**:35–43.

Klohnen, E.C. (1996). Conceptual analysis and measurement of the construct of ego-resiliency. *Journal of Personality and Social Psychology* **70**:1067–1079.

Kolonoff, E.A., Landrine, H. (2000). Revising and improving the African American Acculturation Scale. *Journal of Black Psychology* **26**:235–261.

Kumpfer, K.L., Alvarado, R., Smith, P., Bellamy, N. (2002). Hopeful sensitivity and adaptation in family-based interventions. *Prevention Science* **3**:241–246.

Lafayette de Mente, B. (1996). *NTC's dictionary of Mexican cultural code words*. Chicago, IL: NTC Publishing Group.

LaFromboise, T., Coleman, H.L.K., Gerton, J. (1993). Psychological impact of biculturalism: Evidence and theory. *Psychological Bulletin* **114**:395–412.

LaFromboise, T.D., Trimble, J.E., Mohatt, G.V. (1990). Counseling intervention and American Indian tradition: An integrative approach. *The Counseling Psychologist* **18**:628–654.

Leong, F.T.L., Okazaki, S., Tak, J. (2003). Assessment of depression and anxiety in East Asia. *Psychological Assessment* **15**:290–305.

Lettieri, D.J., Sayers, M., Pearson, H.W. (1984). *Theories on drug abuse: Selected contemporary perspectives*. Washington, DC: National Institute on Drug Abuse.

Locke, D.C. (1998). *Increasing multicultural understanding: A comprehensive model, 2e*. Thousand Oaks, CA: Sage.

Locke, T.F., Newcomb, M.D., Goodyear, R.K. (2005). Childhood experiences and psychosocial influences on risky sexual behavior, condom use, and HIV attitudes-behaviors among Latino males. *Psychology of Men and Masculinity* **6**:25–38.

Marin, G., Gamboa, R.J. (1995). A new measurement of acculturation for Hispanics: The Bidimensional Acculturation Scale for Hispanics (BAS). *Hispanic Journal of Behavioral Sciences* **18**:297–316.

Marin, G., Marin, B.V. (1991). *Research with Hispanic populations*. Newbury Park, CA: Sage.

Marlatt, G.A. (1996). Models of relapse and relapse prevention: A commentary. *Experimental and Clinical Psychopharmacology* **4**:55–60.

Marlatt, G.A., Gordon, J. (1985). *Relapse Prevention: Maintenance Strategies in the Treatment of Addictive Behaviors*. New York: Guilford.

Marsiglia, F.F., Kulis, S., Hecht, M.L., Sills, S. (2004). Ethnicity, and ethnic identity as predictors of drug norms and drug use among preadolescents in the US Southwest. *Substance Use and Misuse* **39**:1061–1094.

Masten, A.S. (2001). Ordinary people: Resilience process in development. *American Psychologist* **56**:227–238.

McKay, J.R., Rutherford, M.J., Alterman, A.I., Cacciola, J.S., Kaplan, M.R. (1995). An examination of the cocaine relapse process. *Drug and Alcohol Dependence* **38**:35–43.

McQueen, A., Getz, G., Bray, J.H. (2003). Acculturation, substance use, and deviant behavior: Examining separation and family conflict as mediators. *Child Development* **74**:1737–1750.

Meyerowitz, B.E., Richardson, J., Hudson, S., Leedham, B. (1998). Ethnicity and cancer outcomes: Behavioral and psychosocial considerations. *Psychological Bulletin* **123**:47–70.

Miller, W.R., Rollnick, S. (1991). *Motivational interviewing: Preparing people to change addictive behaviors.* New York: Guilford Press.

Mirande, A. (1997). *Hombres y machos: Masculinity and Latino culture.* Boulder, CO: Westview.

Moore, J. (1990). Mexican American women addicts: The influence of family background. In Glick, R., Moore, J., eds., *Drugs in Hispanic Communities,* 127–153. New Brunswick: Rutgers University Press.

Morganstern, J., Morgan, T.J., McCrady, B.S., Keller, D.S., Carroll, K.M. (2001). Manual-guided cognitive-behavioral therapy training: A promising method for disseminating empirically supported substance abuse treatments to the practice community. *Psychology of Addictive Behaviors* 15:83–88.

National Institute on Drug Abuse. (1999). Principles of drug addition treatment: A research-based guide. NIH Publication No. 99-4180. Rockville, MD: National Institute on Drug Abuse.

Newcomb, M.D., Bentler, P.M. (1988). *Consequences of adolescent drug use: Impact on the lives of young adults.* Newbury Park, CA: Sage Publications.

Newcomb, M.D., Locke, T. (2005). Childhood adversity and poor mothering: Consequences of polydrug use as a moderator. *Addictive Behaviors* 30:1061–1064.

Norcross, J.C., Beutler, L.E., Levant, R.E. (2006). *Evidence-based practices in mental health: Debate on fundamental questions.* Washington, DC: American Psychological Association.

Obert, J.L., McCann, M.J., Marinelli-Casey, P.M., Weiner, A., Minsky, S., Brethen, P., Rawson, R. (2000). The matrix model of outpatient stimulant abuse treatment: History and description. *Journal of Psychoactive Drugs* 32:157–164.

Oetting, E.R., Bearvais, F. (1987). Peer Cluster Theory: Social characteristics and adolescent drug use: A path analysis. *Journal of Counseling Psychology* 34:205–213.

Oetting, E.R., Bearvais, F. (1990). Orthogonal Cultural Identification Theory: The cultural identification of minority adolescents. *The International Journal of the Addictions* 25:655–685.

Oetting, E.R., Donnermeyer, J.F., Trimble, J.E., Beauvais, F. (1998). Primary Socialization Theory: Culture, ethnicity, and cultural identification. The links between culture and substance use. *Substance Use & Misuse* 33:2075–2107.

Orlandi, M.A., Weston, R., Epstein, L.G. (1992). *Cultural competence for evaluators: A guide for alcohol and other drug abuse prevention practitioners working with ethnic/racial communities.* Rockville, M.D.: Office for Substance Abuse Prevention. U.S. Department of Health and Human Services, Health Resources and Services Administration (2001). *Cultural competence: A journey.* Office of Public Health & Services (USDHHS) Bureau or Primary Care: Washington, DC.

Pandina, R.J., Johnson, V.L. (1999). Why people use, abuse, and become dependent on drugs: Progress toward a heuristic model. In Glantz, M.D., Hartel, C.R., eds., *Drug abuse: Origins & interventions,* 119–147. Washington, DC: American Psychological Association.

Pantin, H., Coatsworth, J.D., Feaster, D.J., Newman, F.L., Briones, E., Prado, G., Schwartz, S.J., Szapocznik, J. (2003). Familias Unidas: The efficacy of an intervention to increase parental investment in Hispanic immigrant families. *Prevention Science* 4:189–201.

Petraitis, J., Flay, B.R., Miller, T.Q. (1995). Reviewing theories of adolescent substance use: Organizing pieces in the puzzle. *Psychological Bulletin* 117:67–86.

Phinney, J.S. (1990). Ethnic identity in adolescents and adults: Review of research. *Psychological Bulletin* 108:499–514.

Portes, A., Rumbaut, R.G. (1996). *Immigrant America: A portrait, 2e.* Berkeley, CA: University of California Press.

Ramirez, M. (1998). *Multicultural/multiracial psychology: Mestizo perspectives in personality and mental health.* Northvale, NJ: Jason Aronson Inc.

Ramierz, M. (1999). *Multicultural psychotherapy: An approach to individual and cultural differences, 2e.* Boston, MA: Allyn & Bacon.

Rebhun, L.A. (1998). Substance use among immigrants to the United States. In Sana, L., ed., *Handbook of immigrant health,* 493–519. New York: Plenum Press.

Resnicow, K., Soler, R., Braithwaite, R.L. (2000). Cultural sensitivity in substance use prevention. *Journal of Community Psychology* **28**:271–290.

Roffman, R.A., Stephens, R.S., Simpson, E.E., Whittaker, D. (1990). Treatment of marijuana dependence: Preliminary results. *Journal of Psychoactive Drugs* **20**:129–137.

Rogler, L.H., Cortés, D.E., Malgady, R.G. (1991). Acculturation and mental health status among Hispanics: Convergence and new directions for research. *American Psychologist* **46**:585–597.

Sabogal, J., Marin, G., Otero-Sabogal, R. (1987). Hispanic familism and acculturation: What changes and what doesn't? *Hispanic Journal of Behavioral Sciences* **9**:397–412.

Schinke, S., Brounstein, P., Gardner, S. (2003). *Science-based prevention programs and principles 2002*. DHHS Pub No. (SMA) 03-3764. Rockville, MD: Center for Substance Abuse Prevention, Substance Abuse and Mental Health Services Administration.

Schwartz, S.J., Montgomery, M.J., Briones, E. (2006). The role of identity in acculturation among immigrant people: Theoretical propositions, empirical questions, and applied recommendations. *Human Development* **49**:1–30.

Shon, S.P., Ja, D.Y. (1982). Asian families. In McGoldrick, M., Pearce, J.K., Giordano, J., eds., *Ethnicity and family therapy*, 208–228. New York: Guilford.

Shulz, A.J., Mullings, L. (2006). *Gender, race, class & health: Intersectional approaches*. San Francisco, CA: Jossey-Bass.

Sue, D.W., Carter, R.T., Casas, J.M., Fouad, N.A., Ivey, A.E., Jensen, M., LaFromboise, T., Manese, J.E., Ponterotto, J.G., Vasquez-Nutall, E. (1998). *Multicultural counseling competencies: Individual and organizational development*. Thousand Oaks, CA: Sage.

Szapocznik, J., Coatsworth, J.D. (1999). An ecodevelopmental framework for organizing the influences on drug abuse: A developmental model of risk and protection. In Glantz, M., Hartel, C., eds., *Drug abuse: Origins & interventions*, 331–366. Washington, DC, American Psychological Association.

Szapocznik, J., Kurtines, W.M. (1989). *Breakthroughs in family therapy with drug abusing and problem youth*. New York: Springer.

Szapocznik, J., Santisteban, D., Rio, A., Perez-Vidal, A. et al. (1989). Family effectiveness training: An intervention to prevent drug abuse and problem behaviors in Hispanic adolescents. *Hispanic Journal of Behavioral Sciences* **11**.4–27.

Szapocznik, J., Williams, R.A. (2000). Brief Strategic Family Therapy: Twenty-five years of interplay among theory, research and practice in adolescent behavior problems and drug abuse. *Clinical Child & Family Psychology Review* **3**:117–134.

Terrell, M.D. (1993). Ethnocultural factors and substance abuse towards culturally sensitive treatment models. *Psychology of Addictive Behaviors* **7**:162–167.

Torres, J.B. (1998). Masculinity and gender roles among Puerto Rican men: Machismo on the U.S. mainland. *American Journal of Orthopsychiatry* **68**:16–26.

Trimble, J.E. (1995). Toward an understanding of ethnicity and ethnic identity, and their relationship to drug use research. In Botvin, G., Schinke, S., Orlandi, M., eds., *Drug abuse prevention with multiethnic youth*, 3–27. Thousand Oaks, CA: Sage.

Trimble, J.E. (2003). Introduction: Social change and acculturation. In Chun, K.M., Organista, P.B., Marin, G., eds., *Acculturation: Advances in theory, measurement, and applied research*, 3–13. Washington, DC: American Psychological Association.

U.S. Census Bureau (2005). Race and Hispanic or Latino Origin of the Population of the United States: 2003 and 2004. Retrieved November 29, 2005, from www.census.gov/Press-Release/www/releases/archives/natrecepop2004_tbl.pdf.

U.S. Census Bureau (2006). Annual estimates of the population by sex, race and Hispanic or Latino origin for the United States: April 1, 2000 to July 1, 2005. Retrieved July 6, 2006, from www.census.gov/popest/national/asrh/NC-EST2005/NC-EST2005-03.xls.

U.S. Department of Health and Human Services (2001). *Mental health: Culture, race, and ethnicity—A supplement to Mental Health: A report of the Surgeon General*. Rockville, MD: U.S. Department of Health and Human Services, Public Health Service, Office of the Surgeon General.

Vega, W., Alderate, E., Kolody, B., Aguilar-Gaxiola, S. (2003). Illicit drug use among Mexican Americans in California: The effects of gender and acculturation. In Aguirre-Molina, M., Molina, C.W., eds., *Latina health in the United States: A public health reader*, 309–326. San Francisco, CA: Jossey-Bass.

Vega, W.A., Gil, A., Warheit, G.J., Zimmerman, R., Apospori, E. (1993). Acculturation and delinquent behavior among Cuban American adolescents: Toward an empirical model. *American Journal of Community Psychology* **21**:113–125.

Vega, W.A., Zimmerman, R.S., Warheit, G.J., Apospori, E., Gil, A.G. (1993). Risk factors for early adolescent drug use in four ethnic and racial groups. *American Journal of Public Health* **83**:185–189.

Walton, M.A., Castro, F.G., Barrington, E.H. (1994). The role of attributions in abstinence, lapse, and relapse following substance abuse treatment. *Addictive Behaviors* **19**:319–331.

Witkiewitz, K., Marlatt, G.A. (2004). Relapse prevention for alcohol and drug problems. *American Psychologist* **59**:224–235.

Zane, N., Mak, W. (2003). Major approaches to the measurement of acculturation among ethnic minority populations: A content analysis and an alternative empirical study. In Chun, K.M., Organista, P.B., Marin, G., eds., *Acculturation: Advances in theory, measurement, and applied research*, 39–60. Washington, DC: American Psychological Association.

INTERNET RESOURCES

- Center for Mental Health Services (CMHS)
  http://www.mentalhealth.samhsa.gov/cmhs/
- Center for Scientific Review 0 (CSR)
  http://cms.csr.nih.gov/
- Center for Substance Abuse Prevention—(CSAP)
  http://prevention.samhsa.gov/
- Center for Substance Abuse Research—(CSAT)
  http://csat.samhsa.gov/
- Centros de Integration Juvenil—(CIJ) (Mexico)
  http://cij.gob.mx/
- National Center on Minority Health and Health Disparities—(NCMHD)
  http://www.ncmhd.nih.gov/
- National Center on Alcohol Abuse and Alcoholism—(NIAAA)
  http://www.niaaa.nih.gov/
- National Institute on Drug Abuse—(NIDA)
  http://www.nida.nih.gov/
- National Institute on Mental Health—(NIMH)
  http://www.nimh.nih.gov/

13

RELAPSE PREVENTION FOR ADOLESCENT SUBSTANCE ABUSE: OVERVIEW AND CASE EXAMPLES

DANIELLE E. RAMO

University of California, San Diego
San Diego State University
La Jolla, California

MARK G. MYERS AND SANDRA A. BROWN

Veterans Affairs San Diego Healthcare System
University of California, San Diego
La Jolla, California

ABSTRACT

Relapse prevention (RP) can be a useful therapeutic resource for clinicians working with adolescents in treatment for substance use disorders (SUDs). This chapter provides an overview of this treatment for SUD youth. We examine the empirical evidence for use of RP techniques with SUD youth, and describe the most important techniques to be used in any RP intervention with SUD youth, including setting goals, identifying high-risk situations, and teaching coping skills. We also put forth some specific considerations when using RP with youth. We describe two clinical case examples to highlight the issues important to RP for youth, including psychiatric comorbidity. Finally, this chapter suggests areas that should be explored further, through clinical trials that focus specifically on RP in youth and generating further evidence on the process of relapse in adolescents over time.

293

INTRODUCTION

Adolescent alcohol and drug use continues to garner national attention as a significant social and public health concern. The Monitoring the Future study, an annual survey of youth funded by the National Institute on Drug Abuse, indicates that 75 percent of high school seniors have used alcohol and 50 percent have used other drugs at least once (Johnston, O'Malley, Bachman & Schulenberg, 2005). Among youth with substance use disorders (SUDs), successful treatment outcomes have eluded both researchers and clinicians in this field, in that approximately half of the adolescents receiving community-based treatment for SUDs return to use within the first three months following treatment (Brown, Mott & Myers, 1990) and two-thirds to four-fifths of youth return to use after six months (Brown, D'Amico, McCarthy & Tapert, 2001; Cornelius et al., 2001). Relapse prevention (RP) is a potentially useful intervention for reducing the high rates of return to substance use among SUD adolescents, either as an adjunct to formal inpatient or outpatient treatment, or as part of a posttreatment aftercare program.

As outlined in earlier chapters in this volume, RP is grounded in cognitive behavioral theory, and was originally described by Marlatt & Gordon (1980, 1985) as a technique to manage alcohol and drug abuse. Multiple studies have described its efficacy in treating these behaviors in adults (e.g., Carroll, 1996; Irvin, Bowers, Dunn & Wang, 1999). RP for adolescents has a similar goal as for adults: helping those with substance abuse problems on the road to recovery to maintain that recovery process without (or despite) the interruptions that tend to occur throughout.

RP may be useful with substance abusing adolescents for a number of reasons. Most notably, it directly addresses the high rate of return to problematic substance use observed among youth treated for SUDs. RP also provides a complementary treatment modality to 12-step approaches (e.g., 12-step facilitation, AA/NA meetings), which tend to be the most available and commonly employed sources of support for abstinence and represent a key component of most substance abuse treatment programs for teens (Kelly, Myers & Brown, 2002). Finally, RP incorporates psychoeducation about the relapse process, including consideration of personal motivation, which can be important for youth who may be early in the addiction recovery process and also allows treatment to be individually tailored to the substance use patterns and needs of adolescents.

Research on RP interventions suggests that it is a promising treatment approach for adolescents, but important developmental considerations must be incorporated in order to address issues specific to younger substance abusers. This chapter provides an overview of RP treatment for SUD youth. We will first review the clinical trials that have addressed relapse prevention in SUD youth. We then describe the major components of the intervention and some important additional considerations for youth. Next, we provide two clinical case examples from our work with youth who have relapsed after inpatient substance abuse treatment.

Finally, we provide suggestions as to future directions for research and clinical applications for RP with adolescents.

REVIEW OF THE LITERATURE

Techniques identified specifically as "relapse prevention" have not been studied extensively with adolescents. However, a number of randomized clinical trials have compared the efficacy of cognitive-behavioral therapy with substance-abusing adolescents to other treatments. A literature search yielded four empirical studies that randomized youth to at least one cognitive behavior therapy-based treatment condition. Each of these treatment conditions included a piece that taught adolescents coping skills to use in situations in which use is common ("high-risk" situations) and ways to prevent a single-use episode from becoming a more prolonged period of use. One study, conducted by Azrin and colleagues (2001) demonstrated that six months of either family behavior therapy (FBT) or individual cognitive problem-solving therapy (ICPS) resulted in similar and significant decreases in substance use six months following treatment in a sample of 56 conduct-disordered substance dependent youth. Almost half of the youth in each treatment condition (45% FBT; 44% ICPS) were abstinent at the six-month follow-up.

Another study compared cognitive-behavioral coping skills (CBS) and psychoeducation (PET) therapies in a sample of 88 adolescents diagnosed with an alcohol or marijuana use disorder, or both (Kaminer, Burleson & Goldberger, 2002). At three months after the eight-week treatment, there was no significant difference in substance use between participants in the two groups, although youth who were younger than 16 were more likely to show a positive drug screen if they had received the PET treatment. At nine months post-treatment, there were no differences in treatment outcomes between the two groups. Youth in both groups tended to improve on domains relevant to adolescent functioning (e.g., family, school, substance use) after treatment. Boys tended to improve more if they were in the CBS group, and girls tended to improve more if they were in the PET group.

A third clinical trial compared cognitive-behavioral therapy (CBT), functional family therapy (FFT), combined CBT/FFT (joint), and a group intervention (Waldron, Slesnick, Brody, Turner & Peterson, 2001). Youth in the joint and group conditions had significantly fewer days of marijuana use from intake to seven months after treatment, but there was no change for the CBT or FFT conditions. There was also a clinically significant change from heavy marijuana use to minimal use (abstinence or near abstinence) in the FFT, joint, and group conditions at the seven-month follow-up.

In a group of two clinical trials, the Cannabis Youth Treatment project (CYT; Dennis et al., 2004) randomized youth ages 12 to 18 years with cannabis use disorders to five treatment conditions across four sites in the United States: 5

sessions of Motivational Enhancement Therapy/Cognitive Behavior Therapy (MET/CBT), 12 sessions of MET/CBT (MET/CBT12), Family Support Network (FSN; including MET/CBT12 along with 6 parent education meetings), the Adolescent Community Reinforcement Approach (ACRA), and Multidimensional Family Therapy (MFT). Both of the MET/CBT conditions involved a component that taught coping skills to handle unanticipated high-risk situations and handling a lapse if one should occur. Results from the two trials indicated that all five CYT interventions demonstrated significant pre- post-treatment effects that were stable in terms of increasing days of abstinence during the 12 months after participants were randomized to a treatment intervention and the percent of adolescents abstinent at the end of the study. Overall, the clinical outcomes were very similar across sites and conditions (Dennis et al., 2004).

Clinical trials considering some aspect of relapse prevention (alone or combined with CBT or another treatment) seem to indicate that this is a promising treatment modality for use with adolescent substance abusers. Overall, it does lead to reduced substance use and improvement on a number of outcome domains relevant to youth (e.g., school, peers, family relations); however, it does not appear to perform better than treatments focused on educating teens about substance use (Kaminer et al., 2002) or involving families (Azrin et al., 2001; Dennis et al., 1994; Waldron et al., 2001). Studies that directly examine relapse prevention techniques in SUD youth are still needed. However, existing outcome studies suggest that we should consider what aspects of RP/CBT might be modified to make the treatment more effective for teens. Research in the process of relapse in youth has uncovered some possible answers to this question.

OVERVIEW OF RP TREATMENT

Relapse prevention treatment for adolescent substance abusers can be thought of as a blend of theory and techniques taken from cognitive therapy of substance abuse (Beck, Wright, Newman & Liese, 1993), RP maintenance treatment (Marlatt & Gordon, 1985), and general therapeutic considerations that are important for working with substance-abusing teens (see Myers, Brown & Vik, 1998, for a detailed review of these considerations). RP with teens should focus on identifying high-risk situations that are emotional and behavioral triggers for use and learning alternative cognitive and behavioral responses to these triggers. The initial stages of treatment focus on enhancing motivation and identifying high risk stimuli for youth (including people, places, and events) and monitoring cognitions that occur in response to those stimuli that have perpetuated substance use over time. Later stages of this intervention focus on providing youth with specific techniques they can use when faced with high-risk situations to avoid using alcohol or drugs, and ways to think about slips when they occur to prevent them from becoming relapses.

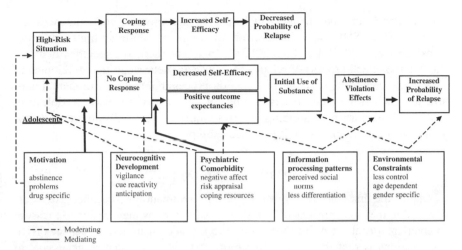

FIGURE 13.1: Youth Addiction Relapse Model
Note: From "Clinical course of youth following treatment for alcohol and drug problems" by S.A. Brown and D.E. Ramo, 2006, in H. Liddle and C. Rowe, eds., *Adolescent Substance Abuse: Research and Clinical Advances*, 79–103. Copyright 2006 by Cambridge University Press. Adapted with permission from the authors.

As described in previous chapters in this volume, the cognitive-behavioral model (see top two rows of Figure 13.1; Marlatt & Gordon, 1985; Witkiewitz & Marlatt, 2004, which views "relapse" as the process of returning to problematic substance use rather than a specific use episode, or "lapse") has been the dominant psychosocial model of addiction relapse for the past two decades. The model suggests that substance abusers often encounter situations with elevated risk for relapse (high-risk situations). If individuals actively employ coping responses other than using (e.g., walking away, thinking about a higher power, calling a sober friend), then they gain confidence in their ability to abstain (increased coping self-efficacy) and are more likely to do so in the future when facing similar situations. By contrast, if individuals do not have adequate coping skills to manage these situations, and hold positive expectations about the effects of using a substance, expectations build that they won't be able to manage high-risk situations without using (reduced self-efficacy) and they will lapse. Lapses may cause negative feelings (e.g., guilt, self-blame), which may make abstinence seem "impossible" (the Abstinence Violation Effect; AVE), and likelihood of future or sustained substance involvement is elevated.

Studies of adolescent substance abuse relapse suggest amendments to the model to make it developmentally appropriate for youth. The Youth Addiction Relapse Model (see Figure 13.1; Brown & Ramo, 2006) proposes ways the cognitive-behavioral model of relapse can be tailored to youth. Motivation for abstinence is a critical construct for SUD youth as studies find that motivation predicts post-treatment use and engagement in the 12-step process, and influences the extent to which SUD youth make effortful coping responses in high-risk situations (Brown, 1999; Kelly et al., 2002). Other constructs that specifically affect the likelihood and process of relapse for youth are neurocognitive development, psychiatric comorbidity, social information processing, and environmental constraints. Each of these constructs will be considered as they relate to adolescent relapse, as we turn to describing the techniques used in RP interventions for youth and then present two clinical case examples.

MOTIVATIONAL ENHANCEMENT

One of the first considerations for youth in treatment for substance use disorders is that they may present with low motivation for abstinence (due to pressure to enter treatment from family, school, etc.). Since an important aspect of RP interventions is that there be a commitment to abstinence, it is necessary to operationalize this goal in the initial stages of treatment, and possibly employ therapeutic techniques such as motivational interviewing (Miller & Rollnick, 2002; O'Leary & Monti, 2004) to build motivation for and self-efficacy regarding abstinence if client and therapist are not in agreement about treatment goals. Motivational interviewing in the first session of adolescent RP treatment creates an opportunity to build personal interest in treatment and commitment to the therapeutic process and will reduce the likelihood of drop-out. Among youth, there are specific challenges to enhancing motivation at treatment outset. For example, motivation for abstinence tends to vary by substance, youth may not be motivated to eliminate using all together, and youth may not be able to anticipate the consequences of abstention (Metrik, McCarthy, Frissell, MacPherson & Brown, 2004). Motivational enhancement in the first session of RP treatment with these factors taken into account will increase the likelihood that the rest of the therapeutic process will be successful.

IDENTIFYING HIGH-RISK SITUATIONS

The next stage of RP with teens involves providing psychoeducation regarding the Youth Addiction Relapse Model and situations that pose a high risk for relapse. Psychoeducation regarding the process of relapse involves outlining the factors involved in relapse, the difference between a lapse and a relapse, and describing cognitive constructs like the Abstinence Violation Effect (AVE). Marlatt and colleagues (Marlatt & Gordon, 1985; Witkiewitz & Marlatt, 2004) identified the AVE as thought patterns that occur as a result of a lapse (e.g., "A lapse means I don't have any control") that make a relapse more likely to occur. Teaching teens that a lapse does not inevitably lead to relapse, that their actions in response to a lapse can influence the outcome, and that cognitive coping skills can decrease the probability of a full-blown relapse when a slip occurs are common therapeutic techniques that can be used at this stage.

The concept of high-risk situations should be presented as part of the psycho-education component of the intervention as they relate to the personal experiences of an adolescent client. Youth tend to relapse most often in situations where peers are present and in the face of direct or perceived social pressure to use. Although less common than for adults, when emotional conflict precedes relapse, it most often involves their parents (Anderson, Frissell & Brown, in press; Brown, Stetson & Beatty, 1989; Myers & Brown, 1990a). Thus, general examples should be provided to teens with these contexts in mind. Information regarding individual use situations can be obtained through a discussion of situations in which an adolescent has had difficulty abstaining or perceives abstention as likely to be difficult. Additional information can be gathered by having the adolescent complete the Inventory of Drug-Taking Situations (IDTS; Turner, Annis & Sklar, 1997) or the Drug-Taking Confidence Questionnaire (DTCQ; Sklar, Annis & Turner, 1997). These paper-and-pencil questionnaires, respectively, assess the frequency of past use across a broad range of situations and examine efficacy for abstinence across these situations, and thus can help generate a list of potential high-risk situations. Then, teens should be given feedback about past frequent use situations that are likely to present a challenge to their abstinence in the future.

We find it helpful at this time to make a list of the situations that are likely to come up in the immediate and more distant future to provide a concrete prioritized list of high-risk situations on which to focus. In addition, youth often fail to anticipate how intense affect (e.g., anxiety, frustration, disappointment, joy) may influence the risk for relapse and thus an introduction to this relationship is particularly important in this phase of RP treatment.

COPING WITH HIGH-RISK SITUATIONS

The next major stage of RP for youth involves helping teens to develop healthy coping strategies that will be effective in the high-risk situations just described. The cognitive and behavioral skills that will work best for a given adolescent depend on the extent to which he or she has been successful at managing situations in the past without using and how well prepared the teen is to face these situations in the future. It is also important to elicit from adolescents their own experiences (if any) at successfully managing temptations to use alcohol and/or drugs in order to build coping self-efficacy (confidence that one can resist the urge to use in a high-risk situation).

When discussing strategies, it is important to recognize that some of the strategies that may have worked with adults are not as applicable to teens. For example, SUD teens report that they are less likely to use cognitive than behavioral or social support-based coping strategies when faced with high-risk situations (Myers & Brown, 1990a). Cognitive strategies are also not as strongly associated with substance use outcomes after treatment as behavioral strategies for teens (Myers, Brown & Mott, 1993). This may be due in part to developmental consequences that are associated with early exposure to alcohol and drug use in youth such as smaller hippocampal volume (DeBellis et al., 2000), and working memory functioning (Brown, Tapert, Granholm & Delis, 2000). As such, cognitive strategies employed with teens must be selected so that they fit the neurocognitive developmental status of adolescence and account for possible further demands placed on the brain from protracted substance use.

Cognitive Strategies

Cognitive coping skills generally include replacing maladaptive thoughts with "control" thoughts that reduce the risk of lapses and relapses (e.g., "I don't need drugs to have fun, A lapse is not equivalent to failure"). Substance-abusing teens tend to exhibit patterns of thinking associated with self-blame and criticism (e.g., "I am a failure"), which are associated with poorer outcomes (Myers et al., 1993). In addition, Peterson & O'Connell (2003), in their description of cognitive therapy for adolescent substance abusers, identified a set of maladaptive cognitions originally described by Emery (1988) that they notice in many of their adolescent patients: "I need others' approval to prove I am worthy; I need to achieve to prove that I am good enough; I need to be in control to avoid feeling helpless; I am powerless to get what I want."

Many cognitive-based substance abuse treatments focus on how thoughts such as these may perpetuate substance use over time, and in RP with teens, it is important to directly address how they may lead to use in high-risk situations. We make sure at this stage of treatment to introduce clients to the "behavior chain" as a way to understand how thoughts lead to substance use and associated consequences if they are not already familiar with this technique (see Myers, Brown & Vik, 1998, for a more detailed discussion of this technique used with SUD youth).

Given the neurocognitive constraints discussed earlier, one of the most important cognitive techniques for youth is distraction, which can be employed as a short-term coping strategy while urges subside. Since substance-dependent youth often exhibit personality characteristics of behavioral disinhibition (Cloninger, Sigvardsson & Bohman, 1988) and youth who relapse exhibit little forethought or "cognitive vigilance" for high-risk situations (Myers & Brown, 1990b), distraction may be more readily available than other cognitive techniques as a tool when faced with an immediate high-risk situation than other coping strategies, and can be used with little rehearsal or warning.

Behavioral Strategies

Adolescents may also require unique behavioral coping strategies to sustain abstinence in the face of the diversified high-risk situations. Behavioral strategies generally tend to include learning and rehearsing techniques to cope with high-risk situations such as social modeling and pressure to use, conflict with parents and peers, and temptations to use, and developing lifestyle patterns that do not support substance use (e.g., affiliation with nonusing peers, pleasant activities other than using).

Socially feasible and acceptable refusal skills are one of the most important behavioral coping strategies to teach adolescent clients in RP treatment, since youth tend to relapse most often in social situations when there is direct or implicit social pressure to use. Youth tend to overestimate the extent to which their friends drink or use drugs (Aas & Klepp, 1992), and perceived norms for use can be associated with relapse in that adolescents may feel indirect pressure to use alcohol or drugs after treatment if they believe a large number of their peers are using. Refusal skills can be rehearsed in sessions and also outside of sessions as homework. An important consideration is that youth may have varied degrees of understanding about assertiveness. Assertiveness training involves describing the differences between assertive, passive, and aggressive communication, and teaching adolescents specific techniques for communicating assertively such as paying attention to body language and using "I" statements (see Myers et al., 1998, for a more detailed description of assertiveness training). Review of assertive communication guidelines can be useful at this point in treatment, even for teens who have had formal training, to increase the likelihood that they will use refusal skills effectively.

Finally, it is important to help youth develop activities that can replace drinking and using drugs. Enjoyable activities can enhance self-esteem, alter self-perceptions, and help teens develop a sense of autonomy and a nonusing peer group. Since research demonstrates that involvement in alternative activities is associated with successful resolution of substance abuse problems for adults and teens (Brown, 1993), this is a particularly useful component of the intervention. Activities should cater to the individual needs/interests of each client in the same fashion as identification of high-risk situations. Teens can be asked their favorite activities before they started using drugs or alcohol and activities they may wish to try for the first time, and then a specific behavioral plan can be made with a therapist to help them get involved in the activities again.

RP with adults may focus on replacing a social network with nonusing social supports. This goal can be particularly challenging with youth. Involvement with substance-using peers is associated with initiation of drug use, and most adolescents in drug and alcohol treatment are likely to have a social network composed of substance-using peers (Chassin, Pillow, Curran, Molina & Barrera, 1993; Swadi, 1999). In addition, adolescents more often identify social motives for drinking (e.g., drinking to enhance a social experience) than coping motives (e.g., drinking to handle worries; Bradizza, Reifman & Barnes, 1999). Thus, for SUD teens developing a nonusing social network may require replacing an existing peer group, which may cause distress and lead to resistance.

SPECIAL CONSIDERATIONS FOR YOUTH

Psychiatric Comorbidity

Among youth, there is a high rate of co-occurrence of other psychiatric disorders, with conduct disorder and mood disorders being most prevalent (e.g.,

Abrantes, Brown & Tomlinson, 2003; Greenbaum, Foster-Johnson & Petrila, 1996). Affective disturbance influences the situations in which youth select for themselves, confidence that they can resist urges to use in those situations (coping self-efficacy), and thus their likelihood of using in those situations. Youth with psychiatric diagnoses have poorer treatment outcomes than their noncomorbid peers (Grella, Hser, Joshi & Rounds-Bryant, 2001; Tomlinson, Brown & Abrantes, 2004). Among comorbid youth, affective symptoms tend to be exacerbated in the two-week period before relapse occurs, with depression symptoms reported most often (McCarthy, Tomlinson, Anderson, Marlatt & Brown, 2005). Elevated affective symptoms in the days preceding relapse make it more likely that relapse will occur in negative intrapersonal contexts (Anderson et al., in press)—a high-risk circumstance reported more frequently for adults than youth. Further, the increased negative affect and emotional lability experienced during adolescence serve as risks for adolescent alcohol and drug use in response to interpersonal stress (Colder & Chassin, 1993). Therefore special consideration should be given to the presence of independent psychiatric symptoms when designing and implementing a RP program for youth.

Family Involvement

It is important to consider the special role that families play in the RP treatment of adolescent substance abuse. An increasing number of therapies for adolescent substance abuse are incorporating families in the process of treatment (see Liddle & Dakoff, 1995, and Waldron, 1997, for reviews). The importance of family involvement suggests that parents/guardians should be involved in RP treatment so as to provide support for teen efforts to make changes that will foster abstinence. This can be accomplished through holding one to two sessions with teens and their parents or family to discuss specific high-risk situations identified for the teen and to discuss concrete ways that the parents can act to facilitate abstinence. The latter includes involving parents and teens together in establishing contingencies of reinforcement for success and consequences of use. Some families may make use of toxicology screens in order to measure outcomes, which should be discussed in the context of treatment. Working with families must take into account the context of substance use for the entire family (e.g., trust issues) and requires helping parents to have realistic expectations about the rate at which their teens can be expected to recover.

Experience with 12-Step-based Interventions

The majority of adolescent substance abuse treatment programs in the United States incorporate the principles and practices of Alcoholics Anonymous (Drug Strategies, 2003), including prescribing participation in 12-step support groups following treatment. The few studies examining this issue suggest that 12-step attendance is associated with better treatment outcomes for youth (e.g., Kelly et al., 2002). However, despite the potential value of youth AA/NA participation, 12-step groups may not be well suited for youth (Brown, 1993). For example, adolescents may benefit more from 12-step groups attended primarily by other youth (Kelly, Myers & Brown, 2005), and parents may resist teen association with people who have had more severe drug and alcohol abuse (Freshman, 2004). Youth ideally should be referred to young-person 12-step meetings when they are available in the community or at treatment facilities. RP therapy with youth can complement the 12-step approach by encouraging youth to use meetings and fellow 12-step members (e.g., sponsors) as means for coping with high-risk situations. Twelve-step fellowships can also provide access to a social network of abstinent teens and alcohol and drug free social activities. Finally, RP can provide a mechanism through which teens can identify with having a substance abuse problem without the pressure of accepting the disease model of addiction.

CASE EXAMPLES

UNSUCCESSFUL CASE EXAMPLE

Cynthia, a 17-year-old high school senior, recently completed inpatient treatment for methamphetamine dependence. She was living with her mother, who had separated from her father several months earlier. Her mother brought her to treatment after she had been repeatedly truant from school and had started spending several nights each week away from home. Cynthia had been a good student, but her grades had deteriorated since starting her senior year in high school. By her own admission, Cynthia had found her parents' separation very difficult and coped by spending much of her time with her boyfriend and his friends, all of whom were older than she and heavy drug and alcohol users. At the time of treatment admission she reported a number of symptoms of depression and anxiety, but these had largely resolved by the time of discharge, consistent with her diagnostic assessment at the facility, which suggested no comorbid psychiatric disorder. Following treatment Cynthia participated weekly in aftercare groups and went to 12-step fellowship meetings three times a week. About a month following her discharge she went to a New Year's Eve party with her boyfriend and ended up having a drink. She felt quite guilty about this lapse, confided in her mother, and together they sought some individual counseling to help support Cynthia's continued abstinence.

The initial RP session began with a brief meeting with Cynthia and her mother, followed by a separate interview with Cynthia. During this time a motivational approach was employed to help engage Cynthia in treatment, with a focus on her experiences of sobriety and her previous period of drug abuse. In addition it was made clear that she had an important role in setting treatment goals. Next the concept of RP was introduced and the therapist inquired as to whether this approach made sense to Cynthia and whether she would like to proceed. Cynthia was then asked to detail the circumstances of her recent lapse so as to illustrate some of the key issues addressed by RP. In reviewing the events that preceded the lapse, Cynthia reported being in a good mood, denied any negative affect or interpersonal conflict, and stated she looked forward to going to the party. She knew alcohol would be present, had planned to drink, and in fact asked for the first drink. She discussed her desire to drink as "wanting to have a good time" and "wanting to fit in." Cynthia stated that she was trying not to drink before the party, but she felt less committed to abstaining after her lapse, and in fact rated as 100 percent the likelihood of drinking again in the next six months; in contrast she rated the likelihood of using other drugs at 1 percent. When queried about the emotional effects of the drinking episode, she acknowledged feeling some guilt over having violated her abstinence and feeling bad that she had stopped spending time with her friends from treatment because "they are supposed to be around sober people."

The discussion of her lapse was used to illustrate the concept of lapse versus relapse, the factors that may lead from lapse to relapse (e.g., AVE, positive expectations for the effects of alcohol), to highlight the importance of identifying high-risk situations, and to explore the factors that appeared to motivate her to drink—peer factors and positive affect. Cynthia's stated expectation that she would continue drinking led the therapist to explore the positive and negative consequences of abstinence versus drinking in an effort to enhance her motivation to maintain abstinence and engage in the RP intervention. In this case, discussion centered on the potential slippery slope effect whereby continued drinking may lead her to situations and temptation to return to methamphetamine use. The initial session ended by bringing Cynthia's mother back into the room, discussing the goals of the RP treatment and the therapist-teen contract and negotiating a contract between Cynthia's mother and the therapist regarding her role in the treatment process. Cynthia's mother identified rewards for her daughter's efforts at maintaining an alcohol- and drug-free lifestyle as well as specific contingencies in the case of continued use. Both Cynthia and her mother agreed that routine drug testing would be implemented to provide evidence of Cynthia's abstinence. As "homework" Cynthia was asked to complete the IDTS and DTCQ and pay attention to her urges or desires to drink and/or use drugs between sessions.

The second session focused on identifying high-risk situations. First, the counselor and Cynthia reviewed her completed IDTS and DTCQ forms. This assessment indicated use predominantly in social and positive affect contexts, and that Cynthia had moderate efficacy for abstaining in these types of situations (50–60 on a 100-point scale). Review of the questionnaires was followed by a discussion of situations that may be particularly challenging to her abstinence (i.e., low self-efficacy for abstaining). Cynthia was asked to rank these situations from most risky to least risky. Her list consisted almost entirely of social situations involving peers and positive affect situations. The therapist recalled to Cynthia that her drug use increased in response to her parent's separation and suggested she add "anger" and "sadness" about her parents' conflict to the bottom of her high-risk situation list as lower priority items "just in case." The homework assignment for this session was for Cynthia to make a list of high risk for relapse situations for the present, the next two weeks, and the next month.

Coping with high risk for relapse situations was introduced in session 3. The therapist reviewed the concept of the behavior chain with Cynthia, highlighting the role of thoughts and feelings in leading to urges in high-risk situations or circumstances. Working from Cynthia's list of present high-risk situations, two were selected to illustrate the behavior change, with a focus on the "irrational" thoughts and feelings that intervened between situation and desire to use. The first situation analyzed involved a social situation with peers. Here, Cynthia identified thinking that "this won't be fun without drinking" and "I won't fit in if I don't drink or use," which led her to feel anxious and self-conscious. Given Cynthia's apparent concern over social issues and situations, the rest of the session focused on various strategies for reducing risk for relapse in these types of circumstances. She acknowledged fears about losing important relationships, in particular her boyfriend, if she chose not to drink. Several options were explored to manage this concern. Working with the therapist, Cynthia agreed to avoid accompanying her boyfriend to social events where alcohol or drugs were present. In addition, she was already regularly attending 12-step meetings and stated her intent to become more socially engaged with members of the fellowship. As homework, she agreed to attend a youth AA function the upcoming weekend.

At the fourth session Cynthia reported having attended a sober dance with her boyfriend and having a good time. She reported having fewer urges to drink over the previous week and felt she was making progress in her self-efficacy for and commitment to abstinence (as supported by her negative drug test results to date). The session centered on additional strategies for managing social high-risk situations, with a focus on assertiveness and refusal skills. In particular, Cynthia and the therapist worked on communicating her needs to her boyfriend in an assertive manner and role-played responding assertively to social-pressure situations. As homework, Cynthia was to request support for her abstinence from her boyfriend in an assertive manner.

When arriving for the fifth session, Cynthia appeared sullen and withdrawn. She reported that when she attempted to assertively request support from her boyfriend he became upset and quite defensive. In response to his anger she tried to reconcile by agreeing to go to a party with him and ended up drinking. The therapist guided Cynthia through a behavior chain analysis of the lapse situation, focusing on the thoughts and feelings that played a role in her drinking. The therapist attempted to frame the lapse as a learning experience rather than as a failure. Cynthia seemed to respond well to the feedback and support, and engaged in further discussion of strategies for managing interpersonal conflict situations. As homework, Cynthia chose to generate a list of activities she and her boyfriend could do that did not involve alcohol and drugs.

Prior to the next session, Cynthia left a message at the therapist's office saying she had to cancel and would call to reschedule. The therapist contacted her and after some hesitation she disclosed that she had used alcohol and drugs the prior weekend and subsequently failed a drug test, which led to an angry confrontation with her mother. She stated that she felt under a lot of pressure and didn't feel counseling was helping. The therapist reviewed the progress she had made during their few sessions and elicited from her the perceived positives and negatives of continuing in therapy in an effort to reengage her. Cynthia was unwilling to reschedule but said she would "call back when I'm ready." As per their contract, the therapist contacted Cynthia's mother to inform her that Cynthia did not want to attend counseling at this time. She informed the therapist that Cynthia had moved out of the home to live with her boyfriend after failing a drug test and had not contacted her since. The therapist did not hear from Cynthia or her mother again.

SUCCESSFUL CASE EXAMPLE

David, a 16-year-old high school sophomore, completed a course of residential substance abuse treatment for marijuana dependence and alcohol abuse two months ago. His admission to treatment followed an arrest for possession of a controlled substance. David's parents had observed increasing oppositional and irresponsible behavior that was in marked contrast to his usual comportment. Prior to his arrest, David had stayed away from home overnight for three days and had not attended school. Previously an above-average student, David's grades had plummeted in the semester prior to his admission for treatment. When admitted for treatment, David was diagnosed with conduct disorder and major depressive disorder. Although many of the conduct symptoms appeared related to substance use, his depression persisted during treatment, suggesting a comorbid condition. David's depressive symptoms improved following a course of medication, which continued following treatment. He had maintained abstinence for 40 days following discharge from treatment and attended aftercare and 12-step meetings weekly. One morning at school he used marijuana before classes. After school he went home and described the lapse to his parents. They were upset that he had used but were supportive and praised his honesty and prior success with abstinence. Because David was on probation as a result of his arrest and subject to routine drug tests, the family had previously agreed to pursue additional counseling if David returned to drug use.

The RP session began with a meeting with David and his parents. David's right to privacy in the counseling process was discussed along with the advantages and disadvantages for the family. Although David preferred to engage primarily in individual counseling, he consented to the therapist informing his parents about session content, since he felt he had "put them through enough," and viewed openness and honesty as an important part of his recovery. The family had previously discussed rewards for abstinence (in the form of increasing freedoms) and consequences (restrictions in time spent with peers and recreational activities). David's probationary drug-testing regimen was the objective source of verification for his drug use status. The second part of the session, conducted with David alone, began with the therapist assessing his motivation for maintaining abstinence, conducting a brief motivational intervention, and negotiating treatment goals. Finally, the rationale for RP was introduced and the therapist and David agreed on the format for future sessions. David agreed to complete the IDTS and DTCQ before the next meeting.

The second session began with David describing the circumstances of his lapse. He reported that he felt substantial pressure to improve his academic performance as well as embarrassment and a sense of stigma related to his arrest, probation, and substance abuse treatment. Following a week in which he had received a large number of class assignments for the weekend, David experienced significant feelings of anxiety. In response, he bought some marijuana over the weekend, and smoked it the following morning at school before class. This use episode acutely exacerbated David's feelings of anxiety and produced additional guilt and a sense of failure: "I felt like I let myself and my family down." This led to a discussion of David's beliefs regarding the effects of marijuana, highlighting the expected versus actual effects on his anxiety.

Next the counselor and David reviewed his completed IDTS and DTCQ. It became apparent from his responses that negative affective situations, especially anxiety, were associated with marijuana and alcohol use. His overall self-efficacy for abstinence was quite high (70–80/100), however, he had low efficacy for coping in solitary and social negative affect situations (30–40/100). In compiling a list of high risk for relapse situations, David ranked anxiety situations at the top of the list, with other negative moods (sadness, anger) next on the list. Although he felt fairly confident in managing social pressure situations, these were added to the list since David recognized that these could present temptation. David agreed to make a list of high risk for relapse situations for the present, the next two weeks, and the next month.

The third session introduced coping with high risk for relapse situations. David had some familiarity with cognitive therapy from his treatment for depression and was able to readily apply the behavior chain to his high-risk situations. The item at the top of his list was anxiety related to school performance. David identified some of the thoughts that fed into his anxiety, such as "This is too hard, I'll never catch up on my school work" and "I'll never get into college with these grades." Given the relevance and immediacy of anxiety-related high-risk situations, the remainder of the session focused on stress-management issues, ranging from cognitive restructuring to relaxation exercises. The therapist and David also discussed practical approaches related to school work such as time management and seeking tutoring. David felt his parents could play an important role with these strategies (e.g., help with rewards and time management) and so they were invited to participate at the end of the session. David and his parents were very receptive to the anxiety-management strategies and agreed to work together on time management and rewards for school work.

At the beginning of the next session David reported that he and his parents worked actively on the "homework" and he made an appointment with a tutor for his challenging math class. David reported experiencing few urges to use, that his drug tests had been clean for the past month, and described that his self-efficacy for abstaining in situations of school-related anxiety had increased "to about 75 percent." The next step was to focus on strategies for managing urges related to social anxiety. Since most of David's friends did not drink or use drugs his concern was primarily about being perceived as a "druggy" and "delinquent." Discussion centered on strategies for managing anxiety-provoking thoughts through cognitive restructuring and thought challenging (e.g., "How do I know they think I'm a druggy—I'm putting words in their mouths"). Assertiveness skills were also reviewed to help David communicate with his close friends regarding these perceptions. He elected to practice assertiveness skills by discussing his fears of being labeled a "druggy" with his best friend.

Over the next month David continued to do well; he continued to have clean drug tests, his parents proved supportive and followed through by rewarding him for his continued abstinence and improvement in school. Sessions moved from short-term to long-term high-risk situations from David's list, including strategies for managing negative feelings such as sadness and anger, and refusal skills for handling social pressures. At the eighth session, David and his parents reviewed the progress to date and agreed that the frequency of sessions could be reduced from weekly to monthly "booster sessions," with periodic reappraisal of the treatment plan and goals. David continued to do well over the subsequent two months, during which he maintained abstinence, his probationary period ended, and his school performance consistently improved. After 10 sessions (over a four-month period) treatment was terminated with a successful outcome.

SUMMARY AND CONCLUSIONS

Relapse prevention tailored to youth can be a particularly useful intervention with SUD teens. There are a number of ways it can be beneficial, including that it directly addresses the high rate of relapse among youth in treatment for substance abuse by catering prevention efforts to the needs and motivation of the individual. RP also offers a complement or an alternative to 12-step-based interventions which, although highly prevalent, may not meet the needs of all SUD adolescents. Research on adult populations suggests that RP works well to curtail substance involvement after treatment. In youth, results of randomized studies using cognitive and behavioral therapies indicate that it tends to work as well as other treatments targeted to SUD youth. The Youth Addiction Relapse Model (Brown & Ramo, 2006) suggests distinctive developmental features that are important considerations in the traditional cognitive behavioral model of relapse that may account for some of the findings in these treatment outcome studies. This chapter has outlined some of the techniques that are important in implementing any RP intervention with youth based on our experience and extant research in this area, and outlined the cases of Cynthia and David to demonstrate some of these techniques.

Clearly studies are needed that test specific RP interventions that have been adapted for youth and take into account some of the variables that have been shown to be important in the relapse process in youth (e.g., neurocognitive development, social information processing, environmental constraints). Additionally, more precise refinement of motivational features will be critical to enhancing youth success through avoidance of high-risk contexts and managing the contexts when they are encountered.

The design of RP interventions for youth is clearly in the developmental stage. It is expected that optimal approaches will need to take into account salient fluctuating needs of youth across gender, age, ethnicities, and personal experience with alcohol and drugs. The flexibility of this approach will be a distinct advantage given the diversity in motivation and resources of youth entering the health service system because of alcohol and drug problems. Overall, RP techniques should be implemented as standard practice in inpatient and outpatient substance abuse treatment programs for youth. Two distinct advantages of RP are outlined in this chapter. First, RP can be used as an adjunct to other common forms of intervention for youth (e.g., family therapy). Second, the motivational focus of RP for youth enhances adherence to behavioral and medical prescriptions as well as works to minimize attrition. Techniques, such as those described in this chapter, will allow professionals in the field of addictive behaviors to influence the change process in youth who are afflicted with problems associated with substance abuse.

REFERENCES

Aas, H., Klepp, K-I. (1992). Adolescents' alcohol use related to perceived norms. *Scandinavian Journal of Psychology* **33**:315–325.

Abrantes, A.M., Brown, S.A., Tomlinson, K.L. (2003). Psychiatric comorbidity and substance use treatment outcomes of adolescents. *Journal of Child & Adolescent Substance Abuse* **13**(2): 83–101.

Anderson, K.G., Frissell, K.C., Brown, S.A. (In press). Contexts of post-treatment use for substance abusing adolescents with comorbid psychopathology. *Journal of Child & Adolescent Substance Abuse*.

Azrin, N.H., Donohoe, B., Teicher, G.A., Crum, T., Howell, J., DeCato, L.A. (2001). A controlled evaluation and description of individual-cognitive problem solving and family-behavior therapies in dually-diagnosed conduct-disordered and substance-dependent youth. *Journal of Child & Adolescent Substance Abuse* **11**:1–43.

Beck, A.T., Wright, F.D., Newman, C.F., Liese, B.S. (1993). *Cognitive Therapy of Substance Abuse*. New York, NY: Guilford Press.

Bradizza, C.M., Reifman, A., Barnes, G.M. (1999). Social and coping reasons for drinking: Predicting alcohol misuse in adolescents. *Journal of Studies on Alcohol* **60**:491–499.

Brown, S.A. (1993). Recovery patterns in adolescent substance abuse. In Baer, J.S., Marlatt, G.A., McMahon, R.J., eds., *Addictive behaviors across the lifespan: Prevention, treatment and policy issues*, 161–183. Beverly Hills, CA: Sage Publications, Inc.

Brown, S.A. (1999). Treatment of adolescent alcohol problems: Research review and appraisal. In National Institute on Alcohol Abuse and Alcoholism extramural scientific advisory board, ed., *Treatment*, 1–26. Bethesda, MD.

Brown, S.A., D'Amico, E.J., McCarthy, D.M., Tapert, S.F. (2001). Four year outcomes from adolescent alcohol and drug treatment. *Journal of Studies on Alcohol* **62**:381–388.

Brown, S.A., Mott, M.A., Myers, M.G. (1990). Adolescent alcohol and drug treatment outcome. In Watson, R.R., ed., *Drug and alcohol abuse prevention*, 373–403. Clifton, NJ: Human Press.

Brown, S.A., Ramo, D.E. (2006). Clinical course of youth following treatment for alcohol and drug problems. In Liddle, H., Rowe, C., eds., *Adolescent substance abuse: Research and clinical advances*, 79–103. Cambridge, UK: Cambridge University Press.

Brown, S.A., Stetson, B.A., Beatty, P. (1989). Cognitive and behavioral features of adolescent coping in high risk drinking situations. *Addictive Behaviors* **14**:43–52.

Brown, S.A., Tapert, S.F., Granholm, E., Delis, D.C. (2000). Neurocognitive functioning of adolescents: Effects of protracted alcohol use. *Alcohol: Clinical and Experimental Research* **24**: 164–171.

Carroll, K.M. (1996). Relapse prevention as a psychosocial treatment: A review of controlled clinical trials. *Experimental and Clinical Psychopharmacology* **4**:46–54.

Chassin, L., Pillow, D., Curran, P., Molina, B., Barrera, M. (1993). The relation of parental alcoholism to adolescent substance use: A test of three mediating mechanisms. *Journal of Abnormal Psychology* **102**:3–19.

Cloninger, C.R., Sigvardsson, S., Bohman, M. (1988). Childhood personality predicts alcohol abuse in young adults. *Alcoholism: Clinical and Experimental Research* **12**:494–505.

Colder, C.R., Chassin, L. (1993). The stress and negative affect model of adolescent alcohol use and the moderating effects of behavioral undercontrol. *Journal of Studies on Alcohol* **54**:326–333.

Cornelius, J.R., Maisto, S.A., Pollock, N.K., Martin, C.S., Salloum, I.M., Lynch, K.G. et al. (2001). Rapid relapse generally follows treatment for substance use disorders among adolescents. *Addictive Behaviors* **27**:1–6.

DeBellis, M.D., Clark, D.B., Beers, S.R., Soloff, P.H., Boring, A.M., Hall, J. et al. (2000). Hippocampal volume in adolescent-onset alcohol use disorders. *American Journal of Psychiatry* **157**:737–744.

Dennis, M., Godley, S.H., Diamond, G., Tims, F.M., Babor, T., Donaldson, J. et al. (2004). The cannabis youth treatment (CYT) study: Main findings from two randomized trials. *Journal of Substance Abuse Treatment* **27**:197–213.

Drug Strategies (2003). *Treating teens: A guide to adolescent programs*. Drug Strategies. Washington, D.C.

Emery, G. (1988). *Dependency free: Rapid cognitive therapy of substance abuse*. Santa Monica, CA: Association for Advanced Training in the Behavioral Sciences.

Freshman, A. (2004). Assessment and treatment of adolescent substance abusers. In Straussner, S.L.A., ed., *Clinical work with substance-abusing clients, 2e*, 305–329. New York: Guilford.

Greenbaum, P.E., Foster-Johnson, L., Petrila, A. (1996). Co-occurring addictive and mental disorders among adolescents: Prevalence research and future directions. *American Journal of Orthopsychiatry* **66**(1):52–60.

Grella, C.E., Hser, Y., Joshi, V., Rounds-Bryant, J. (2001). Drug treatment outcomes for adolescents with comorbid mental and substance use disorders. *Journal of Nervous and Mental Disease* **189**:384–392.

Irvin, J.E., Bowers, C.A., Dunn, M.E., Wang, M.C. (1999). Efficacy of relapse prevention: A meta-analytic review. *Journal of Consulting and Clinical Psychology* **67**:563–570.

Johnston, L.D., O'Malley, P.M., Bachman, J.G., Schulenberg, J.E. (2006). *Monitoring the future national results on adolescent drug use: Overview of key findings, 2005*. NIH Publication No. 06–5882. Bethesda, MD: National Institute on Drug Abuse.

Kaminer, Y., Burleson, J.A., Goldberger, R. (2002). Cognitive-behavioral coping skills and psychoeducation therapies for adolescent substance abuse. *The Journal of Nervous and Mental Disease* **190**:737–745.

Kelly, J.F., Myers, M.G., Brown, S.A. (2002). Do adolescents affiliate with 12-step groups? A multivariate process model of effects. *Journal of Studies on Alcohol* **63**:293–304.

Kelly, J.F., Myers, M.G., Brown, S.A. (2005). The effects of age composition of 12-step groups on adolescent 12-step participation and substance use outcome. *Journal of Child & Adolescent Substance Abuse* **15**(1):63–72.

Liddle, H.A., Dakof, G.A. (1995). Family-based treatment for adolescent drug abuse: State of the science. *NIDA Research Monograph* **156**:218–254.

Marlatt, G.A., Gordon, J.R. (1980). Determinants of relapse: Implications for the maintenance of behavior change. In Davidson, P., Davidson, S.M., eds., *Behavioral medicine: Changing health lifestyles*, 410–452. Elmsford, NY: Pergamon.

Marlatt, G.A., Gordon, J.A. (1985). *Relapse prevention: Maintenance strategies in the treatment of addictive behaviors.* New York: Guilford Press.

McCarthy, D.M., Tomlinson, K.L., Anderson, K.G., Marlatt, G.A., Brown, S.A. (2005). Relapse in alcohol- and drug-disordered adolescents with comorbid psychopathology: Changes in psychiatric symptoms. *Psychology of Addictive Behaviors* **19**:28–34.

Metrik, J., McCarthy, D.M., Frissell, K.C., MacPherson, L., Brown, S.A. (2004). Adolescent alcohol reduction and cessation expectancies. *Journal of Studies on Alcohol* **65**:217–226.

Miller, W.R., Rollnick, S. (2002). *Motivational interviewing: Preparing people for change, 2e.* New York: Guilford.

Myers, M.G., Brown, S.A. (1990a). Coping and appraisal in relapse risk situations among adolescent substance abusers following treatment. *Journal of Adolescent Chemical Dependency* **1**:95–115.

Myers, M.G., Brown, S.A. (1990b). Coping responses and relapse among adolescent substance abusers. *Journal of Substance Abuse* **2**·177–189.

Myers, M.G., Brown, S.A., Mott, M.A. (1993). Coping as a predictor of adolescent substance abuse treatment outcome. *Journal of Substance Abuse* **5**:15–29.

Myers, M.G., Brown, S.A., Vik, P.W. (1998). Adolescent substance use problems. In Mash, E.J., Barkley, R.A., eds., *Treatment of Childhood Disorders, 2e*, 692–730. New York: Guilford.

O'Leary, T.T., Monti, P.M. (2004). Motivational enhancement and other brief interventions for adolescent substance abuse: Foundations, applications, and evaluations. *Addiction* **99**(Suppl. 2): 63–75.

Peterson, H.O., O'Connell, D.F. (2003). Recovery maintenance and relapse prevention with chemically dependent adolescents. In Reinecke, M.A., Dattilio, F.M., Freeman, A., eds., *Cognitive Therapy with Children and Adolescents*, 70–94. New York: Guilford.

Sklar, S.M., Annis, H.M., Turner, N.E. (1997). Development and validation of the Drug-Taking Confidence Questionnaire: A measure of coping self-efficacy. *Addictive Behaviors* **22**:655–670.

Swadi, H. (1999). Individual risk factors for adolescent substance use. *Drug and Alcohol Dependence* **55**:209–224.

Tomlinson, K.L., Brown, S.A., Abrantes, A. (2004). Psychiatric comorbidity and substance use treatment outcomes of adolescents. *Psychology of Addictive Behaviors* **18**:160–169.

Turner, N.E., Annis, H.M., Sklar, S.M. (1997). Measurement of antecedents to drug and alcohol use: Psychometric properties of the Inventory of Drug-Taking Situations (IDTS). *Behavior Research & Therapy* **35**:465–483.

Waldron, H.B. (1997). Adolescent substance abuse and family therapy outcome: A review of randomized trials. *Advances in Clinical Child Psychology* **19**:199–234.

Waldron, H.B., Slesnick, N., Brody, J.L., Turner, C.W., Peterson, T.R. (2001). Treatment outcomes for adolescent substance abuse at 4- and 7-month assessments. *Journal of Consulting and Clinical Psychology* **69**:802–813.

Witkiewitz, K., Marlatt, A.G. (2004). Relapse prevention for alcohol and drug problems: That was Zen, this is Tao. *American Psychologist* **59**:224–235.

14

RELAPSE PREVENTION
WITH OLDER ADULTS

FREDERIC C. BLOW

Department of Psychiatry
University of Michigan and
VA National Serious Mental Illness Treatment Research and
Evaluation Center (SMITREC)
Ann Arbor, Michigan

LAURIE M. BROCKMANN

VA National Serious Mental Illness Treatment Research and
Evaluation Center (SMITREC)
Ann Arbor, Michigan

KRISTEN L. BARRY

Department of Psychiatry
University of Michigan and
VA National Serious Mental Illness Treatment Research and
Evaluation Center (SMITREC)
Ann Arbor, Michigan

INTRODUCTION

A substantial and growing percentage of older adults misuse alcohol, prescription drugs, or other substances. Older adults with alcohol problems are a special and vulnerable population that can benefit from elder-specific relapse prevention strategies focused on the unique issues associated with alcohol abuse and medication misuse in later life.

PREVALENCE AND IMPACT OF SUBSTANCE ABUSE AMONG OLDER ADULTS

Community surveys have estimated the prevalence of problem drinking among older adults to range from 1 to 15 percent (Adams, Barry & Fleming, 1996;

Fleming, Manwell, Barry et al., 1999; Moore et al., 1999). These rates vary widely depending on the definitions of at-risk and problem drinking or alcohol abuse/dependence, and the methodology used in obtaining samples. Estimates of alcohol problems are much higher among healthcare-seeking populations, because problem drinkers are more likely to seek medical care (Beresford, 1979; Institute of Medicine, 1990; Oslin, 2004). Studies in primary care settings found 10 to 15 percent of older patients met criteria for at-risk or problem drinking (Barry et al., 1998; Callahan, 1995). Two studies in nursing homes reported that 29 to 49 percent of residents had a lifetime diagnosis of alcohol abuse or dependence, while 10 to 18 percent reported active dependence symptoms in the past year (Joseph, Ganzini & Atkinson, 1995; Oslin, Streim, Parmelee, Boyce & Katz, 1997). In 2002, over 616,000 adults age 55 and older reported alcohol dependence in the past year (DSM-IV definition): 1.8 percent of those age 55 to 59, 1.5 percent of those age 60 to 64, and 0.5 percent of those age 65 or older (Office of Applied Studies, 2002).

Older adults are at higher risk for inappropriate use of medications than younger groups. Older persons regularly consume on average two to six prescription medications and from one to three over-the-counter medications (Larsen & Martin, 1999). Combined difficulties with alcohol and medication misuse may affect up to 19 percent of older Americans (Bucholz et al., 1995; D'Archangelo, 1993; National Institute on Alcohol Abuse and Alcoholism, 1998). In contrast to younger substance abusers who most often abuse illicit drugs, substance abuse problems among elderly individuals more typically occur from misuse of over-the-counter and prescription drugs. Drug misuse can result from the overuse, underuse, or irregular uses of either prescription or over-the-counter drugs. For some older adults, misuse may become drug abuse (Ellor & Kurz, 1982; Patterson & Jeste, 1999). Factors such as previous or coexisting drug, alcohol, or mental health problems, old age, and being female also increase vulnerability for misusing prescribed medications (Cooperstock & Parnell, 1982; Finlayson, 1995a, 1995b; Finlayson & Davis, 1994; Sheahan, 1989).

Older adults are uniquely vulnerable to substance abuse problems due to the multiple biological, psychological, and social changes that accompany the aging process. These special vulnerabilities include loneliness, diminished mobility, impaired sensory capabilities, chronic pain, poor physical health, and poor economic and social supports (Bucholz et al., 1995; Schonfeld & Dupree, 1995). Compared with younger people, older adults have an increased sensitivity to alcohol as well as to over-the-counter (OTC) and prescription medications. There is an age-related decrease in lean body mass versus total volume of fat, and the resultant decrease in total body volume increases the total distribution of alcohol and other mood-altering chemicals in the body. Liver enzymes that metabolize alcohol and certain other drugs are less efficient with age, and central nervous system sensitivity increases with age.

Alcohol consumption can influence many of the acute and chronic medical and psychiatric conditions that lead to high rates of health care use by older people. These conditions include harmful medication interactions, injury, depression, memory problems, liver disease, cardiovascular disease, cognitive changes, and sleep problems (Gambert & Katsoyannis, 1995; Liberto, Oslin & Ruskin, 1992). The interactions between alcohol and medications are of notable importance to older populations; interactions between psychoactive medications, such as benzodiazepines, barbiturates, and antidepressants are of particular concern. Alcohol use can interfere with the metabolism of many medications and is a leading risk factor for the development of adverse drug reactions (Fraser, 1997; Hylek, 1998; Onder et al., 2002). For some patients, any alcohol use, coupled with the use of specific OTC or prescription medications, can be problematic. Finally, the presence of co-occurring psychiatric conditions (dual diagnosis) including comorbid depression, anxiety disorders, and cognitive impairment, likely represent both a risk factor and a complication of alcohol and medication abuse in older adults (Bartels, 1995).

PROJECTED DEMOGRAPHIC TRENDS

Older adults' higher risk for alcohol and medication, coupled with the rapid growth in this population, highlights the need for targeted relapse prevention strategies. Demographic projections indicate that the aging of the "baby boom" generation will increase the proportion of persons over age 65 from 13 percent currently, to 20 percent by the year 2030 (US Census Bureau, 2000). In addition, the fastest growing segment of the population is composed of individuals age 85 and older (US Census Bureau, 2000). The extent of alcohol and medication misuse is likely to significantly increase as the "baby boom" cohort ages, due to both the growth in the older population as well as cohort-associated lifestyle differences (Spencer, 1989; US Census Bureau, 2000). The projected increase in the number of older adults with substance abuse problems is associated with a 50 percent increase in the number of older adults and a 70 percent increase in the rate of treatment need among older adults (Gfroerer, Penne, Pemberton & Folsom, 2003).

Recent studies of consumption patterns suggest that the baby boom generation, as it continues to age, could maintain a higher level of alcohol consumption than in previous older adult cohorts (Blow, 2002). Rates of heavy alcohol use have been shown to be higher among baby boomers than in earlier cohorts (Hylek, 1998). In addition, drug use is heightened in the baby boomer cohort (Patterson & Jeste, 1999). The increasing rate of problem substance use in this population may be attributed to an increase in problems related to the use of illicit drugs or nonmedical use of prescription drugs (Gfoerer, 2002). Further, these projections may be underestimated, as criteria used to define problem substance use may not be most appropriate for older populations. Increased substance abuse, coupled with the projected increase in the older adult population, will place increasing pressure on the treatment programs and health care resources (Department of

Health and Human Services, 1999). In addition, the population of older adults is expected to become more ethnically and racially diverse in the coming decades. These predicted demographic trends will present new challenges in providing effective treatment strategies and relapse prevention services for older adults.

LIFETIME PATTERNS OF DRINKING

Clinical models of alcoholism and recovery were traditionally thought to follow a natural progression from early signs and symptoms through end stage disease. When patients "hit bottom" they either died or began the long road to recovery ("Jellinek curve"). Most older individuals with alcohol problems do not fit this model. The clinical course of substance use disorders across the life span often is marked by periods of abstinence or low risk use. Variation in substance use over the life span makes a long-term view of relapse prevention essential.

The varying patterns in consumption for persons with problematic use may include the following three different types: early-onset problem drinking marked by heavy use throughout most of adulthood, cyclical heavy drinking, and late-onset problem drinking. Late-onset problem drinkers often begin drinking due to stressors in later life (e.g., retirement, death of spouse, diminished physical capacity). Although original clinical estimates of late-onset problems, based on treatment-seeking individuals, indicated that about one-third of older problem drinkers were in this category (Liberto et al., 1992), some newer research is beginning to place the rate at 10 percent or less (Blow, Gillespie, Barry, Mudd & Hill, 1998). A perspective of potential substance use problems across the life course is of critical importance in sustainable relapse prevention with older adults.

IDENTIFYING SUBSTANCE USE PROBLEMS IN OLDER ADULTS

Many older individuals have unique drinking patterns and alcohol-related consequences, social issues, and treatment needs, compared to their younger counterparts (Atkinson, 1995). Because of this, assessment, intervention, and relapse prevention planning for alcohol problems in late life are likely to require elder-specific approaches. The majority of older adults who are experiencing problems related to their drinking do not meet DSM-IV (American Psychiatric Association, 1994) criteria for alcohol abuse or dependence (Barry, Oslin & Blow, 2001; Blow, 1998b). Alcohol problems are typically thought to occur in persons who consume larger quantities and drink frequently. For some older individuals, any alcohol use can present problems, particularly when coupled with some psychoactive medications. DSM criteria are widely used and distinguish between abuse and dependence. However, these criteria may not be appropriate for many older adults with substance use problems because people in this age group do not often experience the legal, social, or psychological consequences specified in the criteria. Further, a lack of tolerance to alcohol may not be as appropriate an indicator of alcohol-related problems in the elderly as in younger ages. Most DSM criteria for tolerance are based on increased consumption over time. This ignores the physiologic changes of aging that lead to physiologic tolerance at lower levels of alcohol consumption. Another important aspect of the DSM criteria relates to the physical and emotional consequences of alcohol use. These criteria may be especially important in identifying alcohol problems in older adults.

INTERVENTIONS AND TREATMENTS FOR OLDER ADULTS

Most substance abuse treatment settings provide services to very few older individuals. Relatively little is known about treatment outcomes and unique needs of older adults who need help with substance abuse problems, despite the development of elder-specific alcoholism treatment programs in recent years (Atkinson, 1995). The Surgeon General's Report on Mental Health, the Administration of Aging Report on Older Adults (Administration on Aging, 2001), and the Center for Substance Abuse Treatment (CSAT) Treatment Improvement Protocol for Older Adults (TIP #26; Substance Abuse and Mental Health Administration, 1998) underscore some of the positive developments in knowledge over the past decade regarding effective treatments for substance abuse among older adults. An emerging evidence base supports the efficacy of a variety of evidence-based and promising pharmacological and psychotherapeutic interventions for substance abuse problems in older persons (Barry, 1998; Barry et al., 2001; Bartels et al., 2002, 2004; Blow & Barry, 2000; Bruce et al., 2004; Burgio et al., 1995; Cohen-Mansfield, 2001; Doody et al., 2001; Fleming, 2002; Fleming et al., 1999; Gatz, 1998; Gerson, Belin, Kaufman, Mintz & Jarvik, 1999; Pinquart, 2001; Schneider, Pollock & Lyness, 1990; Teri, Logsdon, Uomoto & McCurry, 1997; Thorpe, Whitney, Kutcher & Kennedy, 2001; Willenbring, Johnson & Tan, 1994; Wilson, 2002), but little research has been conducted specifically regarding relapse prevention among this population.

CLINICAL CASE ILLUSTRATION #1

SUCCESSFUL OUTCOME

Sal Franco is a 74-year-old man living alone in an apartment in a complex for older adults. He owned a grocery store with his wife Mary for 44 years. He and Mary sold the business to their son Dominique when Sal was 70 with plans to travel and enjoy their remaining years together. Shortly after their retirement,

Mary was diagnosed with bone cancer and died within six months of the diagnosis. Mr. Franco has been alone for the last three years. Although he was a "hard drinker" as he described it in his 20s and 30s, because of gastritis and high blood pressure, his use of alcohol was limited to his weekly poker games and Sunday family meals for many years. Because Sal and Mary spent most of their time working at the grocery store and involved in family activities, there was little time left for friends. Now he has time on his hands and uses alcohol to alleviate some of the pain and stress of his loneliness, generally having four to five drinks a day. He has developed few outside interests and doesn't know where to start. He came to the clinic for follow-up of his labile hypertension and gastritis. His provider asked Mr. Franco how he was feeling and received this response, "Oh, I guess I'm OK for an old widower. I sometimes think it really doesn't matter how I feel at this age." The provider followed up with some questions about what Mr. Franco does with his time and discovered that he uses alcohol to excess along with taking over-the-counter medication to sleep. The provider, using a brief alcohol intervention model, talked to Mr. Franco about his alcohol use and how it could affect his hypertension and gastritis, as well as his feelings of distress since his wife's death. Mr. Franco told the provider that he thought he could stop using alcohol to see if that helped. One of the clinic nurses also met with Mr. Franco to help him get connected with some senior services in the community. She and Mr. Franco called senior services together to make sure that he could get an appointment and some information on senior activities. The provider followed up with Sal at the next clinic visit to see if he was able to cut down or discontinue his alcohol use and if he was connected to some services in the community. Mr. Franco found that he could stop using alcohol, particularly after he was able to share his loneliness with senior center staff and get more involved in activities at the senior center.

UNSUCCESSFUL OUTCOME

Catherine Jackson is a 67-year old woman living alone in an apartment in a mixed-age housing project. She has one adult son who lives in another state and visits her once or twice a year. She had not worked outside the home until her divorce. After that, she got a job as a clerk in a gift shop and stopped working there five years ago. Mrs. Jackson has had periods of heavy drinking in the past—in early adulthood and again after she was divorced at age 55. She was able to cut back on her alcohol use while seeing a therapist after the divorce. However, her drinking escalated again after she stopped working. Her doctor prescribed Xanax for her anxiety symptoms a few years ago and continues to prescribe this medication for her. They have not discussed her alcohol use. For the past month she has been seen by a visiting nurse. The nurse was assigned upon her discharge from the hospital where she spent one week with the diagnosis of anemia. The nurse noted the smell of alcohol during two of her visits, but Mrs. Jackson did not ever appear intoxicated. When the nurse asked her about her drinking, she said, "Oh, I don't drink very much, really. I just seem so tired all the time and a little drink now and then makes me feel better." She has complained about difficulty sleeping at night. Not counting her stay in the hospital, she has been confined to her apartment for the last two months. The nurse asked more questions about alcohol use but Mrs. Jackson denied heavy use or problems, "I don't know why you are asking all these questions about alcohol. I'm not an alcoholic, you know. I am a little nervous and the doctor helps me with that with the 'nerve pills.'" The nurse suggested to Catherine that she talk to her doctor about her alcohol use with the Xanax. Mrs. Jackson got angry with the nurse. In subsequent visits, the nurse did not ask about alcohol but hoped that Mrs. Jackson would talk to her doctor as advised. As proscribed in the hospital discharge plan, the nurse continued to visit once a week for another month. Mrs. Jackson continued to use alcohol and benzodiazepines, but within two months after the nurse visits stopped, she had a fall, broke her hip, and entered the hospital again.

SUBSTANCE ABUSE TREATMENT OUTCOMES FOR OLDER ADULTS

Research on substance abuse treatment for older adults has examined differences between younger and older treatment populations, compliance/adherence issues, treatment outcomes, and maintenance of treatment gains over time. Older adults entering treatment have been shown to have fewer psychiatric symptoms related to their substance use and less severe substance dependence than their younger counterparts, but typically have more physical impairments (Lemke & Moos, 2003; Oslin, Slaymaker, Blow, Owen & Colleran, 2005; Satre, Mertens, Arean & Weisner, 2004).

Treatment for alcohol use disorders can be effective for older adults. Older adults appear to respond to treatment comparably to younger adults, with some differences that may be associated with age. Lemke and Moos (Lemke and Moos, 2003) found that older patients fared at least as well as younger patients in age-integrated, community-based programs, and they responded in similar ways to treatment experiences and program factors. Oslin and colleagues found that compared with younger adults, older adults had greater attendance at therapy sessions and greater adherence to medication. They concluded that older adults could be treated in mixed-age treatment settings when psychotherapeutic strategies are used that are age-appropriate and delivered on an individual basis (Oslin et al., 2002). Other results from compliance studies have shown that age-specific programming improved treatment completion and resulted in higher rates of attendance at group meetings compared to mixed age treatment (Atkinson, Tolson & Turner, 1993). In a study of treatment matching, Rice and colleagues found that elderly alcoholics responded better to individual-focused interventions, rather than traditional mixed-age, group-oriented treatment (Rice, Longabaugh, Beattie & Noel, 1993).

Satre and colleagues (Satre et al., 2004) found that older adults generally spent longer in treatment than younger adults, and had more favorable long-term outcomes: 52 percent of older adults versus 40 percent of younger adults reported total 30-day abstinence five years after treatment. They concluded that the differences were accounted for by variables associated with age such as type of substance dependence, treatment retention, social networks, and gender. For example, at the five-year follow-up, older adults were less likely than younger adults to have close family or friends who encouraged alcohol or drug use. In addition, older adults with substance use disorders were significantly more likely to complete treatment than younger patients (Schuckit & Pastor, 1978; Wiens, Menustik, Miller & Schmitz, 1982). Atkinson and colleagues also found that the proportion of older male alcoholics completing treatment was twice that of younger men (Atkinson et al., 1993).

In the studies highlighted earlier, similar factors predicted older adults' positive outcomes over time, such as longer treatment retention, older adult engagement in treatment aftercare, and other factors relevant to relapse prevention. For some older adults, traditional outpatient substance abuse post-discharge aftercare is not accepted at the same rates as middle-aged adults. The lower rates of engagement suggest the need for age appropriate treatment options and highlight the risk for relapse in this population (Oslin et al., 2005). To generalize, incorporating some individualized, age-appropriate techniques into substance abuse treatment (even in a predominantly mixed-age, group modality) shows promise as an effective relapse prevention strategy for older adults.

CURRENT RESEARCH ON RELAPSE AMONG OLDER ADULTS

Schutte and colleagues examined long-term risk of relapse among older people with a history of problem drinking (Schutte, Nichols, Brennan & Moos, 2003). Older former problem drinkers (n = 447) were prospectively followed for ten years and compared to lifetime nonproblem drinkers. Relapse was relatively uncommon among the surviving former problem drinkers (11%), although a majority (63%) of former problem drinkers with successfully sustained remission did continue to consume some alcohol. Relapse was associated with a less severe drinking history, heavier baseline alcohol consumption, and lower baseline income. Relapse was defined as experiencing one or more Drinking Problem Index drinking problems at one or more follow-up interviews (Finney, Moos & Brennan, 1991). The majority of former problem drinkers (63%) continued to drink alcohol, at lower levels than older lifetime nonproblem drinkers. Additionally, in the short term, relapse was more common among patients who had the most severe problems related to their use. The authors concluded both current drinking behavior and drinking history are important to consider when making recommendations to older adults about alcohol consumption and preventing relapse.

Older adults have distinctive age-related risks for relapse. Barrick and Connors reviewed the literature regarding relapse prevention among older adults with alcohol use disorders (Barrick & Connors, 2002). The review highlights how psychosocial factors such as social isolation, loneliness, loss and grief, and depression can become antecedents to alcohol use for older adults, and how older drinkers tend to report using alcohol to alleviate negative emotional states (Barrick & Connors, 2002; Brown, Goldman, Inn & Anderson, 1980; Schonfeld & Dupree, 1995). Comorbid medical conditions can place older adults at higher risk for relapse as well. For example, Brennan and colleagues studied the relationship of alcohol use and pain among older adults (Brennan, Schutte & Moos, 2005). The study found that more pain was associated with increased use of alcohol to manage pain, and that this relationship was stronger among older adults with drinking problems than those without.

RELAPSE PREVENTION STRATEGIES AND RECOMMENDATIONS

Effective substance abuse treatment, including relapse prevention, for older adults requires a shift in focus to address the special needs of an older population. Although the following recommendations were intended for general applicability in substance abuse treatment programs, each feature has relevance to late-life relapse prevention treatment planning as well. The TIP Consensus Panel recommends incorporating the following features into substance abuse treatment for older adults (Substance Abuse and Mental Health Administration, 1998; Schonfeld & Dupree, 1995):

(1) Age-specific group treatment that is supportive and nonconfrontational and aims to build or rebuild the patient's self-esteem.
(2) A focus on coping with depression, loneliness, and loss (e.g., death of a spouse, retirement).
(3) A focus on rebuilding the client's social support network.
(4) A pace and content of treatment appropriate for the older person.
(5) Staff members who are interested and experienced in working with older adults.
(6) Linkages with medical services, services for the aging, and institutional settings for referral into and out of treatment, as well as case management.

Further, the Consensus Panel recommended creating a culture of respect for older clients, taking a broad and holistic approach to treatment, keeping the treatment program flexible, and adapting treatment as needed in response to clients' gender. Finally, relapse prevention with older adults requires anticipating and planning for the potential psychosocial and physical health factors that place older adults at risk for relapse. A literature review by Barrick and Connors (2002) summarizes types of relapse prevention treatment approaches such as cognitive-behavioral therapy, group and family therapies, self-help groups, and pharmacological adjuncts.

A GROUP TREATMENT APPROACH TO
SUBSTANCE ABUSE RELAPSE PREVENTION

The Substance Abuse and Mental Health Services Administration recently published a manual entitled *Substance Abuse Relapse Prevention for Older Adults: A Group Treatment Approach* (Center for Substance Abuse Treatment, 2005). This manual describes in detail an approach to relapse prevention that relies on cognitive-behavioral and self-management treatment techniques specifically adapted for use with older adults in a counselor-led group treatment setting. Although this approach was designed for use in outpatient group settings, it can also be adapted for use in other treatment settings such as inpatient, outpatient, or intensive outpatient settings or in other types of treatment such as individual counseling. The stated main goals of this cognitive-behavioral/self-management (CB/SM) relapse prevention approach with older adults are (1) to engage and support clients as they receive skill training, and (2) to analyze, understand, and control the day-to-day factors that have led clients to abuse substances.

The program has four phases:

(1) **Analysis of previous substance use behavior.**
    The CB/SM relapse prevention approach begins with administration of the Substance Abuse Profile for the Elderly (SAPE). The SAPE interview takes approximately two hours. Interview questions include substance use and treatment history, recent substance use patterns, antecedents to substance use, consequences of substance use, and motivation for treatment. The clinician uses the client's responses to the SAPE interview to develop a functional analysis of the individual's "substance use behavior chain": the unique sequence of events that begins with antecedents to substance use, leads to typical initial substance use, and ends with the consequences that commonly follow substance use for that person.
(2) **Identification of high-risk substance abuse situations for each client.**
    The second phase of the CB/SM relapse prevention approach involves client recognition of the "ABCs" of substance abuse. Each older adult learns to identify the individual antecedents (A), behaviors (B), and consequences (C) of his or her own substance use behavior chain. The ABC identification process helps target problem behaviors and select appropriate interventions to prevent relapse in high-risk situations.
(3) **Skills training.**
    The third phase of the CB/SM relapse prevention approach centers on older adults' learning and practicing skills to cope with high-risk situations that

have preceded substance use in the past. Cognitive-behavioral skills may address managing difficult emotions such as depression, grief, anger, frustration, anxiety, and stress as well as how to cope with psychosocial problems such as lack of social support or financial difficulties. A focus on self-management techniques is intended to foster independence and require clients to take responsibility for individual behaviors and actively participate in the treatment process and planning for relapse prevention. This phase typically represents the majority of the treatment sessions, and may vary depending on the number and types of problems identified the characteristics of the group and individual members, and the goals of the broader treatment program.

(4) **Continuing care and follow-up.**
The final phase of the CB/SM relapse prevention approach is designed to provide clients with the support needed to avoid substance abuse. Recommended contact with a client is at least 12 months after successfully leaving the program. Continuing care may include informal support, nonconfrontational methods for handling a relapse, and encouragement to maintain gains made during and after the program. Continuing contact, even as simple as a brief phone call, seems to be valuable for the continued success of older adults in maintaining abstinence or appropriate use of medications, as well as recovering from relapses.

TREATMENT MODULES

The CB/SM relapse prevention approach with older adults consists of nine modules designed to be covered in 16 group sessions. The SAMHSA manual describes the treatment approach in detail, including background and resource information, an implementation guide, and session guides with objectives, step-by-step procedures, materials, classroom exercises, handouts, and suggested homework assignments. The complete treatment manual can be obtained free of charge online at www.ncadi.samhsa.gov or ordered by phone from SAMHSA's National Clearinghouse for Alcohol and Drug Information (NCADI) at 800-729-6686 or 800-487-4889 (TDD).

USE OF BRIEF INTERVENTIONS IN RELAPSE PREVENTION

Low intensity, brief interventions are cost-effective and practical techniques that can be used as an initial approach to at-risk and problem drinkers in primary care settings (Babor, Ritson & Hodgson, 1986). Over the last two decades, there has been an increasing interest in conducting controlled clinical trials to evaluate the effectiveness of early identification and secondary prevention using brief intervention strategies for treating problem drinkers, especially those with relatively mild to moderate alcohol problems who are potentially at-risk for developing more severe problems (Babor & Grant, 1992; Barry & Fleming, 1994; Institute of Medicine, 1990). Brief intervention studies have been conducted in a wide range of health care settings, ranging from hospitals and primary health care locations (Babor & Grant, 1992; Chick, Lloyd & Crombie, 1985; Fleming, Barry, Manwell, Johnson & London, 1997; Wallace, Cutler & Haines, 1988) to mental health clinics (Fleming et al., 1999; Harris & Miller, 1990). More recently, there has been attention given to brief intervention research in older adults. The spectrum of alcohol interventions for older adults range from prevention/education for persons who are abstinent or low-risk drinkers, to minimal advice or brief structured interventions for at-risk or problem drinkers, and formalized alcoholism treatment for drinkers who meet criteria for abuse and/or dependence (Blow, 1998b). Formalized treatment generally is used with persons who meet criteria for alcohol abuse or dependence and cannot discontinue drinking with a brief intervention protocol. Nonetheless, pre-intervention strategies are also appropriate for this high problem population.

Brief interventions for alcohol problems employ various approaches to change drinking behaviors. Strategies have ranged from relatively unstructured counseling and feedback to more formal structured therapy (Fleming et al., 1997; Kristenson, Ohlin, Hulten-Nosslin, Trell & Hood, 1983; Persson & Magnusson, 1989), and have relied heavily on concepts and techniques from the behavioral self-control training (BSCT) literature (Chick et al., 1985; Miller & Hester, 1986; Miller & Munoz, 1976; Miller & Rollnick, 1999; Miller & Taylor, 1980). Both brief interventions and brief therapies have been shown to be effective in a range of clinical settings (Barry, 1999). Brief alcohol interventions have particular usefulness with older adults (Blow, 1998a, 1998b; Blow, Barry & Walton, unpublished; Fleming et al., 1997, 1999; Hayward, Shapiro, Freeman & Corey, 1988). Fleming and colleagues (1999) and Blow and colleagues (unpublished) have conducted randomized clinical brief intervention trials to reduce hazardous drinking in older adults using advice protocols in primary care settings. These large-scale studies have shown that older adults can be engaged in brief intervention protocols, the protocols are acceptable in this population, and there is a substantial reduction in drinking among the at-risk drinkers receiving the interventions compared to a control group. Further, reductions in drinking among at-risk older drinkers who received brief alcohol interventions have been maintained at the one-year follow-up.

BRIEF ALCOHOL INTERVENTION
COMPONENTS WITH OLDER ADULTS

A semi-structured, brief intervention can be conducted following identification of at-risk or problem drinkers through screening techniques. Brief intervention protocols often use a workbook containing opportunities for both patient and practitioner to discuss sections on drinking cues, reasons for drinking, reasons to cut down or quit, a drinking agreement in the form of a prescription, and drinking diary cards for self-monitoring. The content of the intervention needs to be elder-specific and should include identification of the client's future goals, customized feedback on the client's drinking, and coping with risky situations. The approach to patients is nonconfrontational and generally follows motivational interviewing principles as described by Miller and Rollnick (1999). In terms of relapse prevention, identifying individual drinking cues, recommending and agreeing upon limits, and planning for risky situations are all essential elements of relapse prevention in brief alcohol interventions with older adults.

CO-OCCURRING DISORDERS IN OLDER ADULTS

Psychiatric comorbidities complicate treatment and relapse prevention. Studies of older adults with substance use disorders indicate the common presence of co-occurring psychiatric illnesses. Rates of psychiatric illness in older adults with substance use disorders range from 21 to 66 percent (Blazer & Williams, 1980; Blow, Cook, Booth, Falcon & Friedman, 1992; Brennan, Nichols & Moos, 2002; Jinks & Raschko, 1990; Finlayson, 1988; Finlayson & Davis, 1994). Dual diagnoses in older adults are associated with increased suicidality and greater inpatient and outpatient service utilization (Bartels et al., 2002; Brennan, Kagay, Geppert & Moos, 2001; Conwell, 1991; Cook, 1991; Hoff & Rosenheck, 1998; Wu, Ringwalt & Williams, 2003).

Depression and alcohol use are the most commonly cited co-occurring disorders in older adults. For example, approximately 29 percent of older veterans receiving treatment for alcohol use disorders have a co-occurring psychiatric disorder (Brennan et al., 2002), most commonly an affective disorder (Blow et al., 1992). Nearly half of community dwelling older adults with a history of alcohol abuse have co-occurring depressive symptoms (Blazer & Williams, 1980). Among an at-risk population of older adults receiving in-home services, 9.6 percent had an alcohol abuse problem and two-thirds of those individuals (6% of the overall sample) had a comorbid psychiatric illness such as depression or dementia (Jinks & Raschko, 1990). Among older adults with a recognized substance abuse disorder attending an alcohol dependence rehabilitation treatment program, 23 percent had dementia and 12 percent had affective disorders (Finlayson, 1988). Finally, psychiatric comorbidity was prevalent among older persons (age 65+) hospitalized for prescription drug dependence, with indications that 32 percent had a mood disorder and 12 percent had an anxiety disorder (Finlayson & Davis, 1994).

The nature of substance misuse among older adults complicates the relationship between psychiatric illness and substance abuse. As discussed earlier, most older adults who are experiencing problems related to their alcohol consumption do not meet DSM-IV criteria for alcohol abuse or dependence (Barry et al., 2001; Substance Abuse and Mental Health Administration, 1998). However, drinking even small amounts of alcohol can increase risks for developing problems in older adults, particularly when coupled with the use of some over-the-counter or prescription medications. The combination of some psychoactive medications with any alcohol use increases the risk of many unfavorable reactions (Korrapati and Vestal, 1995; Substance Abuse and Mental Health Administration, 1998). Research has indicated how alcohol consumption, as well as at-risk and problem drinking, can aggravate affective disorders, such as depression, among elders (Atkinson, 1999; Coyne & Katz, 2001; Graham & Schmidt, 1999; Saunders et al., 1991). Low and moderate levels of drinking among older adults with psychiatric problems may also influence treatment outcomes for a variety of diagnoses.

COMORBID DEPRESSION

Comorbid depressive symptoms are not only common in late life but are also an important factor in the course and prognosis of psychiatric disorders. Depressed alcoholics have been shown to have a more complicated clinical course of depression with an increased risk of suicide and more social dysfunction than nondepressed alcoholics (Conwell, 1991; Cook, 1991). Moreover, they were shown to seek treatment more often. Relapse rates for those who were alcohol dependent, however, did not appear to be influenced by the presence of depression. Alcohol use prior to late life has also been shown to influence treatment of late life depression. Cook and colleagues (1991) found that a prior history of alcohol abuse predicted a more severe and chronic course for depression. The co-occurrence of alcohol use disorders and depression heightens late-life suicide risk, as does at-risk and problem drinking among elders (Blow, Brockmann & Barry, 2004).

RELAPSE PREVENTION FOR
LATE-LIFE DEPRESSION

Depression can occur with or without substance use disorders. It is often chronic and recurrent among older individuals (Zis, Grof, Webster & Goodwin, 1980). Managing residual or recurrent symptoms and prevention of relapse in later life is of critical importance, as older adults with depression are at high risk for recurrence, disability, and suicide (Bruce et al., 2004; Dietrich et al., 2004; Gray-Toft & Anderson, 1985; Unutzer et al., 1997, 2002). Tailored collaborative care for geriatric patients with depression in primary care settings has shown effectiveness in preventing relapse over time (Hunkeler et al., 2006). The "Improving Mood Promoting Access to Collaborative Care Treatment" (IMPACT) model of collaborative care followed patients aged 60 or older for two years after initial enrollment in a 12-month collaborative care intervention or usual care. Compared to patients receiving usual care, IMPACT patients actively engaged in treatment and experienced less depression, improved physical functioning, and enhanced quality of life one year after study involvement ended. As part of the IMPACT model, patients whose depression improved (50% or decrease in depressive symptoms, fewer than two DSM-IV depression symptoms) created a relapse prevention plan with their depression care manager. Relapse prevention included continuing care, observing early warning signs (i.e., changes in sleep, appetite, social isolation), and utilizing coping strategies such as discussing problems with others, taking medications as prescribed, stress reduction, scheduling positive activities, and contacting help if symptoms reemerged. The relapse prevention plan also included monthly phone calls between patient and depression care manager until the end of the 12-month intervention period. A final meeting at the end of the 12-month period also included review of the relapse prevention plan and shared the plan with the patient's primary care doctor.

In a different clinical trial, Reynolds and colleagues (2006) found that patients 70 years old or older with major depression who responded well to initial treatment with paroxetine and psychotherapy were less likely to experience recurrence when they received two years of maintenance therapy with paroxetine (Reynolds et al., 2006). Monthly maintenance psychotherapy did not prevent recurrence.

ALZHEIMER'S DISEASE (AD)

The relationship between alcohol use and dementing illnesses such as AD is complex. Alcohol-related dementia may be difficult to differentiate from Alzheimer's Disease. Determining whether alcohol use, especially heavy use, influences AD requires autopsy studies that can establish neuropathologic diagnoses of AD. Although the rates of alcohol-related dementia in late life differ according to diagnostic criteria used and the nature of the population studied, there is a consensus that alcohol contributes significantly to the acquired cognitive deficits of late life. Among subjects over the age of 55 evaluated in the Epidemiological Catchment Area (ECA) study, the prevalence of a lifetime history of alcohol abuse or dependence was 1.5 times greater among persons with mild to severe cognitive impairment compared to those with no cognitive impairment (George, 1991). Rains and Ditzler showed that, of 383 patients presenting for assessment of dementia, 9 percent consumed alcohol on a regular basis (Rains & Ditzler, 1993). Similarly, there is a high rate of dementia in alcohol-dependent or alcohol-abusing populations. Finlayson and colleagues found that 49 of 216 (23%) elderly patients presenting for alcohol treatment had dementia associated with alcoholism (Finlayson, 1988). In a study of older veterans presenting for alcohol treatment, Blow and associates found 9 percent of the 60–69 age group (n = 3,986) and 18.4 percent of those over 70 (n = 543) to have comorbid dementia (Blow et al., 1992).

ALCOHOL-ASSOCIATED COGNITIVE IMPAIRMENT

As reviewed by Oslin and colleagues, a complicated relationship exists between alcohol use disorders and cognitive impairment. These disorders span conditions such as acute intoxication states, transient alcohol-induced cognitive impairment, and alcohol-related dementia (ARD) (Oslin & Cary, 2003). However, it is important to note that ARD can be differentiated from other cognitive impairment disorders in older adults and is associated with specific characteristics and different healthcare outcomes (Oslin & Cary, 2003; Oslin, Atkinson, Smith & Hendrie, 1998). Heavy alcohol use is a strong correlate of ARD (Smith & Atkinson, 1995), and higher levels of alcohol use are associated with lower cognitive performance on standardized tests (Smith & Atkinson, 1995). ARD has been reported as the second most common cause of dementia among older adults in institutional settings (Carlen et al., 1994). Of note, in contrast to Alzheimer's dementia and vascular dementia that are characterized by a general decline in cognition and functional status over time, ARD demonstrates stabilization (and in some instances, modest improvement) in cognition and functional status following periods of abstinence (Oslin & Cary, 2003).

SLEEP DISORDERS

Sleep disorders and sleep disturbances represent another group of comorbid disorders exacerbated by alcohol use. Alcohol causes well-established changes in sleep patterns such as decreased sleep latency, decreased stage IV sleep, and precipitation or aggravation of sleep apnea (Wagman, Allen & Upright, 1997). There are also age-associated changes in sleep patterns including increased REM episodes, a decrease in REM length, a decrease in stage III and IV sleep, and increased awakenings. The age-associated changes in sleep can all be worsened by alcohol use and depression. Moeller and colleagues demonstrated in younger subjects that alcohol and depression had additive effects upon sleep disturbances when occurring together (Moeller, 1993). Furthermore, sleep disturbances (especially insomnia) have been implicated as a potential etiologic factor in the development of late life alcohol problems or in precipitating a relapse (Oslin, 1996). This hypothesis is supported by Wagman and colleagues, who demonstrated that abstinent alcoholics did not sleep well because of insomnia, frequent awakenings, and REM fragmentation (Wagman et al., 1997). When these subjects ingested alcohol, however, sleep periodicity normalized and REM sleep was temporarily suppressed, suggesting that alcohol use could be used to self-medicate for sleep disturbances. A common patient anecdote is that alcohol is used to help with sleep problems. Sleep quality and sleep disorders have not been fully examined as factors associated with initiating or maintaining alcohol use in later life. However, addressing sleep problems as precipitants to alcohol use may be an important aspect of relapse prevention for older adults.

CLINICAL CASE ILLUSTRATION #2

SUCCESSFUL OUTCOME

Jack Hendrick is a 64-year-old executive with a large marketing firm. He is a hard-driving person who works long hours and has few hobbies and interests outside of work. Although the company has a policy that employees retire at 65, he has not planned what he will do. He is slightly overweight, does not exercise except for occasionally playing golf, and drinks three drinks a day during the week and four to five drinks a day on the weekends. He has felt somewhat depressed for years but did not want to see a mental health professional because he was afraid that his boss would find out and that it would jeopardize his chances for promotion. He had no diagnosed health problems related to alcohol use but his wife worries about his drinking and worried that he will become more depressed when he retires. She would like him to spend more time in activities with her that do not involve alcohol. He finally went to a psychologist at his wife's urging. In the process of asking how Mr. Hendrick manages stress, he found out more about Mr. Hendrick's alcohol use and, using a motivational, nonjudgmental approach, said,

> You indicated that, on average, you drink alcohol every day and drink two to three drinks at a time during the week and drink more than that on the weekends. You and I have talked about your stresses at work, your wife's concerns about your use of alcohol and feeling "down and angry" a lot, as well as your own worries about retirement. National guidelines recommend that men your age drink no more than seven drinks a week: no more than one drink per day. I am concerned that your pattern of alcohol use fits into the at-risk drinking category. I am also concerned that you have to struggle with depression and anger. One of my concerns is that all of these things can get worse with retirement. I also think that we need to address both of these issues (the alcohol and the depressed feelings) together so that you can have the happier and healthier life that you want. How would you feel about that?

Mr. Hendrick wanted time to think about it so they continued to talk about these issues over the next three sessions. Mr. Hendrick talked to his wife about it and decided to go to the psychiatrist who works with his psychologist to see if medication could help his depression. He also decided to try cutting back on his alcohol use to one drink per day. He started taking antidepressant medications and tried to cut back on alcohol use (he was advised to discontinue using alcohol when taking the antidepressant). After four months, when he was feeling some-what better—less angry, depressed, and anxious—he decided to stop using alcohol to see how that would go. He continues to see the psychologist and Mr. Hendrick and his wife are trying to find new activities in preparation for his retirement.

UNSUCCESSFUL OUTCOME

Joe Thompson is a 68-year-old retired electrician. He was divorced at age 50. He was married for the second time five years ago. He has had chronic abdominal pain and unresolved hypertension for the past ten years. He has a history of alcohol problems and depression, and had an admission to alcohol treatment 15 years ago. Four years ago, after experiencing withdrawal symptoms during a hospital admission for a work-related injury, he again entered an alcohol treat-ment program. He was given a prescription for antidepressant medication by his primary care provider after that hospitalization. After two years of abstinence, Mr. Jackson began drinking again and stopped using the antidepressant medica-tion. He now drinks approximately five beers a day plus some additional liquor once a week. His wife drinks with him. His physician and social worker in the primary care clinic are aware that this is a chronic relapsing disorder and con-tinue to work with Mr. Jackson to help him stabilize his medical conditions, his depressive symptoms, and find longer term help for his primary alcohol dependence.

> Mr. Jackson, your high blood pressure and your stomach pains have not improved. The amount you are drinking can certainly interfere with them getting better and can make other physical and family problems worse. I know you've tried hard to deal with your alcohol problems and that you kept those problems in check for a long time, but now they seem to be getting in the way of your health and well being. You have also indicated that you feel pretty "down" and that "life has not been worth much" lately. I am glad that you are willing to meet with one of the counselors here to talk about working on your alcohol problems and your depressed feeling. I know it takes a lot to stay sober and that relapses can occur when stresses increase.

Mr. Jackson went to the counselor twice and stopped because he was embar-rassed to go. He continued drinking and missed appointments at the primary care clinic. His health deteriorated and he was hospitalized for pancreatitis.

CONCLUSIONS AND FUTURE DIRECTIONS

There are currently a limited number of strategies for identification, interven-tion, treatment, and relapse prevention with older adults who are experiencing problems related to their use of alcohol, medications, and/or other drugs with and without co-occurring mental and physical health disorders. The presence of co-occurring disorders is common in this population, making diagnosis, intervention, and recovery more challenging. However, there are a number of venues in which to detect substance-related problems in this age group, including primary care clinics, specialty care settings, home health care, elder housing, and senior center programs. The range of intervention/treatment/relapse prevention strategies for older adults—minimal advice, structured brief intervention protocols, formalized treatment for older persons with alcohol abuse/dependence, and specialized relapse prevention programs—provides the tools for health care providers to work with older adults across a spectrum of drinking/medication use patterns.

Providers who work with older adults need training and available systems of care in which screening, brief interventions, treatment options, and relapse prevention techniques are essential clinical activities. Both from a public health standpoint and from a clinical perspective, there is a critical need to implement effective treatment and relapse prevention strategies with older drinkers who are at-risk for more serious health, social, and emotional problems.

REFERENCES

Adams, W.L., Barry, K.L., Fleming, M.F. (1996). Screening for problem drinking in older primary care patients. *Journal of the American Medical Association* **276**(24):1964–1967.

Administration on Aging. *Older adults and mental health: Issues and opportunities*. Rockville, MD: Department of Health and Human Services.

American Psychiatric Association. (1994). DSM IV: Diagnostic and Statistical Manual of Mental Disorders. American Psychiatric Association *DSM-IV: Diagnostic and Statistical Manual of Mental Disorders, 4e*. Washington, D.C.: American Psychiatric Association.

Atkinson, R. (1999). Depression, alcoholism and ageing: A brief review. *Int J Geriatr Psychiatry* **14**(11):905–910.

Atkinson, R.M. (1995). Treatment programs for aging alcoholics. In Beresford, T.P., Gomberg, E.S.L., eds., *Alcohol and Aging*, 186–210. New York: Oxford University Press.

Atkinson, R.M., Tolson, R.L., Turner, J.A. (1993). Factors affecting outpatient treatment compliance of older male problem drinkers. *Journal of Studies on Alcohol* **54**(1):102–106.

Babor, T.F., Grant, M. (1992). Geneva: World Health Organization.

Babor, T.F., Ritson, E.B., Hodgson, R.J. (1986). Alcohol-related problems in the primary health care setting: A review of early intervention strategies. *British Journal of Addiction* **81**(1):23–46.

Barrick, C., Connors, G.J. (2002). Relapse prevention and maintaining abstinence in older adults with alcohol-use disorders. *Drugs Aging* **19**(8):583–594.

Barry, K.L. et al. (1998). Elder-specific brief alcohol intervention: 3-month outcomes. Vol. 22:32A.

Barry, K.L. (1999). *Brief interventions and brief therapies for substance abuse* (Treatment Improvement Protocol (TIP) Series No. 34). Rockville, MD: U.S. Department of Health and Human Services, Public Health Service, Substance Abuse and Mental Health Services Administration, Center for Substance Abuse Treatment.

Barry, K.L., Fleming, M.F. (1994). The family physician. *Alcohol Health and Research World* **18**(1):105–109.

Barry, K.L., Oslin, D., Blow, F.C. (2001). *Alcohol problems in older adults: Prevention and management*. New York: Springer Publishing.

Bartels, S.J., Coakley, E.H., Zubritsky, C., Ware, J.H., Miles, K.M., Arean, P.A. et al. (2004). Improving access to geriatric mental health services: A randomized trial comparing treatment engagement with integrated versus enhanced referral care for depression, anxiety, and at-risk alcohol use. *Am J Psychiatry* **161**(8):1455–1462.

Bartels, S.J., Coakley, E., Oxman, T.E., Constantino, G., Oslin, D., Chen, H. et al. (2002). Suicidal and death ideation in older primary care patients with depression, anxiety, and at-risk alcohol use. *Am J Geriatr Psychiatry* **10**(4):417–427.

Bartels, S.J., Dums, A.R., Oxman, T.E., Schneider, L.S., Arean, P.A., Alexopoulos, G.S. et al. (2002). Evidence-based practices in geriatric mental health care. *Psychiatr Serv* **53**(11):1419–1431.

Bartels S.J., L.J. (1995). Dual diagnosis in the elderly. In Lehman AF, D.L., *Substance disorders among persons with chronic mental illness*, 139–157. New York: Harwood Academic Publishers.

Beresford, T.P. (1979). Alcoholism consultation and general hospital psychiatry. *General Hospital Psychiatry* **1**(4):293–300.

Blazer, D., Williams, C.D. (1980). Epidemiology of dysphoria and depression in an elderly population. *American Journal of Psychiatry* **137**(4):439–444.

Blow, F.C. et al. (2002). National longitudinal alcohol epidemiologic survey (NLAES): Alcohol and drug use across age groups. In Korper, S.P., and Cancil, C.L., eds., *Substance Use by Older Adults: Estimate of Future Impact of Treatment System*, Substance Abuse and Mental Health Services Administration Office of Applied Studies, Rockville, MD.

Blow, F.C. (1998a). The spectrum of alcohol interventions for older adults. In E.S.L. Gomberg, A.M. Hegedus & R.A. Zucker, eds., *Alcohol problems and aging*, 373–396. Washington D.C.: U.S. Government Printing Office, National Institute on Alcohol Abuse and Alcoholism.

Blow, F.C. (1998b). *Substance abuse among older adults* (Treatment Improvement Protocol (TIP) Series No. 26). Rockville, MD: U.S. Department of Health and Human Services, Public Health Service, Substance Abuse and Mental Health Services Administration, Center for Substance Abuse Treatment.

Blow, F.C., Barry, K.L. (2000). Older patients with at-risk and problem drinking patterns: New developments in brief interventions. *Journal of Geriatric Psychology and Neurology* **13**(3):115–123.

Blow, F.C., Barry, K.L., Walton, M.A. (Unpublished). The efficacy of elder-specific brief alcohol advice with older at-risk drinkers.

Blow, F.C., Brockmann, L.M., Barry, K.L. (2004). Role of alcohol in late-life suicide. *Alcohol Clin Exp Res* **28**(5 Suppl):48S–56S.

Blow, F.C., Cook, C.A., Booth, B.M., Falcon, S.P., Friedman, M.J. (1992). Age-related psychiatric comorbidities and level of functioning in alcoholic veterans seeking outpatient treatment. *Hospital and Community Psychiatry* **43**(10):990–995.

Blow, F.C., Gillespie, B.W., Barry, K.L., Mudd, S.A., Hill, E.M. (1998). Brief screening for alcohol problems in elderly population using the Short Michigan Alcoholism Screening Test-Geriatric Version (SMAST-G), 20–25.

Brennan, P.L., Kagay, C.R., Geppert, J.J., Moos, R.H. (2001). Predictors and outcomes of outpatient mental health care: A 4-year prospective study of elderly Medicare patients with substance use disorders. *Medical Care* **39**(1):39–49.

Brennan, P.L., Nichols, K.A., Moos, R.H. (2002). Long-term use of VA mental health services by older patients with substance use disorders. *Psychiatr Serv* **53**(7):836–841.

Brennan, P.L., Schutte, K.K., Moos, R.H. (2005). Pain and use of alcohol to manage pain: prevalence and 3-year outcomes among older problem and non-problem drinkers. *Addiction* **100**(6):777–786.

Brown, S.A., Goldman, M.S., Inn, A., Anderson, L.R. (1980). Expectations of reinforcement from alcohol: Their domain and relation to drinking patterns. *J Consult Clin Psychol* **48**(4):419–426.

Bruce, M.L., Ten Have, T.R., Reynolds, C.F.I., Katz, I.I., Schulberg, H.C., Mulsant, B.H. et al. (2004). Reducing suicidal ideation and depressive symptoms in depressed older primary care patients: A randomized controlled trial. *JAMA* **291**(9):1081–1091.

Bucholz, K.K., Hesselbrock, V.M., Shayka, J.J., Nurnberger, J.I. Jr, Schuckit, M.A., Schmidt, I. et al. (1995). Reliability of individual diagnostic criterion items for psychoactive substance dependence and the impact on diagnosis. *J Stud Alcohol* **56**(5):500–505.

Burgio, L.D., Cotter, E.M., Stevens, A.B., Hardin, J.M., Sinnott, J., Hohman, M.J. (1995). Elders' acceptability ratings of behavioral treatments and pharmacotherapy for the management of geriatric behavioral disturbances. *Gerontologist* **35**(5):630–636.

Callahan, C.M.T.W.M. (1995). Health services use and mortality among older primary care patients with alcoholism. *J Am Geriatr Soc* **43**(12):1378–1383.

Carlen, P.L., McAndrews, M.P., Weiss, R.T., Dongier, M., Hill, J.M., Menzano, E. et al. (1994). Alcohol-related dementia in the institutionalized elderly. *Alcohol Clin Exp Res* **18**(6): 1330–1334.

Center for Substance Abuse Treatment. (2005). *Substance abuse relapse prevention for older adults: A group treatment approach.* (Report No. DHHS Publication No. (SMA) 05-4053). Rockville, MD: Substance Abuse and Mental Health Services Administration.

Chick, J., Lloyd, G., Crombie, E. (1985). Counseling problem drinkers in medical wards: A controlled study. *BMJ* **290**(6473):965–967.

Cohen-Mansfield, J. (2001). Nonpharmacologic interventions for inappropriate behaviors in dementia: A review, summary, and critique. *Am J Geriatr Psychiatry* **9**(4):361–381.

Conwell, Y. (1991). Suicide in elderly patients. *Diagnosis and treatment of depression in late life,* 397–418. Washington, DC: American Psychiatric Press.

Cook, B. et al. (1991). Depression and previous alcoholism in the elderly. *British Journal of Psychiatry* **158**:72–75.

Cooperstock, R., Parnell, P. (1982). Research on psychotropic drug use. A review of findings and methods. *Soc Sci Med* **16**(12):1179–1196.

Coyne, J., Katz, I.R. (2001). Improving the primary care treatment of late life depression: Progress and opportunities. *Medical Care* **39**(8):756–759.

D'Archangelo, E. (1993). Substance abuse in later life. *Can Fam Physician* **39**·1986 -1988, 1991 1993.

Department of Health and Human Services. (1999) Washington, DC: National Institute of Health.

Dietrich, A.J., Oxman, T.E., Williams, J.W. Jr, Schulberg, H.C., Bruce, M.L., Lee, P.W. et al. (2004). Re-engineering systems for the treatment of depression in primary care: Cluster randomised controlled trial. *BMJ* **329**(7466):602.

Doody, R.S., Stevens, J.C., Beck, C., Dubinsky, R.M., Kaye, J.A., Gwyther, L. et al. (2001). Practice parameter: Management of dementia (an evidence-based review). Report of the Quality Standards Subcommittee of the American Academy of Neurology. *Neurology* **56**(9):1154–1166.

Ellor, J.R., Kurz, D.J. (1982). Misuse and abuse of prescription and nonprescription drugs by the elderly. *Nurs Clin North Am* **17**(2):319–330.

Finlayson, R.E.A. (1988). Alcoholism in elderly persons: A study of the psychiatric and psychosocial features of 216 inpatients. **63**:761–768.

Finlayson, R.E. (1995a). Comorbidity in elderly alcoholics. In T. Beresford & E.S.L. Gomberg, eds., *Alcohol and aging,* 56–69. New York: Oxford University Press.

Finlayson, R.E. (1995b). Misuse of prescription drugs. *The International Journal of the Addictions* **30**(13–14):1871–1901.

Finlayson, R.E., Davis, L.J. Jr. (1994). Prescription drug dependence in the elderly population: Demographic and clinical features of 100 inpatients. *Mayo Clin Proc* **69**(12):1137–1145.

Finney, J.W., Moos, R.H., Brennan, P.L. (1991). The drinking problems index: A measure to assess alcohol-related problems among older adults. *J Subst Abuse* **3**(4):395–404.

Fleming, M.F. (2002). Identification and treatment of alcohol use disorders in older adults. A.R. Gurnack A.M., eds., *Treating alcohol and drug abuse in the elderly,* 85–108. New York, NY: Springer Publishing.

Fleming, M.F., Barry, K.L., Manwell, L.B., Johnson, K., London, R. (1997). Brief physician advice for problem alcohol drinkers. A randomized controlled trial in community-based primary care practices. *JAMA* **277**(13):1039–1045.

Fleming, M.F., Manwell, L.B., Barry, K.L., Adams, W., Stauffacher, E.A. (1999). Brief physician advice for alcohol problems in older adults: A randomized community-based trial. *J Fam Pract* **48**(5):378–384.

Fraser, A.G. (1997). Pharmacokinetic interactions between alcohol and other drugs. *Clin Pharmacokinet* **33**(2):79–90.

Gambert, S.R., Katsoyannis, K.K. (1995). Alcohol-related medical disorders of older heavy drinkers. In T. Beresford & E. Gomberg, eds., *Alcohol and aging*, 70–81. New York: Oxford University Press.

Gatz, M. et al. (1998). Empirically validated psychological treatments for older adults. *Journal of Mental Health and Aging* **4**(1):9–46.

George, L.K. et al. (1991). Cognitive impairment. *Psychiatric disorders in America: The Epidemiologic Catchment Area Study*, 291–327. New York: Free Press.

Gerson, S., Belin, T.R., Kaufman, A., Mintz, J., Jarvik, L. (1999). Pharmacological and psychological treatments for depressed older patients: A meta-analysis and overview of recent findings. *Harv Rev Psychiatry* **7**(1):1–28.

Gfoerer JC, Penne, M., Pemberton, M. (2002). *The aging baby boom cohort and future prevalence of substance abuse*. (Report No. DHHS Publication No. SMA 03-3763, analytic series A-21). Rockville, MD: Substance Abuse and Mental Health Services Administration, Office of Applied Studies.

Gfroerer, J., Penne, M., Pemberton, M., Folsom, R. (2003). Substance abuse treatment need among older adults in 2020: The impact of the aging baby-boom cohort. *Drug Alcohol Depend* **69**(2):127–135.

Graham, K., Schmidt, G. (1999). Alcohol use and psychosocial well-being among older adults. *Journal of Studies on Alcohol* **60**:345–351.

Gray-Toft, P.A., Anderson, J.G. (1985). Organizational stress in the hospital: Development of a model for diagnosis and prediction. *Health Services Research* **19**(6 Pt 1):753–774.

Harris, K.B., Miller, W.R. (1990). Behavioral self-control training for problem drinkers: Components of efficacy. *Psychology of Addictive Behavior* **4**(2):82–90.

Hayward, R.A., Shapiro, M.F., Freeman, H.E., Corey, C.R. (1988). Inequities in health services among insured Americans. Do working-age adults have less access to medical care than the elderly? *N Engl J Med* **318**(23):1507–1512.

Hoff, R.A., Rosenheck, R.A. (1998). Long-term patterns of service use and cost among patients with both psychiatric and substance abuse disorders. *Med Care* **36**(6):835–843.

Hunkeler, E.M., Katon, W., Tang, L., Williams, J.W. Jr, Kroenke, K., Lin, E.H. et al. (2006). Long term outcomes from the IMPACT randomised trial for depressed elderly patients in primary care. *BMJ* **332**(7536):259–263.

Hylek, E.M. et al. (1998). Acetaminophen and other risk factors for excessive warfarin anticoagulation. *JAMA* **279**(9):657–662.

Institute of Medicine. (1990). Who provides treatment? Committee of the Institute of Medicine (Division of Mental Health and Behavioral Medicine), *Broadening the Base of Treatment for Alcoholism*, 98–141. Washington, DC: National Academy Press.

Jinks, M.J., Raschko, R.R. (1990). A profile of alcohol and prescription drug abuse in a high-risk community-based elderly population. *The Annals of Pharmacotherapy* **24**(10):971–975.

Joseph, C.L., Ganzini, L., Atkinson, R.M. (1995). Screening for alcohol use disorders in the nursing home. *J Am Geriatr Soc* **43**(4):368–373.

Korrapati, M.R., Vestal, R.E. (1995). Alcohol and medications in the elderly: Complex interactions. In Beresford, T.P., Gomberg, E.S.L., eds., *Alcohol and Aging*, 42–55. New York: Oxford University Press.

Kristenson, H., Ohlin, H., Hulten-Nosslin, M.-B., Trell, E., Hood, B. (1983). Identification and intervention of heavy drinking in middle-aged men: Results and follow-up of 24–60 months of long-term study with randomized controls. *Alcoholism: Clinical and Experimental Research* **7**(2):203–209.

Larsen, P.D., Martin, J.L. (1999). Polypharmacy and elderly patients. *Association of Operating Room Nurses Journal* **69**(3):619–622, 625, 627–628.

Lemke, S., Moos, R.H. (2003). Treatment and outcomes of older patients with alcohol use disorders in community residential programs. *J Stud Alcohol* **64**(2):219–226.

Liberto, J.G., Oslin, D.W., Ruskin, P.E. (1992). Alcoholism in older persons: A review of the literature. *Hospital and Community Psychiatry* **43**(10):975–984.

Miller, W.R., Hester, R.K. (1986). *Treating addictive behaviors: Processes of change.* New York: Plenum Press.

Miller, W.R., Munoz, R.F. (1976). *How to control your drinking.* Englewood Cliffs, NJ: Prentice-Hall.

Miller, W.R., Rollnick, S. (1999). *Motivational Interviewing: Preparing people to change addictive behavior.* New York: The Guilford Press.

Miller, W.R., Taylor, C.A. (1980). Relative effectiveness of bibliotherapy, individual and group self-control training in the treatment of problem drinkers. *Addictive Behaviors* **5**(1):13–24.

Moeller, F.G. et al. (1993). A comparison of sleep EEGs in patients with primary major depression and major depression secondary to alcoholism. *Journal of Affective Disorders* **27**:39–42.

Moore, A., Morton, S., Beck, J., Hays, R., Oishi, S., Partridge, J. et al. (1999). A new paradigm for alcohol use in older persons. *Medical Care* **37**(2):165–179.

National Institute on Alcohol Abuse and Alcoholism. (1998). Drinking in the United States. Main findings from the 1992 National Longitudinal Alcohol Epidemiologic Survey (NLAES). *NIH Publication No. 99–3519.*

Office of Applied Studies, S. (2002). *Summary of findings from the 2002 national survey on drug use and health.* Rockville, MD: Substance Abuse and Mental Health Services Administration, Department of Health & Human Services.

Onder, G., Pedone, C., Landi, F., Cesari, M., Della Vedova, C., Bernabei, R. et al. (2002). Adverse drug reactions as cause of hospital admissions: Results from the Italian Group of Pharmacoepidemiology in the Elderly (GIFA). *J Am Geriatr Soc* **50**(12):1962–1968.

Oslin, D., Atkinson, R.M., Smith, D.M., Hendrie, H. (1998). Alcohol related dementia: Proposed clinical criteria. *Int J Geriatr Psychiatry* **13**(4):203–212.

Oslin, D.W. (1996). Alcohol. *Geriatric Secrets.* Philadelphia: Hanley and Belfus.

Oslin, D.W. (2004). Late-life alcoholism: Issues relevant to the geriatric psychiatrist. *Am J Geriatr Psychiatry* **12**(6):571–583.

Oslin, D.W., Cary, M.S. (2003). Alcohol-related dementia: Validation of diagnostic criteria. *Am J Geriatr Psychiatry* **11**(4):441–447.

Oslin, D.W., Pettinati, H., Volpicelli, J.R. (2002). Alcoholism treatment adherence: Older age predicts better adherence and drinking outcomes. *Am J Geriatr Psychiatry* **10**(6):740–747.

Oslin, D.W., Slaymaker, V.J., Blow, F.C., Owen, P.L., Colleran, C. (2005). Treatment outcomes for alcohol dependence among middle-aged and older adults. *Addict Behav* **30**(7):1431–1436.

Oslin, D.W., Streim, J.E., Parmelee, P., Boyce, A.A., Katz, I.R. (1997). Alcohol abuse: A source of reversible functional disability among residents of a VA nursing home. *Int J Geriatr Psychiatry* **12**(8):825–832.

Patterson, T.L., Jeste, D.V. (1999). The potential impact of the baby-boom generation on substance abuse among elderly persons. *Psychiatric Services* **50**(9):1184–1188.

Persson, J., Magnusson, P.-H. (1989). Early intervention in patients with excessive consumption of alcohol: A controlled study. *Alcohol* **6**(5):403–408.

Pinquart, M. (2001). Correlates of subjective health in older adults: A meta-analysis. *Psychol Aging* **16**(3):414–426.

Rains, V., Ditzler, T. (1993). Alcohol use disorders in cognitively impaired patients referred for geriatric assessment. *Journal of Addictive Diseases* **12**:55–64.

Reynolds, C.F. 3rd, Dew, M.A., Pollock, B.G., Mulsant, B.H., Frank, E., Miller, M.D. et al. (2006). Maintenance treatment of major depression in old age. *N Engl J Med* **354**(11):1130–1138.

Rice, C., Longabaugh, R., Beattie, M., Noel, N. (1993). Age group differences in response to treatment for problematic alcohol use. *Addiction* **88**(10):1369–1375.

Satre, D.D., Mertens, J.R., Arean, P.A., Weisner, C. (2004). Five-year alcohol and drug treatment outcomes of older adults versus middle-aged and younger adults in a managed care program. *Addiction* **99**(10):1286–1297.

Saunders, P.A., Copeland, J.R.M., Dewey, M.E., Davidson, I.A., McWilliam, C., Sharma, V. et al. (1991). Heavy drinking as a risk factor for depression and dementia in elderly men. *British Journal of Psychiatry* **159**:213–216.

Schneider, L.S., Pollock, V.E., Lyness, S.A. (1990). A meta-analysis of controlled trials of neuroleptic treatment in dementia. *J Am Geriatr Soc* **38**(5):553–563.

Schonfeld, L., Dupree, L.W. (1995). Treatment approaches for older problem drinkers. *The International Journal of the Addictions* **30**(13–14):1819–1842.

Schuckit, M.A., Pastor, P.A., Jr. (1978). The elderly as a unique population: Alcoholism. *Alcoholism: Clinical and Experimental Research* **2**(1):31–38.

Schutte, K.K., Nichols, K.A., Brennan, P.L., Moos, R.H. (2003). A ten-year follow-up of older former problem drinkers: Risk of relapse and implications of successfully sustained remission. *J Stud Alcohol* **64**(3):367–374.

Sheahan, S.L. et al. (1989). Drug misuse among the elderly: A covert problem. *Health Values* **13**(3):22–29.

Smith, D.M., Atkinson, R.M. (1995). Alcoholism and dementia. *Int J Addict* **30**(13–14):1843–1869.

Spencer, G. (1989). *Projections of the population of the United States by age, sex, and race: 1988–2080*. Vol. Series P-25 (No. 1018). Washington D.C.: U.S. Department of Commerce.

Substance Abuse and Mental Health Administration. (1998). *Substance abuse among older adults: Treatment Improvement Protocol (TIP) Series*. Rockville, MD: U.S. Department of Health and Human Services.

Teri, L., Logsdon, R.G., Uomoto, J., McCurry, S.M. (1997). Behavioral treatment of depression in dementia patients: A controlled clinical trial. *J Gerontol B Psychol Sci Soc Sci* **52**(4): P159–166.

Thorpe, L., Whitney, D.K., Kutcher, S.P., Kennedy, S.H. (2001). Clinical guidelines for the treatment of depressive disorders. VI. Special populations. *Can J Psychiatry* **46**(Suppl 1):63S–76S.

Unutzer, J., Katon, W., Callahan, C.M., Williams, J.W., Hunkeler, E., Harpole, L. et al. (2002). Collaborative care management of late-life depression in the primary care setting. *JAMA* **288**(22):2836–2845.

Unutzer, J., Patrick, D.L., Simon, G., Grembowski, D., Walker, E., Rutter, C. et al. (1997). Depressive symptoms and the cost of health services in HMO patients aged 65 years and older. A 4-year prospective study. *JAMA* **277**(20):1618–1623.

US Census Bureau. *Projections of the Resident Population by Age, Sex, Race, and Hispanic Origin: 1999*. Washington, D.C.

Wagman, A.M., Allen, R.P., Upright, D. (1997). Effects of alcohol consumption upon parameters of ultradian sleep rhythms in alcoholics. *Advances in Experimental Medicine and Biology* **85A**:601–616.

Wallace, P., Cutler, S., Haines, A. (1988). Randomised controlled trial of general practitioner intervention in patients with excessive alcohol consumption. *BMJ* **297**(6649):663–668.

Wiens, A.N., Menustik, C.E., Miller, S.I., Schmitz, R.E. (1982). Medical-behavioral treatment of the older alcoholic patient. *American Journal of Drug and Alcohol Abuse* **9**(4):461–475.

Willenbring, M.L., Johnson, S.B., Tan, E. (1994). Characteristics of male medical patients referred for alcoholism treatment. *Journal of Substance Abuse Treatment* **11**(3):259–265.

Wilson, K., et al. (2002). *Antidepressant versus placebo for depressed elderly*. Cochrane Library: Oxford: Update Software.

Wu, L.T., Ringwalt, C.L., Williams, C.E. (2003). Use of substance abuse treatment services by persons with mental health and substance use problems. *Psychiatr Serv* **54**(3):363–369.

Zis, A.P., Grof, P., Webster, M., Goodwin, F.K. (1980). Prediction of relapse in recurrent affective disorder. *Psychopharmacol Bull* **16**(1):47–49.

INTERNET RESOURCES

- Substance Abuse and Mental Health Services Administration (SAMHSA)
  www.samhsa.gov
  Phone: 301-443-8956
- SAMHSA National Treatment Referral Services
  findtreatment.samhsa.gov
  Phone: 800-662-4357
- SAMHSA National Clearinghouse for Alcohol and Drug Information (NCADI)
  www.ncadi.samhsa.gov
  Phone: 800-729-6686
- National Institute on Alcohol Abuse and Alcoholism (NIAAA)
  www.niaaa.nih.gov
  Phone: 301-496-4000
- Hazelden
  www.hazelden.org
  Phone: 800-257-7810
- National Institute on Aging (NIA)
  www.nia.nih.gov
  Phone: 301-496-1752
- American Society on Aging (ASA)
  www.asaging.org
  Phone: 800-537-9728

These two resources are available via the SAMHSA Clearinghouse:

- Center for Substance Abuse Treatment. *Substance Abuse Relapse Prevention for Older Adults: A Group Treatment Approach.* DHHS Publication No. (SMA) 05-4053. Rockville, MD: Substance Abuse and Mental Health Services Administration, 2005.
- Blow, F.C. (Consensus Panel Chair). Center for Substance Abuse Treatment. *Substance Abuse Among Older Adults: Treatment Improvement Protocol (TIP) Series 26.* Rockville, MD: Substance Abuse and Mental Health Services Administration, 1998.

15

Utilizing Relapse Prevention with Offender Populations: What Works

Craig Dowden and Don A. Andrews

Carleton University
Ottawa, Ontario

INTRODUCTION

Relapse prevention (RP) emerged out of pioneering work conducted in the late 1970s and early 1980s by Alan Marlatt and his colleagues, whose clinical research targeted the processes underlying alcohol and drug-related problems. This research culminated in the publication of the seminal volume *Relapse Prevention*, which outlined how RP techniques could aid in the treatment of a variety of addictive behaviors (Marlatt & Gordon, 1985). However, it should be noted that the initial conceptualization of RP was as a maintenance strategy; in other words, to help individuals maintain the gains they achieved within a treatment program. As described by George and Marlatt (1989, p. 2), it was a "self-control program designed to teach individuals who are trying to change their behavior how to anticipate and cope with the problem of relapse." This definition is significant as it dictates that the individual has already ceased the problematic behavior and is also motivated to maintain this positive behavioral change (Hanson, 2000; Laws, 2003).

Programs incorporating elements of RP focus on teaching an individual how to identify high-risk situations, circumvent habitual coping styles, and enhance feelings of self-efficacy in dealing with these situations (Bakker, Ward, Cryer & Hudson, 2000; Hanson, 2000; Laws, 1999, 2003; Marlatt & Gordon, 1985; Witkiewitz, Marlatt & Walker, 2005). Essentially, RP is a cognitive-behavioral approach to self-management, which teaches individuals alternate responses to high-risk situations (Andrews & Bonta, 2003; Laws, 2003; Marlatt & Gordon, 1985). The development of this treatment concept was based on previous research that demonstrated there are common cognitive, behavioral, and affective pathways associated with the process of relapse, regardless of the type of problem behavior. More specifically, Marlatt and Gordon (1985) demonstrated that three high-risk situations constituted almost 75 percent of relapse episodes. These included negative emotional states, interpersonal conflict, and social pressure. Thus, RP is different from other forms of treatment in that RP strategies can be applied to multiple problem areas, whereas other interventions target a specific issue (e.g., anger management).

As illustrated by the diversity of chapters in this volume, RP has been adopted in wide-ranging settings including the treatment of problem gambling (e.g., Echeburua & Fernandez-Montalvo, 2005; McCown, 2004; Tavares, Zilberman & el-Guebaly, 2003), eating disorders (e.g., Kaplan, 2002; Peterson, Wonderlich, Mitchell & Crow, 2004; Stewart & Williamson, 2003), smoking (e.g., Antonuccio, 2004; Groner, French, Ahijevych & Wewers, 2005; Ramsay & Hoffmann, 2004) and substance abuse (e.g., Hartl, 2005; Stewart & Conrod, 2005; Witkiewitz et al., 2005). Not surprisingly, RP has also been adopted within correctional settings, including programs designed for substance-abusing offenders (Peters, 1993). Other scholars have forwarded that RP should also be applied to the treatment of general offender populations wherever possible (Cullen & Gendreau, 1989; Gendreau, 1996). Arguably, the area in which this approach has been most enthusiastically adopted has been in treatment of sexual offenders (Launay, 2001; Laws, 1999, 2003; Mann, Webster, Schofield & Marshall, 2004; Marques, Wiederanders, Day, Nelson, van Ommeren, 2005; Ward, 2000).[1]

As previously mentioned, although RP initially was formulated as a maintenance strategy for motivated program completers, there are now two forms of this approach (Laws, 1999, 2003). First, and arguably most common, RP is used within the traditional maintenance model to augment treatment services. Second, the RP approach has become the underlying framework within which various treatment services are delivered. This latter approach has been particularly prominent in sexual offender treatment (see Marques et al., 2005 and Pithers, Martin & Cumming, 1989 for examples) where additional program components such as anger management, sexual education, and victim empathy are delivered within the context of a RP framework (Laws, 1999, 2003).

---

[1] It should be noted that there has been an ongoing debate about the utility of the original RP model for treating sexual offenders. This is largely due to concerns regarding the role of lapse and relapse in the model and whether sex offenders are sufficiently motivated for treatment, an essential component of this approach (see Hanson, 2000; Launay, 2001; Laws, 2003; Ward, 2000 for examples). In recent years, to address these concerns, Ward and his colleagues (see Ward & Hudson, 2000; Ward, Hudson & Keenan, 1998) have proposed a self-regulation model of RP, which has also been criticized (see Launay, 2001). It is well beyond the scope of this chapter to review this rich debate, but interested readers are encouraged to review the chapter in this volume by Ward (Chapter 10) as well as the references listed.

One of the major problems with the RP concept is that its popularity led many program designers to claim that their interventions utilized RP strategies, but failed to illustrate precisely what they were doing. For example, Laws (1999) stated that "Virtually any kind of post-treatment intervention has been called relapse prevention" (p. 291). This has created enormous difficulties as it has become increasingly difficult to disentangle RP from other forms of correctional intervention. As Karl Hanson, a preeminent authority in the sex offender treatment literature espoused, "this immense popularity is somewhat puzzling considering that the fundamental principles are not new" (p. 36).

EXPLORING THE QUESTION OF "WHAT WORKS" WITHIN RP: THE ROLE OF META-ANALYSIS

Despite increased attention to this approach within offender rehabilitation, very little controlled outcome research has formally evaluated its effectiveness (Laws, 1999). Given this state of affairs, meta-analytic techniques provide the best mechanism to appropriately and systematically aggregate the results to date while simultaneously highlighting areas in need of further research. A meta-analysis is a statistical technique that aggregates the results of a group of independently conducted studies in order to form a conclusion regarding the strength of the relationship between two variables; in this case, correctional treatment and reduced reoffending (Glass, McGaw & Smith, 1981). The results from each of these studies are converted into a common metric termed an *effect size*[2] to enable cross-study comparison. The ability of meta-analytic techniques to systematically aggregate and compare the findings across several studies is one of its primary advantages.

Meta-analytic reviews essentially replaced traditional narrative reviews given that narrative reviews were typically viewed as more subjective and open to reviewer bias (Rosenthal, 1991; Wolf, 1986). Furthermore, and perhaps more importantly, as highlighted by Glass et al. (1981), individual studies were no more "comprehensible without statistical analysis than the hundreds of data points in one study" (p. 12). A meta-analysis is now the review method of choice within the field of corrections as it addresses each of these concerns within its methodological framework.

Although we recently published a meta-analysis of the RP intervention literature for offenders (Dowden, Antonowicz & Andrews, 2003), it only included papers that were available before 1999, and considerable RP program evaluations have been conducted since that time. Furthermore, and arguably more important, some of the findings we expressed were tentative due to the small number of

---

[2] An effect size is an estimate of the size of the relationship between two variables (Rosenthal, 1991) and is the primary unit of measurement within a meta-analysis.

available studies exploring a specific question. Thus, the purpose of this chapter is to conduct an expanded meta-analysis on a larger sample of studies[3] to explore what works in RP programs and provide some directions for future research.

WHAT WORKS WITHIN RP PROGRAMS: GENERAL TRENDS

Forty-one unique studies contributed 64 tests of the effectiveness of RP elements to the meta-analysis. The vast majority of the effect sizes[4] were derived from studies that were predominantly composed of male (95%), adult (83%) offenders. Interestingly, 39 percent of the included studies were published since 1990, thereby demonstrating the utility of conducting an updated review.[5]

The overall mean effect size for the 41 tests of treatment that had some element of RP was +0.15 (SD = .14) with a 95 percent confidence interval of +0.12 to +0.18. Although the effect sizes ranged from −.21 to +.54, the vast majority (91%) were positive, thus demonstrating the therapeutic potential of these types of programs. Using the Binomial Effect Size Display (BESD) introduced by Rosenthal (1991), the overall mean effect size represents a 42.5 percent recidivism rate for the treatment group and a recidivism rate of 57.5 percent for the control group.

Clearly, treatment programs that incorporated some elements of RP, on average, yielded at least a moderate reduction in recidivism (15%). Notably, however, the mean effect size of approaches incorporating some element of RP was statistically unimpressive relative to the overall mean effect size for human service programs reported by Andrews, Dowden, and Gendreau (1999); that is, .12 (k = 374, SD = 0.19, CI: 0.10–0.14).

However, one of the aspects of RP programs is that they can utilize a variety of techniques to accomplish their therapeutic goals. More specifically, as mentioned at the outset of this chapter, RP programs were designed to assist offenders to identify high-risk situations, to circumvent habitual coping styles, and to enhance feelings of self-efficacy in dealing with these situations. Thus, additional analyses were conducted to explore the most effective RP techniques.

Table 15.1 presents the mean effect sizes for each RP component that was coded for in the present review along with their corresponding definitions. It

---

[3] The set of studies included within the Dowden et al. (2003) meta-analysis were all included in this study (n = 24) as well as other suitable studies that were identified subsequent to 1998 (n = 17). The complete list of studies (n = 41) is available from the first author upon request.

[4] The Pearson Product Moment Correlation Coefficient was the primary effect size measure because the vast majority of the tests of treatment were derived from 2 × 2 contingency tables with two levels of recidivism and two levels of intervention. Multiple effect size estimates were computed if the primary studies allowed separate estimates by case or setting characteristics. Several definitions of recidivism were used with "reconviction" being the preferred measure if multiple indices of recidivism were reported.

[5] All of the coded variables exceeded our interrater acceptability criteria (80% or higher) (see Dowden & Andrews, 1999, 2000, 2004).

TABLE 15.1: The Relationship between Relapse Prevention Components and Effect Size

Relapse Prevention Element	Not Present	Present (k)	Eta
Offense Chain: The offender is taught to recognize his/her offense cycle or the precursory cues that warn an offender that he/she may be in danger of committing a criminal act.	.12 (39)	.19 (25)	.29*
Relapse Rehearsal: Participants are taught to develop skills obtained through corrective feedback received during multiple opportunities for rehearsal of low-risk responses to high-risk situations.	.11 (44)	.24 (20)	.43***
High-Risk Situations: The program teaches the offender to identify situations that are conducive to criminal activity and how to deal with these situations when he/she is placed in one.	.12 (37)	.19 (27)	.26*
Train Significant Others: The program trains significant others such as family, friends, and school and work peers in the program model so the offender is properly reinforced for displaying prosocial behaviors learned in the program.	.14 (57)	.32 (5)	.36**
Booster Sessions: Booster sessions or aftercare focusing on supplementing the program material is made available to the offender within institutional or community settings (Cullen & Gendreau, 1989; Gendreau, 1996; Gendreau & Andrews, 1994).	.15 (48)	.15 (16)	−.02 ns
Failure Situations: The program teaches the offender to deal with failure or relapse constructively and not to lose hope or experience profound discouragement at a setback.	.15 (61)	.07 (3)	−.13 ns
Self-Efficacy: The program aims to instill feelings of self-confidence in the offender that his/her efforts will be successful in avoiding future criminal activity as a result of participating in the program.	.15 (60)	.16 (4)	.01 ns
Coping Skills: One of the explicit targets of the program is to develop or enhance coping skills for the program participants.	.15 (54)	.14 (10)	−.04 ns

should be noted that the list of RP techniques was extracted from Laws (1999), a recognized authority in the field. A wide range of mean effect sizes is presented in this table, with the most effective element of the RP model involving training significant others in the program model. Other promising RP targets included those that focused on identifying the precursors to offense behavior, providing opportunities for relapse rehearsal, and assisting clients identify high-risk situations. The least effective RP elements were providing booster/aftercare sessions and/or developing skills to cope with failure situations.

The additive effect of the number of RP components on program effectiveness was also examined. The simple correlation between the number of RP elements and reduced recidivism was .31 (p < .01). The mean score was 1.66 (SD = 1.8) with a mean inter-item correlation of .23 and an alpha coefficient of .69. The number of RP elements present within a program was categorized using a three-level composite measure (0 = *the program did not identify the specific element(s) used*; 1 = *the program targeted and identified only one element of the model*; 2 = *the program used two or more elements of the RP targets*). A frequency analysis revealed this would be the most appropriate splitting of the data to achieve an approximately equal number of effect sizes in each group. An analysis of variance revealed that significant differences existed within this variable, $F(2, 61)$ = 4.91, p < .05. Follow-up contrasts using the Scheffé correction revealed that programs that overtly identified two or more elements of RP were associated with a significantly higher mean effect size (.22, n = 16) than programs that identified one element (.12, n = 23) or were nonspecific in their RP targets (.11, n = 18) (p < .05).

One final analysis was conducted on the RP model as a whole. More specifically, programs that described their RP strategies in some detail were contrasted to those programs that used only the global term of RP or provided only traditional booster/aftercare sessions that were not judged to be in line with the traditional model for RP. This analysis was quite informative as programs that were specific about their RP strategies were associated with a significantly higher mean effect size (.19, n = 38) than those that failed to describe the strategies used or only provided booster/aftercare sessions (.10, n = 26) (Eta = .31, p < .01).

RISK, NEED, AND RESPONSIVITY: MISSING PIECES IN THE RP PUZZLE?

In one of its earliest critiques, Thornton (1997) identified three fatal flaws surrounding the utilization of RP for sexual offenders. Although his criticisms of RP were specific to sex offenders, he proposed an alternative clinical framework to guide offender treatment. More specifically, he argued that attention should be paid to identifying those risk factors associated with the offending behavior for various categories of offenders through a thorough review of the extant literature and then targeting these specific factors within treatment. This essentially outlines the need principle of correctional treatment proposed by Andrews and his colleagues (Andrews & Bonta, 2003; Andrews, Bonta & Hoge, 1990) in their earlier work on effective correctional treatment. In fact, their risk, need, and responsivity principles have received voluminous meta-analytic support in the treatment of offender populations (see Andrews et al., 1999; Dowden & Andrews, 1999, 2000, 2003 for examples).

Briefly, these principles state that treatment should be reserved for higher risk cases, should predominantly target criminogenic needs, and should use the most powerful social learning and cognitive-behavioral strategies of interpersonal influence outlined by Andrews et al. (1990). The operational definitions for these variables were derived directly from recent meta-analytic reviews of the broader correctional treatment literature conducted by Dowden and Andrews (1999, 2000, 2003). Although significantly enhanced treatment effects were found within RP programs that predominantly targeted criminogenic needs (Eta = .43) and used cognitive-behavioral/social learning strategies (Eta = .34), this was not the case under conditions of appropriate adherence to the risk principle (Eta = .16). More specifically, the risk level of the offender did not impact the effectiveness of the program to a significant degree. Dowden and Andrews (1999, 2000, 2003) created a new composite type-of-treatment variable in their recent meta-analytic reviews of the correctional treatment literature. More specifically, they simply counted the number of principles that were adhered to within a particular program and assigned the corresponding score. In other words, human service programs that targeted each of the principles of risk, need, and responsivity were assigned a score of 3, and human service programs that failed to target any of these principles were coded zero.

For the purposes of this investigation, a three-level composite variable was used where the programs that targeted none or one of the principles were scored in the same category. The analysis revealed that the appropriateness of treatment (as evidenced by the aggregate application of the risk, need, and responsivity principles) was a significant determinant of treatment outcome. More specifically, treatment effectiveness increased in a linear fashion with RP programs having the greatest impact when all three of the principles were adhered to within the program (mean r = .22, k = 31) and having moderate effects when two of these principles were targeted (mean r = .12, k = 23). It should be noted that RP programs offered in the relative absence of these principles (i.e., one or less) had absolutely no impact on recidivism (mean r = .02, k = 8). This finding is worthy of note and suggests that the clinically relevant and psychologically informed principles of risk, need, and responsivity must be addressed within a RP program in order for it to achieve its desired therapeutic impact.

One of the concerns with meta-analytic statistics is that studies of differing quality commonly are combined without any consideration of the methodological rigor with which they were conducted. Consequently, Table 15.2 presents the simple and partial correlation coefficients with effect size (with type of treatment controlled) for each of the strongest methodological variables identified by Andrews et al. (1999). Inspection of Table 15.2 reveals that only the presence of an involved evaluator continued to maintain a significant relationship with effect size once the effects of type of treatment were controlled (see Partial Eta).

OVERALL THOUGHTS AND DIRECTIONS FOR THE FUTURE OF RP WITHIN CORRECTIONAL TREATMENT

Although the present meta-analysis revealed that RP programs were associated with moderate mean reductions in recidivism, these impacts are relatively

TABLE 15.2: Methodological and Control Variables and Effect Size

Methodological Variable	No	Yes	Eta	Partial Eta
CJ Sponsor	.14 (13)	.15 (51)	.03ns	—
CJ Referral	.17 (4)	.15 (60)	−.04ns	—
Nonresidential	.16 (43)	.14 (21)	−.08ns	—
Small Sample (n < 100)	.12 (45)	.23 (19)	.37**	.18ns
New Program (less than 2 years)	.12 (35)	.19 (29)	.23*	.14ns
Involved Evaluator	.11 (46)	.25 (18)	.44**	.28*[1]
Random Assignment	.13 (52)	.18 (12)	.12ns	—

[1] It should be noted that the partial Eta for Appropriate Treatment far outweighs that for Involved Evaluator (e.g., .42 vs. .28).

unimpressive when compared with the mean effect size reported for generic human service programs in past meta-analytic reviews (Dowden & Andrews, 1999a, 1999b, 2000; Lipsey, 1995; Losel, 1995). In other words, RP programs do not seem to "add value" to other forms of correction intervention, as has been argued by Hanson (2000). However, subsequent analyses revealed that this pessimistic conclusion might not be warranted, when one considers the broader array of trends in the evaluation studies. These analyses also identified some issues that must be considered in future RP research.

This investigation revealed that certain elements of the RP model are associated with more positive treatment effects than others. For example, training significant others in the program model is of importance for significantly enhancing program effectiveness. In fact, the value of this type of intervention strategy recently has been recognized in the treatment of juvenile sex offenders (see Zankman & Bonomo, 2004). However, perhaps the strongest support for this can be extracted from the family intervention literature for young offenders. More specifically, a recent meta-analysis (Dowden, Medveduke & Andrews, 2005) reported that family treatment programs that had family members participating in the therapeutic milieu were associated with a significantly higher mean effect size than programs where this was not the case. Given the replication of this finding in another clinical area, the importance of incorporating family members into RP treatment should be seen as of paramount importance for future program success.

Analyses also revealed that other aspects of RP training yielded significantly better programmatic outcomes. More specifically, identifying the offense-chain/ high-risk situations and engaging in relapse rehearsal were associated with significant mean reductions in reoffending. The importance of identifying high-risk situations and offense precursors is listed as a criminogenic need by Andrews and his colleagues (Andrews & Bonta, 2003; Andrews, Bonta & Hoge, 1990). The fact that it has received such strong empirical support in the present review of RP programming is not surprising as the therapeutic benefits of the need principle have been demonstrated across a wide variety of offender populations and programs (e.g., Dowden & Andrews, 1999a, 1999b, 2000, 2003).

In addition, the concept of relapse rehearsal can be seen as equivalent to role playing, which has been forwarded as one of the most crucial elements of Core Correctional Practice (CCP) (Andrews & Carvell, 1998). CCP outlines the characteristics and techniques of effective correctional staff, and again has received strong meta-analytic support regarding its applicability within offender treatment (Dowden & Andrews, 2004).

Conversely, teaching an offender how to deal with failure situations and the provision of booster sessions were not as effective in reducing offender recidivism. Although this may seem surprising, these two aspects of RP do not fit within the criminogenic need principle outlined by Andrews and colleagues. More specifically, teaching an offender skills for appropriately dealing with failure situations does not necessarily mean that the offender has also received appropriate skills training that will help him or her avoid future offending behavior. If the program predominantly or solely targets noncriminogenic needs (e.g., dynamic risk factors that are not related to criminal activity), obtaining skills in coping with failure or the provision of booster sessions (e.g., additional exposure to the program content) will not reduce reoffending. Rather, voluminous meta-analytic evidence suggests programs not adhering to the need principle do not result in reductions in reoffending.

The present study also reveals that increasing the number of RP elements utilized within the program significantly enhances its therapeutic potential in terms of reducing recidivism. It should be noted that this finding supports the multimodal hypothesis (Lipsey, 1995), which argues that offender rehabilitation programs are maximally effective when they address multiple need areas. Past meta-analytic research has supported this hypothesis, but only when the targeting of criminogenic needs is predominant. More specifically, Dowden and Andrews (1999a, 1999b, 2000) have reported a linear increase in the mean effect sizes of programs that target a larger number of criminogenic needs, a trend that does not exist when noncriminogenic needs are considered. Therefore, once again, it is not surprising that increasing the number of RP components would be associated with enhanced program effectiveness.

An additional finding of interest related to how the RP program was described. More specifically, analyses revealed that programs that identified and detailed their RP elements yielded significantly higher means effect sizes than those that were nonspecific in their discussion of RP (i.e., they only used the global term of RP without any further explanation). Therefore, further examination of whether the modest effect of RP programs is due to a weakness in adapting the model to offender rehabilitation or due to the inappropriate labeling of a program as RP when it does not have the necessary components is warranted. Preliminary support for this latter interpretation is provided by Laws (1999), who highlighted that correctional treatment programs commonly are categorized as RP without providing any evidence to support this assertion. Regardless of which interpretation is correct, future RP evaluations must thoroughly describe their treatment elements such that a better understanding of this approach may be obtained.

It should be noted that the importance of articulating treatment strategies and techniques also has been found in meta-analyses of the broader correctional treatment literature. For example, Andrews and Dowden (2005) found that programs that had a program manual and were more specific about the theoretical underpinnings of their treatment model yielded significantly higher mean effect sizes than those that did not. In addition, and more directly related, Dowden and Andrews (2003) uncovered a similar finding in the family treatment literature whereby programs that specifically articulated their program targets (e.g., specifying a particular goal such as increasing family communication/interactions or supervision practices) yielded a significantly higher mean effect size than those programs that mentioned only generic terms (e.g., family counseling).

One possible interpretation of this trend is that in some cases, program developers are using "buzz words" that are *en vogue* at the time to promote the therapeutic benefits of their program, though not really understanding what they entail. In other words, since family programs are some of the most empirically supported types of correctional programs, it makes sense for a developer/administrator to mention that their program includes a family treatment element when marketing the program. However, this creates the danger of combining legitimate and highly specific family treatment programs with those that just offer peripheral services. Additional research exploring the true dynamics of this state of affairs is the next crucial step in the field of correctional rehabilitation research and applies equally well to the RP field.

The present meta-analysis has joined the long line of previous studies providing strong empirical support for the principles of need and general responsivity as these principles made significant contributions to program effectiveness within RP programs. Programs that did not predominantly target criminogenic needs along with RP elements or failed to use cognitive-behavioral/social learning strategies were not associated with reductions in offender recidivism.

The inability of the risk principle to significantly impact effect size magnitude has been reported in a previous meta-analysis (Dowden & Andrews, 2000). A likely explanation is that this is more an issue with coding as opposed to an inherent weakness in the principle itself. For example, primary correctional program evaluations that report treatment outcomes separately for low- and high-risk cases generally provide much stronger empirical evidence for the risk principle (Andrews & Dowden, 2006). Although very few cases separated the results accordingly for this meta-analysis of RP programs, the preliminary results suggest that within this smaller sample of studies, the evidence for the risk principle was much stronger (Eta = .23 as opposed to Eta = .16 in the larger set). Therefore, it is suggested that future RP program evaluations ensure that outcome data are separated according to the risk level of the offender in order to produce a more definitive answer to this question.

The findings regarding the methodological and control variables followed previous meta-analytic research. In fact, it should be noted that for two of the three significant moderating variables, introduction of appropriate treatment (based on the principles of risk, need, and responsivity) reduced their impact to nonsignificant levels. In other words, when the principles of risk, need, and responsivity are introduced into the analysis, the methodological variables that previously held a significant relationship with effect size now have a negligible effect. Thus, adherence to the principles of risk, need, and responsivity are much more important than these methodological characteristics.

When the analyses shifted to involved evaluator, however, both type of treatment and involved evaluator continued to make independent and significant contributions to the magnitude of the mean effect size. Nonetheless, it should be noted that the partial Eta for type of treatment (partial Eta = .15) exceeded that for involved evaluator (partial Eta = .10). Furthermore, and arguably more important, previous researchers (Andrews & Dowden, 2005; Dowden & Andrews, 1999, 2000; Lipsey, 1995) have proposed that an involved evaluator[1] should not be viewed as a form of bias, but rather as a sign of enhanced program integrity, which greatly increases the therapeutic potential of appropriate correctional programs. Further to this point, a recent meta-analysis by Andrews and Dowden (2005) reported that studies in which an evaluator was involved had a significantly higher number of indicators of program integrity present, which suggests involved evaluators take more of an interest in the clinical framework of the program.

There are several directions for future research highlighted within this meta-analysis. First and foremost, we recommend that additional controlled outcome research is still required on the RP model. In particular, program evaluators are strongly encouraged to report on the RP techniques that are being utilized within the program so we can have a better understanding of the "black box" of RP. This is a criticism that has been previously levied against the broader field of correctional treatment and so RP proponents must address these concerns to ensure this approach is widely adopted and accepted within the field or else it may be seen as a buzz word without any legitimate therapeutic value in certain circles.

Finally, and arguably more important, researchers need to start exploring the differential effectiveness of RP across different populations of offenders (defined by offense type or demographic characteristics). Given the recent emphasis on gender-responsive (see Bloom, 1999; Convington, 1999; Dowden & Andrews, 2005) and racially responsive treatment, carefully scrutinizing the effectiveness of RP within these populations is warranted. In addition, given the fact that RP originally was designed to be utilized with addictive behaviors, research into exploring whether this approach is equally effective with substance abusing versus sexual versus general offenders is very much in need of an answer. More importantly, research needs to identify whether certain elements of RP (e.g.,

---

[1] For the purposes of this meta-analysis, an Involved Evaluator is defined as an evaluator who was highly involved in the design and/or implementation of the program being evaluated.

identifying high-risk situations versus teaching coping styles and/or strategies for dealing with failure situations) are more applicable to certain types of offender populations than others. The appropriateness of this form of treatment for sexual offenders also must be addressed in the near future such that all RP programs do not get painted with one correctional brush.

ACKNOWLEDGEMENTS

The authors would like to thank Paul Verbrugge for his assistance in the collection and organization of the studies used in this article.

REFERENCES

Andrews, D.A., Bonta, J. (2003). *The psychology of criminal conduct, 3e.* Cincinnati, OH: Anderson.

Andrews, D.A., Bonta, J., Hoge, R.D. (1990). Classification for effective rehabilitation: Rediscovering psychology. *Criminal Justice and Behavior* **17**:19–52.

Andrews, D.A., Dowden, C. (2005). Managing correctional treatment for reduced recidivism. A meta-analytic review of program integrity. *Legal and Criminological Psychology* **10**:173–187.

Andrews, D.A., Dowden, C. (2006). Risk principle of case classification in correctional treatment: A meta-analytic investigation. *International Journal of Offender Therapy and Comparative Criminology* **50**:88–100.

Andrews, D.A., Dowden, C., Gendreau, P. (1999, November). *New meta-analytic tests of the principles of human service, risk, need and general responsivity.* Symposium presented at the annual meeting of the American Society of Criminology, Toronto, Ontario.

Andrews, D.A., Zinger, I., Hoge, R.D., Bonta, J., Gendreau, P., Cullen, F.T. (1990). Does correctional treatment work? A clinically relevant and psychologically informed meta-analysis. *Criminology* **28**:369–404.

Antonowicz, D.H., Ross, R.R. (1994). Essential components of successful rehabilitation programs for offenders. *International Journal of Offender Therapy and Comparative Criminology* **38**:97–104.

Antonuccio, D. (2004). Integrating behavioral interventions for smoking into primary care. In Cummings, N.A., Duckworth, M.P., O'Donohue, W.T., Ferguson, K.E., eds., *Early detection and treatment of substance abuse within integrated primary care*, 181–195. Reno, NV: Context Press.

Bakker, L., Ward, T., Cryer, M., Hudson, S.M. (2000). Reducing recidivism in driving while disqualified: A treatment evaluation. *Criminal Justice and Behavior* **27**:531–560.

Cullen, F.T., Gendreau, P. (1989). The effectiveness of correctional rehabilitation. In Goodstein, L., MacKenzie, D.L., eds., *The American prison: Issues in research policy*, 23–24. New York: Plenum.

Dowden, C., Andrews, D.A. (1999). What works for female offenders: A meta-analytic review. *Crime and Delinquency* **45**:438–452.

Dowden, C., Andrews, D.A. (1999). What works in young offender treatment: A meta-analysis. *Forum on Corrections Research* **11**(2):21–24.

Dowden, C., Andrews, D.A. (2000). Effective correctional treatment and violent recidivism: A meta-analysis. *Canadian Journal of Criminology* **42**:449–476.

Dowden, C., Andrews, D.A. (2003). Does family intervention work for delinquents? Results of a meta-analysis. *Canadian Journal of Criminology and Criminal Justice* **45**:327–342.

Dowden, C., Andrews, D.A. (2004). The importance of staff practice in delivering effective correctional treatment: A meta-analytic review of Core Correctional Practice. *International Journal of Offender Therapy and Comparative Criminology* **48**:203–214.

Dowden, C., Antonowicz, D.H., Andrews, D.A. (2003). The effectiveness of relapse prevention with offenders: A meta-analysis. *International Journal of Offender Therapy and Comparative Criminology* **47**:516–528.

Dowden, C., Medveduke, D., Andrews, D.A. (2005, May). *The importance of treatment targets and program design for the delivery of effective family treatment to juvenile delinquents: A meta-analysis.* Poster presented at the annual meeting of the Canadian Psychological Association, Montreal, Quebec.

Echeburua, E., Fernandez-Montalvo, J. (2005). Psychological treatment of slot-machine pathological gambling: New perspectives. *Journal of Gambling Studies* **21**:21–26.

George, W.H., Marlatt, G.A. (1989). Introduction. In Laws, D.R., ed., *Relapse prevention with sex offenders*, 1–31. New York, NY: Guilford.

Gendreau, P. (1996). The principles of effective intervention with offenders. In Harland, A., ed., *Choosing correctional options that work*. Thousand Oaks, CA: Sage.

Glass, G.V., McGaw, B., Smith, M.L. (1981). *Meta-analysis of social research*. Beverly Hills: Sage.

Groner, J., French, G., Ahijevych, K., Wewers, M.E. (2005). Process evaluation of a nurse-delivered smoking relapse prevention program for new mothers. *Journal of Community Health Nursing* **22**:157–167.

Hanson, R.K. (2000). What is so special about relapse prevention? In Laws, D.R., Hudson, S.M., Ward, T., eds., *Remaking relapse prevention with sex offenders: A sourcebook*, 27–38. Thousand Oaks, CA: Sage.

Hudson, S.M., Ward, T. (2000). Relapse prevention: Assessment and treatment implications. In Laws, D.R., Hudson, S.M., Ward, T., eds., *Remaking relapse prevention with sex offenders: A sourcebook*, 102–122, Thousand Oaks, CA: Sage.

Kaplan, A.S. (2002). Psychological treatments for anorexia nervosa: A review of published studies and promising new directions. *Canadian Journal of Psychiatry* **47**:235–242.

Launay, G. (2001). Relapse prevention with sex offenders: Practice, theory and research. *Criminal Behaviour and Mental Health* **11**:38–54.

Laws, D.R. (1989). *Relapse prevention with sex offenders*. New York: Guilford.

Laws, D.R. (1999). Relapse prevention: The state of the art. *Journal of Interpersonal Violence* **14**:285–302.

Laws, D.R. (2003). The rise and fall of relapse prevention. *Australian Psychologist* **38**:22–30.

Lipsey, M.W. (1995). What do we learn from 400 research studies on the effectiveness of treatment with juvenile delinquents? In McGuire, J., ed., *What works: Reducing reoffending—Guidelines from research and practice*, 63–78. Chichester, England: Wiley.

Lipsey, M.W., Wilson, D.B. (1998). Effective intervention for serious juvenile offenders: A synthesis of research. In Loeber, R., Farrington, D.P., eds., *Serious and violent juvenile offenders: Risk factors and successful interventions*, 313–345. London: Sage Publications, Inc.

Losel, F. (1995). The efficacy of correctional treatment: A review and synthesis of meta-evaluations. In J. McGuire, ed., *What works: Reducing reoffending—Guidelines from research and practice*, 79–111. Chichester, England: Wiley.

Losel, F. (1996). Effective correctional programming: What empirical research tells us and what it doesn't. *Forum on Corrections Research* **8**:33–36.

Mann, R.E., Webster, S.D., Schofield, C., Marshall, W.L. (2004). Approach versus avoidance goals in relapse prevention with sexual offenders. *Sexual Abuse: A Journal of Research and Treatment* **16**:65–75.

Marlatt, G.A., Gordon, J.R. (1985). *Relapse prevention: Maintenance strategies in the treatment of addictive behaviour.* New York: Guilford.

Marques, J.K., Wiederanders, M., Day, D.M., Nelson, C., van Ommeren, A. (2005). Effects of a relapse prevention program on sexual recidivism: Final results from California's Sex Offender

Treatment and Evaluation (SOTEP) project. *Sexual Abuse: A Journal of Research and Treatment* **17**:79–105.

McCown, W.G. (2004). Treating compulsive and problem gambling. In Holman, R.E., ed., *Handbook of addictive disorders: A practical guide to diagnosis and treatment*, 161–194. John Wiley & Sons. Hoboken, NJ.

Peters, R.H. (1993). Relapse prevention approaches in the criminal justice system. In Gorski, T.T., Kelley, J.M., Havens, L., Peters, R.H., eds., *Relapse prevention and the substance-abusing criminal offender*. Technical Assistance Publication (TAP) Series, Number 8DHHS Pub. N (SMA) 95-3071. Center for Substance Abuse Treatment: U.S. Department of Health and Human Services.

Peterson, C.B., Wonderlich, S.A., Mitchell, J.E., Crow, S.J. (2004). Integrative cognitive therapy for bulimia nervosa. In Thompson, K.J., ed., *Handbook of eating disorders and obesity*, 245–262. Hoboken, NJ: John Wiley & Sons.

Pithers, W.D., Marques, J.K., Gibat, C.C., Marlatt, G.A. (1983). Relapse prevention with sexual aggressiveness: A self-control model of treatment and maintenance of change. In Greer, J.G., Stuart, I.R., eds., *The sexual aggressor*, 214–239. New York: Van Nostrand Reinhold.

Rosenthal, R. (1991) *Meta-analytic procedures for social research* (Revised Edition). Newbury Park, CA: Sage.

Stewart, T.M., Williamson, D.A. (2003). Body positive: A new treatment for persistent body image disturbances in partially recovered eating disorders. *Clinical Case Studies* **2**:154–166.

Tavares, H., Zilberman, M.L., el-Guebaly, N. (2003). Are there cognitive and behavioural approaches specific to the treatment of pathological gambling? *Canadian Journal of Psychiatry* **48**: 22–27.

Ward, T. (2000). Relapse prevention: Critique and reformulation. *The Journal of Sexual Aggression* **5**:118–133.

Ward, T., Hudson, S.M. (1996). Relapse prevention: A critical analysis. *Sexual Abuse: A Journal of Research and Treatment* **8**:177–200.

Ward, T., Hudson, S.M. (2000). A self-regulation model of relapse prevention. In Laws, D.R., Hudson, S.M., Ward, T., eds., *Remaking relapse prevention with sex offenders: A sourcebook*, 177–200. Thousand Oaks, CA: Sage.

Ward, T., Hudson, S.M., Keenan, T. (1998). A self-regulation model of the sexual offense process. *Sexual Abuse: A Journal of Research and Treatment* **10**:141–157.

Witkiewitz, K., Marlatt, A.G., Walker, D. (2005). Mindfulness-based relapse prevention for alcohol and substance use disorders. *Journal of Cognitive Psychotherapy* **19**:211–228.

Wolf, F.M. (1986). *Meta-analysis: Quantitative methods for research synthesis*. Newbury Park, CA: Sage.

Zankman, S., Bonomo, J. (2004). Working with parents to reduce juvenile sex offender recidivism. *Journal of Child Sexual Abuse* **13**:139–154.

16

DRINKING AS AN EPIDEMIC—A SIMPLE MATHEMATICAL MODEL WITH RECOVERY AND RELAPSE

FABIO SÁNCHEZ

Biological Statistics and Computational Biology
Cornell University
Ithaca, New York

XIAOHONG WANG, AND
CARLOS CASTILLO-CHÁVEZ

Department of Mathematics
Arizona State University
Tempe, Arizona

DENNIS M. GORMAN

School of Rural Public Health
Texas A&M Health Science Center
Bryan, Texas

PAUL J. GRUENEWALD

Prevention Research Center
Berkeley, California

INTRODUCTION

The outcomes (patterns) associated with various biological and sociological processes are often the result of interactions or contacts between individuals, groups, subpopulations, or populations. For example, some aspects associated with the process of language acquisition can be thought of as the result of non-specified contacts between those who speak the language and those who have yet to acquire it. Although contacts between individuals in different states are at the heart of these processes, the definition of "contact" (effective contact) is highly dependent on context, population structure, and other factors. Starting with the pioneering work of Ross (1911), researchers who conduct studies of social and health problems in which data are scarce have often relied on *simple* mean field deterministic models to generate insights and understanding on the relative role of various mechanisms of disease spread. The analysis of such mathematical models is used to generate hypotheses or to gain insights (with limited data) on the conversion process (change in epidemiological status) and ways of controlling disease dynamics under clearly specified assumptions (Chowell, Castillo-Chávez, Fenimore et al., 2004; Chowell, Fenimore, Castillo-Garsow & Castillo-Chávez, 2003; Chowell, Hengartner, Castillo-Chávez, Fenimore & Hyman, 2004). In the case of social and behavioral processes, challenges arise from the fact that the dynamics of these processes at the population level are the result of nonlinear interactions between individuals in different states (that is, the whole is not the sum of its parts).

Despite such complexity, epidemiological contact models have also been applied to the study of the dynamics of social and behavioral processes such as eating disorders (González, Huerta-Sánchez, Ortiz-Nieves, Vázquez & Kribs-Zaleta, 2003), drug addictions, treatment, and prevention (Behrens, Caulkins, Tragler, Haunschmied & Feichtinger, 1999; Epstein, 1997; Song, Castillo-Garsow, Castillo-Chávez, et al., 2006; Winkler, Caulkins, Behrens & Tragler, 2004), violence (Patton & Arboleda-Florez, 2004), and even the diffusion of knowledge (Bettencourt, Cintron-Arias, Kaiser & Castillo-Chávez, 2006). Naturally, there are differences in the generation of addictive behaviors and the transmission of infectious diseases but the fact remains that the acquisition of both can be modeled (in the context of specific questions) as the likely result of contacts between individuals in different states in specified environments. For example, the dynamics of alcohol use among young people and the role of "supportive environments" on the development and maintenance of heavy drinking, alcohol abuse and dependence, and alcohol-related problems among adults are predicated upon the combined effects of social influence and access to alcohol (Cox, Yeates, Gilligan & Hosier, 2001; Gorman, 2001; Stockwell & Gruenewald, 2001; Stockwell, Gruenewald, Toumbourou & Loxley, 2005; Treno & Holder, 2001). Thus, additional understanding of the dynamics of drinking behaviors may result from the use of a perspective that models problem drinking as the result of contacts of "at-risk" individuals with individuals in distinct drinking states.

MATHEMATICAL MODEL OF DRINKING LAPSE

Problem drinking is modeled as an "acquired" state, the result of frequent (i.e., high number of contacts) or intense (i.e., high likelihood of conversion) interactions between individuals in three drinking states (susceptible, problem drinkers, and temporarily recovered) within a *specified drinking environment*.

The goal of the model is to identify mechanisms (quantitatively speaking) that facilitate or limit the conversion of a population of nondrinkers to one of drinkers within prespecified environments. The process of quantification helps to understand the role of social forces on the time evolution of drinking. Knowledge of these factors may be useful in the development of effective drinking control policies, in the evaluation of treatment interventions, and in the identification and ranking of mechanisms that facilitate the survival of a culture of drinking.

We describe the dynamics of drinking within the context of the classic SIR (Susceptible-Infected-Recovered) epidemiological framework (Brauer & Castillo-Chávez, 2001). The population in question is divided into the following drinking classes: occasional and moderate drinkers (S); problem drinkers (D); and temporarily recovered (R). It is assumed that the population size remains constant; that is, that the time scale of interest is such that the size of the population under consideration, N, does not change significantly over the length of the study. New recruits join the population as occasional and moderate drinkers (S) and mix at random (i.e., homogeneous mixing) with the rest of the members of the population (see appendix for mathematical details).

The dynamics of the model support two distinct states: the outcomes of the nonlinear interactions between problem drinkers and others in their shared drinking environment. The nature of these distinct outcomes depends in general on the size of the initial proportion of drinkers, the overall average residence time in the drinking environment, and the intensity of the interactions (in this environment) between problem drinkers and the rest of the residents (regulars to this environment). The "invasion" of the environment of a population, composed of moderate drinkers, by a small number of problem drinkers, may increase or decrease the proportion of problem drinkers in the invaded populations. The success or failure of such an invasion process depends on the average total time spent by problem drinkers and residents in this environment and the impact that the interactions between moderate and problem drinkers have on the drinking status of residents. It is assumed that individuals that change their status only do it by moving from moderate to problem drinker or from temporarily recovered back to problem drinker (a class with no members prior to invasion).

The social outcomes that facilitate transmission are modeled by the functions, the incidence "infection" rates, B(S,D) and G(D,R) of the state variables (see appendix for mathematical details). It is assumed that individuals who share a common drinking environment do interact and that such interactions are only frequency-dependent; that is, the larger the proportion of one type, the more likely it is that one will drink with "him" or "her."

TABLE 16.1:   Description of Parameters and Parameter Distribution Functions

Parameter	Description	Min	Max	Median	Std	Distribution Function
β	Transmission rate	0.0012	1.3	0.6434	0.3710	$Unif(0.0001, 0.4)$
μ	Per-person departure rate from drinking environments	0.0001	0.5	0.2553	0.1437	$Unif(0.5, 1)$
ϕ	Per-person recovery rate	$5.43e^{-4}$	0.4646	0.1033	0.0736	$Beta(a = 2, b = 15)$
ρ	Per-person relapse rate	$5e^{-8}$	$3.39e^{-4}$	$3.83e^{-5}$	$5.46e^{-5}$	$exp(5.48e^{-3})$

From the analysis of the "drinking-free" equilibrium—that is, the state where a drinking culture does not exist—we compute the model's basic reproductive number ($\Re_0$), which provides a measure of the resilience of this state to the invasion of problem drinkers. This ratio gives the average number of secondary cases generated by a "typical" problem drinker in a population of moderate drinkers. That is, a population where problem drinkers are so rare that their numbers are insignificant (treatment is not yet needed). $\Re_0$, computed in the situation when the R-class does not yet exist, provides a measure of the capacity for initial growth of drinking behaviors per generation in a population with few problem drinkers. $\Re_0 = \beta L$ where β is a measure of the influence of problem drinkers on S-residents and $L = \dfrac{1}{\mu}$ denotes the average overall total average residence time of individuals in this environment. $\Re_0$ decreases if either L (at-risk window) or β (transmission rate) or both decrease and it increases if either or both increase.

Treatment will affect the ability of problem drinkers to reproduce. Consequently, the reproductive number with recovery via treatment is $\Re_\phi = \dfrac{\beta}{\mu + \phi}$, where β is the influence rate, and $\dfrac{1}{\mu + \phi}$ represents the average time a problem drinker spends on the drinking class D (at-risk window). We observe that $\Re_0 > \Re_\phi$ if $\phi > 0$. SDR dynamics are rather simple. If $\Re_0 < 1$ and the number of problem drinkers in the community is initially low then it is *not* possible to establish a culture of drinking that is $D(t) \to 0$ as $t \to \infty$. However, if $\Re_0 > 1$ even the introduction of a single problem drinker will lead (within this framework) to the establishment of a culture of problem drinkers. The results here are not typical in epidemic models because the outcomes depend not only on the value of $\mathfrak{R}_\phi$ but on the size of the initial population of problem drinkers. Specifically, $\mathfrak{R}_\phi < 1$ does not guarantee the eradication of drinking communities. Why? Because although treatment reduces the residence time of D-individuals in the system as regular drinkers, in the process it can create a second pool of susceptible whose level of susceptibility is measured by the strength of environmentally induced relapse rates. Hence, even when the number of conversions generated by an average typical problem drinker ($\mathfrak{R}_\phi < 1$) is less than one in a community, with treatment a drinking culture can still be established as long as the effectiveness of treatment is low (high relapse rates). However, when $\mathfrak{R}_\phi > 1$ (treatment also not that effective) only one outcome is possible—a drinking community becomes established, that is, the persistence of a regular drinking class over time is guaranteed.

UNCERTAINTY AND SENSITIVITY ANALYSIS

The value of $\mathfrak{R}_\phi$ and the initial conditions determine whether or not a community of problem drinkers can be established in a population under treatment regime ϕ. There is a lot of uncertainty associated with the parameters that enter $\mathfrak{R}_\phi$. Thus, in order to better estimate the impact of variation in parameter ranges on dynamical outcomes, we conduct an uncertainty analysis on three dimensionless quantities, $\mathfrak{R}_\phi$, $\dfrac{\mathfrak{R}_c}{\mathfrak{R}_\phi}$, and $\mathfrak{R}_\rho$. $\mathfrak{R}_\rho$ is the number of secondary drinkers generated by a typical problem drinker in the population of temporarily recovered individuals and $\mathfrak{R}_c$ is the critical value of $\mathfrak{R}_\phi$ that leads to the elimination of a drinking community experiencing treatment regime ϕ (see Figure 16.1). We assigned probability distribution functions[1] to each of the parameters (see Table 16.1) in $\mathfrak{R}_\phi$, $\dfrac{\mathfrak{R}_c}{\mathfrak{R}_\phi}$, and $\mathfrak{R}_\rho$ based on our reading of the relevant literature pertaining to the initiation, maintenance, and cessation of alcohol use, and proceeded to study their impact on the corresponding $\mathfrak{R}_\phi$ and $\dfrac{\mathfrak{R}_c}{\mathfrak{R}_\phi}$ distributions. The level of uncertainty in the model's parameter values is explored via Monte Carlo[2] simulations (based on 1000 realizations). Figures 16.2 and 16.3 show the resulting histograms for $\mathfrak{R}_\phi$ and $\dfrac{\mathfrak{R}_c}{\mathfrak{R}_\phi}$.

[1] A graph of some precise quantitative measure of a character against its frequency of occurrence (helios.bto.ed.ac.uk/bto/glossary/d.htm).

[2] A trial-and-error method of repeated calculations to discover the best solution of a problem. Often used when a great number of variables are present, with interrelationships so extremely complex as to forestall straightforward analytical handling (www.control.co.kr/dic/dic-m.htm).

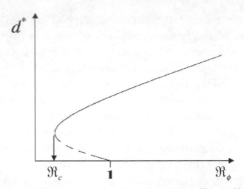

FIGURE 16.1:   Threshold Conditions: $\Re_c$ and $\Re_\phi$

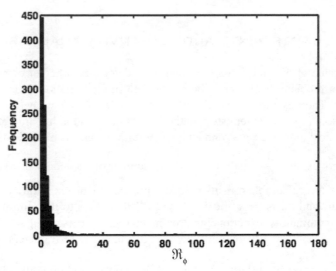

FIGURE 16.2:   Histogram for $\Re_\phi$. The mean is 3.12 with a standard deviation of 7.39 and 71% of $\Re_\phi > 1$

If $\dfrac{\Re_c}{\Re_\phi} < 1$ then the possibility of having two permanent problem drinking states exists. That is if $\dfrac{\Re_c}{\Re_\phi} < 1$, then the initial number of problem drinkers plays a major role on the dynamics of drinking. That is, for prespecified sets of parameter values that satisfy $\dfrac{\Re_c}{\Re_\phi} < 1$, there is a critical mass of problem drinkers that would lead to the establishment of a subpopulation of problem drinkers.

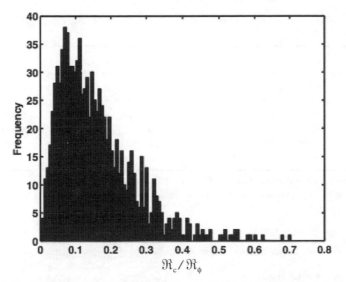

FIGURE 16.3: Histogram for $\mathfrak{R}_c/\mathfrak{R}_\phi$. The mean is 0.16 with a standard deviation of 0.11 and the median is 0.14

Next, we analyze the sensitivity of $\mathfrak{R}_\phi$, $\dfrac{\mathfrak{R}_c}{\mathfrak{R}_\phi}$, and $\mathfrak{R}_\rho$ to parameter variations; that is, we look at parameters that have a positive (increase) or negative (decrease) impact on these ratios. Using the partial rank correlation coefficient (PRCC[3]) we determined the qualitative relationship between the parameters and the threshold quantities previously described. The analysis showed that the alcohol recovery rate was the most significant (sensitive) parameter. Furthermore, if ϕ (recovery rate) is not small and the relapse rate ρ is high enough then the situation can actually worsen despite treatment effectiveness. In other words, whenever the initial rate of recovery from treatment and the subsequent relapse rate are high, then a critical mass of at-risk (highly susceptible) individuals that can reenter the problem drinker class is created.

From Table 16.2 we see that the transmission rate (β) has a negative effect on $\mathfrak{R}_\phi$ and $\dfrac{\mathfrak{R}_c}{\mathfrak{R}_\phi}$. In other words, it decreases both ratios but it has a greater effect on $\mathfrak{R}_\phi$. The relapse rate also (ρ) has a negative effect on $\mathfrak{R}_\rho$ and $\dfrac{\mathfrak{R}_c}{\mathfrak{R}_\phi}$, although it has a relatively strong effect on both ratios. The treatment rate (ϕ) has the

---

[3] The PRCC value indicates the effect (positive or negative) of the parameter in the quantities $\mathfrak{R}_\phi$, $\dfrac{\mathfrak{R}_c}{\mathfrak{R}_\phi}$, and $\mathfrak{R}_\rho$.

TABLE 16.2: Partial Rank Correlation Coefficient of $\mathfrak{R}_\phi$, $\mathfrak{R}_c/\mathfrak{R}_\phi$, and $\mathfrak{R}_\rho$ with Their Respective p-Values[a]

$\mathfrak{R}_\phi$			$\mathfrak{R}_\rho$			$\mathfrak{R}_c/\mathfrak{R}_\phi$		
Parameter	PRCC	p-Value	Parameter	PRCC	p-Value	Parameter	PRCC	p-Value
β	−0.263	0.000	ρ	−0.673	0.000	β	−0.085	0.007
ϕ	0.213	0.000	ϕ	0.079	0.013	ρ	−0.909	0.000
μ	0.066	0.036	μ	−0.031	0.036	ϕ	0.984	0.000
ρ	—	—	β	—	—	μ	0.021	0.500

[a]p-Value indicates the probability that the result attained is due to chance rather than a true relationship between measures. Small p-values indicate that it is highly unlikely that the results are due to chance.

biggest (positive) effect on $\dfrac{\mathfrak{R}_c}{\mathfrak{R}_\phi}$. In other words, if $\dfrac{\mathfrak{R}_c}{\mathfrak{R}_\phi} > 1$ the drinking community becomes established.

NUMERICAL SIMULATIONS

Numerical simulations are used to illustrate our model results on drinking dynamics. The most general model can support two permanent prevalent states when treatment only has short-term effect and relapse rates are high.

If the relapse rate is high, then the probability that we enter the region where we have two prevalent states in the problem drinking class is high and, consequently, the development of successful treatment programs is unlikely. In other words, once a drinking culture is established it is difficult to bring it to a low enough level to completely eliminate it. As soon as a drinking culture is established, the effectiveness of treatment becomes a critical factor in limiting and curtailing its influence. High rates of recovery with high relapse rates will not affect reductions in problem drinking. In fact, a new pool of high-risk "susceptible" previous problem drinkers can become part of such a drinking community. Drinking communities become difficult to eradicate under these circumstances.

In Figure 16.4a we illustrate the scenario where drinking behavior can become quickly established, and getting it under control would require a tremendous effort. We used a range of parameter values that allows for the possibility of two permanent prevalent states. If recovery and relapse rates are equal, $\mathfrak{R}_\phi < 1$, then it is possible to bring the drinking culture under control (see Figure 16.4b).

The number of initial problem drinkers introduced into the population plays a crucial role in the establishment of the drinking community. Figure 16.4c illustrates the role of initial conditions (initial number of occasional and moderate

TABLE 16.3: Estimate of $\Re_\phi$, $\Re_c/\Re_\phi$, and $\Re_\rho$ from 10 Monte Carlo Simulations

	$\Re_\phi$				$\Re_c/\Re_\phi$				$\Re_\rho$		
Realization	Mean	Std	$\Pr(\Re_\phi > 1)$	Realization	Mean	Std	Median	Realization	Mean	Std	$\Pr(\Re_\rho > 1)$
1	3.71	22.24	0.72	1	0.1549	0.1079	0.1278	1	3.68	5.56	0.77
2	3.27	7.80	0.70	2	0.1565	0.1166	0.1382	2	4.26	8.43	0.79
3	3.11	6.11	0.69	3	0.1677	0.1145	0.1399	3	4.07	12.22	0.76
4	2.79	3.86	0.70	4	0.1662	0.1133	0.1403	4	3.89	6.13	0.78
5	3.00	4.47	0.73	5	0.1687	0.1168	0.1413	5	4.07	9.98	0.76
6	3.00	7.23	0.70	6	0.1657	0.1161	0.1373	6	4.30	12.23	0.75
7	2.93	4.07	0.69	7	0.1642	0.1149	0.1564	7	3.71	6.74	0.75
8	2.95	4.96	0.71	8	0.1659	0.1130	0.1397	8	4.22	7.58	0.76
9	3.20	6.43	0.73	9	0.1620	0.1115	0.1363	9	3.78	7.53	0.75
10	3.23	6.73	0.72	10	0.1597	0.1094	0.1354	10	3.73	5.74	0.77
Mean	3.12	7.39	0.71	Mean	0.1642	0.1134	0.1373	Mean	3.97	8.21	0.76
SE	0.0812	1.7049	0.0053	SE	0.0042	0.0003	0.0039	SE	0.0771	0.7880	0.0042
CV	0.0823	0.7296	0.0235	CV	0.0255	0.0267	0.0281	CV	0.0614	0.3034	0.0173

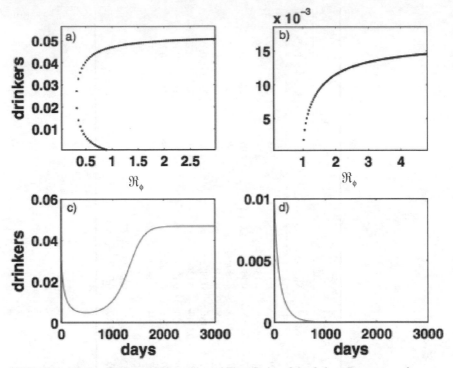

FIGURE 16.4: Backward Bifurcation and Time Series of the d-class. *Parameter values*: $\mu = 0.0000548$, $\phi = 0.2$, $\rho = 0.21$, and $\beta = [0.001,1.3]$. A time series plot of the system with different initial conditions. *Lower left*: $s_0 = 0.97$, $d_0 = 0.03$, and $r_0 = 0$. *Lower right*: $s_0 = 0.99$, $d_0 = 0.01$, and $r_0 = 0$. *Parameter values*: $\mu = 0.0000548$, $\beta = 0.19$, $\phi = 0.2$, and $\rho = 0.21$

drinkers, problem drinkers, and recovered individuals) in the presence of two drinking endemic states (a backward bifurcation). Setting the initial parameter for problem drinkers within the population at just 3 percent is sufficient to establish a community of drinkers. Such a situation might occur, for example, when a new class of freshmen arrives at college, especially if this is comprised of a large number of drinkers with the opportunity to selectively interact with one another in high-risk environments (Duncan, Boisjoly, Kremer, Levy & Eccles, 2005; Weschler & Kuo, 2003). The critical proportion of problem drinkers may determine whether or not a drinking culture becomes endemic (established) even under unfavorable conditions). In contrast, when we start with less than 3 percent of the population as problem drinkers then the drinking community is eliminated (see Figure 16.4d).

DISCUSSION

We introduced a simple mathematical model to describe the dynamics of drinking behaviors generated from contacts between individuals in shared drinking environments. This simple model, despite its limitations, has generated some useful insights. Specifically, the basic reproductive number (as a function of treatment), is not always the key to controlling drinking within the population. This is especially the case when recovery and relapse rates are high. High relapse rates will occur when treatment programs have only short-term positive effects. This finding is in line with the idea that the initial lapse that follows treatment is best represented as a nonlinear dynamic system with abrupt transitions between sobriety and heavy drinking that can be triggered by relatively small changes in risk (Hufford, Witkiewitz, Shields, Kodya & Caruso, 2003; Witkiewitz, 2005). Of course, what is of central importance here is the type of drinking to which individuals return following this initial lapse. One possible outcome is a return to the problematic level of drinking that led them into treatment (relapse), and another is to more moderate and less problematic patterns of consumption (pro-lapse) (Witkiewitz & Marlatt, 2004). As noted by Witkiewitz (2005), engaging in any form of drinking following treatment is nearly always considered as a mark failure, given the abstinence orientation of the vast majority of treatment modalities. However, from a harm reduction perspective, it is the consequences associated with post-treatment drinking that is important rather than drinking *per se* (Marlatt & Witkiewitz, 2002; Witkiewitz, 2005).

Model results and analyses also show that the propagation of drinking behaviors is the result of two conversion processes: *susceptible* to *drinker* and *recovered* to *drinker*. Furthermore, in contrast to classic epidemiology, outbreaks (sudden growth in the number of problem drinkers) are possible. In this last situation, initial conditions (the number of problem drinkers initially introduced into the population) play an essential role in the establishment of drinking communities. The case when the drinking community is established due to the large number of problem drinkers in the population is enhanced by intervention programs with high relapse rates. Under this scenario the control of drinking communities via treatment may be extremely difficult. It may be more effective to try to limit the average residence times of susceptible individuals in drinking environments (i.e., the average time they spend in places in which alcohol is available and drinking is commonplace). Indeed, this may be the most efficient way to proceed until treatments with more sustained effects are identified and widely implemented. This approach would require the extension and refinement of existing local control measures and community-based interventions (Stockwell & Gruenewald, 2001; Treno & Holder, 2001).

Recent findings by Witkiewitz (2006) have shown that within the first year the majority of drinkers that receive treatment lapse to a lighter drinking state (low-risk on S-class). However, some lapse to either moderate or heavy drinking. In the current setting, we have explored a simple model where lapses occur to what we call problem drinkers. Though our current model does not incorporate lapses to different drinking classes we are currently looking at a new model where this is taking into consideration using the recent findings by Witkiewitz (2006).

Finally, it should be noted that a key limitation of our model is that it does not incorporate relapse to different drinking classes following treatment. Rather we explored a simple model in which all the relapses that occurred among problem drinkers were treated as equivalent. However, empirical evidence shows that recovery from problem drinking among both treated and untreated individuals can vary considerably both in terms of the level of drinking involved and types of problems experienced (Dawson, Grant, Stinson, Chou, Huang & Ruan, 2005; Sobell, Sobell, Connors & Agrawal, 2003; Witkiewitz, 2005). For example, recent findings by Witkiewitz (2006) indicate that the majority of drinkers that receive treatment relapse to lighter drinking within the first year. In future models we will take into account this range of possible outcomes among the recovered class and explore the effects of this heterogeneity on the population dynamics.

ACKNOWLEDGEMENTS

This work was conducted under National Institute of Alcohol Abuse and Alcoholism Contract #HHSN281200410012C (P.J. Gruenewald—PI). The first author acknowledges the support of the Alfred P. Sloan Foundation and Cornell University.

REFERENCES

Behrens, D.A., Caulkins, J.P., Tragler, G., Haunschmied, J.L., Feichtinger, G. (1999). A dynamic model of drug initiation: Implications for treatment and drug control. *Mathematical Biosciences* **159**:1–20.

Bettencourt, L.M.A., Cintron-Arias, A., Kaiser, D.I., Castillo-Chávez, C. (2006). The power of a good idea: Quantitative modeling of the spread of ideas from epidemiological models. *Physica A* **364**:513–536.

Booth, B.M., Fortney, S.M., Fortney, J.C., Curran, G.M., Kirchner, J.E. (2001). Short-term course of drinking in an untreated sample of at-risk drinkers. *Journal of Studies on Alcohol* **62**: 580–588.

Borsari, B., Carey, K.B. (2001). Peer influences on college drinking: A review of the research. *Journal of Substance Abuse* **13**:391–424.

Brauer, F., Castillo-Chávez, C. (2001). *Mathematical Models in Population Biology and Epidemiology* (Texts in Applied Mathematics 40). New York: Springer-Verlag.

Chowell, G., Castillo-Chávez, C., Fenimore, P.W., Kribs-Zaleta, C.M., Arriola, L., Hyman, J.M. (2004). Model parameters and outbreak control for SARS, *Emerging Infectious Diseases* **10**: 1258–1263.

Chowell, G., Fenimore, P.W., Castillo-Garsow, M.A., Castillo-Chávez, C. (2003). SARS outbreaks in Ontario, Hong Kong and Singapore: The role of diagnosis and isolation as a control mechanism. *Journal of Theoretical Biology* **224**:1–8.

Chowell, G., Hengartner, N.W., Castillo-Chávez, C., Fenimore, P.W., Hyman, J.M. (2004). The basic reproductive number of Ebola and the effects of public health measures: The cases of Congo and Uganda. *Journal of Theoretical Biology* **229**:119–126.

Cox, W.M., Yeates, G.N., Gilligan, A.T., Hosier, S.G. (2001). Individual differences. In Heather, N., Peters, T.J., Stockwell, T., eds., *International Handbook of Alcohol Dependence and Problems*, 357–374. New York: Wiley.

Daido, K. (2004). Risk-averse agents with peer pressure. *Applied Economics Letters* **11**:383–386.

Dawson, D.A., Grant, B.F., Stinson, F.S., Chou, P.S., Huang, B., Ruan, W.J. (2005). Recovery from DSM-IV alcohol dependence: United States, 2001–2002. *Addiction* **100**:281–292.

Dufour, M.C. (1999). What is moderate drinking? *Alcohol Research & Health* **23**:5–14.

Duncan, G.J., Boisjoly, J., Kremer, M., Levy, D.M., Eccles, J. (2005). Peer effects in drug use and sex among college students. *Journal of Abnormal Child Psychology* **33**:375–385.

Epstein, J.M. (1997). *Nonlinear dynamics*. Mathematical Biology, and Social Science. Boulder, CO: Westview Press.

González, B., Huerta Sánchez, E., Ortiz-Nieves, A., Vázquez-Alvarez, T., Kribs-Zaleta, C. (2003). Am I too fat? Bulimia as an epidemic. *Journal of Mathematical Psychology* **47**:515–526.

Gorman, D.M. (2001). Developmental processes. In Heather, N., Peters, T.J., Stockwell, T., eds., *International Handbook of Alcohol Dependence and Problems*, 339–355. New York: Wiley.

Hufford, M.H., Witkiewitz, K., Shields, A.L., Kodya, S., Caruso, J.C. (2003). Relapse as a nonlinear dynamic system: Application to patients with alcohol use disorders. *Journal of Abnormal Psychology* **112**:219–227.

Kerr, W.C., Fillmore, K.M., Bostrom, A. (2002). Stability of alcohol consumption over time: Evidence from three longitudinal surveys from the United States. *Journal of Studies on Alcohol* **63**:325–333.

Marlatt, G.A., Witkiewitz, K. (2002). Harm reduction approaches to alcohol use: Health promotion, prevention, and treatment. *Addictive Behaviors* **27**:867–886.

McEvoy, P.M., Stritzke, W.G.K., Fronch, D.J., Lang, A.R., Ketterman, R.L. (2003). Comparison of three models of alcohol craving in young adults: A cross-validation. *Addiction* **99**:482–497.

McKay, J.R. (1999). Studies of factors in relapse to alcohol, drug and nicotine use: A critical review of methodologies and findings. *Journal of Studies on Alcohol* **60**:566–576.

Miller, W.R., Walters, S.T., Bennett, M.E. (2001). How effective is alcoholism treatment in the United States. *Journal of Studies of Alcohol* **62**:211–220.

National Institute of Alcohol Abuse and Alcoholism. (2001). Frequently Asked Questions. November, 2001 (http://www.niaaa.nih.gov). *Accessed April 2006*.

Orford, J., Krishnan, M., Balaam, M., Everitt, M., Van der Graaf, K. (2004). University student drinking: The role of motivational and social factors. *Drugs: Education, Prevention & Policy* **11**:407–421.

Patten, S.D.B., Arboleda-Florez, J.A. (2004). Epidemic theory and group violence. *Social Psychiatry and Psychiatric Epidemiology* **39**:853–856.

Ross, R. (1911). *The Prevention of Malaria*. London: John Murray, London.

Sayette, M.A. (1999). Does drinking reduce stress? *Alcohol Research & Health* **23**:250–255.

Schutte, K.K., Nichols, K.A., Brennan, P.L., Moos, R.H. (2003). A ten-year follow-up of older former problem drinkers: Risk of relapse and implications of successfully sustained remission. *Journal of Studies on Alcohol* **64**:367–374.

Sobell, L.C., Sobell, M.B., Connors, G.J., Agrawal, S. (2003). Assessing drinking outcomes in alcohol treatment efficacy studies: Selecting a yardstick of success. *Alcohol: Clinical & Experimental Research* **27**:1661–1666.

Song, B., Castillo-Garsow, M., Castillo-Chávez, C., Rios Soto, K.R., Mejran, M., Henso, L. (2006). Raves, clubs, and ecstasy: the impact of peer pressure. *Mathematical Biosciences & Engineering* **3**:249–266.

Stockwell, T., Gruenewald, P.G. (2001). Controls on the physical availability of alcohol. In Heather, N., Peters, T.J., Stockwell, T., eds., *International handbook of alcohol dependence and problems*, 699–719. New York: Wiley.

Stockwell, T., Gruenewald, P.J., Toumbourou, J., Loxley, W. (2005). *Prevention of harmful substance use: The evidence base for policy and practice*. New York: Wiley.

Treno, A., Holder, H.D. (2001). Prevention at the local level. In Heather, N., Peters, T.J., Stockwell, T., eds., *International handbook of alcohol dependence and problems*, 771–783. New York: Wiley.

Vaillant, G.E. (2003). A 60-year follow-up of alcoholic men. *Addiction* **98**:1043–1051.

Walton, M.A., Reischl, T.M., Ramanathan, C.S. (1995). Social settings and addiction relapse. *Journal of Substance Abuse* **7**:223–233.

Weisner, C., Matzger, H., Kaskutas, L.A. (2003). How important is treatment? One-year outcomes of treated and untreated alcohol-dependent individuals. *Addiction* **98**:901–911.

Weschler, H., Kuo, K. (2003). Watering down the drinks: The moderating effect of college demographics on alcohol use of high-risk groups. *American Journal of Public Health* **93**:1929–1933.

Winkler, D., Caulkins, J.P., Behrens, D.A., Tragler, G. (2004). Estimating the relative efficiency of various forms of prevention at different stages of a drug epidemic. *Socio-Economic Planning Sciences* **38**:43–56.

Witkiewitz, K. (2005). Defining relapse from a harm reduction perspective. *Journal of Evidence-Based Social Work* **2**:191–206.

Witkiewitz, K. (2006). Lapses following community alcohol treatment: Modeling the falls from the wagon. Manuscript under review.

Witkiewitz, K., Marlatt, G.A. (2004). Relapse prevention for alcohol and drug problems: That was Zen, this is Tao. *American Psychologist* **59**:224–235.

APPENDIX

DETERMINISTIC MODEL

Uniform or homogeneous mixing means that the likelihood of coming into contact with members of each class is either $\frac{S}{N} = s$, $\frac{D}{N} = d$, or $\frac{R}{N} = r$, where $N = S + D + R$. Under these assumptions, the process of transmitting drinking behaviors is modeled via the following rescaled (that is, we work with proportions) system of nonlinear differential equations:

$$
\begin{aligned}
s\dot{Y} &= \mu - \beta sd - \mu s, \\
d\dot{Y} &= \beta sd + \rho rd - (\mu + \phi)d, \\
r\dot{Y} &= \phi d - \rho rd - \mu r, \\
1 &= s + d + r.
\end{aligned}
\tag{1}
$$

The rate of conversion from the susceptible state (occasional drinker) to the regular drinking state is assumed to be proportional to the size of the susceptible population, the likelihood of interacting with a randomly selected drinking partner, and both the magnitude and intensity of contacts. The rate of relapse is the result of contacts between R and D individuals.

The fact that individuals can transition to the D class from the S and R classes suggests that conversion is the result of multiple processes; that is, there is not just one way to move into the D-class. The first rate of transfer of individuals to the drinking class is the result of a nonlinear process modeled via a function of S and D, B(S, D). This function must satisfy the following conditions: B(0, D) = B(S, 0) = 0 (in the absence of susceptible drinkers there is no transition).

Homogeneous mixing means that B(S, D) is modeled as $\beta S \frac{D}{N}$ or $B(s, d) = \beta sd$

(in rescaled variables), where β is a measure of the average number of effective interactions between susceptible and drinkers per unit of time. The rate of transfer from R to D is the result of a nonlinear process modeled via the function G(D, R) with G(0, R) = G(D, 0) = 0. That is, in the absence of recovered or problem drinkers transitions from R to D are not possible. In other words, we model the total nonlinear relapse rate by $\rho R \dfrac{D}{N}$ or $\rho r d$ (in rescaled variables), where the parameter ρ is a measure of the average number of effective contacts per unit of time between drinkers and temporarily recovered individuals. This nonlinear process assumes that R and D individuals (as well as S individuals) share the same environments.

POPULATION DYNAMICS OF DRINKING UNDER HIGH RELAPSE RATES

Here the relationship between recovery (ϕ) and relapse (ρ) rates are explored. Ideally, effective treatments should increase recovery and reduce relapse rates to the extent that an epidemic of heavy drinking is reduced or stopped. However, it appears from an analysis of the basic drinking reproductive number (with recovery), $\mathfrak{R}_\phi$, that this may be a difficult task. We have the trivial equilibrium (no drinking state) given (in proportions) by $(s^*, d^*, r^*) = (1, 0, 0)$. Positive solutions $(s^* > 0, d^* > 0, r^* > 0)$, that is, solutions where drinking may become established, are solutions of the quadratic equation $f(d) = d^2 - Bd + C = 0$, where

$$B = 1 - \frac{1}{\mathfrak{R}_0} - \frac{1}{\mathfrak{R}_\rho} \quad \text{and} \quad C = \frac{1}{\mathfrak{R}_0}\left[\frac{1}{\mathfrak{R}_\rho} - \frac{\beta}{\rho}\right] \quad \text{with} \quad \mathfrak{R}_\rho = \frac{\rho}{\mu+\phi}.$$ Two positive solutions d_1^*, d_2^* in (0, 1) exist whenever $B > 0$, $C > 0$, $f'(1) > 0$ and $B^2 - 4C > 0$. From the definition of C it follows that $C > 0$ whenever $\mathfrak{R}_\phi < 1$. The positivity of the discriminant ($B^2 - 4C > 0$) requires the following conditions: $\mathfrak{R}_\rho > 1$ and $0 < \mathfrak{R}_c < \mathfrak{R}_\phi < 1$ ($\mathfrak{R}_c > 0$ whenever $\mathfrak{R}_\phi < 1$) where $\mathfrak{R}_\rho = \dfrac{\rho}{\mu+\phi}$ and

$$\mathfrak{R}_c = \frac{\rho}{\beta}\left[\frac{1}{1+\dfrac{1}{\mathfrak{R}_0}} - 2\sqrt{\frac{1}{\mathfrak{R}_0} - \frac{\mu}{\rho}}\right]$$

If both $0 < \mathfrak{R}_c < \mathfrak{R}_\phi < 1$ and $\mathfrak{R}_\rho < 1$ then drinking dies out. However, whether or not a culture of drinking becomes established ($0 < \mathfrak{R}_c < \mathfrak{R}_\phi < 1$ and $\mathfrak{R}_\rho > 1$) depends on initial conditions (see Figure 16.4c,d); that is, where the system ends up (including the rapid growth and establishment of a D clsass or its elimination) depends on the size of the initial proportion of problem drinkers. In fact, a rapid and large "outbreak" is possible whenever the number (or proportion) of initial drinkers is high. Such an outbreak, the model predicts, will result in the long-term survival of a regular drinking culture despite the fact that $\Re_\phi < 1$. Furthermore, in this last case a community of drinkers not only becomes established but may be nearly impossible to eliminate. In fact, parameters must be modified so that the value of $\Re_0$ is lower than that of $\Re_c$. This result is unexpected since the system has in place parameters that represent the effects of highly effective treatment programs (that is, $\Re_\phi < 1$).

Using current drinking literature pertaining to recovery, relapse, and the social interpersonal influences upon drinking behavior (Booth, Fortney, Fortney, Curran & Kirchner, 2001; Borsari & Carey, 2001; Daido, 2004; Dufour, 1999; Kerr, Fillmore & Bostrom, 2002; McEvoy, Stritzke, French, Lang & Ketterman, 2003; McKay, 1999; Miller, Walters & Bennett, 2001; National Institute of Alcohol Abuse and Alcohilsm, 2001; Orford, Krishnan, Balaam, Everitt & van der Graaf, 2004; Sayette, 1999; Schutte, Nichols, Brennan & Moos, 2003; Vaillant, 2002; Walton, Reischl & Ramanathan, 1995; Weisner, Matzger & Kaskutas, 2003), we have estimated several of the parameters necessary to the initial specification of a simple SDR model of drinking behavior (see Table 16.1). The results of the analysis of the model using these parameter values are discussed further in the numerical simulations section.

REFERENCE

Alcohol Epidemiologic Data System Division of Biometry and Epidemiology, National Institute on Alcohol Abuse and Alcoholism. *Alcohol Epidemiologic Data Directory.* SAMHSA, Office of Applied Studies, National Household Survey on Drug Abuse, 1999–2001. http://www.samhsa. gov/oas/nhsda.htm. Accessed 2005.

INDEX